W9-AQA-017

HEROIC
DIPLOMACY

HEROIC
DIPLOMACY

⁓

SADAT, KISSINGER, CARTER, BEGIN, AND THE QUEST FOR ARAB-ISRAELI PEACE

KENNETH W. STEIN

ROUTLEDGE
NEW YORK   LONDON

Published in 1999 by
Routledge
29 West 35th Street
New York, NY 10001

Published in Great Britain by
Routledge
11 New Fetter Lane
London EC4P 4EE

LIBRARY OF CONGRESS CATALOGING-IN-PUBLICATION DATA

Stein, Kenneth W., 1946–
    Heroic diplomacy : Sadat, Kissinger, Carter, Begin, and the quest
for Arab-Israeli peace / Kenneth W. Stein.
        p.   cm.
    Includes bibliographical references and index.
    ISBN 0-415-92155-4 (pbk.). — ISBN 0-415-92154-6 (cloth)
    1. Arab-Israeli conflict—1973–1993. 2. Diplomatic negotiations
in international disputes. 3. Arab countries—Foreign relations—Israel.
4. Israel—Foreign relations—Arab countries. 5. Israel-Arab war,
1973—Peace. 6. Arab-Israeli conflict—1993—Peace. I. Title.
DS119.7.S6749   1999
956.04—dc21   98-49359
                                                            CIP

Dedicated to my parents,
Tillie and Max Stein,
and
my students

CONTENTS

PREFACE

AFTER ISRAEL'S establishment in May 1948, the Arab world refused to make peace with the new Jewish state. Though Arab states signed armistice agreements with Israel in 1949, a technical state of war remained in effect. Attempts to sign formal peace agreements between Israel and Jordan, and Israel and Syria continually failed, and no Palestinian Arab-Israeli accommodation was seriously considered. The states were locked into a catch-22 situation: Israel would not allow Palestinian refugees to return to the new Jewish state's territory until Arab states recognized it diplomatically; Arab states would not recognize Israel until Israel allowed Palestinians, displaced by Israel's creation, to return to their land within the new state. The Arab world saw Israel as an extension of Western imperial presence in the Middle East. It was also a blight on the Arab character and required removal. Egyptian President Nasser cemented an Arab commitment, which endured for two decades, to seek Israel's destruction. Under pressure to survive in this hostile environment, Israel developed a secure economy, integrated millions of new immigrants, and built an army supported by weapons capable of protecting its national security. For their part, many Arab states, including Egypt, Syria, and Iraq, responded by looking to the Soviet Union for equivalent military hardware. In this manner the cold war further complicated the Arab-Israeli conflict.

In June 1967, mounting tension exploded into war. Without warning, Israel preemptively attacked Syria and Egypt, and then Jordan. Israel's lightening military victories solidified an Arab fear: the unlikelihood of Israel's destruction. The Arab world responded: "No peace, no recognition, no negotiations with Israel." But the international community, working with the United Nations, set forth principles that could govern eventual negotiations. Security Council Resolution 242 of November 1967 became a framework for future negotiations. It called for the sovereignty, independence, and territorial integrity of all states in the region and a solution to the growing refugee problem, and stated an admissibility of the acquisition of territory through war. Along with this general outline, several negotiating mechanisms were tried, among them third-party mediation, great-power talks, private diplomacy, and secret meetings. As Egypt's new president in 1970, Anwar

Sadat sought to alter Nasser's priorities and change Egypt's political orientations: he aimed to lessen Egyptian dependence on the Soviet Union; to turn toward the United States; to right a faltering Egyptian economy; and to remove Israel from its occupation of the Egyptian Sinai. First, Sadat tried to entice American diplomats to pressure an Israeli withdrawal from Sinai, but he failed. Stymied, he surprised Israel with war in October 1973.

Coordinating his war plans with Syrian leaders, Sadat unquestionably launched the October 1973 War to harness American involvement in removing Israel from Sinai. He did not go to war to destroy Israel, because he knew his capabilities were limited and he assumed, correctly, that the United States would not allow Israel's destruction. At the start of the war, Israel lost men and materials but gradually rebounded to push the Syrians off the Golan Heights and to position troops some 25 miles from Damascus and a mere 60 miles from Cairo. Disentangling the armies after the war spawned direct Egyptian-Israeli military talks that led to the convocation of the December 1973 Geneva Middle East Peace Conference, where Sadat used his Arab contemporaries to promote Egyptian national interests, much to their consternation and displeasure. American Secretary of State Henry Kissinger stepped in to knit together Egyptian-Israeli and Syrian-Israeli military disengagement agreements. Kissinger's skill and secretive nature meshed nicely with Sadat's flair for the extraordinary. Sadat gave American administrations and Israel what they had never had previously, a viable Arab negotiating partner who wanted to edge his way toward a diplomatic resolution of the conflict with Israel. For Sadat, making peace with Israel would be a collateral by-product in the process of securing full American support for his objectives to reorient Egypt's priorities. A quarter-century diplomatic process was thus initiated: Washington edged the Soviet Union out of Egypt; dominated the diplomatic process; provided guarantees, verbal assurances, and financial incentives; and inserted third-party personnel as buffers between the former combatants. Step-by-step negotiations succeeded in the phased separation of Israeli and Arab military forces; Israel exchanged land for peace, which entailed a promise of peaceful relations with its neighbors. Indeed, neither the burgeoning domestic problems in Israel nor the intervention of the United States ultimately prevented Egyptian-Israeli agreements from being signed.

The American diplomatic baton, which catalyzed interim agreements, passed from Kissinger to President Jimmy Carter in 1977. Carter was soon consumed with finding the right formulas for convening a Middle East peace conference. Before Menachem Begin unexpectedly became prime minister of Israel in May 1977, he had considered that Israel's best strategic course was to separate Egypt from the larger pan-Arab conflict with Israel. Sadat and Begin began testing each other in secret negotiations and found that, in fact, each would be better off dealing with one another directly, not going through the attempt to resolve the conflict via Washington's preferred method of a comprehensive peace at a conference. Furthermore, each realized a shared common goal: that an agreement between them would serve respective national interests. Sadat's ensuing historic journey to Jerusalem in November 1977 broke psychological barriers, which like his ignition of the October War, catapulted a stagnating diplomatic negotiating process forward. Sadat was angered that Begin did not do something grand in return, like withdraw entirely from Sinai immediately. Sadat's impatience and Begin's limp response created debate and ideas but no agreement. Poles apart in terms of substance, pace, personality, temperament, and style, Begin and Sadat finally came to rely upon Carter's availability and intent to reach an agreement. The Sadat-Carter-Begin triangle provided the drama, procedure, and substance for the ensuing diplomatic negotiating process.

Based upon Begin's idea for Palestinian autonomy, or self-government, Carter's unprecedented personal intervention generated the September 1978 Camp David Accords. Though in the end their discussions about Palestinian autonomy failed, the March 1979 Egyptian-Israeli Peace Treaty created a new reality; the most populous and militarily powerful Arab state established diplomatic relations with Israel. By moving heavy historical blocks, Sadat shocked colleagues and enemies alike, all of whom fretted "Can he be trusted?" or "Where is he going next?" Along the way, he put his political and personal life on the line and was assassinated in October 1981. For a decade, Sadat's accommodation with Israel had made Egypt a pariah among Arab states. Cairo has since aligned itself unequivocally with the United States, which has in turn richly rewarded Egypt with financial assistance, military supplies, and guarantees for its awkward, but necessary, political embrace.

In the 1980s, crises in the Persian Gulf, inter-Arab political squabbles, Jordanian-PLO disagreements, Israeli reluctance to address the Palestinian issue more fully, and other regional issues and conflicts hampered American attention to further progress in Arab-Israeli negotiations. Nevertheless, a series of plans, ideas, and declarations were suggested not only by Americans but also by Arab, Israeli, and European sources to broaden Arab-Israeli negotiations. For a variety of reasons their contents or implementation proved unsuccessful. At the end of the decade, all of Sinai had been returned to Egyptian sovereignty, and Egypt had climbed back into a key position in inter-Arab politics. The "peace process," which Sadat began with Kissinger, Carter, and Begin, continued to unfold, in part because Arabs and Israelis were simply growing weary from the conflict and the resulting expenditure of manpower, time, and money.

Several factors conditioned the Middle Eastern environment for further Arab-Israeli diplomatic progress: the end of the cold war; the decline in Arab oil power; the 1991 Gulf War with protracted American support for the integrity of Arab states demonstrated; and the decided weakening of the PLO in Arab circles because of its embrace of Iraq. With the determination of the Bush administration, the October 1991 Madrid Middle East Peace Conference convened. From it flowed both bilateral talks among Israel and its contiguous Arab neighbors and multilateral talks with other Arab states and countries about transnational issues such as arms control, economic development, environment, refugees, and water supply. Then in September 1993, after secret negotiations with the assistance of the Norwegians, the PLO and Israel signed the Declaration of Principles, setting out how they would share territory and prerogative in the West Bank and Gaza Strip. The area and prerogative circumscribed for Palestinian self-rule were much less ambitious than what Begin and Sadat had agreed upon in the Camp David Accords fifteen years earlier. In October 1994, a Jordanian-Israeli Peace Treaty was signed, further ending the state of war between Israel and its Arab neighbors. With intermittent delays, Israel and the PLO arduously negotiated details affecting the implementation of Palestinian self-rule and Israeli withdrawal from the lives of the Palestinians, who took physical control of Gaza and more than one-third of the West Bank and applied limited self-rule over almost 90 percent of the Palestinian population. In November 1995, Israeli Prime Minister Yitzhak Rabin was assassinated; like Sadat, he was killed because a segment of his country's political culture and environment were not yet fully prepared to accept the outlines of a negotiated Israeli-Palestinian agreement. Even the Israeli Likud government of Benjamin Netanyahu, elected in May 1996, although opposed to the Declaration of Principles—otherwise known as the Oslo Accords—implemented them in part by withdrawing in January 1997 from the religiously important city of Hebron. Under the guidance of President Clinton, Arafat and Netanyahu met for nine days in Maryland in October 1998. Israel agreed to transfer more land to Palestinian control in exchange for reciprocal Palestinian diligence in assuring Israeli security concerns. Both sides agreed to recommence discussions on final status arrangements including the difficult issues of future borders, refugees, water rights, Jerusalem, settlements, and the nature of the Palestinian entity. In the 1990s, with varying degrees of regularity and content, Arab and Muslim states not contiguous to Israel began to normalize relations with the Jewish state. Other countries that once fully supported the Arab cause against Israel also initiated contacts or renewed diplomatic, cultural, and commercial relations with Israel. American diplomacy continued its quarter century of dominance as it mediated PLO-Israeli differences and stimulated Syrian-Israeli diplomatic exchanges. In the late 1990s, Syria and Israel sparred over the terms of an agreement and found it difficult to define a mutually acceptable formula and time frame for implementing the degree of withdrawal from the Golan Heights with the degree of peace to be received by Israel. The Arab-Israeli conflict was becoming a series of Arab-Israeli relationships.

ACKNOWLEDGMENTS

THE IDEA FOR THIS BOOK took shape in the early 1980s, emerging out of my interest in the Arab-Israeli conflict, a topic I studied and taught for a decade at Emory University in Atlanta, Georgia. The book's framework was catalyzed by my association with two extraordinary men, former United States President Jimmy Carter and former ambassador to Israel, Samuel W. Lewis. In 1982, after I had spent five years teaching modern Middle Eastern history courses, President Carter asked me to be associated with the newly developing Carter Center of Emory University. During the subsequent decade, travels and meetings with him allowed me to meet many American and Middle Eastern diplomats and statesmen; I sat in on dozens of face-to-face meetings between Carter and virtually every Middle Eastern head of state and foreign minister throughout the 1980s. I learned how the personalities of the players and the chemistry between them are often bigger keys to essential policy making than the weight of the institutions they represent or the power relationships between those institutions. I also learned about the central role played by professional bureaucrats, ambassadors, and foreign service officers; they not only shape and execute diplomacy but also they remember it rather well. They are virtually the negotiation's archives. President Carter, for example, gave me hours of his time as I relentlessly asked about nuance after nuance related to the Arab-Israeli peace process. Ambassador Lewis encouraged me to inquire of American diplomats who were formerly involved in Arab-Israeli negotiations. When he was president of the United States Institute for Peace, Lewis asked me to organize a study group of these former American practitioners of Middle East diplomacy. From that group, Lewis and I wrote *Making Peace Among Arabs and Israelis: Lessons from Fifty Years of Negotiating Experience* (1991). Then I asked the obvious question: If American civil servants and foreign service officers had such wonderful memories and recollections, then what about their Middle Eastern contemporaries? Slowly, I began conducting interviews, collecting, checking, and organizing oral source material. Many of the civil servants and foreign service officers with whom I spoke had attended the most critical diplomatic meetings as note takers; some wrote the memoranda that later became policy under the name of a president or secretary of state; some had negotiated directly and met dozens of times with foreign and defense ministers, heads of state, presidents, kings, and other foreign cabinet officers; some were detailed with explaining difficult decisions while their superiors attended to other affairs of state; others were like the proverbial fly on the wall, merely attending a meeting or participating in a conversation as an adviser to someone more senior, not realizing then how important that link was in the chain of remembering Arab-Israeli diplomacy.

As usually happens with such undertakings, collecting the information and conducting the interviews in the United States, Europe, and the Middle East took much longer than anticipated. In 1987, I started doing interviews, and I completed the last one in June 1998. (Almost uniformly, I found that most of the career diplomats, foreign service officers, and statesmen associated with Arab-Israeli negotiations had neither written nor had any intention of writing their own memoirs.) The interviews I conducted focused on the period from 1967 to 1991. Invariably each time a two- or three-hour interview was completed, three or four additional interview recommendations were suggested as possible leads. The trail seemed endless. Each interview confirmed that most individuals were only familiar with their particular time frames and had perspectives limited through the eyes of their institution or geographic venue. With the exception of a very few, all those interviewed were stunningly frank, the informational depth and sincerity of the recollections formidable. Most of the interviewees had strong feelings about the people for whom they worked, but by and large they had few axes to grind that would have slanted their recollections. Listening to their attitudes, expressions, and anecdotes was always a pleasure for me. Learning the differences and similarities in perceptions of reality proved vital. Most possessed several colorful anecdotes and insightful recollections about colleagues, events, and bureaucratic tussles. Since most had worked in the bureaucratic trenches and were dedicated to getting a job done, they were not terribly worried about how history would treat them. Their resulting candor was refreshingly different from most of the memoirs and autobiographies written about the diplomacy and statesmen of the period. When they asked that the tape recorder be turned off, or that a story or assessment reach my manuscript anonymously, I honored those requests. In the end, splicing and blending the contents of these tapes together was a lively and enjoyable exercise.

While checking memories and dates for accuracy, expected inconsistencies emerged and omissions appeared. Trying to resolve who used whom and for what purpose and who said what to whom first were recurrent and sometimes unanswered questions. From the research, I believe it is reasonable to assert that self-deprecation or acknowledgment of one's mistakes are rarely found commodities in memoirs or in oral interviews. Likewise, an absence of self-esteem is seldom apparent in autobiographies. As this manuscript was being written, new memoirs were published and recently unclassified national security materials became available. These documents helped refine my earlier assumptions and aligned some interviewees' recollections. As best as I could, I tried to tell the story as these people lived it, saw it, and made it happen. Admittedly both time and language barriers kept me from using several archives, like those in the former Soviet Union, and from interviewing everyone still alive who participated in some significant fashion in this most interesting diplomatic period. Some archives, notably those at the Carter, Ford, and Nixon Libraries, are reportedly rich in detail, but these very sensitive national security materials remain closed to researchers. Some top-secret material was declassified for my use through the Freedom of Information Act. I regret that I did not interview either Richard Nixon or Yitzhak Rabin before they died; I also regret that time and permission did not allow me to see others. Unfortunately, after the collection of the oral source material, many who were interviewed earlier in this undertaking passed away. For many of them, the interviews collected are all that remains of their record in Arab-Israeli diplomacy.

The main focus of this book is the four-year period from October 1973 to November 1977, when Egyptian-Israeli negotiations began in earnest. This was not a smooth, uneventful time. With a broad introduction to 1973 and an epilogue of the subsequent two decades, I have tried to frame these critical years in their unique historical context. In addition, I have provided a separate chapter dealing with the heroic players in this diplomacy. It was fortuitous for those interested in an Arab-Israeli accommodation and a winding down of Soviet involvement in the Middle East that Sadat, Kissinger, Carter, Begin, and some of their key advisers arrived on the historical scene at the same time. Why and how they made their policy choices and how they interacted with one another were telling in the unfolding diplomatic story. Along the way their collective narrative contained duplicity, egos, half-truths, showmanship, and major shifts in the road. Each of them integrated short-term tactics with long-term strategies. They were all dedicated leaders. Each had his guiding ideology or philosophy, which influenced policy choices; each exercised political courage and demonstrated political will. Each made necessary compromises to reach specific objectives. Their common goal was protection of unique national interests; each concluded that an Arab-Israeli accommodation would enhance that interest. These were clever, shrewd, and sometimes devious political leaders. They were not saints by any means. Instead they were seasoned veterans of many skirmishes, and if they were not, then they learned quickly to be calculating in their actions. Each had his or her own unique methods of making and carrying out policy, each used underlings for particular purposes, and each tried, not always successfully, to keep a tight reign on the pace and content of the negotiating process. Unique to all of them was their willingness to go against norms and trends established by predecessors, and a willingness to listen to advisers but always reserve final decisions for themselves. At times each challenged conventional wisdom, bureaucratic recommendations, and the strength of domestic constituencies. Enduring perseverance, vision, and determination were characteristics they all shared. These traits melded well with the diplomatic needs of the moment. At no other time in contemporary Middle Eastern history did the key decision-making personalities align so uniquely to alter the direction of the Arab-Israeli conflict so significantly and therefore the political landscape of the Middle East. With no disrespect intended: Can you imagine Warren Christopher as secretary of state during and after the 1973 war, Nasser flying to Jerusalem, Ronald Reagan carrying on the negotiations at Camp David, or Yitzhak Shamir managing an Israeli response to Sadat?

For several reasons, I have limited the chronological scope of this book. First, I did not realize how extensive the oral source material might be. I thought there would be several dozen interviews; instead I undertook more than eighty separate sessions. Second, excellent books and articles have been written covering the post–1967 War period, though most of them have focused almost exclusively on a rendition from a distinct geographic or political orientation. There was no reason for me to say again what others have said so well. The effort here was to merge recollections with the written available record and blend them into an interactive whole, trying to see the story as it unfolded from the key vantage points along the way. I am sure that not all sides or views to the evolving diplomacy have been covered in this book. Moreover, I am sure there are others who could have made useful additions to the story. Third, narrowing the time span coverage caused me to dig a deeper, rather than a broader, hole. With the lives and memories of those who participated in the diplomacy a quarter century ago diminishing quickly, I simply chose to focus on the earlier period. Though documents will tell us a great deal more in the years to come when national security restrictions are removed and access is provided to the sensitive material huddled in archives, to wait until then to write this history would mean leaving out the memories and recollections of those who were there to make it. For the reader, I hope my effort adds nuance, shades tones, and provides substantive new insight into the people and purposes generating this history.

Many people played significant roles in bringing the enterprise to completion. For all of you who shared stories and recollections with me, I am forever grateful. Each of you had a wonderful slice of history to tell. It was fun probing your memories. I hope my renditions of your recollections are accurate; if not, I apologize in advance if I have presented them other than you had intended. Friends and colleagues made useful suggestions or read parts of the manuscript. Their assistance to me and their mention here illustrates my high regard for their ability to refine my understanding of the Middle East, the diplomatic process, and its peoples. Over the years, I have become indebted to them for their guidance, personal reflections, and insightful assessments. Among others, these people include Mahdi Abdul-Hadi, Kamal Abu-Jaber, Ami Ayalon, Michael Bar-Zohar, Usamah al-Baz, Tahsin Bashir, Uri Bialer, Wolf Blitzer, Neil Caplan, Amnon Cohen, Rafi Danziger, Edward

Djerejian, Abba Eban, Oded Eiran, Hermann Eilts, Adam Garfinkle, Gad Gilbar, Dore Gold, Othman Hallaq, Prince Hassan, Martin Indyk, Mahmud Karem, Rami Khouri, Sami Khouri, Bill Kirby, David Korn, Martin Kramer, Ashraf Kurdi, Dan Kurtzer, Ellen Laipson, Zack Levey, Bruce Maddy-Weitzman, Abdul Salam al-Majali, Alan Makovsky, Moshe Ma'oz, Tahir al-Masri, Phillip Mattar, Ed Medlin, David Menashri, Aaron Miller, Walid Mouallem, Richard Murphy, Yossi Nevo, David Newton, Dan Pattir, Jennie Pickford, Yehoshua Porath, Marwan Qassem, Itamar Rabinovich, Yaacov Rosen, Yuval Rotem, Robert Satloff, Nabil Shaath, Haim Shaked, Shimon Shamir, Gabi Sheffer, Emmanuel Sivan, Steve Spiegel, Farouq al-Shara'a, Rocky Suddarath, Asher Susser, Patrick Theros, Abdullah Touqan, Bernard Wasserstein, David Wasserstein, Werner Weidenfeld, Molly Williamson, Ehud Yaari, and Eyal Zisser. These fine people were never shy or unwilling to help me clarify a point, to find some source material, or to facilitate a better understanding of the Middle East and Washington's diplomatic efforts aimed at resolving the region's conflict. Regardless of how helpful these individuals were to me in understanding various aspects of the conflict or in fine-tuning the detail, none of them bear any responsibility for the contents or analyses provided here. Both are my responsibility alone.

During the last decade, a handful of Emory colleagues and administrators have been extremely supportive of me and my work, especially Juan del Aguila, Bill Chace, Jim Laney, Billy Frye, Eleanor Main, Steven Sanderson, and our former department chairman, J. Russell Major. I am deeply indebted to each of them for their support, collegiality, encouragement, and sage advice. At the United States Institute for Peace, the encouragement of Sheryl Brown, Hrach Gregorian, Barry O'Conor, and Gregg McDonald were greatly appreciated. Deepest thanks are extended to the Foreign Ministry officials in Egypt, Israel, Jordan, and Syria, who helped me arrange interviews and who ensured that my interviews would be conducted on time. Many officials in the U.S. State Department and in American embassies abroad have extended a helping hand, interceding to facilitate this or that interview, providing insight into the contemporary negotiations, and always amenable to hear and share a story about what happened in the 1970s. To all of them: thank you.

The generosity of Arthur Blank, Philip and Ethel Klutznick, and Bernie Marcus has been remarkable. Phil and Ethel gave generously to sustain the Middle East Program at The Carter Center. Since 1987 and 1990 respectively, Arthur Blank and Bernie Marcus have made estimable contributions to my professional life. Their loyalty, unwavering support, and generosity for my research and entire academic career have been extraordinary. Continuously, both have encouraged me and have given me the wherewithal to fulfill aspirations usually only dreamed of by most academics, scholars, and intellectuals. It is not an exaggeration to say that their investment in me made this research possible. The Klutznick, Blank, and Marcus families are exceptional; they are in a class by themselves. I am thankful that they are also my friends.

For their encouragement and friendship over the years, deep appreciation and warm thanks are extended to the Brodzky, Caslow, Chasnov, Copeland, Malkah, Mirmelstein, Murowitz, Porth, Seslowe, and Shaw families. Each of you extended understanding and affection in good and bad times; each opened your hearts and homes with sensitivity, grace, and wise advice. To Nikki and Herb Rosenbaum: for more than half a century you have embraced our family with support, wit, insights, and love. Your students and children, like us, are all better people because of your guidance and compassion.

To the librarians and staff in the Emory University Woodruff Library, I extend sincere thanks for your help to me during the last two decades, with special recognition extended to Marie and Eric Nitschke for their longtime friendship and invaluable assistance. For their constant encouragement and warm friendship over the years, I would like to thank Don Schewe and Martin Elzy at the Carter Presidential Library in Atlanta, Georgia. For assisting in identifying the photographs for the book, I express my appreciation to David Stanhope at the Carter Presidential Library in Atlanta, Georgia; Kenneth G. Hafeli at the Gerald R. Ford Library in Ann Arbor, Michigan; Orna Terlo and Ilana Dayan at the Israel Government Press Office in Jerusalem, Israel; and Bat-Sheva Naftali at the Israel Defense Force Archives in Givatayim, Israel. To all my former students who helped me refine my understanding of the Arab-Israeli conflict, I am forever grateful that you chose my classroom. To former interns and others who transcribed the audiotapes, I offer my sincere thanks for your patience.

Several individuals stand out uniquely in their assistance as friends, secretaries, and administrators. They make the day easier and more productive, and they do it with a caring smile. Amira Margalith, the executive administrator of The Moshe Dayan Center for Middle Eastern and African Studies at Tel Aviv University, did everything humanly possible to assist me in identifying the whereabouts of the key interviewees for the research conducted in Israel in March, August, and November 1992. For twenty years, Amira has been a close friend. Dozens of Israeli scholars and foreign academics have benefited from her wisdom, insight, and efficiency. For the last decade, my own administrative assistant, Diane James, has arranged and managed my professional life in such a way as to give me the time necessary to do the research and to write this and other manuscripts. Without her selfless devotion to me and my work and her dedication to get the job done, the collection and gathering of source material would have been delayed by years, if not indefinitely. I am fortunate to count Amira and Diane as friends. No two people could have been more loyal, more helpful, and more sincere in making the research and writing experience as easy as it was. Every academic, scholar, and researcher should be so entitled.

Acknowledgments

To my mother and late father, I extend my deepest appreciation for their support, patience, and love. In more ways than one, my parents, Max and Tillie Stein, traveled a long way since growing up in central Germany in the early decades of this century. They conveyed to their children and to their grandchildren the love of history, family, and tradition. First, they moved to New York because they had to; then they moved to Atlanta because their grandchildren mattered. In their sojourn through life, they have easily imparted to their descendants the idea that no matter what happens, you take your experience, education, and loyalty with you. No one can deny you these attributes if you want them and cultivate them; no one can take them away. These legacies are invaluable. By example their grandsons have benefited from their wisdom and guidance. With grace, patience, and superb skill, my former wife, Ellen Stein, made the composition of this manuscript clearer and better. For that, I am very thankful, as I am sure the reader is, too. To Laura and Margo, you have brought joy and warmth to me and to our family.

Finally, with enormous gratitude and affection, I recognize the patience of my three sons, Jason, Todd, and Andrew. Each in his own way has nurtured me with his delightful humor, mischievous smile, and love of baseball. Each of them has learned not to take me too seriously; they have kept me and my work in perspective. Each has reminded me that there is something magical about a round ball, a bat, a glove, and a baseball field. They constantly wanted more; no ground ball was hit hard enough, no fly ball was thrown high enough, no discussion of baseball was long enough. In life, too, they have taught me to keep the glove open and in contact with the ground. Together we work and we play in our field of dreams. Their grandparents taught them that by noble example. No father could have been granted more. From generation to generation.

CHAPTER 1

THE KEY PLAYERS
IN ARAB-ISRAELI
DIPLOMACY
1973–1978

FOR ISRAELIS, Egyptian President Gamal Abd al-Nasser personified Arab hatred of Israel. When Nasser died in September 1970, Israelis sighed in relief, but they still faced many other implacable enemies. Israel was victorious in the June 1967 War, devastating Egyptian, Jordanian, and Syrian armed forces. What Israelis did not know then was that their occupation and control of the Sinai Peninsula, Golan Heights, Gaza Strip, West Bank, and east Jerusalem would become the future focus of Arab-Israeli negotiations: Under what circumstances and over what period of time would Israel give back some or all of these territories? and what would Israel receive in return from Arab neighbors in terms of understandings, agreements, and assurances? For the rest of the century, the Arab-Israeli negotiating process was based on delineating Israel's exchange of land and resource assets for less tangible Arab diplomatic promises and agreements. At Nasser's death, Israel's military superiority had been established, and Syrian-Jordanian relations were rancorous. Jordan was slugging it out with the PLO for future control of any of the West Bank that Israel might relinquish. Yet, Israel was still not at ease. Peace treaties did not result from Israel's smashing victory three years earlier; Israelis were not gambling in Cairo, visiting Petra, scuba diving in Aqaba, or taking day trips to Damascus. The war brought more territory but not normalization of Israel's place in the Middle East. Pervasive anti-Israeli feelings transited the war. From the Arab media, Israeli anxiety was reinforced regularly. Constant barrages of rich anti-Israeli sentiment were mixed with nasty political cartoons, many depicting Zionists and Israelis as Nazis. Israel's existential fears thus remained. From the almost twenty years of Nasser's rule, Israelis neither considered nor expected any Arab leader to end the Arab commitment to destroy Israel.

In the early fall of 1970, Israeli decision makers had no reason to believe that

Egypt or its leadership would be any less hostile to the Jewish state. No Arab leader could consider recognizing Israel as a political reality and expect to survive either domestically or in an inter-Arab context. So when Anwar Sadat became Egypt's second president on October 15, 1970, he was viewed by Israelis and Americans alike as someone inextricably bound to the policy priorities of his predecessor—a strong relationship with the Soviet Union, Cairo's leadership in inter-Arab politics, and coordinator of the anti-Israeli caravan. Evidence for Sadat's public antagonism toward Israel came quickly from his speeches and interviews, during which he repeated what Nasser had claimed: Israel was illegitimate, a foreign body artificially implanted in the Middle East by imperial or colonial powers. Sadat's remarks were stereotypical and harshly anti-Jewish. He accused Jews of holding the keys to money and controlling the television and press throughout the world. He denigrated Zionism and acknowledged ruefully that Israel was backed by the United States.[1]

Neither American nor Israeli officials knew much about the new Egyptian president or the subtle changes taking place within Egypt in the waning years of the 1960s. Those in the State Department who dealt with the Middle East considered Sadat not a serious but a minor political player, an interim caretaker, or perhaps a transitional president.[2] Egyptian and foreign analysts postulated that there would be some form of internal political struggle between Sadat and those who were considered leftist or pro-Soviet in their orientation, at least more closely identified with Nasser. Considered a lightweight because he had played a lesser role in Egypt's 1952 revolution, he had no distinguished record of public or military service. After becoming president, Sadat enjoyed the legitimacy of being connected to the Nasser period, but he distanced himself from the mistakes of Nasser's rule. Sadat was part of the officer's group that deposed the corrupt King Farouk in 1952 and went on to rid Egypt of Britain's colonial presence. When Sadat took office, four major issues required attention: the economy was in deep trouble; there was a dominant dependence upon the Soviet Union; Arab states were apprehensive about Cairo's imperious attitudes; and Egyptians remained psychologically hurt by the Israeli victory in the June 1967 War. Sadat saw the need to change Egypt's political course, which he did slowly. First, he consolidated his rule, then he attacked Israel with the purpose of appealing to the United States to help Egypt diplomatically and economically. By the force of his will and with the collaboration of Henry Kissinger and Jimmy Carter, he changed the course of the Arab-Israeli conflict. Sadat aligned with the United States and pushed the Soviet Union out of Egypt. He did what he did for Egypt, neither to please the Americans nor to make peace with Israel. Each agreement with Israel was a building block, an interim step toward the achievement of his objectives. Some of those steps were small, some sudden, others of great magnitude, but each was connected to the next and based upon the previous one. If he could have avoided a peace treaty with Israel, he would have done so. In pursuit of his goal, he provided Israel with what its leaders never expected: in March 1979, the most populous, culturally significant, and militarily powerful Arab state accepted Israel as a legitimate political entity. His heroic and unconventional diplomacy succeeded both because Menachem Begin, a man steeped in Jewish history and horrific memories of the Holocaust, was willing to compromise his own ideology for the good of the Israeli state, and because President Jimmy Carter was determined not to let the possibility of an Egyptian-Israeli agreement slip through his hands. Sadat's turn toward Washington and apparent moderation made it possible for Americans finally to trust an Arab leader. By doing so, Sadat changed the U.S.-Israeli relationship. Legitimately supporting an Arab leader's political requests forced Washington to be a broker and mediator, not just Israel's trusted partner. Israeli leaders were not pleased by this reality, nor were they happy that their carefully defined treaty with Egypt became a cold peace, yet it lasted for the remainder of this century. In his Arab context, Sadat's embrace of Israel sharpened divisions in inter-Arab affairs and also set the pace: the Arab world caught up to Sadat a dozen years later when the 1991 Madrid Peace Conference established the background for eventual Palestinian-Israeli and Jordanian-Israeli agreements and, in turn, a redefinition of general Arab-state attitudes and relations with Israel.

The combination of Sadat's background, flamboyance, disdain for foreign control, secretive style, and impatience redirected Egypt's orientation. Neither Israelis nor Americans saw this change coming. Born on Christmas Day in 1918, Sadat was fifty-two when he became president. Coming from peasant stock, Sadat was raised in the small village of Mit Abul Kom in the Nile River Delta. There a premium was placed on not just belonging to a family but also to the village and the land. In 1925, when Sadat was seven, his family moved to Cairo, where the next quarter century was spent struggling against British imperial presence in Egypt. Protecting Egyptian land and ridding it of foreign domination were core threads in his political fiber. As an Egyptian patriot, he struggled for Egypt's independence, always putting Egypt's national interests first. He had strong beliefs and a vision of what he wanted for Egypt: restructuring the Egyptian economy; moving away from the Soviet Union; moving toward the United States; and restoring Sinai to Egyptian sovereignty. Everything else was negotiable. Possessed with an enormous ego, Sadat intertwined his personal and national priorities so that neither he nor Egypt played second fiddle to anyone. According to Usamah al-Baz, a key official in shaping Egypt's foreign policy for the last quarter of the twentieth century:

Sadat was a man of vision who looked beyond today's constraints and possessed a messianic sense. He had a mystical, almost prophetic feeling that the average Egyptian man supported him no matter how unconventional his choices were. Intellectuals, he felt, were wrapped up in their own ego, rhetoric, and self-interest. And yet he was pragmatic, not a dreamer, nor simple-minded,

3

nor gullible. His willingness and ability to take courageous political steps and unprecedented risks were greater than what Nasser was ever willing to do.[3]

Sadat possessed unalterable objectives, but not fossilized ideologies, as well as a strong will, national pride, and a capacity for enduring until his goals were achieved. Gradually he developed a sense of self-confidence. It evolved after he solidified his grip on power in May 1971, and steadily increased because of his partial victory in the October War and after he secured Kissinger's attention and engagement in Egyptian-Israeli diplomacy. He lacked neither faith in his own judgment nor boldness in execution of his policy choices. When he made a proposal in February 1971 for a staged withdrawal of Israeli forces from Sinai, he did not tell Foreign Minister Mahmoud Riad about the idea before relaying it through Washington to Jerusalem.[4] Neither did he consult with anyone prior to his expulsion of the Soviet advisers in July 1972. Launching the October 1973 War on the Israelis' most holy day of their calendar year was typical Sadat. In planning the war, he did not tell King Hussein exactly when the war would begin and furtively kept from Assad his priority intention to seek only limited military objectives. During the war itself, he intentionally kept Assad uninformed about the state of his military deployment. What he told Kissinger in cable or in person he did not necessarily reveal to Moscow, and when he pleaded with the Soviets about an issue or policy, he shaped his remarks for their ears only. When he decided to go to Jerusalem in November 1977, he kept his own counsel. When he decided to have a preparatory meeting in Cairo prior to returning to a Geneva conference format in December 1977, he told no one in advance and informed the Israelis about it via Cairo radio. Americans and Israelis were repeatedly stunned and perplexed by such unconventional and unexpected actions.

Sadat was a man of extremes and shifts. At times he was simple, austere, and modest; at others complex, autocratic, and egotistical. Sometimes he would think clearly and logically, while at other times he might not be able to articulate a point of view. Sometimes he had an open mind on a subject and could absorb what he heard or read; at other times he might be indifferent, neither caring about nor hearing what was before him. Neither his character nor style were stationary or predictable. If he disagreed with something, then he might just puff on his pipe and grunt quietly. Those who knew him might have assumed this meant assent, though most often it did not. If he had the mind to do something and was asked over and over about his capacity to manage it—such as representing Palestinian interests during the autonomy talks in 1979 and 1980—then he would simply say, "for sure." Even if he could not do what he thought he could do, still he would claim he could, and at least his American interlocutors believed him. Sadat was never hesitant to take a bold initiative even if it did not conform with an accepted norm or philosophical mold. His procedural and substantive preferences were for those that suited his needs at any particular time; ideology was temporarily wedded to pragmatic requirements to meet his long-term objectives. Coming as he did after Nasser, he was, for many Arabs, Israelis, and Americans, a strange breed, a political oxymoron. While Nasser was embedded in almost absolutist ideology—pan-Arabism, anti-Israeli feeling, a deep pro-Soviet orientation, economic socialism, and profound advocacy for Palestinian rights—Sadat adjusted his philosophic commitments to satisfy his political objectives. Going down several paths simultaneously to accomplish a goal was easy for him. He did it all the time. Like his unlikely ascendency to the vice presidency in 1969 and his consolidation of power in 1971, doing things independently, impulsively, and unexpectedly were intrinsic to his nature. Changing the status quo suited his demeanor, personality, and political needs.

Simultaneously, he was a tactician and a strategist. His methods for managing Israel, his Arab peers, his economy, and the superpowers were usually in some form of continuous formulation. His methods were in endless transition; his vision and goals were not. He was secretive and inscrutable about sharing his thoughts, particularly about concepts and initiatives.[5] To most advisers he did not give specific orders, but rather gave underlings a scope within which to operate. At times, he found his Foreign Ministry bureaucracy to be turgid, lacking a broad understanding of politics.[6] He disliked paperwork and details, leaving them to his advisers. He tired of bureaucrats, because they were consensus builders who sought to satisfy several constituencies of objectives simultaneously. When he needed them, he selectively used them as vehicles for propagating or implementing policy, not for making policy. He seldom shared all information on a particular matter. He might float a portion of an idea to someone close to see what would evolve, then allow someone else to react to another segment of the same thought. In this way, he received several responses without any one person knowing all the details. Then he collated the responses, sometimes acting on them, sometimes not. He rarely brought advisers together to discuss or ratify a policy choice. Sadat's meetings with foreign leaders were invariably one-on-one sessions in which his advisers and ministers were not included, thereby causing them inevitable embarrassment and inconvenience. For example, when Sadat and Kissinger met for the first time in November 1973, they talked privately, without advisers or note takers. In negotiating Sinai I, or the first Egyptian-Israeli disengagement agreement, in Aswan, Egypt, in January 1974, though his advisers were nearby, Sadat kept the negotiations with Kissinger to himself. He even admonished his foreign minister for intruding. His foreign minister from January to September 1978 was particularly vexed by being excluded from meetings in which foreign leaders discussed foreign policy issues. When Sadat met with Israeli Defense Minister Ezer Weizman at the end of March 1978, Weizman's counterpart, General el-Gamasy, was absent from the discussions. At times his advisers, like his foreign ministers, were peeved if not downright jealous that they did not enjoy the closeness and trust Sadat had with

Kissinger and later with Carter. That envy gnawed at their already skeptical feelings toward Washington, which was seen as blindly pro-Israeli. Since Sadat disliked the bureaucracy, he avoided its details. But he enjoyed the grand picture and was pleased to find in both Kissinger and Carter not only Americans he could trust but also, to his delight, exceptional minds and draftsmen willing to focus on the details.

Sadat was an actor who believed in grand and sometimes theatrical gestures. He expected others to be equally dramatic. He made the world his stage, kept friends and foes off balance, and used the media to shape public opinion. He was consumed by an eagerness to please and to be accepted by those in power and with authority. Wily and cagey, he played hide-and-seek and made diplomatic scheming his forte.[7] All too often, Sadat played fast and loose with the truth; he was not averse to stretching the boundaries of veracity. He would change his rendition of a story depending largely on the listener. He withheld bits and pieces of the whole story to make a point or create an effect. The rendition he told of an event yesterday was often changed in its telling the following day. Embellishing a story was just as commonplace. Toward the end of the 1973 War, when he exaggerated that something catastrophic was about to happen to the Israeli-surrounded Third Army, Soviet military estimates discounted his overblown assessment. In his speeches, time and time again he overstated and embellished his central role in the 1952 revolution. Soviet Foreign Minister Gromyko felt that Sadat, "had an extraordinary ability to distort facts and blatantly contradict himself [and] suffered from megalomania."[8] His manner thirsted for the daring and spectacular. His penchant for dropping political bombshells startled the Americans, shocked the Israelis, and disconcerted his own advisers. Sadat's foreign minister in 1977–1978, Mohamed Ibrahim Kamel, recalled, "I was mainly concerned with . . . the improvised and impulsive actions of President Sadat which he undertook without prior notice, thus deviating from the political and tactical line we were pursuing."[9] In negotiations, "even on major issues, he would sometimes, to everyone's surprise, give in because this could have a positive effect on the result or the adversary."[10] In appointing aides and ministers, he might ask them whether they wanted a job and then give them time to think about it; but before they responded affirmatively or not, or were even told of appointments, he would have their position announced on Cairo radio or in a press release.[11] In December 1977, he stunned his would-be new and profoundly anti-Israeli foreign minister by swearing him in in front of the first Israeli delegation to visit Cairo. In the Camp David negotiations, Sadat sometimes embarrassed or overruled his own trusted advisers in their presence in order to make a point with a foreign listener. He loved to do the contrary of what his advisers told him.[12] He frequently conceded a point in order to gain assurance of continued American support or to keep the negotiating process moving forward. Abruptly and without warning, he expelled Soviet advisers in July 1972. According to Omar Sirry, an Egyptian Foreign Ministry official, at the time, "It was typical of Sadat not to expect anything from the Americans in return for expelling the Soviet advisers."[13] As he went down the path of diplomacy, he became increasingly willing to sacrifice an asset in order to attain the goal. Eventually that meant giving up uniform Arab hostility to Israel and jettisoning the Palestinian cause, even if only temporarily, for Egyptian national interests. In sustaining Washington's interest in him, Sadat often made necessary compromises with Israel, which his advisers found unnecessary or too forthcoming. In 1978, during the months prior to the signing of the Camp David Accords, White House and State Department officials were constantly afraid that Sadat would give up any real support for the Palestinians just to have the Israelis withdraw from Sinai.

As Sadat's national security adviser noted, Sadat was a man "in a hurry":[14] impatient, wanting results, not wanting to be stymied or held back by the dilly-dallying of others. But Sadat also knew when to let an issue or policy simmer to a conclusion. His political will and courage kept the negotiating process moving forward. He kept his eye on the objective that diplomacy with the Americans meant the return of Sinai. Throughout his eleven years in office, Sadat retained control over this key policy area: relations with the United States and Israel, and dealings with Arab heads of state.

By outsiders, Sadat was seen as mercurial and unpredictable because he did not have a profound ideological base. His motives and actions were difficult to comprehend. These characteristics confounded his Arab contemporaries and Israelis alike. At home, Egyptian political commentators and domestic adversaries considered Sadat a "political clown for making grand but hollow statements, such as 1971 would be the 'year of decision' in the Arab-Israeli conflict."[15] By being both grandiose and erratic, he was able to mask successfully his strategic intentions to other Arabs, Israelis, Soviets, and Americans. His ability to keep his own counsel was also a liability. Sometimes the option Sadat chose was still in intellectual formation, not fully developed, not yet clear. Then he might make a course change along the way before coming to a conclusion. By making such changes, few could confirm or deny his real objectives. By going down several paths simultaneously, he camouflaged his true policy intentions. For him, maintaining parallel courses for action was normal. Consider this trajectory: while flirting with Washington in 1972 and 1973 to create a peaceful change in Sinai through negotiations, Sadat sent his defense minister to Moscow to buy arms. In November 1973, while Sadat directly and vigorously pursued the Kilometer 101 Talks regarding a separation of forces arrangement with the Israelis, he also dispatched Foreign Minister Fahmy to Washington with a detailed outline of the very points being negotiated at Kilometer 101. When Kissinger hit a stalemate in reaching another Egyptian-Israeli agreement in early 1975, Sadat sought out President Ford in an effort to avoid a drift. Constantly averse to allowing the diplomatic process to become fossilized, he repeatedly found ways to keep the negotiating dynamic fluid. At his 1975 meeting with Ford in

Austria, Sadat stressed the import of another Egyptian-Israeli disengagement agreement. Through Kissinger's offices, he told Rabin in 1975 that for every step Israel would make in the negotiations, Egypt would take multiple steps.[16] In late 1976, Sadat sought to probe Israeli readiness for another agreement, but the Israeli parliamentary election process eventually intervened to truncate that overture. In 1977, Sadat maintained a sincere desire to use a conference formula to reignite Arab-Israeli negotiations through American effort, but simultaneously tested the possibilities of direct negotiations by sending his emissary, Hassan Tuhami, to meet secretly first with the head of the Israeli Mossad in August, then a month later with Israeli Foreign Minister Moshe Dayan in Morocco. He went along with Carter's idea for convening a Middle East peace conference in pursuit of a comprehensive peace throughout 1977, but told Carter privately, then said publicly, that he would sign a separate peace treaty with Israel under certain conditions. When procedural knots tied up prospects for a reconvened Geneva Conference, Sadat went directly to the Israelis. While the Americans worked on an illusive declaration of principles in 1978 to engage other Arab parties after Sadat's trip to Jerusalem, he maintained his direct contacts with the Israeli defense establishment so that an agreement over Sinai would not fail to be achieved. When his relationship with Israeli Foreign Minister Dayan went sour, Sadat intentionally tried to use his developing friendship with Israeli Defense Minister Ezer Weizman to change Begin's political positions toward the West Bank and the Palestinians. In public he continuously articulated and defended comprehensive Arab interests, with Egypt taking its traditional leading role. In private, however, Sadat sent messages and undertook actions that clearly indicated Egypt wanted to take the lead in commencing diplomatic negotiations with Israel, leaving Arab counterparts to stew in their procrastination. In these many instances, Sadat lived and managed the middle ground.

Inconsistency, unpredictability, and uncertainty left mistrustful Israelis additionally skeptical about Sadat's intentions. Israel's extraordinarily cautious establishment judged Arab motivation through actions and verbal content analyses, not direct contacts, and found it difficult to read and believe Sadat. He confused the Israelis by keeping their decision makers off balance and inevitably in a quandary about determining the sincerity of his real intentions. Golda Meir, Yitzhak Rabin, and Moshe Dayan all were repeatedly uncertain about his true feelings toward Israel. No one could be sure whether on any given "Wednesday they would wake up and he [Sadat] would withdraw" some earlier idea.[17] For example, in May 1971, within weeks of consolidating power and jailing a pro-Soviet-leaning competitor, Sadat signed a Friendship Treaty with Moscow. Fourteen months later, Sadat calmly and without any warning expelled Soviet advisers from Egypt. For Israelis, as well as for the rest of the world, Sadat's habits with the Soviet Union seemed patternless. The sincerity of his objectives and credibility of his motives were usually in question. In the early 1970s, Israeli intelligence estimates of Sadat's intentions were clouded by the debate of the extent he was prepared to support an agreement with Israel, or to support the Palestinians. It took Israeli leaders a long time to comprehend that Sadat believed in the Palestinian issue and the defense of the Palestinian cause, but not as much as he wanted Sinai returned to Egyptian sovereignty. Israeli leaders repeatedly asked to what degree Sadat wanted to stay under the Arab cover of anti-Zionist sentiment, so aptly developed by Nasser, and use it for abusing Israel. Or was he genuinely interested in breaking with the past in order to go down an independent, but not necessarily separate, path toward an accommodation with Israel? When on November 9, 1977, he announced in the Egyptian Parliament that he would go to "the ends of the earth" to reach an accommodation, no one in Israel believed him. Sadat's inconstant and impetuous style only reinforced Israel's penchant for calibrated and cautious diplomatic reactions; those careful responses added to the prevailing view that Israel was stalling, not willing or capable of responding in kind to the gestures made by Sadat. Not certain about his motivations or direction, Israelis instead frequently asked for opinions about him and for assessments about his intentions from European and Washington policymakers. But no matter what response they received about Sadat, Israelis lived with a historically pervasive doubt about true Arab intentions. Policy shifts caused permanent Israeli consternation about Sadat's motives. His style did little to nullify Israeli anxieties.

Sadat lobbied for Washington's attention and assistance. When he got it, he wanted Kissinger or Carter to translate it into fulfilling requirements of other Arabs. In this way, the needs of other Arab states were important only if Washington kept its Arab focus primarily on Sadat and Egypt. Sadat persuaded Kissinger and Carter that he was serious about reaching a negotiated settlement, but defining a positive working relationship with the United States was always more important than normalizing relations with Israel. Developing the dialogue with Washington could translate into pressure on Israel to return territory, relieve Sadat of having to deal directly with Israel, and obtain financial and military assistance from the United States. Sadat wanted and needed credibility from Washington; he wanted to have America on his side. But he also realized that Washington would not abandon Israel. In essence, he "wanted the lawyer to work for both sides."[18] Since Sadat's long-term policy was predicated on making the United States his close friend, by necessity, that meant getting closer to Israel, a barely acceptable by-product of his grand strategy. In short, Sadat did not *want* to make peace with Israel; rather, he *needed* to make an arrangement with Israel in order to enhance the likelihood of a positive relationship with the United States. He realized he had to show Washington in sharp, graphic, and unmistakable terms that Egypt, under his tenure in office, could be important to American interests. However, Sadat would discover that grand individual gestures toward Washington were insufficient in meeting all of the objectives of American policymakers who still wanted to reduce Soviet influence in the

Middle East and find a comprehensive Arab-Israeli settlement. Sadat's whole philosophy was to create a united Egyptian-American front against the Israelis and channel Washington's role into that of mediator and honest broker and not just of Egypt's advocate.[19] As a case in point, in January 1974, Sadat and Israeli officials agreed on a minimal number of Egyptian tanks that would remain on the relatively small amount of land on the Suez Canal's East Bank, which Egypt had taken with great difficulty during the October War, a move that astonished General el-Gamasy, the Egyptian Army chief of staff. Sadat told el-Gamasy, "My dear General, we are talking about a long period of policy. Peace will not be hurt by ten tanks, or twenty tanks, or thirty tanks. We are planning for peace *with the Americans.*"[20] Sadat understood that if the United States were truly an "honest broker" in fact and in name, then Washington would surely be more sympathetic to the Arab view.

In the end, Sadat was the engine and motivation for Washington's reengagement in Arab-Israeli diplomacy; Sadat made it possible for American foreign policy to deal with an Arab leader. He provided Washington with a splendid package of political enticements: he willingly negotiated with Israel, anointed American mediation, and turned out the Russians. When he sought American engagement in support of an Egyptian view, he constantly corrected the course so it would best suit Cairo's interests. Even after his death in 1981, the United States continued to place its relationship with Egypt at the top of Middle Eastern diplomatic priorities vis-à-vis the Arab world. Close diplomatic relations with Egypt were a cornerstone of America's post–cold war relations with the Middle East. Opening that door was Sadat's long-term legacy to the United States. In a sense, Sadat was an Arab pioneer. He was the first Arab leader to create positive relations with Washington while retaining moorings to the Arab world. Other Arab political leaders were much slower to recognize that these dual relationships were not incompatible, but rather beneficial, to an Arab side that aligned with Washington.

Aligning with Washington meant Sadat was intentionally breaking Egypt's strategic relationship with the Soviet Union. There were two primary reasons for this deliberately planned May 1972 divorce. Sadat was frustrated that he was unable to obtain a supply of quality arms in a timely fashion, something necessary to fight Israel. Secondly, American military power and technology impressed him. Sadat was also taken with America's democratic system, especially its process of government that included listening to the views of the people.[21] But Sadat was no democrat. He believed all that really mattered was direct contact with American presidents.[22] He realized that authority, power, and influence in foreign affairs rested at the White House, first with Nixon and Kissinger and later with Carter. Gradually he came to dismiss the State Department and Secretary of State William Rogers's importance in influencing American foreign policy: he was particularly dismayed by the State Department's inability to find a positive response to his February 1971 initiative for an Egyptian-Israeli interim agreement. In contrast, though

Nixon faced a crescendo of domestic criticism, Sadat was impressed that the Vietnam talks still moved ahead with success.[23] He admired Nixon's resolve and thought Kissinger "was determined, had a sharp mind, was energetic, full of ideas, but at times exaggerated his role that he could do anything he wanted to do."[24]

Willingly, Sadat encouraged, even informally anointed, Kissinger and Carter as "Egypt's ambassadors" to Israel. To both, he needed to appear moderate, never extreme. To this end, his personal preference for traveling several paths suited Kissinger and Carter. Sadat regularly provided them with several options for moving the negotiating process forward, often giving both a front line *and* a fallback position and sometimes a private versus a public position.[25] Personally and professionally, Kissinger and Carter enjoyed the negotiating leeway Sadat provided. Even if Sadat's terms for an agreement were at times inflexible, his tone of moderation, of seeking an accommodation with Israel, could not be ignored by Kissinger or Carter. Sadat did not want history to characterize him as submitting to pressure, so he provided Kissinger and Carter with the parameters of an accepted settlement.[26] Carter particularly enjoyed knowing that Sadat had implicit trust in him. Indeed, their relationship was unique in comparison to all the other relationships Carter had with Middle Eastern leaders. For his part, Kissinger was not only taken by Sadat's character but also by his substantial shift away from Moscow.

Where Nasser's focus was pan-Arabism, Sadat's preference was "Egypt first." Egypt's territorial, economic, and psychological losses from the June 1967 War made its leaders, including Nasser and Sadat, uncomfortable. Sadat was particularly resentful of Egypt's diminished influence in the region.[27] First, Nasser's economic experiment in Arab socialism failed. Then, to worsen matters, after the June 1967 War, Egypt lost income from the Sinai oil fields, tourism, the closure of the Suez Canal, and the abandonment of the cities along the canal. Expenditures rose in absorbing refugees from those canal cities and in rebuilding the shattered army. Sadat disliked Egypt's dependence upon Arab oil states and Moscow. Egypt was aching with underemployment, unemployment, overpopulation, and demanding infrastructure needs. A week before the October 1973 War, Sadat estimated that the Egyptian economy was "at zero, with commitments till the end of the year which we will not be able to fulfill with the banks."[28] Sadat reflected a growing view in Egypt that if a choice had to be made, "Egyptianism" was far more important than pan-Arab commitments. To him, Cairo was the center of the Arab nation: without Egypt, the Arab world was without its core. Egypt was special, culturally unparalleled, more important than the other Arab countries. Indeed, Egypt had more than five thousand years of continuous history. All of this, therefore, made it superior. Sadat wanted to restore Egyptian leadership to its pre–June 1967 War status. He saw himself not only as Egypt's president but also Egypt's "father," an inherent authority not circumstantially bestowed upon him by political or parliamentary power, but his personal gift to his Egyptian family, which would *not* succumb to family or tribal squabbling. If it did, he would by dint of personal force pull the family out of its mire. In 1971, to indicate his beliefs, he changed the country's name from the United Arab Republic to the Arab Republic of Egypt. (Sadat's "Egypt first" policy thus began well before the October War.) Egyptian Foreign Ministry officials recalled that Sadat viewed himself as occupying "a pioneering role. . . . He would be able to move ahead, [and] the Arabs were going to follow; Egypt would lead the caravan."[29] Seeking to resurrect and revitalize Egyptian national dignity after its painful loss in the June 1967 War, he regularly told his advisers that he wanted to prove to the rest of the world, and to the United States in particular, that Egypt was "not a dead horse."[30] His view of putting Egypt first was not shared by many in Egypt's elite, establishment, media, and certainly not by his Foreign Ministry advisers. His Arab contemporaries vilified him for asserting Egypt's primacy.

Whereas Sadat cared only about Egypt, he was neither a lover of other Arabs nor of the Palestinians and used them all to serve his own purposes.[31] The cost of fighting for Palestine was considered at once both an extraordinary statement of Egypt's identity with the Palestinian question and an immense retardant to Egypt's development. In order to rehabilitate Egypt's economy, Egypt could no longer shoulder the main burden of the Arab cause—the Palestinian issue.[32] When he sent a general to negotiate with his Israeli counterpart after the October War, Israelis heard for the first time that Egypt was pragmatically finished with the Palestinian question. When he met with PLO leaders just after the 1973 War, he made them feel he was genuinely interested in their cause by supporting their claims to represent Palestinians politically, yet he never insisted that the PLO participate in the unfolding diplomacy after the war. When Sadat went to Jerusalem in 1977, and in the four years in between, he often spoke about defending Palestinian interests, but he went to Jerusalem to focus on Sinai first, then the remainder of the territories. Publicly, Sadat encouraged full implementation of UNSC Resolution 242 on all fronts and reinforced his commitment to the Palestinian quest for self-determination. What he changed over time was his emphasis on when Israel should withdraw from all the territories and the manner in which the Palestinian issue should be resolved. The looming question for Americans, Egyptians, Israelis, and other Arabs after the signing of the Camp David Accords, which had a Palestinian-Israeli component as well as an Egyptian-Israeli one, was the degree of linkage between the two elements. Sadat's answer was his signature on the March 26, 1979, Egyptian-Israeli Peace Treaty. In his speech at the Israeli Parliament in November 1977, Sadat did not jettison his commitment to the Palestinian question; in fact, he asserted that "ninety percent of the [Egyptian-Israeli] negotiations was on the Palestine problem."[33] But according to Usamah al-Baz, "Sadat had difficulty in finding a formula to propagate the Palestinian cause and promote a solution without speaking for the Palestinians. He felt speaking for them was a hazard. And at the same time, [Sadat] worried that they would not honor the commitments they made to him and he would then lose credibility with others."[34] (Jordan's King Hussein's disengagement from affairs of the West Bank fifteen years later was prompted, in part, by the same skepticism about PLO intentions and credibility.)

Where possible, necessary, and feasible, Sadat did prefer to work in collaboration with his Arab peers in achieving a comprehensive settlement with Israel. (Sadat did not like to incur criticism from his Arab brethren but withstood their censure when it came.) In turn and with surprising consistency, the Nixon, Ford, and Carter administrations were quick to believe that Sadat, or Egypt, could represent Syrian, Palestinian, or Jordanian interests. For his part, though ultimately favoring Syrian, Jordanian, and Palestinian participation in a comprehensive settlement in 1977, Sadat had neither the patience nor the temperament to wait for them to alter their ideology or to overcome their fears. One of the major reasons he had for going to Jerusalem in November 1977 was Washington's inability to find a mechanism for Palestinian representation to a Middle East peace conference. Sadat grew weary of Carter's idea of trying to stitch together a unified Arab delegation that included Palestinian and Syrian participation. He sensed that such a delegation was a sure way for Damascus to constrain his freedom of action in negotiating with the Israelis. Sadat knew well the jealousies, divisions, and shortcomings of Arab-world politics and the difficulty Arab states had in reaching consensus decisions; he also knew that his Arab colleagues would be reluctant to reach an accommodation with Israel. Believing his Arab contemporaries were procrastinators, at times he used inter-Arab wrangling and bickering to Egypt's benefit. Sadat's loudest detractor was Syria, and yet Damascus progressively used Sadat's tilt toward the United States and Israel to bolster its ties to Moscow increasingly on its own terms. On occasion, Sadat cleverly sought political cover from his Arab brothers in order to pursue self-ish Egyptian interests by supporting the PLO against Jordan in inter-Arab counsels. He obtained public credit for supporting their cause, but he knew that a discussion of Jerusalem or the West Bank would never come up, because Israel would not negotiate with the PLO. And to his favor, not discussing the West Bank or Jeru-salem's future kept the focus on Sinai. Neither in 1973 nor 1974 but in 1977 Sadat talked seriously about signing a separate peace with Israel and shared that idea pri-vately with Carter, his prime minister, and his minister of state for foreign affairs.[35] His willingness to break Arab ranks and deal with Israel independently generated a cataclysmic rupture in inter-Arab affairs.

After the October 1973 War, Sadat made all of the key decisions about Egyptian relations with the United States, the Arab world, and Israel. For these critical areas, he was his own foreign minister. With respect to Washington, after the 1973 War, he made two key political appointments that would both influence Cairo's future relationships with Washington and affect how and what decisions Egypt would make during the next four years in Egyptian-American-Israeli diplomacy. Ismail Fahmy became foreign minister; soon thereafter, Ashraf Ghorbal was named as

Egypt's ambassador to Washington. Both men greatly influenced the style and tone, but not the substance, of Egyptian-Israeli negotiations. Fahmy possessed strong views and prejudices. He coveted his status as foreign minister and used his authority and power to deflate the influence of colleagues. Fahmy believed he was important in the scheme of foreign policymaking, but he did not say or do anything unless Sadat knew about it first because Sadat determined the limits of Fahmy's influence on any given matter.[36] Fahmy managed the contacts with the UN and Moscow and was a staunch defender of the Palestinian cause, if not their champion among Sadat's advisers. Sadat did not object to Fahmy's toughness with the Syrians or aggressiveness with the Jordanians and let him implement the technical details surrounding the execution of his foreign policy. In time, because Sadat confided more with Kissinger than with Fahmy in making foreign policy decisions, the Sadat-Kissinger closeness exacerbated Fahmy's fraught relationship with Kissinger. It created envy and jealousy, which in turn reinforced Kissinger's preference for dealing directly with Sadat. In November 1977, Fahmy resigned in protest over Sadat's visit to Jerusalem. In his absence, Fahmy's Foreign Ministry protégés sustained their fervent commitment to the PLO's participation in subsequent negotiations. They philosophically linked up with Carter's Middle East advisers, who until the beginning of the September 1978 Camp David negotiations were intent on Sadat not signing a separate Egyptian-Israeli deal. In these emerging negotiations, Fahmy's departure meant Sadat's key contact with the Soviet Union and the United Nations was gone, tethering Sadat closer to Carter.

Ghorbal had a gentler personality and was much more affable than Fahmy. His experience and personality suited his appointment as Egypt's ambassador to Washington; he had served as head of the Egyptian interests section located under the auspices of the Indian embassy in Washington after the June 1967 break in diplomatic relations. He returned to Egypt and served as deputy national security adviser to Hafez Ismail and then, during the October 1973 War, as head of Sadat's press office. Though Sadat was cordial with Ghorbal, he did not particularly like or trust him. Ghorbal was hurt by Sadat's choice of Fahmy as foreign minister, a wound that lingered. After his appointment, Fahmy continuously considered Ghorbal a potential challenger to his position as foreign minister. Fahmy was nasty to Ghorbal, and their relationship was testy and peevish. Sadat frequently indicated to Americans in Cairo that he did not want Ghorbal involved in certain issues. Fahmy did his best to keep Ghorbal uninformed about certain foreign policy issues. Until the last minute, Fahmy tried to deny Ghorbal the chance to attend the Ford-Sadat meeting in Salzburg in 1975. Later, Fahmy tried unilaterally, without Sadat's knowledge and without success, to shift Ghorbal out of Washington to the less influential position as Egypt's permanent representative to the United Nations. In April 1977, Fahmy went so far as to demand that Kissinger not give Ghorbal Sadat's pending schedule of Washington meetings. Despite their discourteous, if not sometimes hostile, relations, Ghorbal did not resign lest he give Fahmy exactly what he wanted. In Washington, Sadat used Ghorbal's skills to build friendships in Congress, and with the Defense Department, the media, and American Jewish groups. He encouraged American decision makers to visit Cairo and meet their counterparts in an effort to generate a more positive understanding of Egypt's aspirations. While Ghorbal focused on American institutions and the American public, Sadat did not relinquish to him dealing with the American decision makers directly. In instances where it was necessary, Sadat allowed both Ghorbal and Fahmy to absorb the rancor that might come from the constituencies with which they dealt, thereby insulating Sadat's own personal responsibility to policy choices he made. Ultimately, Sadat took it upon himself to initiate, develop, and manage his desired relationship with Washington.

In order to go to war against Israel, Sadat needed at least one other active military front as insurance that Israeli forces would not be entirely concentrated on the Sinai front. Syrian President Hafez al-Assad and Sadat needed each other as partners in the evolving war-diplomacy relationship. Sadat had no doubt about who was the senior and who was the junior partner in this alliance, though Assad believed that it was an equal partnership. Assad was particularly vexed by the loss of the Golan Heights: it was a dishonor to have an Israeli presence on Syrian territory, the retention of which by Israel was absolutely untenable. This status quo had to be reversed. Indeed, Israel's very existence was anathema to Assad. Israel's territorial pressure interfered with Assad's aspiration to control or unite all of the lands contiguous to Syria. Assad was consistently uncompromising toward direct negotiations with Israel. When he took power in 1970, Assad sought to mobilize all resources for the liberation of all the occupied territories, especially the Golan. So committed was Assad to the liberation of Arab land, that according to Israeli military estimates gleaned after the war, Assad was prepared for an all-out war, "including, if necessary, the evacuation of Damascus."[37] The Syrian military needed rebuilding after its shattering loss in 1967; for that, Soviet arms were required and obtained. Assad's battle plan focused on a massive attack on the Golan Heights in the first few days of the war and then a cease-fire to be imposed by the United Nations to secure his military gains. He did not plan on a protracted campaign.[38] Assad's goal, said his foreign minister at the time, Abd al-Halim Khaddam, "was to liberate Syrian land, not to move to political [diplomatic] activity."[39] For Assad, diplomacy meant combining military power with Arab solidarity, securing a new status quo in favor of Syria, and restoring the Golan Heights without seeking an opening to Washington or engaging in negotiations that might normalize relations with Israel. Assad continued to reject UNSC Resolution 242 until 1973 because it legitimized Israel's existence.

From the war, Syria wanted to turn the clock back to the 1947 United Nations partition plan for Palestine and cut the Jewish state down to size if it could not be eliminated. Assad favored comprehensive Arab-Israeli negotiations and never supported separate Arab-Israeli agreements. But supporting negotiations did not mean recognition of Israel; it meant perhaps inking a nonbelligerency agreement at best. Assad wanted to control Sadat's political options and limit his readiness to negotiate with Israel. Both for the planning of the 1973 Geneva Conference and a Carter-planned Middle East conference in 1977, Assad favored a comprehensive format that would require a framework of topical, not geographic, committees. Assad wanted a veto power over Egypt's eagerness to sign agreements with Israel. Geographic committees would facilitate separate and bilateral agreements. In combining war and diplomacy, Assad wanted to execute a successful war against Israel, have Moscow weigh in on the Arab side, assure an early victory through a cease-fire, shift the balance of power significantly in favor of the Arabs, and create conditions necessary to force Israel to withdraw from any territories it still occupied at the end of the war. Assad, though militant in his beliefs, was not an encrusted ideologue. For example, he was committed to the liberation of Palestine, but he never let the Palestinian cause act as a detriment to Syrian interests. Instead, he believed in their cause but also used it to Syrian national advantage. Prior to the war, Assad did not have any plan to replace his Moscow connection with an embrace of Washington. Syria was a key beneficiary of Sadat's expulsion of his Soviet advisers in July 1972. Moscow's influence in Syria rose, and it provided Syria military equipment before, during, and after the war, but Assad did not allow it to influence Syria's sovereign decision making. He was furious when Moscow did not align itself with his priorities during and after the war. As a result, he neither allowed nor insisted that the Soviet Union be a part of Syrian-Israeli negotiations in 1974.[40] Assad's political mix in dealing with Israel was dominated more by force than by diplomacy; he believed that force and additional Israeli casualties would enable him to obtain better terms in his negotiations with Israel. What Assad did not know was that Sadat was eager to use diplomacy, turn heavily toward the United States, and when necessary break Arab ranks against Israel by signing separate agreements with Israel.

In the months before the outbreak of the October 1973 War, high levels of mutual suspicion existed between Egypt, Jordan, and Syria. Though Sadat, Assad, and King Hussein were consensus supporters of Arab unity, each had varying commitments to that goal; these Arab leaders did not get along well. Sadat considered Assad less than a personal or political equal, an expected position because Sadat placed Egypt's interest ahead of the priority of Arab solidarity. Assad believed Egypt would pursue an all-out war against Israel to liberate *all* of Sinai.[41] One observer noted, "Sadat and Assad swore an oath on the Koran, that both would go on fighting until they liberated all the occupied territories, or until Cairo and Damascus were occupied."[42] Assad believed that a coordinated attack against Israel would prevent Israelis from taking on each front separately. Assad recalled that it was decided that the Egyptian Army would move from a point 250 kilometers from the border and the Syrian Army from a point 20 to 30 kilometers from the border.[43] Assad threw all his military capacity into the war because he thought the war would be relatively short and a victory secured quickly; by war's end, his army was severely battered, with almost no strategic reserve left. During the war, there was little coordination of military planning between Syria and Egypt, poor tactical execution after the initial days of the war, and intentional disinformation sent from Egypt to Syria about the war's status or requests for a cease-fire.

Originally, Sadat considered one of two battle plan options, neither of which included the total liberation of Sinai by military force, but which would at least result in an entrenched Egyptian position on the east bank of the canal. Though both battle plan options included the sustained presence of Egyptian troops stretching along the entire 175-kilometer length of the canal, the first plan, known as Granite 1, included stopping the military advance 10 to 20 kilometers east of the canal. The second option, Granite 2, raised the possibility of reaching 65 kilometers into Sinai and taking the strategic Mitla and Gidi Passes, the key access routes through central Sinai, from Israeli control. But Sadat intentionally misled his Syrian ally.[44] He did not inform Assad that he had limited military objectives; Assad was unaware of Sadat's preference to stop his army's military advance after they crossed the canal. During the war, Sadat spurned repeated calls by Politburo and Soviet military leaders to generate some Egyptian-Syrian military coordination. Only as the war progressed did Soviet leaders understand that Sadat was willing to let the Syrians do whatever they liked; they understood that Sadat "was planning his own action."[45] Moreover, Assad did not think that Sadat, after going to war in tandem with Syria, would start a diplomatic offensive without Damascus. In a meeting on November 12, 1973, with Mahmoud Riad, the secretary general of the Arab League, Assad remarked, "The agreement between Sadat and myself before the war laid out that Egypt should occupy the Sinai Passes and not stop ten kilometers east of the canal."[46] Assad also was not privy to the rancorous debate within the Egyptian military over whether the Egyptian objective should be to go for the Sinai passes or simply cross the canal. Then immediately before the war commenced, the Syrians were told that the plan to be activated, Granite 2, involved an advance to the Sinai passes; but the order given to General Ahmad Ismail, the minister of war, was to implement Granite 1, which only envisaged a limited threat into Sinai.[47]

Assad and Sadat both preferred to keep King Hussein uninformed about details surrounding the coming war. Hussein did not know that Sadat wanted to exclude Jordan from a future diplomatic process. Jordanian relations with both Egypt and Syria were generally acrid and strained. In the two years before the October War, Sadat disliked and distrusted Hussein,[48] and Hussein feared Assad. All three disagreed on how to manage and resolve the Palestinian issue and, especially, about what to do about the future of the West Bank and Gaza territories. The Jordanians and the Palestinians were ensnared in angry military and political confrontations. Jordan's crackdown on the Palestinians in 1970–1971 precipitated the prospects for a severe Syrian-Jordanian military clash in September 1970. Syria broke diplomatic relations with Amman in 1971; Egypt did the same a year later. Hussein's 1972 United Kingdom Plan, which asserted Jordanian primacy over the Palestinian issue, the West Bank, and Jerusalem, was viewed antagonistically by Egypt and Syria as an ambitious Jordanian ploy to become the ruler of the land and the people on both sides of the Jordan River.[49] Third, Assad and Sadat knew that King Hussein and Israeli leaders had many "secret talks" about the future of the West Bank and Gaza; perhaps they even knew that since Golda Meir became prime minister in March 1969, she and her closest cabinet colleagues had promised that at some appropriate time in the future "a most sizeable part of the West Bank would revert to [Hussein]."[50]

On September 11, 1973, less than a month before the October War, Hussein met with Assad and Sadat in Egypt, where Egyptian-Jordanian diplomatic relations were restored. Jordanian-Syrian diplomatic relations were renewed in early October of the same year. Still, Jordan was not included in the planning for the October War, and Hussein had no idea that Sadat had limited military objectives. Anyone observing from the outside would have easily interpreted Egypt's restoration of diplomatic relations with Amman in the context of preparations for some still-undefined diplomatic offensive. And yet, Jordan's prime minister, Zaid Rifa'i, claimed that while he did not know that the war was coming, the Jordanians sensed that one was in the offing: "Something was bound to blow."[51] As Sadat devised his war plans, he considered the postwar diplomacy. He did not want the more complicated issue of the West Bank's future or the uncertainty and fractious nature of the Jordanian-Palestinian relationship intruding into his plans for an Egyptian-centered postwar diplomacy and reasoned that if Jordan joined the war in a full-fledged fashion, it would be centrally involved in postwar diplomacy. According to Jordan's Rifa'i, "The best way not to involve Jordan in the negotiations was not to have Jordan as a belligerent."[52]

At their tripartite summit meeting in September, Sadat explored with Hussein the possibility of allowing the Palestinians to use Jordanian territory as a jumping-off point for future guerrilla attacks against Israel. The Jordanians denied the request. Independent of their discussions, Jordanian leadership reasoned that, in the event of war, Amman could not afford to be dragged in like it had been in the June 1967 War. In the October War, when the Syrian military condition on the Golan area greatly deteriorated after a series of Israeli counterattacks, Jordan did send two brigades to assist them; otherwise, Jordan remained out of the war. According to Rifa'i, "During the war itself, Sadat sent messages to us saying, 'Don't get involved in the war, keep out, look after your own boundaries and borders.' . . . Any loss on the Jordanian front would undermine his successes and military victories on his front. And at the same time we were getting continuous telephone calls and messages from the Syrians, telling us, 'What are you waiting for?' Later we understood from the Syrians that Sadat was telling the Syrians to tell us to open another front."[53] The Jordanians constantly questioned Sadat's sincerity. King Hussein believed, after not being told about the exact date for the coming war, that Sadat repeatedly used Jordan to fulfill Egyptian objectives.[54] After the war, Fahmy and his Jordanian counterpart were more than suspicious of one another: they would not even speak in public[55] and were ice-cold toward one another at the December 1973 Middle East Conference at Geneva. For their part, Jordanian leaders felt Sadat was deceptive, if not duplicitous. King Hussein and his prime minister, Zaid Rifa'i, believed Sadat used Jordan to provide Arab cover for the 1973 Geneva Conference and then *intentionally* complicated the Jordanian-Palestinian relationship by supporting the 1974 Rabat Arab Summit Resolution, the result of which was to keep Israel and Washington focused on Egypt and not on fostering a Jordanian-Israeli disengagement agreement. "Sadat," Hussein said, "understood that if the PLO was the sole representative of the Palestinian people, then Israel and Jordan could not work out a separate arrangement between them."[56] Sadat never focused on Jordan's West Bank territorial aspirations, except insofar as it aided Egyptian interests. Said Eilts, "Sadat frankly didn't give a damn about Hussein in Jordan."[57] Some in the Egyptian Foreign Ministry believed that Hussein was also not always scrupulously candid with Sadat or Assad. One American State Department official remarked that many in the Egyptian Foreign Ministry, and particularly Sadat himself, believed that the Jordanian leadership could not be trusted to keep a confidence.

As for Israeli decision making during the October War, it was Meir's so-called "Kitchen Cabinet" that managed policymaking. A handful of people provided critical input to the prime minister. They included Deputy Prime Minister Yigal Allon, Defense Minister Dayan, Finance Minister Pinhas Sapir, Chief of Staff David Elazar, Minister without Portfolio Israel Galili, Ambassador to the United States Simcha Dinitz, and a few others, among them some retired generals. Within that group of Meir's advisers and cabinet ministers, there was a continuous, and often obvious, competition for access to information and policy influence carried out through a network of colleagues, protégés, and political allies. Before the war, Meir was not adverse to making her own critical decisions about the security of the state. She listened carefully to what her military advised her, weighed options and consequences, and then went with her instincts shaped by more than a quarter century of experience in Israeli foreign and domestic affairs. But the shock of the war caused her to be more deliberative and consultative in making decisions affecting Israeli security. After the war, she brought more issues before the cabinet for its perusal, review, and debate.[58] Meir was also limited by domestic political considerations—she feared the loss of her parliamentary plurality and weathered the public anger and trauma from the war. In Washington, she trusted her ambassador to watch and clarify what Kissinger was doing in regard to Israeli interests. By comparison, Israeli Foreign Minister Abba Eban played only a minor role in directing foreign policy and regulating the diplomatic course that unfolded during and after the war. When Rabin was Israel's ambassador in Washington, Meir had intentionally circumvented Eban and the Foreign Ministry in favor of her ambassador as the direct reporting link to the White House. In fact, for much of the war, Eban was out of the country. Meir did not trust Eban, so information was regularly kept from him.[59] She felt that he was not "hawkish" enough on strategic matters and was too often too closely associated with the American viewpoint. Those high up in the Labor Party considered Eban brilliant and extraordinarily eloquent, but he was not considered tactically minded and possessed no sense of administration. Some believed he was not Kissinger's match because he did not have operational practicality to overcome a diplomatic impasse or hurdle. Instead, Eban thought about broader issues. All the important cables to Washington were drafted and sent from the prime minister's office and intentionally shortened for him. Other cables not intended for Eban's eyes were sent via CIA communications, as opposed to regular Foreign Ministry channels. These included daily cables to Kissinger, informing him of the military status during the war. Because Eban was on the sidelines during and after the war, the Foreign Ministry was also on the decision-making periphery, sometimes "completely out of the picture."[60]

On the other hand, Simcha Dinitz, Israeli ambassador in Washington, played a central role in the unfolding diplomacy: Dinitz was Meir's man in Washington, because she trusted him a great deal. Historically, most Israeli prime ministers retained policy formulation for themselves in matters dealing with the Arab world and the United States. With perhaps the notable exception of Moshe Dayan, later as foreign minister under Menachem Begin, the Israeli prime minister always made the final decisions about foreign policy matters, especially vis-à-vis the critical relationship with the United States and when issues of state security were pending. With Dayan, Begin was only occasionally upset or skeptical of his trying to make foreign policy choices on his own. During the October War, Golda Meir had full faith in Dinitz. They had worked together harmoniously when he was the director general of the prime minister's office, before going to Washington in March 1973. Meir's confidence in Dinitz, like Rabin before him, caused Nixon and Kissinger to understand that Israeli Ambassador Dinitz alone spoke authoritatively on behalf of the Israeli prime minister.[61]

When Meir resigned in May 1974 and Yitzhak Rabin replaced her, the Israeli government remained trusting of Arab intentions, even with disengagement agreements signed by then with Egypt and Syria. Rabin's attitude was to rebuild Israel's morale, army, and resolve and to enhance the strategic relationship with the United States. Rabin was in no hurry to negotiate with Jordan. And since Rabin was only appointed as Meir's successor, without an electoral mandate, he was an "accidental" prime minister and moved slowly. To lessen his confidence, Rabin had barely beaten Shimon Peres for the Labor Party leadership. Unlike Meir, however, Rabin brought a strategic view of politics to his new office. Brilliant, somewhat shy, sometimes brutally frank, Rabin was a lone wolf, yet he did believe in the "chain of command." Loyalty was an extraordinarily important virtue for anyone working with him. When Rabin learned that an Israeli Washington embassy official was carrying on discussions behind his back, he summoned the longtime civil servant to his office and summarily sent him back to Israel. Rabin was confident in his own counsel on matters relating to security; he did not have to rely upon generals and analysts for political and military estimates. On several occasions as prime minister when intelligence officials provided him with weighty evidence, maps, and information about a possible Syrian attack, Rabin reviewed the raw data himself and, after listening to their request for a partial mobilization of Israeli forces, simply blurted out, "Bullshit."[62] Thrust as he was into the role of prime minister, his wide experience in the military and his stint in Washington made him ideal to represent Israel in the strategic discussions about future withdrawals that ensued with Kissinger. As for Sadat, Rabin rightly viewed him as fickle. To achieve a successful agreement with him, Rabin believed it important "to establish facts on the ground and structure the deal so that it would pay for him to honor it, or at least hurt him if he did not."[63]

For Israelis and Arabs alike, Moshe Dayan personified Israel's successful struggle against the Arab world. He had one of those unique historical links going back to Israel's prestate period. His public credibility came from his successes in the 1948 Independence War, the October 1956 Sinai campaign, and his leadership in the June 1967 War. Dayan was a true national hero. He possessed an insightful mind and, like Yitzhak Rabin, understood the interrelationships between contemporary tactics and long-term strategy. Tireless, he sought imaginative ways to overcome problems. He exhibited indispensable qualities for a successful negotiator: persistence, tenacity, and creativity to rethink and rework a difficult issue. Self-confident about his knowledge of the Arab world, Dayan believed "he was the best qualified person to negotiate with the Arabs."[64] He was a natural introvert "who never felt that he was part of the inner clique, but his loyalty to Golda, [and later] Begin, or to friends was part of his nature,"[65] and his maverick personality did not make him an easy and close confidant for others. Dayan knew how close Meir was to Galili and was aware of the confidence she had in him. Although Dayan did not like that, he was, nonetheless, a realist; at times, out of necessity to accomplish an objective, he would approach Galili in hopes of winning his approval or endorsement for an idea prior to presenting the notion to Meir. And despite Dayan's detached style, Meir had great faith in his extraordinary ability to conceptualize political issues and lead the Defense Ministry and the war effort. He had his own distinctive views about politics and policies, but he remained loyal to Meir once she made a decision. And though he did not always like the choices she made, he inevitably stood by them, even when they dealt with military matters where he thought he knew better. During and after the October War, Dayan sensed that the Israeli people had lost confidence in him as defense minister. Before the end of the first week of the war, though he told Meir that he was capable of bringing the war to a successful conclusion, he still submitted his resignation to her; she retained her faith in him, particularly in his judgments on military matters, and did not accept his resignation. Meir felt Dayan could do the job as well as anyone. Furthermore, an acceptance of his resignation in the midst of the war would certainly not send a message of confidence to the already traumatized Israeli population.[66] Before the war had ended, Dayan suggested that an investigation be considered regarding the preparations and management of the war. Dayan's thinking on this point was preliminary, but he wanted an inquiry that would satisfy the public's need to know what happened prior to and after the outbreak of the war. Dayan understood the role of accountability and responsibility in political and military matters. He knew such an inquiry would invariably lay some of the responsibility at his own feet; still he wanted a proper investigation that would satisfy the general public. Not everyone in Meir's cabinet agreed with an investigation, but all consented that if one was to be held, then it would be after the parliamentary elections.

Already in 1971, Dayan had publicly stated the importance of removing Egypt from the circle of Arab enemies surrounding Israel. He believed staunchly that any constructively negotiated arrangement had to include the Americans, for only they could persuade Israel's Arab neighbors, only they could continue to provide Israel with its qualitative edge in military equipment. In spite of his differences with Kissinger and later with President Jimmy Carter for their respective "alliances" with Sadat, he instinctively knew that Egypt's physical and political demise as an active opponent of Israel would transform the Arab-Israeli conflict to Israel's advantage. And like the preponderance of Washington's official view, Dayan was also apprehensive about the Soviet presence in the area. During the June 1967 War, he delayed the conquest of the Golan Heights because he feared Soviet intervention.[67] During the 1970 War of Attrition, he found it particularly worrisome that Israeli aircraft had encountered Russian pilots flying Egyptian airplanes over the Suez Canal area. Dayan had no doubts that Israel could defeat the Arab armies eventually, but confronting Soviet pilots was "one of his most difficult moments during the October War."[68] As long as Dayan was involved in shaping Israel's relations with the Arabs, wherever possible he sought to avoid confrontation with Moscow. He wanted to reduce or remove their presence in the area by riding on the coattails of a similar American interest.[69] In much of this, Dayan and Kissinger were protagonists: they did not always trust one another, but they respected each other's motivations and political actions. Dayan appreciated Kissinger's vision, analytical talents, intelligence, and dedication to the cause of peace. Both were shrewd, independent thinkers. But Dayan repeatedly reminded those who would listen that "[Kissinger] was not on Israel's payroll, his advisers were on the American payroll, and though sympathetic to the Jewish people . . . as an American he did not understand the Arab mind."[70] During the October War, though Dayan understood that the Egyptian Third Army should not be destroyed, he still sought its surrender, and he blamed Kissinger for preventing that outcome. Dayan wanted to humble Sadat and felt that Kissinger prevented that from happening. When it came to negotiating the first Egyptian-Israeli disengagement agreement, discussions were frank, sometimes brutal, but commonly based on wanting to reduce significantly Soviet influence and presence in Egypt and the Middle East. Dayan's concern over the Soviets resurfaced in October 1977, when he vigorously repudiated the Carter administration's effort to reintroduce the Soviet Union as an active cochair for a proposed Middle East peace conference.

When Menachem Begin was elected prime minister in May 1977, singularly important to the success of Egyptian-Israeli negotiations was Begin's inclusion of Moshe Dayan as foreign minister. Living with the unpleasant memories of the October 1973 War, Dayan saw this appointment as an opportunity to repair his public image. Although cleared of personal responsibility by the Agranat Commission, which investigated Israel's performance in the October War, the Israeli public still held him accountable for casualties, deaths, and the ill-preparedness of the Israeli Army prior to the war. Dayan knew that he would not be elected as prime minister from the Labor Party, so casting his lot with Begin in this key decision-making role was an advantageous political choice. Dayan's inclusion in Begin's cabinet was an important bridge to the earlier Nixon-Kissinger period of diplomacy. On foreign policy matters, Dayan found himself more compatible with Begin than with his Labor Party contemporaries. Dayan's diplomatic engagement meant that, for the duration of negotiations with the Arabs, Israeli sovereignty would not be extended over the territories. This was a private commitment Dayan obtained from Begin prior to accepting the position of foreign minister.[71]

Leaving open the question of the future sovereignty of the West Bank was an absolute necessity for the success of future negotiations: it made it possible for Sadat and the Americans to negotiate about the territory upon which Palestinian autonomy would be defined and eventually applied. With the West Bank, Dayan did not believe in territorial concessions to Jordan, nor did he support the notion that Israel should retain areas in the Jordan Valley, which he felt could be easily taken in another conflict. Instead, he advocated functional compromise with the Palestinians, including some measure of sharing the territory but providing the Palestinians an opportunity to run their own affairs. (Separating the functions of Palestinian self-rule from Israel's insistence on security responsibility was how Palestinian autonomy was defined after Camp David and again by Israeli and Palestinians in the implementation of the 1993 Israeli-PLO Oslo Accords.) Dayan advocated some form of national referendum in Israel if there was ever to be any consideration of ceding territory. Dayan and Begin found considerable compatibility around the concept of Palestinian autonomy. Dayan supported the idea for practical reasons: the need for coexistence with the Palestinians. Begin supported it because he could not allow foreign sovereignty over any of the land of biblical Israel. Dayan also sensed that at times Begin was moving too slowly in the negotiations with the Egyptians. Begin sensed Dayan's frustrations and even was wary of his foreign minister's willingness to negotiate beyond limitations they mutually established. Begin thought that Dayan would provide access to foreign chancellories, because Dayan had an international reputation, was experienced in dealing with the Arabs, and was a noted soldier. For Begin, who at his election was unknown internationally, it was crucial to appoint someone who had an identity abroad, someone to provide legitimation for the untested Likud leader in the eyes of the United States.[72]

American Secretary of State Cyrus Vance had enormous respect for Dayan, though they frequently disagreed on matters of substance. Dayan considered Vance an honest and straightforward lawyer, a man of integrity. There was an undefinable chemistry between them; in contrast, the Dayan-Carter relationship was strained. Yet, Carter had great respect for Dayan, because he possessed vision and flexibility.[73] Dayan respected Carter's diligence, dedication, and resourcefulness to see agreements concluded. "If not for Carter," said Dayan, "we [Israelis and Egyptians] would not have arrived at a final agreement."[74] Dayan understood that there was a deep philosophical compatability between Washington's Middle Eastern bureaucrats and Sadat's advisers. He tried whenever possible to deal only with Vance, to elevate constantly the level of critical negotiations, keeping them away from the lower bureaucratic ranks, where acceptance of Israel's viewpoints tended to be more rigid.[75]

When Begin initially took office, Sadat was pleased that Dayan was Israel's foreign minister. But as Sadat negotiated with Dayan secretly through third parties, he found him to be less flexible than he had initially hoped. There was mutual respect between them but "no chemistry."[76] It was Dayan with whom Sadat's emissary, Hassan Tuhami, had secret talks in Morocco in September 1977. But when Dayan asked an Egyptian official during Sadat's visit to Jerusalem that same November if Sadat were prepared to sign a separate agreement with Israel, Dayan's star fell and that of Israeli Defense Minister Ezer Weizman correspondingly rose in Sadat's eyes. Sadat might have told Carter and others that he would consider recognition or a separate agreement with Israel, but that question was impertinent for Dayan to ask, let alone for it to be answered. By 1978, Sadat felt that Dayan was devious and untrustworthy. General el-Gamasy felt that Dayan was responsible for the Egyptian defeat in 1967. For Egyptians and most Arabs, Dayan was the "dark side" of Israel.[77] At the end of the day, Sadat and Dayan were pragmatists; Dayan's participation in the negotiations at Camp David, along with legal adviser Aharon Barak and Defense Minister Ezer Weizman in the Israeli negotiating delegation, was critically important in persuading an ideologically committed Begin to make the necessary verbal, if not territorial, concessions over Sinai. And after Camp David concluded and negotiations ensued about defining aspects of Palestinian autonomy, Dayan repeatedly made proposals that were aimed at unblocking negotiations, including a notion later accepted by the PLO and Israel in the 1990s, the application of Palestinian self-rule in Gaza first. Dayan resigned from Begin's cabinet in November 1979 because he felt that Begin was procrastinating in the application of Palestinian autonomy.

For twenty-nine years, until his election as prime minister in May 1977, Menachem Begin led the parliamentary opposition to Israel's dominant Labor Party. Like Meir, Rabin, and Dayan, Begin was an integral part of Zionist history and politics before the state's establishment. He was from the Holocaust generation, whose closest relatives had been killed. He was driven with an emotional fervor to guard against a future holocaust. The image and memory of Nazi destruction of Jews was always paramount in his decision making. When Palestinians attacked Israelis, he likened them to the dreaded Nazis.[78] For Begin, the PLO was anathema; its goal was to destroy Israel and create a Palestinian homeland or state that would, in Begin's eyes, simply become a Soviet outpost. Consumed with Jewish history, he was defensive about any attempt to impugn Israeli legitimacy. His mind-set focused on making decisions based upon one question and one question only: "Is it good or bad for the Jewish people?"[79] That Begin ultimately made any agreement with the Palestinians is truly remarkable; that he actually signed the Camp David Accords, which declared their "legitimate rights," was an ideological compromise and distance whose only remote equivalence was perhaps Sadat's brazen trip to Jerusalem.

In the 1940s, Begin led the Irgun, a small paramilitary Jewish organization that used violence in attacking British soldiers, their installations, and Arab civilians. Begin's Irgun was responsible for bombing British headquarters at the King David Hotel in July 1946 and other acts aimed at forcing the British and Palestinian Arabs from what they considered the historic Jewish homeland. A lawyer by training, Begin possessed an extraordinary, analytical mind with a phenomenal memory. Willingly and eagerly, he immersed himself in every detail and legality associated with policies, politics, and the processes of negotiations. He paid meticulous, if not excessive, attention to specifics. In addition to reading the usual material of cables and intelligence estimates, Begin voraciously devoured the texts of important documents, previous understandings, and agreements. Accuracy and precision epitomized his actions, words, and deeds. He generally kept his own counsel, yet he had implicit trust in those around him and would frequently listen to many opinions and considerable advice before making a decision. He rarely took notes at meetings. His oratorical skills were outstanding, capable of keeping an audience enthralled by his content and tone. When he delivered Israel's response to Sadat's speech at the Knesset in November 1977, he did it without either a note or a prepared text. Begin was a gentleman, but he had a contentious side. He was argumentative and often interrupted others as they spoke. Begin was a skilled politician, but not a seasoned diplomat. He was great at making his point, but less successful at making compromises or trade-offs. In Israel and abroad, he had a reputation of being a hard-line, right-wing Israeli politician who affirmed that the West Bank territories of Judea and Samaria would remain forever connected to Israel.

For Begin, Judea and Samaria were not occupied lands; they were liberated territories. He adamantly rejected any territorial compromise that included the return of Arab sovereignty to the West Bank, which he referred to by the biblically derived geographic names of Judea and Samaria. Retaining Judea and Samaria was not some sophisticated negotiating ploy; it was not an opening position in discussions; Judea and Samaria simply were not on the negotiating agenda. Retaining Judea and Samaria was his closing position; they were the heart of the biblical land of Israel; they were part of its fiber. When he spoke about these territories, there was a reverent, unshakable attachment. Judea and Samaria were inextricably connected to the historical renaissance of Zionism and the geography of modern Israel. Begin carried this ideology with him his entire life; he did not adopt this attitude when he became prime minister in order to be a tough negotiator. In believing that others could hold these views too, Begin was to some degree naive. He felt that if someone did not sense this special feeling about the wholeness Judea and Samaria brought to the Jewish people, if he or she were to listen to Begin's logical and reasoned explanation about why these territories should be integral parts of the state of Israel, that person would automatically understand and clearly accept his just and well-argued viewpoint.[80] Begin thought that once Carter understood that the land of Israel had been liberated by Jews from earlier British occupation, then he would automatically understand why the results of the June 1967 War completed the geographic outline of the Jewish state started in the Independence War of 1948. Besides, the Arabs already had twenty-one states where they exercised political expression; they did not need a twenty-second state in Judea and Samaria. Well before the June 1967 War, Begin had recognized that Jordan was a political reality, even if it sat on what Begin considered part of the land of Israel. Jordan was there, period. Before 1967, Begin asserted that Israel would not wage war to liberate Judea and Samaria, or even Jerusalem; nonetheless, these areas were still part of the land of Israel. Begin would say, "When the Arabs attack us, we are going to repel the enemy, throw them out, and do it on their territory; then we shall fulfill the right that this is our territory."[81] For Begin, the result of the June 1967 War was the logical climax of a clearly articulated vision that would not be reversed by politicians or diplomacy. Sadat's unwavering compulsion to have Sinai fully returned to Egyptian sovereignty was analagous to Begin's absolute intent to keep Judea and Samaria for Israel and the Jewish people.

Sadat and Begin had much in common, but still they could not effectively work together without an intermediary. Each was a fiercely committed nationalist and a proud founding contributor to his country's modern struggle for independence. Each had participated in violent underground activity against the British in his respective country's quest for independence in the 1940s. From the 1940s up through the 1960s, each was relegated to subordinate political status in his country. Nevertheless, each waited patiently, and not always easily, for his turn to influence history. Sadat was a relatively unknown participant in the 1952 revolution and stayed in the shadows even as vice president of Egypt in the late 1960s. Begin too paid his historical dues, but he was active in Israeli politics from, literally, before the beginning. When each achieved the highest political office in his country, each sought peer and foreign recognition for his contribution to the national struggle for independence. In part, both were driven by a need to be accepted by their country-men as worthy stewards defending their countries' national sovereignty. Each needed and wanted respect for the contributions made to his nation's struggle for independence. Both of them sought Washington's approval, acceptance, and diplo-matic involvement in the negotiating process. Both intensely disliked the Soviet Union. Each sought to attain, if not surpass, the political legitimacy and luminary status of his erstwhile predecessor. Each was staunchly adamant about protecting his country's right to make independent sovereign decisions. Outsider coercion or a decision made by another on their country's behalf was unacceptable. On the mat-ter of a conference, for example, neither Sadat nor Begin were great enthusiasts, since each feared losing his individual prerogative to other attendees. Sadat pre-ferred conferences for which agendas or agreements were prenegotiated. Both were willing to make a position speech at a conference, but strongly preferred to have substantive details for an agreement worked out in advance. A conference, in effect, occurred just for show.[82] Each was suspicious and yet familiar with political intrigue. On the other hand, to some degree and at certain times, both were naive about political realities because they were dedicated to the righteous nature of their respective causes. Both were never averse to embellishing reality for political bene-fit and for the objectives they sought. It was not uncommon for each one of them after a meeting with the other, or with Carter, to put their personal spin on an issue, sometimes quite distant from what was actually said between conferring principles. After Sadat's trip to Jerusalem and Begin's return visit to Egypt the fol-lowing month, both leaders endured verbal abuse from domestic opponents. Though some of their lifelong friends abandoned them in opposition to both the peace ini-tiative and Israeli withdrawal from Sinai, they both exhibited political courage and willpower to stay the negotiating course. These disagreements with domestic de-tractors were neither bland nor passing phenomena. They were, in fact, angry and prolonged personal attacks. Nevertheless, Begin and Sadat remained steadfast in seeing agreements made between their two countries.

In the aftermath of Sadat's Jerusalem visit, Begin tried to convince himself that he and Sadat had established a special friendship upon which to build a relationship between Egypt and Israel. At the same time, Sadat now viewed Begin as the obstacle to peace.[83] By the late spring and early summer of 1978, after several meetings with Begin, Sadat simply disliked being in the Israeli prime minister's presence. And though his animosity grew, it did not diminish Sadat's assessment that Begin had "a strong personality and was able to control his cabinet because of his extensive experience."[84] Begin placed enormous emphasis on procedure and the use of terminology, while Sadat was interested in the broader substance and the grand scheme of things. Concurrently, and a definitive sign that he did not want to abandon his initiative despite his differences with Begin, Sadat began to host other Israeli politicians in an intentional effort to circumvent, influence, and circumscribe Begin's seemingly uncompromising attitude. Both leaders were blocked in their ability to compromise with one another because of the recent and tense history between their two nations. They were also hampered by the difference in their political objectives and leadership styles. Sadat sought to restore territory that was rightfully Egyptian, whereas Begin feared that returning land would be an unwelcome precedent for his ideological imperative of retaining Judea and Samaria. Sadat possessed a vision for Egypt's future, whereas Begin was preoccupied with the symbols of recognition long denied Israel as a state. Begin passionately needed to protect his definition of Israel's security and integrity because the lives and well-being of the Jewish people were endangered. Any decision Israel made vis-à-vis Egypt was made in a broader context of what that decision would mean to Israel's strategic relationship with other Arab states; Egypt's task was easier; all it wanted was Sinai, and it did not have much worry in negotiating with Israel about defense and security matters in relation to surrounding Arab neighbors. Sadat always tried to retain the diplomatic initiative and wanted a tangible outcome in the shortest time possible. Since Begin preferred to move more methodically, he often found himself reacting uncomfortably to Sadat's desire for quick progress. Sadat disliked being smothered by a mountain of paper from reports and analyses and was impatient with the technicalities of an issue, whereas Begin crossed every "t."

On those rare official occasions when Begin and Sadat were in each other's presence, they were conscious of how their remarks would be heard by a broader audience. Whatever they decided between them had to be sold to uncertain but attentive domestic listeners and interested constituents beyond their borders. When they discussed sensitive topics or core political questions with one another, these electric moments were almost always cordial and inevitably brief. Based on the historical context of their national animosities, their meetings were constantly overwhelmed by media coverage of two former "anti-imperialist fighters" now speaking directly. When they were together, the personal competition was inevitable and overt. Each was a superb showman and a stylish performer in front of the world audience—both wanted to steal the show, as Sadat did when he went to Jerusalem.[85] When Golda Meir was asked if Begin and Sadat deserved the Nobel Peace Prize after Sadat's trip to Jerusalem, she responded without hesitation, "I do not know if they should get the Nobel, but they certainly deserve an Oscar." When Sadat and Begin tried to negotiate political issues with one another without active American involvement, they created more friction than substantive progress. When left to negotiate political matters alone, they endowed the diplomatic atmosphere with fanfare and inauspicious accents of drama and dislike. The brief moments where they appeared to agree dissipated into misinterpretation and bitterness. In days and weeks following one of their meetings, each man was convinced of the justice and righteousness of his own position and cause. Both felt that their philosophies were insufficiently understood and inadequately appreciated by the other. In the periods between diplomatic meetings, Begin and Sadat would urge American support for their side of an agreement or position. Frequently, headway was made by their advisers, especially on military matters such as troop withdrawals, the boundaries of limited force zones, types of personnel and equipment to be placed in such zones, and timetables for implementation of nonpolitical agenda items. Though they only met formally a few times at Camp David, they did meet on the camp's walking paths; and when Camp David participants broke for a day's intercession to visit the Gettysburg Civil War battlefield, the two of them spent hours in the car together, where even banter and joke telling passed between them. Carter insisted that no Arab-Israeli politics be discussed that day. While others in their delegations discussed the military and political implications of the Gettysburg battle, Begin listened. Then, to everyone's surprise, ever the man of history, while Carter teared up, Begin recited verbatim Lincoln's Gettysburg address. After Camp David, Begin acknowledged that they had "harsh exchanges," but estimated that a "good relationship was established between them."[86] On state occasions, Begin and Sadat met ten times: in Jerusalem in November 1977, in Ismailiya the following month, at Camp David in September 1978, in Washington at the peace treaty signing in March 1979, in Cairo in April 1979, in El-Arish and Beersheba in May 1979, in Alexandria in July 1979, in Haifa in September 1979, at Aswan in January 1980, and near Ophira in southern Sinai in June 1981. None of these meetings fully resolved the key political differences, but Sadat and Begin did agree to continue to exchange ideas with one another, knowing always that American mediation was close by.

Sadat and Begin's inability to get along with one another created the necessary gap for Carter to eventually fill. In addition to his own quest for legitimacy and recognition in Washington, Begin was jealous of the compatibility and closeness in the emerging Carter-Sadat relationship. Begin's view of Carter was that of a "rejected lover who was trying desperately to find a way to get back into the good graces of his beloved. It was difficult for him . . . but Begin suppressed his disappointment about Sadat's prior and preferred position with Carter."[87] Begin appreciated Carter, especially his enormous attention to detail, capacity for work, and commitment to find a settlement between Israelis and Arabs. To his credit, Carter demonstrated his characteristic endurance listening to Begin's frequent, lengthy, and discursive journeys into a review of Jewish suffering in the modern world. Carter understood that Begin needed to explain himself in legal and historical terms. He often soothed Begin's ego and his need for approval by communicating with him through personal letters. Success in the September 1978 Camp David negotiations was positively influenced by the emerging trust Begin developed for Carter and by Begin's yearning for approval from the American president.

Earlier, during the Nixon administration, domestic and foreign policies were centralized in the White House, and the National Security Council office dominated Nixon's foreign policy-making process. This satisfied Kissinger's predilection, if not passion, for secrecy. It also dovetailed nicely with Nixon's personal paranoia. As for Nixon's attitude toward Jews and Israel, he was not a great lover of the Jewish people, but he admired the Israelis for their no-nonsense attitude in defending themselves, even in the face of international public criticism. Kissinger credited Nixon with standing by Israel more firmly than any other president, save Harry Truman, because he respected their leaders' tenacious defense of their national interest.[88] But Anatoly Dobrynin, Moscow's ambassador to Washington, recalled that Nixon believed "most Jews had always voted against him, . . . he did not owe anything to the Jewish vote, . . . that the American media were run by the same Jewish circles who directed the hostile campaign against him over Watergate, and . . . that Israel did not want to end the state of war with the Arabs, and indeed the Cold War, because it wanted to take advantage of permanent confrontation between the United States and the Soviet Union."[89] Nonetheless, Nixon developed great respect for individual Israelis, among them General Yitzhak Rabin. Before Rabin was Israel's ambassador to Washington in 1969, presidential-candidate Nixon visited Israel in 1968. When Rabin, then still Israel's chief of staff, learned that Nixon's trip was not as full or complete as he had wished it to be, he devoted almost a full day to showing Nixon Israel's concern for security via a helicopter tour of Israel's topography and proximity to its enemies. Nixon was very grateful for the day he spent with Rabin. During Rabin's tenure as ambassador, Nixon saw him as "tough, no-nonsense, viewing the Soviet threat as strategic, and a supporter of Nixon's Vietnam policy."[90] In September 1970, when the Syrians threatened to move tanks into Jordan in defense of the Palestinians during the Palestinian-Jordanian uprising in Jordan, Nixon summoned Rabin from New York, where as ambassador he was about to give a speech, and sent a plane to collect him. Because he served as head of Israel's Northern Command before becoming Israel's chief of staff, Rabin was familiar with the detail of every valley, mountain, road, and *wadi* on the Golan Heights; he knew the strategic implications and topographical limitations facing a possible Syrian move into Jordan. For forty-five minutes, Rabin briefed the full U.S. cabinet and members of the defense establishment about the pending military scenarios. It was, perhaps, unheard of for a foreign ambassador to be called to the White House for such a presentation.[91] Later, in 1972, Nixon expressed his gratitude to Meir directly showering praise on Rabin for his wide-ranging strategic understanding of the region.[92] Both Nixon's and Kissinger's trust in Rabin was solidified from Meir's use of her ambassador as the exclusive channel to the White House. When Rabin became Israel's prime minister in June 1974, Kissinger, though sometimes disagreeing deeply with Rabin, had already developed a forth-right working relationship with him. The effect of this highly personalized diplomatic relationship between Washington and Israeli officials centralized key decision making and critical information in the hands of a few. It also meant that when the U.S.-Israeli relationship hit rough times in the spring of 1975, Kissinger and Rabin could rely on their years of previous contact to get through that period.

As national security adviser, Kissinger "mercilessly exploited Secretary of State Rogers' laid-back style and unwillingness to jump into a fray."[93] As a Kissinger aide noted, "Their relationship revealed all the shabby traits of Henry's character: his secretiveness, suspiciousness, and vindictiveness."[94] The under-secretary of state at the time recalled that he spent as much time negotiating between Rogers and Kissinger as he did on the Arab-Israeli conflict.[95] Rabin often found himself in the middle of the bureaucratic scuffling between Kissinger and Rogers. The immediate failure of the 1969 Rogers Plan for a Middle East settlement did not displease Kissinger. Nixon, himself, had little trust in the State Department or its policies,[96] though he used the department to provide a range of policy choices. Except for reliance upon a few individuals whom Kissinger leaned on repeatedly for advice and draftsmanship, rarely were State Department desk officers or ambassadors in the Middle East used by Kissinger to shape policy choices. Kissinger kept all information about the negotiations to himself. American ambassadors abroad rarely had a full picture of what was going on at any one time, even if it affected their ambassadorial post. A major exception was Cairo, where after the restoration of U.S.-Egyptian diplomatic relations in November 1973, the highly talented new American ambassador, Hermann Eilts, played a key role in remaining in contact with Sadat and in helping to represent him accurately to Kissinger, Nixon, and later the Carter administration. In early November 1973, Eilts, a career foreign service officer and World War II veteran, went to Cairo to establish the primary contacts prior to Kissinger's visit on November 7. Eilts became U.S. ambassador to Egypt on February 28, 1974. Eilts was considered by his American colleagues, Egyptian peers, and Sadat as an extraordinarily talented diplomat. By everyone's accounts, the growing nature of American-Egyptian relations in the critical years after the October 1973 War was positively influenced by Eilts's presence in Cairo.

Sadat's first American partner was Henry Kissinger, his second Jimmy Carter.

With President Nixon bounced about by the treacherous winds of Watergate, Kissinger's predisposition for creative and independent action went relatively unchecked. Kissinger relished the power of heading both the Department of State and the National Security Council. When the October War broke out, Kissinger appropriately, and where necessary, showed deference to Nixon. Imbued with an extraordinary ability to manage and relate tactics to strategy in foreign policy, Kissinger eagerly took charge. Early in the war, Kissinger comprehended that three conditions were necessary if the potential of diplomacy was to emerge: avoidance of a unilateral Arab defeat, preservation of Israel's security, and prevention of a superpower confrontation. When Sadat's Third Army was precariously surrounded by Israel at the war's conclusion and Meir was desperate to have Israel's prisoners-of-war returned, Kissinger used both issues to assert, prolong, and deepen Washington's role in the emerging diplomacy. In addition, both Sadat and Meir found it easy to align with Kissinger's goal of reducing Soviet involvement in the region.

Kissinger's constant strategic refrain to the Israelis focused on unwavering American support for Israeli security and the need to limit Soviet presence in the Middle East. He argued that a peace process was in Israel's interest and so was Washington's dominance in it. Repeatedly, he told Meir, "Contribute something . . . pay some price, pay something in order to keep the United States in a dominant position, in the driver's seat, to shield you from pressure, to keep the Soviets out, and the [Arab] radicals off balance."[97] Kissinger also understood that the nature of the territorial conflict between Egypt and Israel had a greater chance of diplomatic success than did the efforts to resolve issues on the Jordanian-Israeli or Syrian-Israeli front. Besides, there was a longer history of attempted negotiating efforts between Cairo and Jerusalem. And as Kissinger would learn from Sadat in their first meeting in early November 1973, the Egyptian president needed Kissinger to implement a disengagement agreement. When Kissinger traveled through the Middle East, he alone knew what each side was telling him; he was able to convey each side's thinking to the other in a part of the world accustomed to dealing with middlemen and back channels (often, the CIA) and emissaries rather than in direct, straightforward communication. A close Kissinger aide said, "He was about as conspiratorial as the people he was dealing with. He was a kindred spirit."[98] He was secretive about his conversations and paranoid about leaks. As a mediator, he befriended each principal by establishing a relationship of sympathy and goodwill with that party's viewpoint; he was able to listen and absorb anger from both sides. At times he let the parties themselves exhaust their own ideas before making suggestions; sometimes he adjusted his style of negotiating to either the objective he was seeking or the principal with whom he was dealing. With Assad he negotiated every word, with Sadat he spoke in greater generalities, and with the Israelis, while not being paternalistic, he was patient with their Talmudic questioning of every detail and concept. With the Soviets in Moscow during the 1973 War, he let them negotiate, but he ultimately did it his way to assure his control over the negotiations then and for the future. To Nixon and Brezhnev, as well as Sadat and Meir, Kissinger easily, but not always pleasingly, interposed himself as the necessary and very indispensable intermediary. In writing diplomatic agreements, memoranda, and understandings, Kissinger made diplomatic ambiguity an art. Throughout his engagement in the emerging diplomacy, he demonstrated a remarkable ability to telegraph a public message while sending a different private one and intended for both to affect certain perceptual ends. If there was a common message to be sent to both sides, Kissinger understood how to include or omit details of its contents or bend a nuance to affect a particular outcome. Where and when possible, he tried to deliver "something" tangible from the other side.

For the Israelis and Egyptians alike, Nixon's embattled domestic condition had little, if any, negative impact upon Kissinger's prestige or his dominating status as the link to a negotiated diplomatic outcome.[99] Structuring of Arab-Israeli negotiations occurred in the midst of the White House turmoil. Sadat already understood that key decision making on foreign policy issues resided in the White House with Nixon and Kissinger. Israeli political leaders realized the degree to which the Watergate crisis had bequeathed to Kissinger, Brent Scowcroft, his national security assistant, and Alexander Haig, Nixon's chief of staff, virtual and exclusive management of American foreign policy. According to Epi Evron, the deputy director general of the Israeli Foreign Ministry at the time, "they had to manage it. The president was practically immobilized; the machinery of government kept going on; they knew they had to handle it [information about certain parts of the crisis]."[100] Though the Watergate affair consumed Nixon and gave Kissinger additional latitude as a negotiator, Kissinger did not forget who was president.[101] And some who participated in Kissinger's negotiating team—State Department officials like Joe Sisco, Roy Atherton, and Hal Saunders—possessed little sense at the time of the depth of Nixon's domestic problems or recognition that those problems might have an adverse impact upon their collective facility to shape the pace and content of negotiations that emerged from the war.[102] As early as January 1974, eight months before Nixon's resignation, Kissinger and others in the White House reckoned the probability of Nixon's departure, with Ford having asked him to stay on as secretary of state. A combination of unique factors merged together to give Kissinger an almost unparalleled opportunity to engage and succeed in Arab-Israeli diplomacy: his enormous intelligence, unparalleled self-confidence, bureaucratic status as head of the NSC and secretary of state, the lack of challenge from Congress, the presence of highly skilled and experienced advisers, knowledge in the Middle East that he represented and spoke authoritatively for the president, and no acceptable international personality from Moscow, the UN, or elsewhere with whom to contend or compete. Neither the UN nor Moscow had the credibility to offset Kissinger's dominance in the negotiating process. By comparison to Kissinger's almost daily contacts with Israeli Ambassador Dinitz, Moscow's policy making was ponderous, unimaginative, stiff. While Moscow had highly skilled Middle East specialists working in the Ministry of Foreign Affairs, all diplomatic steps went through a rigid bureaucratic chain. Foreign Minister Gromyko was the consummate bureaucrat and not a troubleshooter like Kissinger. And the Egyptian and Syrian ambassadors in Moscow had virtually no access to Brezhnev.[103] Moreover, Soviet ambassadors in Syria and Egypt were, for all intents and purposes, postmen, and due to the break in relations in 1967, Moscow had virtually no diplomatic contacts with Jerusalem. With only rare exceptions, as this diplomatic theater unfolded, Kissinger acted and reacted without policy-making constraints, bureaucratic limitations, or personal competition from Moscow.

Central to Kissinger's success was the faith and confidence Meir and Sadat placed in him. Meir had known Kissinger for many years. She regarded him as a friend of Israel and trusted his basic instincts to ensure Israeli security. Despite the delay in American military resupplies sent to Israel during the October War, she believed that he would not let Israel down. "She trusted him, but had her ups and downs with him. She did not always agree with him," noted the director general of her office, Mordechai Gazit.[104] During the war, Kissinger hastily developed a similar sense of mutual trust with Sadat. Sadat understood that because the Israelis trusted Kissinger he was a viable mediator.[105] In pursuing his strategy of trusting the Americans, Sadat enfranchised them with responsibility to achieve progress. If Washington failed to make sufficient diplomatic headway on a particular issue, such as Palestinian representation or the arrangement of procedural issues for holding a peace conference, some of the blame for not achieving an objective could readily be placed on American shoulders. There was enormous significance for American foreign policy making because of Sadat's calculated choice to align with Washington. After so many years of strained contacts with the Arab world because of the Arab-Israeli conflict, Washington focused on building the Egyptian-U.S. relationship. Slowly but formidably, Sadat positioned himself in between the special Israeli-U.S. relationship. Equally relevant for Washington's foreign policy toward the region, American attitudes toward the Arab world and its leaders were, with the exception of oil needs, viewed through an Egyptian prism. By concentrating on Egypt, Washington added to Egypt's isolation and, in turn, increased Sadat's susceptibility to consider separate agreements with Israel.

After the 1973 War commenced, Sadat became increasingly comfortable in dealing with Kissinger. Since 1971, there was an Egyptian predisposition and distinct willingness to enlist American mediation for resolving the conflict and to reduce Soviet influence in Cairo.[106] Kissinger had met three times privately with Hafez Ismail, Sadat's close friend and national security adviser. Without an American ambassador in Cairo, Kissinger had maintained communications with Sadat through the CIA, otherwise known as the "back channel," and specifically via Ismail. After Eilts came to Cairo in November 1973, he was supposed to be Kissinger's primary contact for communications with the Egyptians, but Kissinger's nature and previous experience caused him to continue to communicate with Ismail through the CIA. Eilts remarked that using the CIA as the main channel of communication irritated him: "I was annoyed because it meant that Kissinger was passing things to the Egyptian government through one of my subordinates, the CIA, who wasn't even [my] senior. And then the shit hit the fan. I sent a message to him, on my own, if I'm going to be here as ambassador either you send things like that to me to be passed on or you withdraw me."[107] Kissinger apologized to Eilts and thereafter used the State Department channel for communication with Sadat. Eventually, American diplomatic communication with Washington, whether through the embassy or via the CIA, became a bitter source of competition and "deep personal rivalry" between National Security Council Adviser Ismail and Foreign Minister Fahmy.[108] Receiving all communications through Foreign Ministry and State Department channels enabled Fahmy to diminish Hafez Ismail's role with Sadat, something he was always doing with Ghorbal and other colleagues.

After Kissinger, Sadat courted Carter. In several ways, Jimmy Carter continued the Ford administration's policies of advocating a Palestinian component to an Arab-Israeli settlement and in linking the degree of Washington's commitment to Israel, including military supplies with the degree of Israel's flexibility in negotiating a viable settlement. But Carter went further, deviating from the practiced norm of cuddling Israel. Unlike Ford, he promoted the inclusion of a specific Palestinian dimension to the next proposed Arab-Israeli agreement. Alienating Israel was not Carter's goal; it was the by-product of his objective to achieve a comprehensive Arab-Israeli settlement and the result of his needing Israeli leaders to make compromises. Carter generated enormous consternation from Israelis and from American Jews of all political ilk. But in doing so, he handcuffed Begin and Sadat to agreements in which they agreed to disagree. Historically, Democratic presidents did not usually lean on Israel, but Carter did, and did so publicly. Under Republican administrations, Israeli security was supported. Eisenhower argued for Israel's withdrawal from Sinai after the October 1956 War, and Nixon was tough with Israeli political leaders. Unlike other presidents since Truman, Carter did not have significant exposure in his early political career to Jewish causes or to Israeli issues. Presidents Truman and Eisenhower knew firsthand about the Holocaust. Presidents Ford, Nixon, Johnson, and Kennedy had career experience in Washington and in congressional or national elections; therefore, they were subjected to lobbying and pressures on a variety of foreign policy issues, including matters relating to the Middle East and Israel. As candidates for national office on several occasions, they were exposed to persuasive approaches and enjoyed financial contributions by Jews and non-Jews who had pro-Israeli sympathies. Each of Carter's predecessors had some formative experience in understanding modern Jewish history, with Jews in politics, or intensely with Israel. According to Stuart Eisenstat, Carter's domestic affairs adviser, "I wouldn't say Carter felt uncomfortable in the Jewish crowds, but it clearly was not his element. After all, he was not a northern or northeastern politician who had grown up in a heavily Jewish population. Yes, he knew Jews in Atlanta, but they were not part of his circle."[109]

As a young Congressman, Lyndon Johnson had voiced the need to help Jews escape Nazi persecution in the 1930s; in 1957, he was chairman of the Senate Foreign Revolution Committee, which helped arrange for Israeli withdrawal from Sinai. As president when the Israelis took Sinai in the June 1967 War, Johnson felt somewhat obliged that, if the Israelis were to withdraw again, they would obtain something more tangible, "like a framework or structure for peace."[110] While a student at Harvard in 1939, John Kennedy visited Palestine and understood what the Jews were trying to accomplish there.

As a peanut farmer, state senator, and governor of Georgia, Jimmy Carter had little opportunity to learn about the substance or management of complex foreign policy issues, such as the ones the Middle East raised. Prior to his May 1973 visit to Israel, Jimmy Carter had no direct exposure to Middle Eastern issues at all. On that trip, at the invitation of the former Israeli ambassador to Washington, Yitzhak Rabin, he did not meet with Palestinians or visit an Arab country. He talked with Israeli leaders and toured the Christian holy sites, Jerusalem, Israeli *kibbutzim,* and the Golan Heights. By visiting Israel, Carter aligned his deep biblical knowledge with the geographic reality he witnessed. His religious background had given him a special feeling for the Holy Land and for the Jewish contribution to Christian tradition. Sadat told his ambasssador in Washington that Carter's commitment to his religion gave "them [both] a common element upon which Sadat could rely."[111] Carter was willing to separate his religious sentimentality for Israel's origins from the need to satisfy Palestinian aspirations, which, for Carter, was a human rights issue. In his commitment to human rights, he held the view that the powerful should not persecute the weak. His political laser focused on the right of a people to express themselves freely.[112] In describing Carter's attitude toward Israel, Brzezinski noted that "Carter's feelings on Israel were always ambivalent. On the one hand, he felt that Israel was being intransigent. On the other, he genuinely did have an attachment to the country as 'the land of the Bible.'"[113] While preparing his campaign for the Democratic nomination, he hauled foreign policy specialists down to Plains, "about fifty at a time, for all-day sessions with [him] and Fritz Mondale, talking about what we could do about China, what we could do about the Middle East."[114] By the time Carter was inaugurated, he did not know much about the subtleties of inter-Arab conflicts, the variant expressions of Arab animosities toward Israel, or the inner workings of the PLO. He had little personal knowledge of the differing attitudes Arab states possessed toward the

Palestinians; he sensed that they all promoted Palestinian rights with equal fervor. The pariah status endured by Palestinians in inter-Arab affairs was practically unknown to him, nor did he realize Arab political leaders would use and abuse the Palestinian issue in the promotion of selfish national interests. Carter did not impute responsibility to Arab states for denying Palestinians their rights; and he saw the Israelis as capable of, even responsible for, providing them whatever rights and land they required for self-expression. Only after his first lengthy post-presidency trip to the Middle East in March 1983, when he was a distinguished professor at Emory University, did he admit to first comprehending the various political shades within the fragmented Palestinian community. In hindsight then, he complained that as president he had so many items on his agenda that time did not permit him to understand as fully as he wanted or needed to know the political varieties and variations within the Arab world and within Israel. As 1977 wore on, his storehouse of knowledge about the conflict and its players grew until he developed a mastery of them. But upon taking office, Carter's mind was not cluttered with political experiences, lobbying biases, or historical prejudices that told him a resolution of the Arab-Israeli conflict was not possible. And even when he learned that there were shoals, rocks, or hidden sandbars, he refused to be deterred from finding clear passage to at least partial answers to the conflict's procedural issues or substantive matters.

When his administration began, he could neither understand nor tolerate Arab unwillingness to recognize Israel. For Carter, the Arab economic boycott against Israel was a disgrace; he said it is "not a matter of diplomacy or trade with me; it's a matter of morality."[115] Likewise, he did not accept Israel's dual refusal to stop building settlements or to deal with the PLO. He accepted what he read and heard about the Palestinian desire for a homeland but did not realize how deep PLO antagonism remained toward Israel's very existence. Carter's positive outlook about the world was contagious to the people around him. Problems between peoples and nations were, he believed, based upon misunderstandings that could be properly redefined and reduced to simple terms where agreement could be found between previous hostile adversaries. In this manner, Carter was a problem solver; when there was a problem that he thought was important and that could be solved, he wanted to solve it in a comprehensive manner. According to his Middle East specialist at the National Security Council, William Quandt, "Carter simply thought that every problem had a comprehensive solution, and that we should put our minds to it and come up with one. He was very serious about it. He just tackled the whole thing and started putting the pieces together. Within three or four months, he had pretty much the outlines in his mind of what ought to be done [about Arab-Israeli negotiations]."[116] His penchant to find solutions often combined with an impatience for its resolution. Carter calibrated time with a clock, rather than a calendar, which put him on a collision course with Israel's preference for deliberative decision making. In seeking answers, he sometimes disregarded the fact that all problems or issues are not easily solved; on other occasions, he did not fully comprehend how a particular cultural idiom, a historical precedent, or ideological imperative was associated with the formation and evolution of an attitude or viewpoint. Carter made little, if any, geographical distinctions between the Syrian, Jordanian, or Egyptian desires or rights to have the Golan, West Bank, Sinai, and Gaza returned to each country respectively. Carter did not realize that he was a much more vigorous proponent of a comprehenisve settlement than were most Arab leaders. A comprehensive agreement for Carter meant full application of UNSC Resolution 242 to all of the territories, with only minor border rectifications expected. There was logical symmetry: if Israel returned most of the territories and retained defensible borders, then these Arab countries would proffer Israel peace treaties. Carter was challenged by estimates or predictions that something was impossible to accomplish. Reconciling Anwar Sadat and Menachem Begin's personal and policy differences was precisely the kind of challenge Carter relished. He did not set out to make them friends; he set out to make them negotiate and sign an agreement. It was more than stubbornness; it was a combination of persistence mixed with what he determined to be the "right thing" to do. Carter was guided by his own moral compass in deriving workable formulas for policy making. Indeed, he was not afraid to make a decision based upon what he thought was right and just, even if the political repercussions were unsavory and divisive. Carter disdained political expediency. To say that Carter was naive about politics is too simple an explanation. He understood pragmatic politics and that trade-offs sometimes had to be made. For example, at one point in February–March 1978, when he was concerned about the outcome of the Panama Canal Treaty vote in the Senate, Carter carefully juggled his desire for sales of F-15 airplanes to Saudi Arabia with the possible alienation of senators who favored the treaty but had a pro-Israeli sympathy. In dealing with Begin, Sadat, and their representatives or ministers, he used various combinations of velvet gloves and iron grips, of gentleness, severity, and public threat. His penetrating blue eyes, toothy grin, wry smile, poker face, and southern drawl were often disarming. Carter could, in fact, be very tough, blunt, direct, and steel-like in demeanor. When Carter negotiated with Dayan in October 1977 after the issuance of the U.S.-Soviet Declaration, Dayan called his discussions with Carter some of the toughest he ever endured. During Carter's March 1979 visit to the Middle East to finalize details for the Egyptian-Israeli Peace Treaty, and when he went to Egypt and Israel without any prearranged certainty of presidential success, Carter angrily addressed the Israeli cabinet for its unwillingness to make several necessary compromises. Begin replied, "Mr. President, we will accept what we deem possible to accept. We shall not accept what we do not wish to accept."[117] Carter then backed away, still leaving the impression of an ultimatum.

Carter immersed himself fully in comprehending the substance of an issue. He enjoyed hearing a variety of opinions and was capable of rejecting them as quickly as they were presented. He thrived on receiving information; he consumed and digested it. Because of his ardent interest in studying maps, Carter understood topographical features and geographic relationships. His proclivity was to read and remember reports, memoranda, and estimates; he possessed an almost computer-like ability to recall statistics, information, and concepts. Having information at his fingertips and using it at appropriate moments often gave him advantages as negotiations progressed. His advisers at the State Department and the National Security Council were delighted by his determination and encouraged by both his constant readiness to absorb their memoranda and willingness to listen to their opinions. Using their ideas and opinions, even if infrequently, was inherently different than the Nixon-Ford-Kissinger use of the American foreign policy bureaucracy. His willingness to intervene directly and have the staying power to remain involved uniformly energized his Middle East advisers.[118] For example, in September–October 1977, he stayed current with the various drafts that were proposed for the U.S.-Soviet communiqué; during the negotiations with the Israelis about the procedures for going to Geneva, Carter led the discussions with Dayan, which eventually determined the joint U.S.-Israeli statement about Geneva. Both Dayan and King Hussein were impressed with Carter's involvement and knowledge of the issues. Dayan remarked that Carter "was the central figure and the man who made the decisions, showing great knowledge of the matters as compared to the knowledge shown by other Americans; he knew the various formulations, where the difficulties lie and the different formulations."[119] "He knew more [about the Arab-Israeli] problem than any prior president," recalled King Hussein.[120] In seeking an agreement between Begin and Sadat, Carter had a hands-on attitude. At Camp David, he personally wrote and rewrote several drafts of the Egyptian-Israeli agreement. While Hal Saunders drafted the original framework for the Palestinian autonomy several months earlier and its component elements were developed because of considerable American staff work during the previous eighteen months, Carter set up and chaired a drafting committee at Camp David, made up of senior representatives from Israel (Aharon Barak), Egypt (Usamah al-Baz), and the United States (Cy Vance) to revise the language in the various drafts until it was acceptable to Prime Minister Begin and President Sadat. It is significant that one of the reasons why Sadat and Begin were more, rather than less, susceptible to Carter's suggestions and compromises at Camp David was the absence of individuals in both the Egyptian and Israeli delegations who were rooted in ideology. Instead, both delegations were made up of technocrats, legal advisers, and wordsmiths who were accustomed to finding terminology and phrases that were free of ideological limitations.

Sometimes Carter became frustrated with advisers or bureaucrats who placed self-imposed restraints on achieving results. Here, he was unyielding. If their opinions and options were too limited, he would admonish them for thinking too narrowly. Sometimes he complained that he did not receive innovative ideas from them, especially "about how to modify existing policy in order to meet changing conditions."[121] The most representative case in point was the administration's reluctance and unwillingness to accept Sadat's alteration of the negotiating process with his unexpected trip to Jerusalem. In preparing for Camp David in August 1978, Carter's advisers were deeply interested in connecting an Egyptian-Israeli agreement with progress toward a solution to the Palestinian issue. They felt that Carter had to straddle the Israeli preference for loose or no linkage and the Egyptian preference for overt linkage. His advisers also told him not to focus on achieving a detailed agreement at Camp David, but to establish a coherent basis for a comprehensive settlement. Although Carter admired his Middle East advisers for their skill and knowledge, he felt "they were not aiming high enough. I told them that we can do better than just obtaining broad principles. At a minimum, we can get a framework for an Egyptian-Israeli peace treaty, and that was the issue, not linkage."[122] Carter did not let his advisers' skepticism deter his objective of obtaining an agreement from Begin and Sadat. He was interested in seeing an agreement written and signed and did not allow someone else's potential veto, like that of the Syrians, or noninclusion or participation in an agreement (the Palestinians or Jordanians), to deter an outcome when it was in sight, even if it were not perfect or ideal. Carter did not believe that an earthquake of political instability in the region would be created if the Palestinian issue ultimately were postponed.

As a mediator, Carter had confidence in his ability to arbitrate concessions for what he perceived to be for the benefit of the participants. Frequently, he displayed a tireless commitment to find formulas, definitions, and solutions to the many intricate variables, regardless of perceived or real political limitations, and was capable of soothing fears and anxieties, always with the goal of keeping the negotiations going. Regardless of the tone of a meeting, Carter tried to conclude each one on a positive note. It was part of Carter's negotiating style to take an overly sympathetic view of the person with whom he was speaking.[123] He often created lists, either on paper or in his head, about advantages and disadvantages to one side or the other in pursuing a certain course of action. He was an excellent wordsmith. At Camp David, Carter labored over word choices and came to understand how any combination of adjectives and nouns (for example, choosing either "legitimate," "civil," "national," or "political" as a modifier to either "rights" or "aspirations") made a significant difference to Arabs and Israelis alike. He used his special talent for verbal economy and linguistic precision to suggest compromises. He personally drafted portions of the Camp David Accords on a legal pad, using "the single document method"; taking it back and forth between Sadat, Begin, and their advisers until mutually agreed terminology was found. If a small shaft of light betrayed a potential compromise, then Carter's negotiating skills and relentless determination detected and pursued it. Carter was singularly impressive in his ability to listen attentively, sometimes for hours, while a political leader expounded on an issue or a nation's past. He gradually understood the importance historical events had upon determining personal ideology, but he would not allow it to constrain his political options, and he did not want them to limit the options of those with whom he was negotiating. For example, although he understood the significance of the Holocaust in shaping Israeli Prime Minister Begin's fears and aspirations, Carter would not allow Begin's concern for Israeli security to preclude territorial compromises. Carter did not support Begin's assertion that Judea and Samaria belonged to Israel because of biblical claims. If the Palestinians were to have a place of their own, Carter could not justify retention of the occupied territories nor support the building or expansion of Israeli settlements. Carter constantly urged Begin and Sadat to look beyond the past or present and into the future. At the end of the Camp David talks, when negotiations looked hopeless, he put copies of his signed picture in front of Begin, dedicating each one to Begin's grandchildren at the last moment, successfully appealing to Begin's sentimentality to make the final compromises necessary to reach an agreement for peace in his grandchildren's future.

On several levels, American Jews and Israelis developed a mistrust for Carter and his administration. Between Carter and the American Jewish community feelings ranged from discomfort to antagonism and distrust. Historically, American Jews were generally skeptical of any politician who wore religion on a public sleeve. Carter's "born again" image worried American Jews. In identifying with presidential candidates and with politicians in general, American Jews looked for those with a passionate and unalterable commitment to Israel's interests, security, and policies. Those with religion running through their veins were automatically seen as unlikely friends. When Carter ran for office, his competitor Senator Henry "Scoop" Jackson of Washington received the support of American Jews, which Carter remembered well. "Jackson was their spokesman and was their hero," he recalled, "so, I was looked upon as an alien challenger to their own candidate. . . . So, I didn't feel obligated to them . . . Fritz [Mondale], though, had been immersed in the 'Democratic Party's Liberal Wing,' which was committed to labor reform, that was committed to Israel, and so forth. It was an act just like breathing to him—it wasn't like breathing to me. So, I was willing to break the shell more than he was, or more than Vance was, or people who had been there [in Washington] for a long time."[124]

The manner in which signals and diplomacy were conducted irked Israelis also. Since the Johnson administration, Israel had been accustomed to carrying out all of its policy decisions and discussions with the United States quietly and privately. Kissinger's close-to-the-vest, secretive style was appreciated by Sadat, Hussein, and Rabin. Circumspection and privacy in the conduct of foreign policy was expected. Carter was different. He carried out much of his foreign and domestic policy in naked public view. Carter's tendency was to be open about issues that were considered by others to be sensitive and incubating. Israelis were very unaccustomed to

Carter's shooting unpredicatably from the hip about critical issues. For example, for Carter to suggest that Israel negotiate with the PLO and do so *publicly* in March 1977, demonstrated to them that Carter had a thorough misunderstanding of the depth of real and existential antagonism Israelis possessed for the PLO. Among some Israelis, there was a sense that only a few members of the administration understood Israel. For some, like the Israeli leadership and King Hussein, the unaccustomed frankness and even lack of diplomatic polish that came from the Carter White House was unprecedented. Sadat, by contrast, who often employed the public stage and political shock as a style, was less startled and perturbed by Carter's candor and public revelations. When sensitive Arab-Israeli diplomacy was conducted in a public, and particularly when policies announced were neither cleared nor discussed in advance, Israeli prime ministers were perturbed with Carter. Loosing any perceived independence of political expression, even to the United States, was an adverse consequence, likely to be interpreted by the Arab world as a victory and reason for additional pressure to be applied on Israeli decision makers. Because Carter "had a hard time holding his tongue in public,"[125] Israelis were almost always on edge when he made a remark about the Middle East. Before or after a meeting with a visiting Middle East leader, Carter or a member of his administration would sometimes breach the silence on an issue by announcing something unexpected at a news conference or press briefing. For example, when Secretary of State Vance visited Israel in February 1977, he was uncharacteristically frank with the Israeli leadership. He told them flat out that certain promised weapons would not be coming their way. Kissinger might have meandered on a tough issue, playing for time, saying he needed time to consult with Nixon. Not so with the Carter administration. The next month, when Rabin visited the Carter White House, he was startled by the president's remarks favoring the Palestinians. When Carter asked him whether Israel was prepared for Egyptian tourism, Rabin told an associate, "Doesn't he understand that we are not at peace?" Rabin's unwillingness to be more candid and frank with Carter during that visit about the substance of a possible Israeli arrangement with Egypt stemmed in a major way from the Israeli prime minister's fear that anything said to Carter in private would be made public.[126] Rabin had years of Washington experience that included trust, candor, and disagreement with Kissinger. Neither Rabin nor Begin had that with Carter. Israelis believed that Carter's willingness to make bold, eclectic, and far-reaching statements about the Middle East demonstrated his lack of sophistication about international affairs, the Soviet Union, and Middle Eastern politics.[127] Israel was blindsided by the contents of the October 1977 U.S.-Soviet Declaration, which was issued without consultation with Jerusalem; King Hussein never fully comprehended the lack of diplomatic skill exhibited toward him during Vance's February 1977 visit to Amman or that his initial briefing after the 1978 Camp David Accords came from a relatively junior State Department official.

Israel is a nation consumed by terms, words, and talmudic nuance, a fact the Carter administration during its first year in office did not understand. Every small twist in a phrase or use of a synomyn uttered in public was automatically deciphered by Israeli policymakers as intentional, perhaps a "signal" of a policy shift. Sometimes Carter did intentionally change a word in order to expand or limit an interpretation, depending on the audience that was being addressed or persuaded. Early in 1977, however, he paid little attention to the exactitude of formulas and definitions that had been so tortuously debated and negotiated. Particularly, he did not understand that however small and innocently intended, every public remark about the style or content of Arab-Israeli diplomacy could echo offensively on sensitive Middle Eastern political ears. Any slight deviation articulated in Washington had a crescendo impact in a region where each word and phrase had a history. According to Israel's ambassador to Washington at the time, Epi Evron, the Carter administration did not realize that "Israelis are a people that have a certain degree of paranoia. The administration, the new people around Carter, had few sentiments for it. They seemed to be cold to the issues and looked at them rationally and not sentimentally."[128] For example, after an informal question-and-answer period with Saudi Crown Prince Fahd, Carter said that "there were no disturbing differences at all" between the United States and Saudi Arabia. He also stated then that "all the United Nations resolutions have contemplated a homeland for the Palestinians."[129] There were other examples that, for Israelis and their supporters in the United States, seemed either to be wrong or too frequent. What could a foreign leader do after Carter had a meeting with them and then told the press about promises or agreements discussed? Instead of publicly calling Carter a liar, a Middle East leader would say that there was a misunderstanding between them. As compared to Kissinger, whom he praised for his diplomatic successes, Carter said, "I would rather face a difficult issue at the beginning and tell the truth and try to accommodate the contrary reactions than to hold back bad news or try to mislead the Israelis on what the Egyptian position was, hoping to work it out subsequently. But Kissinger was very effective in what he did, and the bottom result, I must say, was very good."[130] Carter's public diplomacy, content, and style caused Israel great discomfort. When Begin succeeded Rabin after the May 1977 Knesset elections, Israeli anxiety toward Washington did not abate. The Carter administration's direct, shrill, and sometimes callous tones resonated among Jews in the United States and Israel, Carter and his advisers were continuously considered unsympathetic, insensitive, and stubborn about Israel. Said one high-ranking State Department official, there were those in the administration who had an "inadequate understanding of the sort of political psychology of Israel, and how you deal with the Israelis, and what their own complexes and hang-ups were."[131] And yet, in comparison to previous administrations involved in Arab-Israeli diplomacy, Carter's personal commitment and unyielding zeal to impel a negotiated outcome was unequaled. No other

American president before him was willing to put his political life on the line for the achievement of Arab-Israeli agreements. None had such a direct impact on charting new directions for Arab-Israeli relations. The irony was that Jimmy Carter, as president, did more to solidify the state of Israel's existence than any president since Harry Truman, yet his actions put him on a collision course with Israeli political leaders and antagonized the American Jewish community.

As Carter's secretary of state and national security council adviser respectively, Cyrus Vance and Zbigniew Brzezinski generally agreed about the need for a comprehensive Middle East settlement, though they differed about the content and tone of other aspects of foreign policy such as dealing with the Soviet Union. Vance was a lawyer. He was methodical, a good listener, asked questions, and, for his immediate subordinates, proved to be a pleasant colleague. Some suggested that he was rigid, sometimes detached, even "wooden" in manner. Israelis and Arabs alike admired Vance because he was honest, straightforward, and not engaged in the tactical and word maneuvers that had come to personify Kissinger's tenure as secretary of state. And of great significance to Vance's success as secretary of state was the realization that whatever he said or promised, the president and the stature of the presidency stood behind his commitments. Brzezinski, a brilliant and articulate Columbia University professor, was a specialist on the Soviet Union and the cold war. During the 1976 presidential campaign, Brzezinski not only conveyed positive feelings to the Israelis about their security needs but also suggested during his visit there that year that the Carter administration was prepared to find an equitable accommodation for the Palestinians.[132] In a self-assessment of American Jewish attitudes toward his style and personality, Brzezinski understood that he was "not trusted because [he] was Polish, Catholic, and prepared to pursue the peace process by applying pressure on the Arabs, Israelis, and Palestinians."[133] Brzezinski's personal manner did not add to a sense of confidence in the Israeli-U.S. relationship. Israelis had a difficult time coping with what they viewed as his sudden shifts, erratic responses, and aggressively frank and impetuous enthusiasm for various issues. Israeli officials at the Israeli embassy in Washington in 1977 sensed that "Brzezinski was a loose cannon on deck; he would just get an idea and throw it out. We thought it was some devious, well-thought-out policy plan intended perhaps to deceive us. Then, it took us a while to realize that he was just talking as if he was at some university seminar at Columbia, and he probably forgot about his idea an hour after we talked. Once while playing chess with Begin on one of his trips to the United States, Brzezinski offered some idea and later Begin would ask us, 'What did that mean?' Brzezinski would send us into a tizzy and probably had forgotten that he even raised whatever issue it was."[134] Both Vance and Brzezinski were businesslike, and supported Israeli security requirements but not Israeli positions vis-à-vis a negotiated settlement, toward the Palestinians, or toward Soviet participation in the negotiating process.

The differences in analyses and policy options provided Carter the kind of diversity in opinion that he enjoyed in understanding issues. Even with some profound differences between Vance and Brzezinski, there was an environment of cooperation between them as there was between the Department of State and the National Security Council. Some tension remained, but the secretiveness and even disdain that dominated the Kissinger-Rogers era of the early 1970s was gone. Vance was clearly in charge of directing and formulating the steps needed to ignite Arab-Israeli negotiations. Middle Eastern policy advisers to Brzezinski and Vance had worked together compatibly under Presidents Nixon and Ford. Having shared the efforts and exertions of previous administrations, they saw themselves as a team. Their warm and effective working relationship was proudly protected, and their special rapport of trust allowed them to exchange ideas easily. According to Roy Atherton, the assistant secretary of state for Near Eastern and South Asian affairs at the time, "We had about the best collegial team approach that I can remember at any time when I was working on this problem."[135] There was significant continuity, abundant skill, and decades of expertise among these professional bureaucrats who advised Kissinger and Carter in Middle Eastern policy matters. And the lines of open and effective communication in the Washington–Cairo–Jerusalem axis benefited from Eilts's tenure as U.S. ambassador in Cairo and the presence of Samuel W. Lewis as U.S. ambassador in Tel Aviv from 1977 to 1986. Lewis took up his position just before Begin's election and came to understand the intricacies of the personality conflicts in the Israeli political system. Both Eilts and Lewis possessed a sensitivity for Begin and Sadat respectively and both understood the political cultures in which they operated. In the emerging negotiating process, the Lewis-Dayan and Vance-Dayan relationships were critical links between Jerusalem and Washington. Left to their own devices, Begin and Sadat would not have reached an agreement alone. They talked past each other; Sadat the generalist wanting grand gestures, Begin the legalist wanting to inch his way toward an agreement with Egypt. It was the presence of Carter's passionate determination to find an Egyptian-Israeli solution that, finally, made the difference. Coming on the heels of Kissinger's achievements, Carter's tenacity resulted in negotiated results, not perfect by anyone's standard, but signed agreements nonetheless. Begin and Sadat had the vision to understand that another agreement between them was in their respective national interests. And with the United States as umpire, broker, and guarantor, the results stuck and, in turn, laid the foundation for transforming the Arab-Israeli conflict into a series of Arab-Israeli relationships.

⌒

THE ARAB-ISRAELI CONFLICT

1947–1973

IN NOVEMBER 1947, the United Nations General Assembly recommended that the area of Palestine, under a British mandate from the League of Nations since 1922, be partitioned into separate Arab and Jewish states, with an economic union proposed to tie the two states together and an international regime established for the city of Jerusalem. The Arab world vehemently opposed the partition of Palestine into two states, preferring instead the creation of one federal state. For Jews, living among the 1.2 million Arab people who inhabited Palestine would have made them a religious minority of 600,000 in a federal Arab-Jewish state, a minority political status that was not the goal of Zionism.

Zionism, which emerged in late-nineteenth-century Eastern Europe as a Jewish national movement, aimed to create a homeland or territory in which Jews would be free from anti-Semitic persecution. In the 1880s, when Jewish immigrants began to trickle into Palestine, there were less than 30,000 Jews living there. During the next sixty years, a highly diverse group of immigrant Jews purchased land, created autonomous political and social institutions, evolved a small military force, and developed an indigenous economy, all of which would later form the backbone of Israel. At the conclusion of World War I, the British government, after taking Palestine and Syria from the Ottoman Turks, promised in the November 1917 Balfour Declaration to assist Zionists in establishing a national home. The majority Arab population in Palestine protested Britain's protection of the fledgling Jewish minority.

With Arab majority self-rule denied and a weak agricultural economy throughout the 1930s, tensions in Palestine boiled over into protests and civil disturbances. From 1936 to 1939, with the surrounding Arab states of Egypt, Syria, and Iraq focused diligently on their own independence from British and French control, Palestinian Arabs repeatedly rioted against Britain's pro-Zionist policies and the ever-growing Jewish national home. In 1937, Britain suggested that Zionists and

Arabs could jointly occupy Palestine only if they lived apart. However, the idea of Palestine's partition into two distinct political states was immediately scrapped, partly because the proposed Arab state would have been economically unviable. But then Britain gave into Arab demands: with strategic interests in the eastern Mediterranean to protect—namely Egypt and the Suez Canal—Britain moved to protect the Arabs in Palestine against additional Zionist growth. In 1939, Britain imposed severe restrictions on additional Jewish immigration and land purchases in Palestine and promised that a unitary/federal state would be created in Palestine within a decade.

The Zionists were infuriated but had little choice other than to accept Britain's restrictions. In response, a scant number of Zionist zealots, among them Menachem Begin and Yitzhak Shamir, both later prime ministers of Israel, used violence against the British administration. At the moment when Jews needed a haven from the worst persecution in their history, Britain closed almost all the doors to Palestine. Doors to most other countries were also closed to Jewish exiles. Nevertheless, by 1939, before Hitler's invasion of Poland, a geographic nucleus for a Jewish state in Palestine had been established.[1] In the aftermath of the European Holocaust, international public opinion added an emotional imperative to the need to establish the Jewish state already in the making, which would be anchored in the existing Jewish demographic, economic, and physical presence in Palestine. It appeared that indeed a refuge or safe haven for the Jews would be established.

After World War II, the possibility of a Jewish state in Palestine greatly threatened Arab sensibilities. Briefly, during and after World War I, some Arab leaders thought their liberation from four hundred years of Ottoman rule would mean the final emergence of a unified Arab nation. But French and British imperial appetites to create trusteeships for the former Arab provinces of the Ottoman Empire postponed any realization of that truncated dream. Arab disunity was thus blamed upon such foreign occupation and its legacies, without the acknowledgment of local or divergent national interests. Assistance the British had given to the Zionists was also viewed by the Arabs as an intentional Western effort to deny the Arabs' realization of their goal. Greatly angered by the United Nations decision of November 29, 1947, which sanctioned the creation of separate Arab and Jewish states, five Arab states went to war against Israel the same day it declared its independence, May 15, 1948. After the United Nations mediated several cease-fire agreements, four Arab states—Egypt, Jordan, Syria, and Lebanon—signed armistice agreements with Israel in 1949, the same year Israel was admitted into the United Nations. As a result of the war, Israel controlled all of Palestine, with the exception of the Gaza Strip, which was subsequently administered by Egypt, and the so-called West Bank of the Jordan River governed by Jordan, until both areas were taken by Israel in the June 1967 War. The city of Jerusalem itself was divided, with the old city and most Jewish holy sites totally under Jordanian control. Neither an economic union nor a

Palestinian-Arab state were established in the West Bank and Gaza Strip. Approximately 700,000 Palestinians fled Palestine, most of them settling uncomfortably and unwelcome in surrounding Arab states. In the late 1940s and early 1950s, several quiet attempts were made between Zionist leaders in Palestine and Arab leaders in Jordan and Syria to reach a peaceful accommodation between them.[2] Those efforts, however, proved fruitless. No peace treaties were signed and no diplomatic relations were established between Israel and its Arab neighbors. The Arab world remained in a physical and legal state of war with the new Jewish state.

By the early 1950s, the Arab world considered Israel's establishment a heinous crime. For most Arabs, Israel was intentionally inflicted upon them by the same imperial powers that had denied Arab independence and self-determination to the former Arab provinces of the Ottoman Empire after World War I. Zionism was an illegitimate national movement, Israel an artificial offspring of colonialism. Muslim Arab leaders argued that Jews as a people did not constitute a nation. After all, it was recalled, in classical Islam, Jews were only a tolerated minority. Arab anti-Semitism was not directed at Jews, but at Israel as a whole. The elimination of Israel was necessary in order to both right a wrong done to all Arabs and to reverse the "historic injustice" undertaken against the 700,000 displaced Palestinians who had fled villages, homes, and fields after the 1948–1949 War. For Arab political leaders, restoration of the land to these rightful Palestinian owners was required. Israel's destruction would fulfill an even greater purpose: the removal of a foreign element, which contaminated Arab and Muslim homogeneity. In the 1950s and 1960s, the Arab world thus primarily rejected Israel's existence because its very presence blocked the consideration, let alone the fulfillment, of the pan-Arab dream of having a single, united Arab nation. The goal of Israel's destruction acted as a catalyst for assembling Arab states together in a common struggle. To destroy Israel, the Arab world would need to harness all of its economic, political, and military potential. All means would be used: guerilla attacks disrupted civilian life in Israel; diplomatically, Israel was vilified in international forums like the United Nations; an economic boycott was imposed to cripple its strength; and the Great Powers were urged to deny support of Israel. Finally, an Arab military option was required for preparation of the next round of battle against Zionism.

For eighty years Britain occupied and dominated Egypt because its imperial and economic interests dictated control of the Suez Canal. Britain, whose functional imperialist motto was "Good government was better than self-government," intentionally divided Egypt's growing nationalist movement to preserve its control. However, in the early 1950s, nationalists led by Gamel Abd al-Nasser and his military cohorts, including the young Anwar Sadat, hustled the British out of Egypt. In response, a British, French, and Israeli military collusion against Egypt ignited the 1956 Suez War, which in part aimed to topple Nasser. At war's end, President

Eisenhower urged a victorious Israel to withdraw totally from the Sinai Peninsula, which it had captured. Texas Senator Lyndon Johnson, who headed the Senate Foreign Relations Committee, observed Israel's eventual withdrawal from Sinai and the ensuing placement of forces from the United Nations as observers on Egyptian territory. Israel was then promised that the UN peacekeeping troops would not be withdrawn from Sinai unless such action was voted on by the UN Security Council, thus assuring Israel of the unlikelihood of potential counterattacks by Egypt.

Though his army was defeated, Nasser emerged as the staunch defender of Arab territory and national sentiment. His charisma and fiery speeches made him a symbol for achieving pan-Arab aspirations. Egypt, furthermore, now exemplified the Arab quest to rid the Middle East of all vestiges of Western imperialism and, with it, the stinging blight on the Arab character: Israel's continued existence. As president of Egypt, the most powerful Arab state, Nasser became the undisputed leader of the Arab world's objective to destroy Israel. For his part, Nasser made vilifying Israel an art form and repeatedly vowed to destroy the Jewish state. He also helped to sponsor the creation of the Palestinian Liberation Organization in 1964, whose stated purposes were the total liberation of Palestine, the destruction of Israel, and the elimination of Zionism. Achieving these goals was to come through armed struggle and utilization of Arab wealth, manpower, and political unity. The PLO, along with Egypt, Syria, Iraq, and Libya, accepted Moscow's patronage. The U.S. administration was furious. Practically, in the pursuit of Israel's destruction, this patronage meant obtaining weapons, political support, intelligence assistance, and economic aid from the Soviet Union and many Eastern European Soviet Bloc countries. In the Middle East by the 1960s, the cold war between the superpowers and their allies was thus in high gear.

Periodically in the early 1960s, Nasser was criticized by some of his Arab brethren for talking about Israel's destruction but doing little to bring it about. In response, in the spring of 1967, Nasser's verbal antagonism toward Israel reached new levels. Cajoled into action by domestic and regional cohorts, Nasser had United Nations forces stationed in Sinai summarily removed, without the previously promised Security Council permission. By the third week of May 1967, Egypt remilitarized the Sinai Peninsula with five divisions of Egyptian troops. Then, with a naval blockade, the Egyptian president quickly announced the closure of Israel's southern port, Eilat, thereby denying Israel major access to oil supplies that had been coming from the Persian Gulf. At the end of May, Syria and Jordan put their armies under Egyptian military command. With their citizen army already mobilized for almost two weeks, Israelis felt threatened, highly exposed, as if a noose were tightening. Though Nasser might only have intended to rattle his sabers in May 1967, Israel, under great psychological duress and fearful of a crushing defeat, preemptively attacked eleven Egyptian airfields early in the morning of

June 5, 1967. By destroying 189 Egyptian aircraft and 6 airfields by 9:00 A.M., Israel set the tone for the war. After Egyptian tanks in Sinai had lost their air cover, the Israeli Armor Corps quickly swept across the broad peninsula to the Suez Canal. With equal success, Israeli tanks overran the West Bank. Israeli forces also took Jerusalem after the Israeli government had asked the Jordanians to stay out of the war and still Jordanian artillery was fired into Israel. On the Golan Heights, after fierce fighting, the Israeli Army took the city of Kuneitra and came within thirty miles of Damascus. In less than a week, the Egyptian, Syrian, and Jordanian Armies were either devastated or severely damaged. Nasser's political prestige was tarnished. He had offered to resign in the middle of the war, but remained in office after government-orchestrated street demonstrations showed "popular" support for his leadership. The war revealed that conventional Arab military capability was not prepared to fulfill the Arab unity slogan of destroying Israel. The unexpected occurred: Israel increased its territorial dimensions fivefold.

While the results of the war devastated the Arab world, Israel exhibited a sense of relief and new self-esteem, having won a swift and striking military victory. Since gaining independence, Israel had been under a constant state of military threat; its immigrant population, many of whom had survived the Holocaust, possessed an extra measure of insecurity. In the weeks before the June War, Israelis lived in a pressure cooker in which the tension was extraordinary. Then came sudden relief. The war's results caused many Israelis to believe that an Arab soldier was incompetent in battle. Said one American official who served in the region at the time, "To the Israelis everybody was a goy and he's dumb and if he's an Arab goy he's really stupid."[3] Far greater than this attitude of military superiority, the victories over three Arab armies and over contingents from other Arab countries unleashed feelings of triumph along with national euphoria. An impertinent sense of invulnerability became part of Israel's consciousness. There was a sense of complacency and confidence, even "over-whelming arrogance, and a euphoric feeling of well being."[4] With victory came the expectation that the Arabs would have to sue for peace. Said one American diplomat, "Israelis sat around waiting for the telephone to ring, expecting first the Jordanians to step forward." But there was no Arab motivation or compulsion to seek a negotiated settlement with Israel. With unchallenged control over vast new areas of land, Israelis became increasingly comfortable with their territorial spoils of war. They conquered Egypt's Sinai oil fields, developed ski slopes on the Golan Heights, and traveled on off-days to parts of biblical Israel denied them since the 1948 war.

Israel was no longer eleven miles wide at its narrowest point; it now enjoyed occupation of new territory that provided strategic depth to the previously geographically vulnerable Israeli population centers. For Israelis and Jews throughout the world, the unification of Jerusalem under Israeli control contained enormously powerful spiritual and religious value. Jerusalem was no longer a divided city. East Jerusalem, the old city, and the venerated Western Wall (the physical remnant of the Second Jewish Temple), all previously under Jordanian jurisdiction since Israel's Independence War in 1948–1949, were now under exclusive Israeli sovereignty. For many Israelis, dominating portions of the West Bank would become in the years to come demonstrative fulfillment of the long-held Zionist aspiration to reconstitute the Jewish state in all the historic biblical land of Israel. After the 1967 War, the major ideological issue for Israelis did not center around building settlements in these new territories, but on whether and how many Palestinian laborers should be employed in pre-1967 Israel! Encouraged by the Israeli Labor Party, Israelis began to build new settlements in all of the newly acquired territorial areas.

Aside from Israel's many postwar changes were numerous other regional consequences. Attitudes, impressions, and perceptions deepened, reshaped, and were questioned. Israelis, Palestinians, Russians, and Americans all made conceptual adjustments. For the second time in twenty years, Arab states proved unable to defeat Israel; thus the war's results added another layer of cruel cultural and physical punishment. It was a collective Arab emotional setback of stunning proportions. Territorial, economic, and strategic losses from the war were staggering. Israel dominated all of what had been British-mandated Palestine. Before the June 1967 War, Israel was only 8,000 square miles in size. After the war, Israel controlled more than 38,000 square miles of additional Arab land, including all of the Egyptian Sinai Peninsula, the Syrian Golan Heights, east Jerusalem, the Gaza Strip, and the West Bank. After the war, Israel wielded influence over almost one million additional Palestinians, some 350,000 remaining in the population-dense Gaza Strip, the rest in east Jerusalem and the West Bank.

Jordan lost half of its prewar population when the entire West Bank was taken by Israel. The 370,000 Palestinians who crossed the Jordan River to the East Bank added to the refugee population generated by the 1948–1949 War, leaving 650,000 Palestinians in the West Bank and Jerusalem. King Hussein lost control of all the religiously important Muslim holy sites in Jerusalem. One-third of Jordan's gross domestic product and 48 percent of its industrial establishments were lost. The loss of the West Bank meant the loss of half of Jordan's prewar agricultural exports and the loss of 90 percent of tourism revenue.[5] Undoubtedly, the greatest emotional loss to the Arab and Muslim world was Israel's control over all of Jerusalem and the Al-Aqsa Mosque, the third most holy site in Islam. Jerusalem's Muslim and Arab heritage was historically central to Jordan's Hashemite family. Emir Abdullah, who traced his lineage back to the family of Muhammad, the prophet and founder of Islam, founded Transjordan in 1921. Abdullah's father had, with British support, led the 1916 Arab "revolt" against the Turks. During the British mandate for Palestine, Abdullah maintained his own territorial appetite for Palestine, which led him into repeated conflict with Palestinian leaders over that prerogative. In July 1951, young Hussein was standing next to his grandfather at the Al-Aqsa Mosque in Jerusalem when the family patriarch was assassinated by a Palestinian angered that Abdullah had reached the final stages of negotiating an agreement with Israel. After the 1967 War, West Bank political domination by East Bank Hashemite politics, which characterized the 1949–1967 period, did not end immediately. However, the physical removal of Hashemite presence in the West Bank and its replacement by an Israeli military administration saw the birth, evolution, and development of a new assertive Palestinian voice. That voice would be heard twenty years later, when these Palestinians not tethered to Jordan would rebel openly in the 1987 *intifadah* against Israeli occupation.

Before the Golan Heights were captured by Israel, its villages and settlements in the Huleh Valley below suffered from indiscriminate and frequent Syrian shelling; now, they were thoroughly free from that threat. In addition, for the first time Israel controlled the critical headwaters of the Jordan River, a major source of potable water for Israeli domestic consumption and agricultural use. Syria's loss of the Golan Heights put Israeli forces within forty kilometers of Damascus. Eighty thousand Syrians fled the area and became refugees. Since the Golan Heights was a relatively undeveloped region and other damage was not done to Syria's infrastructure, the war had only a limited impact on its economy.

Arab state military failure in the June 1967 War eventually translated into a reemergence of Palestinian national identity and feeling. It generated a rise in the organizational strength and operational activity of the PLO. Most Palestinians saw the Arab state defeat as justification to apply their philosophy of "armed struggle" to the liberation of Palestine. The PLO blossomed as a major force in both inter-Arab affairs and in the battle against Israel. Some Palestinians sought to use Lebanon, Syria, and Jordan as launching pads in their attacks against Israel. In turn, states surrounding Israel found it necessary to limit freedom of Palestinian guerrilla action. Virtually every Palestinian action from sovereign Arab territory against Israel invited an intense Israeli response. Arab states, seeking to curb Israeli retaliation, placed constraints on Palestinian attacks against Israel. Limitations placed on Palestinian action caused friction between PLO and Arab leaders. The latter, however sympathetic to the liberation of Palestine through "armed struggle," were emphatic about protecting their physical and economic infrastructures against Israeli reprisals. Gradually, Arab states focused more and more on defending their national interests and, most particularly, the return of national territories lost in the June War. Jordan and the PLO reignited their competition for the right to retrieve any territory that Israel might return to Arab control. In Egypt, there began a slow rethinking of political priorities: Where should national resources be placed in relation to pan-Arab commitments? Egyptian intellectuals in particular debated the relative importance that the Palestinian question played in defining and setting the priorities for Egypt's national interest. Where and when should Egypt focus on insatiable and staggering domestic problems? When Anwar Sadat succeeded Nasser in 1970, the dominant public debate centered on striking the appropriate balance between satisfying the demands of Egyptian national interests while remaining committed to the restoration of territories lost in the June 1967 War. But unlike before the war, it was not simply the restoration of Palestinian land that was required. Reconstructing the Egyptian economy and restoring Sinai to Egyptian sovereignty became Sadat's mantra.

During the June 1967 War, neither the Soviet Union nor the United States intervened physically on behalf of their Middle Eastern allies, though each made sincere gestures of support. When Israel was conquering the Golan Heights at the end of the war, Moscow sternly impressed upon Washington the need to force Israel to stop its military operations and even threatened military action. The Johnson administration responded by sending the U.S. Sixth Fleet closer to the Syrian coast as a signal that Washington would not be bullied. For Moscow, Israel's victory was traumatic, the defeat of its weapons systems used by Arabs painful. It appeared that a continuing Arab-Israeli confrontation would, once again, reveal the inability of the Soviet Union's friends to produce a victory, and so a continuing Arab-Israeli confrontation presented to Moscow greater dangers than opportunities. Nevertheless, Moscow continued to pour weapons into Syria, Egypt, other Arab clients, and the PLO. In showing solidarity with its Arab friends, Moscow ritually broke diplomatic relations with Israel. Ironically, the massive military defeat of Moscow's Arab clients also allowed it to deepen its relationships with Egypt and Syria.

According to Anatoly Dobrynin, Moscow's ambassador to Washington from 1962 to 1986, Moscow's severance of relations with Israel "proved to be a grave miscalculation because it practically excluded the Soviet Union from any serious role in a Middle East settlement." By favoring the Arabs, Moscow was "left with little flexibility because [Moscow] often blindly followed [their] Arab allies."[6] After the war, Moscow wanted to demonstrate to its Arab clients that it could force Israel's withdrawal via pressure and international censure, while Washington wanted to relieve the Middle East of the conflict, stabilize the region, limit Soviet presence, and secure Israel's existence. In the fracturing of the Middle East, Washington suffered diplomatically too, as numerous Arab states aligned ever more closely with Moscow and severed relations with the United States because of its continued support of Israel. The absence of sufficient and experienced American diplomatic personnel in Egypt and Syria, for example, denied Washington any decided advantage in trying to differentiate Sadat's motivations from that of his predecessor or to assess accurately the degree of tension between Egypt and Jordan and Egypt and Syria.[7]

On the first day of the June War, the State Department announced that the

United States was neutral in "thought, word, and deed." Then on several occasions during the war, Washington claimed it supported the territorial integrity of all states in the region and would support all of the efforts by the Security Council to end the fighting.[8] After the war, President Johnson did not believe Washington should launch a high-level, intensive peace-making effort immediately. Yet on June 19, 1967, he delivered a major public address in which he set forth five major principles for resolving the Middle East conflict: the recognized right to national life; justice for the refugees; innocent maritime passage; limits on the arms race; and political independence and territorial integrity for all. Johnson remembered Israel's total withdrawal from Sinai after the Suez War in 1956. Israel had honored Eisenhower's pressured withdrawal, but it received nothing in return. This time, Johnson's approach placed less emphasis on a total Israeli withdrawal; rather, it encouraged the establishment of a structure where if territory were returned, a framework for peace would be developed. Gradually, the United States and the Soviet Union worked together to devise a diplomatic formula that could be used as a framework to settle the Arab-Israeli conflict.

Initially in working on a United Nations Security Council resolution, the United States supported a resolution that called for complete Israeli withdrawal from the territories taken in the June 1967 War. In this Latin American draft, the Israelis objected to the phraseology of the request for "Israel to withdraw all its forces from all the territories occupied as a result of the recent conflict." By September, the U.S. position no longer favored a full Israeli withdrawal from territories taken in June 1967. The Israelis, for their part, wanted direct negotiations mentioned in any United Nations resolution, but President Nasser specifically rejected any notion or resolution that committed Egypt to face-to-face negotiations with Israel.[9] (Six years later, the idea of direct negotiations was accepted by Egypt in a United Nations resolution at the end of the October 1973 War.) At the end of August 1967, Arab states put down their uncompromising diplomatic markers. At their Arab Summit they "agreed to unite their political efforts on the international and diplomatic level . . . and to ensure the withdrawal of the aggressive Israeli forces from the Arab lands occupied since the June 5 aggression." Moreover, they vowed "no peace with Israel, no recognition of Israel, no negotiations with it, and adherence to the rights of the Palestinian people in their country." In agreeing to these Arab Summit Conference Resolutions, President Nasser and King Hussein obtained subsidies from the oil-producing Arab countries and therefore were more willing not to engage in any political settlement with Israel.[10]

Finally, after prodigious efforts by the U.S. ambassador to the United Nations, Arthur J. Goldberg, and compromise language offered by Soviet Deputy Foreign Minister V. V. Kuznetsov and the British delegate, Lord Caradon, United Nations Security Council (UNSC) Resolution 242 was passed unanimously on November 22, 1967. It read:

UNITED NATIONS SECURITY COUNCIL RESOLUTION 242
22 NOVEMBER 1967

The Security Council,

Expressing its continuing concern with the grave situation in the Middle East,

Emphasizing the inadmissibility of the acquisition of territory by war and the need to work for a just and lasting peace in which every State in the area can live in security,

Emphasizing further that all Member States in their acceptance of the Charter of the United Nations have undertaken a commitment to act in accordance with Article 2 of the Charter,

1. Affirms that the fulfillment of Charter principles requires the establishment of a just and lasting peace in the Middle East which should include the application of both the following principles:
   a. Withdrawal of Israeli armed forces from territories occupied in the recent conflict;
   b. Termination of all claims or states of belligerency and respect for and acknowledgment of the sovereignty, territorial integrity and political independence of every State in the area and their right to live in peace within secure and recognized boundaries free from threats or acts of force;

2. Affirms further the necessity
   a. For guaranteeing freedom of navigation through international waterways in the area;
   b. For achieving a just settlement of the refugee problem;
   c. For guaranteeing the territorial inviolability and political independence of every State in the area, through measures including the establishment of demilitarized zones;

3. Requests the Secretary-General to designate a Special Representative to proceed to the Middle East to establish and maintain contacts with the States concerned in order to promote agreement and assist with efforts to achieve a peaceful and accepted settlement in accordance with the provisions and principles in this resolution;

4. Requests the Secretary-General to report to the Security Council on the progress of the efforts of the Special Representative as soon as possible.

Adopted unanimously at the 1382nd meeting.

For the resolution to pass unanimously, its language was made deliberately ambiguous. Consequently, each side in the Arab-Israeli conflict had its own interpretation of the resolution. None of the countries associated with the conflict embraced it immediately. As a compromise document, depending upon one's viewpoint there were parts of it that contained degrees of acceptability. As a framework, however, its contents were understood as a general outline from which the negotiations of specifics could be defined. The resolution contained all of Johnson's outline except for his call for arms limitations. Its preamble emphasized "the inadmissibility of the acquisition of territory by war," and the text itself called for "withdrawal of Israeli armed forces from territories occupied in the recent conflict, a settlement of the refugee problem, and termination of all claims of belligerency and respect for the territorial integrity and political independence of every State in the area and their right to live in peace within secure and recognized boundaries free from threats or acts of force." The resolution additionally called for UN mediation, a role that fell initially to Sweden's ambassador to Moscow, Gunnar Jarring. Though the resolution did not specifically call for an exchange of territory for peace, this concept evolved from it as a basis of Arab-Israeli negotiations. Several weeks after the resolution's passage, Egypt accepted it, but insisted that withdrawal meant "from all the territories" while ignoring other elements.[11] In May 1968, Israel formally accepted UNSC Resolution 242, but not until May 1970 did Israeli Prime Minister Golda Meir give public endorsement to it. It took Syria more than six years to accept UNSC 242; the PLO finally accepted it in 1988. In both instances withdrawal was defined as "full and complete, including Jerusalem." The resolution posed several serious problems for the PLO. First, it only referred to the refugee problem and did not mention the Palestinians by name; second, it did not call for any political solution for the Palestinians; and third, the resolution called for an end to the state of belligerency and an acceptance of the political independence of every state in the area, which implicitly included Israel.

In 1967 and 1968, the United States worked quietly to support mediation of the conflict, including Jarring's efforts. But there were several reasons why active Middle East diplomacy did not immediately flow from the resolution's passage. First, the United States was not yet fully committed to break the impasse in the Arab-Israeli conflict. Second, neither the Israelis nor the Egyptians had any dire incentive to pursue an agreement between them. Among some Israelis there was even a sense that mediation or action by an intermediary was demeaning: they had won the war and therefore the Arabs should seek peace directly from them. And third, Jarring "didn't have the kind of self-confidence as a negotiator or a mediator that was really required. . . . He had no clout, no means of rewarding the parties. He was a postman, and if he got beyond that he was finished."[12] Moreover, Jarring's mission faltered, in part because he was not a forceful enough mediator and because the Americans were presenting their own plan at the same time.

Early in 1969, immediately after assuming office, President Nixon believed that the Middle East was still potentially explosive and that the United States should support several simultaneous initiatives in seeking a "package settlement." These initiatives included support for Jarring's mediation, bilateral talks with the Soviet Union, four power talks that would include Britain, France, and the Soviet Union, and perhaps an American-led mediation role. In the meetings with the Soviet Union, the United States stressed the need for the parties to sign a peace treaty and the need for final borders to be close to the 1967 lines. Both the United States and the Soviet Union had taken it upon themselves to be proxies for their respective allies; Washington was not officially talking to Cairo, nor did Jerusalem have diplomatic relations with Moscow. Both superpowers were seeking to achieve a comprehensive settlement to the conflict. Nixon wanted to test Soviet intentions in the region: Did Moscow want to pursue "controlled tension" or work with Washington to arrive at a settlement between Egypt and Israel? After a careful review, Nixon concluded that Moscow was not interested in resolving the conflict; he therefore affirmed a policy, from March 1969 forwards, "of a unilateral role for the United States" in resolving the conflict alone, save for limited or ceremonial Soviet participation.[13] If other powers or the UN were to play a role, then it would be a subordinate one to the United States. American foreign policy objectives in the Middle East were tied to the dual apprehension that nonsettlement of the conflict would lead to radicalization of the region and to a deterioration of superpower relations. Nixon's foreign policy in the Middle East vis-à-vis Soviet relations was threefold: to demonstrate Moscow's impotence; to deny them further influence; and to reduce their existing influence whenever possible. At once Nixon wanted to punish Arab countries that enjoyed positive relationships with the Soviet Union and to persuade them to turn to Washington.

In a speech on December 9, 1969, Secretary of State William Rogers offered his plan for a negotiated and comprehensive Arab-Israeli settlement. The so-called Rogers Plan outlined a "package settlement," an end to the state of war between Egypt and Israel, establishment of secure borders and demilitarized zones, a just settlement of the refugee problem, and withdrawal of Israeli armed forces from the Egyptian territory occupied in the June 1967 War. It set forth an Israeli-Jordanian accommodation whereby Jerusalem would be settled by having both countries share Jerusalem's governance. State Department personnel who drafted Rogers's remarks did not discuss the plan's points in advance with the Israelis. Since the Israeli government sensed that the formula for an agreement was being forced upon them, and because its contents were unacceptable, they rejected it within forty-eight hours. Israelis were not going to return to the pre-June 1967 borders that could only be precariously defended. And according to Israeli leaders, there were too many negotiating partners for a comprehensive approach to work. Neither Israelis nor Egyptians wanted a mediator in whom they had no confidence or trust.

Moreover, there was no compelling reason in the regional status quo to precipitate a rush to negotiate an agreement.

From April 1969 through August 1970, during the time when the Rogers Plan was floated and sunk, Egypt and Israel fought the War of Attrition along the Suez Canal. Cairo's goals included inflicting as many casualties on Israel as possible, undermining morale, destroying Israel's newly built Suez Canal length fortification, known as the Bar-Lev line, and bringing the crisis to an apex that would cause the superpowers to force Israel out of Sinai. Egyptian use of artillery bombardments and commando raids were met by Israeli efforts to destroy Egypt's air defense system and batter Egypt's Suez Canal cities into evacuation.[14] So successful were Israel's deep penetration raids into Egypt and against these cities that after Nasser went secretly to Moscow in January 1970, he permitted Soviet control of Egypt's air defenses in the canal zone. The situation in the canal area escalated. In April 1970, Israel detected the participation of Soviet personnel in operational missions over the Suez area, and, in August, when Israeli pilots shot down six Soviet pilots flying Egyptian aircraft, Israel did not allow official publication of it at home but made sure that word got out quickly to the international press. Only later did Egyptian sources publicize the Soviet losses. In mid-June, another Rogers initiative was proposed based on UNSC Resolution 242, tying it to a cease-fire in the War of Attrition. This time there was no specific mention of Israeli withdrawal to the pre-June 1967 War borders. Nasser accepted the cease-fire, but he also cheated by using the ninety-day halt in fighting, which came into effect on August 7, 1970, to construct shelters and move Soviet-made missiles close to the Suez Canal. He accepted this second Rogers initiative because he saw it as an opportunity to halt his devastating military losses and, if possible, stall U.S. delivery of more Phantoms to Israel. Nasser's placement of these missiles was of critical benefit to Sadat. During the October War, they caused Israel devastating aircraft losses, created a protective umbrella for troops that stormed across the canal, and effectively cut off Israeli Air Force action over the battle areas near the canal.[15] In 1970, Israel wanted the United States to force Egypt to remove the missiles, but Washington was unable to do so. As compensation, Israel received from Washington additional Phantom aircraft. For Washington, these fresh aircraft were not meant to extract some diplomatic concession from Israel, but were designed to show the Soviet Union that the United States would assist its ally. Soviet-inspired cease-fire violations undertaken by Egypt, in addition to Israeli partnership in protecting Jordan's political and territorial integrity, caused Washington to view Israel as an important strategic asset.

Despite his public attacks against Israel and Zionism and still less than half a year in office, Sadat sent a cable through the Americans to the Israelis in December 1970, suggesting that he would consider making an agreement with them if they withdrew from all of Sinai. An Israeli Foreign Ministry official showed a colleague Sadat's cable, pointed his hand in the direction of the prime minister's office, and said, "Betach yehargu otah (surely they are going to kill it)."[16] Those apprehensions were realized. Sadat considered the possibility of arriving at some form of phased Israeli withdrawal from Sinai in exchange for something far less than a peace treaty, a military agreement but not a political document. Independently of Sadat's musings, Israeli Defense Minister Moshe Dayan also considered some form or framework for a phased Israeli withdrawal from Sinai. Each wanted a change in the status quo: Sadat wanted his land without having to go to war; Dayan too wanted an agreement without fighting a war. Dayan approached Prime Minister Meir with the idea of a unilateral but only partial withdrawal from Sinai, which would result in some interim arrangement with Egypt. Dayan reasoned that if Israel withdrew from the canal area "far enough so that we do not sit on their [Suez Canal] neck" and receive an Egyptian promise to rebuild the canal cities and open the canal, which had been closed since the June 1967 War, this would be the best assurance that Egypt's intentions were not to launch another war, and perhaps even would bring about negotiations. "On the other hand," Dayan said, "we must be in a position that if they violate our expectations, within hours we will be there to take care of the situation."[17] He floated this idea in front of several Israeli newspaper editors, then repeated it in public. He wanted to see if such a notion of "disengaging" from the Egyptians had any public support. Dayan saw virtue in having the Israelis pull back from the canal both for the maritime users and for Israel's strategic interests. What mattered was that Golda Meir did not approve of Dayan's idea: she said, "We retreat one inch from the canal . . . [we] will in no time land at the international border."[18] Dayan was unable to convince her or their cabinet peers of this idea's merit. Sadat did not discard his readiness to consider a negotiated solution with Israel. Several months into his presidency, Sadat convened the Egyptian National Security Council and extended the first ninety-day cease-fire period for a second ninety-day period, which was to end on February 4, 1971.[19]

Sadat was prepared to recognize Israel, *if* there would be full Israeli withdrawal from all the occupied territories (including east Jerusalem), with the first step being withdrawal from the canal to the strategic Gidi and Mitla Passes in Sinai.[20] Sadat suggested to Israel, through Rogers, that a military disengagement of forces be implemented in some partial manner. Sadat's plan called for partial Israeli withdrawal, first from the Suez Canal by a distance of approximately fifteen kilometers, the stationing of six hundred Egyptian policemen with rifles on the east side of the canal, the reopening of the canal, and then final withdrawal from all of Sinai as part of the full implementation of UNSC Resolution 242.[21] Upon receiving the suggestions, Meir asked Rabin to check with Kissinger about U.S. interest in seeing the canal reopened. She was reasonably sure that because of the Vietnam War and the Soviet Union's desire to use the Suez Canal, Washington would frown upon opening the canal for strategic reasons alone, but she was wrong. Kissinger replied that if the opening of the canal would help bring stability to the Middle East, then that was what the Israelis should consider. Meir was surprised but still did not take positive action on Sadat's initiative,[22] in large measure because its contents contained "the Arabs' maximalist positions."[23]

According to Gideon Rafael, the director general of the Israeli Foreign Ministry at the time, "Meir was more interested in receiving Phantom jet fighters from Washington than in listening to what Sadat was offering. The Israeli political leadership at the time could not accept even the symbolic presence of even a mere token Egyptian police force on the Israeli-occupied east bank of the canal."[24] Three years later, however, Israel did accept an Egyptian presence much greater than a police force. Some of Meir's closest confidants could not believe that Sadat was serious about entering into a separate agreement with Israel. Others, including some in the Israeli military, believed that "Golda Meir's government was still keeping the old holy cows" of refusing to have Egyptian soldiers or policemen on the east (Israeli-held) side of the canal as the first phase of implementing UNSC Resolution 242.[25] Meir did respond to Sadat's overture, but her peace map did not conform with Sadat's absolute requirement of placing Egyptian troops in Sinai after an Israeli withdrawal. Instead, she wanted to retain portions of Sinai and to keep Jerusalem and the Golan Heights under Israeli jurisdiction and control. She would not permit Egyptian forces to cross Sinai, nor would she accept any direct or indirect link of any Sinai arrangement with a commitment to withdrawal on other fronts.[26] Without a commitment for a full peace from Egypt, Israel would not entertain a proposal that made a peace treaty with Egypt contingent upon its withdrawal from the other territories, including east Jerusalem, and some PLO participation in negotiations. Sadat's diplomatic initiatives were spurned by Israel because they contained more territorial concessions than Israel was willing to accept, considering that Sadat was offering much less in return in terms of the nature of peace. For Israel, a nonbelligerent relationship with Egypt without the trappings of full peace and normalization was insufficient compensation for the return of all of Sinai. Israel was determined that this was the end of an era of armistice agreements, of indirect and unwritten understandings, in return for which Israel had to give up territory. Israel was not prepared to accept again vulnerable borders. Israel wanted peace treaties. Israel took the position that Lyndon Johnson had advocated immediately after the June 1967 War: no more Israeli withdrawals without peace treaties.

By February 1971, there were two other diplomatic initiatives that had been pursued, one through Rogers, the other through UN mediator Gunnar Jarring. According to Sadat, "Nobody paid attention to the February 1971 offer of a peace agreement with Israel where Israel could withdraw in stages and Jarring would come and complete the withdrawal between the Arabs and Israel in six months."[27] All three diplomatic initiatives focused on Sinai and the Egyptian-Israeli front. Israel did not consider giving, nor did it receive, any public suggestion for a negotiated settlement on the Golan. Though Israel had proposed a total withdrawal from the Golan Heights after the June 1967 War in exchange for a peace treaty, Syria said no thank you. Recognizing Israel even with the Golan Heights in Syrian possession was not considered in Damascus.[28] Discussion of the West Bank's future was taken up in secret negotiations between Jordanian and Israeli leaders. In this circumstance, Jordan was not going to be the first country to sign a peace treaty with Israel, and Israel was not prepared to return all of the West Bank and east Jerusalem as Jordan wanted. In April 1971, Sadat told American officials that an Israeli withdrawal could be in stages: the details of the depth of withdrawal were unimportant to him; the only thing that mattered was an ultimate Israeli commitment to total withdrawal from all of Sinai. Sadat was not picky about the depth of Israel's first withdrawal or how many stages the withdrawal took; he was more interested in getting Israel to commit itself to a total Israeli withdrawal from Sinai. He told Michael Sterner, the Egyptian desk officer at the Department of State, "The only thing that's important is that I have the ultimate commitment now, before any actions take place, that there is going to be a final withdrawal."[29] Some in the National Security Council believed that in 1971 there was a chance to get a disengagement agreement along the canal because Dayan wanted it and Sadat was tempted. It was, said Quandt, "a doable proposition."[30]

However, in 1971 and 1972, a significant reason why Meir did not take Sadat's overtures seriously was that she knew Kissinger was not interested in putting either his weight or time behind an Egyptian-Israeli negotiating effort. By the middle of 1973, why should Washington or Israel have forced a new diplomatic initiative, if the status quo was not sufficiently troublesome to warrant changing it? There was no real or perceived strategic threat to Israel because of its occupation of the territories, including Sinai. Furthermore, both before and after the October War, the Israeli government was not prepared to accept any linkage between the first and later stages of withdrawal, or to accept linkage between the withdrawal on one front and withdrawal on other fronts. There was no political consensus within Israel about how or where to apply the "withdrawal from territories" notion mentioned in UNSC Resolution 242. In Israel, many believed that after all the wars with the Egyptians, Sinai was now a vital strategic buffer that should not be returned to Egypt. Nonetheless, the discussions from 1969 to 1973 between Washington, Egypt, and Israel, which dealt with the substance and nature of possible withdrawal from Sinai, were quite detailed. Both sides talked in terms of phases or stages of withdrawal; both sides understood that this was a first, or interim, agreement leading to perhaps others. The substance of the exchanges included discussion about establishing demilitarized zones, the depth of withdrawals, and the linkage of territorial withdrawals to a final peace arrangement. Many of these components would reappear in the negotiations for the separation of forces and disengagement agreements signed after the October 1973 War.

The legacy of these unanswered initiatives is that whether from the efforts sponsored by the United Nations, United States, or Dayan/Sadat, the focus of diplomatic attention was on Egypt first, a thought Sadat began to develop in his own mind and then to nurture, and which Israel easily accepted. What is astonishing is that Sadat made his initial suggestions for a diplomatic accommodation with Israel through interim agreements, implemented in phases *before* he removed domestic threats to his own leadership. The so-called "corrective revolution" that took place in May 1971 removed political challenges to his regime, some of which were pro-Moscow in their orientation.

With the comprehensive Rogers Plan summarily dismissed that March, both Israeli and Egyptian leaders considered an interim arrangement in Sinai. By late 1971, the UN's role faded too while U.S.-Israeli relations were strengthened with a long-term military arms supply agreement with the United States. In October, through Donald Bergus, who headed the American interests section under the auspices of the Spanish embassy after Egyptian-U.S. diplomatic relations were severed after the 1967 War, Sadat presented the idea for proximity talks to the United States: Israel and Egypt would not be engaged in direct talks but would be present in the same hotel with the mediator shuttling between the rooms of the delegations. The goal was to be a six-month, renewable-phased agreement with the Israelis. In these potential discussions, Sadat wanted Israel to withdraw to the strategic passes in Sinai with Egyptian troops or forces allowed to cross the canal with some UN supervision;[31] in return, Israel would not receive a nonbelligerency understanding, let alone a peace agreement. When Meir visited Washington in December 1971, she affirmed with Nixon and Kissinger their collective view that interim or phased agreements as suggested by Sadat were, in fact, preferable to a comprehensive agreement. Still, the American foreign policy bureaucracy, especially the State Department, preferred a comprehensive plan that included above all a solution to the Palestinian question. It suspended that institutional preference after the October War when only interim agreements were possible and reaffirmed a comprehensive settlement outlook at the end of the Ford administration and during Carter's first year in office.

For the return of Sinai to Egyptian sovereignty, Sadat developed both a diplomatic and military option in a relative simultaneous and intertwined fashion. With regular diplomatic relations between Cairo and Washington cut since the June 1967 War, Sadat wanted a direct line of communication to Kissinger. He insisted that Kissinger *listen*. In September 1971, Sadat appointed Hafez Ismail as his national security adviser, an appointment intended to create an Egyptian position parallel to that held by Kissinger. Sadat's intentional creation of such an official position did not go unnoticed by Kissinger. By the end of 1971, Sadat had learned from the Saudis that Kissinger was seriously interested in seeing the Soviets expelled from Egypt.[32] Closer collaboration and support for Sadat soon came from the Saudis (who at one point used Assistant Secretary of State Joseph Sisco as their contact) after pro-Soviet elements were expelled from Egypt. At the same time, Sadat needed arms to renew warfare with Israel, but Moscow said no to the Egyptian requests. When, in December 1971, the Soviets rushed arms to India during the Indo-Pakistani War, including shipments dispatched through Cairo, Sadat realized that if the Soviets wanted to send weapons, they could and would. Sadat's impatience with Moscow grew.[33]

His irritation with Moscow did not abate, while the Soviet Union showed no inclination to help Egypt rid Sinai of Israel's presence. Particular displeasure was held for Moscow's unwillingness or inability to apply pressure on Israel through Washington. As early as 1972, Sadat reckoned that the Soviet Union was a declining military power with waning international influence, a revolutionary and prescient assessment. Moscow was benefiting more and Cairo less from Egypt's reliance upon the Soviet Union. There was a sense that Moscow took Egypt for granted; it had repeatedly been arrogant, petty, and stingy in providing military equipment and foreign aid to Egypt.[34]

By General el-Gamasy's recollection, Presidents Sadat and Assad decided by March 1972, four months before the expulsion of Soviet advisers from Egypt and eighteen months before the October War began, that they would plan to go to war in a coordinated manner against Israel, though it would be another year later when they would make the actual decision to go to war. "Before that [March 1972], there were no political consultations about going to war,"[35] except during the last years of Nasser's rule in Egypt, when Damascus and Cairo had agreed in principle to coordinate their political and military efforts to bring about the return of their territories.[36] Nonetheless, in 1972 and 1973, Sadat continued to send military delegations to Moscow and receive high-ranking Soviet military officials in Cairo. In the spring of 1972, Egyptian military officials were purchasing from their Moscow suppliers equipment that could be used to break down the sand walls erected by the Israelis along the east side of the Suez Canal.

Still, Sadat remained perturbed at the results of the U.S.-Soviet Summit in May 1972, because the "Middle East was put on ice."[37] More exactly, the Soviet Union wanted to include in the summit communiqué "some fairly striking language that expressed some urgency [for a diplomatic settlement which] Kissinger evaded, and the Soviets caved in to some rather bland language"[38] because they did not want to disturb detente. The same month, Meir had a meeting with Rumanian President Ceausescu in which he told her that he had heard it from Sadat himself that he was ready to meet with an Israeli—"Maybe with me, maybe not; maybe the meeting would be at a slightly lower level," Ceausescu said, to which Meir replied, "This is the best news I have heard for many years."[39] Nothing ensued from the Rumanian president's suggestion. At the time, Meir's instincts told her not to trust Sadat. According to the estimate of an Israeli intelligence official at the time, "Golda was locked in a ghetto-like perception of the world."[40] Years later, when Sadat made it known that he would come to Israel, Meir did not believe, until the last moment, that he would actually come. She even said to a longtime friend, Israel Galili, "Grass will grow in my hand if he comes to Jerusalem."[41]

Sadat was pursuing several options simultaneously, preparing multiple means to accomplish Sinai's liberation. In developing parallel tracts of force and diplomacy, Sadat was playing his characteristic "hide-and-seek," testing diplomatic openings while preparing for war. He had more surprises in store. In July 1972, Sadat pre-emptively demanded the departure of roughly 15,000 to 20,000 Soviet military advisers from Egypt, the handing over of all Soviet military installations to Egyptian control, and the export or sale to Egypt of all Soviet military equipment. Russia had developed almost an extraterritorial presence in Egypt, including military bases and installations where Egyptians were not wanted or permitted, such as at the port in Alexandria. Sadat detested Soviet haughtiness toward Egypt, and he was not alone in this thinking. Among some junior-level Egyptian generals trained in Moscow, there had developed personal and professional disdain for their Russian hosts, who seemingly always wanted to compromise their training of the Egyptians with women and booze.[42] Sadat's expulsion of the Soviet advisers went unopposed by a significant segment of the Egyptian military elite who, for a good period of time prior to the expulsion, had been ready to see the Russians leave Egypt. Furthermore, there was little political fallout because, save for a few exceptions, Egypt's domestic environment embraced the decision.[43] Some believe that the Soviets were actually planning their departure from Egypt well before Sadat's request and were especially reluctant to maintain their military presence if Sadat was going to war and could possibly drag them into the fight.[44] Regardless, the Soviets complied immediately. They took some sophisticated missile equipment with them and recalled their ambassador from Cairo, but retained some of their naval facilities and privileges.

Sadat's handling of the Soviets was indicative of his political style. He master-minded the operation himself, not consulting with any of his advisers in advance.[45] His actions were motivated by a historical déjà vu: twenty years earlier he and his cohorts had rid Egypt of Britain's heavy-handed colonial control. Russian presence had been constraining Sadat's preparation for military action, including the element of surprise. In reflecting upon the expulsion, Sadat said, "I had endured a great deal of personal insult and national humiliation. All their calculations were based on the fact that I was not their man."[46] In the Middle East, at the time, the Soviets had a large stake in Syria, Libya, Iraq, and Yemen. In order to remain physically in the region, they provided these Arab clients with more arms and supplies. Yet according to Egyptian career foreign service officer Omar Sirry, though the Russians trained Egyptians and gave them arms, "they would never have allowed us to go to war."[47]

By all known accounts, Sadat did not expect the favor of an American reply to his expulsion of the Soviet military advisers. And no Egyptian official, save for Hafez Ismail, indicated that perhaps Sadat was responding to Kissinger's hope to have the Soviet advisers removed from Egypt. At the time, Moshe Dayan believed that Sadat's main purpose in evicting the Soviets "was not just to get them out but to get the Americans in."[48] However, the expulsion of the Soviet advisers was likely a quid pro quo known only to a few in the CIA. Since the late 1960s, Sadat had been apparently receiving direct payments from the CIA.[49] Prior to the May 1972 Soviet-backed plot to unseat Sadat, the CIA alerted him of the attempt on his rule. Therefore, his expulsion of the Soviet advisers two months later was in keeping with an already developed relationship with the CIA and the United States. By comparison, Middle East specialists at the State Department were uniformly surprised that Sadat ejected the Russians from Egypt without prior consultation with Washington for some sort of quid pro quo for such a dramatic political action.[50] Kissinger, for his part, was astounded by Sadat's expulsion of the Soviets; he thought it was bold, brilliant, even a bit wacky. Kissinger asked rhetorically: "Why has Sadat done *me* [*sic*] this favor? Why didn't he get in touch with me? Why didn't he demand of me all kinds of concessions first? We considered him a fool for taking such a major step and not asking anything in return."[51] But this was Sadat's way, and the Americans did not understand that he wanted to be an independent actor. Sadat reckoned that, had he asked the Americans for something in return, it was likely that a Washington leak would have diminished the impact of what he intended to do, or that Kissinger would have bargained with him to a degree that he would have not received very much for the act. What he wanted was Washington's ongoing notice, and he needed to prove his credibility with the White House; surprising U.S. officials seemed to him the best way. The expulsion of the Soviets cleared the way for expanding the highly secret American contacts with Sadat, through the CIA and through the Saudis, contacts known to only a very few in Washington. A meeting of the two national security advisers did not take place until February 1973, in part because Kissinger was consumed with concluding the Vietnam talks, and also because Sadat wanted to redefine first his working relationship with Moscow before embarking on his diplomatic track with Washington.[52] Despite the expulsion of the Soviet advisers, Sadat succeeded in obtaining Soviet weapons necessary for a Sinai operation.[53] Virtually uninterrupted military supply flow from Moscow led support to the notion that Brezhnev wanted to repatriate Soviet advisers and their families and, at the same time, sustain some leverage over Cairo. The official low point in Egyptian-Soviet relations was reached at the end of March 1976, when President Sadat unilaterally abrogated the Egyptian Friendship Treaty with Moscow. In historical perspective, Sadat's expulsion of the Soviets and his turn to Washington might have been the single greatest Third World success for the United States during the entire cold war.

Realistically, Sadat could not rush into Washington's embrace even if he helped to limit Soviet presence in the region. Sadat was perturbed that the Kissinger-Ismail talks were postponed in favor of attention directed toward another world issue. From July 1972 through February 1973, Sadat kept open several channels of communication with Washington. The ongoing CIA channel, opened as early as October 1971, continued after the Ismail-Kissinger talks concluded. Though Sadat generated friction with Moscow, neither Nixon nor Kissinger rewarded Sadat for pursuing Nixon's objective of loosening Arab ties to the Soviet Union. Furthermore, Washington did not demonstrate any interest in applying pressure for an Israeli withdrawal from Sinai. There continued to be an attitude that as there was no issue of crisis proportion, it was acceptable diplomatically to maintain the status quo. Things, however, were not as quiet inside Egypt.

An internal debate between advocates of war and those who believed that war would serve no purpose became rancorous and pointed, unfolding on Egyptian university campuses, among intellectuals, in the media, and at demonstrations. The debate included criticism of Egypt's leadership and its style of autocratic governance. Agreement existed that the status quo needed to be altered, but in which direction? Sadat was angry about American neglect; he expected more from Washington. Only meager and sporadic efforts by the superpowers had been shown toward affecting an Israeli withdrawal. The "no-war, no-peace" situation was becoming less tolerable. In early 1973, Sadat sent Egyptian War Minister Ahmad Ismail to the Soviet Union, where the ongoing venture of squeezing additional military supplies from Moscow continued. At about the same time, in February 1973, Kissinger's first meeting with Hafez Ismail took place in Armonk, New York. Kissinger wanted to conduct discussions to see where they stood before important negotiations could be started. In his conversations with Kissinger, which lasted a full day and a half, Ismail was speaking for Egypt, but he also recalled that he had the rest of the "Arab world on his conscience." Nonetheless, Ismail emphasized primarily Egyptian objectives when he told Kissinger of Sadat's general overview of the region: Egypt had a leading role to play in the future of the Middle East; the United States needed to take a more evenhanded American approach to the Arab-Israeli conflict; and the existing status quo of Israel's occupation of Sinai and other territories was untenable. And once again, Ismail proposed an Israeli withdrawal from Sinai in stages.[54] The concept of an interim agreement, implemented in stages with a guaranteed final outcome, was what Sadat had in mind. Kissinger stressed to Ismail that Sadat had to provide some assurances to Israel. He suggested some permanent overlap between restoration of Egyptian sovereignty and the maintenance of an Israeli presence in civilian garb for security purposes. Kissinger further suggested that there be no diplomatic movement until after Israel's parliamentary elections in October. Ismail had the impression, after both talks with Kissinger, that "Henry was still fully immersed in the conviction that Israel was untouchable. No one could hurt its superiority. No one could do anything to Israel. Egypt might as well just sign on the dotted line and accept the status quo. Kissinger was not responding." "The October War," Ghorbal said, "was the result of the meeting."[55] The concession to Israeli presence on Egyptian territory was totally unacceptable to Sadat. Ismail's talks with Kissinger proved fruitless.

In March, Ismail saw Kissinger again, this time in Paris. Kissinger told him that the United States would not affirm the guarantee of Egyptian sovereign rights over Sinai, and Ismail told Kissinger he did not think there was any reason for them to meet again. Kissinger bluntly told Ismail during these discussions that

> we live in a world of realities and facts. The fact is that you, the Arabs, have been defeated and that Israel has been victorious. You talk as though you were the victors and Israel were the loser. The situation will not change unless you change it militarily. Despite this, I wish you to convey some advice to Sadat and tell him: Beware of attempting to change the situation militarily because you will be defeated again as you were defeated in 1967. There would then be no hope of finding a settlement on the basis of a just peace or anything else. Nobody would be able to speak to Israel.[56]

That same month, a new Egyptian government was formed in which Sadat himself took the position of premier. He reserved all critical decision-making authority for himself while he planned for war and for the diplomatic opening he envisioned would follow it. Ismail was to see Kissinger again in April, but Sadat asked him to postpone the visit until after the new government had time to solidify. Sadat's decision to go to war was made at an Egyptian Cabinet meeting on April 5, 1973. General el-Gamasy delivered the war plan to him that month, and he "was sure that there would be a war between Egypt and Israel within six months."[57]

Then Sadat enlisted Saudi King Feisal's support for use of an oil embargo against the United States and against other Western countries because of their continued support of Israel. Before the war commenced, Sadat had a promise from the Saudis that they would use the oil embargo as part of the political leverage he sought to impose on Washington. But in reality, King Feisal did not want to apply an oil embargo on the United States and the West until he actually saw Sadat initiate the war.[58] Feisal had sent several messages to Washington expressing his profound dissatisfaction with Israel's continued occupation of Arab lands, causing trepidation in Washington that an Arab oil embargo might be used as political leverage against the United States if the status quo remained stagnant. Historically, the Saudis had mistrusted Egypt under Nasser; however, Feisal and Sadat got along reasonably well. Nonetheless, the existence of Arab disharmony, though its degrees were somewhat known to Americans and Israelis alike, was not considered sufficient to see the Arab world as anything but uniformly committed to Israel's destruction. By the summer of 1973, Egypt had mediocre or poor relations with the PLO, many Arab Gulf states, Iraq, Jordan, and Algeria. Guardedly and cleverly, to his own population as well as to his Arab peers and the Israelis, Sadat masked inter-Arab differences and the capabilities of his military.

However, Sadat did not hide his intentions. Whether or not anyone took seriously his public statements about a military option is not certain. Obviously, Israelis and Americans were listening, but they were still encased in a concept that the Arabs would not attack Israel. Sadat told Arnaud de Borchegrave in *Newsweek* of April 9, 1973:

The time has come for a shock. Diplomacy will continue before, during, and after the battle. All West Europeans are telling us that everybody has fallen asleep over the Middle East crisis. But they will soon wake up to the fact that America has left us no other way out. The resumption of the hostilities is the only way out. Everything is now being mobilized in concert for the resumption of the battle which is inevitable.[59]

That month he met secretly with President Assad in Egypt and told him, "Hafez, I am going to war this year. What do you think? He said: I am with you."[60] Only Egyptian War Minister Ahmed Ismail and General el-Gamasy knew about this visit. War Minister Ismail presented Sadat and Assad with el-Gamasy's handwritten copy of the proposed operational war plan. Three possible time frames were considered for launching the proposed Egyptian-Syrian attack: May 1973, September 1973, or October 1973. Undertaking a war anytime after October 1973 was deemed unsuitable because of the projected poor weather conditions on the Golan Heights. They dismissed the May 1973 date as too soon, primarily because Syria still wanted to obtain additional weapons from the Soviet Union.

However, in May 1973, Egypt deployed its forces along the canal in such a manner that Israeli military intelligence thought that Sadat would go to the brink of war, but not actually launch one. Yet the possibility of a pending Egyptian military attack caused the Israeli Chief of Staff, David Elazar, to expand Israel's military infrastructure including the establishment of new divisions. He also ordered a partial mobilization of Israel's citizen army, which cost Israel approximately eleven million dollars. But the Egyptian attack did not materialize, and Israeli military intelligence felt vindicated by their estimate that this was a threat and not the real thing pending.[61] When the Egyptians moved into similar military formations in October 1973, Israeli military intelligence again took the view that Sadat was saber-rattling. The Israelis decided not to mobilize their citizen army this time because of the great cost of the May false alarm. From August 21 to 23, Syrian and Egyptian military officials met in Cairo and sharpened their war plans, providing Assad and Sadat a choice of either September 7–11 or October 5–10 for a suitable D Day.

Syrian and Egyptian generals asked from their presidents a fifteen-day notice for preparation prior to the date chosen for an attack.[62]

In relation to Egypt, Israel had become rather comfortable with its defense on the east bank of the canal and with what it believed to be the impregnable line of fortifications known as the Bar-Lev line. Constructed immediately adjacent to the canal in 1969 during the War of Attrition, and named for the Israeli chief of staff at the time, it consisted of thirty strong points, approximately three kilometers apart joined together by a continuous sandbank rising twelve to thirty meters in height and ten meters across the top. The Bar-Lev line was meant to be a trip wire for the prevention or tracking down and destruction of Egyptian infiltrators into Sinai. Because the Egyptians made no serious attempt to cross the canal and because during the War of Attrition it withstood artillery attacks, Israelis were lulled into a false belief that it was some kind of impassable barrier. By the time the war broke out, only half of the strong points were manned. Inside the Bar-Lev line were shelters that housed troops and fortifications against 1,000-pound bombs. Surrounding the Bar-Lev line were perimeter defenses. Under two of the strong points were a series of oil tanks leading to a system of pipes and pumps that when activated were intended to spray a thin film of oil over the surface of the Suez Canal. When operational and ignited, fire would deter and likely incinerate any assaulting force. Because of military leaves granted for Yom Kippur, the normal strength of eight hundred personnel was only at six hundred when the Egyptians attacked. Israeli military and political leaders believed that its Suez Canal defensive line, air power, qualitative military superiority, along with Egypt's corresponding military combat deficiency in the latter two areas, meant that Egypt would not go to war. And if it did, it would not be successful. Israeli military intelligence did assess correctly that the Egyptian Army was well armed from the Soviet Union and other suppliers. However, overall estimates made by Israeli intelligence sources succumbed to a general concept which said that although there "was a possibility that Egypt and Syria would start a war against us [they would] not start a war as long as counterweight to our military advantage" did not exist. Israel's military and political leaders, including Dayan, "accepted the concept that the chance of war in October 1973 was low."[63]

Israeli military intelligence had accurately assessed Egypt's capabilities but did not accurately estimate Egypt's intentions. Recalling those last days of September and early October, the deputy chief of mission at the American embassy in Tel Aviv, Nicholis A. Veliotes, remarked, "For weeks before the outbreak of the October War our military guys were going in to their intelligence people and asking 'What about this, what about that, aren't you worried about this,' and they said, 'No, forget about it, we are not worried about it.'"[64] On September 25, ten days before the war, Jordan's King Hussein had a secret meeting with the Israeli prime minister.[65] A difference of opinion exists among Israelis about what Meir learned from this meeting. Gazit, who attended that meeting, asserted that "Hussein did not tell us nor did we hear from any other source that a Syrian-Egyptian coordinated attack was forthcoming."[66] Other Israeli military and intelligence sources claim otherwise. According to General Peled, "Golda knew exactly from Hussein that Syria and Egypt would attack."[67] With this information, Meir still unexplicably left Israel for quick visits to France and Austria.

On October 2, 1973, when Meir inquired about the meaning of Egypt's increase in troop deployment along the west side of the canal, she was told that Egypt had the capability to go to war and to cross the canal, but that Israeli intelligence discounted the probability of war.[68] On October 4, when Mordechai Kidron, the deputy director general of the Israeli Foreign Ministry, asked a military intelligence officer whether the Arab military preparations were something to be concerned about, he was told, "Nothing is going to happen. You go to London as scheduled."[69] The same day, Israeli intelligence sources noted that the Soviet Union had evacuated three thousand dependents of Soviet personnel from Syria and Egypt. For the Politburo, it was simple: the lives of the Soviet people were dearer than whether they were tipping off either the Israelis or Americans that a war was imminent.[70] When on October 5 the Americans had still not inquired from Moscow about the evacuation of Soviet personnel, Vasilli V. Kuznetsov, the first deputy minister of Soviet foreign affairs, reasoned that "there is so much evidence of Arab military preparations that only a stone-blind person could miss it."[71] That evening, a select few ministers in Meir's government understood definitively that the Egyptians and Syrians were prepared to attack, but "the probability of war breaking out was regarded as the lowest of the low."[72] Early the next morning, Meir was told that an attack would take place at 6 P.M. that day. At a cabinet meeting called for 8 A.M., along with her military advisers and close cabinet ministers in Tel Aviv, Meir decided not to launch a preemptive strike against either Arab army. She told those in attendance, "Look, this war is only beginning now. We do not know how long it will take, we don't know if we will be in dire need of ammunition, and so on. And if I know the world, if we begin, no one will give us a pin; they will say, "How did you know that they [the Arabs] would have attacked?"[73]

Through the Israeli Foreign Ministry, Meir summoned U.S. Ambassador Keating and Deputy Chief of Mission Veliotes to a meeting around 9 A.M. She told the Americans that Israel "had word" that the Egyptians and Syrians were about to attack, but that Israel, although mobilizing its ground forces, would not take the initiative and launch a preemptive air strike. Meir asked Keating to try to head off the war by having the Russians or Americans persuade the Egyptians and Syrians to step back from their offensive preparations because "it would be a mistake."[74] After their meeting, Veliotes returned to the U.S. embassy, where, before drafting a cable to the State Department intended to summarize the meeting with Meir, he called the State Department via an unsecured telephone line, a move "intended so that the Russians and the Arabs could listen." An unbelieving State Department Israeli desk officer answered around 4 A.M. Veliotes told him, "Wake up Roy [Atherton], wake up Joe

Sisco, all of you get down to the department." The desk officer kept interrupting Veliotes, saying that this was classified information. Finally, Veliotes wanting to make his point with whomever was listening, said, "Shut up and listen, the Syrians and Egyptians are about to attack the Israelis. Get to the Russians and tell them that this [war] is going to be terrible for them."[75] Though Veliotes had done as Meir had requested, the plea to the Egyptians and Syrians via the Russians was not heeded.

Instead of launching a preemptive air strike as Israel had done prior to the June 1967 War, it mobilized 100,000 troops, a compromise number taken from the high and low suggestions of the chief of staff and the defense minister. Elazar was in favor of a preemptive air strike against, at least, the Syrians and also in favor of a general mobilization. On the other side of the issue was Dayan, who only wanted "mobilization of 50,000 troops solely for defensive purposes."[76] In supporting the decision not to strike preemptively surrounding Arab forces, Dayan believed that "when that message was sent to the Egyptians through the Americans, Sadat would realize that their attack would not be a surprise, and that there was a real possibility that the Egyptians might not attack. Dayan, like Meir, wanted to be sure that the Americans understood that the Israelis did not initiate the war."[77] Dayan wanted no mistaken identity about who the aggressor was in this war. Though Israel decided to mobilize its citizen army, it only mobilized a portion of it, waiting until 9 A.M. on October 6 to do so, though four hours earlier Israeli military intelligence confirmed that war would occur and estimated that the war would begin that evening. The war started at 2 P.M. on October 6, 1973. It was Yom Kippur; much of Israel was at home or at worship, fasting, with Israeli radio and television off the air. It took Israel forty-eight to seventy-two hours to mobilize its army.

Meanwhile, Washington was totally unprepared for the coming war. On September 22, 1973, Kissinger had become secretary of state, successfully terminating his long-term rivalry with William Rogers. He also still headed the National Security Council. Several days later, he was in New York for the opening of the United Nations General Assembly where, among other activities, he attended a luncheon for Arab foreign ministers. At that luncheon, he acknowledged that the Middle East problem was a complex one, involving legitimate concerns for both the security of Israel and justice for the Palestinians. The problem, he said, "should be approached gradually piece by piece." He implied that he would launch a new initiative at the end of 1973, obviously implying to the Arab foreign ministers that he had to await the outcome of Israel's parliamentary elections, then scheduled for October, and afterward wait further for the new Israeli government to be formed. He mentioned UNSC Resolution 242, but the Egyptian representative to the UN and other Arab ambassadors there had the impression that Kissinger did not really know the contents of the resolution. Meguid characterized Kissinger's luncheon talk as "grandiose simplicity."[78] About ten days later, on October 5, Kissinger held a meeting with Abdel Meguid and Egyptian Foreign Minister Muhammad Zayyat in his suite in the Waldorf Astoria. There, Kissinger reiterated to the Egyptian diplomats that he would initiate a diplomatic effort after the new Israeli government was formed, most likely in early 1974. Kissinger was "so self-assured and so relaxed, leaving the Middle East question on his back burner."[79] Eban also remembered Kissinger's serenity and contentment with the status quo just before the October War.[80]

On October 6, at 7 A.M. New York time, Meguid received a phone call from Zayyat telling him that Hafez Ismail had informed him that Egyptian troops had launched an attack against several islands in the Red Sea, and a state of emergency had been declared in Egypt. Before Zayyat called Meguid, he had received a phone call from Kissinger "who was very angry, asking Zayyat what was going on, why?"[81] Kissinger also tried to reach the Syrian foreign minister by telephone, but had to settle instead for a perfunctory conversation with the Syrian deputy foreign minister. Syrian Foreign Minister Abd-al Halim Khaddam was already en route back to Damascus. Kissinger did reach Soviet Ambassador Dobrynin in Washington. Dobrynin was totally surprised by the call and completely unaware of the level of tension in the Arab-Israeli theater. Moscow's Washington embassy was not informed at all about Sadat's meetings with the Soviet ambassador in Cairo, which suggested pending hostilities, nor informed about the evacuation of Soviet families from Syria and Egypt.[82] Though Moscow knew that the war was imminent, Brezhnev and members of the Politburo believed it was a "gross miscalculation . . . [a] major political error" with "certain and speedy defeat for the Arabs." This conclusion was based on the mistaken belief held by Soviet experts and advisers that "the Arab soldier, not only was insufficiently trained technically, but also lacked courage under battle conditions."[83] As for Kissinger, he was "stunned" when he learned about the Syrian and Egyptian surprise attack.[84] Kissinger's first reaction was, "What do the Arabs think they can gain? Everyone had the illusion that this would be a short war, another Arab humiliation, and there was no way they could obtain significant territories."[85] American intelligence estimates confirmed the Israeli view that without a prospect of aerial advantage, Egypt would not risk storming the Suez Canal and Bar-Lev fortifications.[86] By October 8, Sadat communicated with Washington and told Kissinger that he wanted American intervention to resolve diplomatically the conflict with Israel.[87] Sadat said, "I want you to understand I'm not out to defeat Israel or to conquer Israeli territory. I'm out to get back my territory, and to go on that basis to negotiations."[88] The Syrians possessed no knowledge of Sadat's CIA contacts, nor did Damascus know that it was Sadat's intention to launch only a limited war. Sadat's actions intrigued Kissinger because the Egyptian president wanted to use military force to chart a course for a clear political outcome. These Egyptian-U.S. contacts continued regularly throughout the war. What remains unknown is to what degree these communications established confidence between Sadat and Kissinger, if it was Kissinger's decision to squire Sadat during and after the war, and to what degree Sadat's comunications with Kissinger influenced American policy choices during the war. For example, was the decision to move slowly in the resupply of material to Israel in any way affected by Kissinger's unfolding relationship with Sadat and an emerging American desired outcome from the war? ("No victor; no vanquished"?) No one in Washington understood that the joint Egyptian-Syrian attack against Israel would ultimately, via unintended twists and unforeseen consequences, transform the political map of the Middle East for the remainder of the century.

⌒〜⌐

THE
OCTOBER 1973
WAR

OR THE FIRST two or three days of the October War, Israel's military position on the Golan and Sinai fronts was strained; some observers even defined it
as "hopeless."[1] Using Soviet supplied sophisticated air defense systems, the Syrians
and Egyptians effectively limited the superiority of Israel's Air Force. Egyptian
ground forces overwhelmed and destroyed Israel's defensive line on the Suez Canal
running from the Mediterranean to the Red Sea. Syrian divisions penetrated to the
edge of the Golan Heights until they overlooked the Sea of Galilee and the Israeli
settlements in the valley below. At one point during the first ten days of the war,
Israel lost almost two-thirds of its mechanized forces. According to General Avraham Adan, who commanded an Israeli division in Sinai, Egypt succeeded because
Israel was "heavily outnumbered and had made mistakes at the tactical, operational,
and strategic levels."[2] Of the approximately 300 tanks stationed at the canal, 200 of
them were actually fifty or sixty miles from the canal. The remainder faced five
Egyptian infantry divisions, three mechanized divisions, two armored divisions,
and more than 1,400 tanks. For the Egyptian and Syrian armies, the first days were
the most successful segment of the war. In contrast, for Israel, the first days equalled
shock, trauma, disbelief, and very extensive losses of men and military equipment.
The combination of an air of invincibility and incredulity, incomplete intelligence
assessments or assessments not passed through the chain of command, being
caught off guard, bickering between Israeli generals about turf and tactics, and facing down better-trained and better-equipped Arab soldiers left Israelis stunned.
Israel lost 200 tanks in the first twenty-four hours of fighting alone as it sought to
repel the Egyptian advance. Israel also lost dozens of aircraft to the sophisticated
missile system brought originally to the canal area by Nasser a month before his
death. Commanding the Egyptian Air Force during the war was its chief of staff,
Husni Mubarak, who would later succeed Sadat. On the second day of the war,
when Israeli General Ariel Sharon wanted to have his armed division rescue those

still alive at the canal, Chief of Staff Elezar remarked, "We can't do that, . . . the only force we have between this spot (central Sinai) and Tel Aviv right now is your division."[3]

The Egyptian infantry faced the Israelis in Sinai and did not melt away in front of an Israeli tank attack; it was "the first truly modern infantry equipped and trained to fight and even hunt tanks with their own organic weapons."[4] Egyptian commandos had disabled or found inoperative the oil pipe mechanisms aimed at layering the canal with a burning inferno. By using water under high pressure, the Egyptian engineering corps opened sixty gaps in the sand walls set up at the canal's edge in front of the Bar-Lev line. The use by individual Egyptian infantrymen of handheld missiles systematically cut down dozens of Israeli tanks and armed personnel carriers; likewise, Egypt's antiaircraft batteries and missiles rendered ineffective Israel's low-flying air-to-ground support tactics. Throughout the war, that same umbrella of missile protection made it costly and difficult for Israel to attack the Egyptian ground troops with air strikes. By establishing ten bridges and fifty ferries across the canal within nine hours of the war's beginning, the Egyptian Army easily overran the Bar-Lev line. The Egyptians had gained ground combat superiority over the Israelis. By the end of the first night of the war, Egypt had 250 tanks, other armor, missiles, jeeps, artillery batteries, and troops in Sinai. It was a superb first day for the Egyptian Army.

Rather than pushing toward the strategic Sinai passes immediately as the Israelis had expected, the Egyptian high command chose to use their initial battlefield successes to create a continuous bridgehead along the east bank of the canal, with only small gaps remaining between the Egyptian Second and Third Army concentrations across the canal. By October 12, Egypt's military line stretched from Port Said to Suez City, though some areas of the continuous bridgehead were thinly manned. At this point in the war, Egyptian military behavior suggested that Sadat had limited strategic objectives: he kept several of his mechanized divisions on the canal's west bank. At the very moment when the Israelis were successfully completing the counterattack against the Syrians, the Egyptians halted their advance into Sinai; the Egyptian Army did not keep Israel off balance by exploiting its initial successes. And it did not coordinate its military moves with Syria. Rather than being offensive, Egypt's restraint allowed Israel to recover from initial setbacks along the canal and take the offensive.[5] Egyptian Minister of War Ahmed Ismail, who originally argued for going to the strategic passes in Sinai, now asserted that the Egyptian soldiers could not succeed in taking them. He feared that if his soldiers moved out from under their protective antiaircraft missile umbrella, they would be destroyed by counterstrikes from the Israeli Air Force. El-Gamasy, the Egyptian chief of operations, contended that even without the missile umbrella, the Egyptian Army could have reached and held the passes before Israel could muster a sufficient number of its reserve troops for a counterattack.[6] Arguing the folly of trying to get to the passes was Army Chief of Staff General El-Shazly, who "opposed the idea passionately, continuously, and in front of many people."[7] When the Egyptians broke out to the passes, they confronted an array of Israeli reserve units, resulting in a rout of the Egyptians. The Israelis destroyed more than 250 Egyptian tanks in the breakout, five times as many tanks as the Egyptians had lost in the war already.[8] According to Muhammad Baysuni, who was Egypt's liaison for military coordination with Syria, the Egyptian counterattack "failed because El-Shazly sent his reserve units at the Israeli salient in small numbers, rather than all at once, thereby not executing War Minister Ismail's orders to launch a full counterattack."[9] The absence of strategic harmony from Sadat's generals on how the war should be prosecuted, especially during the second week of the war, limited the possible expansion of Egypt's initial military successes. Ostensibly for his opposition to take the passes in general and then his failure to do so completely, along with his wrongful commitment of Egyptian tanks and outspoken manner, El-Shazly was dismissed as chief of staff on October 19. He was replaced immediately by al-Gamasy. El-Shazly's dismissal was not made public until after the war ended in order to preserve military morale and the public's confidence in the army.[10]

With the Syrians, the Israelis reeled and sputtered during the first days of the war. Problems existed in equipping Israeli forces on the Golan Heights. Mobilization went slowly. Units from different formations rushed to the front with little organization. Some equipment was out of date; some just simply was not where it was supposed to be. Sophisticated night-fighting optical equipment was lacking; tanks were ready for battle but ammunition was not. Meanwhile, in huge numbers, Syrian troops poured over the Golan Heights. Syria stormed more than 1,200 of their 1,700 tanks into the Israeli-held Golan Heights, 300 of which were the newer Soviet-supplied T-62s. The Syrian Army on the Golan Heights was built around five divisions. Compared to the Israelis, who had no more than 400 tanks at any point during the war, the Syrian forces were overwhelming. Deciding to delay initial mobilization of the army cost the Israeli Army surprise in tactics and a heavy loss of life. Successfully piercing Israeli defenses, the Syrians penetrated the Heights. The scattered Israeli brigade units were forced to fight defensive and static battles. Barrages of constant Syrian shelling, including rockets fired at northern Israeli settlements by Palestinians in southern Lebanon, inflicted huge and sudden Israeli casualties. At one point, the Syrians were a ten-minute drive from where the Jordan River meets the Sea of Galilee and a three-minute ride from the kibbutz at Ein Gev. Dayan remarked to General Moshe Peled that the situation on the Golan Heights was very grave, and that the "fate of the Third Temple" was at stake.[11] Soviet General Chief of Staff Victor Kulikov reportedly believed that the early tactical successes of the Syrians on the Golan Heights could have been turned into a decisive military victory, but the Syrians stopped during the first days of the war for reasons he could not explain.[12]

From an Israeli strategic standpoint, defense of the Golan Heights received top priority. As compared to Sinai, there was much less territorial depth to protect Israeli population centers. Furthermore, Israelis feared that Arab reinforcements from Iraq, Saudi Arabia, Morocco, and Jordan might become involved on the Golan front. By the end of the first thirty-six hours, Israel planned and then executed a successful counterattack against the Syrians. The war on the Golan Heights turned as fast against the Syrians as it had initially devastated the Israeli forces. In a span of five days, Israel repulsed the Syrian advance through the Golan Heights, destroying the bulk of the Syrian tank corps. The Syrians left behind more than 800 or 900 tanks, including new T-62s. Israel made repairs to these captured tanks and used them later in the war. The full counterattack against Syria, which ended on October 11–12, included Israel's recapture of all the territory it had lost at the beginning of the war, plus more. Israel decided not to take Damascus, some twenty-five miles away because its military value would, at best, be dubious; Dayan believed that there was "absolutely no reasonable purpose for occupying an Arab capital."[13] Israel continued to pound Syrian positions with artillery shelling of Damascus. During the Israeli counterattack, the Israeli Air Force reasserted itself, bombing strategic Syrian targets, including airfields, oil depots, power stations, and highways. Israeli commandos destroyed a bridge 100 kilometers northeast of Damascus on the night of October 12–13, crippling the ability of 16,000 Iraqi troops and 250 tanks that were destined to join the Syrians against the Israelis on the Golan.[14] According to General Peled, "It took only sixty artillery shells to land near Damascus for the Syrians to request a cease-fire."[15] Syria replied by launching surface-to-surface missiles at Israeli civilian targets in the Galilee. Because Syria remained threatened by the constant possibility of Israeli artillery fire and unimpeded Israeli access to Damascus, the Syrians pressed for a cease-fire, but not before Moscow indicated to Washington that Soviet airborne forces were put on alert to defend Damascus while Moscow opened a military resupply conduit to the Syrians.[16]

Along the Jordanian front, Israel's longest border with any Arab state, there was virtually no fighting. According to several Israeli sources who preferred anonymity, had King Hussein crossed the Jordan River, there would have been virtually no Israeli troops there to stop him. Said one Israeli intelligence officer, "Only forty Sherman tanks were along the entire length of that border." In addition, during the first days of the war, Israel engaged in an extensive propaganda campaign aimed at keeping the Jordanians on edge and disinterested in joining the war. During the early days of the war, via the United States, Israel informed Hussein that if he sent his army across the Jordan River, Israel would retaliate by going to Amman. There was also an Israeli understanding with Hussein that if he joined the war, he would send his troops to fight with the Syrians on the Golan Heights. If Presidents Assad and Sadat had told Hussein about the timing of the war and encouraged and obtained his participation, even in a limited fashion, then they would have diverted much-needed Israeli men, equipment, and supplies from their two fronts. Had Jordan joined the war in some limited fashion, the war's outcome might have been different.

These were some of the darkest days in Israel's military history. Israel was in emotional agony and in need of physical assistance. Simultaneously in Tel Aviv and Washington, Israel requested assistance from the United States and provided the American embassy in Tel Aviv with a lengthy list of needed military equipment, while Dinitz requested the resupply of both ammunition and equipment. Israeli leaders were not sure that a resupply operation could be mustered, but they asked anyway. What the Israelis wanted were the supplies and material "already in the pipeline." "During the war Kissinger told us—hit them, don't spare your ammunition. You'll get everything back. Don't wait for us, you cannot get the tanks overnight. You will get everything back."[17] Kissinger did not want to use American planes to ferry supplies to Israel, lest it upset Washington's relationship with Moscow or humiliate the Arabs. By the second week of the war, when the full military resupply airlift started to Israel, neither Cairo nor Moscow perceived it as an American provocation, but rather as a response to the Soviet Union's resupply and "the biggest airlift in its history."[18] Early in the war, Moscow supplied Syria by sea; reluctantly, Israel capitulated to the American request not to bomb these Soviet transport vessels,[19] yet at least one was hit off the Syrian coast.

There were several reasons why the resupply to Israel was delayed. First, Kissinger intentionally "withheld major deliveries to Israel so long as the Russians exercised restraint and so long as Sadat would accept a cease-fire in place."[20] Kissinger wanted to ensure an opening to Sadat, prevent his army's defeat, prevent an Arab oil embargo, prevent violent anti-American reprisals from the Arab world, and prevent alienation of NATO partners. Second, military estimates suggested that while Israelis needed resupply, their critical condition was prematurely overstated.[21] Moreover, on October 9, when Israeli officials handed the Americans another list of requested ammunition and supplies, they were informed by the Israelis that the Syrians were stopped on the Golan Heights; officials at the American embassy in Tel Aviv were told the crisis was over in that theater of battle and therefore resupply was not urgent. Furthermore, the United States did not have in its stocks the quantities of weapons Israel needed. For example, Washington could provide Israel with only six TOW missile launchers from NATO warehouses. When the huge C5A aircraft landed in Israel for the first time (after the major battles were fought in Sinai and the Golan Heights, but before Israel's countercrossing of the canal on October 15–16), it only had one M-60 battle tank in its belly. Also, Defense Secretary James Schlesinger asserted that it was initially Washington's intention "to provide Israel with supplies but not major equipment, but to do so in such a way that the U.S. would not be overtly identified with Israel. . . . [T]here was fear of another Arab humiliation like 1967, concern for implementation of an Arab oil embargo, and worry about its impact on U.S. relations with the Soviet Union and NATO allies."[22] In any event, the American resupply mission of ammunition and supplies (only four Sky Hawk aircraft and a maximum of two tanks were sent via airlift) to Israel had military, strategic, and psychological implications. According to Wat Cluverius, a junior-level State Department desk officer who then worked in the operations center, "Nobody believed that Israel was in any kind of mortal danger whatever. Hurt, yes; frightened, yes. It was pretty quickly clear that what we had to have out of the war was no unchallenged victor and no humiliated loser, and we all agreed. I don't think anyone in that operations [center] could ever believe that we had anything but a situation that had to be manipulated."[23]

Once the airlift of military equipment started, Israel wanted it to go faster. For Israeli morale the resupply was terribly important. Sitting at the U.S. embassy, Veliotes said, "The show for resupply was more for show than for blow."[24] Once the decision was made to use American aircraft to bring supplies to Israel, the U.S. and Israel were told that the planes would land under the cover of darkness, unload their contents, and depart before daybreak. However, unexpected head winds at the refueling air base in the Azores caused the aircraft to be delayed in their refueling; therefore, they were plainly seen landing in Israel during the daylight hours. In the middle of the war, Israel wanted to demonstrate to the Arabs the measure of Washington's friendship. U.S. military resupply was confirmation for Sadat that Washington indeed possessed strong physical and moral support for the Jewish state. But Sadat expected that, even included it in his reasoning: Israel felt beholden to the United States and therefore obliged to at least listen to Washington's entreaties about withdrawal from Arab lands. Ultimately, the unwillingness of America's NATO allies to allow use of their airspace and airfields to affect the American resupply mission created for Moscow welcome gaps in the North Atlantic alliance. The massive resupply to Israel justified the subsequent action by Arab oil producers, lined up in advance of the war, to embargo oil sales to the United States and other Western countries deemed sympathetic to Israel. According to Peter Rodman, for the Arabs, "the American airlift to Israel drove them crazy. The American-Israeli alliance was considered formidable; the Americans did not allow the Israelis to be defeated."[25] In 1977, when Meir was asked whether she believed that Kissinger intentionally held back the needed military resupply, she responded, "I honestly still do not know."[26]

At the end of the first week of the war, after repelling the Syrians on the Golan, Israel redirected its attention toward the Egyptian front, moving from the defensive to the offensive, transferring additional men and equipment from the northern to the southern front. During the second week of the war, Israel tried to break through the new line of defense that Egypt had created on the ashes of the destroyed Bar-Lev line. Due to the high-casualty loss of Israeli personnel in the frontal armored tank assaults in Sinai, Israeli military planners opted for the more delicate effort of establishing a bridgehead across the canal as a way to neutralize the Egyptian success and to minimize casualties. Time was required to traverse the distance from where reserves and their material were located to the canal. Israeli political leaders were still pessimistic because of the level of their losses and slow ability to regain any military initiative. Israel had no reason to believe that Sadat wanted to use diplomacy after the war. The wrangling for arms supply from the United States continued. By the end of the first week of the war, Israel almost consented to a cease-fire sponsored by the United Nations, hoping that negotiations based upon UNSC Resolution 242 would emerge from the war. When Israel felt besieged and Egypt had achieved a limited, but noticeable, military success, leaders of the Soviet Union and the United States "decided that a continuation of the war ran the risk of endangering their mutually advantageous policy of detente and embroiling them in war."[27] Before the end of the war's first week, the Syrian Army was in retreat. Not during the first several days of the war, but by the end of the first week, Syria wanted the Soviet Union to press for a cease-fire. Throughout the war Assad reproached Moscow for not having responded to his cease-fire appeal; he portrayed Moscow's unwillingness to seek a cease-fire as "treasonous." The Politburo was willing to endorse a cease-fire and would only veto it if *both* Egypt and Syria disapproved; if Egypt and Syria disagreed, Moscow's representative at the United Nations was to act in accordance with Egypt's position.[28] Not only did Assad not have Sadat's backing for a cease-fire, and therefore Moscow's support, but Assad was not able to convince Sadat to sustain a counterattack against Israel in Sinai. Assad wanted such an attack to divert Israeli men and material to Sinai and away from the Golan. On October 11, Syria sent an envoy to Cairo making this request. Partially in response to the Syrian request, the Egyptians tried but failed to move out of their entrenched positions in order to take the strategic passes, but that did little to divert Israeli pressure on the Golan. Egypt's motivation was to regain national territory, not to take pressure off the Syrian front. By the end of the first week of the war, Moscow began to confront the prospect of an Arab defeat in Sinai and the Golan.[29] According to General Peled, Syrian "interest in a cease-fire increased" after artillery shells fell on Damascus. Moscow's ambassador in Cairo, Vladamir Vinogradov, apparently communicated to Sadat on October 12 that the Syrians wanted a Russian-supported cease-fire. Because his army had achieved early battlefield successes across the Suez Canal, Sadat was incredulous at the Soviet suggestion and spurned the idea.[30]

On October 16, Sadat addressed a special session of the Egyptian Parliament. This speech was, by far, the most important one he had yet delivered since coming to office three years earlier. Its contents were derived almost exclusively from the initial successes of the Egyptian military. Sadat could claim that the vaunted Israeli Army was not impregnable. He told his countrymen that he was fulfilling his pledge to show that the military defeat in 1967 was an exception, that the Egyptian

military's humiliation then would not now be handed down to the next generation. He paid tribute to the successes of the Egyptian armed forces and what could
be considered lip service to the Syrian Army fighting one of the most glorious battles in Arab history. His suggestion for an international conference under the
umbrella of the United Nations apparently came from various communications he
had with Moscow during the war. Though he had direct contact with Kissinger as
the war progressed, "Sadat still had not developed enough confidence" that Washington would engage itself fully in the diplomatic process after the war.[31] After
describing this war as a fight for peace with justice, Sadat specified five objectives to
his parliamentary audience: (1) to liberate all the lands occupied by Israel since 1967
and to find a way to restore the legitimate rights of the Palestinian people; (2) to
accept a cease-fire on the basis of full and immediate Israeli withdrawal from all
occupied territories, under international supervision, to the pre–June 5, 1967,
lines; (3) to take part, subsequent to the completion of withdrawal from all these
territories, in an international peace conference under UN auspices; (4) to start
clearing the Suez Canal and reopening it to international navigation; and (5) not to
accept any nebulous pledges or elastic definitions that could be subjected to all
kinds of interpretations, but instead see the above objectives met.[32] In the middle of
a fierce war with unbearable casualties, the Israelis paid little attention to his speech,
which contained nothing new save for the international conference idea. No one
in the Israeli prime minister's office or Foreign Ministry took serious notice of it or
of Sadat's call for an international conference under UN auspices.[33] For Israelis,
"restoration of the legitimate rights of the Palestinian people" was the typical Arab
blueprint to return to the 1947 plan to partition Palestine into Arab and Jewish
states with an international regime in Jerusalem; calling for an international conference *after* Israeli withdrawal was a precondition for negotiations without either
nonbelligerency or peace promised from the Egyptian side. Sadat certainly was not
signaling compromise to Israeli listeners. Sadat's content and tone were distinctively
more antagonistic toward Israel than the proposal he had made to the Israeli government in February 1971. By the time Sadat had finished addressing the Egyptian
Parliament, Israel had already crossed the canal with a small expeditionary force. At
twilight on October 15, Israeli armor, under Sharon's command, exploited the gap
between the Egyptian Second in the north and Third Armies to its south. Sharon
had found the seam on October 9 and wanted to move across the canal two days
later but was ordered not to do so. Withstanding a heavy barrage of Egyptian
artillery and air attacks where Sharon himself was slightly wounded, by the morning of the 16th, Israel began ferrying tanks to the west side of the canal. By noon,
twenty-seven Israeli tanks, reinforced by paratroopers, were moving along the Cairo
side of the canal, destroying Egyptian tanks, missile sites, communication facilities,
and ammunition depots. By the afternoon of the 17th, Israel's bridge across the
canal was finished, yet it took the Israelis two days since the original crossing and

seven hours after the bridge was in place for a large complement of tanks to cross. During that time, the Egyptians did not confront Sharon's crossing, except for the initial artillery and air attacks. Israel was met with less resistance because when Egyptian forces tried to move toward the Sinai passes several days earlier, El-Shazly committed and lost his strategic manpower and tank reserve originally held on the west bank to the fight. The absence of that reserve reduced Egypt's ability to thwart Israel's crossing of the canal on October 16.[34] By the evening of the 18th, Israel's bridgehead on the west bank was secure; Israel's plan was to encircle the Egyptian Third Army.[35] Egyptian military leaders at the front intentionally belittled the importance and danger of a small Israeli counterattack and breakthrough to the west bank of the Suez Canal.[36] Sadat's intelligence evaluations from the front were understated in terms of the seriousness of Israel's canal countercrossing. For the remainder of the war, intentional Egyptian disinformation was presented to the media, downplaying the nature of the Israeli breakthrough and emphasizing the "satisfactory" condition of the Third Army.[37] Sadat shaded the truth for his domestic audience as it was unfolding. He needed to protect the sanctity of the original canal crossing, which meant Egyptian Defense Minister Ismail was feeding Syria with false information too.[38] Confirming this point, Khaddam recalled, "When there was the [Israeli] breakthrough, we were really given incorrect information [by the Egyptians]. This really caused a bitter heart."[39]

The goals of the Soviet premier's secret visit to Cairo from October 16 to 19 were to end the fighting and show Moscow's loyalty to its most important Arab ally. Kosygin presented Egyptian President Sadat with a four-point "peace" proposal that called for: (1) "a cease-fire in place"; (2) Israeli withdrawal to the 1967 boundaries, after some minor changes; (3) an international peace conference, at which the final agreement would be negotiated and ratified; and (4) a "guarantee" of the entire agreement by the Soviet Union and the United States, including the cease-fire.[40] The Soviet Union wanted to bring the war to an immediate end through a cease-fire acceptable to the Americans.[41] Kosygin told Sadat that the Syrians wanted a cease-fire, a claim Sadat believed was false. When Kosygin raised the serious nature of Israel's presence on the west bank of the canal, Sadat dismissed the Soviet premier's assertion, claiming at one point that the Israeli counterattack across the canal "would have no impact on the course of the war in general" and "no threat posed to Cairo."[42] A totally different assessment was provided by the Soviet military attaché in Moscow, who told Kosygin while he was there that "from a military point of view it would *not* be very difficult for Israel to seize the Egyptian capital."[43] As for a conference, the idea apparently crystallized in Sadat's mind during and after the unsuccessful efforts by UN mediator Gunnar Jarring to affect Egyptian-Israeli negotiations earlier in the 1970s. Then, Egypt preferred a multilateral solution to the conflict, not the achievement of a bilateral agreement. For Sadat, an international conference was the next logical step, following either successful or failed UN negotiating efforts.[44] But Sadat only wanted a conference if there was full-fledged cooperation and promises made by Moscow and Washington to bring about a full Israeli withdrawal from all of the occupied territories. Without that cooperation, a conference could only work if it were a political shield behind which Sadat could maneuver an Israeli withdrawal.

On October 17, while Kosygin was in Egypt, Arab oil producers announced a seventeen percent increase in the price of oil and announced that oil exports to countries "unfriendly" to the Arab cause would be reduced by 5 percent each month until Israel evacuated the territories it took in the 1967 War. On October 19, Nixon asked the U.S. Congress for 2.2 billion dollars in emergency aid for Israel.

Secretly, Kosygin met with Sadat three times during his four-day visit. Only a few of Sadat's closest advisers were privy to the contents of these meetings. On October 18, the Soviet ambassador to the United States, Anotoly Dobrynin, told Kissinger that Moscow wanted a rapid end to the fighting, followed by a staged Israeli withdrawal to the 1967 lines.[45] Several days earlier, Soviet General Secretary Brezhnev had written Nixon a detailed assessment of American and Soviet interests in the Middle East, seeking collaboration with Washington in bringing an end to the fighting. Brezhnev was disappointed that Nixon avoided responding to key issues in his reply. The absence of a substantive American reply, the coincidental timely request made by Soviet Ambassador Dobrynin to the Kremlin to invite Kissinger to Moscow, and Kissinger's almost instant acceptance of the invitation through Nixon does not rule out the possibility that it was Kissinger's preconceived intention to take charge of the war's diplomatic outcome by "soliciting" a Kremlin invitation.

Brezhnev invited Kissinger to come to Moscow to discuss drafting and implementing a cease-fire. While Arab partners were talking pros and cons of a cease-fire, Israel was not near ready for such an agreement. For their part, the Soviet Union had five motivations for seeking a cease-fire and therefore for inviting Kissinger to Moscow for consultation. As the Israelis slowly but successfully surrounded the Egyptian Third Army, Moscow was gravely concerned that a military disaster was about to befall their Egyptian client. A crushing Egyptian military defeat would occur if the Third Army was destroyed. An Arab surrender would damage their image in many Third World countries. Moscow did not want the war to affect adversely its working relationship with Washington. Preserving detente was important. Also, the Kremlin was opposed to any military action that could involve the Soviet Union in the war.[46] Moreover, Moscow's policymakers wanted to assure themselves equal status with Washington in any emerging postwar diplomacy, an objective that Kissinger wanted to deny or limit both for American and Israeli interests. By the time Kissinger arrived in Moscow on the evening of October 20, the Soviet Union had drafted a UN cease-fire resolution. The Kremlin, unable to obtain Sadat's agreement on a cease-fire during Kosygin's visit, worked independently of him. With the Israelis rapidly expanding their bridgehead on the west bank of the canal but not yet fully surrounding the Third Army and Israeli presence less than sixty miles from Cairo, Sadat was sufficiently anxious to now want a cease-fire. Meanwhile in Washington, just prior to Kissinger's meeting with Brezhnev at the Kremlin, Nixon fired Watergate special prosecutor Archibald Cox. Cox had wanted the audiotapes of Oval Office conversations relating to Watergate and not just the summaries offered by the White House. Along with Cox's firing came the dismissals of Attorney General Elliot Richardson and Deputy Attorney General Ruckelshaus in what came to be known as "The Saturday Night Massacre." While negotiating in the Kremlin, Kissinger had no information about the domestic head-rolling occurring in Washington and, to his chagrin, did not receive the up-to-the-minute military reports from the Israelis through the White House that he had requested from Dinitz prior to his departure.

By October 20, Sadat accepted a cease-fire. Now, Assad did not want to stop fighting until Israel evacuated at least all of the Golan Heights occupied by Israel in the October 1973 War.[47] In separate messages to Kissinger and Brezhnev, Sadat indicated that he wanted a cease-fire, while at the same time seeking King Hussein's permission to have fifty Egyptian commandos cross from Syria into Jordan and then strike at Israeli installations in Sinai.[48] According to a junior American diplomat in Amman at the time, Sadat's request for the commando action through Jordanian territory came well after the establishment of the Israeli bridgehead on the west bank of the canal.[49] King Hussein did not give permission to the proposed Egyptian commando foray. When the war ended and Sadat traveled to several capitals in the Arab Gulf, he privately told those who would listen that a reason "for his military *defeat* in Sinai and the reason that the Israelis were able to cross the canal was because Jordan would not allow [Egyptian] commandos to attack the Israelis from the east."[50]

When Kissinger and his advisers arrived in Moscow on October 21, they were in a powerful negotiating position. Brezhnev naively believed that Sadat only relied upon the Kremlin;[51] he did not understand that Kissinger was emerging as the only policymaker who had communication lines, influence, and something to offer Egypt, Israel, and the Kremlin. While Israel seemed poised to achieve a decisive victory, Kissinger understood that his goal was to limit that success, exclude the Soviets as much as possible from key decisions, and enhance his evolving relationship with Sadat. Sisco said, "A cease-fire was much more important to the Soviets at that point, because the situation militarily on the ground favored us—meaning the Israelis."[52] Encirclement of the Third Army, according to Riad, "was the trump card that Israel was using to pressure Egypt" and "as a consequence of the deterioration of the military situation along the Egyptian front, Brezhnev was unable to enforce the Arab demands [for Israeli withdrawal]; the best he could achieve was an agreement for a cease-fire."[53] The Soviets believed that "the gap Israel had succeeded in opening in the Egyptian front and its establishment of a pocket [the breakthrough to the west bank of the Suez Canal] had in fact done away with the success Egypt had achieved in the first ten days of the war."[54] For their part, when Israeli leaders learned that Kissinger was going to Moscow, they believed that his intention was to "work out a denouement for the war's conclusion."[55] In fact, Kissinger told Dinitz before his departure, "Israel would be well advised to conduct operations in the knowledge that we would not be able to stall a cease-fire proposal for more than forty-eight hours." With current intelligence available from American sources about battlefield realities, Kissinger wanted either to delay or accelerate in Moscow the cease-fire resolution's implementation. By informing Brezhnev that he needed to await a "power of attorney" from Nixon, he could stall initialing any document by saying he had to refer its contents to Washington. Nixon, however, either as show of bravado or fear that Kissinger would protect the Israelis, deliberately undermined Kissinger's desire to control the clock.[56] On Kissinger's way to Moscow, Nixon told both Brezhnev and Kissinger that his secretary of state enjoyed the president's "full power to negotiate" on behalf of the United States.[57] Learning that these instructions had been sent to Brezhnev, Kissinger was angry. These instructions, known to Brezhnev too, meant that Kissinger *could be* deprived any capacity to filibuster. But the signal was also sent to Moscow that Kissinger was in charge of these negotiations and implied that he could negotiate and impose an overall settlement and not just negotiate a cease-fire.[58] Kissinger recalled, "History will not record that I resisted many grants of authority. This one I resented bitterly; it was a classic example of how 'full powers' can inhibit rather than enhance negotiating flexibility."[59] Peter Rodman recalled, "Even as it was, Kissinger went to Moscow trying to stall. He did not want to sign the cease-fire, but Nixon undermined Kissinger, either deliberately or stupidly, in sending this message while they were airborne, saying that Kissinger had full authority to sign the cease-fire. Kissinger wanted the option of at least not signing and claiming he could not because he lacked the authority of the president. Nixon was getting a little nervous that Kissinger was protecting the Israelis too much."[60] In fact, while Kissinger complained about Nixon giving him power to draft, to initial an agreement, and to negotiate fully, Kissinger still stalled. Kissinger's preflight suggestion to Dinitz seeped through to the Israeli military command. Dayan noted that as intense negotiations were about to proceed in Moscow, Israel hurried "to secure her essential military objectives with the utmost speed."[61]

Three meetings were held in Moscow from October 20 to 22 between the Soviet and American delegations. The first, in Brezhnev's office in the Kremlin, the evening Kissinger arrived, focused on the common objective to bring about an end to the war, because that was "extremely important" to the superpower relationship. The second meeting, also in Brezhnev's office on October 21, focused on the word-by-word drafting of what came to be the UNSC [cease-fire] Resolution 338,

and mutual understandings between the Kremlin and Washington on how the resolution would be presented and implemented. The third meeting, over breakfast
on October 22, covered a substantive discussion about other members of the Security Council and how they might be informed about the Soviet-American draft
cease-fire resolution. Spotlighting the necessity for a cease-fire on the Egyptian-
Israeli front did not postpone Soviet interest for an equal role with the United
States in the postwar diplomacy. Brezhnev did not want to impose a solution on the
Arabs and Israelis. He complained to Kissinger that instead he wanted "to bring to
an end all slanderous allegations about the superpowers wanting to dictate their will
to others" to impose a solution. Nixon, on the other hand, told Kissinger to tell
Brezhnev that the United States wanted to "use the end of the war to impose a
comprehensive peace in the Middle East."[62] Kissinger in his first meeting with
Brezhnev concurred more with the Soviet general secretary than with his own
boss. Why? Kissinger believed if he could separate a cease-fire from a postwar settlement, then he would be able to use Soviet pressure to bring about the cease-fire
with the Israelis at a distinct military advantage and relegate Soviet participation
in the subsequent diplomacy to a formal role of bystander. For its part, Moscow
had no idea to what degree Sadat was entrusting the process of Sinai's return to
Kissinger; they did not know about the frequency or depth of communications
Sadat already had with Kissinger via CIA channels nor did they know that
Kissinger and Nixon differed significantly in attitude about dealing with Israel.
Most of all, the Kremlin did not know that Nixon was willing to apply pressure on
the Israelis to assure survival of the Third Army. Nixon had told Kissinger, "U.S.
political considerations will have absolutely no, repeat no, influences on our decisions in this regard. I want you to know that I am prepared to pressure the Israelis to
the extent required, regardless of the domestic political consequences."[63]

The American-compiled minutes of the three meetings that Kissinger attended
with Brezhnev unequivocally show that he accurately and repeatedly represented
Israeli interests to Moscow, almost totally contrary to Nixon's preferences. Kissinger
delayed, while Nixon wanted a quicker pace in moving toward discussions about a
final diplomatic settlement. In Damascus, eight months later, Kissinger would again
vigorously disagree with Nixon's desire to put pressure on the Israelis, but this time
he would speak his mind in front of President Assad and Foreign Minister Khaddam. The Soviet draft of what would eventually become UNSC Resolution 338
was presented to Kissinger on October 20, with an earlier copy sent to Nixon in
Washington. The resolution was based on three principles: (1) neither the U.S. nor
the Soviet Union would seek unilateral advantage over the other; (2) there should
be an immediate cease-fire, withdrawal of Israeli troops from the occupied territories [to the 1967 borders], and appropriate Soviet-U.S. consultations; and (3) and
the direction of the discussions between Moscow and Washington should not be
shaped by the changing situation at the war fronts.[64] Kissinger prevailed in his

determination not to link broader issues of Israeli withdrawal with negotiating a cease-fire. He made it clear to his Soviet interlocutors that Israel would not be pleased with a cease-fire resolution that contained just general mention of UNSC 242; it wanted direct negotiations with the Arabs. Israel had of course gained more territory in 1973, so it would be opposed to withdrawal to lines close to the 1967 borders. Kissinger's preference was to find common agreement in Moscow, discuss the agreement with the parties, exercise influence over them, and submit the agreement to the Security Council. Then, after the cease-fire, Moscow and Washington could discuss how to move toward a final solution. Brezhnev opposed asking either the Arabs or the Israelis for their opinions on what might be agreed in Moscow because "the Israelis will confront you with so many questions as the Arabs will us; our agreement will be worth nothing."[65] Throughout the discussions with Kissinger, Brezhnev wanted to be sure that whatever emanated from the cease-fire would flow directly into negotiations conducted under "our" joint or appropriate auspices. When Brezhnev said, "I believe that both the Israelis and the Arabs will be pleased that we, the Great Powers, will be acting to promote a settlement," Kissinger replied instantly, "Not Israel, believe me. If you want to mention 242, which the Israelis violently object to, we have to mention negotiations 'between the parties' or something like it, something that can be pointed to as a process of negotiation. The Israelis, I know, will demand a release of prisoners [of war] as a condition of [accepting] the cease fire."[66] On October 21, the Kremlin was told by their ambassador in Cairo that Sadat was despairing of a cease-fire. By putting a territorial noose around the Third Army and sitting about sixty miles from Cairo, Israeli forces had open terrain and no opposition to move on Cairo; had they done so Sadat's rule might have ended. Quickly, Sadat, and therefore the Soviets, had to concentrate on saving the Third Army from Israeli retribution. Kissinger had time working in his favor; Brezhnev did not.

Despite Nixon's interest in a broader Arab-Israeli settlement, on October 21, Kissinger, Brezhnev, and their respective advisers drafted and reworked the final version of a cease-fire resolution, which called upon the parties to terminate all military activity no later than twelve hours after the adoption of the resolution, to start immediately after the cease-fire with the implementation of UNSC Resolution 242 in all of its parts. Concurrently with the cease-fire, *negotiations would start between the parties under appropriate auspices* aimed at establishing a just and durable peace in the Middle East. The proposed resolution did not contain mention of any mechanism for enforcing its contents or for guarantees to the negotiating parties. According to Kissinger, his Soviet counterparts agreed with the American view that "appropriate auspices" meant Soviet and American diplomats at the opening of negotiations at a peace conference and at the foreign minister's level.[67] Kissinger obtained from Brezhnev a written explanation of "appropriate auspices" by which the secretary could prove to Israeli leaders that nothing was being imposed upon them. But Kissinger disagreed with Brezhnev over the Soviet's desire to have a broader role at key moments in the negotiations. The dialogue at the end of the meeting on October 21, 1973, went thusly:[68]

KISSINGER: Let me sum up so we are very sure. Our understanding of "auspices" is that at the opening of negotiations and at some crucial moments the U.S. and the Soviet Union will be participants in the process of negotiations.

BREZHNEV: We will participate.

KISSINGER: Right, not at every session, but at key points. This is our understanding. The actual implementation we will have to work out afterwards, because we cannot get it accepted tonight.

BREZHNEV: In short, the U.S. and the Soviet Union are active participants in the negotiations.

KISSINGER: Not in every detail, but in the opening phase and at crucial points throughout.

BREZHNEV: Perhaps we could formulate it in this way. The Soviet Union and the United States are active participants in the negotiations which shall be conducted under their auspices. Details of what particular moments will be worked out in the process of actual negotiations, but also with a view to not letting the process of negotiations slip out of our hands.

KISSINGER: I must tell you honestly the Israelis will violently object to Soviet participation.

BREZHNEV: But that is something I would like to have laid down as an understanding jointly reached on our interpretation of the meaning of the word "auspices."

KISSINGER: What I have written out is that the negotiations will be conducted under our auspices and we will participate in them at crucial moments.

BREZHNEV: In other words in the solution for all the key issues.

KISSINGER: Yes.

At the conclusion of this second meeting, though Kissinger and Brezhnev agreed that they "absolutely reached agreement," Kissinger turned to the Soviet general secretary and said, "I technically have to ask the president's approval. The president could overrule me. It could happen, but I tell you as a friend, it won't happen." Kissinger still wanted "wiggle room," not for altering the content of the agreed-upon draft cease-fire resolution but to use time to his advantage.

Once the draft resolution was initialed by Soviet and U.S. officials, Kissinger and Foreign Minister Gromyko sent telegrams to the American and Soviet ambassadors at the United Nations with identical instructions that the resolution be introduced by the superpowers jointly. Both Charles Malik, the Soviet representative, and John

Scali, his American counterpart, were told by Kissinger and Gromyko not to accept any amendments to the draft except by mutual agreement. Said Sisco, this was "not exactly standard operating procedure in those days [of the cold war]."[69] Kissinger did not want a comma changed in the resolution. His deputy at the NSC, General Alexander Haig, called Dinitz to the White House, gave him the text of 338, and "added that its words were etched in stone and could not be changed."[70] In a separate cable to Scali, headed, "STRICTLY EYES ONLY FOR SCALI FROM THE SECRETARY," Kissinger wrote to his UN ambassador on October 21 that "this is a private message just for you. It has not been discussed with the Soviets. Your joint instruction says we would like the resolution adopted by midnight if possible. You should proceed at a deliberate pace in the Security Council. I do not mean delaying matter or appearing to delay matter. We agreed with the Soviets to midnight as a target for adoption of the resolution because of the stress Soviets put on speed. *We do not have the same interest in such speed* [my emphasis]."[71] The resolution was unanimously passed 14–0 at 12:52 A.M. on October 22, 1973. Neither the Egyptians, Syrians, nor the Israelis received a draft of the resolution for their comment. A few minutes before the cease-fire went into effect, which was also just prior to Kissinger's third meeting in the Kremlin at 8:45 A.M. Moscow time, SCUD missiles, ostensibly under Soviet military control in Cairo, were harmlessly launched against Israeli positions in Sinai. Permission to launch them was provided by the Soviet minister of defense[72] apparently without the knowledge of Kremlin political leaders. Even though UNSC Resolution 338 called for a prompt cease-fire within twelve hours of the adoption of the resolution and despite the scare that the SCUDs were to provide, Israel continued to enlarge and solidify its presence sixty miles from Cairo. Moscow was satisfied with the achievement of the cease-fire resolution and its general talks with Kissinger: "Good feelings and satisfaction prevailed."[73]

The resolution read:

UNITED NATIONS SECURITY COUNCIL RESOLUTION 338
22 OCTOBER 1973

The Security Council,

1. Calls upon all parties to the present fighting to cease all firing and terminate all military activity immediately, no later than 12 hours after the moment of the adoption of this decision, in the position they now occupy;

2. Calls upon the parties concerned to start immediately after the cease-fire the implementation of Security Council Resolution 242 (1967) in all of its parts;

3. Decides that, immediately and concurrently with the cease-fire, negotiations start between the parties concerned under appropriate auspices aimed at establishing a just and durable peace in the Middle East.

Israel had some input in choosing the wording for the resolution. But apparently,
the Israeli Foreign Ministry did not know that Meir had communicated with
Kissinger directly before he completed his visit in Moscow and made the request to
include a phrase about negotiations "between the parties," a concept that Sadat
reportedly also endorsed before Kissinger's trip to Moscow.[74] Where the Foreign
Ministry was excluded, the prime minister's office was engaged. Mordechai Gazit, in
the prime minister's office, explicitly recalled that "she said, I want the resolution to
say peace between them, negotiations between them. And she got it."[75] Despite
Israel's input into the resolution's contents, the Israelis felt slighted and annoyed by
Kissinger's imperious actions in Moscow in shaping the United Nations resolution.
Israel had felt violated by the surprise Egyptian-Syrian attack just weeks earlier; now
the Israeli leadership was incensed when they witnessed Moscow and Washington
working together to find a formula or solution to an aspect of the Arab-Israeli conflict. In this case, as Rodman remembered, "Israel felt [it] had been shafted [in
Moscow] by the United States."[76] Foreign Minister Eban felt this was a "dictate"
because Israel "had to give an ultimatum answer to a document which [it] had no
part in drafting or formulating."[77] Evron recalled that "all of a sudden the cease-fire
was materializing but there had been no U.S. discussions with Israel about [its] concerns."[78] In fact, Kissinger, while not representing Israel to the Kremlin, certainly presented Israel's concerns, including written understandings about the term "auspices"
and Moscow's agreement to use their maximum influence to ensure that all POWs
would be released no later than seventy-two hours following the cease-fire. Logistically accomplishing that objective was not possible, but it indicated Kissinger's understanding and sympathizing with the human dimension of Israel's trauma.

On his way back to Washington, Kissinger stopped in Israel, but not in Egypt.
Prior to leaving Moscow, Kissinger asked Gromyko if he could tell newsmen at the
airport that he was going to Israel. "Psychologically," replied Gromyko, "it would
be preferable if you not tell your destination from Moscow." Kissinger told his
counterpart that he had to go to Israel for two reasons—"They [the Israelis] had to
accept the resolution and there had to be substantial compliance with the resolution."[79] Though Golda Meir had requested the visit, there is no confirmation that
she accepted the premise that Kissinger put before Gromyko. Less than four hours
before his Moscow departure, Kissinger notified Sadat, Hussein, and NATO
ambassadors of the cease-fire resolution. But when the Israeli Foreign Ministry
planned logistics for Kissinger's arrival in Israel and wanted to know his plane's
markings, U.S. Ambassador to Israel Kenneth Keating had no idea that such a visit

was even scheduled. The American deputy chief of mission in Tel Aviv, Nicholis Veliotes, learned of the Kissinger visit from an Israeli Foreign Ministry counterpart.[80] More important to Kissinger than informing the U.S. embassy in Tel Aviv of his pending trip was notice given to the commander of the U.S. Mediterranean Sixth Fleet, which provided the secretary's plane with escort service to Israeli airspace. Kissinger doled out information only to those who needed to know and then only when he thought they needed to know it. When Kissinger arrived in Israel, he was in a rather upbeat, even optimistic, mood, because he knew that the Egyptians were ready to negotiate while he personally possessed exclusive control of the negotiating process. Yet, he could not help but sense the wrenching national loss of self-confidence that hung like a cloud over the general public and its political leadership. Evron recalled,

> We were suffering. Henry noticed this right away. He said this. He wrote about it later. He spoke about it. I think he realized this was an historic moment. But he saw the yearning in the eyes of the people. The nervous soldiers. They were tired. It did not take him long to sense that the country did not want to go through this experience again. [He sensed that] the generals wanted another round, . . . something like the immediate capture of Ismailiya. But the country as a whole wanted an end to the war. That was something he could sense right away, and he did.[81]

Kissinger's short meeting with Meir, Dayan, Elezar, and others gave him a detailed understanding of the unfolding drama and tension Israel was sustaining. He knew from cables received from Dinitz before the Moscow trip that "the Israeli Army was exhausted."[82] There was a raw and exposed sense of national sullenness. Much Israeli blood was spilled during the war. The casualty count was huge. More than 2,200 Israelis were killed in the war, a percentage equivalent to 200,000 Americans. The number of Israelis killed was four times as many as Israelis killed in the June 1967 War. Over 5,600 more were maimed or wounded. By comparison, 61,000 Arabs were killed in the 1967 War and 8,500 in the October War.

According to Evron, when Meir saw him, "she was absolutely mad with Kissinger."[83] In public at least, Kissinger was forcing Israel to pay a political price, because it still wanted to encircle the Third Army.[84] Less than a week later, Kissinger and Nixon warned Meir that American arms deliveries would be suspended if the Israelis pursued their assault on the Third Army; apparently, Kissinger also threatened to send in food and medicine to the Third Army (by American helicopters) if Israel did not allow the Egyptians to establish their own relief corridor. When Dayan met Kissinger, he told him that the Israelis wanted several more days, at least, to complete the encirclement of the Third Army, even though the United Nations

Security Council had just called for implementation within twelve hours after the cease-fire resolution's passage. According to Rodman, Kissinger would have delayed in Moscow to allow the Israelis to finish surrounding the Third Army, but not to defeat it, *if* he had known, before leaving Washington, that their military intentions were strictly that. Israel was faced with a political fait accompli: to stop the fighting. Yet, Kissinger gave Dayan tacit approval to continue the Third Army's encirclement, but nothing more drastic. Kissinger told Israeli leaders that if it was their intention to starve out the Egyptian Third Army, the United States would "dissociate itself from it."[85] But Kissinger did not tell the Israelis not to better their military field advantage. Dayan wanted another seventy-two hours, and Kissinger acquiesced. Finally when Kissinger left Israel, Golda felt better.[86] Kissinger was not finished, but neither were Meir or Sadat, leaving solution of their problems solely to him or the White House. Instead, they found direct negotiations necessary and plausible.

The war was not over yet. Israel's decision to inflict pain and damage on the Egyptian Third Army was a strategic choice; surrounding and entrapping it were considered easier and less costly than dislodging the Egyptians from the east bank of the canal.[87] During these final days of the October War, deep apprehension gripped Sadat because of Israeli presence on the west side of the canal. With impunity and Kissinger's sanction, of which Sadat was not aware, Israel violated the cease-fire resolution. The Israeli bulge grew larger as troops were advancing south along the west side of the canal. The Third Army was surrounded, its supply lines slowly and completely cut. Egyptian civilians in Suez City were displaced and homeless; the Israeli army enjoyed virtually unimpeded access to the Suez City-Cairo road. Already, Egypt had used the bulk of its fighting reserves; there was nothing west of the canal to obstruct a possible Israeli advance toward Cairo. Fired Egyptian General Saad El-Shazly said, "the Third Army was on the brink of collapse."[88] Sadat sensed a desperate immediacy;[89] he repeatedly told Kissinger and the Soviets that a cease-fire had to be observed without delay, implying that after the Third Army, his capital was next on the Israeli agenda. President Nixon promised Sadat "to do whatever was necessary to stop the war,"[90] which meant creating an enforceable cease-fire and ensuring the survival of the Third Army. Since the Egyptians as well as the Syrians continued to breach the cease-fire, the Israelis willingly accommodated the renewal of fighting. As the Israelis improved their positions on the ground, mostly west of the canal, Kissinger could not savor achievement of the cease-fire resolution and defining Moscow's future diplomatic role. Instead, he had to prevent the destruction and human deterioration of the Egyptian Third Army.

In violation of the cease-fire, Israel poured men and equipment across the canal, and artillery exchanges continued between Egyptian and Israeli forces. In an effort to end the fighting, on October 23, the United Nations Security Council passed its second cease-fire resolution. UNSC Resolution 339 called for a cessation of the hostilities, a return to the October 22 lines, and the prompt dispatch of United

Nations observers. Unlike UNSC Resolution 338, UNSC Resolution 339 contained a mechanism for enforcing the proposed cease-fire. On October 24, Sadat publicly requested the dispatch of Soviet and American observers to the battle zones to monitor the cease-fire. Sadat suggested having the Soviets intervene because he believed that American observers were already on the Israeli side in Sinai; Sadat wanted to have the superpowers return Israel to its prewar positions, without Egypt doing the same. Moscow presented a proposal to Nixon and Kissinger in which the Soviet Union and the United States would position their own forces on both sides of the canal, forcing Israel to withdraw.[91] Nixon and Kissinger were of the same mind, fearing any dispatch of American troops would be met with a corresponding Soviet reply; implanting contingents of American and Soviet soldiers into the battle zone to halt the fighting and to separate the forces would, in Kissinger's mind, increase the prospects of a superpower confrontation. According to Ismail, Nixon sent a message to Sadat telling him that the United States would not intervene with American troops. The fluidity of the battle lines, combined with the entangled nature of the two armies, deterred Kissinger from any serious consideration of the idea. Furthermore, if Kissinger wanted to seal off Soviet engagement in the postwar diplomacy, then inviting or sanctioning their physical peacekeeping presence before the negotiations began was out of the question. But even *before* Sadat asked publicly for the American and Soviet cease-fire observers, Moscow had sent four dozen of them along with twenty interpreters to Cairo, where they were greeted by Fahmy. After a few days, they returned to the Soviet Union.[92] What motivated them to dispatch the observers quickly and return them equally as fast remains to be explained fully.

Israel continued to improve its military positions on both fronts, despite the two cease-fire resolutions. The Israelis surrounded Suez City, but they did not take it; likewise, Israeli forces were tightening the clamps around the Third Army with its 15,000 men and 300 tanks. Egyptian supply lines were fully cut. On October 24, after Soviet President Brezhnev heard Sadat beg "to save me and the Egyptian capital encircled by Israeli tanks," he checked with the Soviet military representative in Cairo, who said that "Sadat had completely lost his head" in exaggeration.[93] By then, Moscow had sent several very stern messages to the White House "urging," not "requesting," decisive American pressure to halt Israeli military actions. Each message sent on October 23 and 24 contained progressively more explicit language regarding Soviet impatience with Israeli military action and Soviet preparedness to respond aggressively. Senator Jackson described these messages as "brutal and threatening."[94] Finally, Anatoly Dobrynin called Kissinger to convey the most strident message sent that day from President Brezhnev to President Nixon: "I will say it straight, that if you find it impossible to act jointly with us in this matter, we should be faced with the necessity urgently to consider the question of taking steps *unilaterally* [my emphasis]. We cannot allow arbitrariness on the part of Israel."[95]

The inability to achieve an enforceable cease-fire temporarily altered Moscow-Washington relations. Only four days earlier at the Kremlin, Brezhnev showed extreme satisfaction at Washington's collaboration in drafting the cease-fire resolution. Brezhnev increasingly believed that there was overt American collusion with Israel against Egypt. No one in the Soviet Foreign Ministry's Department of International Organizations, which consulted with the Politburo throughout the war, believed even after the message was sent to Nixon that Brezhnev or others would have undertaken "unilateral Soviet military action." The Kremlin estimated that Nixon's response to the Brezhnev note would have been at worst some temporary deterioration in Soviet-American relations or a joint political remonstrance from NATO. According to Victor Israelyan, who participated in those discussions, "how wrong was our forecast of the American reaction!"[96]

Israel continued to focus on Egypt because the Third Army's fate could be translated into political currency.[97] Besides, Egypt had ambushed Israel. Some in the Israeli military establishment wanted to exact revenge. They kept up the pressure on Suez City and the Third Army. Just seventy-two hours after the first cease-fire resolution was passed, the unanticipated prospect of military confrontation between the Soviet Union and the United States over the fate of the Egyptian Third Army appeared real. According to Eban, "the globalization of the Arab-Israeli conflict had always been the American nightmare." This was according to him the gravest portent of a superpower confrontation since the Cuban Missile Crisis of October 1962; it almost started World War III.[98] Apparently, Washington made it publicly known that Moscow was willing to move troops unilaterally into the Middle East in order to save Egypt's precariously encircled Third Army. Noticing a reduction of Soviet air flights to Egypt, American intelligence circles calculated out loud that instead of sending military resupply to Sadat's army, the Soviets were preparing to fly troops to the battle zone. According to Hafez Ismail, the Soviets were indeed "preparing to send a division of airborne troops to Egypt,"[99] but was Moscow actually ready to dispatch them? Moshe Dayan predicted that "the Russians [would] not do anything."[100] Those familiar with Soviet decision making at the time said, "Nobody in the Kremlin liked the idea of sending in troops unilaterally. . . . [T]he only way [to preserve the Third Army] was to exert effective pressure on Washington and force the Americans to pressure Israel. Some even believed that sending troops to the Middle East would inevitably lead to a confrontation with the United States."[101] Dobrynin concurred that it "would have been reckless both politically and militarily. . . . [I]t would have transformed the Arab-Israeli War into a direct clash between the Soviet Union and the United States. Nobody in Moscow wanted that."[102] Said Kosygin at the Politburo meeting on October 25, "It is not reasonable to become engaged in a war with the United States because of Egypt and Syria."[103]

Nonetheless, late in the evening on October 24, Washington "reacted" to possible Soviet intervention by going on a worldwide "nuclear military alert." According to Peter Rodman, "It was our strategy to deliberately overreact . . . facing down the Russians . . . you had to scare them off."[104] Privately, Kissinger reassured the Soviets. That day Kissinger and Dobrynin had a detailed conversation about the organization of the proposed Middle East peace conference following a cease-fire, including reaffirmation of coequal status at the conference.[105] Before the public, however, the added drama of a possible superpower showdown sent a message to the Israelis to desist in violating the cease-fires and warned the Soviets not to intervene; it also enhanced the status of the American negotiating role. Although there was a confirmed account of Moscow routing at least one freighter with nuclear weapons toward Egypt, the Soviets reportedly decided against delivering the cargo into Egyptian hands.[106] Given the Soviet Union's close control over nuclear weapons, the Soviets were not prepared to provide them to the Egyptians. On October 24, according to Moscow's ambassador to Washington, Kissinger told him that the instructions for limited combat readiness should not be taken by Moscow as a hostile action but instead were mostly determined by "domestic considerations." The White House wanted a clear message sent to Moscow that the American government was not stalemated because of Nixon's Watergate problem. Kissinger apparently assured Dobrynin that the order about combat readiness would be revoked the next day, "and that in the meanwhile [Dobrynin] could urgently inform Brezhnev about it in strict confidence."[107] Again, it was typical of Kissinger's style not to inform in a prior manner either the American embassy in Tel Aviv or the Israeli government of the intent to go on nuclear alert.[108] For Kissinger, the alert was intended to send a message to the Soviets and Israelis alike, not to inform some bureaucrat in Tel Aviv of an Oval Office decision.

On October 25, Washington leaked information about its troops in Europe being prepared for possible action. The following day, the United States backed off its alert status, quickly reducing the threat of a Soviet-American confrontation. At his press conference on October 26, Nixon said, "This was a precautionary alert . . . to indicate to the Soviet Union that we would not accept any unilateral move on their part to move military forces into the Middle East." By the time the press conference was held, American troops were beginning to stand down from the alert. Cease-fires called for on October 22 and October 23 by the United Nations were finally observed with intermittent interruptions, at least on the Egyptian-Israeli front.[109] In short, Kissinger's actions were really meant for Moscow's and secondarily Israel's consumption. Kissinger did not want Moscow intervening militarily; he intentionally raised real and perceived tensions between Washington and Moscow in order to remind them who was in charge. He told Dinitz, "I do not want Egypt to have any advantages from the war, either psychological or territorial."[110] Neither did he want Israel to destroy the Third Army. According to Eban, "None [who] took part in the all-night meeting of the Israeli cabinet on October 25–26 will ever forget the tension."[111] Kissinger enhanced

American prestige in the Middle East by reacting to the Soviet threat and gained currency with Sadat for his ability to prevent the possible destruction of the Third Army. Ironically, Kissinger earned that currency through Israel's performance on the battlefield. Though the resupply of material to Israel was slow, Kissinger and Nixon could not tolerate Israel's defeat; that would not reinforce Sadat's choice of moderation toward Israel via American diplomatic intervention.

~~~~~

FROM WAR
TO DIPLOMACY
THE KILOMETER 101 TALKS

A N UNBEARABLE status quo along with domestic priorities drove both
Meir and Sadat to engage in immediate negotiations. Each needed resolution of his or her respective problems. Israel yearned to repatriate its prisoners-
of-war and war dead. Also, Meir did not want to enter any controversial
negotiations or reach any political arrangement with Egypt before the newly
rescheduled December parliamentary elections. With Israel mobilized for war, its
economy had come to a screeching halt; that had to be reversed. And weapons and
supplies lost in the war needed to be replaced. For his part, Sadat needed to redirect
momentum from the war into substantive diplomacy. Failure to save the Third
Army from annihilation could have brought his rule to an end. The Egyptian crossing had been a spectacular accomplishment: its blemishes needed to be denied, its
success overstated. To this end, Sadat blamed others for mistakes made, but took the
credit for the crossing's achievement. Depending upon the constituency addressed,
Sadat told the story of the Third Army differently: to his Arab brethren in general
and to his domestic audience, he would not admit publicly that his army was surrounded or in peril. To Brezhnev and Kissinger, he pleaded the cause and certainly
exaggerated its precarious condition. Privately, he understood it was bad, but not
catastrophic. On October 31, a day after Egyptian-Israeli military talks began, Sadat
refuted Israel's claim of surrounding the Third Army; he said that Israel's presence
on the west bank of the Suez Canal was a fabrication.[1] In public, Sadat said that
Cairo opened direct military talks with the Israelis because they had refused to
revert to the October 22 cease-fire lines. That is what made disengagement of
Egyptian and Israeli forces necessary.[2] *Sadat contended that the Israelis wanted their
enclave removed from the west bank of the canal in order to gain a better bargaining position.*
He readily blamed the Israelis for his military predicament, especially their violations of both cease-fire resolutions. He added the Americans to his list of culprits
for their resupply of Israel during the war, citing as alleged evidence to Eilts that

tanks with low odometer readings were delivered to the Israelis directly in Sinai. With this he threw up his hands and said, "I cannot fight the U.S."[3] Later he would blame the Jordanians too for their inaction at the end of the war. With all of this Sadat was protecting his image and putting his "spin" on events. Until he died in October 1981, time after time, speech after speech, he repeated his rendition of the "great October War victory"; listening to Sadat one would never have known that the Israelis had crossed the canal. Some of Sadat's detractors criticized him for failing to recognize the magnitude of the victory that was now in his grasp. Said Heikal, "He held all the trumps . . . instead he opted for the victory parades and the cameras, . . . resolved that he would rebuild the area alone with his new friend, Henry Kissinger."[4] Sadat saw negotiations with the Israelis as a way to ingratiate himself with Kissinger, assure the political spotlight, and keep the momentum from the war moving forward.

On the Israeli side of negotiations, a source for the idea of direct Egyptian-Israeli talks came from the director general of the Israeli prime minister's office, Mordechai Gazit.[5] Gazit persuaded Meir that there was no reason why Israel should not negotiate directly with Egypt on military matters. As originally conceived, the purpose of the talks was to separate the forces in general. Ultimately, though, the talks focused on achieving and maintaining a cease-fire and dealt with exchanging prisoners-of-war, finding soldiers who were missing-in-action, providing supplies to the Third Army, and deciding on whether and where the United Nations or Israel controlled the roads and checkpoints that entwined the two armies. After the standdown from the nuclear alert, Sadat pushed Nixon and Kissinger to stop the war and resolve the supply issue to the Third Army.[6] Kissinger felt that Egypt would not even accept participation in the direct military talks the Israelis proposed for Kilometer 101 (the distance from Cairo) because the distrust between the belligerents was too great.[7] He was surprised then by the Egyptian readiness to hold military talks and did not anticipate that Egyptian and Israeli generals would eventually hold political discussions as well.[8] Though Kissinger was not personally in favor of direct Egyptian-Israeli talks, on October 27, 1973, he conveyed Sadat's unexpected and eager consent to the Israeli negotiating initiative. There was no indication at the beginning of the Kilometer 101 Talks that Meir or other important Israeli governmental officials were contemplating detailed discussions about anything more than a separation of the forces. Unlike some of her generals, such as Sharon, who were willing to stay on the west side of the canal for perhaps up to a year, Meir did not want to stay there longer than was absolutely necessary. From the beginning of the talks, the Israeli representatives were instructed to "suggest, request, and demand" that there be a future meeting of Israelis with Egyptians on the political level.[9] But Meir's government did not want to do anything immediately that would create additional skittishness among the Israeli voting public already disoriented and angered by the war's surprise and outcome. Moreover, the Israeli government and public were not yet psychologically ready to debate either the contents or the implications of a formal peace with Egypt. In the end, neither Israeli nor Egyptian Foreign Ministry officials played any role in the substantive evolution or outcome of these talks, though some officials attended the talks with both overt or covert identities. West of the canal, the Kilometer 101 Talks were conducted officially between Egypt's General el-Gamasy and Israel's General Yariv.[10] With their respective generals as envoys, the talks were closely managed and monitored by Sadat and Meir.

General el-Gamasy was an extremely proud Egyptian with a superb military career that included fighting Israel in four wars. He was honest, principled, and had great difficulty in making compromises that required deviousness. Israelis who negotiated with him considered him an excellent professional soldier, dedicated to the restoration of Egyptian land and national pride lost in the June 1967 War. According to el-Gamasy, "In the October War, we took revenge for the Six Day War. It was personal from me to Dayan. The Six Day War hurt us to the utmost. We got back our prestige from Dayan. When I say Dayan, I mean Dayan. I hated Dayan more than I hated Sharon or Bar-Lev."[11] El-Gamasy equally and strongly supported Sadat's desire to end the conflict with Israel, but in the subsequent diplomatic negotiations after the October 1973 War, he sometimes disagreed with Sadat's concessions to the Americans or Israelis where felt Egyptian pride, honor, or accomplishments were in his estimation unnecessarily compromised. El-Gamasy remained loyal to Sadat throughout the subsequent negotiations with Israel and the Americans; despite his loyalty, in 1978 when Egyptian-Israeli negotiations were in the pre–Camp David stage, el-Gamasy lost out in a scenario of political intrigue to Husni Mubarak for the chance to succeed Sadat.[12]

On October 27, General Ahmed Ismail, the Egyptian minister of war, told el-Gamasy that he was to meet with the Israelis at Kilometer 101. Later that day, el-Gamasy was accompanied to the talks by Omar Sirry, the German-born Egyptian career foreign service officer, and by Brigadier General Howeidi, an Egyptian military intelligence officer. During the war, Sirry served as deputy chief of operations in the Foreign Ministry. He also had previous experience in international organizations, including United Nations affairs. On October 27, Sirry was beckoned to see Acting-Foreign Minister Fahmy, who told him to "get a toothbrush and a pajama and be ready!" Sirry then inquired about what he should be ready to do and what his guidelines were for these discussions. Hesitating at each of Sirry's questions and avoiding a reply, Fahmy was quite reluctant to tell Sirry what his exact mission would be. Not only was Fahmy personally uncomfortable about having any discussions with the Israelis but also he was not fully informed about Sadat's objectives. After a pause, Fahmy told Sirry that he was to go to military headquarters, meet General el-Gamasy, and become el-Gamasy's political adviser. Sirry replied, "I have never heard of him before." Fahmy continued to be oblique, but volunteered that Sirry had to be prepared to go to Suez. "But Suez is totally surrounded by Israeli troops," he responded. Sirry continued to inquire, Fahmy remained circumspect, perhaps even ashamed. Fahmy's extreme reluctance to define for Sirry his exact assignment was, according to Sirry, "indicative of the psychological attitude that was prevailing at the time in Egypt because, after so many years of fighting and opposing the Israelis, Fahmy found it very difficult to tell me that I was going to talk to them."[13] Sirry astonished Fahmy with his reply: "Hooray." "Hooray what?" asked Fahmy. "We are finally talking,"[14] replied Sirry. Sirry then received additional instructions not to wear civilian clothes nor to let anyone know that he was the foreign minister's representative, because the talks were to be purely military. In the end, Sirry only attended the first meeting at Kilometer 101, because when Fahmy took the permanent position of foreign minister on October 31, Sirry became his chief of cabinet. That left Fawzi al-Ibrashi, another Egyptian Foreign Ministry official, and several other Egyptian soldiers to join el-Gamasy in the approximately eighteen meetings that he and Yariv would conduct during the next month.

Earlier in 1973, Israeli General Aharon Yariv had retired as head of Israeli military intelligence. During the October War, he undertook several ad hoc assignments as special assistant to Israel's military chief of staff, David Elazar. Yariv was in the Sinai when he was summoned to Tel Aviv late in the morning on Saturday, October 27. A few hours later, Meir told him that he would be negotiating with an Egyptian counterpart at Kilometer 101. Yariv, chosen because he was knowledgeable about military matters, had observed the war closely, and was considered politically independent of any particular Israeli cabinet minister, would be accompanied by Dov Tsion, Dayan's son-in-law, who had served in the strategic planning division of the general staff. Only an elite few around Meir knew about the pending talks with the Egyptians. Yariv understood that Dayan and members of the Defense Ministry were less than committed to making life easy for the Third Army. An advocate of "Dayan's view" at the Kilometer 101 Talks would have brought sternness in dealing with the future of the Third Army. Unlike Dayan, Yariv had not held an official military position during the war. Had he done so, he might have been motivated to be retributive against the Egyptians. Moreover, Yariv's character was neither arrogant nor vengeful. Dayan was not thrilled that military talks were about to take place and that he was not in charge.

From Israel Galili, a very close confidant of Meir and minister without portfolio in her cabinet, Yariv received his instructions. Galili made sure that Yariv did not give, say, propose, or affirm *anything* without prior approval and knowledge of the government, including the prime minister, defense minister, Committee of Ministers on Defense Issues, and even the Foreign Affairs and Defense Committee of the Knesset.[15] Galili directed Yariv that Israel wanted a firm cease-fire, an exchange of prisoners-of-war, and a lifting of the Egyptian naval blockade of Israeli shipping at the Bab al-Mandab Straits. Other than the regular assessments he read about the disposition of the Egyptian military forces, Yariv's preparation for the Kilometer 101 Talks was very limited. He was expected not to stray from directives provided him. He received brief evaluations from Israeli military intelligence about el-Gamasy's personal profile and other matters relating to the surrounded Third Army, which Yariv described as "hard pressed." These pending talks were unique in their belligerent relationship: Egyptian and Israeli military officials were about to negotiate the separation of their forces without a third party in a mediation role and with the United Nations assisting only in implementing the understandings. Although Israel was reeling in agony from the war, a superpower confrontation had recently been avoided, and the Israeli political system was engaged in the run-up to parliamentary elections, only Galili, Gazit, and a few others actually realized that direct Egyptian-Israeli military talks were truly unprecedented. Likewise, on the Egyptian side, "no one understood the political significance of what we were doing."[16]

Just three weeks after the war began, in a military convoy the small Egyptian negotiating team headed to Suez City. Talks with the Israelis were scheduled to begin at seven o'clock in the evening on October 27, 1973. On the way to Suez, the Egyptian convoy of several jeeps accidentally met UN General Ensio Siilasvuo, who was returning from a meeting with an Israeli near Suez City. When el-Gamasy asked Siilasvuo if his party was expected by the Israelis, the head of the United Nations Emergency Force (UNEF) told el-Gamasy, "I know nothing about such a meeting; I have come from their headquarters in Suez; there is no indication that a meeting is to take place; no one is there to meet you."[17] El-Gamasy and his entourage returned to Cairo and reported to General Ahmed Ismail what had happened. After several hours, contact was reestablished with Kissinger in order to clarify the problem and reset the meeting time for one o'clock in the morning. The Egyptians understood the scheduling for local time, but the Israelis assumed the scheduling was in accordance with New York time (that is, seven hours later). Thus, when Siilasvuo was in Suez City with the Israelis, he still did not know that the separation-of-forces talks were to take place. Simultaneously and unrelated, the Israelis mistakenly ended up at Kilometer 105 and then had to return to Kilometer 101, where they awaited el-Gamasy's arrival. Remaining "in alert," el-Gamasy and his small party were called again, this time around midnight, to go again to Suez City to meet the Israelis. This time, two Austrian UN drivers took the Egyptian delegation toward Suez. On a very dark night, the two cars passed through the Egyptian lines, onto the desert road that el-Gamasy believed was mined. They were traveling to Israeli-controlled territory. To avoid possible injury to the civilians, el-Gamasy put them in the second vehicle and instructed the driver to stay on the tracks of the first, in case they did encounter mines. Sirry recalled that those in the Egyptian delegation were very apprehensive in anticipation of how the Israelis would behave at the first meeting. "There was a fear that the Israelis would be obnoxious or act in a superior fashion, and we debated among ourselves how we should behave in such a situation. Fortunately, the Israelis chose very well in sending [General] Yariv. He was absolutely the right man; the Israelis could not have chosen better."[18]

On the way to their meeting on the west bank of the canal, Yariv cautioned the Israeli members of his small delegation that under no circumstances were they to do anything that would embarrass the Egyptians about the besieged status of the Third Army. He impressed upon them that they treat the Egyptian representatives with respect and make no references to Israel's military successes. Rather than present General el-Gamasy with a handshake greeting, which might have been construed by the Egyptians as humiliating due to the critical status of the Third Army, Yariv chose to salute el-Gamasy when they met. While traveling from Cairo to his first meeting with Yariv, el-Gamasy also was not sure whether he should greet Yariv with a handshake or a salute. El-Gamasy decided before the meeting that he would do what Yariv did. Finally, on the bitter cold morning of Sunday, October 28, shortly after 1 A.M., the initial Egyptian-Israeli negotiating session took place at a wooden table under a camouflage canopy stretched between four Israeli tanks. Very dim lights were provided by a portable generator, which proved sufficient light for taking notes. The first meeting took place in Israeli-controlled territory, as opposed to what later came to be known as *no-man's land*. When the Egyptians finally arrived, the six or seven Israelis were standing in a line and salutes were exchanged, followed by handshakes. Recalling his first impressions of the Israelis, el-Gamasy said, "It was a good show from them."[19] There were no embarrassing diplomatic incidents, though the Egyptians were somewhat perturbed by the sight of the Israeli flag.[20] To the slight irritation of the Israelis, the Egyptians introduced themselves by their first names only, frustrating Israeli eagerness to know exactly with whom they were negotiating. When the Israelis inquired further about Sirry, el-Gamasy did not indicate that he was a Foreign Ministry official, but instead told the Israelis that he was his "political consultant."

Once the first session began, one member of the Israeli team thought that the Egyptians were "shivering in fright" from anxiety engendered by their first negotiations with the Israelis. But Yariv knew that really the temperature was the issue. When el-Gamasy acknowledged that he and his team were physically quite cold, Yariv offered them Israeli Air Force jackets, which, according to Yariv, some of the Egyptians gladly donned. El-Gamasy apparently did not. Sirry recalled that it was so frightfully cold that he could not take notes and was glad to sip hot coffee during the two-hour session.[21] Each general started by making short remarks with introductory statements noting that both armies had fought well and honorably and that both sides should now perform admirably in making peace. The content and tone of Yariv's comments alleviated the apprehension among the Egyptians that the Israelis would be arrogant. Sirry described Yariv as "sophisticated and calm. He did not shove anything down our throats. Had he been otherwise, the Egyptian delegation would not have accepted it."[22] El-Gamasy considered Yariv "a very fine man who knew his work very well."[23] Yariv believed el-Gamasy to be "a pedantic man, but a proud officer, Egyptian, and Arab."[24] Even while the separation of forces discussions took place, elements of the two armies remained engaged. As the talks continued that first night until approximately four o'clock in the morning, there were intermittent intrusions of shooting, gun fire, rockets, and flares. For weeks after the commencement of the Kilometer 101 negotiations, the cease-fire was periodically broken. El-Gamasy acknowledged that most of those violations came from the Egyptian side.[25] The primary issue raised by the Egyptians was selecting, securing, and delivering supplies to the Third Army. For Israel, logistically, this was not a major problem.[26] Israel's absolute priority was effecting a swift exchange of war prisoners and arranging the return of the soldiers who had been killed.

Replying to Yariv, el-Gamasy deflected many answers by saying he had to refer to Cairo. The Egyptians found it unusual that during this first negotiating session, Yariv repeatedly excused himself to phone his superiors in order to report information and to receive further instructions.[27] While military men were negotiating, their civilian superiors were essentially making the decisions about the content of the talks, which obviously contained political implications, including their respective relationships with Washington. Yariv sensed that his direct communications with Meir and Galili gave the Israelis a certain advantage. Likewise, el-Gamasy customarily reported back directly to President Sadat in the form of both verbal and written assessments of Israeli views on a variety of issues under negotiation and the direction in which he thought they were heading. After the end of the first negotiating session, Sirry and al-Ibrashi, a legal specialist in the Egyptian Foreign Ministry, finished their report around six o'clock in the morning and apparently hand-delivered it to President Sadat. After a short nap, Sirry was summoned by Sadat for a 9:00 A.M. meeting with Air Force General Husni Mubarak, Ahmed Ismail, Hafez Ismail, Ismail Fahmy, Abd al-Ghani el-Gamasy, and several others. Abruptly, Sadat informed Fahmy that he would immediately go to Washington to meet with Kissinger and told Fahmy exactly what he wanted from the trip. In his memoirs, Fahmy claimed that he conceived the ideas that eventually became the operational outline for the tactics and strategy of Egyptian negotiating policy. But Sirry, who took the notes in this meeting, said that Sadat provided the original detailed framework for the agreement he was seeking with the Israelis. When Sirry sent the typed text to Sadat for final review, Sadat inserted several words that had been omitted from Sirry's version, an indication of Sadat's attention to the specific detail of the substantive Egyptian positions destined to be part of the coming negotiations with the United States. Apparently, not until that meeting did Sadat have a written text of what he wanted to accomplish. The framework, which Sadat dictated and Fahmy took to Washington, included the following steps: "Israel would withdraw to the October 22 lines; all prisoners-of-war would be released; Israel would then withdraw to a line inside Sinai east of the passes, while Egypt's forces remained in place; UN forces would be deployed between the Egyptian and Israeli forces; after Israel started withdrawing to the disengagement line, Egypt would lift the blockade of the Straits of Bab el-Mandeb; once the disengagement was completed, Egypt would start clearing the Suez Canal; within an agreed time, Israel would withdraw to the international frontier; at this point belligerency would end."[28] Also included in the framework was an outline of steps to be taken to obtain a similar disengagement on the Syrian front, to convene an international conference, and to restore diplomatic relations between Egypt and the United States. From the outset of Egypt's diplomatic effort, Sadat wanted all the detailed issues agreed upon before going to a conference for their ratification.

Of particular sensitivity in the negotiations was the scheduled pace of resupply and then ultimately the release of the Egyptian Third Army. Through el-Gamasy, Sadat clearly communicated to the Americans and the Israelis that he did not want all his soldiers released at once. He sought to avoid an unwanted publicity problem. Few people in Egypt understood the quantity of surrounded soldiers or the severity of the Third Army's condition. For political reasons, some Israeli leaders still wanted to find a way to neutralize the despair that Israel had suffered at the beginning of the war. Holding on to the encircled Third Army was symbolic for some Israeli politicians; others wanted the destruction of the Third Army in order to finish the war on a high note. Dayan did not mind releasing all of the Egyptian soldiers in a short period of time (such as in large convoys of 5,000 men) in order to make Sadat suffer open humiliation for their acknowledged entrapment by Israel.[29] Meir wanted the Third Army speedily released so Israel could have their prisoners-of-war returned. In order to lessen potential embarrassment because of the numbers of Egyptian prisoners-of-war requiring repatriation, some of the exchanges apparently took place via air through Cyprus; but most exchanges were conducted overland via bus transport. For its part, the United Nations conveyed prisoners-of-war to the military lines separating the respective armies and handled their return in a timely fashion. Dayan still wanted to find ways to spite the Egyptians for their surprise attack—not to destroy them, but to convey an unmistakable message that Israel was in charge.[30] As the negotiations continued about managing the fate of the Third Army, the legal adviser to the Israeli Foreign Ministry, Meir Rosenne, was asked to find historical precedents regarding possible Israeli legal responsibility for provision of supplies to an army that had not yet given itself up, was not yet in the status of war prisoners, and still had the status of "combatants." Because no legal precedent was found, the issue of Israel supplying or starving the Third Army needed to be resolved on humanitarian not political grounds.[31]

Simultaneous to the ongoing Kilometer 101 Talks, Egyptian Brigadier General Taha El Magdoob and Major General Herzel Shafir, head of the manpower and training branch of the Israeli Army, negotiated issues pertaining to military personnel, prisoners-of-war, and soldiers missing-in-action. Magdoob and Shafir handled some of the operational discussions involving details of restoring soldiers to their respective sides, while Yariv and el-Gamasy focused on other issues of military disengagement. In describing Magdoob, Shafir recalled him as highly professional, cooperative, and polite, "but from time to time, one had the feeling that he was not providing us all the information we wanted, not because he did not want to give [it] to us, but because he was ordered to withhold such information [about Israelis missing-in-action and the prisoners-of-war] as a weapon against us all the time. The Egyptians recognized immediately our sensitivity to this point [the missing-in-action and the prisoners-of-war]."[32] In the separation of forces discussion, maps were designed and exchanged by Egyptian and Israeli officers. Yariv raised a series of issues, which included the importance of an effective cease-fire based upon United Nations participation, an undelayed prisoners-of-war exchange, free navigation through the Suez Canal and Bab el-Mandeb Straits, establishment of communications between local commanders, the quick definition of cease-fire lines, the establishment of a ten-kilometer-wide buffer zone between the armies, and a ban on the fortification of frontline positions. Additionally, el-Gamasy wanted United Nations forces to interpose themselves between the armies, quick resupply for the Third Army and supplies to Suez City (then cut off by the Israeli presence), and an Israeli withdrawal to the cease-fire lines of October 22. El-Gamasy was not sure about the size of the buffer zone, but wanted instead to discuss the contents of UNSC Resolution 338, "the withdrawal of Israel to the 1967 border."[33] Sadat instructed el-Gamasy not only to discuss prompt solutions to problems created by the October 1973 War but also to have Yariv and the Israelis understand the urgency of discussing the broader issue of "liquidating" Israel's total presence from Sinai. During the first week in November, when Yariv accompanied Meir to Washington, General Israel Tal, the Israeli deputy chief of staff, filled in for Yariv at the Kilometer 101 Talks. Tal and el-Gamasy had detailed discussions about how the prisoners-of-war would be returned. As el-Gamasy recalled, "We started drawing [withdrawal] lines in the sand and he accepted the idea that the Israeli troops on the western bank should move to the east. Tal said 'For us this is not a problem, but what will you do?' Then we started discussing so many political things. This was a turning point in relations between Egypt and Israel. I was talking as President Sadat and he [Tal] was talking as Meir."[34] El-Gamasy returned to Cairo and told a surprised Sadat that, based on what Tal said, the Israelis were willing to withdraw to the east side of the canal. So before Kissinger made his first trip to Cairo on November 7, Sadat knew from el-Gamasy that the Israelis would withdraw from the western side of the canal. Sadat understood that a separation of forces agreement was possible and the Third Army would be spared.

To this point, Kissinger was not privy to the scope or detail of the negotiations. He did not have timely information about what was happening on the ground between the armies, and he had no clue about who said what to whom. Only in late

November and early December did the State Department receive extremely short summaries of the el-Gamasy–Yariv sessions. Kissinger was unrestrained in his anger during his talks with Meir at Blair House in Washington, apparently not knowing that Egyptian-Israeli military discussions on the separation of forces and prisoners-of-war exchanges were going well with agreements being reached. In retrospect, Meir described these meetings as "bitter; they were a terrible two nights of discussion."[35] Through cable communications, Kissinger had apparently promised Sadat that he would obtain UN control of the roads leading to Suez and the Third Army. According to Meir, "Sadat and Kissinger demanded that we return to the October 22 cease-fire lines, but the Egyptians kept on shooting, we kept on shooting, and we moved to our advantage. And I said no. We will not go back. He begged for supplies for the Third Army."[36] On the issue of control of the supply corridor, Meir said she would not budge until she received all her prisoners-of-war back. Kissinger had Nelson Rockefeller, Alexander Haig, and others call Meir in an effort to have her turn control of the roads over to the United Nations. Showing his frustration over Meir's apparent stubbornness about the control of the roads and their checkpoints, Kissinger told her, "You are not giving me anything to go to Cairo with. I have nothing to offer them."[37] While Kissinger did not know what was transpiring at Kilometer 101, Sadat and Meir did. Their generals had reached workable understandings.

When the Kilometer 101 Talks began, the United Nations was present in the person of a junior official, an Irish captain named Joseph Fallon. By the end of the first week of the talks, Fallon was responsible for having the United Nations drive the resupply convoys to the Egyptian Third Army. The convoys were usually loaded by Egyptian soldiers at the points of origin and were inspected by Israeli soldiers as they passed into Israeli-held territory. Joining the talks in mid-November, General Siilasvuo witnessed the signing of the six-point Egyptian-Israeli accord on November 11, which outlined the cease-fire agreement. This was the day *after* the Kilometer 101 cease-fire agreement was concluded and almost three weeks after the first cease-fire resolution had been passed unanimously in the United Nations Security Council. Shafir and Magdoob negotiated the manpower understandings, and the United Nations and Red Cross were useful and cooperative in managing and implementing the process of prisoners-of-war exchange. While the United Nations set up inspection checkpoints for the supply columns to the Third Army, the Israelis undertook the inspection and retained control of the roads. Repeatedly, Israel through Yariv sought to restrict the UN's mediation role. When Yariv or el-Gamasy wanted to clarify an issue or reach an understanding with one another during their eighteen sessions, the two of them, or those in their delegation, would leave the table and confer privately, beyond the hearing range of United Nations personnel. As the negotiations continued, an excellent rapport developed between Yariv and el-Gamasy. El-Gamasy later told Hermann Eilts, "We were able to sit down and talk about things as two soldiers to one another and, to my surprise, work out the disengagement between the forces and the arrangements to assure that."[38]

To Yariv, the most startling revelation during the talks was el-Gamasy's assertion at the second meeting that "halasna Filastin"—"We are finished with Palestine."[39] El-Gamasy told Yariv, "We started the war to liberate Sinai. We did not do anything for the Palestinians during this war. And the Syrians did not do anything [for them]. I told [Yariv] that we started the war not to liberate all of Sinai, because we did not have the capability to do it. But, as a result of the war, we will liberate Sinai."[40] El-Gamasy also said that peace would come to Israel if all the Sinai were returned. When Yariv asked el-Gamasy about the other Arab countries, el-Gamasy replied, "They do not matter."[41] What is very significant is that neither Yariv nor others in the Israeli political or intelligence elite comprehended at that moment that Egypt and Sadat might be prepared to move independently or at least ahead of the rest of the Arab world in achieving interim arrangements with Israel. According to Avraham Sela, who at the time evaluated Palestinian affairs in Israeli military intelligence,

> In the trauma from the war we only saw the Arabs as strong, and then we saw Arab unity from the oil embargo and feared Israel being blamed for it by the whole world; we did not see the differences that existed between the Arabs; for us Israelis, it was too good to be true what el-Gamasy told Yariv—that the Egyptians were finished with the Palestinians. That Egypt wanted to advance its own interests first, we could not absorb something like this, it just would not penetrate our cognizance at the time.[42]

Sela continued, "Toward the end of the war, when Yasir Arafat, the chairman of the PLO, visited the Third Army, Egyptian soldiers embraced him and his presence." No distinctions were made at the time between what Sadat wanted or el-Gamasy said on the one hand, and what Israelis read, saw, and heard from Egyptians not close to Sadat's entourage. Only toward the end of 1976 did Israeli military intelligence consider making political estimates that suggested Sadat might consider a nonmilitary solution to remaining differences with Israel.

In the fortnight between the evening of October 28 and 29 and November 11, 1973, Yariv and el-Gamasy negotiated a separation of forces agreement. Fahmy claimed that when he met with Kissinger on October 29 in Washington, the six points were "all agreed upon," a statement that has been disputed by Saunders, Sisco, and Yariv.[43] What Fahmy brought to Washington was the ambitious Egyptian proposal that Sadat had dictated during the morning meeting on October 28, which included a unilateral Israeli withdrawal east of the canal, perhaps as far as the strategic passes, while Egypt would keep its troops west of the canal. The cease-fire arrangement was negotiated with input from several sources: it originated from Sadat's dictated brief to Fahmy; was discussed by Kissinger in his talks with Meir (without Foreign Minister Eban) in Washington in early November; reworked during the Sadat-Kissinger talks in Cairo on November 7; and supplemented by the Sisco-Saunders discussions with the Israelis immediately after the Sadat-Kissinger meeting. What neither Fahmy nor Kissinger's American advisers knew was that Sadat previously had el-Gamasy present the same "strategic" plan to Yariv at Kilometer 101.[44] It was what Tal and el-Gamasy discussed while Meir was in Washington. She presented Kissinger with the same six points at their meeting in Washington on Saturday, November 3, at Blair House, and Kissinger told Meir that he would take the six points to Sadat for his approval, but did not think Sadat would agree.[45] Kissinger did not know that the six-point document was already a consensus understanding in the process of being defined by the Israelis and Egyptians at the Kilometer 101 Talks. Sadat did not seem to mind that UN personnel would also learn about his cease-fire plan of having the Israelis withdraw to the east bank of the canal and his broader intention of negotiating Israel's full but staged withdrawal from Sinai. When Kissinger, Fahmy, and other Egyptian foreign service officers found out that el-Gamasy had given Yariv Egypt's strategic plan, they were perturbed because they felt their diplomatic status as negotiators was somehow compromised. This was Sadat's way: to use several channels to be sure his objective was accomplished. Sadat used the reports from el-Gamasy's meetings with Yariv to glean information about Israeli intentions and objectives, allowing him to develop impressions of the Israelis separate and independent from what Kissinger and the Americans were telling him. By making the plan of an initial and partial Israeli withdrawal easily available to the Israelis—willfully or not—Sadat was forcing Kissinger to develop a sole and proprietary role over the negotiations. Otherwise, Yariv and el-Gamasy would continue their avid political discussions.[46] After some last-minute dickering between Israel and the American negotiators, the disengagement agreement drafted by Generals Yariv and el-Gamasy on November 11, 1973, contained the following general six points:[47]

1. Egypt and Israel agree to observe scrupulously the cease-fire called for by the UN Security Council.
2. Both sides agree that discussion between them will begin immediately to settle the question of the return to the October 22 positions in the framework of agreement on the disengagement and separation of forces under the auspices of the United Nations.
3. The town of Suez will receive daily supplies of food, water, and medicine. All wounded civilians in the town of Suez will be evacuated.
4. There will be no impediment to the movement of nonmilitary supplies to the east bank.
5. The Israeli checkpoints on the Cairo-Suez road will be replaced by UN checkpoints. At the Suez end of the road, Israeli officers can participate with the UN to supervise the nonmilitary nature of the cargo at the bank of the canal.

6. As soon as the UN checkpoints are established on the Cairo-Suez road, there will be an exchange of all prisoners-of-war, including wounded.

In the moments after the signing ceremony was completed at Kilometer 101, and while the international media were taking pictures, the dialogue between Yariv and el-Gamasy went approximately as follows: Yariv said, "My dear General, what do you mean by disengagement agreement? It is listed in the six-point agreement, that phrase." To which el-Gamasy replied, "I said it means to place the troops away from one another." Yariv replied, "No. . . . It is a Harvard expression and it is Kissinger who will put the explanation for it, and you and I will not be able to do anything about it until Kissinger says what he means by it."[48] El-Gamasy acknowledged the relevance of Yariv's assessment. Both generals understood that the diplomatic negotiations involving political discussions would be ultimately transferred to Kissinger's control, but neither knew when or how that would happen. Neither general was yet prepared to deliver the negotiating prerogative to him.

After the signing ceremony on November 11, 1973, the environment of the talks became more formal and more detailed, the UN role more obvious but not more substantive. Siilasvuo became the de facto and unappointed mediator. Instead of meetings taking place under one canopy stretched between four tanks, there were three tents set up: one tent for each military delegation and one tent in the middle hosted by the United Nations. But the increased bureaucratic and physical structure of the setting did not diminish the informality in which Yariv and el-Gamasy wanted to carry on their conversations with one another. The next day Siilasvuo tried to interpose himself as the middleman between Yariv and el-Gamasy. Yariv, polite but firm, would not have it and told Siilasvuo, "El-Gamasy and I get along just fine. Don't try to be a mediator. Your patronage and auspices, yes. But please, sir, don't be a mediator."[49] Siilasvuo was not pleased; perhaps he was even offended. In recalling this conversation with Siilasvuo, Yariv added, "If you have ever seen a carrot, it was pale compared to the redness on his face."[50]

As would occur with subsequent Egyptian-Israeli agreements, disputes arose about implementation. How were the six points to be linked? What were to be the amounts and quantities of supplies to be provided? How long would the prisoner and dead body exchanges last?[51] A cease-fire had been signed, but thereafter disagreeable negotiations ensued about how the agreement would be applied, how the prisoners-of-war would be exchanged, and how quickly this exchange would occur. (The first prisoners-of-war were exchanged on November 15.) Israel wanted its 240 prisoners-of-war returned as soon as possible. The details pertaining to the volume and nature of supplies to the Third Army and to Suez City (also under partial Israeli siege) were delegated directly for management to Generals Magdoob and Shafir. In providing access to the supplies to be administered to the Egyptian soldiers of the Third Army and to Suez City, Israel continued to search the supply convoys in order

to avoid the smuggling of military equipment, which might be used against the surrounding Israeli forces. El-Gamasy refuted the notion that the Third Army was in as
much peril as reported when the war ended. "It had its personnel, equipment,
ammunition, food, and water—it had emergency rations for one week."[52]

At one of the negotiating sessions in early November, el-Gamasy returned a
captured Israeli soldier to Yariv, hoping to demonstrate to the Israelis at least his
own sincerity in saying that Egypt wanted peaceful relations with Israel. Yariv's
opening negotiating position was for Egyptian and Israeli Armies to "swap
banks"—that Israel leave "Africa" and Egypt leave "Asia." Meir wanted the mutual
retreat to the prewar status quo. Prior to the negotiations, she repeatedly said to
Kissinger, "How come they start a war and they get rewarded. [It] is not fair. They
start a war and we withdraw from their territory."[53] El-Gamasy, the quintessential
Egyptian nationalist and military man who refused to take the same land twice,
replied, "Withdrawing Egyptian forces to the eastern bank was nonsense. Both
sides of the canal are our land. You move from the west to the east, but we will
never move from the east to the west. You move to the international borders."[54] In
suggesting that the Israelis retreat ten to twelve kilometers, Yariv counterproposed
that the Egyptians thin out their forces within thirty kilometers of the canal. But
el-Gamasy could not accept such a proposal after taking territory and proving the
competence of the Egyptian soldier. For Egypt, the Suez Canal represented a physical as well as a psychological median: if the Egyptians moved eastward, then they
were gaining; if they moved westward, then they were losing. At subsequent sessions, the Egyptians suggested an Israeli withdrawal of thirty-five kilometers deep
into Sinai, with UN observers separating the belligerent forces and a zone for the
drawn-down forces of both armies. The Egyptians worked out time schedules for a
full Israeli withdrawal accompanied by one for Suez Canal repair.

As meetings continued after November 11 in an increasingly friendly atmosphere, Yariv replied with even more specifics.[55] From then on, their meetings took
place at least every two or three days for several hours or more. Progressively, discussions at the meetings became more and more detailed. They included give-and-
take about force levels in main and thinned-out buffer zones, the number of buffer
zones and their sizes, the number of UN personnel and where they would be stationed, what authority the UN would enjoy in relationship to Israeli forces, when
Egyptian civilians would return to the canal zone, and so on. El-Gamasy and Yariv
went further, beyond the scope of a cease-fire and the issues of manpower movement and transfer. They strayed far past the supposedly strict limits provided them
when they were initially asked to undertake the military disengagement negotiations. Considerable detail about the size of the buffer zones to be established was
made public in a television interview given by Meir on November 16 and repeated
by Dayan to a U.S. congressional delegation on November 19. Three days later,
Yariv and el-Gamasy agreed that "disengagement and separation of forces should

be held for three to six months followed by successive Israeli withdrawals until a line agreed upon in peace negotiations is reached."[56] At the same meeting, Yariv dropped Israel's insistence that the Egyptian armies on the east bank of the canal return to the prewar lines; el-Gamasy and Yariv agreed that the main Israeli force should be somewhere between thirty-five and forty-five kilometers east of the canal; disengagement and separation of forces should take place within six months, with Egypt wanting the first disengagement completed by January 15, 1974; and the United Nations would man the different buffer zones to be set up between their respective armies.

At their November 26 meeting, Yariv and el-Gamasy had concluded several options pertaining to the content and implementation of the disengagement agreement. There were five or six different proposals for the depth of Israeli withdrawal in Sinai. Yariv stated that Israel was ready to withdraw even beyond the strategic passes if Egypt would minimize its number of troops, tanks, and artillery on the western bank of the canal. Maps were exchanged at virtually every meeting in efforts to reach implementable compromises. From the pace of negotiations and the detail discussed at meetings between November 19 and November 26, some key disagreements remained over the number of forces each side would have in the different buffer zones and the number, range capability, and kinds of weapons each could have in those zones. Nonetheless, the talks were progressing well.

On November 28, 1973, quite abruptly, Yariv told el-Gamasy that he could no longer discuss matters pertaining to the separation of forces. Siilasvuo was bewildered, and el-Gamasy was upset. El-Gamasy asked Yariv, "Why can't you discuss the separation of forces issue? We have spoken about ten principles on which we have agreed."[57] When Yariv departed the Kilometer 101 Talks, he too was disappointed that he suddenly had to break off his personal contacts with el-Gamasy. On the same day, Sadat publicly claimed that he was discontinuing them because the agreements were "not to his liking, led nowhere, and were characterized by Israeli schemes and intrigues."[58] Many Egyptian officials, including Foreign Minister Fahmy and General el-Gamasy, saw the sudden Israeli withdrawal from the Kilometer 101 Talks as a case of Israeli duplicity—making agreements one day and suspending their meaning the next.[59] El-Gamasy had no idea that Kissinger had asked Meir to stop the negotiations. At the conclusion of the talks, Sadat's advisers, who were already predisposed negatively toward Israel, saw the breakdown of the talks as another indication of the lack of Israeli sincerity and trustworthiness. However, when they ended on November 29, 1973, virtually all the details for a full disengagement agreement had been discussed and made public.

The Kilometer 101 Talks ended because Kissinger wanted them to end. In his memoirs, Kissinger noted that he was "not eager for a breakthrough at Kilometer 101 before the Geneva Conference . . . [it] tested our patience. . . . We never knew exactly what was happening at Kilometer 101. . . . If disengagement disappeared from the agenda, we would be forced into endless skirmishing over broader issues on which I knew we would not be able to deliver quickly. As I cautioned Ambassador Dinitz on December 3: Suppose Yariv comes out a great hero on disengagement, what do you discuss [at Geneva]?"[60] Dinitz added, "Kissinger did not value direct discussions at [Kilometer] 101 because he believed that they would be making [political] concessions there to each other without actually eliciting the full price" he could have obtained had he been choreographing the negotiations.[61] Kissinger told Eban, "For God's sake, stop the Yariv/el-Gamasy thing—put it on the Geneva level. Otherwise, we don't have an agenda in Geneva."[62] Kissinger asked Fahmy later in Washington, "What are you doing? Why did you present this [disengagement plan] to the Israelis [at Kilometer 101]?"[63] At one point Kissinger told Meir, "You don't seem to understand that they are making mistakes [at Kilometer 101]. Let me do it."[64] According to Eilts, political discussions had to be avoided because they "would potentially incapacitate [Kissinger's] direct and incipient intervention"; "he wanted all the reigns in his own hands, and was uneasy about all this progress being made and the military working group where he wasn't present."[65] The Israelis and the United States agreed to pull the rug out from under Kilometer 101. The cease-fire remained in effect, but all of the details—withdrawal, how far, and who did what to whom—were to be the subject of the Geneva Conference. "We knew," said Veliotes, "Geneva would be window dressing for what had already been achieved in the Kilometer 101 negotiations."[66] Yariv remembered it this way: "Kissinger said, 'What is he [Yariv] doing there at Kilometer 101? He is proposing disengagement. I need a disengagement agreement at Geneva.' Kissinger told the whole Israeli government, 'I do not want a disengagement agreement now.' And thus Yariv got instructions to say good-bye to el-Gamasy. Kissinger pressured us to be sure that we arrived at an impasse."[67]

"This was," said Peter Rodman, "the classical Kissinger back-channel approach. . . . Kissinger was willing to let the military technicians explore the ground, define and sharpen the key issues at Kilometer 101, but then he wanted deadlock to set in, and then allow the negotiations to escalate to the higher political level, allowing the politicians to make the trade-offs."[68] But in this case, deadlock had not set in: progress had won the day. Whether intended or not, Kissinger understood that the greater Egypt's mistrust toward Israel, the greater role he could play in mediating their differences. Furthermore, progress in the Kilometer 101 Talks allowed Israel to free itself from American tutelage.

Kissinger was not alone in wanting the Kilometer 101 Talks to stall after an agreement was all but signed; Sadat, Dayan, Meir, and Moscow—all for different reasons—wanted the negotiations to stop short of a signed agreement. Sadat needed the fanfare of the international conference to give himself cover for what was essentially a bilateral interim arrangement with Israel. Sadat through el-Gamasy had received Israel's commitment for disengagement at Kilometer 101. Now, he could blame the Israelis for bad faith for breaking off the talks he wanted ended anyway and could offer Kissinger "a done deal" in advance of Geneva, guaranteeing Washington's direct involvement in the negotiating process, which had been one of the central reasons for going to war in the first place. Dayan "opposed the negotiations at Kilometer 101 from the very beginning because the United States was not taking part in them." He told Eban at one point, "we're negotiating directly with them. This is terrible. We have to have them [U.S.] as the mediator, because we have to have a guarantor [of what is agreed]."[69] On a personal level, he did not like Yariv reporting to Meir about political-military matters. Moreover, Dayan was still angry at Kissinger for curtailing his military options at the end of the war and shared a broader objective with Sadat: putting the United States at the center of Egyptian-Israeli negotiations and reducing Soviet involvement in the diplomacy. Meir and Dayan understood that while establishing the cease-fire lines and military alignments were important, the contents of the American political assurances, amount of military supply, and degree of economic aid to Israel that would emerge from Washington as a result of a soon to be negotiated agreement(s) was even more important. Four years later, in early November 1977, Dayan asserted a somewhat different view when he said that the United States had missed an opportunity to pressure Sadat into making peace with Israel when the Israeli Army was at Kilometer 101.[70] Moscow, for its part, was so obsessed with getting an equal piece of the diplomatic action that it, too, preferred delaying disengagement to the Geneva Conference.

In November, simultaneous to the Kilometer 101 Talks, Kissinger engaged in a series of meetings with Egyptian, Israeli, and Jordanian officials. In Washington and in the Middle East, Kissinger needed time to meet the players, build the set, do the lighting, and arrange the choreography for Washington's dominance in the negotiations. He needed time to shape, solidify, and build working relationships with the other Arab leaders and tackle the oil embargo. Sadat and Kissinger were compatible on five independent but interrelated points: strategic assessment of the conflict's overall resolution via diplomatic means; deep common interest in coaxing the Soviet Union to the sidelines and keeping their capacity for obstruction to a minimum;[71] the dominant role that each wanted the United States to play in the negotiations; their common understanding of the interconnection between immediate tactics with longer-term strategy; and a penchant for secrecy, if not conspiracy. Each worked with the other in relative harmony, but each was also willing to pursue parallel diplomatic courses to assure success. Sadat did not mind if Kissinger saw himself as the chief diplomatic choreographer because he wanted Kissinger to represent Egyptian interests to the Israelis. Sadat wanted the United States to become the "honest broker," a surefire position that would force the United States away from taking Israel's position in current and future negotiations. For public consumption, Kissinger maintained the image and made himself increasingly responsible for persuading Sadat to look at issues broader than the immediate resolution of the problems that emerged from the October 1973 War. Sadat, with his proposal for strategic coordination between Egypt and America, gained Kissinger's confidence and an increasing degree of faith from Washington bureaucrats.

In his two-and-one-half-hour meeting with Sadat on November 7, Kissinger "persuaded" an already predisposed Sadat not to settle just for a separation of forces agreement reflective of the October 22 cease-fire lines, but to aim for a larger disengagement agreement, one with considerable more significance.[72] This visit was pivotal in crystallizing the concept of step-by-step diplomacy because "Sadat and Kissinger began to devise a strategy which became ultimately a strategy of interim steps . . . under the mantle of a conference to bless the interim steps."[73] Activation of the interim approach came about because Sadat assented to Kissinger's wish for patience and for an agreement with the Israelis more substantive than just military disengagement. Kissinger also indicated to Sadat that the Palestinians could be invited to participate in a conference. For his part, Sadat did not need to be convinced of the merit of the step-by-step approach; the notion of liberating Sinai through stages or phases was inherent in the Sadat-Dayan exchange via Washington two years earlier. He accepted such a notion because he saw it as analogous to an interim agreement he had conceptually accepted in early 1973. Now the step-by-step process was revisited and accepted because both Israel and Egypt demanded changing the status quo. The significant differences for Sadat's acceptance of an interim agreement after the 1973 War were his willingness to pursue such an agreement *without* guarantees for full withdrawal from all fronts and the fact that he was willing to "throw himself into the arms of the United States to tell him how to do it."[74] Combined, the prestige his army garnered from its limited successes during the war, his priority for "Egypt first," and the faith he put in Kissinger allowed for the "interim agreement disguised as disengagement."[75] The details would be prepackaged for an international conference where Sadat and Kissinger would use the other Arab delegations as cover for Sadat's separate agreement with Israel. During this meeting with Sadat, it also became clear that the military and political issues could be separated, with the former being easier to discuss and implement. Kissinger also discussed with Sadat elements of the six-point plan he had reviewed with Meir in Washington, which would be signed a week later in Sinai at Kilometer 101. Kissinger was apparently surprised that Sadat accepted the six-point plan so quickly.[76] Officially, Sadat told Kissinger that this plan would be communicated to el-Gamasy for discussion with Yariv at Kilometer 101, but actually he was simply assenting to a plan he had initially outlined to the Israelis a week earlier. Sadat knew he could interest the Israelis in discussions about the six points of disengagement, because Israel needed accurate and timely knowledge regarding Egyptian-held Israeli prisoners-of-war. Sadat knowingly dangled or withheld various bits of information on the Israeli prisoners-of-war in order to soften Israel's possible unwillingness to discuss the ideas of his disengagement plan. El-Gamasy claimed that it was "Sadat who presented to Kissinger [at this November meeting] a strategic plan for how to solve the [Arab-Israeli] problem as a whole."[77] Core parts of what became the January 1974 Egyptian-Israeli Disengagement Agreement were brought to Washington at the end of October by Fahmy, at the same time that el-Gamasy offered the core ideas to Yariv at Kilometer 101. Kissinger had heard Israel's acceptance of a force separation agreement via steps just days earlier from Mordechai Gazit in discussions at Blair House.[78] The six-point plan agreed on November 11 and the subsequent Yariv–el-Gamasy agreements at Kilometer 101 were not a Kissinger original: they were a hybrid parented by Sadat and Meir.

Assad could smell it. During the Kilometer 101 Talks, Sadat represented to the outside world that these Egyptian-Israeli negotiations were strictly military and not political talks. They were, in fact, both. Betrayed by Sadat during the war and in bringing the war to a conclusion, Assad increased his anger toward the Egyptian president, as Sadat embraced Kissinger and the Americans. Assad believed that the Americans represented Israeli interests, and therefore Sadat was joining the same camp; and that while the two countries had entered the war together to liberate *both* Golan and Sinai, Sadat had not carried out his part of the bargain. According to Assad, they should have ended the war together, not independent of the other's military condition. Furthermore, he felt that diplomacy was a march to be done in tandem, that separate and bilateral arrangements with Israel were not remotely considered as part of the prewar collaborative planning. Assad vigorously asserted these opinions to Sadat when they met in Kuwait on November 1 and again in Cairo on November 24 (when both leaders were on their way to the Algiers Arab Summit meeting).[79] When Sadat told Assad that these apprehensions were unfounded, Assad was not persuaded. Assad's deep antagonism toward Sadat's independent diplomacy with Israel was severe and constant. With Sadat venturing along his separate path and Israeli forces thirty to forty kilometers from Damascus, the Syrians were, according to Khaddam, "outraged. We felt bitterness. This kind of action by Sadat was just treason."[80] Assad's anger did not change Syria's own strategic problem of Israeli presence within artillery range of Damascus. United Nations official Brian Urquhart recalled that the Syrians also desperately needed a disengagement of forces agreement with the Israelis, "but did not know how to do it without losing public face."[81]

Sadat wanted dual protection: against Syrian diplomatic procrastination, and a public Arab umbrella that showed Egypt was not traveling a separate route with Israel. In order to placate Assad, Sadat sent him a letter after meeting with Kissinger on November 7, in which he told Assad that "he [Sadat] was trying to obtain the withdrawal from the two fronts and there would be disengagement agreements about which Kissinger had agreed, including withdrawal,"[82] which the Syrians interpreted as withdrawal from the Golan Heights. By the end of November, Sadat's main concern was keeping Kissinger focused on the Geneva Conference, not on fostering a Syrian-Israeli disengagement agreement on the Golan Heights.

The danger points with the Third Army had passed with minimum Israeli compliance in supplying provisions to the Third Army. Kissinger wanted Sadat to sign the disengagement agreement only *after* the Geneva Conference convened.[83] From the end of November until the convocation of the Geneva talks on December 21, there were no official Egyptian-Israeli disengagement negotiations under UN auspices—merely liaison talks where procedures were adopted to implement the cease-fire agreement, exchange prisoners, and provide supplies for the Third Army. For Egypt and Israel, Washington was the trusted intermediary for both sides. Meir and Sadat wanted Kissinger to parachute into their talks. Moscow had no leverage on Israel; it had to rely on Kissinger's "goodwill," which meant letting the fox determine detente in the hen house. By December 1973, the pre-October lull in Arab-Israeli negotiations was a distant memory.

CHAPTER 5

THE 1973
GENEVA MIDDLE EAST
PEACE CONFERENCE
AND THE BUILDUP
TO SINAI I

T HE INCONCLUSIVE military result of the war, the near disaster for Israel, the threat to the Third Army's well-being, the precariously entangled armed forces, and the quick need to resolve the POW issue made negotiations imperative. The success of the Kilometer 101 Talks had proven that Egyptian and Israeli leaders wanted and needed a disengagement agreement.[1] According to Peter Rodman, "There were two governments who really wanted to settle somehow, and who were groping for a procedure that was feasible. We sold Sadat on the idea of step-by-step, because we knew this was the only process that was digestible on the Israeli side. There was great confidence in the United States"[2] to make an agreement happen. As Kissinger noted, the Americans wanted "one symbolic act, to enable each side to pursue a separate course. . . . Our [U.S.] strategy required first that we assemble the conference to defuse the situation and symbolize progress, but then we use its auspices to establish our central role."[3] Kissinger had absolutely no interest in continuing the conference after it met briefly; he had every intention of limiting Soviet participation in the evolving diplomacy. He did not believe in something called a "comprehensive settlement." Instead, his approach was not to tackle the problems all at once; the outstanding political issues were too complex and explosive.[4] Built into this pessimistic psychology, which said political problems are never truly solved, Kissinger possessed a gradualist approach aimed at reducing their complexity. Easing Moscow away from the core of Arab-Israeli diplomacy through a slow process was easier and more practical than doing or saying something bluntly about their exclusion.

For Sadat and Meir, the convocation of the December 1973 Geneva Middle East Peace Conference served several purposes. For Sadat, it would demonstrate to his countrymen that his combination of war and diplomacy would harvest an Israeli withdrawal from Sinai; keep the negotiating momentum moving forward; deepen his relationship with the United States and Kissinger; push Moscow further to the diplomatic edges; express appropriate concern for resolution of the Palestinian issue and territorial withdrawals from other fronts; and provide some shield from domestic and Arab criticism for pursuing an Egypt-first deal with Israel.[5] For Meir, participating in the Geneva Conference would also serve several purposes: it would bring political normalization with Egypt closer to the international community's desire for peace between Israel and the Arabs; raise the level of the discussions to the nature of peace, not just the future of the territories; and create encounters with Arab and Soviet delegates. It could persuade an emotionally lacerated Israeli population that, despite the shortcomings and even the culpability ascribed to Meir's Labor government, the conference remained Israel's best alternative for sustaining good relations with Washington and for the unfolding diplomatic process with the Arabs. All arrows pointed to a post-conference Egyptian-Israeli limited military disengagement. On the other hand, agreement with Jordan was neither simple nor desirable because it would involve withdrawals, settlements, and discussion about Jerusalem; an agreement with Syria was not considered seriously because of the geographic limitations on political and physical maneuvers the Golan presented. The success of the Kilometer 101 Talks, in contrast to these other situations, meant that a difficult agreement was 90 percent completed. Sadat and Meir colluded with Kissinger to present the public appearance of a full-fledged conference without a prearranged agenda. In so doing, Kissinger provided Sadat with his required political cover. No serious business would take place at the conference.[6] A secret understanding was reached between them in late November 1973, which said that the conference would have "a ceiling" in terms of its content, on what would and would not happen at Geneva and afterward. The understanding noted that the conference would be held only to set up the disengagement committees and to strengthen the cease-fire, not to discuss *substance*. With regard to Jordan, "there was no precooking prior for the conference."[7]

The idea of an international Middle East peace conference as a means to discuss a Middle East settlement was raised initially by Hafez Ismail in his meetings with Kissinger during their 1973 secret meeting in Paris.[8] After the October War started, Kissinger told Sadat on October 10, via the CIA, that "the situation had now reached a point which offered a good chance for a satisfactory settlement based on a cease-fire and some sort of international conference."[9] Sadat then mentioned the idea publicly in his October 16 speech to the Egyptian Parliament. He also raised the idea of an international conference with Alexei Kosygin during the latter's visit to Cairo from October 16 to 19. Neither Harold Saunders nor Bill Quandt at the

NSC and neither Michael Sterner nor Joe Sisco at the State Department recalled that the idea of a conference as a mechanism for Arab-Israeli negotiations had been discussed among American policymakers prior to Sadat's speech. Washington, which was still interested in seeing the Soviet Union play a constructive, though limited, role in evolving diplomacy, quickly came to view a conference as a potential mechanism for fulfilling such a controlled outcome. Egyptian Foreign Minister Fahmy was more adamant than Sadat in wanting a central and instrumental role for the United Nations; Sadat saw the United Nations as providing international legitimacy, but not actual involvement, in the coming diplomacy. For him, the UN Security Council was too cumbersome and ultimately could not (in comparison to Washington) deliver or guarantee results. According to Sadat's national security adviser, "Sadat wanted the United Nations to act just as an umbrella, like they did at the Rhodes discussions in 1949."[10]

Like the UN and Europe, the Soviet Union was only partially and intermittently informed about what would take place. Initially, during Kissinger's October meeting in Moscow, Gromyko believed that UNSC Resolution 338 would guarantee the Soviet Union an equal role with the United States, at least at the beginning of the conference. Kissinger said that "the original idea . . . was for a conference of Arabs and Israelis under American and Soviet auspices to discuss a comprehensive peace settlement."[11] According to Kissinger, Moscow's objectives at the conference were threefold: to reduce the freedom of action of the United States in shaping a Middle East diplomatic outcome; to receive credit for any progress by riding on America's coattails; and in the more likely eventuality of a deadlock, to shift the onus for it onto U.S. shoulders.[12] In addition, the Soviets saw the conference as a means to present Arab demands and therefore enhance their standing with Arab allies. Evidently, the Soviets did not fully comprehend what was Sadat's duplicity when he anointed Kissinger and Washington, not Moscow, to disentangle what Kissinger exaggeratingly termed the "precarious, dangerous, and intolerable military dispositions." Since Moscow knew that the Third Army had to be saved, the Soviet Union could not sabotage a rescue process, be it a cease-fire, disengagement agreement, or other separate arrangement between Egypt and Israel. Moreover, for their own national reasons, recalled Rodman, "the Arabs were listening to us, and the Soviets had no entree. The Arabs . . . were having to come to . . . our court, to take their chances on their own. The Soviets had no opening. The Arabs did not trust the Soviets. We were struck, to our pleasant surprise, by how much the Egyptians did not want the Soviets involved."[13]

Sadat and Kissinger concurred in their desire to limit the Soviet Union's role in the evolving diplomacy.[14] In October, at the Kremlin, Kissinger wanted Moscow's participation only at the beginning of the conference. By November 8, when Kissinger and Fahmy met in Cairo, the term "appropriate auspices" was then interpreted to deny Moscow any kind of veto over the unfolding process.[15] Kissinger put it succinctly: "Detente did not prevent us from seeking to reduce the Soviet role in the Middle East nor the Soviets from scoring points with the Arabs now and then. But fairness compels the recognition that Moscow never launched an all-out campaign against us. And we took pains not to humiliate the Soviet Union overtly even while weakening its influence. Detente is the mitigation of conflict among adversaries, not the cultivation of friendship."[16] Dinitz also noted, "One has to be mad to suffer all the consequences of the war and share the fruits of the loom with the Soviets. Kissinger was very suspicious of them [the Soviets]. But it was important that the war have a pacifying effect between the superpowers."[17] Eban judged it better to have Moscow involved rather than sidelined and sniping at the process. In a rather graphic description of Kissinger's preference for Soviet participation at Geneva, Eban quoted a Lyndon Johnson expression, "I would rather have them inside my tent pissing outward, than outside my tent pissing inward."[18]

The Soviet Union's restraint in the postwar negotiating phase came from Moscow's commitment to preserve detente with the United States. Soviet caution was viewed by most Arab states as Moscow's greater concern for its relationship with Washington than for helping the Arabs. In contrast, Washington demonstrated that its interests in the Middle East were not solely determined by its relationship with either Moscow or Israel. Furthermore, the Soviet Union did not help bolster its role as a close friend of Egypt; nor did Moscow have recourse to counteract Kissinger's enforcement of Israel's precondition of no Palestinian presence at the conference.[19] In November 1973, when Sadat wanted more and better military resupplies for his army, Moscow had refused, and when Sadat needed incentives from Moscow in the form of arms, he did not receive them.[20] The Syrians did not press the Americans to involve the Soviets in the decision-making process in planning for the conference, despite the massive military resupply the Soviets had provided to Egypt and Syria during the war. Assad knew that only Kissinger could broker a deal that would remove Israeli presence in Syrian-held territory.

In the end there was no significant participation by Moscow or the United Nations in putting the conference together, aside from the actual issuance of invitations to attend. At the conference neither had a primary part in determining the content or pace of negotiations. Waldheim's adviser, UN Under-Secretary-General Brian Urquhart, understood that he had to be a figurehead. Waldheim himself was the conference coordinator. Kissinger asked that the UN handle logistics, prepare the conference facilities, convene the conference's opening, and act as the communication conduit to the other Security Council members. As Urquhart said, "That was the point of having Waldheim in Geneva. There was a UN involvement without involving the whole Security Council, which the Israelis [didn't] like."[21] UN involvement represented something "obnoxious" to the Israelis. By Dinitz's recollections, the Israeli goal was to give the UN secretary-general only a "dummy" role.[22] Another Israeli who attended the conference categorized Waldheim "as walking around like a head-waiter in a restaurant. The only thing he was missing was a towel and a hat."[23] Earlier in December 1973, the United States (and, in particular, Kissinger) had decided to have the United Nations issue the invitations to the Geneva Conference. Although American officials did not request the Security Council to authorize the dispatch of those invitations, the United Nations sent them. Indeed, Kissinger had no intention of seeking authorization from the United Nations. It was a matter of the United States informing the United Nations through the secretary-general and informally persuading him or his representatives to attend the Geneva Conference.[24] Urquhart recalled that the United Nations was not ideal for the kind of diplomacy Kissinger was practicing. Kissinger "used to come here once a week and meet Waldheim and me and, I must say, it worked extremely well. He was very, very good. . . . I think he used [the United Nations] exactly right: he used it to do things he could not do, and we could get him to do the things we couldn't do."[25] Official purview for convening the conference was, therefore, voluntarily given to the United Nations, but everyone understood that the UN role lacked any substance as a mediator.

When Meir first learned that the conference would be in Geneva, she asked Kissinger[26] whether the term "appropriate auspices" would mean imposition. "He explained that she should not be too much afraid, he would take care of Geneva,"[27] Gazit recalled. When Kissinger left Israel on October 22, the Israeli prime minister was only marginally mollified by his explanations. With more compelling issues before Meir's cabinet, however, the Israeli Foreign Ministry was not even informed about the need to define or prepare for a conference. In fact, the nature, procedure, agenda, and substance of the proposed conference were not considered by Foreign Ministry officials until late November. Public trauma from the war remained naked, raw, and profound. Media debate daily covered what went wrong and why. The Israeli people still had not assigned political responsibility for military failures and fatalities. Any discussion about withdrawal or territorial concessions in the midst of an election campaign, especially before all the prisoners-of-war were returned, would have been political suicide. Meir's major concern was to avoid any conference that would complicate further the Labor Party's public standing prior to the rescheduled December 1973 Knesset parliamentary elections. Kissinger understood Meir's domestic political concerns. "My advice to you," he said, "if we can time [the conference] in such a way that all that happens before the election, the symbolism of sitting around the conference table with the Arab foreign ministers, that would be a terrific bonanza point. Everyone agrees that nothing substantive, none of the detailed negotiations, would happen until after [the conference]."[28] Kissinger's own predisposition for a slow pace, controlled and managed by Washington, meshed nicely with Israeli caution. Already heartily disposed to merely a ceremonial forum, he suggested a short conference with opening speeches, to be followed by substantive discussions immediately after Israel's election.[29] Meir wanted a short conference because the Israelis were sure they would not gain any-thing positive from a long format.[30] A brief ceremonial conference would guaran-tee that the Arab states would make individual appeals protecting national interests rather than having time to coordinate goals and gang up on Israel. He made it quite plain to Meir that "there would be no political decisions taken at Geneva. It would be just a show with speeches: the international media would have a field day, Israel would benefit from the show, and then we would go to work on the Egyptian dis-engagement agreement."[31] Dinitz recalled that "Geneva was a disease that one had to go through."[32]

Those at the Israeli Foreign Ministry, including Foreign Minister Abba Eban, enthusiastically but naively believed that the conference would be a major turning point in the Egyptian-Israeli relationship, one that would lead to further negotia-tions after the conference ended.[33] Israeli Foreign Ministry officials hoped that the conference would not result merely in a list of abstentions from firing, terrorism, hostile propaganda, boycott, and blockade, but would be able to establish a new order of regional relations.[34] When in late November it began to prepare for the Geneva Conference, the Israeli Foreign Ministry drafted peace treaties for Egypt, Syria, and Jordan. Israeli officials made arrangements in Geneva for an ongoing peace process; the Israeli Foreign Ministry did not rent rooms at a hotel for several days, but rented a whole building in Geneva to house a large Israeli delegation for a long period of time. Preparations were also made to handle the international media in an expansive way. To put Israel's best public foot forward, the Foreign Ministry selected a number of prominent Israeli professors and intellectuals familiar with the Middle East, Europe, and the United States and sent them abroad immediately after the war in an effort to promote the view that Israel needed the sympathy of world opinion. Some of the professors, such as Dr. Shaul Friedlander, had been very crit-ical of the prior unwillingness on the part of the Israeli government to entertain seriously Sadat's diplomatic initiatives in the 1970s.[35] Intellectuals, such as Zvi Yavitz, Moshe Ma'oz, and Shimon Shamir, gave public lectures in European cities and were interviewed on television and in newspapers. Despite their personal political preferences, these professors sensed that, because Israel had been in mortal danger, they were obliged to influence European public opinion in favor of Israel during and after the war. Later, a number of these prominent Israeli academics became part of Israel's delegation to Geneva. At Geneva, they gave more interviews to the international media, gossiped with Egyptian and other journalists, and compared stories on how the war had transpired. Their task was to mingle, establish contact, start a dialogue, learn about Egyptian perceptions, and generally be attentive to what was going on.[36]

As the Egyptian Foreign Ministry prepared for the conference, the idea of direct negotiations with Israelis had no appeal because of what the greater Arab world would say and think; an international conference under UN auspices with the superpowers present was better, but Sadat also did not want a peace conference to lead to some kind of a veto over Egypt.[37] For this reason, Egypt wanted all committee discussions that might emerge from a conference to be defined on a geographic and not on a functional basis. The benefits and liabilities of both methods were apparent. Functional committees would mean a greater degree of coordination between the Arab sides on issues such as withdrawal and recognition, which, for Syria, meant a measure of inter-Arab consensus would give Damascus some control over Egyptian negotiating options; geographic committees would allow each country to reach its own independent arrangement with Israel. The goal of Sinai's return would therefore not be held hostage to some topical or functional committee dealing with "territories," or "withdrawal," or "the Palestinian question" in which all participating Arab parties could exercise a veto over Egypt's prerogative. Furthermore, a conference could be legally justified to the Egyptian public, because it would be Cairo's adherence to international legitimacy as contained in UNSC Resolutions 338 and 242, both of which Egypt still interpreted to mean Israeli withdrawal from all the territories taken in the June 1967 War. In organizing themselves for the 1973 Geneva Conference, Egyptian Foreign Ministry bureaucrats were instructed by Sadat through Ismail Fahmy to prepare concept papers that went beyond a disengagement accord to include political elements. They did not write the elements of a peace treaty with Israel, but fashioned a plan to include "the elements of withdrawal, exchange [of territory] . . . on the basis of 242—withdrawal vs. recognition—acknowledgment of [Israel's] existence."[38] Sadat contemplated full Israeli withdrawal from all the territories, which Egyptian Foreign Ministry officials clearly understood. Sadat did not waiver from that goal; he merely decided to implement it in stages.

The "sting" was on. Sadat was integrally involved in putting in place the elements of the conference charade. When Kissinger visited Amman, after Cairo, on his early November 1973 trip to the Middle East, he told King Hussein that he wanted Jordan to be a "founding member of the Geneva Conference so *it* would be the spokesman for the Palestinians." In response, Hussein gladly accepted Kissinger's invitation because it emphatically rejected any role for the PLO as a legitimate representative speaking especially on behalf of Palestinians living in Jordan. Moreover, Hussein possessed his historical imperative of entitlement to negotiate for the return of the West Bank and East Jerusalem to his sovereignty. The PLO and Jordan were at opposite poles on two contentious issues: who spoke for which Palestinians, and who would be the rightful benefactor of any West Bank territory ceded by Israel to Arab stewardship. In November 1973, Israel's preference was to create a negotiating formula through which King Hussein would have considerable influence and connection in shaping the future of the territories. But that did not mean Israel was actually prepared to negotiate the return of Gaza, the West Bank, or any portion of East Jerusalem. Kissinger reminded the Israelis and confided in King Hussein that if they ignored reaching a Jordanian-Israeli agreement, both sides would have to deal with Arafat. Yet, before the conference convened, Kissinger said that he would not force the Israelis to make an agreement with Jordan, but neither did he want them to neglect consideration of one.[39] For Amman, the Arab Summit's denial of Jordan's political prerogative to represent the Palestinians had a positive impact upon many Jordanians who hailed from the east bank: these pro-Jordanian royalists viewed the Algiers Resolution "as a way to get rid of the Palestinian question and leave it to [the PLO]."[40] However, catering to what King Hussein wanted to hear, Kissinger publicly stated that a conference would be a way to bring Jordan back onto the West Bank.[41] On November 27, 1973, Jordan announced that it would boycott the proposed peace conference with Israel if the Arab Summit Conference, which concluded its meetings several days later, endorsed the PLO as the legitimate representative of the Palestinian people, which is precisely what the Summit Conference did. King Hussein did not attend the Algiers Summit Conference because of the deep political differences concerning PLO participation and what for public explanation were described as "undisclosed security problems." Despite the diplomatic black eye received at Algiers, Jordan, nonetheless, ignored its own threat not to participate in the Geneva Conference. Amman needed to reassert its Arab claim to negotiate for the territories. A conference would shut out PLO participation. Washington made no commitment to King Hussein to focus on an agreement between Jordan and Israel after the war; but according to King Hussein, the Jordanians were dearly interested in achieving an agreement with the Israelis.[42] Since direct public negotiations with Israel were impossible as a starting point, a conference provided Jordan with a proper framework and, most of all, international legitimacy that could permit movement toward bilateral talks and international sanction to speak about the West Bank and Jerusalem. In preparing for Geneva, Jordan, like Egypt, anticipated moving from the conference opening to bilateral geographic committee talks because it did not want any other Arab state, specifically Syria, from inhibiting or participating in discussions about the future of the West Bank, Gaza, and Jerusalem.[43] King Hussein strongly believed that the conference would permit negotiations regarding the West Bank and east Jerusalem under a comprehensive settlement.[44]

Whereas King Hussein disliked the PLO, Sadat intentionally misused and abused the organization. On October 26, Sadat met with two top leaders in the PLO, Salah Khalaf and Farouk Qaddumi. As the meeting commenced, Sadat told them that it was important for them to participate in the Geneva Peace Conference. Based on discussions held with other PLO leaders in Beirut, Khalaf recalled the following:

> Sadat had placed us in a difficult, not to say impossible, situation. Everyone
> was agreed not to reject the principle of a peace conference out of hand, but it
> would have been just as imprudent to reply affirmatively. We couldn't simply

overlook the fact that the cease-fire had been established on the basis of Resolution 242, which denied the Palestinians their most elementary rights. So we decided not to reply either way until we received a formal invitation. It was only then that we would be in a position to define our position in a clear and precise manner.[45]

Sadat argued to the PLO leaders that they should ignore the stipulations in UNSC Resolution 242, which only made mention of "refugees," and that they should submit the Palestinian point of view at a peace conference. Kissinger had agreed during his meeting with Sadat in Cairo on November 7 that there could be Palestinian, but not PLO, participation at the conference. Though Arafat sensed that Sadat was disinterested in PLO participation in the Geneva meeting, Sadat was certainly interested in Palestinian involvement in the evolving diplomacy. He had a genuine interest in seeing their aspirations met, however, because for his and Egypt's requirements, their participation in a conference would provide useful cover against those who said he was entering into a separate agreement with the Israelis. And yet Sadat was not going to let Palestinian absence either prevent the convocation of the conference or delay his attainment of the conference's intended results. Arafat's advisers were quick to blame Sadat for succumbing to Kissinger's diplomatic priorities, not realizing that it was Sadat who was in a hurry and not willing to stop the diplomatic process simply because the PLO was not ready. PLO leaders also did not realize that the Israeli-Egyptian Kilometer 101 Talks had, by the end of the second week in November, essentially outlined agreements on force separation and a broader military disengagement. Neither did the PLO leadership know that Egypt, as well as Syria and eventually Moscow, would not keep the conference from meeting because the PLO or other Palestinians were not invited. As for themselves, PLO leaders refused to assume any responsibility for not accepting the advice of other Arab leaders to join the diplomatic process at this juncture. In addition, the terms of general reference of the Geneva Conference were to be UNSC Resolutions 242 and 338—political definitions that even accommodating elements within the PLO were yet unable to accept. The PLO opposed all political compromise that might eventually lead to the recognition of Israel's existence.

Kissinger's shuttle team paid little, if any, attention to the contents or resolutions of the Arab states gathered at their summit meeting in Algiers at the end of November.[46] Their tunnel vision was evolving to a distinct focus: developing the diplomatic scaffolding support for an Egyptian-Israeli agreement through a conference. Sadat took it upon himself to manage the "Arab" team. In so doing, Egypt's president did not mind that the Arab Summit had reinforced the political distance between Jordan and the PLO, a result that increased Jordanian likelihood to participate in the coming conference. For Sadat, the Algiers Arab Summit Resolutions successfully alienated Jordan and mollified the PLO, without allowing the PLO to be an obstacle to Sadat's interest in reaching an arrangement with Israel through Washington. Outside of inter-Arab discussions, Sadat privately abandoned the PLO in order to focus on Sinai. Israeli estimates at the time never doubted that Sadat was speaking from the heart about the centrality of the Palestinian question to Egyptian political priorities. Sadat encouraged his foreign minister's undisguised personal disdain for Jordan and strong support of the PLO, both of which suited Sadat's scheme of quietly doing his private diplomacy while allowing his foreign minister to toe the Arab line in public. With Meir, Sadat, Hussein, and later Assad, Kissinger had discussions about PLO participation at a conference. Arab world debate focused on whether the Palestinians should be a separate delegation or be part of a joint Palestinian-Jordanian delegation, or be present at all. The Arab Summit Resolutions did not take a formal position regarding the Geneva Conference, nor did they establish preconditions for negotiations with Israel or give a specific endorsement for PLO participation at Geneva.[47] They did, however, endorse the concept of a "phased strategy" or "interim aims" in dealing with Israel and recognize the PLO as the sole representative of the Palestinian people. With these public Arab endorsements, Egypt could not be assailed for usurping the prerogative of Palestinian or PLO representation. Sadat reckoned that if the PLO could sense a victory over King Hussein on the Palestinian representation issue, then Egypt could move forward at its own pace because Israel would never attend a conference where the PLO participated. In the post–October War period, the PLO was more concerned with *who* would represent Palestinian interests, and the Jordanian challenge to it, than with *when and how* those interests could be expressed. Through Egypt's efforts, Kissinger's incremental approach to Egyptian-Israeli movement in negotiations was not condemned by the Arab Summit. There was no clearly stated Arab opposition to the convocation of a Middle East peace conference; the absence of a stated opposition became the functional equivalent of a tacit endorsement. As a nonstate actor, the PLO's preoccupation with its legitimacy in inter-Arab counsels, such as its perennial struggles with Jordan over representation, allowed Sadat the prerogative to claim that he had roped Palestinian interests to Cairo's objectives. And each time he did in the subsequent six years of diplomacy with Washington, not surprisingly, Cairo's interests prevailed. Sadat's sincerity for the Palestinian cause did not diminish, but Sadat was an Egyptian nationalist, not a Palestinian; therefore, Cairo's objectives came first. Quite ironically, this was a lesson that took a long time for Israel to understand and for the PLO to recognize.

During their meeting in Cairo on December 11 about the conference's terms of reference, Assad and Sadat agreed to go to the conference on the basis of a list of conditions. Having summoned the American and Soviet ambassadors to tell them, according to Eilts, Fahmy did not know that the list of conditions he was reading was one drawn up by the Americans.[48] Neither Syria nor Egypt were going to stay away from the conference because the PLO was not invited; if Assad stayed away, it would be primarily for other reasons. Then Vinogradov and Eilts took a walk along the Nile. In that conversation, the Soviet ambassador explained that Moscow wanted the PLO at the conference from its outset, not invited at some later juncture in the conference or negotiations as agreed by the Egyptian and Syrian foreign ministers. According to Eilts, Vinogradov said, "You know this [non-Palestinian representation] is unacceptable, surely the U.S. is not going to accept it."[49] Vinogradov's disappointment notwithstanding, the Soviets ultimately swallowed non-PLO and non-Palestinian participation because Moscow wanted to be part of the emerging diplomacy. They did not know then that Kissinger had maneuvered the PLO out.

When Kissinger met with Sadat in Cairo on December 14, it was understood between them that Egypt was not prepared to let the conference fall apart because of no PLO or Palestinian presence. Fahmy was furious, and he told Eilts, "You really pulled a fast one. You pulled it on the president. You knew you were going to do this [omit the PLO]."[50] What Fahmy did not know was that Sadat had consented to the omission of the PLO; it was "easier" for Sadat to let Kissinger take the blame. Sadat was disappointed but pragmatic about the PLO not coming to Geneva; the significance of the PLO absence from Geneva meant that Israel would deal directly with Egypt. Though Fahmy's view of PLO participation at Geneva did not prevail, he doggedly retained his commitment to the PLO, a position that continuously fueled an already dicey Jordanian-Egyptian relationship. Several days later, when Waldheim sent out the invitations on behalf of the cochairmen, Kissinger had renegotiated the letter's contents with Jordanian Prime Minister Rifa'i. Kissinger told Rifa'i that

> the Israelis refuse to come to the conference unless we change the invitation. . . . There [will] be just three changes. In the invitation there is the implication that the negotiations will be in committees that will discuss subjects—an Arab-Israeli committee to discuss borders, an Arab-Israeli committee to discuss withdrawal, peace by subject by groupings. The Israelis insist on geographic committees—a Jordanian-Israeli committee to discuss everything. . . . The second amendment is that the invitation said that Palestinian participants [will] be invited in a later stage. And the Israelis objected to the word "Palestinian" So we [Kissinger and the Israelis] would like to change it and say "other participants" will come at a later stage. The convocation date was also changed to the 21st.[51]

Jordan did not balk at any of the word changes proposed for the amended invitations. Jordan's Rifa'i recalled, "We had planned to stay in Geneva for months. We rented apartments for our delegation, and we had no idea that we were just needed there to give legitimacy to the Egyptian-Israeli negotiations. By including pro-Jordanian Palestinians in the Jordanian delegation, King Hussein made a prominent statement in opposition to the Algiers Summit Resolutions."[52] The Jordanian dele-gation went to Geneva expecting that there would be a full-fledged international conference, that it would be continuous, and that agreements would be reached. The Jordanians were unaware that the Geneva Conference would be merely a pub-lic relations ploy for a predetermined and privately prearranged Egyptian-Israeli deal that would emerge afterward. In the week before the Geneva Conference convened, Kissinger told Fahmy and his Foreign Ministry advisers that only an Egyptian-Israeli disengagement would be negotiated, "so do not support one with the Jordanians."[53] Jordanian government officials "considered Kissinger and Sadat equally deceitful."[54] Assad, however, understood that Sadat and Kissinger were engaged in a not-so-subtle political charade that eventually would result in an Egyptian-Israeli agreement.

On December 6, 1973, Gerald Ford took the oath of office as the U.S. vice pres-ident, just two weeks after Spiro Agnew's resignation. The same day, Syrian Deputy Foreign Minister Zakariyya Ismail noted that his country would not attend the Geneva Conference unless there was some prior Israeli withdrawal to cease-fire lines of October 22. Syria and Israel squared off over the exchange of prisoners-of-war and prisoners-of-war lists. Syria wanted to discuss the release of Israeli prison-ers only in the framework of a total Israeli withdrawal from Arab land, to which Israeli Defense Minister Dayan replied that Israel would not enter peace talks unless Syria disclosed the fate of Israeli prisoners-of-war.[55] After the Sadat-Assad meeting in December, Eilts and Vinogradov were summoned to the Egyptian Foreign Min-istry where they were informed in the presence of both the Egyptian and Syrian foreign ministers that Egypt and Syria agreed to attend an international conference in accordance with UNSC Resolutions 242 and 338. Substantial disagreements existed between Cairo and Damascus over conference procedures: Egypt contin-ued to insist on having geographic committees, while the Syrians preferred to have functional ones.

Initially, Syria considered attending the Geneva Conference. During the October 1973 War, there had been no contact between Washington and Damascus;[56] Syria, however, wanted to reestablish diplomatic relations broken after the June 1967 War. Since Kissinger was choreographing the postwar diplomacy, Assad did not want to be excluded from the political aftermath of the war. Second, Assad's engagement in discussions about the conference was aimed at reducing the rapid pace of the diplo-matic progress that flowed too quickly from the war. When Assad learned that mil-itary separation of forces discussions held at Kilometer 101 had not only touched on military topics, but included discussion of political issues, and by November 11th outlined an Egyptian-Israeli disengagement agreement, he was enraged; re-ducing Sadat's pace was important, and going to a conference would give Assad the ability to slow down Sadat's clock. Just as Assad believed that Syria and Egypt had entered the war together in order to liberate both Golan and Sinai, he also viewed diplomacy as a march to be done in tandem, that separate and bilateral arrangements with Israel were not to be part of the postwar negotiations. Assad wanted the Egyptian-Syrian alliance to continue "and [to] never allow Kissinger to undermine it."[57] Though white with anger at the lack of military coordination during the war, Assad still wanted collaborative negotiations to take place about military disengagement. Assad was the champion of categoric Arab rejection of Israel's legitimacy. Negotiations with Israel that led to its recognition were not acceptable, but if Assad could retrieve his territory through American pressure and the Arab oil embargo, that option needed to be pursued.

Assad also wanted to show the Soviet Union that he was not its lapdog even though he had received vast quantities of arms supply from it during the war. There were mutual interests between Moscow and Damascus, but Assad prided himself on being fiercely independent and not part of the "Socialist Block." In fact, Syrian officials bristled when Americans categorized Syria as part of the Soviet orbit.[58] Any remote inching by Syria toward Washington would make Moscow more attentive to Syria's needs. Assad was certainly not averse to using Moscow's jealousy for Washington's attention and quest for diplomatic parity to satisfy Syrian interests. He understood that his intimate discussions with Kissinger caused Moscow to realize that Syria's relationship with the Soviets could not be taken for granted. Assad was displeased that the Soviets had failed to meet his request for an early cease-fire; it damaged Soviet-Syrian relations.[59] Syria still wanted Moscow as its patron, giving unqualified support to Damascus, but not dictating priorities. Assad balanced, as best he could, reliance but not dependence upon the Soviet Union. When Moscow did not give him political support or acted contrary to what Assad saw as Syrian national interests, he was incensed. Their ultimate decision to attend the Geneva Conference, for example, angered Assad.[60] During the Kissinger-driven Syrian-Israeli negotiations in early 1974, Assad held Moscow in contempt.[61] Moscow, for its part, was "terribly worried that this ingenious Henry Kissinger could dislodge the Syrians from [Moscow's] orbit."[62] Syrian Foreign Minister Abd al-Halim Khaddam contended, "It was Kissinger's intention to widen the gap between Moscow and Damascus."[63] But Assad chose to meet Kissinger and interview him because Israeli forces were only twenty-five miles from Damascus. "Assad respected and feared Israeli power,"[64] but he was not going to be bullied, not ever. He needed a conduit of communications through Washington about a future Israeli withdrawal, not dictated by Sadat's schedule or priorities but by Assad's interest to move the Israelis from their proximity to Damascus.

From Assad's meetings with Sadat in Kuwait on November 1, in Cairo on November 24, and for a third time in early December, through Syrian-Egyptian discussions held at Foreign Ministry channels, and by way of visits of envoys to each other's capitals, Assad remained well informed about Sadat's inclination to make a deal with the Israelis independent of Syria. When Sadat told Assad that those apprehensions about a separate deal with Israel were unfounded, Assad was not convinced.

Sadat had used Assad; Egypt had trumped Syria. The preconditioned hostile Syrian-Egyptian atmosphere hovered above Kissinger's visit to Damascus.

Kissinger knew very little about the deep personal or political rifts that divided Sadat and Assad. Lacking an understanding of the resentment between Cairo and Damascus, or even the intricacies of inter-Arab jealousies, was a detriment to American policymakers. Even if Washington had registered a full understanding of their mutual distrust, it would not have altered Kissinger's objective to focus on Egypt and Sadat. In fact, the differences between Damascus and Cairo made it easier for Washington to concentrate on nurturing an Egyptian-Israeli relationship. Like Moscow, Washington's decision makers viewed Arab politics through glasses framed in Cairo. Washington was conceptually mesmerized by Egypt. When Kissinger arrived in Damascus in mid-December, he was predisposed by his pre–October War attitudes to concentrate on Egypt. This was greatly reinforced by his meeting with Sadat on November 7 in Cairo. Through Sadat, the United States had an unprecedented opportunity to move Moscow to the sidelines and to move Arab-Israeli diplomacy forward. "The focus was predominately on Egypt," said Joseph Sisco,[65] Sadat loved it. This fact was on Kissinger's mind when he saw Assad in Damascus on December 15, 1973. Kissinger had only a passing interest in responding to Assad's aspirations. If the resentment Assad held for Sadat was realized, it was not apparent in Kissinger's remarks to Assad. Though Kissinger acknowledged that the Soviets had resupplied Syria with weapons during the recent war, Kissinger did not understand the degree to which Assad faulted the United States for Syria's lesser military position when the cease-fire resolutions were passed by the United Nations on October 22 and 23, 1973.

In preparing for Kissinger's Damascus visit, David Korn, the State Department's office director for northern Arab affairs, was dispatched to the Syrian capital to arrange the logistics and prepare for the meetings with Assad. Arriving in Beirut, Korn motored to the Lebanese-Syrian border, where he was escorted to Damascus by members of the Syrian Foreign Ministry. Prior to going to Syria, Kissinger asked the Syrian ambassador to the United Nations to come to Washington for some preliminary discussions. He had already met with Sadat on several occasions, and momentum for the conference's convocation was picking up speed. Kissinger believed that his negotiation train, already moving, could pick up Assad at the station, and the Syrian president would gladly jump aboard. Assad was in a foul mood about Sadat's actions the previous two months. Now came the train's engineer. Before Kissinger arrived in Damascus, he believed Assad would attend the proposed international conference, which he had heard from both the Soviets and via diplomatic cable traffic from Cairo. The questions to be answered for Kissinger were primarily procedural: the timing of the conference, the content and manner in which the letters of invitation to the conference would be sent, and whether Assad could/would provide "Arab cover" for the prenegotiated Egyptian-Israeli disengagement agreement. As for Kissinger, recalled Korn, the secretary of state was not bound by a cautious self-estimate of his competency as a negotiator. He calmly remarked to Korn that his "experience in the Vietnam negotiations qualified him to undertake these [Middle East] negotiations. It is my destiny."[66] Korn thought that Kissinger's "my destiny" comment was so ridiculously pompous, he almost burst out laughing. After a lunch hosted by Syrian Foreign Minister Khaddam, Kissinger reflected, "It is my destiny which has brought me to this place." Clearly Kissinger did not lack immodesty, and he relished this chance. Korn was not as sanguine about Assad either taking a ticket from Kissinger or about his willingness to have it punched. Kissinger was about to obtain a dose of Assad's political reality: he would learn that Assad was not Sadat, and that he would be his own political engineer.

When his meeting with Assad began, Kissinger was surprised to learn that Syria's willingness to attend the conference would depend on the outcome of their discussions. So from the beginning of their exchange, Kissinger was on the defensive, trying to persuade Assad. Syrian presence at the conference was preferred; indeed, Kissinger knew that failing to persuade Assad would not keep the conference from convening. Assad listened intently for well over an hour to what Kissinger had to say. Finally, more than halfway through their meeting, Assad looked at Kissinger and said, "Mr. Secretary, is it now my turn to speak?" Assad, with tongue in cheek, told Kissinger that Syria "did not know what the conference will be and what it will achieve and that we are not dreaming about going to conference."[67] As a consequence, Assad admitted that no preparations were yet made to form a Syrian delegation. By contrast, the Israelis, Jordanians, and Egyptians were already engaged in making in-depth arrangements to prepare for and attend the Geneva Conference.

To Assad, Kissinger was on a mission, in a hurry, Egypt's "ambassador," and Syria was peripheral to his goals. They talked past each other. Kissinger's focus was on the procedure of convening the Geneva Conference; Assad wanted to speak about the substance of Israel's "aggression," how it would be liquidated in general, and what the United States was prepared to do about it in particular. Kissinger willingly informed the Syrian president that "the peace conference provides [a] legal front within which negotiating activity can go on. Real solutions," said Kissinger, "will occur outside the conference. . . . We can use the conference to provide scenery and framework. The conference is a mechanism for moving from war to peace. We will attempt to get separation of forces in the first phase," meaning some Israeli withdrawal. "This would be followed by another stage of withdrawal and discussions on security, borders, Jerusalem, and the fate of the Palestinians."[68] On the Palestinian representation issue, Kissinger said, "I recognize that the Palestine movement [*sic*] needs to be discussed, but not in the first phase. You have seen the letter to the [UN] Secretary General we [*sic*] intend to send to the participants. Our problem is that the Israelis don't want reference to the Palestinians in that letter, particularly because of their elections. Our view is that it would be a mistake to take up the Palestinian question now in the conference. We recognize the problem cannot be solved without taking into account interests of the Palestinians. We are not opposed in principle to contact with the Palestinians. . . . There are so many Palestinian groups, we don't know who to deal with. You might advise us as to which might be the authentic group. Sadat is willing to have invitations go without any specific mention of the Palestinians."[69]

As was Assad's habit, he would glean and learn from the discourse of others; he did not know for sure by then that Sadat had taken the position of no Palestinian representation at Geneva, though he did know from various sources that Sadat had agreed with Kissinger on an interim withdrawal. Though Kissinger wanted Assad to assent to the contents of the letter of invitation that would omit mention of the Palestinians, he knew that it would not be easy to convince Assad to accept the Palestinians' absence. With almost naive candor, he told Assad, "Everybody says that of all the Arabs, you Syrians are the most impossible to deal with."[70] While listening to Kissinger, besides knowing about the negotiated separation of forces agreement at Kilometer 101, Assad was informed that the conference would serve Sadat's interests alone. Confirmation of this point came to Assad when he compared the inconsistency in Kissinger's early remarks, which suggested that so far there was no agreement on substance on any issue, and when he later contradicted himself with the detail about the Egyptian-Israeli disengagement discussions. When Assad told Kissinger that he wanted the Israelis to withdraw beyond the new areas they occupied during the October War, Kissinger acknowledged that he had not yet discussed a Golan withdrawal with the Israelis. In responding to what the United States was prepared to do for Syria, Kissinger said that diplomatic interests sections and direct communications would be established, using the model just begun with the appointment of Eilts as U.S. ambassador in Cairo. The secretary acknowledged that "there are strong domestic pressures in the U.S. in favor of support of Israel. We have to manage our domestic situation in order to be helpful. Don't put us in a position," asked Kissinger, "where we have to take final positions, when what is required is first steps."[71]

Naturally, Assad was not pleased that Kissinger was only making a general commitment to find a phased Israeli withdrawal from the Golan, especially when he said that getting "Israel to withdraw from something . . . was more important than any legal interpretation of [UNSC] 242."[72] Kissinger did not understand that Syria's acceptance of UNSC Resolution 242 and Assad's willingness to negotiate with Israel was centrally predicated on the legal interpretation of UNSC Resolution 242. Assad made his positions clear:

We are against Zionism as an expansionist move, but we are not against Jews or the Jewish religion. . . . No leaders of a regime can give up sovereignty. We cannot compromise one inch of territory. It should all be restored. . . . Israel does not want peace and cannot realize her dream without the U.S.-Israel talks about secure borders. The invalidity of this theory is obvious. Modern weapons show that there are no real secure borders. This theory is invalid. We need a just peace. We are serious. We want to build our own country. There can be no peace with justice unless the Arab Palestinian question is settled. The Arab people of Palestine were driven out by force and are now living in camps. How can there be peace without settling their problem? We believe that the U.S. is a major factor to check the aggressive Israeli spirit. I believe that when the U.S. tells Israel to go back, it will do so without hesitation. Are we to go to a peace conference for implementation of the points that we cannot give up one inch of territory and that there can't be a solution without the peoples of Palestine?[73]

Later in their exchange, Assad gave Kissinger the bottom line, "I know we lost this war, so we shall have another one, and another one, a third, a fourth, a fifth. We can take it. Finally, we shall drive them into the sea, because the Israelis cannot take casualties, even if they win a war."[74]

Kissinger was correctly informed by Sadat that a Syrian-Israeli disengagement should be discussed, but what Sadat failed to convey, or perhaps convey firmly enough, to Kissinger was that the question of an Israeli-Syrian disengagement had to be settled before the convening of such a conference. Assad told Kissinger directly, "The conference should only be a framework . . . that the question of disengagement must be settled beforehand. If we go to a conference without deciding things [in advance], our losses would be very great," to which Kissinger replied, "I did not know a prior disengagement agreement was a condition of your attendance at Geneva. I came here under a misapprehension. I did not think that your attendance [at the conference] was conditional on anything."[75] What seems to have happened is that Sadat told two different versions to instigate an Assad-Kissinger meeting. Sadat told the Syrians that Kissinger might be able to reach a settlement about the Golan,[76] while he told Kissinger that Assad had no prerequisites for going to the Geneva Conference. Concluding their six-hour conversation, Assad assented to all the amendments Kissinger proposed and patiently reviewed the letter of invitation line-by-line. Assad smiled and said he agreed with the letter of invitation. Breathing a sigh of relief, Kissinger turned to Sisco with a pleased expression. The American delegation had not expected an affirmative reply so readily and so easily.[77] Kissinger thought he would have to fire everyone in the State Department who had predicted that Assad would be difficult. Not wanting to overstay his welcome, Kissinger prepared to leave and was given an open invitation by Assad to return as an honored guest. When the meetings were ending and Kissinger remarked to the Syrian foreign minister, "I shall see you in Geneva," Assad replied, "What Geneva?" Somewhat startled, Kissinger replied, "The conference in Geneva," to which Assad quickly replied, "You are certainly not going to see my foreign minister there." "What do you mean, Mr. President?" inquired Kissinger. Assad responded, "We have no intention of accepting the invitation or of going to Geneva." Kissinger responded, "But Mr. President, you have just accepted all the amendments to the text." "Yes," said Assad, "I accept them and any other amendment which you like, because I refuse the whole invitation. So you can amend it any way you like now. It doesn't concern me. You can put the wording any way you [and Sadat] like. We will not go."[78] Assad had no intention of going to a conference that would suit only Egypt's needs. The precooking for Geneva contained no Syrian ingredient; Assad found no compartment to his liking on this train, at least not yet. The only substantive result of the Kissinger-Assad exchange was the decision that the United States should open a diplomatic interest section in Damascus. It would be six more months before full diplomatic relations were established between Damascus and Washington.

Assad had accurately sized up Kissinger and his motivations. He understood that when Kissinger told him, "There can be no settlement you don't agree to and we will not force you," that regardless of whether the conference were convened or not, whether it reached an Egyptian-Israeli understanding or not, Kissinger would have to return to Damascus at some point to negotiate ultimately a Syrian-Israeli agreement. Assad understood how intent Israeli Prime Minister Golda Meir was on having Israel's POWs returned; if Kissinger or Sadat wanted or desired additional Arab endorsement for an Egyptian-Israeli agreement today, then that need would not diminish in the future. Time was Assad's ally, so why hurry now? Why help either Sadat or the United States by going to Geneva, with no apparent benefit in store for Syria? To what degree Assad's decision not to attend the Geneva Conference was due to internal Syrian domestic pressures remains open to question,[79] but clearly Kissinger had not brought Assad any incentive to attend the conference. During the next week, Sadat was unsuccessful in his perfunctory effort in sending General el-Gamasy to Damascus to persuade Assad to change his mind. In response, Assad sent word to Sadat that "he would send two officers to be part of the Egyptian delegation, but not as Syrian delegates."[80] Years later, Dayan recalled that at the Geneva Conference, "the Syrians sat with the Egyptian delegation."[81] With Syria not going to Geneva, prospects soared for a relatively uncomplicated conclusion to an Egyptian-Israeli agreement channeled through Geneva. According to Kissinger, the Syrian nonparticipation decision was satisfactory—"a blessing in disguise."[82] Khaddam acknowledged that at that moment, "Assad knew that Kissinger was not totally sincere in his effort to have Syria come to Geneva."[83] Was it luck or careful planning by the secretary of state to have Assad say no?

For several reasons, Assad chose not to send an official delegation to Geneva. First, he sensed the negotiations contained nothing for him or for Syria at that time[84] and correctly calculated that, for the time being, Syrian interests would be adequately met by establishing open and direct communications with Kissinger. Therefore, Assad did not need to go to Geneva to urge Washington to put pressure on Israel for withdrawal on the Golan Heights, or to open a dialogue with Washington. Neither did he need to make a big fuss about the conference after the meeting with Kissinger, because he knew that eventually Kissinger would have to negotiate a Syrian-Israeli disengagement agreement after completing the Egyptian-Israeli negotiation. Assad also knew that Sadat needed an additional Arab cover, which a Syrian-Israeli agreement could partially provide. Assad was not going to Geneva to be only a passenger and neither a conductor nor an engineer. For that matter, he wasn't even sure of his destination.

Second, Assad did not attend the conference because he felt that Sadat was acting in a deceitful, impatient, and premature manner. Most particularly, Sadat continued to break Assad's absolute cardinal rule: he was voiding Arab unity, solidarity, and complete coordination by negotiating with Israel for Egypt's interests first. In Assad's view, whether in war or diplomacy, the Arab world would be irreparably weakened if individual Arab-state interests prevailed over collective action. Separate Arab negotiations with Israel could not be condoned. According to Mahmoud Raid, "After what Assad heard [from Kissinger] about differentiating between withdrawals on the two fronts and that disengagement on the Egyptian front would be announced independently, he could not agree to Syria's participation in the Geneva Conference."[85] In Assad's view, over the previous ten weeks, there were too many examples of deviousness on Sadat's part, and he suspected that Sadat "had not informed him of all the agreements concluded with Kissinger."[86] Assad understood the substance and direction of the Kilometer 101 Talks, but when he saw them "collapse unexpectedly," he inferred there was a logical reason: Kissinger wanted it that way. Assad had the initial intention of going to Geneva, but, in his own words, "there was not enough time to resolve the issue[s] before the first session."[87] The pace was too quick for Assad; he preferred to make important decisions through reflection, rather than upon impulse.

Third, Assad was not yet prepared for the public symbolism of Arabs negotiating with Israelis. Assad's deep mistrust and fear of the Israelis led him to believe that no accommodation could be negotiated quickly at Geneva. In a meeting on December 19, Assad told King Hussein that nothing would come out of this conference, that Jordan would be used only as a decorative Arab presence. Jordan still tried to convince Syria to attend.[88]

Fourth, there was some concern on Assad's part that his regime might become destabilized if he went to Geneva.[89] Since he had been in power for only three years, his grip on the country was not yet totally solidified, particularly with the army after the losses sustained in the October 1973 War. Going to Geneva could be perceived as a political concession, which could be self-debilitating. There was no need to take the risk. Instead, by not going to Geneva, Assad preserved his leading position among those against any accommodation with Israel.

Fifth, Assad did not want to appear as an adjunct of or corollary to an American initiative. He had just met Henry Kissinger for the first time. The Syrian-American connection was very new. Assad had not yet enjoyed the series of contacts with Washington that Sadat had experienced since coming to office in 1970. Further-more, because of Assad's style and personality, he needed to have confidence and trust in a person empowered to mediate and influence political issues affecting Syria's present and future. It was still too sudden for Assad to measure Kissinger's style and motivations. What he saw in Kissinger's motivations was not encouraging. For Assad, Sadat was traveling at an impulsive pace with Israel and the United States; he needed to evaluate closely how Sadat's policy choices would influence his relations with the Soviet Union, other Arab states, Lebanon, and the Palestinians. At that moment, for Assad, reflection was required to clarify a new reality of dissi-pating Arab unity against Israel. If given more time to decide on when or how to participate in negotiations, Assad realized he could extract concessions and obtain rewards as the process unfolded. Of particular relevance to him was how the oil embargo might be used to pressure the United States into forcing Israeli withdrawal from the Golan Heights. In a 1990 interview, Assad recounted Kissinger's efforts to persuade the Syrians to participate in the Geneva Conference and described why he did not go to Geneva:

> Syria did not attend the conference, not because it was against it, but because President Anwar al-Sadat did not abide by the agreement we reached together that the disengagement of forces in Sinai and the Golan be reached and defined on maps before we go to Geneva. Former U.S. Secretary of State Henry Kissinger failed to change our position although he was insistent. I did abide by my agreement with Sadat concerning his proposal to carry out the disengagement on both fronts at the same time, although I was not thinking of disengagement, because I was of the view that either we reached a compre-hensive peace or we continued the war. Sadat did not abide by the agreement. He went alone to Geneva and had his separate plan. Sadat theoretically fol-lowed a joint plan, but in practice he adopted a unilateral plan. We, therefore, did not go to Geneva. Had we gone, the Egyptian and Syrian delegations would have appeared to be at odds instead of facing the Israeli delegation together. Had this happened, it would have been a tragedy, because we had just come out of the war, and the soldiers were still engaged.[90]

He could have also said, "I would have been dragged into recognizing Israel, which I did not want to do."

Though the Soviet Union wanted diplomatic parity with the United States, Kissinger never gave it to them. By designating Soviet Foreign Minister Gromyko as a coconvener, the United States considerably mollified Arab apprehensions about Washington's domination of the conference. Of course, any joint sponsorship related to procedure, not to substance. As Urquhart said, the "Russians were really playing second fiddle, they were just anxious to be there. It gave the Russians exactly what the U.S. wanted—the formal cochairmanship and absolutely no involvement or responsibility at all."[91] Without their major client participating, Moscow lost its potentially persuasive influence with and through Damascus. Assad's rejection of participation at the Geneva Conference did not cause Kissinger to call off the conference; on the contrary, for several reasons Kissinger decided to hold the conference as soon as possible.[92] He knew that the Egyptians and Israelis wanted an agreement immediately, and recognized Jordan's strong motivation to represent its interests at a conference over the surging PLO claim to represent *all* Palestinians. Syria's absence meant that Moscow's role would be negligible; Damascus would only be a passing verbal nuisance to the signature of an Egyptian-Israeli agreement. American, Egyptian, Jordanian, and Israeli national interests were all commonly served by attending the conference, while Moscow went to save some prestige. Although Kissinger kept the Europeans informed through periodic visits to their capitals, he denied them substantive involvement in shaping either the agenda or form of the conference. Suffering from the oil embargo, European countries wanted to be apprised of the diplomatic process, but in general, they chose to be distant politically from the center of negotiations in order to increase the chances of lifting the embargo. The British and French did want to attend the conference, with the French more intent on doing so and only grudgingly giving up their insistence. Europe's general voluntary detachment did not displease Kissinger. As Sisco said, "Throughout the whole period, candidly, we tended to either try to keep the Europeans out, or to just absolutely minimize their role."[93]

On November 17, more than one month before the conference was to convene and within two weeks of truncating the Kilometer 101 Talks, Kissinger discussed with Dobrynin the contents of the conference invitation. Kissinger wanted a joint U.S.-Soviet letter to the UN secretary-general, who would in turn issue the formal invitations to the parties, which Kissinger listed as Egypt, Syria, Jordan, and Israel, but not the Palestinians. On November 21, Kissinger sent the proposed draft letter through Waldheim to Dobrynin. The letter stated that the United States and the Soviet Union, "having canvassed the principal parties requested the UN secretary-general to invite Jordan, Israel, Egypt, and Syria to a conference in Geneva beginning December 17 or 18, under the co-chairmanship of the United States and the Soviet Union."[94] On December 14, the United States appointed Ellsworth Bunker as the U.S. delegate to the Geneva Conference. The next day, Kissinger met Assad in Damascus and the Security Council passed UNSC Resolution 344. The resolution was intended to provide political cover for the secretary-general's association with the conference, since he was nervous about any role that he might play without proper authorization. Waldheim and the nonpermanent members of the Security Council were also concerned about "full Security Council authorization" for the secretary-general's participation in the conference. In fact, as mentioned earlier, neither the UNSC nor the secretary-general did more than extend conference invitations, call the session to order, and chair the two-day meeting. In defining the role of the United Nations at the Geneva Conference, there was to be no UNSC authorization of the process, production, or postscript of Geneva. UNSC Resolution 344 was passed specifically for "cosmetic" purposes because it defined the term "appropriate auspices," which was significantly present in UNSC Resolution 338.[95] According to the Americans and Israelis, aside from this point, the UNSC Resolution had little meaning.[96] Rather than writing a joint letter, the Soviet Union and the United States sent identical letters to the secretary-general on December 18, stating who would be invited and that "the parties also agreed that the question of other participants from the Middle East will be discussed during the first stage of the conference." Even to the United Nations, Kissinger made it appear as if Moscow and Washington were coequals. According to Rodman, "Negotiating the letter of invitation turned into a farce, plunging into theology in defining every phrase, haggling, costing us weeks. But the letters of invitation meant little after the conference was convened."[97]

Specifics about seating arrangements and exact conference procedures only gelled after Syria's decision not to participate. Refining them came after Kissinger had another meeting with Israeli, Jordanian, Soviet, or Egyptian officials. Discussions about procedural wrangling did not dominate the conversations. Kissinger's State Department assistants handled the last-minute details, while he shuttled between Jerusalem, Cairo, and Damascus. The "lack of predetermined agreement on procedural issues allowed a measure of flexibility once the conference actually began."[98] By contrast to the vast, complex, and lengthy public discussion about the procedures that would predate the 1991 Madrid Middle East Peace Conference, the plans for the Geneva meeting were hastily prepared. Not hastily prepared, however, were the promises Kissinger gave to Meir, outlined in a December 20 Memorandum of Understanding. On nonconference matters, the United States committed itself to achieve a prompt and satisfactory solution to the Israeli-Syrian POW problem and a commitment to ensure Israel's uninterrupted passage of ships through the Bab al-Mandab Straits. Israel promised to observe scrupulously the cease-fire and observe existing arrangements for nonmilitary supply to the Third Army. With regard to the conference, it was stipulated that negotiations were to be conducted between the parties with the secretary-general participating in the opening sessions in a "nonsubstantive capacity"; that there would be no discussion or any action taken on any substantive issue prior to the elections in Israel, other than the question of disengagement and separation of forces, with reconvening of the conference to take place only after the new Israeli cabinet was formed; discussions would take place between the parties; and the participation at a subsequent phase of the conference of any possible additional state, group, or organization would require the agreement of all the initial participants.

The night before the conference convened, Waldheim and Eban sought to resolve the problematic seating arrangement. Waldheim suggested that the delegations meet in the secretary-general's suite of rooms immediately before the conference for a short exchange of pleasantries. But the next morning, Eban was told by Waldheim that the Arab states would not meet the Israelis socially before the conference, nor were they prepared to sit next to the Israelis at the conference. Previously, when the Soviet Union had suggested a seating arrangement, the placements symbolically demonstrated Moscow's anti-Israeli attitude. Gromyko proposed that the Soviet Union, Egypt, and Syria be seated to the right of Waldheim, and that the United States, Israel, and Jordan be to the left. Jordan would thereby be segregated from the Arab fold, and the Soviet Union would be posed as the champion of the genuine Arab cause. The configuration was rejected. Egypt and Jordan refused the placement of the countries in alphabetical order, because then Israel would be seated between them.[99] Establishing seating arrangements for the conference ballooned into an almost insurmountable problem. Insisting that they were not to sit next to the Israelis, the Egyptians wanted an empty table placed between their delegations. Foreign Minister Eban had no intention of fostering public ostracism. After agitated consultations with the delegations, which were scattered in different corners of the same large room, Kissinger devised a "buffer" solution: secretary-general Waldheim sat in the middle with Foreign Minister Eban on his left and Egyptian Foreign Minister Fahmy on his right. On Israel's left was Gromyko; on Fahmy's right was Kissinger. Beyond the Soviet chair was an empty place for the absent Syrians and then the Jordanian chair, occupied by Prime Minister Zaid Rifa'i. Less than thirty minutes before the conference began, it was agreed that no decisions, whether procedural or substantive, could be made at the conference without the unanimous consent of the participants.[100] At the conference itself and in potential photo opportunities on the periphery of the conference, Arab delegates were extraordinarily self-conscious about media coverage, especially (as Eban noted in his autobiography) with regard to the televised "tint of shame" of shaking hands with the Israelis. In his speech to the Israeli Parliament on November 20, 1977, Sadat acknowledged that Egyptian delegates to the Geneva Conference had not exchanged a direct word with Israelis.[101] Fahmy was afraid to be seen in public with the Israelis and told the UN secretary-general that if there were cocktail parties, then he hoped that the Israelis would be on the other side of the room.[102] Even though some of the Egyptian delegates were personal friends with members of the Jordanian delegation, they were instructed by Fahmy not to have any contact with the Jordanian delegation—"none whatsoever."[103] Thus, there was little Arab coordination at all before the Geneva Conference. However difficult it was to seat the delegations, there was great symbolism for Israel when the Egyptians and Jordanians agreed to sit in public with the Israelis.[104] Egyptian and Israeli generals meeting privately under a canopy and in tents in the Egyptian desert on a daily basis for almost a month was fine, but in public it was imperative for the Egyptian and all Arab delegates to maximize their physical distance from the Israelis. Seventeen years later, at the Madrid Middle East Peace Conference in 1991, Israel and all the Arab delegations sat in the same room and at the same table. This seating arrangement was in stark contrast to the British-sponsored 1939 St. James Arab-Zionist Conference, and the 1949 UN-directed Rhodes and Lausanne Armistice Talks, when the host or mediator alternated between delegations and where there were off-the-record but direct contacts between Arabs and Israelis. In Geneva and later in Madrid, the seating dispute clouded the potential of visual acceptance that Israeli delegates wanted from their Arab counterparts.

On December 21 at ten o'clock in the morning, when the conference was scheduled to begin, the various delegations were still standing as they waited for the seating issue to be resolved. The conference was designed to commence with public speeches on Friday morning, bilateral consultations Friday afternoon, and a second open session on Saturday to conclude the speeches. As it turned out, all the speeches were given on Friday, and the Saturday session was closed to the public. With Gromyko and Kissinger as cochairmen, Waldheim opened the conference. Gromyko spoke first, followed by Kissinger, Fahmy, Rifa'i, and Eban. Each delegation sat formally and stiffly behind its delegation head. Each delegation leader had carefully prepared his speech to be well received at home. Written for "domestic consumption," as Rifa'i described it, the speeches were intended first to neutralize possible criticisms about conference participation and then to stake out important political and strategic positions. Somewhat surprisingly, the Soviet foreign minister's speech firmly endorsed the Arab side without being unremittingly hostile toward Israel. Gromyko emphasized the need for achievement of a political settlement of the conflict. Kissinger categorized Gromyko's speech as "offering no new perspectives, but also doing nothing to exacerbate the situation."[105] The Soviet foreign minister cited detente as a reason and as a precondition for facilitating a stable political outcome to the war. He did not ignore the Palestinian problem in his remarks, but neither did he state that the Palestinian issue was the central problem. In fact, he made specific reference to the language of UNSC Resolution 242, which called for "respect for and recognition of the sovereignty, territorial integrity and political independence of states in the Middle East and their right to live in peace." He continued, saying that "the Soviet Union harbors no hostility towards the State of Israel as such. The practical task of the conference consists of working out a concrete and realistic program of implementing the resolution of the Security Council [242] in all its parts, . . . agreements arrived at by the interested parties with respect to such a settlement be reinforced at the conference in appropriate documents, and . . . the Soviet Union is ready, together with the other appropriate powers, to assume suitable commitments."[106] Gromyko reminded his listeners that *both* Moscow and Washington were responsible for the UN resolutions dealing with the potential resolution of the Arab-Israeli conflict. Although an active Geneva framework protected Moscow's interests as a central diplomatic player, it also preserved Washington's role as prime maestro. From the Geneva Conference up through convocation of the 1991 Madrid Middle East Peace Conference, Moscow used "the return to Geneva" as its claim to be a coequal participant with Washington in attempts to rejuvinate periodic doldrums in Arab-Israeli negotiations. That claim received its most serious American endorsement from the Carter administration in 1977. Thereafter, Moscow repeatedly used its status as the conference coconvener to sustain Arab clientage for Soviet support to convene another conference.

Following Gromyko's speech, Kissinger asserted four essential points: maintenance of the cease-fire; a realistic assessment of what could be accomplished; the need for early disengagement of forces; and the importance of further negotiations. His strategy was to frame the conflict in terms all sides could respect. He said, "One side seeks the recovery of sovereignty and the redress of grievances suffered by a displaced people. The other seeks security and recognition of its legitimacy as a nation. The common goal of peace must surely be broad enough to embrace all these aspirations. . . . Peace will require that we relate the imperative of withdrawals to the necessities of security, the requirement of guarantees to the sovereignty of the parties, the hopes of the displaced to the realities now existing."[107] In his public statement of U.S. goals, Kissinger anticipated the outcome of negotiations as peace agreements that contained withdrawals, recognized frontiers, security arrangements, guarantees, a settlement of the legitimate interests of the Palestinians, and a recognition of the holy sites in Jerusalem.[108] Such a comprehensive peace was envisioned, but it could only come about through a series of interim steps. Of course, Kissinger's privately orchestrated diplomatic choreography was much different than what he expressed in public.

Following Kissinger's presentation, Egyptian Foreign Minister Fahmy expounded uncompromising positions. He demanded total Israeli withdrawal to pre–1967 War borders, the return of Jerusalem, the exercise of Palestinian self-determination, and provision of international guarantees by the superpowers or the United Nations. In noting that these requirements were consistent with the resolutions of the recently held Algiers Summit Conference, Fahmy demonstrated that Cairo was not breaking Arab ranks by negotiating directly with Israel at a conference. Egypt, he said, was at the conference to conduct itself in a businesslike manner. Fahmy said that "although matters of substance were to be discussed on the second day of the conference, he refused to do so because of the absence of the Syrian and Palestinian delegations."[109] (Twenty years after the conference, Fahmy either forgot or still had no idea that Sadat and Kissinger agreed to no substantive discussions at Geneva.) In his 1973 speech, Fahmy said that Egypt would be prepared to use "other means to liberate our lands and to restore the legitimate rights of the Palestinians." Fahmy's staunch public defense of the Palestinians was clearly incompatible with el-Gamasy's "finished with Palestine" statement to Yariv at the Kilometer 101 Talks. In this manner, Fahmy and el-Gamasy reflected two contrasting but forceful tenets in Egyptian political thinking: one emphasized Egypt's needs; the other stressed Cairo's historic devotion to the Palestinian cause. What Sadat did with his advisers at the Geneva Conference, he would do repeatedly in his subsequent execution of policy options toward Israel. He would deny strategic information to his own foreign minister but permit him to, or at least not discourage him from, stating a hardline public position that was less ideologically strident than his private views. Four years later, when Fahmy spoke about reconvening the Geneva Conference in 1977, he still believed that the 1973 Geneva Conference had been held without sufficient preparation.[110]

Most uncompromising in his public remarks toward Israel was Jordanian Prime Minister Zaid Rifa'i. Rifa'i later told Kissinger that his harsh tone had reflected the "necessities of Arab politics."[111] Rifa'i and Eban remembered that, despite public statements to the contrary, Jordan dearly wanted an agreement with Israel.[112] Again, Jordan's public statements were harsher than its private remarks to Israelis in secret talks. After expounding the public rhetoric, Rifa'i recalled that Jordan was prepared to negotiate seriously. Initially, Jordan wanted the return of only a small amount of the territory taken by Israel in the June 1967 War. This small recovery of land would give King Hussein a negotiating toehold to affirm the Hashemite presence in the territories and demonstrate to the PLO that Amman was the only address to which the Israelis would return land. But Israelis who had met with Hussein secretly on dozens of occasions, both before and after the October 1973 War, knew that he wanted all of the West Bank and East Jerusalem returned to his control. They had no illusions that Hussein would change his objective of securing total Israeli withdrawal,[113] even if it were to begin in stages. Though wanting an agreement privately, the Jordanian prime minister publicly recounted a fierce litany of Israeli culpability and shortcomings in preventing peace. The list was as extensive as it was shrill. Rifa'i called Israel "an authority of terror and aggression, the conduct of which is always characterized with defiance and arrogance. The seeds of oppression which it planted in the Arab soil grew up with hatred." Like Fahmy, Rifa'i called for the restoration of the pre–June 1967 War borders, the right of every state in the area to live in peace, fulfillment of the legitimate rights of the Palestinian people, and the restoration of Arab sovereignty over Jerusalem. He made it clear that Jordan was unprepared to conclude any partial settlement on matters that were not of joint interest with the Arab world. For Jordan, the conference gave legitimacy to the negotiations, because they were based on implementation of UN Security Council Resolutions 242 and 338. Jordan also wanted to use the conference to counteract the anticipated and inevitable Arab opposition that might emerge should Amman negotiate an arrangement with Israel. Hashemite genuflection toward Arab unity did not camouflage the necessity to protect national interests.

Like Sadat, King Hussein was motivated to negotiate with Israel seriously; he did not want broader issues debated (like Palestinian political rights or the Palestinian relationship to Jordan) that would impede achieving satisfactory arrangement with Israel over the West Bank and East Jerusalem. Hussein's definition of a settlement with Israel was considerably different from what the Israelis wanted from Jordan; his consistent goals were to promote Jordanian interests and to prevent Palestinian and Syrian priorities from occluding his options. In subsequent years, Jordan preferred and promoted the conference framework for negotiations as the most viable mechanism for reaching a negotiated agreement with Israel, always emphasizing procedures that protected independent Jordanian decision making from becoming subsumed by larger pan-Arab interests.

Unlike Egypt, Jordanian Foreign Minister Rifa'i specifically mentioned Palestinian repatriation and compensation, but did not explicitly call for Palestinian self-determination. In his reference to the Palestinians, Rifa'i only went so far as to say that the legitimate rights of the Arab people of Palestine must be fulfilled in accordance with resolutions of the United Nations. Jordan wanted resolution of the Palestinian issue on Palestinian soil (Israel, the West Bank, and Gaza areas) and, therefore, wanted protection against encroachment on Jordanian sovereignty by Palestinian resettlement east of the Jordan River. Israel's Eban recalled that the shortcoming of the Geneva Conference was the inability to arrive at an agreement with Jordan. "Looking back," said Eban, "I confess that it was an error on everybody's part not to take the Jordanian aspect of the peace conference more seriously. If there had been an Israeli deal with [King] Hussein, he wouldn't have been humiliated when he went to Rabat"[114] in October 1974, when the PLO was anointed as the sole legitimate representative of the Palestinian people.

Eban was scheduled to speak on Saturday, December 22. But after listening to Fahmy's tough and vitriolic anti-Israeli speech, Eban and his Foreign Ministry advisers decided to reply immediately. To wait until Saturday would give the Egyptians an undue propaganda advantage, Eban thought, especially with the vast number of international media assembled. Responding on Friday enabled more Israelis to watch Eban on the evening television news. He made the decision in consultation with Meir, who felt an immediate and vigorous reply would benefit the Labor Party's electoral considerations.[115] With his characteristic genius for oration, Eban clearly stated that Israel's goal "at the conference is a peace treaty defining the terms of our [Arab-Israeli] coexistence in future years. [Peace] was not a mere cease-fire or armistice. Its meaning is not exhausted by the absence of war. Peace commits us not only to abstention from violence but also to positive obligations which neighboring states owe to each other by virtue of their very proximity. . . . The ultimate guarantee of a peace agreement lies in the creation of common regional interests in such degree of intensity, in such multiplicity of interaction, in such entanglement of reciprocal advantage, in such mutual accessibility of human contact, as to put the possibility of future war beyond rational contingency."[116] Eban's theme was the requirement for complementary and dual responsibility in peaceful relations. As an idealist, he envisioned a peace treaty negotiated with each Arab neighbor, with agreement on boundaries and their defensibility, territorial compromise, security arrangements, resolution of the refugee problem in a regional context, compensation for the refugees, and a unified Jerusalem under Israeli control. Fahmy took rebuttal time and escalated his anger to the one established earlier by Rifa'i. Like Jordan's delegate, he accused Israel of atrocities against farmers and children and asserted that Eban had spoken merely for domestic consumption due to the Israeli election campaign.

It had been one of Eban's objectives at the conference to engage in some public discussion with Gromyko. As much as Fahmy wanted nothing to do with the Israelis, no such hesitancy restrained the Soviet foreign minister. When Eban entered the conference hall, Gromyko shook Eban's hand as cameras clicked enthusiastically. Again, during the lunch break on Friday, Gromyko took the initiative to shake Eban's hand without rebuff and to exchange pleasantries. In a meeting on Friday evening, they spoke for about an hour. They discussed the need for a troop disengagement agreement and the possibility of a renewal of Israeli-Soviet diplomatic relations. Gromyko reaffirmed the Soviet Union's 1948 position in support of Israel's right to sovereign existence and independence.[117] These were the first public meetings between high-ranking Israeli and Soviet officials since the break in diplomatic relations after the June 1967 War. Although diplomatic relations with Israel were not restored as a consequence of Geneva, the taboo of speaking to the Israelis was broken.

During the conference, as negotiations continued about Egyptian-Israeli disengagement of forces, there were almost daily violations of the cease-fire with small arms fire exchanged along the Suez front. Sporadic fighting also continued along the Syrian-Israeli front. At the end of the session on Friday, Kissinger suggested that the conference be suspended until January 10. Fahmy was uneasy about the postponement because he had not been informed about the arrangements that Sadat had made with Kissinger. Equally surprised, the Jordanians objected to the turn of events that made them uninvited spectators to the Egyptian-Israeli military and political committee talks that flowed out of the 1973 Geneva Conference. When Rifa'i asked for a Jordanian-Israeli political committee to convene, Eban objected on the basis that the discussion would be about territorial issues remnant from the June 1967 War rather than those recently contested in the October 1973 War. Rifa'i rhetorically asked Eban if Jordanians were now to be penalized for not joining the October 1973 War.[118] The Soviets were likewise frustrated by Kissinger's success at persuading Sadat to let the United States function independently through a shuttle effort.[119]

Eban's recollection was that the conference ended too quickly; he believed that Kissinger could have achieved more political substance from the conference and its immediate aftermath than merely a disengagement agreement, including more concrete Egyptian political acceptance of Israel.[120] Since the main speeches were given, the Saturday session was closed. A brief communiqué issued at the end of the conference noted that "the conference at the Foreign Minister's level will reconvene in Geneva as needed in the light of developments." On December 22, the five foreign ministers and their assistants met privately away from the media. Eban characterized these discussions as the most important result of the conference.[121] What Eban did not know was that Kissinger had already predetermined that political and military committee talks would be the next procedural mechanism to flow from the conference. Waldheim told the foreign ministers "that the conference would continue its work through setting up discussions on disengagement of forces, with the conference itself to continue at an ambassadorial level and reconvene at the foreign minister's level as needed in light of developments."[122] Waldheim announced that since it was consensus that the most urgent task facing the conference was disengagement of forces, it would be the subject of discussion by a military working group that would be set up as soon as possible. Not by coincidence, Kissinger agreed with Waldheim. In speaking for Jordan, Rifa'i, while concurring that the first order of business was the disengagement of forces, also "hoped that disengagement would not be limited to one front only." Rifa'i was still under the impression that Jordanian-Israeli disengagement talks would follow. Eban revealed his absence from the Israeli decision-making loop when he suggested to those assembled that one should not "rule out establishment of other committees to discuss other aspects of a peace settlement at an appropriate time." At the conclusion of the meeting, Kissinger thanked Waldheim for "convening the conference, [for the] impartial spirit in which he had presided, and [for the] excellent arrangements which the UN had made for the conference."[123]

CHAPTER 6

THE SYRIAN-ISRAELI AGREEMENT, SINAI I AND II, AND DEFINING A COMPREHENSIVE PEACE

1974–1977

K ISSINGER maneuvered Egypt and Israel into negotiating an agreement
they both needed, while solidifying the centrality of the American mediation role. Once the Geneva Conference was over, Moscow, Syria, the PLO, Jordan,
the UN, and most European countries had been shuffled out of the picture, were
leaving the picture, or were already on the sidelines. From the Geneva meetings
came political and military committee talks meant to be equally unchallenging to
Kissinger's passion to control the content and pace. The presence of the United
States's Ellsworth Bunker and the Soviet Union's Sergei Vinogradov in Geneva as
official delegation heads to the political committee talks, and Israeli General Gur
and Egyptian General Magdoob as delegation heads to the military talks, provided
Kissinger all the cover he needed. For the United Nations, General Siilasvuo
presided at the military committee talks, but he had neither authority nor influence. The possibility of direct talks (between Egyptians and Israelis, or between
Israelis and the Soviets) outside of Kissinger's influence was not only greatly dis-
couraged but also unlikely to occur. Epi Evron noted, "It was the kind of thing that
Henry did not want at all."[1] Vinogradov was upset because he was stonewalled by
Sterner per Kissinger's instructions; the Soviet delegate "had absolutely no idea
what was going on."[2] No one except the Egyptians was telling Vinogradov anything about the nature or content of the political committee discussions. Bunker
wanted to go home for Christmas and spend New Year's on his farm in Vermont,
but he waited until early January to leave the Geneva talks. Sterner could not get

146

permission from Kissinger to leave "because he wanted this symbol that we were still in this bond in the Geneva Conference; he wanted to get committee talks going, but there was always an element of saying to himself . . . a bunch of Israelis and Egyptians sitting down are not going to get anywhere."[3] Sterner spent forty days in Geneva and discussed no detail whatsoever.

Between December 26, 1973, and January 9, 1974, there were six meetings of the Egyptian-Israeli military committee. The first three meetings on December 26, 28, and January 2 focused on "Principles of Disengagement." It was commonly agreed to have buffer zones and UN observers. Disagreement between the sides ensued about the distance between forces, buffer zone width, depth of withdrawal, whether Israel in the first stage should withdraw forces from east of the canal, and whether there should be an Israeli withdrawal from territory taken in 1967. Israel demanded "reciprocity," or some Egyptian withdrawal. Egypt finally agreed to reciprocity as a "thinning out" of its forces east of the canal. At the final three meetings on January 4, 7, and 9, detailed maps and plans were exchanged. With some minor modifications, much of what was discussed about the disengagement had been previously concluded in the Kilometer 101 Talks. On January 9, 1974, the military and political committee talks in Geneva were suspended, pending the outcome of political decisions in Cairo and Jerusalem.[4]

Prior to Dayan's visit to Washington on January 4, Israel had tweaked the Egyptians; they periodically stopped nonmilitary supplies to the Third Army. Israeli leaders enjoyed reminding both the United States and Egypt that it still held the fate of the Third Army in its hands; coincidentally when Dayan reached Washington, the supply convoys were again weaving their way through Israeli lines. In Washington, Dayan presented Kissinger with Israel's disengagement plan: Egypt would retain a zone of approximately six to ten kilometers on the east bank of the canal; Israel would withdraw to a new line twenty kilometers east of the canal. Israel would give up its bridgehead on the west bank of the canal, and there would be a six- to twenty-kilometer UN buffer zone between the Egyptian and Israeli Armies. The number of troops and armaments of both armies would be sharply limited. Dayan did not want a single Egyptian tank east of the canal and wanted all Egyptian troops returned west of the canal. However, he was willing to accept a ceiling of 250 to 300 Egyptian tanks on the east bank accompanied by an Egyptian withdrawal of more than 70,000 men, 720 tanks, and approximately 1,000 artillery pieces. To prevent another war of attrition, each side's artillery and surface-to-air missiles were to be out of range of the other's. Meir's government wanted the state of belligerency with Egypt ended, the blockade at Bab al-Mandeb lifted, a pledge made to reopen the Suez Canal to Israeli vessels, and an assurance of long-term arms supply from Washington. According to Kissinger, "In characteristic Israeli negotiating style, he [Dayan] presented the scheme as one without flexibility. The Cabinet insisted that there would be little margin left for negotiation."[5] Kissinger thought the plan had many shortcomings, especially regarding the depth of Israeli withdrawal, the degree of Egyptian military presence, whether the state of belligerency would cease, and how freedom of navigation would be stated. Kissinger thought that he might present the Dayan plan to Sadat as a reworked American idea. While in Washington, Dayan also met with Defense Secretary Schlesinger to discuss military supply issues. An Egyptian-Israeli troop disengagement was a prerequisite for lifting the Arab oil embargo.

However, before Kissinger could submit details of a disengagement agreement to Sadat, Dayan's plan was made public by General Gur at the military committee talks in Geneva. Both Kissinger and Dayan were stunned by Gur's presentation.[6] Israel did not intentionally decide to make its proposals public in order to embarrass either Kissinger or Sadat, nor to demonstrate Israel's military superiority at the end of the war. By accident, Gur publicized a feasible plan without coordination from the Israeli Defense Ministry; Dayan had not told him the contents of the Dayan-Kissinger-Sadat discussions. Somewhat perturbed, Dayan told Gur to stop hypothesizing aloud. "Your job," said Dayan, "is not to make models or speculate. That is my job."[7] Sadat called the Egyptian delegate to instruct him likewise to stop negotiating with Gur. When Kissinger met with Dayan in Washington in early January, he upbraided the Israeli defense minister again for allowing Gur to negotiate, to which Dayan angrily replied, "So what do you want me to do about it?" It was simply unacceptable for Kissinger to lose any handle on the negotiations, and he rarely shied away from saying so.

On January 12, Kissinger traveled to Egypt and Israel to hammer out the final details of the disengagement agreement. From his daily travels between Aswan and Jerusalem, the term *shuttle diplomacy* was coined by the journalists traveling with him. Prior to his departure, several memoranda were prepared for the secretary by White House and Department of State staff. One focused on the Palestinian issue, the other on where this disengagement agreement fit into a longer-term U.S. effort of moving the negotiations forward. Kissinger's advisers were focused quite accurately on the combination of the tactics and strategy in negotiations. What were the immediate stumbling blocks and what were the longer-term objectives? Quandt, at the National Security Council, recommended that Kissinger urge "President Sadat to go slow in pushing the Palestinian case. Peace negotiations could be adversely affected by such a development [creation of a Palestinian provisional government] at this stage."[8] Complications with the Palestinian component of the conflict could stymie an Egyptian-Israeli agreement. By contrast, four years later, when Quandt was working for Brzenzinski at the NSC in the Carter White House, though he was still aware of how the Palestinian issue entangled Egyptian-Israeli negotiations, he was resistant to Sadat's desire to divorce himself from the Palestinian issue. In 1974, for Sadat, the contents of the disengagement agreement were not as important as building a relationship that contained trust with *Washington*.

A second memorandum prepared at the State Department evaluated how this disengagement agreement would fit into the next Egyptian-Israeli agreement, where the "negotiating momemtum is maintained without radically altering the security situation. Testing the viability of peacekeeping and demilitarization arrangements on a small scale would then be expanded to larger areas [in Sinai] and become the basis of long-term security arrangements in a peace settlement."[9] The mind-set in Washington was clearly focused on small interconnected steps that would slowly lead to another interim but a larger step in disengaging Egypt and Israel from war and returning most or all of Sinai to Egyptian sovereignty. This is what Sadat had wanted, but, at that moment, the pace was too slow for Sadat. Impatient, he wanted this first agreement signed before he left on a trip to Arab capitals on January 18, 1974. Furthermore, since Assad would always find some pretext for delay or put forward impossible demands, Sadat still wanted Egypt to proceed alone.[10]

Sadat's deadline guaranteed that he would go to the limit in possible concessions to the Israelis. In fact, he went on to agree that a total of 8,000 men would remain on the east bank, meaning Egypt would withdraw more than ninety percent of its army that had crossed the canal! There were no conclusions regarding the timetable of Israeli withdrawals until after the signing of the agreement on January 18. Sadat ultimately agreed that the Israelis could remain west of the strategic Sinai passes. Sadat told Kissinger that thirty tanks east of the canal would be sufficient, one-tenth the number in Dayan's original proposal. However, Sadat was not prepared to accept nonbelligerency with Israel or a formal obligation to open the Suez Canal. Sadat did not raise the Palestinian issue during these disengagement discussions. The Israelis dropped their insistence that a nonbelligerency understanding be included in the agreement.

On January 14, 1974, various meetings took place in Aswan between Kissinger, Sadat, and their advisers involving final discussion of the disengagement agreement. Sadat left formulation of the agreement's details to his military and political advisers. The next morning, Sadat had a private meeting with Kissinger to review Israel's disengagement plan. To Kissinger's surprise, Sadat did not haggle with him about the plan's details and, at one point in this session, requested that they be joined by their respective aides. When Sadat phoned Fahmy to tell him that there would be a meeting of both delegations, the negotiations were promptly institutionalized. Sadat wanted their presence, not for their input, but to have them "validate" the agreement. After hearing Kissinger's rendition of the Israeli disengagement scheme, the Egyptians "grew frosty." Kissinger then submitted a U.S. proposal, which became the outline for the first disengagement agreement.[11] At these meetings, Sadat had Kissinger deliver the "compromising" news to a conjoint meeting of the American and Egyptian delegations. With Kissinger as his messenger, Sadat avoided any discussion of his own decisions and left the impression that Egypt had no choice but to accept the American proposals.

Sadat, likewise, maneuvered around political and military advisers who opposed portions of the agreement. Essentially, Sadat accepted Dayan's proposal, presented as an American plan, for the depth of the buffer zones between the armies and the prescribed limitations on the number of troops, tanks, and missiles in the limited force zones.[12] Prior to his arrival in Aswan to participate in the talks, Sadat had not informed el-Gamasy of any prior agreement between him and Kissinger.[13] When he was suddenly told of the Israeli arms limitations, el-Gamasy considered them outrageous. After Sadat adjourned the session, Sadat and Kissinger continued talking privately until early afternoon. At the end of their meeting, Sadat summoned el-Gamasy to tell him that "Dr. Kissinger and I have agreed on how to proceed to an agreement. *You*, el-Gamasy, will sign it."[14] When Kissinger and Sadat rejoined their colleagues, two documents were prepared: one was to be signed at Kilometer 101, and the other was an American proposal to specify some of the force and arms limitations. After a four-hour meeting where the delegations hammered out details, Kissinger flew off to Israel the same evening. There, too, he negotiated the details with Israeli leaders on the disposition of Egyptian and Israeli troops and their numbers in relation to the disengagement lines that were to separate the forces. In addition to the disengagement agreement itself, Kissinger provided to each side letters of understanding and assurances about the agreement and future arms procurement. Kissinger continued the precedent set for Israel prior to the holding of the Geneva Conference a month earlier, providing assurances to and guarantees for Egyptians and the Israelis alike to ensure more discussions through Washington than with each other.

Kissinger returned to Aswan on January 16 and saw Sadat that same afternoon. In the early evening, Sadat reviewed with el-Gamasy and Fahmy all the final texts of the agreement. El-Gamasy reacted angrily. He wanted three hundred Egyptian tanks on the east side of the canal, but Sadat had agreed to between twenty-nine and thirty. "Impossible. No," said el-Gamasy. "This is Egyptian land conquered by the Egyptian forces, with the price of blood, of sacrifice. How can I withdraw my army like this? I can't defend that in front of my troops. I cannot, as chief of staff of the armed forces, justify it to our forces. I don't accept that."[15] In a very emotional response and with tears in his eyes, el-Gamasy excused himself from the tent where the meeting with Kissinger was being held.[16] When el-Gamasy returned to the meeting, he apologized to those in attendance by explaining that he was a military man, that his duty was to obey his political superiors, and that it would not be easy for him to face the highly motivated Egyptian military leadership. Then Fahmy met with Kissinger separately from Sadat and took it upon himself to renegotiate the disengagement terms upon which Sadat, Kissinger, and the Israelis had agreed. Kissinger was not moved. After a while, a phone call came from Sadat with the inquiry, "Where is Henry?" When he was told that Kissinger was negotiating with the Egyptians, Sadat ended the meeting abruptly by saying, "There [is] nothing to negotiate. Only I negotiate."[17]

Public perceptions that held that Ismail Fahmy, Hafez Ismail, and General el-Gamasy were participants in the final negotiations about the contents of the disengagement agreement were wrong. Sadat did all the key negotiating with Kissinger alone, though Fahmy claimed otherwise to assert his mythical importance. So it was not surprising in January 1974, during the last round of negotiations between Kissinger and Sadat in Aswan, that Fahmy "cooled his heels" in his rest house while Kissinger and Sadat negotiated.[18] Later, during a meeting with Sadat, el-Gamasy stated that it was a proper moment for him to leave his post. He told Sadat, "If the Israelis start an offensive against us now, we will lose what we won in the October War:"[19] El-Gamasy stayed in his post. Sadat refused el-Gamasy's request to reconsider the troop and tank sizes or to call War Minister Ahmad Ismail in Cairo for his opinion. He then charged el-Gamasy with drawing up an appropriate plan for defense of the canal's east side and for monitoring and executing the overall disengagement plan.[20]

On January 17, the Israeli Cabinet approved the disengagement agreement. That same afternoon in Washington, President Nixon announced in a press conference that the agreement would be signed the next day. Sadat told Kissinger, "Never forget, I am making this [disengagement] agreement with the United States, not with Israel."[21] Nonetheless, Hafez Ismail, General el-Gamasy, Fahmy, and other high-ranking Egyptian officials were very upset at Egypt's modest presence in Sinai, which resulted from the agreement, and Egypt's great success in the October War.

On January 18, 1974, in separate ceremonies in Egypt and Israel, Sadat and Meir initialed the disengagement agreement, or what was called "Sinai I." Meir signed in her apartment on a snowy day in Jerusalem. Because of inclement weather, in order to convene the appropriate cabinet members and other officials in Meir's home, the Israeli Army fetched each person in heavy vehicles. To transport the American delegation to Lod Airport, a special train had to be assembled for the Americans and their Israeli escorts. During that train ride, Kissinger told Eban that Israel would have to consider a disengagement agreement with Jordan within six months or otherwise deal with the PLO.[22] An American legal adviser hand-carried the Israeli text from Jerusalem to Tel Aviv in the snow, flew to Cyprus, and then flew to Cairo to deliver the original documents to the American team. On the same day, at Kilometer 101, General el-Gamasy, now the Egyptian Army chief of staff, and his Israeli counterpart, David Elazar, also signed Sinai I.

As part of the disengagement agreement, the United States signed a ten-point memorandum of understanding. Similarly, President Nixon sent letters to both Sadat and Meir detailing the agreed-upon force limitations. In the memorandum with Israel,[23] the United States received assurances from Egypt to complete the disengagement agreement, to open the Suez Canal, and to rehabilitate the cities and towns along its length; the United States promised to oppose the presence of UN observers from the Soviet Union or from other communist countries that did not have diplomatic relations with Israel; the United States promised to perform aerial reconnaissance missions at least fortnightly over the areas covered by the agreement, making photographs available to Israel *and* Egypt; the United States promised "to strongly support" Israel's free passage of shipping through the Bab al-Mandab Straits; the United States would make every effort to be fully responsive on a continuing long-term basis to Israel's military equipment requirements; and, "in case of Egyptian violation" of the agreement, the United States and Israel would consult regarding the necessary reaction. Israel might have signed a disengagement agreement with Egypt, but its core premises were strengthening American monitoring of the negotiating process and deepening American relations with Israel. The quest for an Arab-Israeli peace became a series of Egyptian and Israeli accommodations channeled through Washington.

Sadat's first priority was the size of the territory returned, not the size of Egyptian forces stationed there. He knew that the Israelis would want to determine the issues related to security: the size of the forces; nature and number of weapons apportioned; and depth of the limited force zones. There was no reason to argue over issues about which he knew the Israelis would not compromise. Sadat was interested *only* in the restoration of land to Egyptian sovereignty and could, therefore, afford to let the Israelis determine security matters. As for Egyptian officials, such as Fahmy, el-Gamasy, and Ismail, they considered the agreement a "disgrace to what Egypt had done in the war and were bitterly disappointed" because Sinai I was "so much less than what they thought they ought to get for having gone through the Bar-Lev line, never mind [the survival] of the Third Army."[24] In retrospect, however, Hafez Ismail recalled that this separation of forces agreement "was not bad. It was the implementation of the first part of the [February 1971] Sadat initiative, putting UN troops between the forces and having limited force areas."[25] Similarly, Kissinger noted to Sisco in late January 1974, "Joe, this [disengagement agreement] is essentially what you tried to get in the interim canal negotiations in 1971. . . . [Y]ou got remarkably far without White House support."[26]

Four days after Sinai I was signed, by a vote of seventy-six to thirty-five, Israel's Knesset approved the disengagement agreement. Two days later, a detailed agreement was reached between the Israeli chief of staff, David Elazar, and General el-Gamasy on a timetable for troop withdrawal. After the signing of Sinai I, Egyptian Brigadier General Magdoob and Israeli Major General Herzl Shafir, along with their aides, met in Geneva about the agreement's implementation. Presiding again on behalf of the United Nations was General Siilasvuo. In these negotiations dealing with disengagement procedures (and in the later discussions with the Syrians), the documents, maps, and timetables, with few exceptions, were of Israeli origin, but they were presented as UN papers. (In ensuing military discussions involving Egypt and Syria, the United Nations established the subject agenda, but only after consultation and consensus with the Israelis.) The core of the Sinai I disengagement agreement outlined a series of Israeli withdrawals leading ultimately to their position of a distance of twenty miles from the Suez Canal; a limited Egyptian force occupation of the east side of the canal; and a UN truce force stationed between the two armies. Israel withdrew its forces in stages, beginning on January 15 and ending on January 25, completing a second phase on February 4, and ending a third stage on February 12. Israel's withdrawal from the west bank of the Suez began on February 21 and concluded on March 3. By March 20, Egypt had opened the Suez gulf harbors of Adabiya and Port Ibrahim.

Meanwhile, anger and frustration consumed the Syrian leadership. Assad and other Arab leaders engaged in an overt campaign to discredit Sadat and Egypt. Assad tried to have Arab leaders intervene to prevent Sadat from signing the agreement; a procession of Arab foreign ministers arrived in Aswan to try to stop Sadat. On the day the disengagement agreement was signed, Assad personally called Sadat to plead for postponement of the signing. The Egyptian-Syrian wartime alliance, which cracked during the war, further splintered after the signing of Sinai I.[27] Immediately after the signing, Sadat countered Syrian objections and lobbied hard for other Arab leaders to support the agreement. During a five-day trip to selected Arab capitals, Sadat explained the nature, meaning, and contents of the agreement. At each stop, he reassured his hosts that he was still pursuing a comprehensive, not a separatist, approach in resolving the Arab-Israeli conflict. Before returning to Cairo on January 23, Sadat explained the accord to leaders in Saudi Arabia, Syria, Kuwait, Algiers, and Morocco. Aspiring to sustain and bolster Egypt's public centrality in inter-Arab affairs, Egyptian Foreign Minister Fahmy affirmed the need for a comprehensive solution. At the end of January 1974, he stated that Egypt would sign a peace agreement with Israel if "Israel would withdraw from the land captured in 1967 *and recognize* the national rights of the Palestinians."[28] Fahmy went to Moscow to explain the agreement to Soviet leaders, a clear reaffirmation that Moscow had indeed not been party to the negotiations or to the conclusions reached in Sinai I.

For Americans, their management of disengaging Egyptian and Israeli troops deserved praise, though little came. Far more important and pressing upon Nixon was the American public's dismay with the broadly felt negative effects of the oil embargo and ensuing price rises. On December 23, the day the Geneva Conference ended, OPEC raised the price of oil again; it was already 387 percent higher than it had been before the October War! Whether hyperbole or not, Kissinger called this jump "one of the pivotal events in the history of this century . . . a colossal blow to balance of payments, economic growth, employment, price stability, and social cohesion."[29] Ultimately, the embargo cost the United States

500,000 jobs, more than $10 billion in national production, and induced rampant inflation.[30] Long gas lines evolved into newly devised "self-serve" pumps at gasoline stations, and oil conservation measures were adopted. Meanwhile, a truckers' strike, a national obsession with Nixon's (un)paid taxes, skyrocketing consumer prices, and a severe dip in the Dow Jones average compounded Nixon's troubles with the Watergate crisis. While Sadat traversed the Middle East explaining or justifying his agreement with Israel, Nixon gave a nationwide radio address during which he declared, "Scare stories that the American people will soon be paying a dollar a gallon of gas are just as ridiculous as the stories that say that we will be paying a dollar for a loaf of bread. . . . I can assure you that we will not have to pay them."[31] Nixon was wrong. Kissinger immediately traveled to Syria and Jordan to explain the details of the disengagement agreement; his driving motivation was to thus push along Israeli-Syrian negotiations to obtain relief from the oil embargo. Publicly, Kissinger stated that similar arrangements could be negotiated between Israel and these countries. But, he was less than sincere in his advocacy of an Israeli-Jordanian agreement. Sadat showed no interest either in Jordanian or Palestinian agreements with Israel; there was no demand by either the Egyptians or the Saudis to link suspension of the oil embargo with a political arrangement for the Jordanians; nor, said one American negotiator, was "the lifting of the embargo tied to progress on the Palestinian issue."[32]

Achieving an Israeli-Syrian agreement was most imperative: indeed, it was tied directly both to removing the oil embargo and to helping Sadat. Saudi Arabia's King Feisal lent strong support to Sadat, which meant that only further diplomatic progress would end the oil embargo. Kissinger believed he had a commitment from Feisal that "if we [Washington] got some kind of agreement between Syria and Israel, the Saudis would lift the oil embargo."[33] Sadat wanted and needed at least a semblance of diplomatic movement on the Syrian-Israeli front to fend off repeated criticism that he was duplicitously involved in separate arrangements with Israel. After the disengagement agreement was signed, he said to Kissinger, "Now you have to get a similar disengagement agreement for Syria."[34] Kissinger understood that Sadat could not be perceived as "going it alone" with the Israelis. Sadat even told Kissinger that he would persuade the Arab oil-producing countries to lift the embargo if a disengagement agreement were finalized with the Syrians. Moreover, for Sadat, developing the Egyptian-U.S. relationship was best served by focusing on a Syrian-Israeli deal. Damascus was key to adjusting Sadat's standing within the Arab world. Though he led the effort to retrieve lands from Israel diplomatically and still did not trust Assad, Sadat could not get too far out in front of Assad. Kissinger, therefore, set about to "cover Sadat's rear end with a Syrian-Israeli agreement."[35]

Catalyzing discussion about a Syrian-Israeli agreement was the entangled nature of their respective forces, but there was no immediate crisis facing either Israel or

Syria, like the fate of Egypt's Third Army. The incentives to reach an agreement were that Israel wanted its POWs returned, and Assad was not happy with the Israeli Army's proximity to Damascus. Despite his disadvantaged strategic condition vis-à-vis Israel, Assad used the knowledge that Kissinger needed a Syrian-Israeli agreement to enhance Syrian national interests. Assad was not about to be stampeded into any disengagement agreement; he intended to understand its national and pan-Arab implications, and personally negotiated every detail, using Kissinger's impatience to his advantage all along. Assad used a calendar; Kissinger, a clock. Assad prevailed. On January 27, ten days after Kissinger departed Damascus, sporadic skirmishes, artillery duels, and a Syrian war of attrition was imposed on Israeli troops in the Golan area. Israeli military analysts believed that Assad thus sought sustained Israeli losses in order to force the Meir government to withdraw from the Golan Heights and from all of the territory Syria lost in the June 1967 War.[36]

When Assad visited Saudi Arabia, he sought to use relief from the oil embargo as leverage against the Americans and wanted Riyadh to apply pressure on the United States for Israel's withdrawal from the Golan. During a meeting with King Feisal on February 2, Assad reminded him that "if you lift the embargo, they [the Israelis and the Americans] are not going to do anything with us."[37] But Kissinger did not want Washington perceived as succumbing to political pressure from Arab oil producers; he did not want the Saudis to "have the impression that they had a veto, that he was sort of a puppet at the end of their string. On the other hand, he recognized that one test of the success of his negotiations was getting the oil embargo lifted, [getting] oil production back to normal."[38] Kissinger told Sadat, "I cannot do anything for Syria as long as you have an embargo. I cannot go to Congress and tell them that in spite of the embargo, I shall deliver Israel to Hafez al-Assad."[39] In fact, before the embargo was officially lifted in March and three months before the signing of the Syrian-Israeli disengagement agreement, oil supplies were quietly placed into American stocks, including those for the U.S. military and, especially, for the Sixth Fleet in the Mediterranean. The embargo was lifted because of a U.S. commitment to seek a Syrian-Israeli disengagement accord similar to that between the Egyptians and Israelis. Step-by-step diplomacy developed a definite geographic aspect—one country negotiating with Israel at a time. It seems that neither the Saudis nor other OPEC oil producers truly realized the extraordinary leverage they could have exercised on Washington because of the domestic impact of the oil crisis when it was potentially mixed in with the other paralyzing problems confounding the Nixon presidency.

On February 17, representatives from Egypt, Saudi Arabia, and Syria met with Kissinger in Washington to discuss details for a proposed Syrian-Israeli disengagement agreement. Items on the negotiating agenda included the status of the Israeli prisoners-of-war, lifting the oil embargo, and the future disposition of Israeli forces close to Damascus. After numerous meetings with Middle East envoys in Washington, at the end of the month, Kissinger returned to his diplomatic shuttle. (The United States had no ambassador in the Syrian capital, but was ably represented by a charge d'affaires, Thomas Skotes.) But Assad was not yet prepared to carry on serious negotiations with the secretary of state. Assad still had not developed confidence in Henry Kissinger as an honest broker or mediator, nor was he any less passionately incensed at Sadat's abandonment of Arab solidarity in favor of an Egypt-first policy. Assad was reluctant to negotiate a separate agreement with Israel, despite the presence of Israeli troops on the outskirts of Damascus. In an interview in the *New York Times* in early February 1974, Syrian Foreign Minister Khaddam said that a disengagement by itself, without a *commitment* for total Israeli withdrawal and assurance of Palestinian rights, was not acceptable to Syria under any circumstances. He said that Syria would accept a military disengagement only "as part of a plan for a total Israeli withdrawal from Arab territories taken in the 1967 and 1973 Wars."[40] Though Israeli generals believed that Assad was "eager to put an end to their awkward military position,"[41] Assad did not rush to an agreement. The Syrians effectively created the impression that they were apathetic about an agreement, notwithstanding Israel's close military proximity to Damascus.[42] On February 26, at a meeting between Kissinger and Assad, an outline of a draft Syrian-Israeli disengagement agreement was discussed. Based on what Skotes had told him about the Syrian president's objections, Kissinger referred to Assad's reservations about certain provisions in the agreement. "No," said Assad, sitting perfectly immobile, "Mr. Kissinger, I don't object to these. I object to the whole agreement."[43]

The next day, Kissinger arrived in Israel with a list of Syrian-held Israeli POWs. On March 2, American officials announced that Israel and Syria would send delegations, not merely representatives or envoys, to Washington to continue independent talks with Kissinger aimed at achieving a separation of troops agreement for the Golan Heights.

For the Israelis, Assad was the most enigmatic of Arab leaders.[44] More than any other Arab leader, he was fervidly anti-Zionist, and his regime had treated Israeli prisoners-of-war in the harshest fashion imaginable. In contrast to the Egyptian attitude on the prisoners-of-war issue, the Syrians were more strident and "used their information about Israeli prisoners-of-war as a weapon [against Israel]."[45] Before the June 1967 War, Syria had hurt Israel physically and economically, both by attacking Israel's northern settlements from the Golan Heights and by blocking Israeli access to the Jordan River water sources that substantially originated in Syria. Since Nasser's death in September 1970, Assad had been committed to creating a public image of himself as the philosophical leader of Arab solidarity. For Israel, the Golan Heights, as compared to Sinai, were more strategically valuable; there was less room for physical compromise in reaching a negotiated settlement with Syria. Typifying Israeli establishment views about the Golan Heights, Meir

View from west bank of east bank of the Suez Canal—Egyptian soldiers unloading relief supplies for the Third Army, November 1, 1973. *(Courtesy of Israeli Government Press Office)*

An Israeli supply convoy crossing one of the bridges to the west bank of the Suez Canal, October 19, 1973. *(Courtesy of Israeli Government Press Office)*

Kilometer 101 Talks, November 1973. Second to left of pole: General Yariv; Third to right of pole: General el-Gamasy; UN General Siilasuvo in middle. *(Courtesy of Israel Sun Ltd.)*

Israeli Prime Minister Golda Meir with Defense Minister Dayan and General Hofi speaking to troops on the Golan Heights, November 21, 1973. *(Courtesy of Israeli Government Press Office)*

Egyptians carrying coffins from the Israeli Army vehicles past an Israeli and Egyptian guard of honor during the exchange of bodies on the Baluza-Kantara Road, November 25, 1973. *(Courtesy of Israeli Government Press Office)*

Israeli Chief of Staff Elazar and Egyptian Chief of Staff General el-Gamasy leaving the tent at Kilometer 101 after the signature of the agreement of disengagement and separation of Israeli and Egyptian forces, January 18, 1974. *(Courtesy of Israeli Government Press Office)*

Soviet Ambassador to the United States Anatoly Dobrynin, President Gerald Ford, General Secretary Leonid Brezhnev, Secretary of State Henry Kissinger, and Foreign Minister Andrei Gromyko exchange pleasantries following the arrival of President Ford at the airport in Vladivostok, USSR, November 23, 1974. *(Courtesy of Gerald R. Ford Library)*

Signing of U.S.-Israeli Memorandum of Understanding at the Prime Minister's Office in Jerusalem, September 1, 1975. From left to right: Prime Minister Rabin; Defense Minister Peres; Ambassador Dinitz; Secretary of State Kissinger; Press spokesman Pattir; Foreign Ministry Legal Adviser Rosenne; Foreign Minister Allon; behind Allon, Assistant Secretary of State Atherton and National Security Council member Saunders. *(Courtesy of Israeli Government Press Office)*

President Ford meets with King Hussein of Jordan and Ziad Rifai, Jordanian Prime Minister and Minister of Foreign Affairs, in the Oval Office, March 30, 1976. *(Courtesy of Gerald R. Ford Library)*

President Carter and President Assad waiting to begin press conference at the end of their meeting in Geneva, Switzerland, May 9, 1977. *(Courtesy of Jimmy Carter Library)*

Moshe Dayan listening to President Carter at the conclusion of their meeting at the United Nations, October 4, 1977. Standing behind Dayan: Naftali Lavi, his press officer. *(Courtesy of Jimmy Carter Library)*

Prime Minister Begin welcoming President Sadat with Israeli President Katzir looking on from right, and Mustapha Khalil behind Sadat, at Lod Airport, November 19, 1977. *(Courtesy of Israeli Government Press Office)*

Opening session of political committee talks in Jerusalem, with American, Egyptian, and Israeli delegations headed by foreign ministers. From far left, moving counterclockwise: American delegation—David Korn, Cyrus Vance, Roy Atherton [back to camera], and Michael Sterner; Israeli delegation—Ephraim Evron, Moshe Dayan, Aharon Barak, Meir Rosenne; Egyptian delegation—Dr. Esmat Abdel Meguid, Mohamed Kamel, Dr. Boutros-Ghali, and Dr. Usamah al-Baz, January 16, 1978. *(Courtesy of Israeli Government Press Office)*

Prime Minister Begin and Presidents Carter and Sadat meeting at
Camp David, September 7, 1978. *(Courtesy of Jimmy Carter Library)*

Menachem Begin and Zbigniew Brzezinski playing chess at Camp David,
September 9, 1978. *(Courtesy of Jimmy Carter Library)*

Working session at Camp David, from left to right: Americans—Roy Atherton,
Hal Saunders, Cyrus Vance, Zbigniew Brzezinski, Bill Quandt; Nabil al-Arabi,
Egyptian Foreign Ministry; September 12, 1978. *(Courtesy of Jimmy Carter Library)*

President Sadat, Prime Minister Begin, and President Carter at Camp David signing ceremony, White House, September 17, 1978. *(Courtesy of Jimmy Carter Library)*

Camp David signing ceremony, White House, September 17, 1978.
(Courtesy of Jimmy Carter Library)

Presidents Carter and Sadat conferring during their meeting in Cairo, March 9, 1979.
(Courtesy of Jimmy Carter Library)

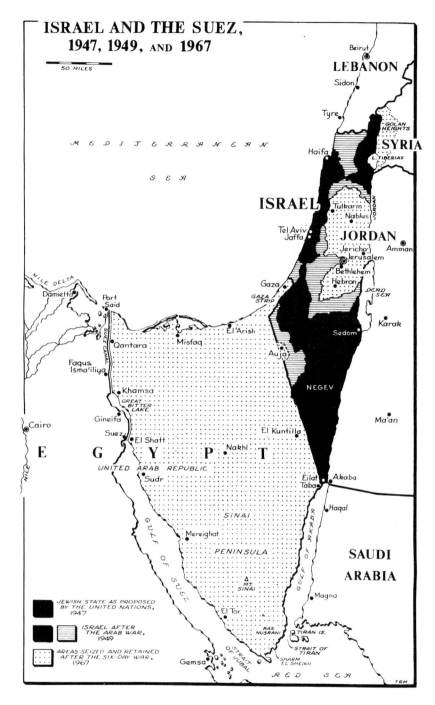

Israel and the Suez, 1947, 1949, and 1967. (From *The Middle East: A History* by Sidney Nettleton Fisher, Copyright © 1959, 1969, 1979 by Sidney Nettleton Fisher, Reprinted by permission of Alfred A. Knopf, Inc.)

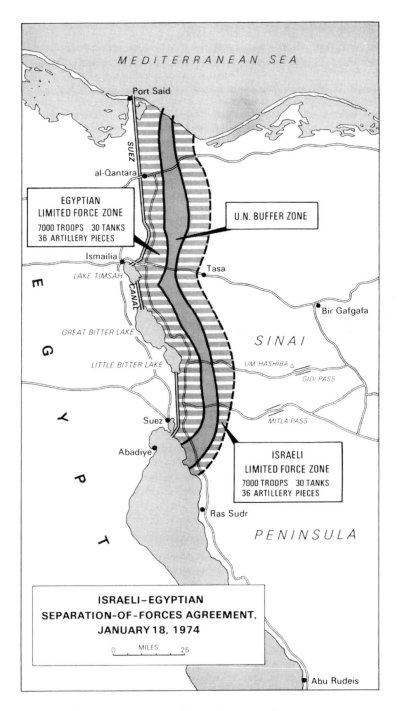

MEDITERRANEAN SEA

Port Said

al-Qantara

EGYPTIAN
LIMITED FORCE ZONE
7000 TROOPS   30 TANKS
36 ARTILLERY PIECES

U.N. BUFFER ZONE

Ismailia

Tasa

LAKE TIMSAH

Bir Gafgafa

GREAT BITTER LAKE

SINAI

LITTLE BITTER LAKE

UM HASHIBA △

GIDI PASS

Suez

MITLA PASS

Abadiye

ISRAELI
LIMITED FORCE ZONE
7000 TROOPS   30 TANKS
36 ARTILLERY PIECES

Ras Sudr

PENINSULA

EGYPT

SUEZ

CANAL

ISRAELI–EGYPTIAN
SEPARATION-OF-FORCES AGREEMENT,
JANUARY 18, 1974

0   MILES   25

Abu Rudeis

Israeli-Egyptian Separation-of-Forces Agreement, January 18, 1974.
(From *A History of Israel* by Howard M. Sachar, Copyright © 1976 by
Howard M. Sachar, Reprinted by permission of Alfred A. Knopf, Inc.)

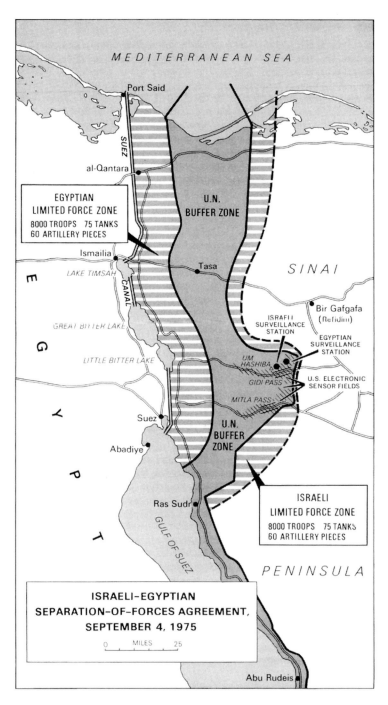

Israeli-Egyptian Separation-of-Forces Agreement, September 4, 1975.
(From *A History of Israel* by Howard M. Sachar, Copyright © 1976 by
Howard M. Sachar, Reprinted by permission of Alfred A. Knopf, Inc.)

recalled, "I have yet to find anybody who believes that the Syrians would not have gone through the Jezreel Valley if we had not been on the Golan Heights before the 1973 War."[46] After the October War, Israel not only had a newfound assertive military presence on the Golan Heights but also it had more settlements established there than in Sinai. By the spring of 1974, Israeli leaders realized that an agreement with Syria was a precondition for another agreement with Egypt. Because Assad needed to receive something substantial in return for negotiations with Israel, an agreement with Assad required a territorial withdrawal. A Golan agreement could not be achieved until Assad was ready, which meant meeting his twin criteria for Israeli military withdrawal: no implication of any Syrian recognition of Israel, but some clear link to Israel's withdrawal from all the occupied territories.[47] The critical point in the negotiations was the Syrian Golan Heights city of Kuneitra, in Israel's control, bereft of population, and abandoned after the June 1967 War. In making concessions to Syria in these negotiations, Israel did not want to imply any eventual return of all of the Golan Heights. Because Syria wanted to be sure that this agreement with Israel could falter, it insisted on biannual renewal of the mandate for the UN force monitoring the agreement.

After the late December 1973 parliamentary elections, Meir finally, on March 10, formed her new government, which lasted only one month. Israel's political leadership was investigated for shortcomings associated with the preparation and prosecution of the war. On April 2, 1974, the Agranat Commission unveiled the contents of its inquiry into the omissions and failures surrounding the conduct of the Israeli Army prior to and during the October 1973 War. Public pressure for their resignations mounted against Meir and Dayan. The Agranat Commission Report questioned the competence of the military intelligence services and the Israeli Army commanders in Sinai, and the military's slow reaction to advance warnings of an enemy offensive. Its conclusions made clear that senior army officers have an inseparable responsibility in the field of security, which the political echelon cannot remove; while the political echelon, though sharing responsibility for decisions made, were not required to resign. Nonetheless, Meir resigned on April 10. Dayan resigned because of the combination of adverse public feeling, Labor Party pressure from Deputy Prime Minister Yigal Allon and Labor Minister Yitzhak Rabin, and what Dayan saw as only partial exoneration by the commission.[48] The Agranat Commission also called for the resignation of the Israeli chief of staff and chief of military intelligence. Two weeks after Meir's resignation, the central committee of the Israeli Labor Party chose Yitzhak Rabin to succeed her as prime minister. On May 28, Rabin announced the formation of his new Cabinet, without Dayan as defense minister. Negotiations for a Syrian-Israeli agreement continued despite Israeli and American domestic political turmoil.

Shuttle diplomacy had two emerging venues: Arab leaders traveling to Washington and Kissinger traveling to capitals in the Middle East. On April 10, Syrian officials met with Kissinger in Washington. The head of Syrian military intelligence, Brigadier General Hikmat Shihabi, was Syria's chief military negotiator, and Salah al-din Tarazi was the head of the political delegation. Shihabi and the Syrian delegation arrived in Washington as scheduled, and four days later, on April 14, Kissinger presented Israeli Ambassador Dinitz with Syria's most recent proposals for troop separation. Two weeks later, Kissinger left Washington for a Middle East trip that lasted until the Syrian-Israeli agreement was signed.

Twice during the next thirty-plus days, Kissinger met with Soviet Foreign Minister Gromyko, once in Geneva on April 28–29 and once in Cyprus on May 4–5. In a joint communiqué issued after the Cyprus meeting, Kissinger and Gromyko favored an early resumption of the "work of the Geneva Conference," but not the Geneva Conference itself. Although the Soviets were consulted, Kissinger cherished orchestrating the diplomacy alone. Because these sensitive negotiations involved more than a political agreement, military advisers on both sides played significant roles in shaping the outcome. During the negotiations, the Americans who traveled with Kissinger sensed that "the Syrians were quite independent of the Soviets, and in fact were disdainful [of them]. At no time did the Syrians press [the United States] to include the Soviets."[49] At one point, Gromyko arrived in Damascus and did not even see Assad. The situation became embarrassing for the Soviets because they had to rubber-stamp the Golan agreement.[50] Though the Russians were trying to share in the spectacle of mediation, they did not play a concrete role as mediator, nor did they know the details of the negotiations.[51]

For members of the American negotiating team, the month-plus shuttle negotiations with Assad were extremely tiring. Although he gained respect for Assad as a truly intelligent and practical person, Kissinger did not cultivate the same closeness with Assad that he did with Sadat. For his part, Assad continued to distrust Kissinger.[52] Each time Kissinger came from Israel to negotiate another issue or narrow another difference, he gave Assad a political precis of the current political mood in Israel. For many members of Kissinger's entourage, "the details of the negotiations which [he] had carried around in his head"[53] were not known until Kissinger spoke with Assad. On both the macro- and microlevels of political negotiations, Kissinger and Assad assessed one another through sophisticated discourse. One on one, with minimal participation by advisers, they discussed minute details about the disposition of the Golan Heights: each surrounding hill; map coordinates; the strategic high ground west of Kuneitra; the frequency and location of observation points; and the number of tanks and personnel permissible in various demilitarized zones. In comparison to Egyptian-Israeli negotiations over Sinai and the Suez Canal area, the Golan discussions were far more difficult. From an American perspective, there was greater incentive to assure fulfillment of Sadat's requests because Washington was entering a new strategic and, hopefully, long-term relationship with Egypt. By contrast, Washington's motivations with Syria were more tactical. Although Syria did not want warm relations with Washington, neither did it want Moscow to become too complacent or overconfident about Syrian-Soviet relations. In dealing with Assad, Washington altered the style that had been used with Sadat. To Assad, every detail personally mattered, every rock was important.[54] In order to obtain an agreement, Kissinger adapted to Assad's more tedious negotiating style. Said Rodman:

> The [negotiating] relationship with Syria was . . . to free up another step with Egypt. We understood then that Sadat was something phenomenal, and that this could be the beginning of something important with Egypt, but Henry was totally honest. He never pretended that there were no risks with the Syrians. He said, "I don't trust the Syrians." This is not an agreement that has anything to do with trust or confidence in some wonderful political evolution with Syria. It's tactical. It's a marriage of convenience. You will not trust each other afterwards, but it can be done. And with Egypt, it's something different.[55]

Assad wanted to be sure that this agreement was viewed only as a step toward a comprehensive peace and as neither a separate agreement nor a step toward any political recognition of Israel. To this end an effort was made to use terms and language similar to the Egyptian-Israeli disengagement agreement. It was critical for him that every definition of the disengagement include a symbolic recovery of territory taken in the June 1967 War. Assad had wanted all of the Golan returned; he had to settle "for meters and essentially the city of Kuneitra."[56] But Kuneitra's return to Syrian control was nevertheless extremely important to Assad. During the negotiations, Assad repeatedly mentioned the Palestinian issue but not a simultaneous Jordanian-Israeli disengagement arrangement. Assad's method for handling the Jordanian front was to implore Kissinger to deal with the Palestinian issue. First and foremost, Assad wanted the protection of Syrian national interests. From a strategic viewpoint, he wanted Israel's removal from artillery range of the distant suburbs of Damascus; the United States was singularly capable of delivering that reality. "Assad made the U.S. sweat for thirty-four days, acting as if he didn't care and keeping the agreement out of reach. He would make us wait until the last minute . . . make us sweat until the end of a six-hour meeting, and then he'd say, 'Okay, I'll agree to that.'"[57] Joe Sisco remembered it this way:

> About the 23rd or 24th day, all of us were saying, "Henry, we can't keep flying . . . between Damascus and Jerusalem every day. You've been away as secretary of state, it's over twenty days." And so, I remember myself suggesting to him that I write out a short sentence which said, I'm sorry, in effect, we can't really come to an agreement, and we are going to suspend the talks. And, I

actually gave that to Henry in my long hand, and I said, "Henry, at the key point, hand it to Assad," because this guy personified brinkmanship. So, we went through it another two, three, four hours, and Henry, in effect, says, "Well, I guess we can't get any further, and I was thinking of making a statement along these lines." And Assad said, "Just a minute," and he gave us a few more feet right at the end of that particular meeting. . . . This is literally the way it happened, and we went back to Jerusalem for another round.[58]

Recalling the tones of the Jerusalem-Damascus shuttle, Golda Meir said, "Kissinger found it difficult to move a lot. Assad would say another hundred meters, and we would say no. Kissinger would come back and say twenty meters, and we would say ten. Finally, Dr. Kissinger said to me, 'I know exactly what my future will be, I shall be a peddler of notions.'"[59] The sheer force of Assad's will, his ability to retain a veto over progress, and his status as an uncharted enigma provided the Syrian president with enormous prestige and influence over the negotiating process. Peter Rodman described Assad's tactic as "to flaunt his ability to block"[60] negotiations or an agreement.

As the frequency and intensity of Kissinger's diplomatic effort increased, there was an escalation in Arab-Israeli violence. During the last month of the negotiations, the level of fighting between Israel and Syria increased dramatically; however, the new artillery exchanges with Israel did not affect Israel's willingness to reach an agreement with Syria. Whether by coincidence or in coordination with Syria, the Damascus-based Palestinian guerrilla organization, the Popular Democratic Front for the Liberation of Palestine, attacked an Israeli schoolhouse at Maalot in northern Israel. The attack resulted in the death of sixteen Israeli schoolchildren and the wounding of more than seventy others. Israeli war planes responded by bombing Palestinian refugee camps and suspected terrorist hideouts in Lebanon, where more than 50 were reported killed and 170 injured. As the signing of a Syrian-Israeli agreement seemed more likely, the Soviet media grumpily emphasized "the negative value of partial solutions and the need to return to Geneva."[61] Finally, the Syrian-Israeli separation of forces agreement was signed on May 31, 1974, within days of the Rabin government taking office. Though Meir and Nixon would resign within four months of each other, Rabin's and Kissinger's previous contact sustained a working, if not always amicable, U.S.-Israeli relationship.

Present at the signing of the Syrian-Israeli agreement were personnel from the Israeli and Syrian military and Foreign Ministries, and representatives from the United Nations, the United States, and the Soviet Union. According to Israeli Foreign Ministry officials, the agreement was not signed by the Syrian officers who were present in Geneva. Instead, it was signed by Egyptian General Magdoob, who was given authority by Damascus to initial the agreement in the context of the framework of the Egyptian-Israeli military committee of the Geneva Conference.[62] Magdoob's experience in the Sinai I negotiations helped him immeasurably in understanding what the Israelis wanted in terms of security assurances. According to Shafir and Rosenne, the Syrians were very "closed, professional, with a lot of pride, and not willing to engage in side talks with the Israelis."[63] There were numerous interruptions in the discussions about the agreement's implementation because all issues were tediously referred to Damascus for final resolution. The agreement itself called for a disengagement of Syrian and Israeli forces and a complete withdrawal of Israeli forces from the area occupied in the October 1973 War and a small portion of land occupied in the June 1967 War, including Kuneitra. A buffer zone, policed by the United Nations, was established in the area of separation. To supervise the cease-fire and to verify inspections of the limitations on armaments and forces, the United Nations established the Defense Observation Forces (UNDOF), comprised of roughly 1,200 soldiers and 90 observers. Israeli officials assert that the Syrians rarely kept a full complement of soldiers in the limited force zones and never violated the agreement.[64] At the request of the Syrians, a portion of the agreement, which dealt with the number of troops and forces permitted on the Golan Heights, was kept secret and was not published.[65] Implementation of the negotiations was managed by American officials with the United Nations present but without any Soviet diplomatic representation. A two-week time limit was set to fulfill the agreement; when that lapsed, Syrian, Israeli, and American participants actually disconnected the Swiss clock to extend the deadline. Although the agreement did not immediately halt Syrian and Israeli artillery exchanges, Assad had reportedly, privately, but not in writing, assured Israel that Syria would not allow Palestinian guerrillas to infiltrate into Israel through Syria.[66] Despite the artillery exchanges, Syria and Israel swapped prisoners-of-war a week after the agreement was signed. By June 14, Israel evacuated approximately one-third of the Golan salient captured during the October 1973 War.

Though a modest arrangement, the Syrian-Israeli disengagement agreement was significant for several international, regional, and local reasons. As the second Arab belligerent of the October 1973 War, Syria entered into a nonpolitical agreement with Israel. The United States again affirmed its role as the primary mediator in Arab-Israeli negotiations, whereas both the United Nations and Moscow were relegated to observer or witness status in the negotiations. And as it had done with the Egyptian-Israeli agreement the previous January, the U.S. flew reconnaissance flights to monitor the implementation of the agreement. As a result of the negotiations, full U.S.-Syrian diplomatic relations were restored. Damascus accepted the agreement because Syria received all of the territory it lost in the October 1973 War and a small segment of land lost in the June 1967 War. Having reluctantly had this agreement signed on its behalf, Damascus still did not recognize Israeli legitimacy, thus Syria retained its commitment to restore a measure of unity and solidarity to the Arab front, already passionately splintered by the conduct and out-come of the October 1973 War. In the negotiations, Damascus asserted its rele-vance as an essential focus in any Arab-Israeli negotiation effort. To some degree, this agreement offset the previously intense diplomatic concentration on what appeared to be exclusively Egyptian-Israeli negotiations. For a change, the spotlight was not on Sadat, but on Assad. For Egyptian President Sadat, this agreement gave him credibility with the Saudis and other oil producers, whom he had lobbied to remove the oil embargo. They agreed to do so if a Syrian-Israeli agreement would eventuate in Israeli territorial withdrawal. The Syrian-Israeli agreement deflected some Arab criticism that Egypt was pursuing a separate course with Israel. As for the negotiating process, it was not held hostage or postponed because the Ameri-can presidency was ensnared by the Watergate affair. It was, as Kissinger remarked, "the last major achievement of the Nixon administration."[67] Likewise, negotiations were not delayed because of the political leadership changes taking place in Israel. Though there was the public assignment of culpability for the Israeli government's management of the war, Israeli strategic interest demanded signing such an agree-ment with the Syrians. Intense Syrian-Israeli negotiations that took place while Israel was forming a new government were handled by Dayan, who already was under intense public pressure to leave office. It was a great achievement for Dayan as he left office, especially as Rabin found the agreement acceptable. Assad could not help notice that there would be a measure of continuity in commitment to this agreement by the new Israeli leadership. Finally, neither Assad nor Sadat had made negotiating their agreements or reaching them with Israel contingent on resolving the Palestinian component of the conflict.

In the four-month interval between the signing of the two disengagement agreements, under the congressional and media scrutiny of the Watergate cover-up, the political noose around Nixon's neck tightened. Gasping for relief, he dis-suaded a dejected Kissinger from giving up during his Jerusalem-Damascus shuttle; Nixon wanted this foreign policy success so he could gain a respite from Watergate, bask in a presidential visit to the Middle East, and receive a measure of reflected glory.[68] As much as Nixon was vilified by the media, Kissinger was praised for his completion of the Syrian-Israeli agreement. And then Kissinger was accused in the American press of wiretapping NSC staffers, which the secretary refuted. Nixon refused to defend Kissinger publicly. On the eve of his last visit abroad as president, Nixon was virtually not on speaking terms with Kissinger. Not an insignificant amount of jealousy existed between them. When Kissinger threatened to resign unless his name was cleared from the wiretap controversy, American and world politicians extolled his successes and virtues as much as they attacked Nixon's.

On June 10, Nixon headed for the Middle East to visit Egypt, Saudi Arabia, Syria, Israel, and Jordan, seeking to divert attention away from his besieged presi-dency. As Nixon traveled through the Middle East, tapes of his White House conversations were heard by the House Judiciary Committee. During his trip, Nixon was suffering from phlebitis, one leg swollen almost double its normal size. American embassy officials in the Middle East who were responsible for planning Nixon's trip found it hectic, chaotic, and lacking cohesion. Tensions between Nixon and Kissinger percolated down to their respective advisers in planning the trip's logistics. How events were planned would depict Nixon's "usurpation" of Kissinger's accomplishments of the previous half year. It seems that at each stop, or at least in Egypt, Israel, and Syria, in private meetings, Nixon spoke or behaved in a manner that surprised either his hosts or American officials. On the trip, Kissinger was reminded that despite his diplomatic successes, he was not the president. But Kissinger knew Nixon's days were numbered; he had already agreed to stay on with Ford as secretary of state. Sadat turned out huge crowds to greet the first American president to visit Egypt. In their private discussions and public remarks, among other points, Sadat insisted on a "political solution to the Palestinian problem," one that met "their national aspirations." Nixon and Sadat took a train from Cairo to Alexandria, where the public adulation delighted Nixon. He promised to provide Egypt with additional economic aid, suggested Egypt could purchase a nuclear reactor for energy production, promised to restore the international frontier as the Egyptian-Israeli border, and offered to bring the Palestinians into the negotiations at an early date.[69] "What is needed," Nixon reportedly said, "is the step-by-step approach, not because we want to go slow, but because we want to get there."[70] When Sadat was asked if he foresaw direct discussions with Israel, he replied, "No, not at all," then after a pause he added, "Not yet."[71]

Sadat stated his preferences, including not opening the Palestinian drama which would not mesh with his timetable, for further negotiations known to Kissinger. Rather than pursuing a disengagement agreement with Jordan, Sadat wanted to give priority to the Egyptian front and not defer his own claim to another slice of the Sinai; the process of Jordanian disengagement involved too many pitfalls. Sadat knew that the new Rabin government, with only a one-vote majority in Parliament, could not discuss the West Bank without going to new elections and, above all, would not negotiate with the PLO. Kissinger understood Sadat's attitudes toward further negotiations, but perhaps did not see Sadat's planned intention to bolt the door on any Israeli-Jordanian and Israeli-Palestinian negotiations by his advocacy later in the fall of the PLO as the sole legitimate representative of the Palestinian people. In concluding the visit to Egypt, a protocol was signed by the two presidents calling for cooperation and exchanges in scientific and cultural fields, in pursuit of Middle East peace, and in efforts to reopen the Suez Canal. Nixon's next stops were in Saudi Arabia, Israel, Syria, and Jordan.

In Damascus on June 15, Nixon met with Assad for several hours; the following day Washington restored diplomatic relations with Damascus. At that meeting, Nixon indicated a desire to see the Geneva Conference reconvened as early as

September. From the Syrian perspective, a conference venue for additional agreements with Israel would provide a structure for controlling Sadat's propensity for independent diplomacy. But a definite date for a conference was not set immediately because of differences regarding the date and procedures for a conference and for Palestinian representation. Syria wanted a conference immediately after May 1974 and wanted full and immediate implementation of UNSC Resolutions 242 and 338. Israel wanted to wait at least until September, since the new government under Yitzhak Rabin had recently been formed; Egypt preferred to wait until after the Arab Summit in the fall "so as to give the Arab countries time to agree on future steps."[72]

At their meeting, Assad cross-examined the president about the next stage in negotiations: How would "step-by-step" be defined? How did the United States see the final borders of Israel? And how synchronized should Israeli withdrawal be expected from Sinai and Golan? Syria wanted Arab coordination in planning future Israeli withdrawals, and Damascus did not want any more separate or unilateral acts similar to the Egyptian-Israeli agreement. Without revealing the actual contents of the Nixon-Assad discussions, Kissinger recalled in his memoirs, "Assad . . . would not have been far off the mark if he distilled from the conversation the idea that Nixon, in his own elliptical way, was agreeing to total Israeli withdrawal from the Golan."[73] Though apparently accurate, Kissinger's rendition was nonetheless diluted. After Assad asked Nixon three or four times about America's position on the future of the Golan Heights, Nixon gave a "stark commitment" for full Israeli withdrawal from all the occupied Arab territories, including the Golan Heights. According to Khaddam, Nixon stated clearly, "The United States of America will never agree to allowing Israel to annex any of the occupied territories. Israel should withdraw from all the occupied territories," at which point Kissinger then entered the conversation in a gross manner and said, "You are an elected president by the people and you will be held responsible."[74] Nevertheless, the Syrian leadership heard a highly valued commitment from an American president. Did it embolden Syrians to believe that, if they remained steadfast in their quest to have all of the territories returned, they would ultimately triumph? Assad was astonished and delighted to hear that the purpose of step-by-step diplomacy was to persuade the Israelis to pull back until they returned to previous borders.[75] After hearing President Nixon's promise just weeks after the signing of the Syrian-Israeli agreement, President Assad could only be buoyed by the possibility that Washington would pressure Israel. According to Khaddam, Nixon's remarks led Assad to conclude that Nixon's political demise several months later was due, at least partially, to his commitment to see Israel withdraw from all the occupied territories. Even if Watergate was ultimately responsible for Nixon's resignation, it is important to note that, however obtuse the logic, the Syrian leadership believed that American presidents would directly suffer their loss of office because of the commitments they made in opposing Israeli policies.[76]

Though this was the first visit by an American president to Israel, by the time

Nixon arrived there, his remarks in Arab countries and with Arab leaders made his reception chilly. Nixon recalled, "Our reception in Israel, although warm by ordinary standards, was the most restrained of the trip."[77] In addition, on his ride from the airport he saw signs that reminded him of what he had left at home: "You Can't Run from Justice," "Welcome President Ford," and "We are all Jew Boys" (a reference to remarks that were reported to be on the White House tapes).[78] The Israeli government wanted at least symmetrical treatment from Washington but did not want to hasten the pace of the negotiations. If Egypt was to receive nuclear reactors, Jerusalem wanted them too, and so Nixon promised them to Rabin. Nixon urged Rabin to deal with Jordan's King Hussein now, rather than later with Arafat's PLO.[79] At an assembled Israeli Cabinet meeting, when discussing a way to deal with terrorists, Nixon leaped out of his seat and fired an imaginary submachine gun at his startled listeners. Then there was the "hat" incident: stopping at Yad Vashem to pay tribute to the memory of the six million Jews who died in the Holocaust was an almost obligatory stop for every politician or dignitary who visited Israel, yet Nixon absolutely did not want to visit the Yad Vashem memorial. The American DCM told the White House that, in effect, if Nixon did not visit Yad Vashem, then the prospects for the Israelis canceling his visit were real. When he arrived in Israel, Nixon had not been told that he would be visiting the memorial. He arrived at the memorial, a hat (*kippa*) was put on his head, as is custom, and he was ushered inside. Later Nixon's reticence to visit Yad Vashem was explained: it was not that Nixon did not want to visit the memorial but that he "was so far gone; he was paranoid about wearing a hat because he had recalled that in his campaign against Kennedy [in 1960], a picture was taken of him wearing a hat and he blamed that picture as contributing to his election defeat, and after that he was never going to wear another hat."[80]

In their private talks, Rabin negotiated an arms package for Israel, and Nixon worked to secure an Israeli commitment to further negotiations with the Arabs. The substance of this Nixon-Rabin exchange was historic: Israel learned that its relationship with the United States was changing and would essentially not be the same as it once was; the United States learned, in emphatic terms, that peace for Israel required security and reciprocity. Nixon said that "the days when Israel felt very comfortable with a relationship . . . where we supported Israel . . . were going to be Israel's best friend . . . where your immediate warlike neighbors, Syria and Egypt, were considered enemies of the United States, those days [are over]. I don't think that's a policy. I don't think it is viable for the future . . . time will run out."[81] Nixon openly acknowledged to Israeli leaders that Sadat's opening to the United States had significantly changed the Israeli-U.S. relationship. Rabin outlined Israel's outlook. In the context of the moment, his views seemed reasonable, but his words could have been uttered exactly by Israeli Prime Minister Benjamin Netanyahu twenty-two years later. According to Kissinger's recollection, Rabin told Nixon,

"Peace had to be related to security. . . . [I]t could not consist simply of a series of Israeli withdrawals; there had to be reciprocity; Israel would not tolerate terrorist attacks; it was essential that Israel's strength be maintained."[82] Nixon's trip ended in Amman, with the Jordanians out of sorts, in part because Kissinger chose to return to the semiannual meeting of NATO foreign ministers in Ottawa, and as Kissinger would acknowledge, "no decisions were required in Amman." They had been relegated to a secondary role.[83]

When Kissinger traveled to Amman in January 1974 after Sinai I was signed, the Jordanians presented him with a draft of a Jordanian-Israeli disengagement agreement to give to the Israelis. The proposal called for an Israeli withdrawal ten kilometers west of the Jordan River, to the Judean and Samarian foothills. When Kissinger returned to Washington from Israel, he said that they had rejected the Jordanian proposal and had put forth a counterproposal: "The Israelis proposed to return ninety-five percent of the population and ninety percent of the land, but wanted to retain their presence along the Jordan River and in East Jerusalem."[84] The Israelis saw this as a proposal for a final peace treaty. Rifa'i contests Quandt's assertion that no Jordanian-Israeli agreement was negotiated in early 1974 because a disengagement accord would have been a political step that King Hussein was not prepared to make. To the contrary, Rifa'i recalled, "We did our best to get a disengagement agreement. We pressured Kissinger as much as we could. The Israelis refused. It was not because we were not prepared."[85] King Hussein bears some of the responsibility for not acquiescing to a partial withdrawal as an interim agreement, especially his insistence that Israel's first withdrawal be from the Jordan River. By summer, when Yitzhak Rabin was prime minister, neither he, Defense Minister Shimon Peres, nor Foreign Minister Yigal Allon were willing to discuss seriously with the rest of their government an agreement with Jordan based initially on Israel's withdrawal from the river. Kissinger kept the Israelis thinking about an agreement with Jordan. But he did not force it upon them. As for the king, Quandt recalled that Hussein wanted treatment equal to Sadat's. "I'm supposed to be your closest friend. You've got a disengagement here with the Egyptians. . . . [H]ow am I going to look as your closest friend without comparable treatment . . . for anything much less than ninety-nine percent of the territory. . . . I've got real problems, because I'm going to be attacked for what I didn't get, not praised for what I did get."[86] The same motivation—fear of severe criticism for obtaining less than the Palestinians wanted—caused King Hussein, in July 1988, to disengage politically from the West Bank. Throughout 1974, Washington's entertainment of a Jordanian-Israeli agreement was sincere. But it was a lukewarm priority as compared to the prinicipal priorities given earlier to Sadat and then focused on Assad.[87] Immediately after the Syrian-Israeli agreement was signed in May, Jordan wanted a disengagement agreement reached with Israel before any international conference was held and certainly before an Arab Summit again supported the PLO's negotiating privileges.[88]

Israel had a long history of negotiating and meeting secretly with Jordan's leaders, including the king's visit to Meir just prior to the 1973 War. All during 1974, these regular secret talks continued. They were known as "Operation Lift," with minutes of these meetings routinely sent to Kissinger, both from Jordanian and Israeli sources. After Rabin's assumption as prime minister, these talks included Allon, Peres, the prime minister, and often Amos Eiran, the director-general of Rabin's office. Both King Hussein and Ziad al-Rifa'i, whether or not the latter held official office, represented the Jordanian side. Eiran described Rifa'i as "straightforward, eloquent, and always more holier than the pope" [meaning King Hussein]. Inevitably in explaining Jordan's positions in these meetings, the king spoke, sometimes for a prolonged period of time, usually sounding mild, accommodating, as the "good cop," while al-Rifa'i was the "bad cop" in criticizing Israel and its policies. It was routine for the Israeli team to meet prior to each session of these secret talks in order to coordinate their statements and replies.[89] From these meetings, Rabin and King Hussein developed a respect and fondness for one another, and a trust that would carry them through two decades, until Jordan and Israel signed their peace treaty in October 1994. When Begin took office in June 1977, he was briefed and provided the protocols of these secret meetings; he was not unaware that they had occurred.[90]

Earlier in June, the 12th Palestinian National Council (PNC) meeting took place in Cairo, where the PLO accepted the notion of a "phased political program and the establishment of a national authority on any territory liberated" from Israel. Since the October 1973 War, the PLO leadership, particularly those in Arafat's al-Fatah organization, were engaged in internal debate about how the new realities of diplomacy should affect them. Once an agreement was made between Syria and Israel, the PLO could indicate without sacrificing its long-term goals, an intent to be part of a diplomatic process, but only under certain defined conditions. The PNC resolutions in Cairo granted the PLO leadership the right to participate in Geneva-type peace talks if the Palestine question were regarded as a national cause, as long as they did not betray their strategic goal of liberating all of Palestine. The PLO would be permitted to participate in the conference if the invitation recognized the PLO as the "sole representative of the Palestinians."[91] But the issue of Palestinian representation continued to plague efforts to reconvene the Geneva Conference in pursuit of a preferred comprehensive settlement. For the remainder of 1974, while seeking to sustain a reduction of Soviet influence in the Middle East, Washington made several pro forma public gestures aimed at reconvening Geneva, yet clearly rewarded countries individually for accepting the road toward separate negotiations. In the Soviet-U.S. communiqué at the end of President Nixon's visit to Moscow on July 3, 1974, the United States and the Soviet Union were described as cochairmen of the Geneva Peace Conference on the Middle East: "The USA and the U.S.S.R. consider it important that the conference resume its work as soon as possible, with the question of other participants from the Middle

East area to be discussed at the conference. Both sides see the main purpose of the Geneva peace conference, the achievement of which they will promote in every way, as the establishment of a just and stable peace in the Middle East."[92]

No formulas were agreed on by the superpowers for Palestinian participation or representation at a conference. Neither was there consensus between Jordan and the PLO, nor was Sadat motivated to bridge the gap between them on this seemingly insoluble issue. Thus, because both Israel and Jordan wanted to deny the PLO access to the negotiating process and because the PLO was not yet prepared to negotiate with Israel, the PLO could do little more than reassert its status within inter-Arab politics. In the absence of progress on the Palestinian representation issue, Kissinger had the continued incentive to seek bilateral arrangements with Egypt, Israel, and Jordan. It was understood that another substantial sum of foreign assistance would be available in "assisting those countries in the areas which have accepted that goal [of a negotiated settlement],"[93] which presumably meant possible aid to Syria.

Given competing interests within the Arab world and domestic stumbling blocks within Israel, creating a Jordanian-Israeli agreement was next to impossible. Though Kissinger and Sadat agreed in the summer of 1974 that there should be a Jordanian-Israeli accord for the West Bank, the issue that separated Washington and Cairo was timing. Sadat argued that, since the first Egyptian-Israeli agreement was so modest and it had caused him domestic problems, he needed another Sinai agreement before a Jordanian-Israeli agreement. Aligning PLO-Jordanian interests was next to impossible also. Both wanted to control any territory relinquished by Israel as a consequence of future negotiations. To ensure the demographic integrity of his kingdom, King Hussein could not relinquish to the PLO any political rights to represent Palestinians living in Jordan.

During the late spring of 1974, Israeli Foreign Minister Allon was again talking about implementation of his plan for territorial compromise with Jordan over the West Bank. Submitted to several Israeli Cabinets for approval but not officially endorsed, the Allon Plan was initially presented in July 1967. The plan's core assumptions included defensible borders as defined by Israel, a return of the densely populated areas to a "Jordanian-Palestinian state" with Israel retaining control of the Jordan Rift Valley and mountain ridges to the west from Nablus to Hebron. Under the plan, Israel would assert and sustain military presence over the West Bank up to the Jordan River, the West Bank would be demilitarized, the Palestinians would be provided self-administration in an autonomous or semiautonomous region, and Israel would remain in full control over a united Jerusalem, with perhaps a Jordanian status in the Muslim quarter of the Old City. Israeli leaders then ruled out the possibility of incorporating the West Bank Palestinian population into a greater Israel because it would have dramatically changed the state's Jewish demographic orientation. When the Allon Plan was officially offered to the king in cordial and secret talks in September 1968, Hussein rejected it because he felt it "infringed on Jordanian sovereignty."[94] Nonetheless, the Allon Plan served as a basis for the Labor Party election platforms in 1974, 1977, 1981, 1984, and 1987. The concept of providing autonomy or self-administration for the Palestinians was offered by Israeli Prime Minister Begin to Sadat in December 1977 and enshrined in both the September 1978 Camp David and the September 1993 Oslo Accords.

By the spring of 1974, discussions focused on implementing an amended version of Allon's plan by first returning Jericho to Jordan, with Israel retaining a security strip along the Jordan River. Hussein was willing to accept a partial Israeli withdrawal as part of a total withdrawal, first from a small salient beginning on the Jordan River and then farther inland. The Israelis were not interested in either total withdrawal from the West Bank nor in returning the strip of settlements along the Jordan River, both of which were integral to Hussein's plan that dictated an Israeli withdrawal to begin from the river. Kissinger believed the Israelis would not accept this proposal. According to Quandt, "The thing that mattered to [Hussein] was to get the Israelis pulling back from the river. He really meant it. He wanted to demonstrate that he could get something that mattered, and what he was being offered was the chance to police the West Bank under Israeli supervision, because they made it very clear that there would be a little narrow neck allowing Jordan entree to the West Bank."[95]

Later in the spring and summer of 1974, Sadat made only a perfunctory effort to achieve Jordanian-PLO coordination so that a Geneva Conference could be reconvened. The Egyptian-Jordanian communiqué issued in Alexandria in July 1974 stated that "both sides see eye to eye on the need to include the PLO at an appropriate time, as an independent delegation to the Geneva Conference, in order to stress the [Palestinians'] right to self-determination."[96] During Hussein's visit to Washington in August, he pressed for an Israeli-Jordanian disengagement agreement and repeated his threat to boycott a reconvened Geneva Middle East Peace Conference until at least a partial withdrawal from the West Bank had been achieved.[97] In mid-August, the Israeli Parliament rejected an opposition Likud Party motion to have a national referendum on the future of the West Bank. Diplomats who worked in the Israeli Foreign Ministry at the time described Israeli Prime Minister Rabin as "timid [and] lacking self-confidence, courage, and vision" in seeking an agreement with Hussein. Most all of those bureaucrats and civil servants had no clue how extensive the secret Jordanian-Israeli contacts were at the time, or what ideas were bandied about in these meetings. Rabin resisted an agreement with King Hussein because it would have necessitated either Israeli withdrawal from part or all of the West Bank and opening the sensitive Jerusalem issue to public debate, or going to new parliamentary elections to elicit endorsement for such an agreement. None of the options were palatable for Rabin.

Less than a month after Nixon resigned, Hussein had secret talks with Yigal Allon, Shimon Peres, and Yitzhak Rabin near Tel Aviv on August 29, 1974, where he rejected an Israeli proposal for their return of a small area around Jericho as part of a Jordanian-Israeli interim ageement. In September, Jordan again announced that it was "freezing all activities . . . which stem from Jordan's consent to participate in the . . . Geneva Conference."[98] Two issues were problematic for Hussein: he could not be assured of representing the Palestinians even resident in his kingdom, and Israel's territorial withdrawal offer was too little in proportion to the concession of political recognition Israel required. Jordan's demand for initial withdrawal was in the context of full Israeli withdrawal from the West Bank and East Jerusalem, but Rabin remained steadfast in not accepting full Israeli withdrawal for a full peace agreement. Other factors conspired against a Jordanian-Israeli agreement: Sadat's pro forma, if not insincere, interest in a Jordanian-Israeli agreement; Israel's chronically lingering war trauma and introspective national catharsis; its unwillingness to withdraw initially from the river that, for Hussein, was "something that mattered"; Jordan's lack of interest in becoming the policeman of the West Bank's Arab populated areas; and Israel's insistence of remaining in control of East Jerusalem.[99] Furthermore, Rabin strongly preferred another Egyptian-Israeli agreement to one with Jordan. Kissinger's decision to focus on Egypt and not Jordan further promoted the PLO, at least within Arab political circles, as the proper negotiating address for the Palestinians.

As he would over and over again, Sadat insisted that the diplomatic focus remain on Egypt; he was tiring and growing impatient with inter-Arab bickering. In the summer of 1974, he really did not want a Jordanian-Israeli agreement. Diplomatic cables to the State Department from Kissinger indicated beyond any doubt that "Sadat had asked that the Americans not work on a Palesinian issue [a Jordanian-Israeli agreement] which would complicate his life."[100] Sadat realized that finding a formula for Palestinian representation to a reconvened Geneva Conference was next to impossible. He knew that the PLO was unwilling to accept UNSC Resolution 242 and to go to Geneva, and he did not want to speak for the Palestinians. He knew that Israel insisted on upholding the December 1973 United States promise not to include the PLO in a future conference.

At the November 1973 Arab Summit in Algiers, Egyptian Foreign Minister Fahmy enthusiastically supported the notion that the PLO be recognized by the Arab countries as the legitimate representative of the Palestinian people. Then the Jordanian reaction was "complete silence and Rifa'i was so pale he looked frozen."[101] A year later, to the consternation of Jordan again, that resolution was confirmed. On October 28, 1974, the Arab Summit endorsed the PLO as the sole legitimate representative of the Palestinian people with the endorsement to establish a national authority on any liberated territory.

The Arab Summit Resolution at Rabat stated that it:

1. Affirms the right of the Palestinian people to return to their homeland and to self-determination.
2. Affirms the right of the Palestinian people to establish an independent national authority, under the leadership of the PLO in its capacity as the sole legitimate representative of the Palestinian people, over all liberated territory. The Arab States are pledged to uphold this authority, when it is established, in all spheres and at all levels.
3. Supports the PLO in the exercise of its national and international responsibilities, within the context of the principle of Arab solidarity.
4. Invites the kingdoms of Jordan, Syria and Egypt to formalize their relations in the light of these decisions and in order that they be implemented.
5. Affirms the obligation of all Arab States to preserve Palestinian unity and not to interfere in Palestinian internal affairs.

Jordan was stunned, again. The Jordanian leadership believed that Sadat had "intentionally deceived" them into believing that Cairo would not endorse the resolution that was adopted at Rabat.[102] Reluctantly, Sadat "caved in" to pressure from Saudi Arabia, the PLO, and Syria to back the PLO vis-à-vis Hussein. By doing so, Sadat could restore some lost luster in inter-Arab circles for negotiating with Israel and for reaching the first disengagement agreement; he gained public opinion points by supporting the PLO vis-à-vis Jordan. Sadat's advisers claim that he was sincere in his support of the PLO and Palestinian self-determination, but he also was a political pragmatist whose goal remained regaining all of Sinai. Sadat's endorsement of the PLO smothered any opportunity in an inter-Arab context for further discussion about an Israeli-Jordanian agreement about the West Bank and Jerusalem. In that context, Hussein did not consider himself a free agent to negotiate for the West Bank.[103] It was a diplomatic fact that Israel would not negotiate with the PLO over the West Bank, or with them as a negotiating partner over anything else. King Hussein understood more than the Israelis did that the passage of the Rabat Summit Resolution would inevitably allow Egypt to focus on reaching another agreement with Israel.[104] Sadat proved once again to the wary Jordanians that he could not be trusted, and Sadat, for all intents and purposes, forced American diplomacy to refocus on another Egyptian-Israeli agreement. Syria was delighted to tie Hussein's hands by forcing Hussein to weigh Jordanian interests in reaching a separate agreement with Israel in favor of pan-Arab consensus toward the Palestinians.

In the aftermath of the Rabat Resolution, Syria dismissed out-of-hand an Israeli proposal for a second Syrian-Israeli agreement, in which in return for several kilometers on the Golan Heights Israel wanted a commitment for the end of belligerency from Damascus. Said one Israeli intelligence official, "For a lousy few kilometers, Assad would not give an end to belligerency with Israel."[105] Rabin now observed Sadat with greater caution, in whom he saw great inconsistency, as Sadat easily drifted from the Alexandria communiqué in which he supported Hussein's claim to be at Geneva, a stance of promoting *his* Palestinians, to excluding Hussein entirely. Rabin recalled this about Sadat: "No trace of this [Alexandria] agreement remained in the Egyptian position at Rabat. When Sadat realized which way the wind was blowing, he threw his vigorous support behind the PLO. . . . His move was a warning signal to me. The most important part of any agreement with Egypt must not be the commitments it contained, but the concrete conditions it established on the ground."[106] Furthermore, the Nixon and Ford administrations also misread Sadat's apparent support for King Hussein.[107] Kissinger, privy to the conversations of the secret Israeli-Jordanian talks, was led to believe that this dialogue might, of its own pace, reach a positive conclusion. He did not factor in Sadat's impatience and meddling desire to keep that from happening. American policymakers and diplomats traveling with Kissinger on his visits to the region believed that an opportunity to persuade the king to accept "the Jericho sausage" was sacrificed when the Rabat Summit Resolution favored the PLO.[108] Kissinger himself admitted that, rather than push vigorously for another Egyptian-Israeli agreement or for a first Jordanian-Israeli disengagement agreement, he played for time and committed to neither, thereby creating the Israeli-Jordanian-Palestinian stalemate.[109] For misreading Sadat's intentions about alleged support for a Jordanian-Israeli agreement, Kissinger later apologized to Jordanian Prime Minister Rifa'i, saying, "Ziad, I am sorry. We miscalculated our manipulative capabilities."[110] By this time, Kissinger's frustrations toward Rabin were also evident, "We are racking our brains to find some formula, and there sits a Prime Minister shivering in fear every time I mention the word Jordan. It [was] a lost cause."[111] Kissinger knew that Rabin was told by Hussein that he could have face-to-face negotiations with an Arab leader that could result in a peace treaty with full diplomatic, tourist, and commercial relations, but Israel had to give back completely whatever was captured in the Six-Day War, including Jerusalem, with the situation restored to exactly the way it was one day before the war. Hussein reportedly told Rabin that "he could not afford anything less than that. If you think you can get a better deal with the PLO, you should try."[112] But Kissinger and Rabin had different priorities. Rabin had domestic constraints working on him, the most salient of which was the political risk of taking such an idea of full withdrawal to the Israeli people less than a year after the war. "Shimon Peres at the time was the hawk behind most of the settlements; at every turn he was prepared to challenge Rabin for the Labor Party leadership. Israel was not ready for an agreement with Jordan. If Rabin did it, it would have been political suicide."[113]

After Rabat, Sadat of course preferred step-by-step negotiatons, though he proclaimed in public his commitment to a reconvened Geneva Conference. The United States was not, as Eilts recalled, "going to fool around with Geneva, except as a stamping of approval authority."[114] In early November 1974, Kissinger made another trip through the Middle East, where he did the usual rounds with Israeli and Arab leaders. Kissinger still wanted to emphasize the step-by-step approach, but he found most Arab leaders eager to "return to Geneva."[115] A year after he and Sadat accepted the notion of a phased or staged Israeli withdrawal from Sinai, Kissinger was eager to have Sadat support a series of political objectives: stop denigrating Israel in the Egyptian media; stop pressuring African states to boycott diplomatic relations with Israel; stop preventing Israeli access to the Suez Canal; and end the state of belligerency with Israel. According to Eilts, Sadat "hit the ceiling" when he was presented Kissinger's requests. Kissinger wanted these Egyptian concessions as demanded by Israel so that he could persuade the Israelis to give up the strategic Gidi and Mitla Passes in Sinai and later the Egyptian oil fields, as part of the next Egyptian-Israeli agreement. In response, Sadat said that Egypt's commitment to nonbelligerency would require Israel to pull back almost entirely to the international borders.[116]

As for the Soviets, after Rabat, they were as Kissinger had wanted, nowhere to be found in Arab-Israeli negotiations. They did not participate in any fashion in either the first Egyptian-Israeli disengagement agreement or in the Syrian-Israeli agreement. Having previously and severely slowed down its military and economic assistance to Egypt, the Soviet Union virtually stopped providing aid by October 1974. Omar Sirry recalled, "The Soviets were feeling very strongly that they were losing ground in Egypt and in the Middle East. They were beginning to feel their own weakness. They were marginal. They could not deliver the goods the way the Americans would. And they were upset about that. But Fahmy managed to continue to get arms from them."[117] While Kissinger pursued bilateral agreements, the Soviets had to be content with issuing statements with the Arabs and Americans about the need to get back to Geneva. No party, except perhaps the Syrians and the PLO, took the idea seriously. In Fahmy's October 1974 trip to Moscow, details were arranged for a visit by Brezhnev to Egypt in January 1975. When Fahmy left Moscow, the Egyptian-Soviet communiqué noted that "a complete and final settlement to the Middle East crisis can be achieved only within the framework of the Geneva Conference and . . . the PLO should take part in the Geneva Conference on an equal footing with the other participants."[118] During Nixon's meeting with Brezhnev in July, agreement emerged about reconvening a Geneva Conference. In the late November 1974 Vladisvostok U.S.-U.S.S.R. Summit meeting, Ford and Brezhnev called for a lasting peace in the Middle East based upon UNSC Resolution 338, including "due account taken of the legitimate interests of all peoples of the area including the Palestinians, and respect for the right of all the states of the area to independent existence. The sides believe that the Geneva Conference should play an important part in the establishment of a just and lasting peace in the Middle East and should resume its work as soon as possible."[119] By the end of 1974, after Ford's meeting with Brezhnev, Sadat was increasingly disillusioned by the United States and beginning to sense that the first disengagement agreement was it; there would be no more.

When the Soviet Union hosted the Egyptian minister of defense and minister of economy in Moscow in late December, the Egyptians received tempting but conditional options: military and economic assistance would be available *only* if Brezhnev could visit Egypt in January 1975, *only* if the Egyptians would be prepared to jettison step-by-step diplomacy, and *only* if any further peace efforts would be solely through the Geneva forum.[120] But the Soviets also wanted increased Egyptian payment on the military debt due Moscow, and they used the debt as an excuse for not providing additional weapons or spare parts needed by the Egyptian Army.[121] Not surprisingly, Sadat declined Soviet demands for a major shift away from his American leanings. Moscow's preconditions for rewarming the Moscow-Cairo relationship were objectionable; moreover, Sadat was increasingly angered by the fact that Moscow was making Syria its most important ally in the Middle East.[122] In late December 1974, Brezhnev's visit to Egypt was canceled, and Sadat continued to resist the Soviet preconditions. He told Eilts, "Tell Henry we have got to move, we cannot continue" without another agreement.[123]

At the end of 1974, Israel and the United States were on compatible terms with Sadat's interest in seeing another negotiated Egyptian-Israeli agreement. In an interview in *Ha'aretz* in early December 1974, Rabin said that Israel's goals were "to separate Egypt from Syria, to delay negotiations until after the 1976 U.S. Presidential elections, and to delay talks until the West was less dependent on Middle Eastern oil."[124] In his late January 1975 visit to the region, Kissinger came away from Israel believing that there was a firm Israeli commitment to retreat from the strategic Sinai passes and, with several exceptions, return the Gulf of Suez oil fields; Kissinger had no such firm commitment, because Egypt was still not prepared to provide Israel with a promise to leave the conflict. On February 7, 1975, Rabin revealed Israel's conditions for an agreement with Egypt: "In exchange for an Egyptian commitment not to go to war and not to use the threat to use force, the Egyptians could get even the passes and the oil fields." Clarifying his negotiating position, Rabin told the Israeli Parliament four days later that Israel would not withdraw from the passes or the oil fields "unless Egypt withdrew from the war."[125] Like his stance with Jordan, Rabin wanted, in exchange for territory, a changed Arab attitude toward Israel. Another agreement with Syria was remote in Rabin's thinking, and Jordan's demand to have all the territories taken in 1967 returned was a nonstarter, even if a peace treaty and direct negotiations with an Arab leader were the results. Ford became involved in seeking another Egyptian-Israeli agreement, but only after floating the idea of a more comprehensive approach. In response,

State Department specialists, many Arab leaders, and some of Sadat's advisers warned him not to advance too fast without movement on the Palestinian-Jordanian front with Israel. Immediately after the Rabat Resolution, Ford said that the United States hoped to see movement toward a settlement between Israel, Jordan, and the PLO. Israelis were irate when they heard Ford's suggestion, unprecedented by an American president, that Israel should deal directly with the PLO. Six months earlier, Nixon had told Rabin that the U.S.-Israeli relationship was changing. There was substantial continuity in Ford's remarks to Rabin, as there would be in Jimmy Carter's urgings to Israeli prime ministers in 1977. While the Israeli-U.S. relationship continued to chill, Ford intimated a cut in financial aid to Israel. He also suggested the possibility of abandoning the step-by-step approach in favor of going back to Geneva, a point included in the Syrian-Soviet communiqué of February 1, 1975. The concept of "going back to Geneva" was defined by those who traveled with Kissinger as a symbolic step to achieve further small steps and to scare the Israelis.[126] Ford tried to find procedural formulas for progress on the Israeli-Jordanian-Palestinian front, but was stymied. An astute politician, Ford ultimately sensed the infeasibility of making the process broader and more comprehensive. Ford turned his attention toward reaching a less ambitious diplomatic conclusion, a second Sinai agreement. By the spring, a two-track strategy had clearly developed in Washington's pursuit of additional Middle East diplomatic progress: achievement of another Egyptian-Israeli agreement as soon as possible, and laying the groundwork for negotiations on the West Bank at a slower pace.[127] Washington's revision and redefinition of the special U.S.-Israeli relationship was underway.

In February and March 1975, Kissinger shuttled through the region under the shadow of Geneva. No one wanted another conference, especially the Jordanians and the Israelis. Greater Soviet involvement through Geneva was vigorously opposed by Egypt and Israel. The Syrians, who wanted Moscow to offset Washington's influence internationally, refused to be dictated to politically by the Soviet Union. The focus remained on obtaining another Egyptian-Israeli agreement. In early March, to everyone's surprise, Sadat announced that he was going to reopen the Suez Canal on June 5, the anniversary of the June War. Israel responded by unilaterally withdrawing troops from the limited force zone established under the first disengagement accord. Egypt and Israel were accommodating each other in bilateral actions that did not go through Washington; this would be a pattern that would repeat itself again in 1977 and 1978. Overarching and far-ranging disagreements existed between Egypt and Israel, but underlying interests in not going to war again prevailed. Still, the March 1975 negotiations on another Egyptian-Israeli interim agreement broke down for three reasons, as noted by Rabin: "The depth of Israel's withdrawal and the extent of the Egyptian [Army] advance; [control of] the Israeli early warning installation; and the duration of the agreement."[128] Israel did not want to accept an ultimatum from Egypt in which the strategic passes and oil fields were exchanged for a mere statement about either "nonbelligerency"[129] or Sadat's preference for a "nonuse of force" clause in the agreement being negotiated. Israel wanted its ships to use the Suez Canal; Sadat replied only cargoes bound for Israel should be allowed. Israel wanted a halt to the Egyptian media attacks against it; Sadat agreed only to ease the "militant" attacks. Israel was not prepared to give back the oil fields and preferred a peace treaty with Egypt. At one point, Rabin asked Kissinger to probe Sadat privately about whether he would agree to conclude a separate and full peace agreement with Israel in return for most—or possibly all—of the Sinai. Kissinger told Rabin upon his return from Egypt that "Sadat can't conclude a separate peace agreement, so the question of what Israel is prepared to pay in return is not relevant now."[130] Rabin noticed that Sadat did not say he would *not* sign a separate peace agreement.

Nonetheless, with Ford's consent, Kissinger terminated the negotiations with Rabin and painted a bleaker and exaggerated picture of the ramifications of the failed talks. The Americans wanted to use the break in negotiations to pressure Israel to be more flexible in negotiations. The stark break in negotiations did have a salutary effect of neutralizing some of Sadat's domestic critics who were very vocal about Sadat's pro-U.S. tilt. On the evening of March 22, 1974, Kissinger announced from Israel that Washington was prepared to enter a "reassessment" of U.S. relations with Israel. With more emotion and exaggeration than a sense of reality, Kissinger told Rabin:

The Arab leader who banked on the U.S. is discredited; the Arab leader who attempted a separate deal has failed. We will see a greater emphasis on the Palestinians. There will be no propositions about the Sinai separated from propositions about the Golan. The Soviets will step into the area at least as equals of the U.S. We are losing control over events in the Middle East. There is no further chance for separate American efforts. They would not be accepted by the Arabs or tolerated by the Soviets. . . . We will not oppose the resumption of the Geneva Conference. . . . Ask yourselves what the position of the U.S. can be at Geneva without a plan, even the most benevolent American president. That is my nightmare—what I now see marching toward you. Compared to that, ten kilometers in Sinai is trivial.[131]

Kissinger had thought he could deliver Israel; he could not, and so he blamed the Israelis. Israeli and U.S. positions diverged, leaving Rabin to decide that Israel would determine what was in *its* best strategic interest.

When Kissinger left the next day, he and Rabin had engaged in the toughest, most emotional, and most painful conversation they had ever had. For personal and national reasons, Rabin told Kissinger how deeply he regretted the failure of his mission. Rabin was aware that a breakdown in negotiations might lead to hostilities between Egypt and Israel, though it was not very likely. Rabin's rebuff of Kissinger did not turn out to be apocalyptic. Although Kissinger could not be characterized as impatient, he was perturbed that the expiration of time would negate Sadat's orientation toward Washington and toward a negotiated accommodation. Kissinger, however, misread that time was running out on Sadat. For his part, Sadat was not displeased about the tension in the U.S.-Israeli relationship. It appeared in public that Washington was willing to exert influence on Israel for another agreement in Sinai. When Israeli Foreign Minister Allon was in Washington in April 1975, Kissinger threatened him, "We've attempted to reconcile our support for you with our other interests in the Middle East, so that you wouldn't have to make your decisions all at once. Our strategy was to save you from dealing with all those pressures all at once. If we wanted the 1967 borders we could do it with all of the world opinion and considerable domestic opinion behind us."[132] Washington's policy of "reassessment," which took place vis-à-vis Israel during the spring of 1975, included a restriction in arms supply and suspended consideration of economic assistance to Israel.[133] It did not mean abandoning Israel, nor did it permit Egypt to plan and execute a military option against Israel. The immediate impact of reassessment did not effect the breadth or strength in U.S.-Israeli relations or suspend the search for another Egyptian-Israeli agreement. Ford and Kissinger wanted another Egyptian-Israeli agreement, and Rabin knew it.

Weighing in heavily on behalf of Israel and undercutting the Ford-Kissinger reassessment was a letter signed by seventy-six senators calling for undiminished military and economic aid to Israel. Israel's support in the Senate was unchallenged, and any impression that Sadat could pressure Israel into concessions was erased. "Withholding military equipment from Israel," said the letter, "would be dangerous [and] discouraging accommodation by Israel's neighbors and encouraging a resort to force."[134] Bipartisan in support, it challenged the administration's policy in a strikingly powerful fashion. It angered Ford but made the statement that Israel was not going to be bulldozed by the Kissinger-Ford tandem. Despite the testiness and wrangling, Israeli-Egyptian-American discussions continued in efforts to reconcile differences. In June, Ford met with Sadat in Salzburg and later in the month with Rabin in Washington. At the White House, Ford told Rabin that "reassessment was not intended to penalize Israel."[135] Rabin told Ford that Israel could not return to the pre–June War borders since they were not defensible. Kissinger sensed that Rabin was overstating the strategic and political significance of the Israeli withdrawal from the strategic passes. When Kissinger again tried to pressure Rabin with the possibility "of a return to Geneva," Rabin finally said, "Don't threaten me with the Geneva Conference."[136] For three major reasons, a reconvened Geneva Conference was simply not a viable or serious negotiating mechanism: first, there was no acceptable compromise for Palestinian representation, especially after the Rabat Summit Resolution; second, creating a unified Arab delegation with compatible views was not possible; and third, any conference would require at least a ceremonial, if not substantial, Soviet role, and the United States, after all its efforts to deposit Moscow on the side of the diplomatic road, was not about to welcome the Russians back so easily.

When Rabin left the United States, he still refused to give up control of the eastern ridge of the Mitla and Gidi Passes in Sinai. The major sticking point for Rabin and Sadat was control of the passes. Other items discussed in great detail included Israel's deployment line in relation to the two strategic Sinai passes; Egypt's forward movement into the evacuated zone; the proximity of Israeli and Egyptian forces near the Abu Rodeis oil fields in Sinai; the line of Israeli withdrawal north of the mountains in Sinai; the manning and operation of the early-warning stations; specific Egyptian steps to ease the economic boycott against Israel; Israeli use of a reopened Suez Canal; financial assistance and weapons supply to Israel; and defining an Israeli-U.S. understanding on the future strategy of the peace process (including nonrecognition of the PLO and Israel's opposition to an international conference). Control of the passes was resolved with a proposal, initially frowned upon by Ford, that the American military take control of early-warning stations at the passes and operate them on behalf of both Egypt and Israel.[137] The original proposal for five to nine American military posts was reduced to encompass American civilians in what came to be known as the Sinai Field Mission. Several years after Sinai II was signed, Rabin said that he accepted the placement of Americans there "not as an act of Egyptian-Israeli reconciliation—but in order to strengthen the U.S.-Israeli bond and to buttress the new Egyptian pro-American orientation, and introduce a wedge in the Egyptian-Syrian war coalition."[138]

All summer, negotiations continued, including another trip to the region by Kissinger in August. On September 1, 1975, the documents for the second Egyptian-Israeli disengagement agreement were initialed by representatives of Israel in Jerusalem and representatives of Egypt in Alexandria. Otherwise known as Sinai II, it was signed at Geneva on September 4, 1975. Details concerning the operational implementation, timing, and phasing of the agreement were worked out in Geneva under the auspices of the United Nations and General Siilasvuo. Proposed U.S. manning of early-warning stations was given consent by Congress in a joint resolution on October 13, 1975. The second Egyptian-Israeli disengagement agreement set important precedents in Arab-Israeli negotiations: it was the first Arab-Israeli agreement not negotiated at the conclusion of a war. Israel exchanged tangible assets in return for confidence that Egypt could be trusted to make further agreements. Unlike Sinai I, which essentially dealt with only a disengagement of forces resulting from the October 1973 War, Sinai II broadened the Egyptian-Israeli nonbelligerency relationship; it was a signed statement of nonuse of force. It also provided for U.S. civilian observers to work in conjunction with UN monitors. For Israel, Sinai II made the possibility of a confrontation with Egypt not completely impossible, but extremely unlikely. It moved Egypt further away from Moscow, limiting Soviet supply of weapons to Egypt, and widened hostilities between Syria and Egypt. For Egypt, Sinai II maintained the sense of progress and momentum that Sadat needed. The Suez Canal had been reopened, cities along the canal were undergoing repair, and the oil fields were returned. Sadat sensed that more activity on the negotiating process could wait until after the 1976 U.S. presidential elections.[139]

However, the American pause in the diplomatic process did not give Sadat a reprieve from serious criticism from his Arab brethren. The Syrians faulted Sadat for betraying them again. According to Hafez Ismail, "Hard feelings developed further from the Syrians toward Sadat, especially after the second disengagement agreement. Since they had done the war together, Assad felt that they should engage in the political action together."[140] Assad had been informed through letters written by Ford that there would be another Israeli-Syrian agreement, a Golan II Agreement.[141] But such an agreement did not materialize, because Assad refused to negotiate; in part, he thought any Israeli withdrawal would only be cosmetic, and Israel had no pressing reason to withdraw from the Golan Heights. Sadat's pro-American and pro-negotiation policy gave Syria the opportunity to "outbid" Egypt for the leading position in the struggle against Israel.[142]

Sinai II contained explicit side assurances in the form of letters and memoranda of understandings between Egypt and Israel. To Jerusalem, these included promises about weapons acquisitions, financial assistance, oil supplies, and the nature of future negotiations. Washington promised Israel that it "would not recognize or negotiate with the PLO as long as the PLO did not recognize Israel's right to exist and did not accept UNSC Resolutions 242 and 338." Another memorandum dealt with Washington's willingness to guarantee Israel's future oil supplies, without an expiration date, if Israel were unable to purchase oil from other sources.[143] Another assured Israel of acquisition of the most sophisticated aircraft in the American arsenal. Additional U.S. commitments to Israel included the statement that "no American proposal would be put forward without first consulting on it with the Israelis."[144] In a commitment to Israel about the Golan Heights, Ford said:

> The U.S. will support the position that an overall settlement with Syria in the framework of a peace agreement must assure Israel's security from attack from the Golan Heights. The U.S. further supports the position that a just and lasting peace, which remains our objective, must be acceptable to both sides. The U.S. has not developed a final position on the borders. Should it do so it will give great weight to Israel's position that any peace agreement with Syria must be predicated on Israel remaining on the Golan Heights. My view in this regard was stated in our conversation of September 13, 1974.[145]

The Egyptians were not informed about this U.S. memorandum to Israel; when they found out about it much later, they were, not surprisingly, upset by its contents.

Ford's private memorandum was in stark contrast to Nixon's remarks to Assad fifteen months earlier. Indeed, Ford's own earlier remarks that Israel should consider negotiating with the PLO had caused the Israelis to demand from the United States that the PLO not be included in future negotiations with Israel. In drafting the memorandum defining PLO–U.S. relations, it was neither Kissinger's intent nor desire to give Israel a veto power over a future Washington prerogative to speak to the PLO. Nevertheless, for the next twenty years, that was the effect the memorandum had on American involvement in the Arab-Israeli negotiating process. Assistant Secretary of State Roy Atherton, who drafted the memorandum, recalled that Kissinger did not want to "abandon the freedom of the United States to talk to anybody who wants to talk. We would coordinate with the Israelis in terms of reconvening the Geneva Conference, that we would not negotiate with or recognize the PLO *at Geneva,* meaning as the representative of the Palestinians, unless they accept Resolution 242 and Israel's right to exist."[146]

U.S.–Israel Memorandum of Agreement
Dealing with Geneva
17 September 1975

1. The Geneva Peace Conference will be reconvened at a time coordinated between the United States and Israel.

2. The United States will continue to adhere to its present policy with respect to the Palestine Liberation Organization, whereby it will not recognize or negotiate with the Palestine Liberation Organization so long as the Palestine Liberation Organization does not recognize Israel's right to exist and does not accept Security Council Resolutions 242 and 338. The United States Government will consult fully and seek to concert its position and strategy at the Geneva Peace Conference on this issue with the Government of Israel. Similarly, the United States will consult fully and seek to concert its position and strategy with Israel with regard to the participation of any other additional states. It is understood that the participation at a subsequent phase of the conference of any possible additional state, group or organization will require the agreement of all the initial participants.

3. The United States will make every effort to insure at the conference that all the substantive negotiations will be on a bilateral basis.

4. The United States will oppose and, if necessary, vote against any initiative in the Security Council to alter adversely the terms of refer-

ence of the Geneva Peace Conference or to change Resolutions 242 and 338 in ways which are incompatible with their original purpose.

5. The United States will seek to insure that the role of the co-sponsors will be consistent with what was agreed in the memorandum of understanding between the United States Government and the Government of Israel of December 20, 1973.

6. The United States and Israel will concert action to assure that the conference will be conducted in a manner consonant with the objectives of this document and with the declared purpose of the conference, namely the advancement of a negotiated peace between Israel and its neighbors.[147]

There were two secret undertakings made by the United States to Egypt when Sinai II was negotiated: commitments both to conclude a second disengagement agreement with Syria and to provide some settlement for the Palestinians. Sadat later claimed that there was a third commitment for the United States not to attack Syria, but there is no independent confirmation of such an American promise in writing.[148] Unlike the specifics guaranteed Israel, promises made to Egypt were politically broad and lacking real substance. After Sinai II was signed, Syria opened up its propaganda guns to underscore its traditional leadership of the Arab nationalist movement. After the signing of Sinai II in September 1975, Rabin made a secret two-day visit to Morocco. There, Moroccan King Hassan and Rabin took each other's measure. From that visit and with King Hassan's knowledge, Israel placed a Mossad agent in residence under a commercial cover to sustain and open contacts with different parts of the Arab world. For Rabin, the major purpose of this secret visit was to learn more about Egypt, particularly about Sadat's intentions.[149] It seems that after going through the tough period of reassessment with the United States, Rabin was inclined to open additional pathways to Arab leaders, lines that did not necessarily travel through Washington.

While Gerald Ford focused on the 1976 presidential elections, the State Department and Kissinger concentrated on other foreign policy issues, like developing American positions toward the Law of the Sea and another arms control agreement with the Soviet Union. Said Rabin, "1976 will not be remembered as a year of much progress in Middle East diplomacy."[150] There was no pressing need from parties in the Middle East to obtain another Arab-Israeli agreement immediately. Forging a Jordanian-Israeli agreement was almost impossible. Furthermore, a series of events reinforced Israeli discomfort with their international standing and relationship with the United States. On November 10, 1975, the United Nations General Assembly passed a resolution defining Zionism as a "form of racism or racial discrimination." The resolution not only offended Israeli and Diaspora Jews alike but also reinforced Israel's predisposition to mistrust the United Nations as an institutional forum for sponsorship or conduct of Arab-Israeli negotiations. Two days later, Deputy Assistant Secretary of State for Near Eastern Affairs Harold Saunders appeared before the House Subcommittee on Near Eastern Affairs and stated that "the legitimate interests of the Palestinian Arabs must be taken into account in the negotiating of an Arab-Israeli peace." Kissinger had cleared Saunder's statement. Almost immediately, the PLO formally registered with the Justice Department, the first step toward opening a diplomatic office in Washington. And then the prestigious Brookings Institution in Washington, D.C., issued what the Israeli government saw as an offensive blueprint for an Arab-Israeli settlement. *Toward Peace in the Middle East* called for peace agreements between the parties, "extensive Palestinian political autonomy or a Palestinian entity federated with Jordan," resettlement of the Palestinian refugees, an Israeli withdrawal to almost the June 5, 1967, borders, stages for implementing agreements, provision of UN guarantees, and constructive Soviet involvement in the negotiations. The method for achieving these diplomatic outcomes would be determined through a general conference or informal multilateral meetings. This was a comprehensive approach. To some Israelis, much of the Brookings report content was fine, but to most, the call to return to 1967 borders was unacceptable. Most of all, Israelis reacted negatively to the Brookings report because it circumscribed their prerogative by defining an outcome in advance of the negotiations. With the environments at the UN and in Washington drifting emphatically toward a negotiating role for the PLO, Israel was in no mood for further discussions, let alone possible territorial concessions.

Sadat was pleased that there were negative feelings in the U.S.-Israeli relationship and that there was a respite in the negotiating process. Having obtained Washington's physical involvement in negotiating and in implementing the agreement, Sadat "needed coverage from the Arab world, a declaration of principles governing the Palestinian issue."[151] Inadvertently, the Brookings report provided Sadat an opportunity to coordinate closely with Assad, the possibility of a comprehensively achieved diplomatic outcome, publicly advocated by one of Washington's most prestigious think tanks. Meanwhile, in late 1975, the State Department proceeded to develop preparatory suggestions for the next stage of negotiations. Recommendations included the definition of agenda and procedural items relevant to a reconvened conference, while interagency working groups were established on several technical subjects. Topics of these functional working groups included the use of international waterways, refugee compensation, arms limitation, enforcement of demilitarized zones, and post-settlement relationships. A vast amount of American bureaucratic work focused on preparing various proposals for the resumption of the Geneva Conference.[152]

After Sinai II, the Soviet Union also presented the U.S. administration with a

series of overtures focused on reconvening Geneva, none of which went anywhere. On November 9, 1975, Moscow again asked for the reconvention of the
Geneva Conference, with full participation of the PLO. Washington's judicious
reply of December 1 showed the lack of enthusiasm Washington had for resuming
the conference at that juncture and on the terms described by Moscow.[153] While
politically acknowledging Moscow's desire to reconvene Geneva, the United States
noted that "only after careful preparation" could the Geneva Peace Conference
"serve the goal of achieving progress in the settlement of the conflict." Second, in
response to Moscow's request that the United States and the Soviet Union act as
cochairmen and "take a joint initiative to reconvene the Geneva Peace Conference," Washington responded that it "is consulting the parties to determine their
views . . . on how best to prepare the agenda and procedures for a reconvened conference." Third, in answer to the Soviet interest to have the PLO participate in a
conference, the United States repeated its view "that legitimate Palestinian interests
must be taken into account in an overall settlement," but the United States "cannot
agree . . . that the co-chairmen of the conference can alter the definition of the
participants in the conference initially agreed to by the original participants."
Finally, Washington proposed that a practical way of proceeding would be through
a preparatory conference of

> those who have participated so far in the negotiations toward a settlement
> within the Geneva Conference framework. In addition to the United States
> and the Soviet Union, such a preparatory conference could include Egypt,
> Jordan, Syria, and Israel, and could consider agenda, procedures, and the mat-
> ter of participation in a subsequent full conference, with a view toward laying
> a foundation for negotiation for an overall settlement. The United States is
> also prepared to consider holding bilateral consultations with the U.S.S.R. in
> advance of such a preparatory conference, and solicits the views of the Soviet
> Union on this possible approach.[154]

Kissinger had promised Sadat that, once Ford was re-elected, an effort would be
made to find a comprehensive settlement. After Sinai II, Ford sent a letter to Sadat
that Eilts recalled as saying, "Mr. President, next year is a presidential election year,
I can't do anything, which you will appreciate. But when I'm re-elected, we're going
to drop the step-by-step approach for a comprehensive settlement."[154] Kissinger
also told Sadat that disengagement stages would be transformed or merged for a
comprehensive peace. In March 1976, Egyptian Foreign Ministry officials were asked
to prepare a peace agreement for use after the American presidential elections.[156]

In the region, the Lebanese civil war erupted in 1975. With a weak central government, Lebanon's precarious division of power along Christian and Muslim religious lines unraveled in a context of exploding inflation, unemployment, and a

reinvigorated PLO assertiveness to protect its politically autonomous presence in southern Lebanon. Syria's Assad considered Lebanon to be part of his country's national strategic depth and was determined to keep control, if not influence, over Lebanon through whatever political or military means were necessary. Though the quest for political and physical control of Lebanon wrenched its history for the next fifteen years, the struggle in Lebanon did not keep either Syria or the PLO so preoccupied that they refrained from upbraiding Sadat for going his separate way with Israel through Washington. Israeli society in 1976 was still skeptical of Arab intentions, and Rabin in particular was skeptical of Sadat's motivations. While a demoralized feeling still lingered from the 1973 War, Israelis injected a needed dose of self-confidence about themselves when their army rescued one hundred Jews who had been kidnapped and hijacked to Entebbe Airport in Uganda. The daring July 4, 1976, rescue mission restored some lost faith in the political and military leadership. Throughout 1976, Washington pursued two tracks for a comprehensive Arab-Israeli settlement, while focusing intently on solidifying Egypt's agreements with Israel.

Sadat and Rabin continued to probe each other's respective readiness and content of resumed negotiations through several venues, among them Washington, Morocco, and Rumania. In Washington, talks occurred at different levels: in the White House, State Department, and Congress. In late October and early November 1976, Sadat spoke to visiting American senators about making peace with Israel. In Israel, Prime Minister Rabin said in response, "We had to regard President Sadat's latest remarks on peace carefully and with skepticism."[157] In late December 1976, uncommonly arranged on a Saturday afternoon, the Rumanian ambassador to Israel asked to see Israeli Foreign Minister Allon at his home in Kibbutz Ginossar. There, he reminded Allon that an annual subministerial-level exchange visit between their countries was customary and that none had taken place in 1976. Allon asked the director general of the Foreign Ministry, Shlomo Avineri, to go to Rumania as requested. Allon and Avineri thought it strange that such a request was made on the Sabbath. There was nothing special about Avineri's trip until he was headed back to the airport in Bucharest for the flight home. In the car, "strong terms" were used to suggest the importance of a visit by Prime Minister Rabin to Rumania soon. Avineri responded by explaining the improbability of a visit during an election campaign in which Rabin would be challenged for his party's leadership. He also told his cordial hosts that the Israeli prime minister's next visit abroad would almost certainly be to meet the new American president. When Allon and Avineri explained to Rabin that this invitation might be a hidden Soviet initiative, Rabin was unreceptive. He did not want to hear another lecture from Nicolai Ceausescu about establishing Israeli contacts with the PLO, and he did not want to strain his schedule by taking even one day off from the election campaign to go to Rumania.

Rabin probably knew that Prime Minister Meir had spent fourteen hours with Ceausescu in the early 1970s, well before the October 1973 War. Talks then continued through emissaries, as suggested by the Rumanian president, but nothing substantive transpired between Egypt and Israel.[158] Although Rabin did not go to Rumania for a day, he did find time to meet on February 4, 1977, with Ivory Coast President Félix Houphouët-Bouigny, in Geneva. Nothing more ensued with the Rumanians until the day after the Labor Party lost the election in May, when Avineri was asked by the Rumanian ambassador to inquire about arranging an appointment with the new foreign minister. At the July 4, 1977, American Embassy Independence Day reception for diplomats and dignitaries, newly installed Israeli Prime Minister Menachem Begin was introduced to the Rumanian ambassador to Israel. Avineri recalls, "On the spot, in the presence of some other people, the Rumanian ambassador invited Begin to Rumania. Begin said that this a welcome invitation."[159] Several days later, the visit was scheduled for the end of August. Sadat had asked Ceausescu to probe Begin's readiness for an agreement between them.[160] The question today is: How would the history of Egyptian-Israeli negotiations have been different if Rabin had seen Ceausescu in January 1977, and perhaps learned directly from the Rumanian president that Sadat was prepared to do something dramatic after the Israeli parliamentary election? Avineri again claimed that Austrian President Kriskey had told him later in 1977 that Sadat had been prepared, before the May 1977 Israeli elections, to do something dramatic immediately following the elections.[161] Whether probing Begin's readiness to negotiate or showing an eagerness to be dramatic, Sadat was ready to move negotiations forward with Israel in some continuing bilateral manner in 1977, regardless of who was Israel's prime minister.

Ford's defeat and Carter's victory were viewed differently in Damascus, Cairo, and Jerusalem. In Damascus, the Syrian media indicated doubt that there could or would be any appreciable change between Ford and Carter. "The USA is the USA. . . . Ford and the new president, Carter, both tried during the election campaign to outdo each other in giving promises to Israel."[162] Sadat told Eilts that "to his disappointment Ford was not reelected and Carter's election was a great shock."[163] Sadat had anticipated Ford's reelection in part because Ford promised Sadat that the United States would pursue a comprehensive settlement. Sadat had come to the conclusion that "if one continued with an interim agreement, he would give too much away and not recover everything he wanted recovered."[164] Sadat knew very little about Jimmy Carter. What he did know, he was not sure he liked. Somewhat apprehensive about the new president, Sadat was aware that Carter's presidential campaign included several pro-Israeli statements. He was thus concerned that Carter would feel obliged to be attentive to supporters of Israel.[165] Fearing that Carter would not pursue Ford's promise of a comprehensive settlement, Sadat worried that another interim agreement would be the administration's priority.

Out of the Arab Summit meeting in Riyadh in October 1976, Sadat regained some of the political prestige in Arab affairs that he had lost by negotiating directly with Israel. Furthermore, after Assad's meeting with Sadat in Cairo in mid-December, Syria announced its readiness to attend a reconvened Geneva Conference "as part of the struggle against the Zionist enemy."[166] During the Ford-Carter transition period, Sadat gave an extensive interview to *Newsweek* magazine, in which he stated that step-by-step diplomacy had ended and asserted that 1977 should be the year of a durable peace, which could only be established in Geneva. Sadat noted that Cairo's differences with Damascus were repaired and that the new state of Arab rapprochement was appropriate for the United States to launch a peace initiative.[167] During the transition period from Republican to Democratic administrations, Phil Habib, the designate for the position of under-secretary of state for political affairs, ascertained by consensus that the top priority in the Middle East would be to find a comprehensive settlement.[168] Consequently, Carter sent a message to Sadat saying, "We'd like to move toward a comprehensive settlement."[169] Consideration for the active reconvention of the Geneva Conference was taking place, but Sadat was interested in a conference only if the format did not obstruct his objective of having another portion of Sinai returned. And in Jerusalem, though much attention was paid to Carter's election, it was overshadowed by Rabin's decision in December 1976 to move the scheduled autumn parliamentary elections forward to May.

CHAPTER 7

༄ ༄༅ ༄

UNINTENDED CONSEQUENCES

THE 1977 ROAD TO GENEVA
ENDS IN JERUSALEM

WHEN Jimmy Carter became president, there was no crisis in the Middle East and therefore no immediate reason to engage in diplomacy. The negotiating process had stalemated. Nevertheless, Washington was still concerned that Arab-Israeli nonbelligerency could degenerate into conflict, and there was also concern about the high price of oil. Another oil embargo did not seem likely, but in Washington, the threat of it lingered as a possibility. Where there was any urgency driving policy, it centered on the belief that if Arab support could be enlisted for a comprehensive Arab-Israeli agreement, then Arab attempts at blackmailing the United States could be avoided.[1] If, after taking office in January 1977, Carter had told Vance and Brzezinski that before the end of the year he expected Sadat to visit Israel and Begin to reciprocate with a visit to Egypt, then both advisers would have thought that the commander-in-chief knew very little about the dynamics of the Arab-Israeli conflict. The new year was to start with the goal of finding a comprehensive Middle East settlement via another conference at Geneva, not with responding to an Israeli government request for Egypt's national anthem so it could be played properly upon Sadat's arrival in Jerusalem!

Carter's propensity to search for total solutions to problems meshed very nicely with Ford's promise to Sadat to pursue a comprehensive settlement. Brzezinski and Vance fully agreed with Carter that "the step-by-step approach had run out of steam."[2] They considered the conclusion of Sinai II a major expenditure of time for a relatively minor diplomatic outcome, and they did not want to acquire consecutive slices of Sinai through the same numerical process (Sinai III, Sinai IV, and Sinai V, etc.). Vance believed that if a comprehensive method did not work, then a step-by-step approach could set the outlines for comprehensive settlement. All agreed that a negotiated settlement should be based on UNSC Resolution 242, include almost full Israeli withdrawal to the June 1967 borders, and contain a solution for Palestinian political rights and aspirations. No time was expended in interagency debates about the outline of a settlement; there was now a common clear purpose. Among the members of the Middle East foreign policy team, Brzezinski thought globally and ambitiously, believing that the first year of the administration would offer the best opportunity for major progress.[3] Carter opted to pursue a negotiated comprehensive settlement via another Middle East conference with Moscow playing the role of coconvener. The Brookings Institution's 1975 monograph, *Toward Peace in the Middle East,* which Brzezinski, Quandt, and Vance had key roles in drafting, became the administration's objective framework. The monograph's contents were singularly important because they reinforced Carter's engineering preference for a comprehensive settlement. For Carter, this was an evenhanded, logical, and capable approach. Seeking a comprehensive peace "comprehensively," Carter aligned himself more with Sadat and, eventually, in direct opposition to Prime Ministers Rabin and Begin.

Neither Rabin nor Begin wanted either a comprehensive settlement or a conference, though each was willing to listen to options that pertained to both. And neither Israeli leader was willing to commit to making substantive political decisions in advance of a conference because each feared pressure would be exerted upon them to negotiate with the PLO. Rabin and Begin sensed that a conference was an Arab excuse to avoid direct negotiations. Therefore, if there was to be a conference, then procedures had to lead to direct negotiations. Eventually, Israel's vigorous opposition to a comprehensive settlement caused Carter to become impatient with its leaders; he saw Israelis limiting their focus to another incremental step with the Egyptians. Early on, Carter did not know that the 1973 Geneva Middle East Peace Conference was a cloak for a prearranged Egyptian-Israeli agreement. Its lack of success, he believed, was due to its short duration. How a conference would operate was not yet part of Carter's mind-set. Said Carter, "We never got to the point of asking what's going to be the order of events and what's going to be the way negotiations will take place, will there be mediators, who will finance the outcome. We never got into that."[4] But as 1977 progressed, Vance chaired a working group of specialists who studied and suggested procedural methods for Geneva, with both the NSC and State Department doing the staff work. By spring, details were worked out on how the proposed conference would divide into bilateral working groups. Carter envisioned himself or the secretary of state presiding over the conference to be held in either September or October, foreshadowing his personal involvement in the diplomatic process. Brzezinski differed slightly with Carter on what a Geneva Conference might accomplish. Brzezinski believed that before Geneva, a substantive set of principles would be negotiated and agreed upon, and "Geneva itself would not be used for negotiations as such but should be held to legitimize any agreement previously reached by the parties through U.S. efforts."[5]

Sadat very much wanted a conference, and his views were similar to Brzezinski's,

namely that there should be some prearranged agreement or set of principles negotiated prior to the conference. Sadat wanted Vance to handle all the prenegotiations
and, at Geneva, to manage the execution of the prenegotiated principles. Sadat had
liked how the 1973 Geneva Conference worked; it gave him an umbrella under
which to operate without sacrificing independent Egyptian decision making. He
believed this model could be duplicated. Carter, on the other hand, sensed that
successful negotiations were possible at a conference, thus he was less interested
in the need to agree on principles in advance. Indeed, he was even willing to have
the agenda for the negotiations debated *at* the conference. Carter tended to thus
emphasize a focus on a comprehensive settlement among all parties. Sadat was not
opposed to this position, except in those instances where prenegotiations or procedures might provoke inter-Arab polemics, diminish Egypt's role as Washington's
primary Arab friend, or slow the negotiating process to a snail's pace. Mutually
committed to a comprehensive peace and a reconvened Geneva Conference, Sadat
and Carter were compatible because of respective expectations: Carter's innate
impatience to solve the "problem," and Sadat's desire to have Sinai returned sooner
rather than later. Neither political realities nor political expediency restrained either
one of them. In general terms, neither Sadat nor Carter were opposed to limited
Soviet participation at a Geneva Conference; yet Carter, more than Sadat, was confident about Soviet inclusion in renewed Arab-Israeli negotiations. As for the
United Nations, Carter saw them "authenticating it through the Security Council,
with the UN providing fairly extensive UN peacekeeping efforts in the Golan
Heights and in the Sinai, and maybe even in the occupied territories."[6] Preparations were made with the Soviets for their participation, but the White House
alone, much like Kissinger, had sought to narrow differences on substance between
the respective sides.

While the bureaucracy churned out procedural options for convening and managing a conference, Carter, Vance, and Brzezinski set out to learn firsthand from
the region's leaders their views, and what would be feasible to accomplish. Preparations for Vance's February 1977 Middle East trip began during the transition
period. Vance went to the Middle East carrying Carter's ambitious decision to convene an international Middle East peace conference and seek a comprehensive
peace. He questioned Middle East leaders in Amman, Cairo, Damascus, Jerusalem,
and Riyadh about their willingness to engage in direct or indirect negotiations and
about what principles would guide their discussions.[7] In Egypt, Sadat suggested to
Vance that Jordan and the PLO consider establishing a confederation between
them in administering the West Bank. In Israel, Prime Minister Rabin reviewed
Israel's priorities for the nature of peace and the Palestinian problem. Vance told
Rabin that the visit was a preparatory and exploratory mission, "that no great issues
were going to be discussed in detail."[8] Yet Vance also told Rabin that Washington
would not honor President Ford's commitment to deliver high-percussion cluster

bombs to Israel. According to Hal Saunders, who was sitting in the room, the Israelis were dumbfounded. Rather than the secretary of state saying to Rabin, as Kissinger might have done, "I shall report your views to the president," Vance replied immediately with a "no" response.[9] Rabin was angered that Washington would unilaterally renege from an earlier commitment to Israel. In response, he said, "If it is cluster bombs today, tomorrow it will be something else."[10] Washington had already strained the U.S.-Israeli relationship by forbidding Israel to sell twenty-four Israeli-built Kfir fighter bombers to Ecuador because the planes were equipped with U.S.-made engines. The administration did not sense that, for Rabin at least, military and strategic matters took immediate precedent over political issues, such as the negotiating process. Israeli leaders knew Vance from his previous service in the Department of Defense and thought him to be very honorable. As foreign minister, Moshe Dayan later developed confidence in Vance, admired his integrity, and considered him as someone in the administration upon whom Israel could rely and through whom difficulties with Carter could be corrected. But Vance's fine human characteristics did not camouflage the disagreements on substance which Israelis had with him on this trip and on future occasions. Many Israeli officials were vexed by the tone of Vance's first visit. When he returned in August, they were no more satisfied with either the content or tone of his remarks. Israelis had become accustomed to Kissinger's diplomatic style; they were very unaccustomed to Vance, the lawyer, working for Carter, the engineer. Epi Evron characterized Vance's February 1977 visit as "terrible."[11]

The meetings in Amman were scarred by two unrelated issues: the death of King Hussein's twenty-eight-year-old wife, Alia, in a helicopter crash a week before Vance's visit, and newspaper revelations in Washington reporting Hussein's ties to the CIA. Though the positions of Amman and Washington on a reconvened Middle East peace conference were similar, a crisis of confidence between Hussein and Carter was emerging. On February 18, the day Vance arrived in Amman, the *Washington Post* reported that King Hussein had received approximately $1 million a year for twenty years from the CIA as "walking around" money, not connected to either economic or military aid. Those funds were reportedly used to sponsor the king's lifestyle, defray costs of bodyguards for his children, and for his female companionship. Cash payments were made directly to Hussein by the CIA station chief in Amman.[12] Apparently during the transition period of 1976–1977, neither Ford, Kissinger, nor former CIA Director George Bush, mentioned to Carter the existence of this financial tether to Hussein. In an Oval Office meeting where the *Post* sought White House confirmation of the story, Carter told *Post* editor Ben Bradlee that while Jordan was vital to the Middle East peace process, the payments would be stopped. Carter hoped that Bradlee would not run the story, especially while Vance was in the Middle East and about to visit Amman. After the *Post* ran the article, Carter penned a personal note to Bradlee telling him that "the publication of the CIA story as the secretary of state was on his Middle East mission and about to arrive in Jordan was irresponsible." Bradlee told Jody Powell, Carter's press secretary, that he was upset with Carter's note, to which Carter replied, "Well, fuck him."[13] Upon hearing the story of Hussein's connection to the CIA, the PLO was gleeful; not unexpectedly, the Jordanian government called the *Post* story a distortion and fabrication. In a series of articles appearing the following week about the Hussein-CIA connection, it was reported that the CIA had provided funds to half-a-dozen other heads of state over the years. Included among others as a recipient of those funds, said the *Post,* was Kamal Adham, Saudi Arabia's head of national security and brother-in-law of the former Saudi King Faisal. The *Post* also reported that in the 1960s, Adham had cultivated a positive relationship with Anwar Sadat while he was Egypt's vice president, in part to balance or offset Nasser's anti-Saudi attitude, and, said the *Post,* Adham provided Sadat "a steady private income."[14]

For different reasons, Vance's visit to both Israel and Jordan were marred. Rabin and Hussein had real cause to be perturbed with the content and style of Washington's diplomacy, which was direct, rough, and embarrassingly public. King Hussein would again be stung by a string of what were considered insensitive acts by the Carter administration: Carter's endorsement of a Palestinian homeland in March 1977, without considering the political fallout such a statement would have in Amman; and the impolitic manner in which Hussein was handled during and after the September 1978 Camp David negotiations. While the Israelis may have expected more from Vance, the Syrians received him well. As Carter's representative, Vance affirmed that the U.S. administration was serious about pushing forward an Arab-Israeli negotiating process. In their meeting, Syrian Foreign Minister Abd al-Halim Khaddam grew increasingly aware that Vance, "with his notebook full of ideas about how to resume the Geneva Conference,"[15] was seriously interested in finding a way to start negotiations. Khaddam was pleased that the Carter administration was focused on going to a Geneva Conference because, as he noted, "it was an obstacle to a unilateral solution [wanted by Egypt]."[16] Since the administration was advocating Syria's preferred method, the Syrian government was comfortable with the idea of Carter possibly meeting Assad several months later. Moreover, Vance told Assad that Carter wanted to meet with the Syrian president, which would be the first such meeting since Nixon had been to Damascus in June 1974. The Syrians, always mindful of Cairo's edge in keeping Washington's attention, were extremely pleased by the invitation.

Having extended invitations to each Middle Eastern leader to visit President Carter, the White House and State Department began to define areas of difference and common ground that would be the focus of these meetings when they commenced just two weeks after Vance's return. The pilgrimages to the Oval Office began on March 7 with Rabin, followed by Sadat on April 4, Hussein on April 25, and Saudi Crown Prince Fahd on May 24. Sandwiched in between the Hussein and Fahd meetings, Carter met with Syrian President Assad on May 9.[17]

Carter and Rabin were on a collision course. In private, Carter presented to the Israeli prime minister the American outline for a settlement: the Brookings report recommendations. Rabin described the report as having "absolutely nothing in common with Israel's views about final borders."[18] In communicating with Carter, Rabin was cautious, fearing in part that anything he said in the White House or to the president would find its way to the media. With the elections upcoming, Rabin could not afford a White House disclosure about possible withdrawals, which the Labor Party could accept and that might be communicated privately to Carter. Rabin still preferred Kissinger's step-by-step approach and wanted to negotiate with Egypt first.[19] Carter made several dramatic suggestions to Rabin that an American president had not yet made to an Israeli prime minister. First, he told Rabin, "It would be a blow to U.S. support for Israel if you refused to participate in the Geneva talks over the technicality of the PLO being in the negotiations."[20] Second, Carter told Rabin that Israel needed to withdraw essentially to the 1967 borders and to consider going to a conference with a single unified Arab delegation. For the Israelis, a unified Arab delegation meant dealing with an Arab viewpoint, which would be most uncompromising; a unified delegation would deny Israel the opportunity to exploit the parochial differences among Arab states. Third, Carter bluntly told Rabin, as he repeated later in October to Foreign Minister Dayan, Israeli recalcitrance in the peace process would be sharply rebuked by the American people. When they were alone at Blair House on the evening of their first meeting, Carter pressed Rabin for Israel's "real or fallback position." Rabin, who wanted peace treaties as the next diplomatic objective, felt trapped by Carter. Carter felt that Rabin was not totally candid with him. Indeed, Rabin did *not* reveal his inner thoughts, fearful that if he did Carter might somehow make them public.[21] For Israelis, the discussions were dealing with highly sensitive issues regarding legitimacy and security, to which Carter was giving his own ad hoc interpretation. Not only was Carter telling Israel what to do, but he was also giving explicit warnings that failure to cooperate would jeopardize U.S.-Israeli relations. This was *not* the accustomed "Kissingerian" way. Kissinger was tough and angry with Israeli leaders, but he never told Israelis to swallow discomforting ideological positions. By contrast, Carter took the conclusions of a consensus document, which had been drafted without any Israeli input, and imposed them on Rabin, believing them to be fair, equitable, and adequately acceptable. Recalling his high expectations about the prime minister's visit, Carter said, "I was looking forward to meeting with Rabin as kind of a peg on which I could hang my whole Mideast peace ambitions. And Rabin was absolutely and totally uninterested, very timid, very stubborn, and somewhat ill-at-ease. The fact was he had no interest at all in talking about negotiations. It was just like talking to a dead fish."[22]

On March 9, immediately after his meetings with Rabin, Carter said publicly that there would have to be a substantial Israeli withdrawal with only some minor adjustments to Israel's 1967 borders. Rabin and other Israelis were shocked by Carter's remarks and did not understand why Carter would publicly outline the geographic map for a settlement when there were major differences between his views and Israel's. Immediately after receiving an honorary degree from American University, Rabin was told about Carter's remarks by an Israeli embassy official, to which he responded, "You are fantasizing."[23] Before Rabin departed from the Washington airport, Vance told him that Carter's statement was intended. Israeli embassy official Bar-On recalled telling Assistant Secretary of State Atherton that Carter's remarks would surely hurt the Labor Party in the May parliamentary elections. Atherton concurred. Carter did not consider that his frank style and meddlesomeness could have an impact on the Israeli electorate. Certainly the sour fermentation in the U.S.-Israeli relationship, which had begun during the Ford administration, facilitated Menachem Begin's campaign for Israeli votes: the Rabin government could not successfully manage Jerusalem's most critical foreign relations priority. Nevertheless, Carter's policy toward Israel was not the factor that drove the Labor Party from office. Instead, the issues that had accumulated in favor of the Likud Party were domestic in origin: scandals; improprieties; rancorous competition for the Labor Party leadership; public recuperation from Labor's stewardship of the October 1973 War; Rabin's inability to project strong internal party leadership; evolution of a newly competing political party; a skillfully managed Likud Party election campaign; and a change in traditional voter preference.[24] When Rabin left Washington, it would be his last time visiting there as prime minister until he returned in 1992. He departed with deep anxiety about Carter's motivations, which reinforced preexistent Israeli confusion and trepidation about the Carter administration. Rabin saw no continuity in form, substance, or tone between Carter and his predecessors. Not only had Carter disagreed with Israeli policy in public but also had unilaterally proposed Washington's own outline for a settlement, told the Israelis that they had to deal with the PLO, and expressed his feelings in what Israelis viewed as shrill tones.

Israelis were angry and chalked up Carter's public diplomacy to inexperience. For them, Carter's beating drum was too loud, too resonant, too relentless. On March 16, 1977, a week after meeting Rabin, Carter held a town hall meeting in Clinton, Massachusetts. Responding to a question on the Middle East, Carter said, "There has to be a homeland provided for the Palestinian refugees who have suffered for many, many years."[25] Rabin and most Israelis were astounded by Carter's remarks. But the Palestine National Council, which was meeting in Cairo at the same time, welcomed the unprecedented public call by an American president for a political solution to the Palestinians' plight. When he heard Carter's remarks, Arafat apparently "had tears in his eyes."[26] According to Atherton, "It was a statement which no one in the State Department had put in his briefing books. Those of us who were in the trenches read it with surprise."[27] Veliotes, who worked with Atherton at the time, recalled, "We were stunned, furious; that Carter should give this [public endorsement of a Palestinian homeland] away to the Palestinians and the Arabs for nothing. It was dumb, utterly stupid."[28] Carter recalled that he had discussed using the term *homeland* with Vice President Mondale and others before using it. The words *community* and *nation* were discarded; Mondale also did not like the use of *homeland,* which he felt was too strong. But Carter decided to use the term either without considering or disregarding the degree of impact it would have internationally in the Middle East or domestically in the United States. Those in the Egyptian Foreign Ministry who dealt with the Palestinian issue believed that Carter's remarks were a sign of more positive things to come. And although Carter obviously realized that the PLO would respond positively, he did not consider the degree of Israeli or Jordanian displeasure.[29] Amman was vexed that Carter was outlining a political solution based on a new geographic entity that could be problematic for the Hashemite Kingdom. Amman's relationship with the PLO remained strained and distant. Only a week before Carter's remarks in Massachusetts, Hussein and PLO leaders had met for the first time since Amman's crackdown on the PLO in Jordan in 1970–1971. With their historic interest in the West Bank, the Jordanians wanted to know what their relationship would be to the "homeland." As soon as the "Palestinian homeland" remarks were made, Carter told Vance and Brzezinski that "no elaborations or clarifications were to be issued" on the matter.[30] Only *after* Carter created this verbal firestorm did he ask his Middle East advisers for the history of Washington's voting record on all UN resolutions dealing with Palestine. He looked for a possible historical footnote to defend his use of the term. Meanwhile, Eilts reported to Washington that Sadat was pleased with the "homeland" remark. Steadily, Carter came to realize that what was for him such an obvious human right for the Palestinians created enormous credibility for him in parts of the Arab world.[31] Without asking them for any concessions toward the Israelis, Carter awarded American support to the PLO.

Giving minimal attention to the impact of his remarks, Carter laid out specific markers on the diplomatic field. This was vintage Carter: ready, shoot, aim. Immediately after the "homeland" remark, American Jewish leaders descended upon Carter and, through Vance, upon Warren Christopher, Vance's deputy at the State Department. Christopher gave reassurances that Israel was not being betrayed by the use of the controversial term.[32] By the end of March 1977, Washington was replete with rumors about Brzezinski's public definitions of Israel's final borders, something closely akin to the pre–June 1967 War armistice lines. In spite of what Brzezinski said or did not say, in spite of what he did or did not clarify in discussion with Israel's ambassador to Washington, the tones around Washington suggested that Israel's relationship with the Carter administration was deteriorating. Israelis were stunned by Brzezinski's reported comment that Carter's Clinton, Massachusetts, speech was the "Palestinians' Balfour Declaration."[33] Compounding the increasingly polluted relationship, Israelis and American Jews took no comfort in Carter's embrace of Sadat and then Assad.

Prior to his turn to visit Carter, Sadat was uneasy and uncertain about what he would find. He had a working relationship with Kissinger and had become accustomed to Kissinger's friendship, shrewdness, and flamboyance; Sadat had come to expect American mediation, intervention, and assistance in moving Israel out of all of Sinai. He expected that to continue and, therefore, preferred Ford's re-election. Recognizing that Carter was a man of religion, however, he told Eilts that Carter "must not be all that bad."[34] When Sadat met Carter for the first time on April 4, Carter had developed fairly clear and specific thoughts about the mutual advantages to Egypt and Israel of a comprehensive agreement. Recalling their encounter in the White House's private quarters, Carter beamed, "I was as overwhelmed with joy as I had been overwhelmed with despair when I met with Rabin."[35] Carter recalled that in the meeting where they talked about recognizing Israel and opening the Suez Canal to Israeli ships, Sadat acknowledged the possibility, but he said to Carter, "Not in my lifetime." Although he told Carter there might be peace in five years, Sadat's first response was that he was only prepared to end the state of war. Carter forcefully told Sadat that Egypt's recognition of Israel would have to happen simultaneously with Israeli withdrawal. If Sadat expected to receive all of Sinai back, Carter said firmly, then Egypt would have to recognize Israel formally and establish diplomatic relations with the Jewish state. As Eilts notes, this was an extraordinary request made by an American president to any Arab leader. Carter further told Sadat that a formal status of no-war, or nonbelligerency, was inadequate and unacceptable; the concept of a full peace with Israel was required.[36] Sadat was surprised that Carter addressed him directly and with such frankness. But, by the end of the meetings, he was willing to explore every alternative, including "the recognition of Israel,"[37] if Carter could make progress toward peace. At this juncture, Sadat was willing to attend a conference and support a joint Arab delegation, since that was the only way the Palestinians could possibly participate, given Israel's opposition to a separate Palestinian delegation. The meeting showed Sadat that Carter was not going to wallow in the trivial or dwell on the margins. Carter told him essentially: if you want Sinai, then you will have to grant Israel recognition; waiting for the next generation will not make a deal possible now. Carter felt that the Egyptian president had shown "adequate flexibility" to pursue serious negotiations with the Israelis. He recalled that Sadat had told him privately and in confidence that he would contemplate signing a separate agreement *without* completely resolving the Palestinian issue or worrying about Jordan's refusal to join subsequent talks.[38] In a published interview recounting this April visit with Carter, Sadat said that he had told Carter by the end of their meetings that "the most that we can do is to agree on a peace treaty."[39] Sadat also told Carter that Egypt's national defense requirements necessitated acquisition of U.S. weapons. Carter left a very positive impression on Sadat when he estimated that in ten years U.S.-Egyptian relations could be like U.S.-Israeli relations. When he finished his discussions with Carter, Sadat had a clearer understanding that if Egypt waited until the next generation to establish full diplomatic relations with Israel, then Israel would wait until then to relinquish all of Sinai.

Carter believed that "a rare harmony" was created between him and Sadat.[40] An affectionate trust also developed between them. Eilts said, "Sadat was mesmerized by Carter, a personal relationship of unprecedented proportions which I had not seen before."[41] In contrast, recalling the meeting, Brzezinski believed that Sadat was a wonderful human manipulator; both he and Eisenstat believed "Sadat played Carter like a violin."[42] After the April meeting, Sadat continued to be impressed with Carter and saw him as a decent and moral man. Sadat became "very dedicated, very convinced that, in contrast to some of the people he had known before in the U.S. government, Carter was a person on whom he could rely."[43] And Carter said of Sadat:

> He put faith in me to protect Egypt's interests. No matter what I did, he felt that I would never lie to him. He felt that if I told him something that the Israelis said or the United States would do, that he could depend on it. And it wasn't something that I had to build or orchestrate. It was kind of an immediate sharing of trust. And when somebody puts implicit faith in you, you are just not going to betray them. And I felt the same way with him. And so, I thought after that meeting, that as far as Egypt and Israel were concerned, I had a card to play in my pocket named Anwar Sadat. And when the time came where I really needed some help, that I could depend on him. Sadat was acting under a duality of pressures that were interconnected but conflicting [his preoccupation with Egypt and his commitments to the Palestinian issue/Arab world]. Sadat saw himself as the bold leader who would make history. And he saw me as an eager ally.[44]

Comparatively speaking, Carter bestowed faith on Sadat in a manner not previously expressed by any American president toward an Arab political leader. With all sincerity, Carter once told Brzezinski, "Sadat was like a brother."[45]

In turn, Sadat in a certain sense bequeathed to Carter a responsibility of representing Egypt in negotiations with the Israelis, though he kept some of that negotiating prerogative for himself. Focus was diminishing about what could be done about the Golan Heights or the West Bank, Gaza, and Jerusalem in part because Sadat and Carter had a special developing rapport not matched by any relationship Carter would have with another Middle East leader, or with other contemporary political leader for that matter. The issue of Sinai thus grew in proportion.

One difference between Sadat and Rabin was that Sadat was very good at getting people to feel that he agreed with them and saw their point of view. Another difference was that Sadat believed Carter was going to get Sinai back for him, while Rabin believed that Carter was going to take it away from Israel. For Egypt, Carter was evolving as an envoy to Israel; for Israel, Carter was quickly becoming an adversary. In response to the Sadat-Carter meeting, Israeli trepidation soared about the positive interactions developing between the two presidents.

The parade of Middle Eastern leaders to Washington continued: King Hussein, Assad, then the Saudis. In their late April 1997 meeting, Carter and King Hussein concurred that Jordan's role would be less active and public than Egypt's. Hussein was prepared to come to an international conference and would be "adequately constructive."[46] With Syria, Carter knew that Assad's participation in a reconvened Geneva Conference was more problematic. When they met in Geneva on May 9, Assad had paid close attention to Carter's public remarks about the Palestinians, the need to go to a conference, and the desire to achieve a comprehensive agreement. Emerging from Washington, these positions were hopeful and positive signs. Still, Assad needed to take Carter's measure. Assad, at the time, was nowhere close to where Sadat was in readiness for direct negotiations with the Israelis. Carter's view of Assad was rather stark: he was "sitting way on the outside, totally removed, a puppet of the Soviet Union, and not consulted except as it concerned the Golan Heights."[47] An international conference was a way for Assad to play a substantial role in the negotiating process. It seems that Carter and elements of his administration misunderstood Assad's political objectives. Assad refuted the notion of Syria serving merely as an instrument of the Soviet Union or participating only from the sidelines. Assad's political or independent Arab nationalist role did not depend on efforts to resolve the Arab-Israeli conflict. For Assad, an international conference was not a mechanism to instigate Arab-Israeli talks, but a vehicle to restrain Sadat's movement toward negotiating another separate agreement with Israel. It was a means with which Assad could reemphasize Arab solidarity. Assad was not disappointed with what he heard from Carter. Syrian Foreign Minister Abd al-Halim Khaddam attended and recalled that Carter told Assad the Palestinians could be represented at an international conference, not by "first rank" PLO members, but by those of a lesser rank. Carter reaffirmed to Assad that he was supportive of a Palestinian homeland.[48] On procedure, Carter was willing to consider conference committees that were functional as well as geographic, which would have given Assad some control over the terms and content of the subsequent negotiations. "Carter left a very comfortable impression, an impression that showed he wanted to obtain a solution on a moral basis,"[49] but a moral basis to the Syrians meant the Israelis giving and the Arabs taking. Without knowing the contents of the private discussions between them which would have angered the Israelis, Carter's particularly effusive and public embrace of Assad caused Israelis great trepidation.

Like Nixon, Carter was extremely accommodating to Assad. Brzezinski remarked that, while Carter pushed Assad into greater flexibility on such issues as the Palestinians or security arrangements, some of his remarks could have been misunderstood by the Israelis because Carter was being overly sympathetic to Syrian aspirations and overly critical of the Israelis.[50] Nixon had similarly ingratiated himself with Assad in June 1974, and Kissinger's reaction then was similar to Brzezinski's: the American president was promising too much to Assad. Carter noted that his relationship with Assad "was not built on trust,"[51] as was his relationship with Sadat. Carter's early embrace of Assad turned to distance, because, as Carter noted, Assad "would soon sabotage the Geneva peace talks by refusing to attend under any reasonable circumstances, and . . . would, still later, do everything possible to prevent the Camp David Accords from being fulfilled."[52]

Thus, in the spring of 1977, all efforts were aimed at achieving a comprehensive Middle East settlement: all the heads of state were interviewed in Washington and in the region; discussion commenced about including the Soviet Union in some manner; a conference format was elaborated; Egypt's leading role was established; and there was even some initial discussion about some transitional period where territories would move in stages from Israeli to Arab control. Now everyone waited for the Labor Party's re-election. As unexpected as the October War and Sadat's visit to Jerusalem was later in the year, Menachem Begin's election as Israel's sixth prime minister startled the U.S. government. Sadat was equally chagrined by the result, and King Hussein, who had secret meetings with Labor Party leaders during more than a dozen years, was wary. All of a sudden, Washington's twenty-nine-year policy of cooperation with the Israeli Labor Party abruptly ended. At the State Department, Begin's election "knocked everyone out of whack."[53] Referring to how little was known about Begin, Quandt said, "We didn't know where he was coming from. We weren't prepared for [his election]."[54] As Brzezinski explained in a briefing to Carter after the Israeli election, Begin was a totally different kettle of fish."[55] Said Sam Lewis, who came to know Begin as well as any American official, "Begin was a new figure regarded as a total disaster by the American government. Few knew him, and the ones who did thought of him as a terrorist, because of his pre–Israeli state association with the underground that fought against the British."[56] Unlike Rabin, Begin was not a social democrat, and his contrary views were more than political differences; they were based on firm ideological commitment.

When he took over the prime minister's office in June 1977, Begin carefully read the protocols of Rabin's talks with Carter and all of Carter's statements and declarations on the Middle East. He knew that Carter and Rabin were distant and discordant, that "they were at loggerheads with each other."[57] In recalling the preparations for his July trip to Washington, Ben-Elisar, the director general of Begin's office, remarked that "Begin, of course, did not like the Palestinian homeland statement. None of us liked it very much. We resented it. In fact, we hated it. Begin considered it a major shift in U.S. policy."[58] At the time, Begin was privy to an Israeli intelligence estimate suggesting very rough times ahead in which "U.S.-Israeli relations would sink to the deepest ebb since the foundation of the state of Israel."[59] Additionally, the estimate portrayed the prospects of Carter violating the Kissinger pledge not to negotiate with the PLO, or some stoppage in the flow of economic or military assistance. Recognizing his deep philosophical and political disagreement with the president, Begin was well aware of the lack of compatibility of Carter's positions on the peace process with his own. In preparing for his visit on July 17, Begin was obviously apprehensive about having a tense exchange with Carter and his advisers.[60]

Begin was perceived as an outsider in Israeli politics. For decades, he had been publicly disparaged by Israel's first prime minister, David Ben-Gurion. For this and other reasons, he craved acceptance from his countrymen and from the United States. Carter came to understand Begin's yearning for this approval. Susceptible to flattery, Begin also desperately wanted to be accepted as a legitimate prime minister.[61] Among Carter's Middle East advisers, there was considerable debate about how to handle Begin and his visit to Washington.[62] In Brzezinski's opinion, Begin "was very tough himself and, therefore, took people who were tough seriously. He would not take people who were soft seriously."[63] Lewis suggested that Begin be treated "with honey, not vinegar."[64] Based on Lewis's recommendations, Carter did not enter into an immediate showdown with Begin over the territorial issue or the settlements, but rather provided Begin honor and legitimacy. Carter's previous and negative experience with Rabin suggested that if the United States gave Begin support, then Begin would prove to be a strong leader and quite different from Rabin. Whereas he had expected Rabin to be flexible instead of rigid, Carter accurately anticipated and properly prepared for Begin's tenacity, but he was not prepared for what he saw as Begin's stubbornness. Sitting intently and saying nothing, Carter listened to Begin's historical rendition of the history of the Jewish people and the primacy of Judea and Samaria to Israel's future. Begin later spoke to the press about the compatibility of views between him and the American president. Carter, thereby, began learning that silence during one of Begin's "ritual" presentations was interpreted as tacit acquiescence to Begin's perspective. In subsequent dealings with Begin, Carter took copious notes on every issue in Begin's presence and, if necessary, debated each point. Begin could not then walk away from a meeting with him, give a press conference on the White House lawn, and say that there is American agreement or harmony in Israeli positions and attitudes.[65]

When Begin presented his ideas about how the negotiations should precede, Washington saw far more flexibility in substance and procedure than they had anticipated. On procedural matters, Begin suggested a reconvened Geneva Conference by October 10, 1977, with geographic committees established to discuss bilateral differences between Israel and Arab states. If the committee structure were to fail, he proposed proximity or rapprochement talks where there would be direct negotiations with the aid of a mediator, or the mediator would move between the delegations gathered together in the same area. Proximity talks were an American suggestion made in 1972 as a mechanism for possible Arab-Israeli negotiations.[66] For the first time, Begin also raised ideas about Palestinian self-rule. Although Begin's thoughts were not yet fully developed, he did stipulate that there were areas of governance where the Palestinians could and should make their own decisions. He specified that the political future of the Palestinians would be linked to Jordan and that there would be no foreign sovereignty over the West Bank. (This autonomy plan for the Palestinians was not presented until Begin's December 1977 visit to Carter.) Begin told Carter that Israel was prepared to go to Geneva on the basis of UNSC Resolution 338, which referred to UNSC Resolution 242. Begin's interpretation of UNSC Resolution 242 was simple: because there was no reference to Israeli withdrawal from *all the territories,* only certain territories were negotiable and should be returned.[67] Thus, Begin tended to emphasize UNSC Resolution 338 because it referred specifically to negotiation between the parties; participants in the reconvened conference were to be accredited representatives of Israel, Egypt, Syria, and Jordan, and they were not to present preconditions of any kind for their participation. At the proposed inaugural conference session, the representatives of all the parties would make public opening addresses. Thereafter, three separate geographic committees would be established—Egyptian-Israeli, Syrian-Israeli, and Jordanian-Israeli—to finalize the peace treaties between Israel and its neighbors.[68] This was precisely the structure that emerged after the opening of the 1991 Madrid Peace Conference. By insisting on no preconditions, Begin left open the possibility that both Jerusalem and the West Bank could be discussed, which were for him otherwise nonnegotiable issues. Begin recognized Jordan as a fact, but he never said Jordan was a Palestinian state. Although Jordan contained parts of historic Eretz Yisrael, Israel would not try to take it. As compared to the Labor Party, which focused on a solution with Jordan, Begin felt that maintaining Israeli presence in Judea and Samaria was integral because the West Bank was part of Israel's national patrimony. Since he was ideologically committed to Judea and Samaria, no political solution offered by Begin for these areas would be acceptable to the Americans. Instead, he proposed the possibility of reaching peace agreements with Egypt and Syria in return for territories Israel held since the June 1967 War. Proposing new ideas for American reaction did not eliminate the obstacles to participating in Geneva, especially those concerning Palestinian representation. Syria's only acceptable options were a unified Arab delegation to represent Arab interests, or where independent delegations were, as Assad said, "coordinated fully among themselves."[69]

After Begin's visit to Washington, Assad said that there were three elements of peace: "withdrawal from the territories occupied in 1967, self-determination and restoration of the property of the Palestinian Arab people, and the termination of the state of war."[70] Significantly, in this July 1977 interview where he spelled out his views, Assad did not call for withdrawal from all the territories, but that was a casual omission; his complete unwillingness to have peace treaties as the diplomatic goal exposed Syria's continuing reluctance to accept Israel as a reality. Nonbelligerency was all that he was willing to consider, and that could only come after total withdrawal. These points were unacceptable to Israel, but when Carter presented Begin with a concept of peace, Dayan, who did not accompany Begin on this visit, sensed it was of "the highest significance."[71] Carter had widened the meaning of UNSC Resolution 242 to oblige the parties to conclude a full peace agreement, not merely to end belligerency. The American view was to have open borders, free movement of peoples and cargoes, diplomatic ties, and the establishment of normal relations ratified by full peace agreements. Carter wanted the peace to be with all of Israel's neighbors, involve Israel's withdrawal from "occupied territory to secure borders, and see the creation of a Palestinian entity (not independent nation)." Begin told Carter that he could agree with all of these points except the Palestinian entity; he felt that every Israeli and Jew possessed the legitimate right to settle in Judea and Samaria. Thus, the nucleus of the disagreement between Carter and Begin was the future of the West Bank. Carter told Begin that the Israeli settlements established within the occupied territories were serious obstacles to peace and to initiating Palestinian political rights.[72] Carter believed that all the territories needed to be returned if there was going to be a comprehensive negotiated settlement. From his view, Begin's ideology and the building of settlements adversely affected the prospects for the comprehensive peace Washington was seeking. Begin's attitude toward Judea and Samaria limited the geographic substance that could be discussed in reaching an arrangement with the Jordanians or Palestinians. This profound disagreement over the future of the West Bank and the settlements there was fully established by the end of the Camp David negotiations. They bitterly infected U.S.-Israeli relations until Carter left office.

Though the political distance about the future of the territories might have been greater between Carter and Begin than between Carter and Rabin, the personal warmth between Carter and Begin more than neutralized that gap. Carter believed that Begin was much more far-reaching in offering an accommodation with Egypt than his predecessor. For his part, Begin had a positive sense of his meetings because he had established an emotional and functional rapport with the U.S. president. Upon his return to Israel from Washington, Begin said, "I was deeply impressed by President Carter's exceptional personality."[73] Significantly, Begin had not only avoided a confrontation between the United States and Israel on political issues, but had even achieved what Dayan termed a "mutual understanding."[74] "Perhaps Begin intentionally flattered Carter," recalled Begin's personal secretary Yahiel Kadishai.[75] Regardless, from Begin's viewpoint, their talks were positive, including Begin quoting from the Bible, "something Rabin would never had done."[76] From Brzezinski's account, the first Carter-Begin meeting "did little to advance the prospects for peace,"[77] because Carter was too soft on Begin. However, a significant consensus was reached in the Begin-Carter meetings: a growing recognition that another Egyptian-Israeli agreement was possible.

Years before Begin was elected, his view was that Egypt, not Jordan, should be the first country to make peace with Israel. When he became prime minister, "he went looking for Sadat."[78] Before going to Washington, Begin seriously considered a "far-reaching territorial compromise" in Sinai,[79] a strong preference he expressed to Carter, Vance, and other U.S. officials. He had no emotional resistance to territorial compromise in Sinai; his only difficulty in returning Sinai was the dismantling of Israeli settlements. Begin's reasoning was simple; if Israel returned Sinai, he told Kadishai, then "we did our share in fulfilling UNSC 242."[80] After he left Washington, Carter informed Sadat by private letter that Begin was willing to make a significant withdrawal from Sinai. Though Carter still advocated a comprehensive settlement at a conference, he became a willing, though inadvertent, accomplice to the evolving understanding between Begin and Sadat. Begin used Carter to confirm information gleaned from other sources that an agreement could be reached over Sinai. A ripening negotiating environment developed on the Egyptian-Israeli front. Secretly, Washington and Moscow were concluding a common statement that would be an outline for a negotiated settlement and the framework upon which another conference could be convened. Both Sadat and Begin were telling Carter that significant progress could be made through Washington in swapping Sinai for a peace agreement. Washington spent time narrowing differences on substance. However, neither leader gave himself over to total American control of the negotiating process; instead, each tested the other's intentions.

No matter how much faith Sadat put in Carter, no matter how important Israel's strategic relationship was with Washington, Begin and Sadat seriously tested the possibility of reaching an agreement independently of the United States. Though the exact details of the conversations are not known, when the head of the Israeli Mossad met Sadat's envoy in Morocco in July, and in subsequent secret exchanges through Morocco and Rumania, and before Vance's August Middle East trip, Israelis and Egyptians had measured each other sufficiently to realize that a deal might be struck between them. If not by early September, then certainly by the end of the month, through private channels, Begin and Sadat were fairly clear with one another about the general outlines of what was possible or expected in the next diplomatic agreement between them.

As the fall approached, the public possibilities of another Egyptian-Israeli agreement grew as the other parties to the conflict, one by one, removed themselves from consideration as candidates to participate in a comprehensive settlement. After Begin's July visit, the administration began to expand its focus from substantive consideration of what could be ratified at a Geneva Conference to procedural discussions of how to convene a conference. With the determination reflective of Carter himself, representatives of his administration tried to thread a diplomatic needle with a rope, seeking to find workable formulas and understandings that would enable a conference convocation and a comprehensive settlement. The administration's talented civil servants worked diligently: they adamantly resisted Israeli pressure to exclude Judea and Samaria in future negotiations for a comprehensive settlement; sent secret emissaries to Arafat to have the PLO recognize Israel and accept UNSC Resolution 242; negotiated a formula for Moscow's participation in convening a conference; and tinkered in every way possible to solicit Syrian participation. During the summer, the Carter administration, in short, narrowed differences on substance between Israel and its neighbors. The NSC and State Department churned out position papers and memoranda suggesting compromises. Though their effort and successes were quite remarkable, still they were insufficient, yet reflective of the Brookings Institution general outline. On substantive issues, Egypt, Jordan, and Israel (not Syria or the PLO) agreed on the following terms for the conference: (1) there would be no preconditions required prior to the conference's convocation; (2) peace treaties would be the negotiating objective in exchange for territory held by Israel since the June 1967 War; (3) a unified Arab delegation would include Palestinians (but not PLO members) and would represent the Arab side at a ceremonial opening session; (4) the conference would evolve immediately into bilateral talks between Israel and the respective Arab states; (5) West Bank and Gaza (but not Syrian) issues would be discussed in a working group of parties attending the conference; (6) the agreed basis of the negotiations would be UNSC Resolutions 242 and 338; and (7) the Soviet Union would convene the conference along with the United States.

Despite all of this, nettlesome issues could not be overcome: the nature of peace; the definition of Palestinian representation; the degree of "comprehensiveness" desired by Egypt and Israel; Begin's refusal to transfer any of the West Bank to a foreign sovereignty and unwillingness to halt the building and expansion of Israeli settlements; and Syria's adamant refusal to recognize Israel. These were too broad, too complicated, and too ideologically motivated to succumb to modification. No one factor or political leader was responsible for keeping the administration's effort from progressing, but collectively their weight sunk the conference idea and the objective of a comprehensive settlement. The PLO refused to accept UNSC Resolution 242 or to participate in any negotiations in which it would not be a separate and independent delegation. For his part, King Hussein questioned Yasir Arafat's ability to lead a Palestinian delegation to a reconvened Geneva Conference and affirmed Jordan's opposition to accept representatives from the PLO within the Jordanian delegation.[81] Egypt wanted a prior commitment (not a precondition) from Israel for full withdrawal from Sinai, including dismantling of settlements in exchange for a peace treaty. But Syria played the most devilish role: it set out to scuttle any conference. Assad refused to accept Israel's right to exist, was adamantly opposed to another separate Egyptian-Israeli agreement, and lobbied hard against Carter's concerted effort. A determined Damascus thwarted the American effort to engage the PLO. Arafat's al-Fatah Palestinian organization went as far as accepting a formula in which it would accept the contents of UNSC 242 "with reservations," if Washington would accept the principle of Palestinian self-determination and develop a dialogue with the PLO without the Carter administration committing itself to any other diplomatic outcome. For Palestinian representation, the PLO accepted a formula for nonprominent members of the PLO to be nominated by the PLO through the decision of their executive committee and ratified by Arafat's signature. While the U.S. goal was to initiate a Palestinian-Israeli negotiating process, the PLO goal was to assure its centrality and maintain its validity as the sole representative of the Palestinian people, two very different sorts of objectives. The PLO's goal was not Washington's, but the PLO wanted Washington's recognition to round out its quest for legitimacy. The concept of a U.S.-PLO dialogue became a reality eleven years later when the PLO finally accepted UNSC 242. But in September 1977, Syrian Foreign Minister Khaddam asked rhetorically of al-Fatah leaders, "Why accept a dialogue without any concrete political commitments from the United States?" The PLO did not rescind its demand for an "assured presence" at a reconvened Geneva Conference; in 1991 at the Madrid Middle East Peace Conference, the PLO accepted Palestinian (not PLO) presence in a joint Palestinian-Jordanian delegation. On September 20, in a long and stormy session with his PLO colleagues, Arafat apparently cut his hand on a glass trying to persuade them to accept the American offer.[82] Arafat was not then the ostensible moderate he would become two decades later, but he was seeking a way for the PLO to nose its way into the negotiating tent. Brutal Syrian pressure kept the PLO from accepting the American formula. Assad, in a remarkably candid interview at the end of August 1977, said, "In light of what is being said and put forth by Israel, it is very difficult to be very enthusiastic . . . or optimistic about convening or the results of the Geneva Conference. I believe that if the conference does not convene it will not be bad in all aspects, particularly with regard to Arab unity. If the conference is not convened, this would lead to further Arab solidarity and unity. When we sign the agreement ending the state of war, Israel would be an established fact. For Israel to be an established fact is one thing and forcing us to recognize Israel is something else."[83]

When Secretary of State Vance went to the Middle East in August 1977, he focused on finding compromises but came home empty. In fact, Vance returned home with renewed and unintended Israeli irritation for the Carter administration. Israeli leaders anticipated a philosophical and political slugfest and they got it. The day before his departure, Vance received a phone call from Israeli Ambassador

Dinitz, asking him "not to mention American views on the 1967 frontiers, nor the points of the U.S. package for Geneva, which dealt with Palestinian representation and the question of a Palestinian entity."[84] Begin had made a similar request of Carter at the White House, specifically asking that the administration no longer talk publicly about Israeli withdrawals to the 1967 borders or use the phrase "Palestinian homeland." Vance was very tough with the Israelis, and, emboldened by Carter, would not relent. In turn, Vance wanted Carter to stand firm against the Israelis, which he did. So lathered by the Israeli request was Vance that he said he would consider resigning if Carter did not stand firm against the Israeli pressure. The official American position was an Israeli withdrawal to the 1967 lines with minor border adjustments. Said Vance, "The administration was committed to evenhandedness in the search for peace; and although it could consult closely with Israel, they were not going to concert with us against the Arabs."[85]

Israelis were angry because the United States was all at once trying to find a formula for PLO representation or other Palestinians to be at the Geneva Conference, continued to be critical of Israeli settlement activity, and wanted Begin to compromise on his determination to hold on to the West Bank at all costs. The Carter administration was thus turning up the heat. After Vance's return, on September 13, 1977, the administration said that Palestinian representatives would have to be at Geneva for the Palestinian question to be solved. When the Carter administration announced with the Soviet Union on October 1, 1997, in their joint declaration about the Middle East, that the legitimate rights of the Palestinians be ensured, Israelis and American Jews were apoplectic, accusing the administration of "betraying their basic commitments,"[86] and ultimately causing the administration to back down in an unprecedented public fight with Israelis and American Jews.

By the first weeks of September, a comprehensive settlement seemed unlikely. An Israeli-Jordanian agreement was improbable, finding the formula for Palestinian representation not feasible, and generating Syrian-Israeli negotiations impossible. However, the Egyptian-Israeli track still looked promising, but the the administration did not know how promising it was because it was excluded from detail passing between Cairo and Jerusalem. Washington's conceptual focus switched to getting to Geneva, whatever the cost. Thinking shifted to just getting the parties together, because once there, no one would want to leave.[87] A conference became an end in itself, rather than a device to pressure or induce the parties on substantive issues before a conference. Failing to synthesize opinions on substance and pace, the Carter administration sought to harmonize matters of procedure, which was not what Sadat preferred. For him, going to Geneva without a guaranteed outcome or an assured success could mean "negotiating there for ten years."[88] He also disliked the diplomatic slowdown, so he added unexpected wood to the smoldering fire. Out of the blue, he volunteered to Vance a draft peace treaty between Egypt and Israel. In the draft document's margins, he noted his fallback position on certain points. He then requested that Vance obtain similar treaties from the other parties to the conflict, telling him to "stitch them together, propose them to us, and we'll go to Geneva to work out the details."[89] Typical of Sadat was his request that the Egyptian draft treaty not be shown to the Israelis, leaving the Americans with the impression that they were the only postmen. By September 2, 1977, Dayan had provided Washington a rough copy of an Israeli draft for a treaty with Egypt and then presented a more polished version to Carter later in that month.[90] Quandt noted that the examination of these draft treaties was to be "handled with utmost care and secrecy, since the Carter administration had said repeatedly that it would not try to impose a blueprint of its own,"[91] except, of course, the Brookings Institution outline. And, Vance's August Middle Eastern trip was chock-full of American formulas and frameworks for procedural and substantive matters.

Unknowingly, precisely when the administration was more forceful, demanding, and exact in what it wanted from a conference and how the conference would be conducted, Begin and Sadat continued to contact each other privately. Unknown to Washington at the time, Egyptians and Israelis were conducting high-level secret talks and carrying on communications through third parties. After Dayan secretly met King Hussein in London in late August, the Israeli foreign minister sensed that there was no pending diplomatic breakthrough with the Jordanians.[92] On September 4, 1977, Dayan flew to Morocco to discuss with King Hassan, apparently at the king's instigation, the possibility of finding an Arab-Israeli settlement. King Hassan seemed to want to play a more active role in the politics and diplomacy of the conflict's resolution and suggested another meeting between Israeli and Egyptian representatives.

By September 9, four days after conversing with King Hassan, Dayan received word that the Egyptians preferred a meeting between Dayan and Egyptian Deputy Prime Minister Dr. Hassan Tuhami, as compared to the Israeli preference of a meeting between Begin and Sadat or Vice President Mubarak. On September 15, on his way to Washington, Dayan was clandestinely rerouted to Paris and then to Rabat, where he met Tuhami on September 16. Of Begin's close advisers, apparently Ben-Elisar and Kadishai did not know in advance about the proposed secret meeting and neither did Defense Minister Ezer Weizman.[93] On the Egyptian side, only President Sadat and Mubarak were aware of the meeting. At Sadat's insistence, significant details of the meeting were kept from the Americans.[94] Egyptian Foreign Minister Fahmy was not informed, and his successor, Mohamed Ibrahim Kamel, inadvertently learned about them in July 1978, seven months after taking office. In addition, from a variety of sources, Sadat obtained opinions and assurances from Austrian Prime Minister Kreisky and Rumanian President Ceausescu that Begin was prepared for serious negotiations with Egypt. Sadat learned about Begin's readiness and conditions for parting with Sinai. According to Tuhami, Sadat's reason for sending him as a personal envoy was to ascertain "proof of Israel's good intent in seeking a just peace."[95] Among his contemporaries, Tuhami was not taken seriously; on the contrary he was considered eccentric, a court jester.

When they met for the first time, Tuhami did not shake Dayan's hand. After several hours of informal and "get acquainted" talks, they discussed substantive issues: withdrawal from territories; sovereignty questions; the Palestinian issue; the nature of coexistence; and Jerusalem. King Hassan then suggested that "it was up to Tuhami and Dayan to prepare the way for Begin to come and talk to Sadat."[96] When Sadat saw Vance in August, he indicated a desire to meet Begin.[97] Tuhami made it clear to Dayan that Sadat wanted peace, was willing to meet with Begin, and would provide guarantees for Israeli security, if Begin agreed in principle to total withdrawal from all the territories. Tuhami proposed that Egypt and Israel conclude their substantive negotiations with the help of King Hassan and then go to Geneva merely to sign the document. Tuhami suggested that the two sides complete the deal there—with all the difficulties worked out, not in a partial arrangement, not in public, and not at Geneva.[98] Sadat remained consistent in his intent to have a conference as a forum for signing or ratifying a document, but not for negotiating. From all available sources, Dayan did not promise or signal to Tuhami any Israeli willingness to return immediately or eventually all of Sinai or any of the territories. Dayan said that he "did not promise anything because I was not authorized to promise him anything."[99] Kadishai, recalling what Begin later told him about the Dayan-Tuhami meetings, emphatically reported that "Dayan promised Tuhami nothing."[100] All Dayan promised was that, if Sadat visited Begin, he would be accorded the highest dignity of any head of state, and there was no explicit commitment made at these meetings for full Israeli withdrawal from Sinai.[101] Nonetheless, Tuhami had the impression that Israel would exchange territory for peace, knew that their discussions had to be referred back to Begin, and still reported to Sadat that Egypt would receive Sinai.[102] Dayan was not excessively encouraged by these secret talks, but he did tell Begin "that something new had opened, that there could be another meeting, and that the Egyptians wanted Sinai back."[103] Dayan suggested and Begin accepted three points resulting from the Dayan-Tuhami meeting: that Israel and Egypt exchange proposals for a peace treaty (a process that was underway before Dayan's first visit to Morocco); that another meeting with Tuhami be scheduled in a fortnight; and that if there were an imminent Begin-Sadat meeting, then no prior commitment be made to withdraw from all the occupied territories.[104]

After hearing a report of the meetings with Tuhami, Begin continued to be more optimistic than Dayan about the possibilities of reaching an early agreement with Egypt. Sadat had publicly spoken about a treaty with Israel in his speech before the Arab Socialist Union in July and had mentioned it to American congressional leaders visiting Cairo the same month. He had also mentioned it to Carter, but it is unclear whether Carter actually told Begin in July or afterward about such a prospect. After reporting to Begin about the talks with Tuhami, Dayan went to the United States. Two weeks later, Dayan and Tuhami had a second meeting in which Tuhami accused Dayan of starting "a plan for negotiation and procrastination, in the traditional Jewish style of wheeling and dealing in time of sale or purchase. I rejected this style and told him [Dayan]: 'Go back to your Chief and demand clear-cut responses for every item I have mentioned to you in the previous meeting.'"[105] If Sadat had originally intended to withhold the content of the Tuhami-Dayan talks from the Americans, then he violated his own intentions. Dayan certainly told Vance, who in turn told Carter, that the meetings took place, though Dayan did not give a full account of his discussions to the Americans. While Sadat did not directly tell Carter about the Tuhami-Dayan talks, Sadat sent him a letter on October 4, urging the United States not to do anything "to prevent Israel and Egypt from negotiating directly, with the United States serving as an intermediary either before or after the Geneva Conference is convened."[106] Before choosing to go to Jerusalem, Sadat had considered the possibility of meeting Begin in several locations. These included the island of Rhodes or at Rafah in Sinai. Sadat moved quickly toward the decision of meeting Begin soon, and he still wanted Geneva to be a place where agreements were ratified, not negotiated. Fahmy, Sadat's foreign minister, differed from his boss, wanting the conference to negotiate practical matters; Sadat was growing impatient with all the time-consuming discussion about Palestinian representation. He told the American ambassador in Cairo, "Peace is slipping through my fingers for procedural reasons."[107]

Dayan went to the United States in mid-September to attend the opening session of the UN General Assembly. He used the occasion to go to Washington to take his first personal measure of Carter, Vance, and Brzezinski. (Dayan had not accompanied Begin on the July trip, which had been Begin's selfish moment in the spotlight.) Wanting their meetings to focus on the peace process, Dayan engaged in substantive discussions about convening Geneva—he reviewed the contents of Israel's proposed draft treaty with Egypt and Israeli attitudes toward the other territories, Jerusalem, and the Palestinian representation issue. On the eve of his visit, Dayan was disturbed by the Likud Party decision to establish six new settlements in Judea and Samaria; he knew that it would trigger a new argument with the administration and give Carter another excuse to criticize Israel.[108] Prior to his meeting with Carter and other American officials on September 19, Dayan spoke with Vance at the State Department. Unlike his American counterparts, Dayan was not tied to a particular procedure, such as a conference; "he just wanted a breakthrough somewhere."[109] On the matter of Palestinian representation, Dayan was equally flexible and was not going to examine passports or identity cards; he wanted the negotiations to commence and acceptable conclusions to be reached. Although more pragmatic than Begin, Dayan still reflected Begin's view that there would be no negotiations with the PLO. At the State Department, Dayan and the Carter administration ventilated, candidly if not bluntly, their major differences about the substance of a final settlement and the procedures necessary to initiate a new round of negotiations. On matters of substance, Washington angrily opposed Israeli settlement policy, still favored a return to the 1967 borders with minor modifications, was prepared to initiate a dialogue with the PLO, and wanted negotiations about a "Palestinian entity" raised at the conference. On matters of procedure, Washington sought a unified Arab delegation to the proposed Geneva Conference, including, perhaps, low-level PLO members.[110] Dayan was pleased with Vance's statement that the United States was prepared to guarantee Israeli security and sensed that this protection was offered in exchange for Israeli willingness to return almost all the territories it held from the June 1967 War. Vance told Dayan that although the Arab states were not yet prepared to sign peace treaties with Israel, they wanted the territories back immediately. Vance, who had several proposed draft treaties in hand and yet seemed to understand Arab reluctance to sign them, did not seem to know the level of Sadat's readiness to reach a separate arrangement with Israel. And it is unclear how much Carter had told Vance of Sadat's readiness. At the State Department, Dayan was questioned about the kind of "home rule" Israel would grant to the Palestinians, the nature of Palestinian representation that Israel would accept, the issue of future sovereignty for the territories, and the timetable and structure for a withdrawal from Sinai. There was less discussion about the Golan.[111]

Dayan's White House meetings with Carter that September afternoon were distinctly unpleasant. The first meeting began with Carter, Mondale, and Dayan in a private session and then incorporated their respective staffs and advisers. Carter and Dayan clashed over the settlements issue. Unlike Begin, whose view about settlements was based on ideology, Dayan preferred not to encourage the building of settlements except where they served military or strategic purposes.[112] Carter told the Israeli foreign minister that continued establishment of any kind of settlements was liable to prevent the Palestinian Arabs from joining the peace talks. Dayan demurred, saying that "there never was and never could be a government in Israel that would fail to establish Israeli settlements in the territories." In response, Carter said, "You are more stubborn than the Arabs, and you put obstacles on the path to peace."[113] In the private Dayan-Carter meetings, there was little mention of the prospects of progress toward an agreement with Syria or over the Golan Heights, except the expressed American view that Israel should settle for the pre–June 1967 War borders, with slight or minor modifications. In the larger staff meeting, Carter again did not hide his anger and disappointment over the settlements. When issues of procedure were discussed about convening a Geneva Conference, Carter wanted Israel to accept his definition of Palestinian representation: a unified Arab delegation composed of "not-well-known PLO members." Carter repeated what Begin had said to him in July, that "Israel would not check the credentials of the Palestinians who will participate."[114] Liberally interpreting Begin's remarks, Carter deduced that Begin would not mind if there were PLO members. Carter was trying to find a thin line of overlap between what he said to Assad in Geneva and what Begin had said to him in July. Characteristic of his style as a problem solver, Carter was determined to reconcile the opposing perspectives about the Palestinian representation issue. He said that the United States did not expect Israel to negotiate with the Arabs as a collective whole, as the Syrians preferred. Arafat and his colleagues were particularly perturbed that all the Arab states had now consented to a unified Arab delegation, thereby preventing the PLO from having the independent voice it had been seeking. The president agreed with Begin's premise that Jordan and Israel, along with the "not-well-known" PLO members, would discuss the West Bank. Dayan said the Geneva agenda would not include a discussion of territory with the Palestinians, but only a discussion of the status of the Palestinian refugees. Furthermore, noted Dayan, Palestinian representation would have to be part of a Jordanian delegation; there could not be either a separate Palestinian delegation or a PLO delegation. Carter responded that the Israeli position on Palestinian representation was too intransigent. In the end, Dayan, who was not enthusiastic about a conference because he saw it as a counterweight working against Sadat's ability to act independently, sensed that anything that required Sadat to consult with the PLO or Soviets was doomed to failure.[115] Nonetheless, Dayan clarified his preference about how a conference might proceed, if it were convened: after an opening session, there would be negotiations with the heads of state, followed by talks elsewhere than in Geneva.[116] The notion of separate bilateral talks flowing from the plenary session was congealing as accepted procedure. Vance generally agreed with Dayan's projection that if "agreement was reached in these secret talks, the parties could return to Geneva to sign."[117] But from the American viewpoint, a conference was still to have a comprehensive quality. Finally, in the larger session, Dayan was adamant about Israel not allowing the West Bank to be annexed to Jordan and to become, therefore, a PLO-run territory and a security nightmare for Israel. Reading from a text, Vance said that the Americans were intent to have the Israeli borders closely identical to those prior to the June 1967 War.[118] There was little conversation between Dayan and Carter about Egyptian readiness to reach an agreement with Israel; that fact was understood because Dayan had heard from Tuhami firsthand what Egypt wanted and needed. With Israeli Foreign Ministry officials in Washington, "Dayan was very closemouthed about those meetings and said little also about his recent private meeting with King Hussein in London."[119] The meetings with Dayan were an opportunity for the Americans to place their ideas, culled and developed since Vance's trip, directly before the Israelis. By rejecting many of them, Dayan rebuffed the Carter administration's desire to play the role of active interlocutor. Angered by Dayan's disfavor, Carter provided no information to the Israelis about discussions or preparations for a communiqué to be offered soon by Moscow and Washington. Failure to keep Israel apprised led to an even more heated exchange between Carter and Dayan in early October. In spite of the escalating discord, the United States did not stop promoting ideas that Israel opposed with great vehemence. The heat kept on being turned up. First Dayan and then Begin disliked the message, the style, and now, the messenger. But because of his preeminent priority to sustain a positive relationship between Jerusalem and Washington, Dayan constantly tried to avoid lingering rancor between the two countries.

For the ten days after Dayan's visit, the Carter administration focused even more intently on defining an agenda and procedural arrangements for convening the conference. Using a version of shuttle diplomacy in Washington, foreign ministers and other officials of Egypt, Jordan, and Syria met periodically with Vance and other American bureaucrats. These sessions were the prenegotiations and clarification talks on Geneva's terms of reference for the conference representatives, but consensus conclusions proved impossible to achieve. Sadat's level of impatience was again tested. In the lengthy letter delivered by Fahmy in late September, Sadat told Carter that time was running out and the parties should stop haggling over procedures; Fahmy contradicted Sadat's tone by saying that Egypt was not in a hurry to go to Geneva. Fahmy tried to negotiate for Sadat like he had done just prior to the signing of Sinai I. This time he revisited the Palestinian representation issue, requesting a UN resolution to confirm the PLO's participation at a peace conference, to which Carter replied that the United States would veto it. Carter also told Fahmy, that he, himself, would worry about Assad and Hussein, and that the Soviets would neither be excluded nor given a major role.[120]

On September 25, the Israeli Cabinet agreed that Palestinian representatives could constitute part of a unified Arab delegation at the opening session of a reconvened Geneva Conference. This was a shift in Israel's position, but it did not change Israel's total opposition to PLO participation. Israel clearly stated that it would not negotiate with this unified delegation at the ceremonial opening session, but that it would subsequently negotiate with individual Arab states. The Israeli cabinet also rejected any attempt to change the contents of UNSC Resolution 242 or to legitimize the PLO as a negotiating partner, because that would mean Israel would have a "partner in a debate about the establishment of a state."[121]

When Syrian Foreign Minister Khaddam met with Carter on September 28, Khaddam expressed Assad's misgivings that a Geneva Conference would be a cover for Egypt negotiating a separate peace with Israel. Like Fahmy, Khaddam suggested that another UN resolution be passed to give the PLO an opportunity to participate at a conference. Carter told Khaddam that the Arabs were responsible for deciding how much coordination they wanted prior to Geneva and that a series of bilateral agreements could emerge from a Geneva Conference. Again, Syria did not want an assemblage of geographic committees, which would procedurally facilitate separate, unilateral, or bilateral agreements. Syria wanted to veto the possibility of another Egyptian-Israeli agreement. Syria had not altered its view that Israel was simply illegitimate, an "unprecedented aggression" against the Arabs.[122] Though deeply enmeshed in trying to get to the conference, the Carter administration did not accurately gauge the sensibilities and the political priorities of Begin and Sadat. The administration failed to comprehend four important variables in Sadat's thinking: the magnitude of his impatience for progress; the extent of his willingness to deal directly with the Israelis; the degree of his anxiety about a Syrian veto of his actions; and the level of his cynicism toward the Soviet Union. Washington's motivation to include a Soviet role at Geneva was based on Russia's cochairmanship there in December 1973 and the influence Washington perceived Moscow had with the PLO and Syria.

From the outset, Carter did not see any alternative but to invite Soviet participation in the Arab-Israeli negotiating process. In the early days of Carter's administration, Brzezinski had advocated that the Soviets be kept informed of Washington's efforts to convene a Geneva Middle East Peace Conference. In February 1977, Brzezinski further argued that going to Geneva would be a concession to the Soviet Union, and in return, Soviets would use their influence to assist the negotiating process. He noted, until "we have an understanding with the Soviets that they will, in fact, play a constructive role, we should avoid getting publicly committed to holding a Geneva Conference. In other words, we should hold out the promise of a Geneva Conference this fall and work toward it, but stop short of being committed to holding it."[123] In a February 23 National Security Council meeting, Brzezinski warned, "If we only resolve procedural questions before going to Geneva, Geneva will break down, and the Soviets will try and exploit the situation; they could be spoilers while Vance thought they could be partners."[124] Beginning in May 1977, Washington channeled part of its attention on how to bring Moscow into a distinctively limited role in a portended Middle East peace conference. While Washington wanted to allow the Soviets into the negotiating scheme, it did not want to give them control or too much influence over the outcome. By late summer, Carter felt that the movement to involve the Soviets was influenced more by Vance than Brzezinski.[125] Vance was committed to getting to Geneva and would not be dissuaded about the need for the Soviets to be included in some carefully defined, if not restricted, role. Vance was concerned that if they were not included, then they could cause problems.[126] In late August, Vance asked Dobrynin to obtain ideas from Soviet Foreign Minister Gromyko about the statement to be made in conjunction with the joint U.S.-Soviet communiqué on the Middle East. The presence of Gromyko in New York for the opening of the annual session of the United Nations gave Vance the opportunity to speak to the Soviet foreign minister about a variety of issues, including an update about Washington's progress in writing terms of reference and an agenda for the conference. In negotiating the contents of the U.S.-Soviet communiqué, there was an air of casualness and "business as usual." The communiqué itself was expected to be a product of normal diplomatic dialogue and exchange, generated through the usual procedure for a U.S. draft document to be turned over to the Soviets for comment. But, in this case, according to the State Department officials, "This was not an idea that was staffed out. We were not consulted about it in advance. Vance gave us our marching orders together . . . and our job [was] to salute like good soldiers and . . . try to make it work."[127] Vance simply informed Atherton and Saunders to comment on the original Soviet version and work primarily with Mikhail Sytenko, a Soviet diplomat. They both had some reservations in drafting the communiqué, wondering whether Vance had sufficiently considered how the Israelis would respond. Atherton said, "We both had sort of an uneasy feeling. I won't say we articulated it in great detail. We had an uneasy feeling that this was starting down a path that might cause problems; it might blow up."[128] In drafting the communiqué, Saunders and Atherton stayed in close contact with Quandt at the White House to confirm that their terminology corresponded to Brzezinski's concepts. There was also close coordination between the State Department and the White House to determine if Vance and Brzezinski were in agreement on the contents.

Finally, the communiqué was a consensus document; sentences and paragraphs were lashed together, inevitably creating compromises on terms and definitions about substance and procedure. Like UNSC Resolution 338, Moscow offered the first draft and Washington policymakers redrafted it. The carefully worded U.S.-Soviet communiqué of October 1, 1977, contained the acceptable phrases from UNSC 242, but without mentioning 242 by name. For the United States, the major new formulation referred to "legitimate rights of the Palestinian people," in contrast to Washington's previous statement about the "legitimate interests" of the Palestinians. Although the Soviets wanted "national rights," the United States would not concede to that extent. Washington succeeded in describing the goal of the negotiations as "normal peaceful relations," rather than just "peaceful relations." A legalistic tone dominated the communiqué's textural evolution. Except in general terms, it was not written to satisfy the concerns or trepidations of the parties to the conflict, especially Israel; it was crafted to reach an understanding with Moscow and not blow the Arabs out of the water.[129] American officials who worked on the text believed that it phrased the content more favorably than might have otherwise been expected from Moscow because the Soviets were so eager to get into the diplomatic game. Recalled David Korn, who was working in the State Department's policy planning staff at the time, "The Russians caved in on just about everything we wanted because they were concerned that Sadat was going to leave them out."[130] The Soviet first draft did not contain the cold war rhetoric such as a demand for PLO recognition or for a Palestinian state. Moscow was also willing to use compromise language because they wanted an agreement.[131] In the days before issuance of the communiqué, Vance shuttled with his advisers to the Soviets and negotiated directly with Gromyko to achieve the right language. Except for

Vance and few others who knew about the drafting with the Soviets, no one in the State Department was informed that Carter wanted the Soviets involved.[132] Moscow wanted to renew its influence with Arab allies, to return to an important role in the diplomatic process. Carter, Brzezinski, and Quandt all believed that if this were a balanced multinational approach, Moscow "could help" with the Syrians and the PLO. Neither Carter nor his advisers explained how Moscow could have possibly modified either the Syrians' or the PLO's hatred toward Israel.[133] There was a sense that this joint communiqué would catapult the administration to Geneva, where the dynamic of the moment would force substantial changes on the principles. Carter knew that there was political sacrifice on his part in issuing the communiqué because, by advocating legitimate Palestinian rights, this was a step toward a Palestinian homeland the Israelis disliked.[134]

Joint U.S.-Soviet Statement on the Middle East
1 October 1977

Having exchanged views regarding the unsafe situation which remains in the Middle East, U.S. Secretary of State Cyrus Vance and Member of the Politburo of the Central Committee of the CPSU, Minister for Foreign Affairs of the U.S.S.R. A. A. Gromyko have the following statement to make on behalf of their countries, which are co-chairmen of the Geneva Peace Conference on the Middle East.

1. Both governments are convinced that vital interest of the peoples of this area, as well as the interests of strengthening peace and international security in general, urgently dictate the necessity of achieving, as soon as possible, a just and lasting settlement of the Arab-Israeli conflict. This settlement should be comprehensive, incorporating all parties concerned and all questions.

   The United States and the Soviet Union believe that, within the framework of a comprehensive settlement of the Middle East problem, all specific questions of the settlement should be resolved, including such key issues as withdrawal of Israeli Armed Forces from territories occupied in the 1967 conflict; the resolution of the Palestinian question, including insuring the legitimate rights of the Palestinian people; termination of the state of war and establishment of normal peaceful relations on the basis of mutual recognition of the principles of sovereignty, territorial integrity, and political independence.

   The two governments believe that, in addition to such measures for insuring the security of the borders between Israel and the neighboring Arab states as the establishment of demilitarized zones and the agreed stationing in them of U.N. troops or observers, international guarantees of such borders as well as the observance of the terms of the settlement can also be established should the contracting parties so desire. The United States and the Soviet Union are ready to participate in these guarantees subject to their constitutional processes.

2. The United States and the Soviet Union believe that the only right and effective way for achieving a fundamental solution to all aspects of the Middle East problem in its entirety is negotiations within the framework of the Geneva Peace Conference, specially convened for these purposes, with participation in its work of the representatives of all parties involved in the conflict including those of the Palestinian people, and legal and contractual formalization of the decisions reached at the conference.

   In their capacity as co-chairmen of the Geneva Conference, the United States and the U.S.S.R. affirm their intention, through joint efforts and in their contacts with the parties concerned, to facilitate in every way the resumption of the work of the conference not later than December 1977. The co-chairmen note that there still exist several questions of a procedural and organizational nature which remain to be agreed upon by the participants to the conference.

3. Guided by the goal of achieving a just political settlement in the Middle East and of eliminating the explosive situation in this area of the world, the United States and the U.S.S.R. appeal to all parties in the conflict to understand the necessity for careful consideration of each other's legitimate rights and interests and to demonstrate mutual readiness to act accordingly.

So absorbed in securing a Soviet-American understanding as the key framework for a Geneva conference, the administration failed to foresee how the communiqué could have a deleterious impact upon its intended course. Just as Egypt and Israel were not forthcoming with the Americans about the Dayan-Tuhami talks, the administration did not feel obliged to share the contents of the communiqué with any side. Washington felt that the communiqué was in the interests of American foreign policy and, therefore, did not require either prior Egyptian or Israeli consultation or approval. But reintroducing an active role for the Soviet Union gave Sadat, Begin, and supporters of Israel an unexpected jolt. First, the communiqué was in direct contradiction to an understanding Tuhami and Dayan had reached in Morocco, that the United States would be the prime mediator, and "the Soviets would not play any positive or constructive role in future negotiations."[135] The communiqué itself did not drive Sadat's decision to go to Jerusalem, but his relations with Moscow had worsened all summer long and he was acutely angry at Moscow's insistence that Cairo pay for all military spare parts in hard currency and for not rescheduling Egypt's debt with them. These stringent disputes over weapons supply and payment method dated back to the pre–1973 War period. In 1977, Moscow again told Cairo that it would not sell Egypt replacements for arms lost in the October War as it had to Syria. Sadat felt that the Soviet Union had behaved "very rudely" toward Egypt. Relations between Moscow and Cairo had so severely deteriorated in August that Gromyko's proposed visit did not materialize, and the Brezhnev-Sadat Summit scheduled for September was canceled.[136]

Second, though Carter knew that "Sadat's only expressed concern was [over] bringing the Soviet Union back into a prominent role in the Middle East,"[137] the administration did it anyway. When Sadat went to Jerusalem seven weeks later, he remarked to Dayan, "Why did they [the United States] have to get the Russians involved that way?"[138] This was more of vintage Sadat: telling Eilts he was not upset about the communiqué, but telling the Americans and the Israelis that he was.

Third, the administration tried to mollify Israeli reaction. Dayan would not have any part in sanctioning the communiqué. When Vance saw Dayan in New York on September 28, Vance wanted to give Dayan a copy of the communiqué. Atherton placed several copies of the communiqué in front of him, and he replied, "If this paper has to deal with us and you did not consult with us, we do not want to see it. It is none of our business."[139] Dayan asked his aide Naftali Lavi to give him back the papers; he did as Dayan requested, but managed to keep one copy by sliding it under his own sheaf of papers. Dayan realized that such a communiqué might be necessary for there to be a common outlook by the conference cochairmen. Dayan told Vance that Israel would not take the communiqué lightly and would appeal directly to the American people, Congress, and the American Jewish community. Because of Dayan's moderate public response to the issuance of the communiqué, the administration expected Israel's reaction to be less severe than it was. The Israelis reacted negatively for two reasons: they hated the communiqué's contents, and they were not consulted in the drafting process. The administration knew full well that had the Israelis been consulted, there would have been a public outrage about issuing such a communiqué and tedious discussion about the terminology to be used. One State Department official recalled that for the Israelis, Moscow's invited participation at any level was "a great shock and a disappointment."[140] In publicly castigating the administration after the issuance of the communiqué, Dayan said, "The minute a Soviet-American agreement exists, our room to maneuver diminishes. We will be confronted with a single-minded Soviet-American fortress. The agreement will make the discussions in Geneva difficult."[141]

In Israel, the political leadership felt ambushed by the Carter administration, again. Some in Begin's office believed, as did Begin, that the communiqué's issuance "was an act of delusion. Begin had believed the Americans, at this juncture, had become almost traitors. They knew that we were pursuing this direct path with the Egyptians."[142] The Americans knew of the Egyptian-Israeli contacts, but did not know the depth, duration, and level of content of their discussions. Nonetheless, it was seen by Begin as an American effort to forestall those direct contacts, which would by definition have limited American choreography and engagement. In Israel, there was a feeling that Carter had succumbed to Soviet interests. According to Hanan Bar-on, "In a way, we thought that this was an enormous Soviet coup."[143] Knesset member Yitzhak Rabin called it "the beginning of a process aimed at political solution imposed by the two powers, with the coercion directed primarily against Israel. It is known today that the Soviet and American positions are identical, that is, withdrawal to the lines of 4 June 1967."[144] Israelis were specifically offended by the language and several key phrases used in the communiqué, in which new diplomatic formulations were employed and traditionally expected phrases were omitted. Instead of having the goal of a "just and lasting peace" as stated in UNSC Resolution 242, the communiqué spoke about a "just and lasting settlement." It specified inclusion of "representatives of the Palestinian people," a clearly implied reference to the PLO. The term *legitimate rights* was a marked shift in favor of Palestinian claims. UNSC Resolutions 242 and 338 were neither mentioned nor fully quoted, causing the Israelis to be dazed by the impact of omission.

Fourth, the communiqué did nothing to make either the PLO or Syria feel better. Two points were objectionable to both the PLO and Syria. The joint communiqué spoke about withdrawal, but not about withdrawal from all the occupied territories. And, the text specifically addressed the nature of peace, defining the subject of normalization as guaranteed through contractual international documents. The same day the communiqué was published, the PLO coincidentally issued a statement to affirm its right as the unquestioned representative of the Palestinian people inside and outside the occupied territory, to assert its participation at the conference on "the same footing with the other parties concerned," and to support the idea of the Security Council to "issue a new resolution endorsing the right of the Palestinian people to establish an independent state and return to their homeland."[145]

Fifth, Carter and his advisers failed to anticipate the negative response that would come from the communiqué. Stu Eisenstat, the domestic affairs adviser, acknowledged that up until the issuance of the communiqué there was very little if any interchange at the Carter White House between foreign and domestic policies.[146] It came like a bombshell on supporters of Israel. Brzezinski said, "I, for one, did not quite appreciate the extent to which it was at all that inflammatory."[147] Atherton recalled that it was "a little innocent, perhaps, to have not prepared the groundwork better. We made the . . . mistake . . . with the Soviet [communiqué]. . . . We hadn't prepared it [the groundwork] at all in terms of congressional reaction, public reaction, Israeli reaction, Jewish community reaction; and it suddenly broke all around everybody's head."[148] Scoop Jackson, one of Israel's leading advocates in the U.S. Senate, "was livid, and it was not us [the Israelis] that made him go livid."[149] Dayan improvised a public relations campaign to kill and bury the U.S.–Soviet communiqué. The thrust of Dayan's message to the American people was that the administration had reneged on its commitments to Israel after a long and tedious period of negotiations preparing for the Geneva Conference.

Dayan's promised media blitz across the country made the administration sufficiently uneasy that it asked Dayan to meet with Carter at the United Nations Plaza Hotel during the evening of October 4, where, rightly or wrongly, the administration ultimately caved in to Dayan's promise of pressure. Carter and Dayan discussed the procedures that were to be employed at a conference. The identified draft procedures tilted favorably toward Arab preconditions for a conference. The draft called for low-level PLO participation, the same formula promised to Assad in Geneva in May. It recommended that the Palestinian question should be on the conference agenda as a topic for discussions in a multilateral format. In suggesting that the opening plenum involve a unified Arab delegation and Israel, the draft specified that the plenum remain in session throughout the conference, even after the multilateral and bilateral working groups were established. Adamantly objecting, Israel did not want to give the conference plenum any power, jurisdiction, or authority to resolve an impasse between the parties. Instead, Israel wanted the plenum to dissolve quickly into bilateral working groups and to be impotent to impose or force a decision on the participants. The original draft noted that Israel would "negotiate" over the future of the West Bank and the Gaza Strip, but there was little, if any, mention about the future status of Jerusalem. At the United Nations Plaza Hotel, the Dayan-Carter exchanges were unprecedented in terms of difficulty and rancor. In these sessions, which lasted from 7:00 P.M. to 1:30 A.M., the United States was represented by Carter, Vance, Brzezinski, Atherton, Quandt, and Sterner (the policy planning staff); Israel was represented by Dayan, Dinitz, Meir Rosenne (a Foreign Ministry legal adviser), and Naftali Lavi (Dayan's press spokesman).[150] Dayan sensed the pressure that Secretary of State Vance and President Carter were applying upon Israel. The administration wanted Israel to accept the contents of the U.S.–Soviet communiqué, as well as the conference formulations and procedures devised and basically accepted by Syrian, Jordanian, and Egyptian ministers in the conversations with Vance and Brzezinski during the previous fortnight. In his recollection of that evening's discussion with Carter, Dayan remembered the president's initial tough words, "Understand the significance of our not reaching agreement. You will be isolated from the whole world."[151] Rosenne recalled that, for the first and only time, he heard Dayan refer to his physical infirmity in responding bluntly to Carter's demand for Israeli flexibility: "Mr. President, I only have one eye, but I am not blind."[152] Brzezinski remembered that "what appalled [him] was the way Dayan intimidated Carter, by saying that he was going to take this issue to American Jewish opinion in this country. Instead of Carter stomping on him and telling Dayan that he was quite capable of facing a challenge, he leaned over backwards to be reassuring, accommodating, pleasant, and gave Dayan the impression that he was not dealing with someone who was very tough."[153] The final version of a U.S.-Israeli understanding was drafted after Carter left the discussions around 1:30 A.M.

Having gathered all evening, three hundred members of the press were waiting for conclusive information from Dayan and Vance. During the evening's discussion, Carter periodically asked what Dayan would tell the press and what Dayan would tell his audiences during the cross-country trip immediately after their discussions. Before and after Carter left the meetings, several Americans and Israelis (including Atherton, Lavi, and Bar-On) put together several drafts of a joint statement to be issued to the press. When they finally greeted the press, Dayan intentionally deferred to Vance to announce it. When the press statement was read to the world media it was dubbed the "U.S.-Israeli working paper" and was substantiated by the "weight and signature" of the American secretary of state's presentation. Dayan carefully orchestrated Vance to the podium to announce their "agreement." The Israelis had negotiated in a strenuous fashion, used the thirst of the media to portray consonance with Washington, and buried the U.S.-Soviet communiqué in the process.

The U.S.-Israeli working paper included the following six elements:[154]

1. The Arab parties will be represented by a unified Arab delegation, which will include Palestinian Arabs. After the opening sessions, the conference will split into working groups.
2. The working groups for the negotiations and conclusion of peace treaties will be formed as follows: Egypt-Israel, Jordan-Israel, Syria-Israel, Lebanon-Israel. (All the parties agree that Lebanon may join the conference when it so requests.)
3. The West Bank and Gaza issues will be discussed in a working group to consist of Israel, Egypt, Jordan and Palestinian Arabs.
4. The solution of the problem of Arab refugees and of the Jewish refugees will be discussed in accordance with the terms to be agreed upon.
5. The agreed bases for the negotiations at the Geneva Conference on the Middle East are U.N. Security Council Resolutions 242 and 338.
6. All the initial terms of reference of the Geneva Peace Conference remain in force, except as may be agreed by the parties.

In addition, there were bilateral clarifications appended to these elements to stipulate that Israel could object to any attempt made in the course of the conference to have the PLO participate or have the issue of a Palestinian entity discussed. This American promise did not have the diplomatic weight of the memorandum of understanding of the Sinai II Agreement; it was, however, sufficiently effective in reassuring the Israelis that they would not be steamrolled by the United States into attending a conference with PLO members participating. Israel had the United States reaffirm its commitment that "no innovations or changes [in procedure] could be introduced without Israel's agreement, just as in the first Geneva session. This question, though seemingly technical, was substantive and substantial. In his public remarks, Dayan strongly reasserted that "there cannot be a Geneva without Israel; we shall not go if the PLO is there. We shall not negotiate with the PLO. And if the Arabs will not be willing to go to Geneva without the PLO, then there will not be Geneva."[155] Israeli leaders did not exclude Palestinians who lived in the territories, just representatives of the PLO.[156] The administration also promised that if Israel exercised the right not to attend a conference, then the administration would not adopt any sanctions against it.[157] Israel was pleased that UNSC Resolutions 242 and 338 were reaffirmed as the basis for a conference, and that the U.S.-Soviet communiqué was not a precondition for determining participation in a Geneva Conference. At this juncture, Israel restated its interpretation of UNSC Resolution 242, noting that it "does not call for the return to former borders, but to recognized and secure borders."[158] The final version of the U.S.-Israeli working paper was ratified by the Israeli Cabinet on October 11. However, Begin was angry that Dayan had agreed to provide separate recognition to the Palestinian Arabs in paragraph 3 of the drafted working paper.[159] Furthermore, Begin was not pleased that Egypt was designated to participate in the discussions about the future of the West Bank and Gaza Strip, but he ultimately relented on this point.

Unresolved issues surrounding procedures for the conference included questions of who would convene it, who would receive the invitation for the unified Arab delegation, who would speak for the unified Arab delegation (or would each Arab foreign minister address the plenum), and how would the Palestinian representatives from the territories be elected and invited. With these issues weighing in, Dayan publicly presented Israel's staunch opposition to the communiqué, taking correspondents from *Time* and *Newsweek* on his plane as he and his staff barnstormed Chicago, Los Angeles, Atlanta, Miami, and then New York again. He spoke before Jewish audiences, held press conferences, gave network interviews, and provided editorial boards with private briefings. Deftly and with unrestrained vigor, the Israelis consigned the U.S.-Soviet communiqué to the diplomatic refuse bin. Its legacy was another example of the Carter administration trying to usurp Israeli prerogative to determine security interests and political concessions by itself.

Sadat was more displeased with the U.S.-Israeli working paper than he was with the U.S.-Soviet communiqué, which he saw as confirmation that even his trusted friend Jimmy Carter could not neutralize the repercussions from Israel, the American Jewish community, and Israel's friends in Congress. From Sadat's viewpoint, Carter had yielded to Israeli demands, and his administration was too intensely focused on Geneva and had succumbed to Syria's procedural preference for a joint delegation. He sensed that too much time and energy were focused on getting to Geneva and not enough effort was expended on the substance of the issue. Diplomatic momentum without Israel's movement from Sinai frustrated Sadat. Sadat complained that the road to Geneva got lost in the bureaucratic papers, inter-Arab fighting, and in arranging for the sundry logistics for a conference.[160] The Syrians, too, openly opposed the contents of the U.S.-Israeli working paper. For them, Arab solidarity was vital; recalled Veliotes, "The conference became a crapper, not because the Russians were the bad guys, but because the Syrians wanted to have a veto power over essentially the Egyptians."[161] And by favoring the unified Arab delegation and the linkage of all working groups, the Syrians opposed the bilateral geographic committees. Khaddam feared any procedural mechanism that encouraged Sadat's preferences for independent Egyptian action that would not result in a comprehensive solution would enable Israel to "take everything that it wants."[162]

Having already considered the idea of going to Jerusalem, Sadat received a confidential, handwritten letter from Carter, dated October 27 and sent via a special Egyptian courier from Washington, in which Carter urged Sadat to consider some "dramatic action because Carter had come to the end of the [diplomatic] road" and had reached an impasse.[163] Carter suggested that some bold measure was needed to move the negotiating process forward, though he did not specifically suggest or encourage Sadat to visit Jerusalem. In fact, he said on many occasions that "Sadat decided on his own to go to Jerusalem."[164] Carter hoped that Sadat might find a way to modify Syrian and PLO resistance to an agreement and recognition of Israel. Elements of the administration had a misinformed view that Syria or the PLO could be influenced to change their attitudes; Vance had believed that was a reason to include the Soviets in preparation for the Geneva Conference, and Carter had the same faith in Sadat. There was a misreading of Syrian and PLO steadfastness and an overestimation of Soviet influence over their friends. Carter's letter reminded Sadat of the president's inability to shape an agenda or agreement prior to the Geneva Conference. The letter also told Sadat that Carter was prepared "to make an unequivocal public statement that the Palestinian question, as well as the question of withdrawal and borders of peace, must be dealt with seriously at the conference with the aim of finding a comprehensive solution to all aspects of the Arab-Israeli conflict."[165]

Simultaneous to hearing Carter's frustrations and promises, Sadat continued to seek the advice of several foreign political leaders. He traveled to Rumania to meet President Ceausescu near Bucharest on October 30, to Iran to meet with the Shah, and to Saudi Arabia to meet with King Khalid in Riyadh on November 2. In his conversation with Ceausescu, Sadat stated his desire to test Israeli intentions directly. The Rumanian president reconfirmed for Sadat his view that an agreement with Begin could be reached, that Sadat could trust Begin, and that Begin, "once he agrees to something, will implement it to the last comma and period."[166] During Sadat's visit to Rumania, Arab ambassadors in Bucharest sensed vague evidence of momentum between Egypt and Israel. Walid Mouallem, who was then Syria's ambassador to Rumania, recalled, "There was a feeling that something was afoot; something was cooking between Israel and Egypt."[167] During the visit, both Ceausescu and Sadat asserted the need to resume the Geneva Conference, but Sadat said, "I prefer not to go to Geneva if there are not good preparations for the conference."[168] While no answer came from the Syrians, Sadat, at this point, accepted going to Geneva without an agreed agenda. In Saudi Arabia, Sadat apparently did not tell the king of his intention to go to Jerusalem, partially out of respect for the Saudi relationship to the Muslim holy places. Sadat did not want to have the Saudis oppose his trip before he actually went there.[169] If he had told the Saudis and then ignored their negative response, Sadat would have affronted them, which he preferred not to do. But Sadat did not seek approval for his visit from either his cabinet or from his National Security Council. According to Mustapha Khalil, who was at that time secretary-general of the Arab Socialist Union, Egypt's majority political party, when Sadat returned from this trip he told the Egyptian Committee on Higher Security that "Begin is ready to make peace."[170]

On November 3, Sadat publicly offered to convene a multilateral peace conference in East Jerusalem to be attended by the United States, the Soviet Union, China, France, Great Britain, Israel, Syria, Jordan, Egypt, and the PLO. Sadat wanted to have the conclusions known in advance, or at least most of them; he did not want to go to Geneva simply to go to a conference. On November 4, he said, "We will not go to Geneva in a vacuum."[171]

The Carter administration was stunned by Sadat's announcement. Within the administration there was agreement that "Sadat's suggestion [the East Jerusalem conference] was not likely to prove constructive. All of us felt that such a summit would be sterile, quite apart from the specific PLO problem. We worried about Sadat and wondered whether he was not losing his sense of reality,"[172] Brzezinski said. "It was a bizarre and eccentric idea. . . . [A]fter the Americans shot it down, Sadat realized that Washington was not going to back him on this grandiose multilateral initiative, that Washington was not going to push the Israelis, and that Washington was not going to work cooperatively with the Soviets to impose a two-power settlement."[173] Sadat was doing what he did best: in a flurry of diplomatic activity in early November he conducted meetings in Cairo and in the Middle East, fired various political volleys, and touched as many politically necessary and correct bases as he could. No, he had not lost his sense of reality as Brzezinski asserted. But the administration, which had its laser beam aimed at getting to Geneva at virtually any cost, did not see Sadat's Arab context and his frustration, nor did they understand where he was headed. On November 3, Sadat announced that strategic cooperation with Saudi Arabia had been achieved. The next day, Sadat mentioned unqualified praise for Carter, calling him "honest, not one who gives blind support to Israel, . . . he will play a very good role for peace in this area."[174] Sadat met with King Hussein on November 6 and Yasir Arafat the day before he announced in the Egyptian Parliament on November 9, 1977, that he was prepared to go to Jerusalem. When his speech was initially drafted it did not contain mention of a possible trip to Jerusalem; it was a point Sadat added. He had sent his presidential plane to Libya to transport Arafat to Cairo so the PLO leader could hear the speech. Some PLO members who heard the speech live were predictably uncomfortable, but Arafat actually joined in the applause with the rest of the audience after the announcement was made that he would consider going to Israel.[175]

Visiting Cairo at the time were two congressional delegations. Sadat reaffirmed with them Egypt's alliance with the United States, reminding eager congressional ears that the United States held ninety-nine percent of the cards in this game, while the Soviet Union had very few. Sadat also told them that he considered his visit to the Israeli Parliament as part of the preparations for reconvening the Geneva Conference, but that he could not sign a separate agreement with Israel. Sadat lavished unrestrained praise for Carter, calling him "honest and worthy of confidence," boasted proudly that a personal relationship had been established between them, and hoped that Begin had the same confidence in Carter as he did.[176] Sadat told Eilts that any invitation that came from the Israelis would have to come through the Americans because he could not accept such an invitation from Begin directly. When Eilts told Sadat he had an oral invitation, which Begin issued over Jerusalem media on November 13 and again on November 14, Sadat responded that he had to have a written invitation. Only then did the Israeli leadership take Sadat's intent to visit Jerusalem as something more than a rhetorical flourish.

Speculation in the Israeli press had Sadat's visit scheduled from November 24 onward. Begin canceled a trip to London. In the grandiosity of the moment, Begin also invited the presidents of Lebanon and Syria, and Jordan's King Hussein, to visit Israel, open negotiations, and sign peace treaties.[177] Dampening the enthusiasm of the moment were the remarks of Israel's chief of staff, Mordechai Gur, who welcomed Sadat to Israel but also stated in a widely debated interview that appeared in the Israeli newspaper *Yediot Aharanot* on November 15, that if Sadat "is planning another fraud like the Yom Kippur War, his intentions are clear to us because the Egyptian Army is at the peak of preparations to begin a war against Israel." Gur took note that the Egyptians had extended the UN observer force mandate in Sinai the previous month as required by Sinai II, but still had twice the number of battalions permitted under the September 1975 agreement. Israeli military intelligence convened a meeting at the office of their chief, Shlomo Gazit, offering skeptical and gloomy assessments of Sadat's intentions. Information had been gleaned from a variety of sources that suggested the Egyptian Army was put in a state of readiness with ammunition stocks taken from depots. Some at this meeting saw the Sadat visit as a trick to deflect preplanned Egyptian military objectives against Israel. In reality, Sadat had merely prepared a portion of his army for what he saw as negative domestic fallout anticipated from his visit to Jerusalem.[178] Though Foreign Minister Dayan did not dismiss Gur's warnings, especially if Sadat returned from Damascus saying that he decided to postpone his intention to visit Jerusalem, Dayan provided an extraordinary prescient review of what Sadat was doing: Sadat would come to Jerusalem to announce the Arab viewpoint; make the basic Arab demands for a return of all the territories and the right of the Palestinians to establish a state; not negotiate with the Israelis; not sign a separate peace (though Dayan knew of the exchanges of peace treaties earlier in September); and see the visit in the context of getting to Geneva. Despite his dour forecast, Dayan acknowledged that Sadat's visit would have important symbolic meaning since it would reduce Israel's international isolation because an Arab leader was now ready for public dialogue with Israel even though Israel held Arab territory, a precondition for not negotiating earlier with Israel. Indeed, Dayan was surprised that such a visit was contemplated; he was delighted by it but also aware of the negotiating distance that still needed to be traversed in order to reach an agreement or agreements between Egypt and Israel.[179]

Preparations for Sadat's visit moved apace. On Wednesday, November 16, the written invitation to visit Israel was cabled from Lewis to Eilts. Upon receiving it early in the morning, Eilts woke up Sadat, wanting him to see the invitation before his scheduled trip to Damascus that day. Also seeing the invitation that morning was Vice President Husni Mubarak, who cautioned Sadat that if he decided to accept the invitation, it would be prudent of him "not to say anything about the visit until you come back from Damascus, because if something is said about this before you go to Damascus, you may not come back from Damascus!"[180] When Eilts inquired of Mubarak about when Sadat intended to go to Israel, Mubarak told him Saturday. But Mubarak asked Eilts not to tell the Israelis yet. Eilts reminded Mubarak that proper preparations had to be made for such a state visit. Still, Mubarak insisted that the Israelis not yet be informed. Finally persuaded by Eilts, Mubarak conceded and asked Eilts to send the following message to the Israeli government: "If a certain president wants to visit Israel, what is the earliest time on Saturday that he should arrive?" In reply, Sam Lewis's cable to Eilts read, "If a certain president wants to visit Israel on a Saturday, he should come anytime after six o'clock in the afternoon." Sadat went that day to Damascus to tell Assad about the visit, and that he was not going to forget the Palestinian issue or the other Arab countries in his solution. "Sadat was not seeking his permission or endorsement of that decision, because they cannot control me concerning relations between Egypt and Israel."[181] As Sadat would later tell Moshe Sasson, Israel's second ambassador to Egypt, "When I decided to go to Jerusalem, I knew that I had a chance to be successful only if I [would] have Assad out. If he will be in, he will spoil everything. So how to have him out? I went to Damascus; I invited him. He said, no, I was sure he would say no."[182] Sadat promised Eilts that he would receive the official answer to the Begin invitation when he returned to Ismailiya from Damascus on Thursday. Eilts met him in Ismailiya, along with other high-ranking Egyptian officials. Sadat told Eilts that he would indeed go on Saturday. Sensing that the public air had been filled with speculation about whether he would go to Jerusalem or not, the media and photographers gathered to obtain Sadat's answer.

In the garden of his home in Ismailiya, Sadat asked Eilts to show him the invitation again. However, Eilts had already given the invitation to Sadat. Sadat, who could not remember where it was, worriedly asked, "What did I do with it?" Eilts replied, "You gave it to the vice president." "Husni, what have you done with the invitation, where is it?" Mubarak said, "I left it in Cairo." Always resourceful, Eilts pulled from his pocket a one-page letter, customarily written by the Egyptian president to him and to other ambassadors announcing the arrival and celebration of an annual Muslim holiday. Sadat, the actor, seated himself in the corner of a room so no one would get behind him, admitted the photographers, puffed his pipe, and "asked" Eilts, "What do you have here?" Eilts replied, "An invitation from Mr. Begin." Sadat opened the letter, puffed his pipe again, nodded, and said, "Please tell Mr. Begin through President Carter, I accept."[183] War Minister el-Gamasy did not approve of Sadat's decision, but stood by it nonetheless. Most other Egyptian officials were either furious at his decision or delighted by it. Some actually believed that Sadat, upon arrival in Israel, would be killed.

In the ten days from the time Sadat announced his trip to Jerusalem to his actual arrival there, the Carter administration debated whether to dissuade Sadat from going to Jerusalem and to get him back on the Geneva track. In Washington there was a sense of disarray and surprise, because Carter and Brzezinski were particularly immersed in getting to Geneva. The administration had not been consulted, and the American game plan was thrown out of kilter, perhaps even endangering the whole possibility of peace negotiations.[184] The White House communicated a view to Sadat that merely by his going to Jerusalem, Begin was not going to give back the West Bank; he might not even provide Sinai, and Sadat was advised not to forget the Palestinian issue.[185] Meanwhile, the State Department encouraged its ambassadors to be as helpful as possible in arranging the logistics for Sadat's visit. In preparing for the Jerusalem visit, Boutros-Ghali tried to brief Sadat for technical, procedural, substantive, and agenda questions. When he presented these issues to Sadat, the Egyptian president rejected them, saying, "My only agenda is coming to Jerusalem."[186] Dayan got it right. Sadat did not want to negotiate the specific details of sensitive issues; instead, he wanted to engage Begin in a discussion of general principles. In his Jerusalem visit, Sadat wanted to lead other Arabs toward negotiations. He did not want to negotiate specifically for them, lest they would have to pass, judge, sanction, and therefore possibly further delay his aim of achieving Sinai's return. Upon returning from a meeting of Arab foreign ministers in Tunis, just days before the Jerusalem visit, Fahmy reported to Sadat that he had been able to have the Arab Summit postponed until early 1978 so that the Geneva Peace Conference could take place as scheduled in December. Although appreciative of these scheduling efforts, Sadat stunned Fahmy by explaining the trip to Jerusalem. Fahmy then responded by submitting his resignation in writing, totally opposing Sadat's visit and Egypt's recognition of Israel.[187] In anticipation of Sadat's visit, many details required attention. Motorcades, lodging, communications, schedules, security checks, invitation lists, and a host of other logistical arrangements had to be set in place. The handling of the number of requests for the international media alone was unprecedented in scope. For public use and distribution, small and large Egyptian flags were quickly produced. A photo of Egypt's flag was provided to the Israeli Foreign Ministry by the American ambassador's wife by cutting out a page of flags from her personal copy of the World Book Encyclopedia. In frantic preparation, the Israeli Foreign Ministry tried unsuccessfully to obtain the music sheets of the Egyptian national anthem. Even without the music sheets, the anthem was played when Sadat arrived. Using his musical skill and ingenuity, the head of the Israel Defense Force Band had taped the Egyptian national anthem when Cairo radio and television went off the air the night before and then transcribed it for the band's use during the welcoming ceremony.

Egyptian President Sadat's plane arrived at Ben-Gurion Airport in the outskirts of Tel Aviv, Israel, in the early evening of November 19, 1977. Upon arrival, Sadat met Israeli dignitaries at the airport. After greeting Israeli and Arab politicians and religious leaders, he shook Mrs. Meir's hand and said, "I have waited a long time to meet you," to which she replied, "Nu, so what?"[188] He rode in a motorcade that took him and Israeli President Ephraim Qatzir to the King David Hotel in Jerusalem. At the hotel, Sadat and Begin conducted a short, private meeting. The next morning, Sadat visited the Al-Aqsa Mosque, the Dome of the Rock, and the Church of the Holy Sepulcher. On the afternoon of November 20, 1977, Sadat addressed the Israeli Parliament and pulled no punches. Confirming that he did not consult with Arab heads of state and acknowledging "the feeling of utter suspicion and absolute lack of confidence between the Arab states and the Palestinian people on the one hand, and Israel on the other," he said that he had come to Israel "not to forge a unilateral agreement between Egypt and Israel, seek a partial peace," nor to sign "a third disengagement agreement." In his speech, Sadat mentioned the Palestinians or the Palestinian problem no less than a dozen times. Claiming that he undertook this trip on behalf of the Egyptian people, the Arab nation, and the Palestinian people, he stipulated his desire to live in peace with Israel, to accept Israel as a reality, and to allow Israel to enjoy any guarantees it wanted for its security. He spoke of "the need for Palestinian self-determination including their right to establish their own state." Not up for debate if Israel wanted to live in peace, he insisted "complete withdrawal from all the Arab territories occupied in 1967 is a logical and undisputed fact, . . . including Arab Jerusalem." By doing this, Sadat affirmed a consequential central core of future Arab negotiations with Israel: the land-for-peace concept. He gave public notice that UNSC Resolution 242 meant "all the territories"; anything less would be unacceptable to the Arab world. In reply to Sadat's speech, Begin welcomed the Egyptian president with an out-stretched hand of peace, acknowledging Sadat's courageous crossing from Cairo to Jerusalem. Begin called for negotiations without prior conditions to achieve "real peace with complete reconciliation between Jewish and Arab peoples."

Begin requested peace treaties with all of Israel's Arab neighbors, and economic cooperation, and invited both President Assad and King Hussein to follow in Sadat's footsteps. Begin made no reference to the Palestinians or the Palestinian people; instead he referred to them as the "Arabs of Eretz Yisrael," inviting them to hold talks with the Israelis about "their common future." On Jerusalem, Begin did not even speak about Arab or East Jerusalem, merely noting that it was a unified city, and Israel would guarantee free access of every faith to it. He went on to say, "We are ready to sit together at a peace conference in Geneva. Sadat proposed that the Geneva Conference be renewed, on the basis of the two Security Council Res-olutions: 242 and 338. If there are problems between us by convening the Geneva Conference, we will be able to clarify them . . . in Cairo [or] in a neutral place, there is no objection."[189] The day ended with Sadat having closed sessions with leading Israeli politicians and the news media, participating in a festive dinner, and then meeting privately with Begin. On Monday, November 21, 1977, before leav-ing for Cairo at midday, Sadat talked with various members of the Israeli Parlia-ment and a delegation of West Bank and Gaza Palestinians.

Israel and the international community were captured by the drama of Sadat's visit and by the significance of his remarks about "no more war." Everyone focused on the euphoria of the moment, the joyous fulfillment of Israel's century-long quest for acceptance. Golda Meir characterized Sadat's visit "as if the Messiah had almost arrived. Sadat was really touched by the emotional Israeli response to his visit."[190] In their excitement and exhilaration, the Israelis did not fully comprehend Sadat's demand that this new reality be linked to full territorial withdrawal and a solution to the Palestinian issue. Moving cautiously, Begin directed discussion about territorial withdrawal almost exclusively toward Sinai. According to Begin's recounting of his private conversations with Sadat at the King David Hotel, Sadat issued a specific promise that the Egyptian Army would not cross the Mitla and Gidi Passes in Sinai.[191] Sadat's willingness to recognize Israel diplomatically before obtaining a firm and explicit commitment about full withdrawal did not reduce his interest, intent, and expectation that Israel was reciprocally obligated. Begin did not offer any concessions to Sadat, though Sadat had vowed that the October 1973 War was the last Arab-Israeli assault. It took less than three months for Sadat to realize two unwanted and unanticipated conclusions: Israel was not ready to withdraw from all the territories, especially Sinai, as he had thought his Jerusalem visit would justify; and American engagement in the negotiating process was necessary in order to catalyze withdrawal and to shape a suitable outline for a Palestinian solution. Not realizing that his grand gesture needed a sequential step, Sadat felt that the contents and delivery of his message were sufficient. Said Epi Evron, "He made his speech. Then what? He took everyone by surprise, and no one had the courage to say no to him. But then what?"[192] In reaction to Sadat's visit, Israelis in general, including most politicians, had high expectations that peace would come to them *immediately*. Many Israelis had regarded Egypt as the primary enemy, and now its leader was in Jerusalem. Many had developed an unrealistic belief that if Egypt recognized Israel, then other Arab states would possibly and similarly comply. In terms of future relations with Egypt, Israelis were immediately talking about open borders, commercial links, and diplomatic exchanges—the full range of contacts enjoyed by two sovereign states with normalized relations. Egypt, the central voice of pan-Arab and anti-Israeli feeling in the 1950s and 1960s, was now conferring recognition and legitimacy upon Israel. According to Sam Lewis, Israelis "had a very heady feeling because they had finally achieved this breakthrough, and they didn't need the United States. . . . They needed our support, obviously, but they really hoped and many of them thought that they could translate Sadat's trip into a quick bilateral agreement."[193] Abba Eban sensed that Sadat's visit "changed the entire psychological and emotional context in which our relationship has been conducted." Speaking more realistically, Yitzhak Rabin noted that Sadat's visit could create a new era in the region. Peace "is not peace that will remain a piece of paper; it has to be translated to the daily life of every citizen of the countries of the area." Dayan, for his part, noted that Sadat had not come to Israel with "an Egyptian shopping basket to fill. He told us that the question of the Palestinians, the West Bank, the refugees in general, and Jerusalem were less a priority than occupied Sinai."[194] In public, Sadat wanted all discussions to start with the Palestinians and their aspirations, because he did not want to be accused of looking after Egypt's interests first. During the next several weeks and months, Dayan reinforced his view that Sadat's visit would require Israelis to decide on their borders and that achieving peace would involve concessions about the territories Israel had captured in the June 1967 War.

As it had been prior to the October War, Sadat's dilemma was how to ensure and promote Egyptian interests while not sacrificing the demands of the other Arab states and the Palestinians. Dayan and Begin were eager to disconnect Sadat and Egypt from these commitments, while Sadat's advisers and the Carter administration were resistant. Carter, in his determination to find a solution to that dilemma, helped formulate the 1978 Camp David Accords, in which Begin and Sadat agreed to disagree.

◦─────✦

CHAPTER 8

FROM JERUSALEM
TO OSLO
AND BEYOND
1978–1998

A T THE END of 1977, all attention was focused on Sadat. His brazen and unexpected act demonstrated, once again, that he was a showman, a statesman, and a daring risk taker. He did what no other Arab leader had done in thirty years: he broke the Arab psychological barrier by recognizing the existence and legitimacy of the Jewish state. Given both the historical context of Arab enmity toward Israel and what Israel represented as a Western nation-state in the middle of the Muslim and Arab heartland, Sadat's was an extraordinary act. Sadat did not wake up one morning believing Zionism was the path to righteousness and fulfillment. He did not necessarily *want* to go to Jerusalem, but he *needed* to go to continue his march for Sinai's return. His ego, Egyptian chauvinism, personal flamboyance, steadfast motivation, and the dilly-dallying of the other players in a stagnating diplomatic environment all forced both the consideration of the visit and the visit itself. If he had fears about his personal safety as a consequence of his trip, he did not show them. In catalyzing a moribund negotiating process, he enraged his Arab contemporaries, forced the Arab world to punish Egypt with isolation, transferred the diplomatic initiative to Begin, and caused initial American consternation. Although Sadat broke a small hole in the Arab barrier of refusal to deal with Israel in a protracted face-to-face and public manner, he did not have a similar effect of changing Israel's passionately held ideological attitudes or historically-based sense of physical insecurity. No matter how welcome Sadat's visit was to the Israelis, it did not overturn deeply embedded fears about Arabs, in general, or remove anxieties that Israelis possessed for Egypt's leadership role in the Arab world. The most immediate response catalyzed by the visit was the transfer of the negotiating process onto the shoulders of the protagonists; the geographic locus of diplomatic activity, at least temporarily, shifted to the region. A series of bilateral and direct Egyptian-Israeli contacts expanded. Washington was still a venue and a participant in consultations, but meetings in Cairo and Jerusalem became a more integral part of the negotiating format, at least until Begin and Sadat realized that they were talking past each other and needed American mediation and, eventually, Carter's personal intervention.

When Sadat returned to Cairo, masses of people lined the streets to welcome his overture for peace. He quickly tried to blunt Arab criticism by telling all who would listen what he had said in public before his trip and again at Knesset: he did not go to Israel to sign a separate peace agreement.[1] Indeed, if he had wanted to do so, then he probably could have begun discussions for a separate deal with the Israelis during the visit. Nonetheless, in the weeks, months, and years after his visit, virtually every Arab leader and media outlet brutalized him for speaking to the Israelis directly and in public. A constant barrage of verbal abuse was hurled at him; its level of intensity peaked in the immediate aftermaths of the Jerusalem visit, the signing of the Camp David Accords, and the Egyptian-Israeli Peace Treaty. His Arab contemporaries variously labeled him as an "honorary Zionist," and characterized his visit to Jerusalem as "a day of humiliation and submission to the Zionists," "an act of capitulation and treason," "a sell out of pan-Arab dignity and the Egyptian people's Arabism." Given Assad's opposition to the Jerusalem trip and his unwavering commitment to Arab solidarity, Arab leaders flocked to Damascus to persuade an easily inclined Assad to confront Sadat's objective. At the United Nations, the Syrian representative, Mouaffak el-Allaf (who fourteen years later headed the Syrian delegation to the Arab-Israeli talks after the 1991 Madrid Middle East Peace Conference), vehemently attacked Sadat and Egypt. He said, "Could this be the hero of the July 23 revolution, the successor of Gamal Abdel Nasser, the same man who shook the hand of the terrorist Menachem Begin, the one who shook the hand of the war criminal Moshe Dayan, who planted a kiss on the cheek of the racist Golda Meir? What has happened?"[2] The Syrian response to the visit was summarized in Syria's domestic service, which described Sadat's betrayal as giving "Israel a golden opportunity to intensify its inflexibility, hard line, arrogance, denial of the Palestinian people's rights, and its scorn of the Arabs."[3] More restrained in its criticism was the Jordanian reaction, which reminded Arab detractors that what Sadat said from the rostrum of the Israeli Parliament was no deviation from the Arab position of seeking Israel's full withdrawal from the occupied territories.

For his visit, Sadat expected a grand Israeli gesture equivalent in significance to his Jerusalem journey. He did not get it. He believed that his visit would lead to reaching an agreement within a week.[4] Upon his return from Jerusalem, Sadat told Eilts, "We will be in Geneva in two weeks. You'll see, I have done it."[5] To the Americans, "Sadat talked as if, once he had broken the psychological barrier, the Israelis will have no excuse, he was not going to need [the Americans] anymore."[6] However, Sadat did not realize that Begin would not provide the far-ranging response he was seeking. An unintended result of Sadat's visit was to push Begin to center stage, where he relished the opportunistic spotlight and grabbed the diplomatic offensive. Thus, rather than the Americans responding to Sadat's initiative, Washington was forced to respond to Begin's reply.

Begin's response was the outline of a two-part Egyptian-Israeli agreement: Sinai's return for a peace treaty and some self-rule or autonomy for the Palestinians, but no allocation of Judea and Samaria to a foreign sovereignty. Begin wanted an agreement with Egypt, but not at any price. And Judea and Samaria were not on the negotiating table. Sadat had provided the general opening, and now Begin went right for the details, making clear what was not negotiable. As Sadat would soon realize, the emotional luster of his visit quickly trailed off into hard realities. And, Begin was up to the task of defending his position, in which no Israeli settlements would be dismantled to honor Sadat's desire to receive Sinai free of Jewish physical presence. Ultimately, Begin *would* pay that price because the greater reward of a peace agreement with Egypt was possible. But for the moment, Sadat was growing impatient, even exasperated, with the slowness of Begin's response. One imposing problem was that Begin still did not trust Sadat, and when they met personally, no working chemistry emerged between them.

From the Jerusalem visit until their meetings at Camp David in September 1978, narrowing their differences proved enormously difficult. Their direct contacts became visually more intense and verbally more ill tempered. Between their meetings, they each used the media to defend their historic positions. Yet, for different reasons, they each wanted an agreement. Their earlier diplomatic contacts were quiet and furtive, known to only a few. Once they went public, a domestic political price was attached for talking to the other and for not reaching an agreement. It was quite remarkable that neither was prepared to walk away totally from the big-splash opening of the Sadat visit. Of course, neither wanted to waste the opportunity, even if they had every reason to do so: most of all, their personalities clashed; and each was not prepared to sacrifice core territorial national interests. Sadat was not "in love" with the idea of signing a peace treaty with Israel, and Begin did not relish returning Sinai or uprooting Israeli settlements there. They constantly bickered over the substance, pace, and procedure of the negotiations; their respective domestic opponents salivated when failure loomed likely. Ironically, those nay-sayers, in a certain sense, helped drive Sadat and Begin to reach their compromise agreement at Camp David. Once Egypt and Israel captured the spotlight, barely any attention was paid to Israel's other neighbors as possible negotiating partners. Even after Israel signed a peace treaty with Egypt in 1979, it remained unsure about Sadat's intentions. His character, actions, and words still suggested the potential for more surprises; on one level, he wanted an agreement; on another, he continuously propounded an unceasing public commitment to Palestinian political aspirations.

Carter administration officials were stunned and had difficulty adjusting to the new reality created by Sadat's visit. Washington strongly preferred to pull Sadat back from the bilateral diplomacy in which he was increasingly engaged. Not only was the Washington bureaucracy temporarily bypassed as the diplomatic catalyst, but also there was silence, some incoherence, and resistance to what blatantly appeared to be another bilateral Egyptian-Israeli agreement in the making. According to Sam Lewis, "Washington feared that Sadat was going to give away the Palestinian cause, pay lip service to them, and feared that Begin would buy him off with Sinai."[7] From the NSC, Quandt acknowledged that "it took many more months for the Americans to realize fully that Sadat's priorities were shifting."[8] Though conceptually disheveled by Sadat's visit, Washington never suspended its functions as diplomatic coach and postman. Immediately, Washington wanted to get Sadat back on the comprehensive settlement track that the United States had momentarily lost. If possible, Washington would try to knit a negotiated agreement that would be something more than another bilateral understanding. By the end of December, Carter believed that Sadat's visit canceled the Geneva Peace Conference, but it did not immediately kill the hope of achieving a comprehensive settlement. Carter, perhaps unlike his advisers, who were still clinging to the prospects of a broader settlement, wanted the negotiating focus and responsibility to be on Begin and Sadat.[9] There was a paradox running through American diplomatic action: on the one hand, American officials tried to lower expectations of what could be accomplished and in what time frame, while on the other hand, Washington continued to urge upon Sadat a broader agreement that would include a substantial political solution for the Palestinians.

Not wanting the momentum of his visit to stagnate, Sadat announced on November 27 over Cairo radio his decision to host a preliminary meeting that would prepare the agenda for a Geneva-like conference. He had broken the pyschological barrier, but proper preparations for a conference were still required, something Begin acknowledged in his Knesset response to Sadat. Sadat's decision to have a preparatory conference in Cairo was the first of half a dozen major efforts or mechanisms undertaken between the November visit and the Camp David meetings, all intended to keep the negotiating process going, either directly with the Israelis or through Washington. Vance traveled to the Middle East in early December. That visit was followed by a preparatory conference in Cairo, otherwise known as the Mena House Talks, held December 13–15, 1977. The conference occurred simultaneously with Begin's visit to Washington. Then the Begin-Sadat summit was held in Ismailiya on Sadat's birthday, Christmas Day, 1977. This was immediately followed by talks between Israeli and Egyptian political and military committees respectively held in Jerusalem and Cairo in January and February 1978, followed by foreign minister–level diplomatic meetings at Leeds Castle in England in July 1978. Connecting these various meetings were numerous trips to the region by Assistant Secretary of Near Eastern and South Asian Affairs Atherton, a brief stop in Cairo by President Carter in early January 1978, a visit by Sadat and Begin to Washington in the spring, and numerous exchanges between foreign and defense ministers and other U.S. envoys. In the ten months between the Jerusalem visit and the Camp David meetings, a very significant amount of progress was made in narrowing differences between Israeli and Egyptian views, but not sufficient for an agreement to be reached without the direct, continuous, and active support of the White House and the president of the United States. The five substantive areas where positions narrowed were: (1) the meaning of Palestinian rights in the context of Begin's offer of Palestinian self-rule; (2) agreement on an illusive declaration of principles that would govern future negotiations and especially defining a mutually suitable interpretation of UNSC Resolution 242; (3) the military details and associated guarantees related to Israel's withdrawal from Sinai and the contents of an Egyptian-Israeli peace treaty; (4) an understanding about Israeli settlements in Sinai and the Gaza Strip, West Bank, and Golan Heights; and (5) a way to discern the level of philosophical commitment, legal connection, or political linkage between a possible Israeli-Egyptian peace treaty and what might be decided for the management of Palestinian rights in the West Bank and Gaza.

Already in the early spring of 1977, American Middle Eastern policymakers were evolving ideas for a transitional period to devolve power from Israeli to Palestinian control in the West Bank.[10] This dovetailed with Begin's own notion of Palestinian autonomy, an idea Begin had been percolating in his mind since the 1950s. Begin knew, for example, that the Austrian-Hungarian empire handled their minority problems through the use of autonomy. Furthermore, the notion was present in the writings of his ideological mentor, Ze'ev Jabotinsky, and had been considered in earlier centuries as a way for Jews to express themselves in foreign lands. Jabotinsky believed that the Arabs living in the land of Israel were, in fact, a nation with legitimate claims that could never be reconciled with Zionism and, therefore, would have to be granted minority self-rule.[11] For Begin, Palestinian autonomy was the only acceptable formula that would not compromise his philosophical requirements of keeping Judea and Samaria under Israeli control while not providing the Palestinians with full political rights in the Jewish state. Begin did not consider Israel to be occupying Judea, Samaria, and the Gaza district; instead, Israel had liberated that land from Arab control. Though a substantial Arab population was living there, Israel could not give them independence in that area because it "belonged" to Israel. At the same time, Israel could not give them citizenship, since that would alter the demography of the Jewish state. Moreover, the Palestinian Arab population *did not want* to be Israeli citizens. The only solution was to separate the land from the people. As compared to Dayan, Begin wanted tighter Israeli control over the West Bank and Gaza and more freedom for Israelis settling in, what was for Begin, the Land of Israel. For Begin, autonomy relieved him publicly of being considered an occupier of what he considered to be his own land; political autonomy gave full equality to the Arabs living in the West Bank and Gaza without allowing sovereignty in these areas to slip to a foreign power. Begin first raised the idea of Palestinian autonomy during his visit with Carter at the White House in July 1977.

The Israeli definition given to autonomy was, in a sense, a compromise formula arrived at between Begin and Dayan. Dayan was willing to cede to the Palestinians greater control of their daily lives than was Begin's intention. In 1974, Dayan raised with Kissinger the idea of *functional partition* of the West Bank.[12] He made a distinction between the local Palestinians who would control their daily lives and with Jordan and Israel who would retain control over the land. In short, Dayan was suggesting that citizenship be severed from territory—Israel would remove itself from the quotidian lives of the people. Dayan took the position that it was Israel's responsibility to raise the standard of living of the Arabs in Judea and Samaria, because ultimately Israelis would have to live side by side with them. Ultimately, he felt that Israelis should be allowed to live in the territories as long as Arabs were not being pushed out and as long as Jews did not settle directly in their midst. Functional partition, if adopted, would result in the development and perpetuation of two types of citizens living side by side. But Dayan was pragmatic and believed that "no matter what we [Israelis] do for them, in their eyes, we shall always be seen as conquerors."[13] Therefore, as minister of defense, he was deliberately nonintrusive in Palestinian affairs.[14] Instead, he wanted them to manage their own problems, except for security and foreign affairs issues.

In December, when Vance visited the Middle East for the third time in 1977, Begin told him that he wanted to see Carter to present him with his ideas about a solution to the Palestinian issue. Begin understood that some progress had to be made in the Palestinian theater, but progress to him meant distinguishing between providing rights to the Palestinian population (which he repeatedly referred to as "the Arabs of Eretz Yisrael") without providing territorial withdrawal from Judea and Samaria. Begin wanted to continue to focus on Sinai and divert attention away from the Geneva path.[15] A trip to Washington to visit Carter would allow Begin to achieve four additional objectives: recapture the international focus; further bury the Geneva Conference idea; provide enough political movement on the Palestinian issue to sustain the Egyptian-Israeli dialogue; and hopefully enlist Carter's support to pressure Sadat to accept Begin's notion of Palestinian autonomy. Begin wanted to reach a quick bilateral deal directly with Sadat, optimally with minimum U.S. involvement but with maximum U.S. support. According to Quandt, "Begin was a very shrewd politician; [he] realized that it was going to be difficult for us to distance ourselves from a formal Israeli [Palestinian self-rule] proposal that looked like it was forthcoming."[16] Just before visiting Carter at the White House on December 16 and 17, Begin dictated the original twenty-six points of the autonomy plan to his personal assistant, Yahiel Kadishai, in the prime minister's office of the Israeli Parliament. How much of the self-rule proposal he showed to Carter is still unclear, but he did emphatically tell Carter what Israel would not do, including not leaving the West Bank.

After the Americans listened to Begin's self-rule proposal, they realized Begin's ideas were not the grand gesture that Sadat wanted; they intimated to Begin that perhaps he should not even present this idea to Sadat, in part because it was not far-reaching enough. Toward the end of his meeting with Begin, Carter phoned Sadat and suggested that he take Begin's proposal seriously, though it would not meet all his expectations about the Palestinians. Because of this call, Sadat was not surprised by the proposal's concept when Begin arrived a week later.[17] Carter was convinced that by the time Begin offered the autonomy idea and the Sinai withdrawal proposals to Sadat in Ismailiya on December 25, the Israeli prime minister had altered their contents. This left the impression with Sadat that Carter had endorsed Begin's proposals, though Carter noted that the plan that Begin presented to Sadat "was attenuated substantially."[18] By taking a more forthcoming position with Carter, then retreating even a small bit because of what his Israeli Cabinet demanded, Begin was able to explain later to Carter that domestic constraints forced such changes. Since Begin drew criticism from Israeli settlers because of the prospects of having to live under Egyptian sovereignty if Sinai were returned, after leaving Washington he added an additional idea to the autonomy scheme that included a provision enabling the settlements to be defended by Israeli forces and linked to Israeli administration and jurisdiction.[19] Carter thought he had obtained something more forthcoming from Begin than he had given, and Begin thought he had received Carter's endorsement for his Palestinian self-rule proposals.[20] But Ben-Elisar claims that there were no *significant* changes made between the document handed to Carter and the one Sadat received after amendments were made to it by Begin's cabinet.[21] Indeed, changes *were* made, and for those Americans dealing with the negotiations, they were considered significant. Carter felt that Begin manipulated what he heard and what he did not hear for his own purposes. The administration was peeved that Begin was prepared to present his autonomy idea to congressional leaders and thereby put the White House on the defensive against a Begin-proposed idea. By having Carter focus on the definition of Palestinian self-rule, Begin succeeded in deflecting attention away from the broader territorial withdrawal issues[22] and, of course, the dreaded conference, Russian involvement, and a comprehensive settlement. This would not be the last time that Carter and the administration thought they heard Begin say one thing and found out later it meant something else.

Begin was never averse to taking someone's silence as tacit agreement with a position he took, or to taking a lukewarm response to an idea he felt had enormous merit and exaggerating agreement to it for political effect. The most serious misunderstanding between Carter and Begin came at the end of the Camp David negotiations when Carter thought Begin had committed himself to a settlement freeze of prolonged duration, when, in fact, Begin said he never made such a commitment. (Some detail of that disagreement follows.) At the conclusion of the Begin visit to Carter in December, Brzezinski was suspicious of Begin's autonomy definition, which he strongly believed would not be sufficient for the Palestinians and certainly not sufficient for Sadat. Brzezinski wanted to find a way to use Begin's idea for Palestinian self-rule, making it not the final point in negotiations but a place or step along a broader continuum that would lead to something closer to Palestinian self-determination. When Begin left Washington, Carter still wanted to focus on a final outcome for the territories and their inhabitants, rather than another incremental step,[23] which was inherent in political autonomy.

By the time Begin arrived in Washington, the Cairo Conference, otherwise known as the Mena House Talks, had already begun. This conference was to serve as a platform for preparatory talks leading up to the Geneva Conference. A preparatory conference was first referred to publicly by Sadat on November 3, 1977, when he returned from Saudi Arabia and said he wanted a working committee to prepare the topics to be discussed at a conference, because without sound preparations it "was destined to fail."[24] The notion of such a conference was also suggested to Begin when Sadat was in Jerusalem. From November to mid-December, the purpose of the preparatory conference idea changed; whereas initially it was meant to provide a place to work on details, after the dramatic Jerusalem trip, the preparatory conference became a mere tactical ploy. Sadat, hearing the viscerally negative reaction from the Arab media for breaking Arab ranks and for recognizing Israel, wanted to show that he was being inclusive by inviting all Arab parties, especially the Palestinians, to participate in negotiations with Israel. In announcing this proposed Cairo meeting, Sadat surprised the Israelis, other Arab states, and the Americans alike. He did not care which diplomatic or political rank participated in the conference; he simply wanted the conference to commence as early as December 3, 1977. When Begin initially heard about the preparatory conference from the Cairo radio reports, his first reaction was that it was no way to conduct negotiations. Dayan wanted nothing to do with this conference because he had no idea "what Sadat had in mind and was absolutely certain that the conference would fail."[25] Furthermore, Dayan rejected the preparatory conference idea because Begin and the prime minister's office rather than the foreign minister were engaged in the diplomacy of the moment. Sadat sent invitations for the proposed conference to Israel, Jordan, Lebanon, the PLO, Syria, the Soviet Union, the United Nations, and the United States. Sadat was not sincere, nor did he expect the other Arab parties to participate, because if they had, then his political options would have been restrained by their reluctance to deal with Israel. For its part, Washington was generally apprehensive because it could not stage-manage the conference from afar and viewed the drift toward a separate arrangement between Cairo and Jerusalem as inherently unstable for the region. Carter's administration steadily held on to the view, even after Sadat's Jerusalem visit, that unless the Palestinian issue was properly addressed, no real Arab-Israeli settlement was stable. Begin accepted Sadat's offer to attend this preparatory conference because he wanted the benefit from the symbolism of an Israeli delegation in Cairo, but he did nothing to empower the conference to negotiate substantive matters. Begin's substantive response was given to Carter, not in the form of a declaration of general principles, but as an outline of how the Palestinian issue should be treated as an exchange for an Israeli withdrawal from Sinai. It remained Israel's intention to keep Sadat's beam locked onto Washington for his wanted and needed answers. Strategically for Israel, Washington had to be the source of mediation, compromise, guarantees, and assurances. If an Israeli priority had to be set for the emerging public diplomacy, symbolism was as important as were changes in Egyptian public attitudes toward Israel. But they were not as important as Sadat's sustained and unshakeable link to Washington, where Israel felt it could sustain its political positions with the American public, media, and Congress.

Of the principal Middle Eastern adversaries, only Egypt and Israel actually sat down together at Mena House, though also attending were American and United Nations representatives. Before the conference was to open at 11 A.M. on December 15, the head of the Israeli delegation, Eliyahu Ben-Elisar, the director-general of the Israel prime minister's office, somewhat cautious in his first public meeting with the Egyptians, dispatched a member of his delegation to review the layout of the meeting room before he entered. When Ben-Elisar was late in coming to the opening of the conference, Esmat Abdel-Meguid, the Egyptian delegation head, sent someone to inquire if all was in order. Ben-Elisar replied that he could not come because the room had been arranged for additional delegations, with unrecognized flags displayed in front of certain chairs. Ben-Elisar then told his Israeli colleagues to start packing; a message was sent to the Egyptians that the Israelis might need their airplane to return to Israel. Suddenly, all the flags were removed from the conference room, including the PLO flag. But the truth was, said Ben-Elisar, "I did not know and no one [in our delegation] knew what the flag of the PLO looked like!"[26] So the Israeli delegation contacted the foreign office in Jerusalem and ascertained that it was indeed the PLO flag in the conference room and also outside the Mena House, where the delegates were to have lunch. During lunch, Ben-Elisar informed the head of Egyptian protocol that he was not happy with the Mena House hospitality and wanted to change hotels. The Egyptians inquired about Ben-Elisar's discomfort, and the second PLO flag was removed from the premises. It is not clear what Israel's response would have been if the PLO had accepted the invitation to attend the Mena House Talks; it is likely they would have gone to Cairo, but avoided meeting the PLO.[27] Sadat later indicated that the PLO refused to come because they were subjected to pressure from Syria and the Soviet

Union.[28] For their own reasons of not wanting to sanctify Sadat's policies toward Israel, they did not attend.

When the conference began, there was no preset agenda. Each delegation head made opening remarks. No substantive breakthrough was achieved, and though there was some discussion of the meaning of UNSC Resolution 242, they reached no agreement on interpretation.[29] The respective delegations at the Mena House Talks realized that nothing substantive would be negotiated until Begin and Sadat met again. According to Abdel Meguid, "We were never pretending to reach an agreement; it would be a real exaggeration to say so."[30] One American attending recalled that "it was path-breaking because the Israelis were in Cairo, but the talks were terribly unproductive. The two sides talked past each other."[31] However, Israeli and Egyptian generals were afforded an opportunity to learn the essence of the security arrangements needed in Sinai.

For Begin, the presence of an Israeli delegation in Egypt's capital was too good an opportunity to pass up.[32] Watching from Washington, Begin saw the Israeli delegation on television and expressed great delight that they were being hosted so warmly. Likewise, Israelis at home were glued to television sets, catching every possible moment of the official Israeli delegation in Cairo. The El-Al Airline crew that took the Israeli delegation to Cairo was composed of Israelis who were of Egyptian-Jewish origin; in fact, some of the pilots had actually spent time in an Egyptian prison camp. At the Tel-Aviv Airport, the Israeli delegation members found it surreal to see Cairo as an El-Al destination on the flight departure board and, upon arrival at the Cairo Airport, to see the Israeli flag. Without kosher food available in Cairo, the Israeli delegation was provided kosher box lunches from Austrian Airlines.[33] Israeli officials visited the main synagogue in Cairo—an event covered by more than 2,000 journalists. Ben-Elisar waded deep into the crowd, shaking hands with Egyptian spectators, and was greeted warmly by the general public.

Two useful by-products of Egyptian-Israeli negotiations emerged from the Mena House Talks. A secure and direct communication line was established between Cairo and Jerusalem, which was used effectively in early 1978 when bilateral relations were quickly deteriorating over the lack of diplomatic progress. And Egyptians and Israelis, though not on the same negotiating page, began to see each other as Yariv and el-Gamasy had four years earlier at the Kilometer 101 Talks. Information was traded and exchanged directly between them, a process that would continue, albeit sporadically, through Camp David, up to and after the signing of their peace treaty in 1979. Generals, Foreign Ministry officials, media specialists, and other civil servants from both sides began to see a human dimension in their protagonists, which while not causing mutual physical or political embrace, broke the icy chill that otherwise personified their relations before Sadat's Jerusalem visit.

On December 25, Begin visited Sadat at Ismailiya, where he presented his ideas about Palestinian autonomy and the substance of future Egyptian-Israeli relations.

Though Sadat still expected a grand gesture from Begin, the Israeli prime minister could not even begin to contemplate something as dramatic as unilateral Israeli withdrawal from some or all of Sinai, in part because the Israelis still did not fully trust Sadat. Even Ezer Weizman, who became as close to Sadat as any Israeli official, later told him bluntly, "Do you really imagine that because of [your Jerusalem visit] we can place all our trust in your hands? Today, you are president, and tomorrow not. Israel's existence cannot be dependent upon you."[34] Israeli leaders understood that this negotiating process was embodied in a thin reed called Sadat. Resignations and appointments of ministers because of Sadat's policies and whims did not create additional confidence about the breadth of Egyptian governmental support for his policy shift toward Israel. When he replaced Foreign Minister Fahmy over his opposition to the Jerusalem visit, he chose a longtime friend, Mohamed Ibrahim Kamel. Although Fahmy might have strongly opposed Sadat's policies, Sadat had confidence in Fahmy's ability to communicate with Assad and Hussein, both of whom found Kamel a lesser talent than Fahmy. Hence a casualty of the Jerusalem visit was less confident and familiar communication with Arab leaders already angry at Sadat's one-man diplomacy. While waiting for the Israelis to arrive at Ismailiya, Sadat told Kamel that the Arab leaders, especially Assad, had tried his patience and that he "could not maintain a policy which tied Egypt to the Arab present course, with its jealousies and struggles for leadership."[35] Kamel was both particularly troubled by Sadat's steady inclination to place the return of Sinai above the Palestinian issue and regularly at odds with Sadat because of his tilt toward Israel and away from the Arab world.[36] Kamel simply did not believe in anything that Sadat wanted to do with the Israelis and was perturbed by the manner in which he was appointed. Sadat had given Kamel a twenty-four-hour notice that he would be appointed foreign minister. After a pause in the conversation, where Sadat went to greet Begin and the visiting Israeli delegation, to Kamel's consternation, Sadat proceeded to swear in Kamel as Egypt's foreign minister. For Kamel, the swearing-in ceremony was emotionally wrenching because it was done in front of the visiting Israelis.

Begin presented Sadat with two documents: one outlining an Egyptian-Israeli peace treaty; the other, Begin's self-rule plan for the Palestinians in the West Bank and Gaza Strip. Some of the conceptual seeds for the September 1978 Camp David Accords were thus planted: discussion of a framework governing Egyptian-Israeli relations and a definition of intent for Palestinian association with the negotiations. Begin apparently said that "when the peace agreement is signed, the Egyptian Army may be established on a line which will not reach beyond the Mitla and Gidi Passes."[37] Begin later claimed that he based his suggested plan about Egyptian military presence in Sinai according to what Sadat told him in a one-on-one meeting in Jerusalem in November: "my [Egyptian] Army will not cross the passes."[38] As for the rest of Sinai, Begin suggested that it be demilitarized; Israel would retain its military airports in Sinai, and the settlements would become civilian settlements. In addition, Begin spoke about the establishment of full normalization of relations, including diplomatic relations. He suggested that the Israelis withdraw in two stages over a two- to five-year period, with Israel retaining a presence in a zone to be controlled by the United Nations but subject to Israeli jurisdiction and administration, the presence of early-warning stations in Sinai under Israeli control, Israel's custody and civilian use of three key military airfields in Sinai, and guaranteed open navigation through the Straits of Tiran and the Gulf of Aqaba.[39]

Begin went into considerable detail in describing to Sadat how his autonomy scheme for the Palestinians would work. His discourse focused on separating the future Egyptian-Israeli relationship from the West Bank/Gaza Palestinian issue. Although Sadat did not dissuade or oppose Begin's interest in treating the two ideas separately, he said that Begin's "peace proposals were unacceptable."[40] The key elements of Begin's proposal for self-rule in the West Bank and Gaza were:[41]

1. The military government in the West Bank would be dismantled and the Palestinian Arab inhabitants of these territories would be granted self-rule under an elected administrative council, located in Bethlehem.
2. Israel would be responsible for security and public order in the territories.
3. The Arab inhabitants would be given a choice between Israeli or Jordanian citizenship.
4. A committee would be established including representatives of Israel, Jordan and the elected administrative council, which would examine existing legislation in the territories and would determine, by consent, which laws would remain in force, and what authority the administrative council would have to determine regulations.
5. Israeli citizens would be entitled to buy land in the territories. Those Arab residents accepting Israeli citizenship would also be entitled to purchase land and settle anywhere in Israel.
6. A committee comprising representatives of Israel, Jordan and the administrative council would determine regulations for the admission of Arab refugees to the territories in reasonable numbers.
7. Freedom of movement and of economic activity in Israel, the West Bank and the Gaza Strip would be assured for all their inhabitants.
8. Israel would maintain its claim to sovereignty over these territories while being fully aware that there were other claims to them. Israel, however, proposed that, in order to reach a peace settlement, the question of sovereignty should remain open.
9. Regarding Jerusalem—Israel would present a separate proposal for the administration of the holy places of the three religions. This proposal would ensure freedom of access to the sites to members of each faith.

The above principles would be subject to reassessment after a period of five years. Equally important was the degree to which agreement on the Palestinian issue would be linked to progress in defining the Egyptian-Israeli relationship. The major sticking point was Egypt's nonacceptance of any continuing Israeli civilian or military presence in Sinai. Begin told Sadat, that "not only the settlements would stay, but they will be defended by an Israeli contingent."[42] Just as Golda Meir was driven to have her POWs returned in the shortest possible time frame after the October War, and Sadat and Kissinger used her impatience for their purposes, now Begin proposed dragging out the time period when Sinai, and then only half of it, would be returned. Begin eventually used Sadat's insatiable thirst for Sinai's return to dislodge and redefine Sadat's commitment to the Palestinians. Among Sadat's advisers, there was a strong commitment to see the Palestinian Arabs achieve self-determination and statehood, rather than merely self-rule, as Israel had proposed; the American position was, as Brzezinski had hoped after Begin's visit with Carter, that self-rule would just be a place along the way to something more concrete like Palestinian self-determination.

At the Ismailiya Summit, the development of a declaration of principles that would govern their future negotiations was broached but not finalized. Sadat was more enthusiastic for a declaration of principles than was Begin, because he wanted the principles to outline an Arab-Israeli settlement, with specific reference to the Palestinian issue. He told Begin that Egypt was bound by the Arab Summit Conference Resolutions, especially those that referred to Israeli withdrawal from the territories and a solution to the Palestinian problem on the basis of the legitimate rights of the Palestinians. If there was going to be a declaration of principles, Begin wanted one that would be much more vague, without an explicit Israeli promise to withdraw to the 1967 borders and certainly without any mention of Palestinian self-determination. There was no hint of a unilateral withdrawal from Sinai offered by the Israeli side. However, in fashioning an outline for a declaration of principles, Sadat and Begin reached three points of agreement: a commitment to achieve a comprehensive peace settlement; a willingness to negotiate peace treaties based upon UNSC Resolutions 242 and 338; and the fulfillment of all the specific contents of UNSC Resolution 242. Sadat told the Israelis that UNSC Resolution 242 required Israel to return all territories taken by force and return to the pre-1967 armistice lines.[43] There was no declaration published because a formula for the Palestinian Arabs could not be agreed upon. There was little agreement between the Israeli and Egyptian viewpoints on Begin's presentation. According to Vice President Mubarak, who attended the Begin presentation, Begin drew a line across Sinai; "they take half and we take the other half. We all revolted, including President al-Sadat."[44]

No Americans attended the Ismailiya Summit. What the Americans learned from the summit was provided to their respective ambassadors in Cairo and Tel Aviv.

There were two diametrically conflicting reports. "Begin called the meeting a big success. . . . Sadat thought the meeting was a complete failure, a real setback for the peace initiative."[45] The State Department cables, which came from Lewis in Tel-Aviv and Eilts in Cairo, relayed completely dissimilar reports. Each ambassador faithfully couched his cable with his secondhand impression of the summit. Lewis reported that Begin and Sadat were close to an agreement, but Sadat's advisers held him back from endorsing the self-rule idea. Eilts's cable reported that Sadat said, "This was the most insulting meeting. I'm never going to see this man again. He was my guest, so I had to be polite to him, but don't ever expect me to talk to him again. I will talk to [the Americans], but not to him, because he's a shop keeper, a nickel and dime. He has these little proposals about self-rule and so forth. I just offered him peace and no more war. I've gone to Jerusalem, and he comes here, and he gives me this lousy piece of paper."[46] Typical of Sadat putting on a different public face than what he claimed in private, a week later in an interview on Cairo radio, he said, "Ismailiya was successful."[47] Not surprisingly, the PLO rejected the concept of political autonomy; Arafat said in January 1978, "What is Begin offering us now, Bantustans, not more."[48] Arab mayors from West Bank and Gaza Strip cities also rejected the Palestinian self-rule plan, categorizing it as a means to legitimize and legalize "Zionist occupation of Arab territory."[49]

At the Israeli airport ceremony on the prime minister's return from Ismailiya, Begin was positive in summing up his talks with Sadat. Dayan, on the other hand, when he stepped off the plane from the summit, was "convinced that the whole thing had been a disaster . . . [and] that there was no alternative now, but to turn to the Americans, and get us into the act à la Kissinger. . . . [W]e're not going to get anywhere this way."[50] Dayan remained unsure about whether the Egyptians would sign a separate peace with Israel; at almost every negotiating opportunity with the Egyptians until Camp David and even subsequently, Dayan asked this same question. And if the answer came up positive, he always asked, "At what price?" Given the deep residual interest of the Carter administration to manage the negotiations, Washington warmly received Dayan's strong reservations about Begin and Sadat making progress on their own. After Ismailiya, the Carter administration tried to keep Sadat focused on an agreement that would be broader than another strictly Egyptian-Israeli understanding and, at the same time, tried to pry Begin from his ideological grip on the West Bank and Gaza. After the summit meeting, there was considerable worry among some at the White House that Sadat was so disappointed with Begin and his response that he just might scrap the whole adventure of seeking an agreement with Israel. But Sadat had come too far with Washington to abandon his quest for Sinai's return. For its part, the administration was still not willing to jettison its own keen philosophical commitment to find a workable solution for the Palestinian dimension of the conflict, something broader than Begin's self-rule. The administration did not want Sadat to act impulsively; there was a fear that he was in too much of a hurry to have Sinai returned. American policymakers worried that Sadat would make verbal concessions to Begin that would compromise the chances for withdrawal from the West Bank and Gaza and thereby forfeit an opportunity to provide territory for the Palestinians. And Washington knew that Begin was steering the negotiations toward Sinai and away from an agreement with Jordan, because he did not want an agreement with Jordan, which would necessitate the unthinkable: discussion about possession and use of the West Bank and Jerusalem. Begin's feelings about the West Bank were unmistakable. In a meeting between Secretary of State Vance and Begin on January 15, 1978, Vance told Begin that Israel's position on UNSC Resolution 242, namely their claim that it did not apply to the West Bank and Gaza, was untenable. According to Atherton and Quandt, who recalled the same conversation, Begin viscerally replied that "this [Judea and Samaria] is the land of Israel; I can never agree to give it up. But I won't be prime minister in five years; who knows who'll be here. I will never be the prime minister who will agree to relinquish—maybe my successor will. . . . I won't annex the territory; I won't claim sovereignty, but I'm not going to be the one who ever gives up [the West Bank]."[51] Several days earlier, Begin said in an interview in a Paris publication that "self-determination means a Palestinian state. A Palestinian state would be mortal danger to Israel. Such a Palestinian state would, in no time, be a Soviet base."[52] It was readily clear that Begin had red lines that he would not cross; slowly, very slowly, Washington and Sadat absorbed that reality.

Issues that separated Begin and Sadat were starkly apparent. Begin did not want to remove Israeli settlements from Sinai; Sadat insisted upon it. Sadat wanted a specific commitment for Israeli withdrawal from the territories acquired in the 1967 War or an Israeli commitment to have UNSC Resolution 242 apply to all fronts; Begin refused. Begin wanted Sadat to keep his military from repopulating all of Sinai; Sadat wanted absolutely no restrictions on the sovereign use of Egyptian territory. Sadat wanted self-determination and a state for the Palestinians; Begin offered autonomy with Israel in control of the land. For the Carter administration, the next goal was to narrow these differences and to identify common language that would define the agenda and principles for future negotiations. For the next eight months, the administration focused on devising such a framework. Neither side was opposed to such a declaration, but given the political distance between Begin and Sadat, a combination of determination and linguistic expertise was necessary in writing definitions suitable to both sides. When sensitive, emotional, or contentious issues were broached in their subsequent discussions, both sides intentionally dropped the toughest issues from the negotiating agenda so that they might achieve a consensus over issues in which there was potential agreement. Compromises could not be found on the issues of Israeli settlements, the disposition of East

Jerusalem, or an agreed definition of UNSC Resolution 242. Instead, constructive verbal ambiguity was used to paper over those differences.

After the Ismailiya Summit, Sadat accepted Begin's suggestion that the next round of talks be held as separate military and political committee discussions, with the former taking place in Cairo and the latter in Jerusalem. The political committee talks were headed by foreign ministers, the military committee talks by defense ministers. The United States participated in the former talks, but not in the latter ones. Both sets of talks were considered a natural negotiating progression from the Mena House Talks. "The idea of the political committee talks," said a member of the Egyptian delegation, "was to give a political context to the military committee talks, provide a road map that would govern Egyptian-Israeli negotiations, and specifically achieve some generally accepted principles."[53] Dayan did not think Egypt would have formed the military and political committees if Sadat had not wanted to make peace with Israel.[54] By segregating military and political issues into separate meetings, Egypt and Israel acknowledged that they were not willing to give up. In his opening remarks at the military committee talks on January 11, 1978, General el-Gamasy, by then Egypt's deputy prime minister and minister of defense and war production, was emphatic about Egypt's desire for "complete Israeli withdrawal from Sinai, including the elimination of Israeli settlements from Sinai. We do not accept their existence because they violate Egyptian sovereignty."[55] Egypt was ready to provide Israel with whatever security guarantees it wished, as long as it was prepared to withdraw fully from Sinai. In reply, Israeli Defense Minister Weizman proposed a five-point agenda for discussion: (1) phased withdrawal of Israeli forces from Sinai; (2) geographical designations of demilitarized zones for Sinai; (3) the status of Israeli military airports in Sinai; (4) implementation of reciprocal observations and inspection measures, including early-warning systems; and (5) the state of Israeli settlements in Sinai and determination of their future status. Egyptian and Israeli military views concurred on several issues: the establishment of buffer zones where only UN presence was permitted; the creation of limited-force zones where the Egyptian Army was to be stationed; and the institution of demilitarized zones where only civilian activity would be allowed. Disagreement between Egyptian and Israeli negotiators continued over the depth of each demilitarized zone, Israel's desire to retain the Sinai airfields for a three- to five-year period, and the status of Israeli settlements. But what the Israelis took from the military talks was extraordinarily important. Moshe Sasson, an Israeli Foreign Ministry official and later Israel's ambassador to Egypt, reported to Foreign Minister Dayan upon his return from Cairo, "I am sure that the Egyptians will sign a separate peace agreement and will remain committed to it, provided that there be something very vague related to the whole [Arab-Israeli-Palestinian] question."[56] General Avraham Tamir, who was the primary Israeli negotiator at the military committee talks, agreed with Sasson's conclusion: "Egypt would be prepared to make a separate peace with Israel on [the] condition that a declaration of principles be agreed [upon] providing for self-determination for the Palestinian Arabs after a period of autonomy under Egyptian and Jordanian supervision."[57] Only after Weizman returned from Cairo and his meetings with Sadat at the end of March 1978 had a consensus developed among Israeli decision makers that Sadat indeed was willing in clear and unambiguous terms to sign a separate agreement with Israel. Weizman reported that though Egypt would try and get something for the Palestinians, he would, if necessary, go it alone with Israel.[58] A year had passed since Sadat told Carter privately at their first White House meeting that Egypt would be inclined, if necessary, to sign a separate peace with Israel.

Though the participating American, Egyptian, and Israeli delegations to the political committee talks, which opened in Jerusalem on January 16, 1978, expected their deliberations to go on for some time, they were abruptly shortened by rancor and dispute. In his opening remarks, Israeli Foreign Minister Dayan commented favorably on the precedent-setting nature of the discussions, which he termed *peace talks.* He acknowledged that a great distance had to be traversed from peace talks to peace treaties, but negotiations were a step in the right direction. Dayan had singular praise for Secretary of State Vance. Foreign Minister Kamel also praised Vance's presence and negotiating efforts. Kamel went on to call for full Israeli withdrawal from all the territories taken in the June 1967 War, including Jerusalem, and asked for self-determination for the Palestinians. He presented a six-point proposal for a declaration of principles, which included Egypt's interpretation of UNSC Resolution 242, namely withdrawal from all the territories; guarantees for the political independence, sovereignty, territorial integrity of every state in the area; achievement of a just solution for the Palestinian question on the basis of the right of self-determination through negotiations with Egypt, Jordan, Israel, and the representatives of the Palestinian people; termination of all the claims or states of war and establishment of peaceful relations among all the states in the region through peace treaties; the establishment of demilitarized zones, areas with reduced arms on both sides, early-warning stations; and the establishment of a joint commission to supervise implementation of this agreement.[59] Kamel was not at ease. This was his first overseas assignment, and he was presenting Egypt's declaration of principles to the Israelis in Jerusalem. For him, it was a nerve-wracking experience.[60]

After the opening statements by the respective foreign ministers, the talks were briefly adjourned; they commenced again in two brief, closed sessions. The meetings that were held later in the day were mainly proximity talks, engineered primarily by Secretary of State Vance. There were very few meetings held between the members of Egyptian and Israeli delegations, though legal specialists from both sides met to reconcile the language of the pertinent documents. At the noon session, a three-clause agenda for the talks was presented for acceptance by Secretary of State Vance, including a declaration of principles intended to guide the negotiations toward a comprehensive peace in the Middle East, guidelines for the negotiations concerning issues of the West Bank and Gaza Strip (the Israeli foreign minister remarked that the Israeli terminology was "Judea and Samaria" instead of "the West Bank"), and a summary of the components of a suggested peace treaty between Israel and its neighbors according to the principles of UNSC Resolution 242. The Egyptians and Israelis exchanged documents and the session was adjourned until 3:00 P.M. on January 17. When Kamel returned to his hotel room after lunch, he found a cable from Vice President Mubarak stating that Sadat congratulated him on the opening session of the talks and hoped that he would "maintain [his] calm, and that [his] speech be deliberate and controlled."[61] Kamel was astonished to have received such an admonition.

Late in the afternoon, Kamel met privately with Begin. With Dayan and Epi Evron present, Begin explained to Kamel that he was disappointed that Sadat had created a crisis over the settlements, as if it were a new issue. Angrily, Begin told Kamel that he was highly offended by articles in the Egyptian press that categorized him as a shylock and a fascist. In front of the Knesset six days later, Begin repeated the litany of vicious anti-Israeli comments and anti-Semitic innuendos that had appeared most recently in the Egyptian press. Kamel said that he had been offended by Israeli radio broadcasts that quoted Sadat as saying, "the leaders of the PLO were agents of the Soviet Union." Begin replied that was precisely what Sadat had said to him. Kamel responded that he doubted that these were Sadat's words, but "even if they were, there were certain conversations that should, under the circumstances, not be disclosed."[62]

That evening, all three delegations attended a dinner hosted by Prime Minister Begin. The atmosphere between Begin and his Egyptian visitors was tense and highly charged due to the sharp exchange of ideas, quips, and barbs in the afternoon meeting. Begin's dinner speech was a reply to Kamel's arrival statement, which had demanded, among other things, Israel's return of Jerusalem to Arab control, as well as all the territories taken in the June 1967 War. Perturbed by Kamel's earlier remarks, Begin offered a toast during dinner to the Egyptian foreign minister, in which he referred to Kamel as a "young man" who did not understand history and obviously implied he was inexperienced, if not inept, as a diplomat. Begin also made reference to the misuse of the concept of self-determination, which he believed had launched the destruction in Europe in the 1930s. According to David Korn's recollection of the evening,

We were sitting [at] a table with Egyptians and Israelis, and Begin got up to speak. We all felt like we wanted to crawl under the table; Kamel's flesh was crawling. The Egyptians looked like they were about to die. Kamel got up and he was shaking. Suddenly we were all adjourning. Begin was so obnoxious. [Kamel] wanted to go back to Cairo. Kamel had not slept for one second, as long as he had been in Jerusalem; he had not wanted to go in the first place, and he was out of his league. You really had to be at that dinner to see how awful it was. He was so nervous that Begin's speech pushed him over the edge. Kamel called Sadat, and Sadat felt sorry for him and asked him to return to Cairo.[63]

At this point, according to Atherton, Kamel "was crestfallen."[64] In reply to Begin, Kamel did not offer the traditional toast. Ben-Elisar, who was present too, said, "Begin did not intend to insult or to demean Kamel, but he was not 100 percent tactful and was a *little* paternalistic, as he so often was, but we did not pay any attention to it."[65] Sadat used Begin's undiplomatic toasting of Kamel as an excuse to suspend the political talks; meanwhile, Egyptian and Israeli military officials continued their informal talks in Cairo. Though talks were suspended, the political committee had already agreed on five out of seven paragraphs that were to be part of that illusive declaration of principles that would guide the negotiations. Five days later, on January 22, 1978, the Israeli Cabinet authorized Defense Minister Weizman to resume participation in the military committee talks. On the following day, Begin commented to the Israeli Parliament that "we made progress, and President Sadat stopped it suddenly. With all due respect, there was no justification for this."[66]

Was Sadat truly impatient with Begin and the lack of progress on withdrawal from Sinai? Why did the political committee talks end so abruptly? Several plausible explanations are likely. First, most Israelis who were associated with the political committee talks believed that Sadat pulled the plug on the discussions because he neither liked their content nor their pace. Second, Sadat wanted to be back in control of the negotiations and not leave them to his underlings. Third, according to General el-Gamasy, the Saudis were exerting pressure on Sadat to stop the Jerusalem negotiations, threatening that if he did not halt the talks with Israel, moderate Arab states would immediately sever relations with Egypt and join an anti-Egyptian boycott.[67] Finally, Ahmed Maher, an Egyptian Foreign Ministry official who would later join the Egyptian delegation at Camp David, was of the opinion that withdrawing the delegation really had nothing to do with content. The Egyptians felt that they were on a dangerous downward negotiating slope. They sensed that Vance was offering new formulations entirely unacceptable to Egypt's political positions. According to el-Sayeed, Sadat withdrew the Egyptian delegation because Vance could not find compromise language satisfactory to Egypt. Rather than embarrassing Vance by having to say no to him, and therefore to Carter, Sadat recalled his delegation.[68] Egypt was not prepared to renounce its right to have all of Sinai returned, and Vance's formulations might have presaged that possibility. By withdrawing his delegation, Sadat sent a message to the Americans that the talks had reached a crisis and were in need of rescue. Sadat, according to el-Sayeed, did not want the Americans seeking a middle ground between the Egyptian and Israeli viewpoints, certainly not about Sinai.[69] He wanted Washington to advocate Egypt's position and its position only. The issues for the American administration now became: (1) how to provide a sufficient degree of progress or enough public protection for Sadat to reach an agreement on the Palestinian/West Bank territorial issue; and (2) how to keep the pressure on Israel to make additional compromises for the return of all of Sinai. With the collapse of the political committee talks, Carter began to sense that whatever Egypt and Israel agreed would be fine with him, even if that meant not resolving the Palestinian question.[70] Twice in a month, the negotiating atmosphere was clouded by extraordinarily bad feelings; the pace and content of the negotiations was, as Ben-Elisar noted, like "giving gas in neutral."[71]

U.S. hopes for an appropriate Israeli reply to Sadat's initiative diminished quickly, and the focus shifted to the definition of the transitional authority. From early January, Carter took it upon himself to keep the negotiating process moving and to try to broaden the circle of negotiations to include Arab partners other than Egypt. Carter met with King Hussein in Tehran on New Year's Day and with the Saudi leadership two days later. He told them that he favored Palestinian self-determination and hoped that King Hussein would join the negotiations, but the king remained noncommittal. Flying home via Egypt, Carter stopped in Aswan, where he met Sadat and publicly stated a formula much less amorphous than his "Palestinian homeland" remark of ten months earlier. He said, "There must be a resolution of the Palestinian problem in all its aspects. The solution must recognize the legitimate rights of the Palestinian people and enable the Palestinians to participate in the determination of their own future." Carter's public position was the middle ground between Sadat's affirmed objective of an independent Palestinian state and Begin's autonomy proposal. He staked it out to encourage Saudi support for Sadat's initiative, but going any further would have alienated Begin altogether. For some in Israel, Carter's endorsement of Palestinian self-determination was another example of the American shift away from Israeli views. From their point of view, more such tilting was in the offing. Carter, however, was not deterred by criticism from Israel or from American Jews sympathetic to Israel. When Sadat visited Washington in February, the administration presented to Congress an aircraft arms sale for Egypt, Israel, and Saudi Arabia in a package deal. Presented in this manner, if Israeli supporters in Washington opposed aircraft sales to Cairo and Riyadh, then Israel would be denied its arms acquisition request as well. During Sadat's visit, the White House issued a statement emphasizing that UNSC Resolution 242 was "applicable to all fronts of the conflict" and "Israeli settlements in occupied territory are contrary to international law and an obstacle to peace, and that further settlement activity would be inconsistent with the effort to reach a peace settlement."[72] The same month, in a discussion with Mrs. Carter, President Carter conceived of the idea of inviting Begin and Sadat to Camp David for a summit meeting.[73] When Israeli Defense Minister Weizman visited Washington in early March, Carter offered the idea that the Palestinians be given the right to hold a referendum or plebiscite at the end of the five-year transitional period to determine their future. Carter remained relentless in keeping the pressure on all sides, in offering new and revised ideas, in forcing Egypt, Israel, and perhaps, Jordan and the Saudis to endorse the negotiating process. Public statements and the definition of negotiating parameters went along with Carter-Sadat and Carter-Begin summit meetings in Washington in February and March.

Additionally, during Sadat's visit, officials at the White House tried to entice him into a collusive U.S.-Egyptian ruse: its core operating principle would be for him to make some staunch demand or put forth a fairly tough position, like the necessity to create a Palestinian state; then the Americans would "force" Sadat to back down from that demand after a very intense public disagreement with him. This, in turn, might allow the Americans to use the opportunity to force Begin to back away from one of his uncompromising positions, such as continuing to build settlements. Sadat, ever the actor and not shy in being devious when it suited him, relished the idea of the Americans applying pressure on Begin. The Americans *still* thought they could change the political dynamics on the Israeli side by "apparent" reciprocity from Sadat. As it turned out, however, the unfolding ruse took too long to implement, Sadat lost patience for its evolution, and other issues intervened to prevent the ruse from being actually made operative.[74] Weizman saw Carter on March 10, 1978; the next day, PLO terrorists attacked an Israeli bus along the Haifa-Tel Aviv coastal road, killing thirty-five people. Several days later, Israel reacted militarily with a major incursion into the Lebanese south. Its objectives were to destroy the PLO bases near Israel's northern border used as launching pads for attacks against Israeli villages and settlements. More than 1,000 Lebanese were reportedly killed by the Israeli action and more than 100,000 fled their homes. Carter believed Israel's response to be "a terrible overreaction" and instructed Vance to vote for a UN resolution calling for Israel's withdrawal and the establishment of a United Nations peacekeeping force in southern Lebanon. Carter was also perturbed by Israel's use in the attack of American-made cluster bombs.[75] For the remainder of the spring, the negotiating process was full of mutual accusations about the absence of sincerity, honesty, and commitment to reach an understanding. Dayan said, "difficulties facing us are many."[76] Weizman described Begin's March talks with Carter as a "severe confrontation, a serious one, the like of which Israel has never known, and cannot be compared to any in the past. If President Carter has made up his mind to enter such a severe and dangerous confrontation with Israel, the Israeli response should be a united nation, ready to fight like the United States."[77]

The administration's futility in dealing with Sadat as a negotiating partner was evident in Quandt's memorandum sent to Brzezinski in mid-May. He wrote:

> In February, we tried to develop a joint approach with Sadat. With the passage of several months, it is unclear how much of a common strategy remains. Sadat takes initiatives without informing us in advance; he holds back on what

he is saying to Weizman; he lets his officials turn out worthless legalistic documents in the guise of serious negotiating proposals; and yet he seems to be disappointed with our reluctance to become a full partner. We do not have a satisfactory political understanding with Sadat as we enter a crucial phase of the negotiations. The reason, in my view, is that he has little idea of how to proceed and counts on us to bail him out. His impatience with details is becoming a real problem, as is his reluctance to engage in sustained negotiations.[78]

Nonetheless, the State Department, and in particular Roy Atherton, now the ambassador-at-large for negotiations, knitted existing common threads together throughout the spring in a series of shuttle visits between Cairo and Jerusalem. By the beginning of the summer, Egypt and Israel agreed on nine points for guiding a West Bank/Gaza Strip solution. These included ideas for a transitional authority; deferral of sovereignty; a Palestinian self-rule arrangement and its establishment; withdrawal of Israeli armed forces to specified areas; negotiations to be held between Israel, Jordan, Egypt, and Palestinians freely elected by the inhabitants of the West Bank and Gaza; negotiations to be conducted within a five-year period to determine the future of the territories, with the residents there consenting to whatever agreement was reached by the negotiating parties; and some regional economic development plan launched between Jordan, the West Bank/Gaza authority, Israel, and Egypt.

From July 17–19, 1978, American, Egyptian, and Israeli foreign ministers met at Leeds Castle in Kent, England. From these talks, Hal Saunders, the assistant secretary of state for Near Eastern and South Asian affairs, drafted a new document, which became the basis of the Camp David Accords.[79] The document contained a combination of notions and ideas from months of staff work, layered onto Begin's autonomy proposal, Carter's Aswan definition of Palestinian rights, and clarifications emerging from Atherton's spring shuttle missions. Although Begin and Sadat were still not prepared to relinquish control of the negotiations to their respective foreign ministers, at Leeds, Egyptian and Israeli officials, who had traded barbs for months previously, were suddenly reenergized. Dayan heard from Usamah al-Baz, a political adviser to Sadat, a moving understanding of Israeli security needs; Dayan told those assembled what was not possible; and when the talks broke, key personalities who would be central to engineering verbal compromises at Camp David two months later found themselves on the same negotiating page. Saunders said the talks at Leeds were "some of the best, freest, farthest ranging and honest discussions of underlying issues."[80] According to Atherton, "Leeds was a very important breakthrough in a lot of ways, not in terms of issues, but in terms of people getting to begin to perceive each other's points of view . . . and locking them up inside of a castle with a moat around it, symbolically, the press was on the other side of the moat, and they couldn't get in."[81] By comparison, Carter, who was not at Leeds, did not believe that positions were changed there;[82] however, in speaking frankly, dining together, going arm-in-arm for walks, even feeling relieved that one did not have to make a critical negotiating decision because the "boss" was back home, all allowed some misperceptions to be ironed out before more serious talks would take place at Camp David and after. By early August, Sadat, Begin, and Carter were antsy to have an agreement. Sadat by now considered Carter a dear friend in whom he had absolute faith, but he sensed that all of the momentum from his trip ten months earlier had dissipated. He had told Atherton and Sterner in Cairo in July, "I want some action."[83] Quandt noted, "Carter, too, was intensely irritated with the slow pace of the Middle East peace negotiations. Sadat and Begin continued to be deeply distrustful of each other, and diplomatic exchanges continued to be sterile."[84] By then, only Brzezinski, Vance, Mondale, Mrs. Carter, and Hamilton Jordan were privy to the idea of holding a Camp David summit meeting with the two leaders. When Vance went to the Middle East in August 1978, he delivered Carter's handwritten Camp David invitations to Begin and Sadat, who were both pleased with the invitation. According to Sam Lewis, "both principals jumped immediately to accept. . . . [T]hey were both delighted that the invitation suggested that this was the only way they were going to get any further."[85]

Despite their respective frustrations about dealing with each other, Carter, Begin, and Sadat sensed that an Egyptian-Israeli agreement on Sinai could be finalized. Indeed, without the real prospect of Sinai's full return to Egyptian sovereignty and a peace treaty recognizing Israeli existence, neither Egypt nor Israel would have been motivated to come to Camp David. In the days before the Camp David meetings, Carter knew that Sadat was prepared to sign a peace treaty with Israel if all of Sinai could be returned and if Israel could make a statement about withdrawal from the other fronts.[86] Both Begin and Sadat were prepared to reach a compromise arrangement on the Palestinian/West Bank–Gaza dimension of the conflict. In preparation for the Camp David meetings, Carter's advisers still had not dropped their concern that Sadat would sign a separate peace with Israel. They strongly advocated that Carter be sure of explicit linkage between the two areas under negotiation. But Carter paid less attention to the linkage issue than his advisers advocated. Even in the briefing materials prepared for Carter for the Camp David meetings, little attention was paid to Sinai because the potential for a successful resolution was almost taken for granted. Instead, almost all of the American effort was aimed at breaking the impasse on the Palestinian/West Bank–Gaza dimension.[87] Begin went to Camp David knowing that he would have to make some compromises, including a readiness to go back to the international frontier with Egypt; he still hoped Israel could retain its Sinai settlements. According to Ben-Elisar, Begin had two linked objectives: "to let a situation be created where Israel's presence and Zionist continuation in Judea and Samaria would continue; and [in return] to pay a high price in Sinai, not dismantling the settlements, but return[ing] sovereignty [to

Egypt]."[88] And at Camp David, Begin did everything in his power to make certain that what he did in Sinai absolutely would not set a precedent for Israeli withdrawals from Judea and Samaria. For that and other reasons, Begin was staunchly opposed to an independent Palestinian entity or any agreement that might restrict any Israeli prerogative to continue to populate the occupied territories, especially in the West Bank and Gaza. Two or three times at Camp David, when considering major compromises, he asked rhetorically of his personal aide, Yahiel Kadishai, "Are our people close members with our ideology, are our people going to live with it?"[89]

After thirteen days of negotiations, the Camp David meetings ended at the White House with the signing of the Camp David Accords on Sunday evening, September 17, 1978. Many of the concepts and substantive ideas that were discussed in the previous eighteen months percolated into them. It seemed like light years away from discussions of less than eleven months earlier about a comprehensive peace, a full-fledged conference, or Soviet participation. At Camp David, Begin and Sadat met occasionally on walks on the paths that wound around the series of small cottages that made up the central living areas. But for the most part, except for the first few days, their day trip to the Gettysburg battlefield and again toward the end of their meetings, Begin and Sadat did not spend prolonged periods of time together. Success at Camp David was due to Carter's commitment to see Egyptian-Israeli negotiations reach a conclusion. For two consecutive weeks, the president of the United States focused on resolving one international problem. This was unprecedented. Carter displayed an extraordinary command of detail and stamina. His dogged determination and faith pushed him to find compromises when others might have willingly and easily relented. Without those qualities, the Camp David Accords would not have been signed.[90] Additionally, Carter was the beneficiary of a very talented American foreign policy team that was creative, experienced, knowledgeable, and task-oriented. Likewise, the Israeli delegation had a stable of excellent talent in Ministers Dayan and Weizman and the legal brain power of Meir Rosenne and Aharon Barak. Adding to Camp David's success was the absence of the media. There were no opportunities for either Begin or Sadat to reassure domestic constituencies or be driven to conclusions by nay-sayers. While there were doubters in the Egyptian and Israeli delegations, absent were nay-sayers like Ismail Fahmy or hard-line Likud ideologues. There were numerous moments when both Begin and Sadat wanted to scrap their negotiations. But each time they considered doing so, they had to listen to an inner voice that told them they were deviating from a broader strategic national objective; if they bolted from Camp David, then they were assured of being blamed for the summit's failure, of disappointing the American president, and with that, risking frosty relations with the White House in coming months and years. Ultimately, neither Begin nor Sadat were willing to risk those eventualities. Both of them had invested enormous amounts of political capital and time to reach

Camp David. Under the auspices of an American president, the prize for succeeding was much greater than the price for failing.

The Camp David Accords were not a treaty; instead, they enshrined two negotiating tracks. Three main parts—a preamble, an Egyptian-Israeli section, and a framework outlining agreement on the Palestinian/West Bank–Gaza dimension—comprised the document. The preamble mentioned Resolution 242 by name along with all of the important terminology from it, but did not say that it applied to all fronts. If it had, Begin would never have signed. In the Accords, Egypt obtained a commitment from Israel for full withdrawal from Sinai, a process that would be completed in three years, and Israel obtained an Egyptian commitment to "normalize relations." Egypt and Israel agreed to reach a "just, comprehensive, and durable settlement of the Middle East conflict through the conclusion of peace treaties." On the Palestinian/West Bank segment of the Accords, the "legitimate rights of the Palestinian people" were acknowledged, and a process was to be set up to implement "full autonomy" within a period of five years. Begin insisted on the word "full" as an adjective prior to the word autonomy to indicate that this was the maximum political rights the Palestinians would attain. Negotiations regarding how autonomy was to occur, in what fields of self-rule, were to be worked out between Israel, Egypt, Jordan, and the Palestinians. In the Accords, the Palestinians were defined in various ways, but most specifically, reference was made to them as those "from the West Bank and Gaza or other Palestinians as mutually agreed." No reference was made to the PLO. As for Judea and Samaria, it was stipulated that once a Palestinian self-governing authority was established, a transitional period of five years would commence. It was anticipated that at the end of the third year of the transitional phase, negotiations would be resumed to determine the final status of "the West Bank and Gaza and its relationship with its neighbors." Nowhere in the framework was it stipulated *when* the autonomy period would begin. Likewise, there was no specific Israeli commitment for any full withdrawal from the West Bank and Gaza, other than "withdrawal of the Israeli military government and its civilian administration . . . as soon as a self-governing authority was freely elected by the inhabitants of these areas to replace the military government." The elections therefore were to be the trigger mechanism that initiated Israel's withdrawal of its government and administration. No mention was made of withdrawal of civilian settlements, dismantling of settlements, a settlements freeze, or the future status of Jerusalem. The settlements issue was handled in an understanding between Carter and Begin, but its interpretation blew up into immediate controversy. Mention was made of creating a committee to review the "modalities of admission of persons displaced from the West Bank and Gaza in 1967," but no commitment was made to actually return such persons. The portion of the Camp David Accords focused on the Palestinian/West Bank–Gaza dimension was only an interim outline or framework of what might be done immediately, without any commitment for a final determination on the future sovereignty of the territories. The Accords did not mention the Golan Heights, Syria, or Lebanon. This was not the comprehensive peace that Kissinger, Ford, Carter, or Sadat had in mind during the previous American presidential transition. Instead, the Accords were another interim agreement or step, but negotiations that flowed from the Accords slowed for several reasons. These included an inability to bring the Jordanians into the discussions; the controversy over settlements; the inconclusive nature of the subsequent autonomy talks; domestic opposition sustained by both Begin and Sadat and, in Sadat's case, ostracism and anger from the Arab world; the emergence of a what became a cold peace between Egypt and Israel; and changes in foreign policy priorities including discontinuity in personnel committed to sustaining the negotiating process.

When the Camp David Accords were signed, King Hussein saw it as a slap in the face of Jordanian sovereignty. Sadat volunteered Jordan's participation in deciding how functional autonomy would work and, more specifically, effectively said that Jordan would have a role in how the West Bank would be administered. Like the Rabat Summit Resolution, the Camp David Accords circumscribed Jordan's objective to reassert its control over the West Bank. Focusing as it did on Egypt, the Carter administration accepted Sadat's claim that he could deliver Hussein. Once again, Jordan remained the spurned suitor. And with a crescendo of Arab world opposition building against Sadat, Jordan could not risk accepting the Accords, without the support from powerful Arab neighbors, like Iraq, Saudi Arabia, and Syria. The dispatch of high-ranking administration officials to Amman to clarify the contents of the Accords did little to mollify Hussein's apprehensions: this was another Egyptian-Israeli agreement done behind Jordan's back. Hussein felt diplomatically snubbed by Carter's focus on Egypt. Carter admitted in early 1979 that perhaps one of the mistakes made at Camp David was to allow Sadat to claim that he could speak for Hussein if Jordan refused to join the talks.[91] But by then the damage was done with the Jordanians. After Camp David, according to the U.S. ambassador at the time, "It took us more than two years to overcome the animosity Hussein held for Carter."[92] Most of that bad feeling dissipated, but when Carter, as a private citizen, visited Jordan in 1983, some of the residue of bad taste remained evident. At least one positive result emerged for Jordan from the Camp David Accords: a firm commitment by Israel not to permit the evolution of an independent Palestinian state and an unstated commitment not to annex or apply Israeli sovereignty to the West Bank. During the 1980s, King Hussein continued his secret meetings with Israeli leaders; however, no public agreements were struck between Jordan and Israel. This was due to a series of interrelated factors, among them Hussein's regular hesitancy to join negotiations, doubt about whether the engine for the diplomatic process should come from Amman or Washington, a lack of strong Israeli political leadership, a fear of public leaks from the Israeli media about secret negotiations, a lack of clarity about what Jordan might receive from Israel if they engaged in public talks, Jordan's on-again off-again relationship with the PLO, and Arab financial incentives and political pressures to stay away from direct negotiations.

No unresolved issue clouded U.S.-Israeli relations more than the settlements controversy. Building of Israeli settlements was not halted. Their construction, expansion, and development continuously bedeviled U.S.-Israeli relations while antagonizing Arab world attitudes toward Israel. For two decades after Camp David, the inability of the United States to curb the building and expansion of Israeli settlements kept burning embers smouldering in Jerusalem-Washington relations. Arab interlocutors would repeatedly ask American officials to halt or curb Israeli settlement activity. Washington's inability to stop the settlements was perceived as American bias for Israel. Begin considered it a right for Jews to settle in the territories; Carter believed that the settlements were an obstacle to peace and said so publicly. Carter believed that after he had met with Begin on September 16, he had a commitment from the Israeli prime minister to halt them for the duration of the negotiations. According to Carter's memoir, "No new Israeli settlements would be established after the signing of this Framework for Peace, and . . . the issue of additional settlements would be resolved by the parties during the negotiations. This would be stated in a letter to be made public, from Begin to me. . . . My notes are clear—that the settlements freeze would continue until all negotiations were completed—and Cy Vance confirms my interpretation of what we decided."[93] Not exactly. Carter wanted a freeze on settlement activity not just for the duration of the talks on the Egyptian-Israeli relationship but until the end of the negotiations on autonomy as well. What seems to have happened is that at their Saturday night exchanges, Begin intimated consideration of a freeze, and then only for a limited period. Carter understood that to mean he had a firm commitment for no additional building of settlements encompassing the duration of both sets of negotiations. According to Quandt and Sol Linowitz (who later became the special American negotiator for the autonomy talks), who were both familiar with the different sets of notes of what transpired over the settlements that night, there was ambiguity in what Begin promised.[94] The next day, in a morning walk with Sadat, Carter told him that he had obtained Begin's promise about the settlements; later in the day, Begin's promise as stated in a letter to Carter did not stipulate an indefinite period for a settlements freeze, rather only for a three-month period and tied to the Egyptian-Israeli negotiations. Thus Carter's prestige was on the line with Sadat for having made a promise he thought he had before finding out that he did not have that *exact* promise. Toward the afternoon of September 17, agreement on the settlements issue was not concluded; Sadat at that point apparently did not care very much about the settlements freeze, but it became a major issue between Carter and Begin. The signing ceremony took place that night at the White House. The next day, Begin sent the same letter on settlements to Carter again. Begin was unwilling to accept Dayan's public remarks that no new settlements would be authorized in the West Bank and Gaza during the period to establish the self-governing authority. Though Begin had agreed that the Israeli Parliament could vote on the matter of withdrawal of Israeli settlements from Sinai, itself a major concession for him to even consider, he was not going to allow anyone to veto the Israeli right to settle in Judea and Samaria. Just two days after the Accords were signed, Sadat also said that the freeze on settlements was only for three months.[95] On Monday evening, September 19, with Begin and Sadat in the balcony of the House of Representatives, Carter delivered his report to the nation about the success at Camp David. It was perhaps the high point of Carter's presidency. But Carter felt Begin betrayed him on the settlements issue. "I think Begin deliberately sabotaged the whole thing with the damn settlements. He knows he lied. He hadn't left Camp David twelve hours before he was under tremendous [domestic] pressure. And when Begin and Sadat and I walked into the Capitol Monday night to give my report to the world, Sadat and I took Begin to the side and really gave him a hard time because he had just totally betrayed the spirit of the commitments of Camp David. There was never any equivocation when we left Camp David about the fact that there would be no settlements during the interim period, during which we would be negotiating the final peace agreement. That was absolutely and totally understood."[96] This disagreement soured their relations for the remainder of Carter's administration and thereafter. Because Carter openly and publicly disagreed with the Israeli prime minister over a highly sensitive issue of Israeli prerogative, the settlements controversy repeatedly soiled Carter's already suspicious relationship with the American Jewish community as well.

Most Israelis supported Begin's overtures toward Egypt, but a vocal minority adamantly opposed Begin's willingness to establish Palestinian autonomy, withdraw from Sinai, give back the airfields and oil fields, and dismantle Sinai settlements as part of the final arrangement with Egypt. Politicians on the Israeli right opposed in varying degrees any return of land or compromises to be made over Israeli prerogatives for Judea and Samaria. When the Israeli Parliament ratified the Camp David Accords on September 27, 1978, only two-thirds of those belonging to the government coalition endorsed them. The vote was eighty-four in favor and nineteen opposed, with seventeen abstentions. Begin's closest political friends were most pronounced in their opposition to returning territory and uprooting settlements. Many of those who opposed him were ideological colleagues of more than thirty years, men and women who had fought with him in the underground against British administration during the mandate. To many of these ideological stalwarts, Palestinian autonomy was interpreted as an overt compromise of total Israeli control over the Land of Israel. When talks at the Blair House commenced on October 12, 1978, Israeli and Egyptian delegations discussed the nature of Palestinian autonomy and finalized the details associated with an Egyptian-Israeli treaty. Gradually, details about Palestinian autonomy became secondary to finalizing details for the treaty.

In treaty negotiations, the most contentious issues included timing of Israeli withdrawals in Sinai in relation to establishment of diplomatic relations with Egypt; the possibilities of revising a treaty between Israel and Egypt after five years; U.S. financial and military commitments to both Cairo and Jerusalem; problems relating to Israel's demand for guaranteed oil supplies; compensation to Israel for withdrawing from strategic airfields in Sinai; and Egypt's request for a timetable for ending the Israeli military government in the West Bank and Gaza. In order to solidify progress and keep the talks headed in a positive direction, Carter intervened directly in these Washington talks. On October 20, a draft of an Egyptian-Israeli treaty was agreed upon and ratified with modifications by the Israeli Cabinet five days later. A second round of talks ensued in Washington, in which Dayan and Weizman appeared more willing to sign the treaty than Begin, who was in Jerusalem. Vance met with Dayan and Egyptian Prime Minister Khalil in Brussels to narrow differences, but no real progress was made. Still, Carter did not give up. Begin again sensed that Dayan was too eager to reach an agreement with the Egyptians and therefore restrained his foreign minister's prerogatives to negotiate on behalf of the government. When the final treaty details could not be completed, Carter invited Sadat and Begin to Camp David again. That summit did not materialize, so Begin went to Washington separately at the end of February to see Carter. Some head-way was made, but major gaps still existed. Determined to see an Egyptian-Israeli treaty signed, Carter went to Israel on March 10. He noted in his memoirs that his proposal to go to Egypt and Israel was "an act of desperation."[97] There were numerous outstanding issues, the most significant for Israel pertained to its insistence that the treaty with Egypt supersede all other commitments Egypt had with the Arab world, including the 1950 Collective Arab Defense Agreement that said that one Arab country would come to the aid of another if attacked. (When Israel invaded Lebanon in June 1982, it tested the Egyptian commitment to Lebanon; Cairo did not send troops.) In his March visit with Begin, Carter had difficult talks, including an unprecedented meeting at Begin's private residence. Recalled Carter, "Begin said no until the last day. And it was only because of intense pressure from his own cabinet members that Begin ever agreed to go to that final little step in having a peace treaty. He did not want to do it. And it took a hell of an effort for him."[98] From the time Carter left Israel on March 13 until the Israeli parliament ratified the proposed treaty on March 21 (ninety-five in favor, eighteen against, two abstentions, and five not participating), the pockets of opposition to the peace treaty with Egypt became increasingly vocal and antagonistic toward Begin. The Egyptian-Israeli Peace Treaty was signed on the White House lawn on March 26, 1979.

Attention thereafter shifted toward defining autonomy. Throughout 1979 and 1980, considerable progress was made in defining twenty-five separate areas of Palestinian self-governing responsibility. And then, again, difficulty arose in detailing responsibilities in the areas of self-rule. The areas of Egyptian-Israeli agreement on Palestinian self-rule included the administration of agriculture, budget, civil service, commerce, culture, ecology, education, finance, health, housing and construction, industry, internal communications and post, internal transportation, justice, labor, local police and prisons, manpower, municipal affairs, nature preserves and parks, public works, refugee rehabilitation, religious affairs, social welfare, taxation, and tourism. Five areas not agreed upon were the issues of settlements, division of water, responsibility for external security, powers granted to the Palestinian self-governing authority, and whether Palestinians in East Jerusalem should vote for that authority.[99] At the time, autonomy was viewed by the staunch Israeli political right as a basis for eventual territorial compromise that would mean turning West Bank land over to another's authority. That is exactly what the 1993 Oslo Accords and their subsequent implementation agreements accomplished, and it was precisely what Israeli Prime Ministers Rabin, Peres, and Netanyahu did in turning over political and physical control to the Palestinians of the urban and rural areas in the West Bank and Gaza Strip from 1995 through 1998. In terms of making a compromise with its longtime ideology in combination with other causes, including Begin's own departure from public life in 1983, the political right in Israel fragmented. The ideology that was once so sacred and unalterable was amended to accommodate contemporary consensus political realities: Israel was not going to annex the territories with two million Palestinian residents and offer them Israeli citizenship; Israel was not going to rule a foreign population without continued and large human, political, and financial costs. The legacy of the Camp David Accords was a step, an interim phase as Brzezinski had postulated, to keep open the possibility of the Palestinian quest for self-determination being satisfied at some future time in the West Bank and Gaza Strip.

Though the Egyptian media hailed his trip to Jerusalem, it also vilified Begin and Israel for not doing what Sadat had wanted: full withdrawal from all the territories. A perceptual gap developed within the Egyptian public between what Sadat said was possible and what actually materialized. In Egypt, the initial euphoria of his claim of "no more war" wore off. Once the various diplomatic meetings, summits, and fanfare passed, reality began to set in. External distractions could not hide Egypt's domestic problems. Many high expectations went unfulfilled at home. Sadat's economic reform policies of encouraging private-sector growth had not fully taken root, and there was no peace dividend felt by the Egyptian middle class. With vengeance, most of the Arab world lashed out at Sadat and Egypt for signing the Camp David Accords and a peace treaty with Israel. Cairo was skewered by its Arab neighbors. In Baghdad at the November 1978 Arab Summit meeting and the meeting of Arab foreign ministers in March 1979, Egypt was vilified and condemned for signing agreements with Israel. From the November 1978 meeting, an Arab delegation went to Cairo seeking to convince Sadat that if he dropped this initiative with Israel, large sums of economic aid would be offered to Cairo. Sadat turned down the offer of what was rumored to be $5 billion annually for ten years.[100] The day after the Egyptian-Israeli Peace Treaty was signed, Arab foreign ministers met in Baghdad, where Arafat called upon Arab countries to adhere to their pan-Arab commitments, punish the United States, confront the "ugly conspiracy," and punish the Egyptian regime.[101] Said Dr. George Habbash, head of a militant Palestinian organization under the PLO umbrella, "We can and must direct military blows against the Zionist entity, al-Sadat's regime, and U.S. imperialism."[102] Syrian Deputy Prime Minister and Foreign Minister Khaddam categorized Camp David as " reorganizing Israeli occupation," and called upon the Arab masses "to stifle, bring down, and punish the Egyptian regime."[103] At the conclusion of the Arab ministerial conference, the Arab League Council, short of declaring war, decided on the widest range of sanctions that could be possibly applied to Egypt. It decided to withdraw its ambassadors from Egypt immediately, recommended the severance of diplomatic relations with the Egyptian government, suspended Egypt's membership in the Arab League, made Tunis the temporary headquarters of the Arab League, and took recourse against Egypt if Cairo hindered the transfer of the Arab League headquarters. Transferring the Arab League from Cairo meant moving dozens of Arab organizations as varied as the Arab Telecommunications Union to the Joint Arab Defense Council that were under the Arab League's umbrella. Branch offices in Cairo of Arab companies, such as investment, banking, insurance, agriculture, and every conceivable Arab business or labor enterprise, were likewise to be shut or transferred, with all bank loans, deposits, and financial facilities in Egypt to be closed. And the Arab boycott of Arab goods to Israel, in effect since the late 1940s, was applied to Egyptian companies that dealt directly or indirectly with Israel. A ban on Egyptian newspapers and periodicals to the rest of the Arab world was also applied. Arab League member states also worked to isolate Egypt politically from other international organizations, such as the Islamic Conference Organization and the Organization of African Unity. The PLO wanted the toughest of sanctions applied against Egypt; Saudi Arabia and other Arab states wanted the sanctions to be of a low level of formality; tough and private, Egypt was punished. Three months later only three Arab countries—Sudan, Oman, and Somalia—had not severed diplomatic relations with Cairo. Nasser's Egypt, once the epicenter of Arab unity and inter-Arab politics, was now ostracized in a manner and magnitude never anticipated and accompanied by constant verbal attacks for making a separate peace with Israel. These were extraordinary political and economic prices for Sadat to pay. And then in May 1980, the autonomy talks were suspended.

Sadat expressed his frustrations publicly, but in 1981 the Reagan administration did not have the same penchant to narrow Egyptian and Israeli differences. Inside Egypt, religious tensions flamed between Muslims and Copts, government restrictions were placed on what was supposed to be a liberalizing political environment, leftists were still carping at Sadat for turning toward the United States, the flow of capital that was to go into investment was engulfed by consumerism, and the conduit of funds from Arab states stopped. Inspired in part by the successful overthrow of a secular leader in Iran, Muslim groups in Egypt, already part of Egypt's domestic opposition for fifty years, attacked his policies, especially his embrace of the United States and Israel. In late summer 1981, Sadat arrested more than three thousand of his most vocal domestic opponents. On October 6, 1981, as he reviewed the military parade celebrating the eighth anniversary of the October War, Sadat was assassinated by a young Egyptian lieutenant who belonged to a Muslim fundamentalist organization. Western, but not Arab, political leaders attended Sadat's funeral. In most of the Arab world and for a portion of Egypt, he was not a hero, but he had engaged in heroic diplomacy. Israel completed its withdrawal from Sinai, with the exception of a small piece of land near the southern Israeli port of Eilat, on April 25, 1982.

The public spotlight, document-signing ceremonies, and media fanfare did not diminish many of the mutually distrustful perceptions Israelis and Egyptians possessed for one another. Though Egypt and Israel possessed a peace treaty, it was not marked by warmth and cordial relations. Instead, a cold nonbelligerency characterized their subsequent relationship. Though ostracized from the Arab world for the treaty with Israel, Sadat had believed that Egypt was leading the Arab world in restoring the lands taken in the 1967 War. In his view, the treaty did not remove Egypt from its natural Arab orbit. On the other hand, Israel's priority remained keeping Egypt away from any future military involvement in a future Arab-Israeli conflict. Israel remained focused on its security, national defense, and fear of the next war. Israelis often doubted whether they had signed an agreement with a man or a country; they had self-doubts about giving up Sinai, an asset of strategic depth, and about returning the oil fields and the airfields. But Israel and Israelis wanted and expected more. Those self-imposed and unrealistic expectations for Israeli leaders and the Israeli public were met by disillusionment and profound reassessment about exchanging land for a hollow contextual peace. Land was returned, but no one demanded that Egypt give Israel peace, at least the way Israelis expected it. Israelis never had any doubts about Egypt's legitimacy. But many Egyptians, even after the treaty was signed, were still in a quandary about Israel's right to exist. Habits of the heart and mind did not abruptly end because a president and prime minister signed a document not to go to war again. The Egyptian press was merciless against Begin. Articles, anecdotes, and cartoons in the Egyptian media depicted Jews as immoral, hypocritical, unreliable, unmanly, intransigent, insecure, greedy, ill-intentioned, and chronically suspicious of everyone.[104] When Israel invaded

Lebanon in March 1978, the Egyptian daily *Akhbar al-Yawm* described Begin as "intransigent and defiant," and the invasion itself as a "Hitlerite military adventure."[105] Cairo's *al-Jumhuriyah* described the invasion as "part of the Zionist [mandate] to annihilate the Palestinian people, whose principles were laid down by Herzl."[106] In 1980, Israel's first ambassador to Egypt was socially boycotted, and the Israeli embassy staff faced difficulties in renting apartments in Cairo. Almost no tourism from Egypt to Israel materialized, and few commercial deals were negotiated. Academic and cultural exchanges were stillborn. Major professional associations in Egypt, like those of lawyers, engineers, and physicians and the General Federation of Trade Unionists, formally boycotted agreements with Israel and banned participation in the normalization process. Egyptian tourists and businessmen were not encouraged to visit Israel. And so it went through the 1980s; Egyptian-Israeli relations were cool, if not at times frozen. Had the peace treaty with Israel not been in Egypt's national interest, there were sufficient reasons for Cairo to break it. On numerous occassions, President Mubarak made it clear that the peace treaty and support of the Camp David Accords was in the interest of Egypt and the Arab world.[107] To break the treaty meant not only raising the prospects of war with Israel again but also alienating the United States, which made no sense for economic, financial, and military assistance reasons.

Israeli policies toward the rest of the Arab world in the 1980s greatly dismayed Egypt, particularly when Israel tried to alter physically its surrounding neighborhood. Israel pursued a security axiom toward Arab neighbors that was the obverse of the Golden Rule: "Do Unto Others Before They Do Unto You." Israeli actions included the June 1981 bombing of the Iraqi reactor; the December 1981 application of Israeli law to the Golan Heights; the June 1982 invasion of Lebanon and its prolonged presence there; continued growth and expansion of Jewish settlements; the bombing of the PLO headquarters in Tunis in October 1985; and the outbreak and Israel's management of the Palestinian uprising, or *intifadah,* against Israeli administration and rule in the territories after November 1987. Egyptian anger with Israeli policies continued in the 1990s with the deportation of Hamas activists to Lebanon in 1992; the killing of Palestinians by a crazed Israeli fanatic at the mosque in Hebron in 1993; Israel's unwillingness to sign the nuclear nonproliferation treaty; the opening of the Western Wall tunnel in 1996; plans to build new Jewish settlements at Har Homa near Jerusalem in 1997; and delay in implementing the second major Israeli withdrawal from West Bank areas as promised by the Oslo Accords.

Only for a brief period in the early 1990s was there a temporary warming of relations, after the Labor Party returned to power in 1992, and the Oslo Accords were signed the next year. Israel essentially was uncurbed in its choice and implementation of policies. Egypt's frustration was an inability to thwart Israeli actions directly and a lack of success to have the United States stop Israel's expansion of settlements. A series of weak Israeli governments in the 1980s contributed to a lack of Arab-Israeli negotiating progress. Some real efforts were made to find an accomodation with Jordan, but each initiative failed. In the 1980s, the Likud and Labor Parties continuously jockeyed for power, either ruling with razor-thin majorities in the Israeli Parliament, or as a national unity government, itself a blueprint for political inaction. Additionally, Israel's leaders focused on reducing triple-digit inflation, removing Israeli troops from Lebanon, and absorbing well over 800,000 Jewish immigrants from Eastern Europe, Ethiopia, and the former Soviet Union.

In June 1992, when Rabin became prime minister for the second time, a majority of Israelis had grown weary of continuing to control and administer the lives of the Palestinians in the West Bank and Gaza Strip. For most Israelis, Rabin personified a reasonably comfortable middle ground. In their minds, his military cum political career inspired trust that he would take the appropriate steps necessary for, and commensurate with, ensuring Israeli security. He used that public mandate to negotiate the 1993 Oslo Accords and their subsequent implementation agreements. However, by negotiating and recognizing the legitimacy of each other, Rabin and Arafat faced enormous criticism from respective domestic opponents who felt that their leaders had no right to reach a compromise for sharing the land of historic Palestine. Claiming that Rabin had no right to give up a portion of the Land of Israel as promised by G-d, in November 1995 a right-wing Israeli law student, Yigal Amir, assassinated Rabin. His death put the future pace of the Arab-Israeli peace process in doubt. In February and March 1996, four Palestinian terrorist bombings killed hundreds of Israelis, further compounding deep Israeli mistrust for Arafat, his motives, and his ability to provide Israelis with the personal security they wanted. The bombings undertaken by extremist Palestinian groups that opposed the Oslo Accords also put Arafat on notice that a segment of his community was violent and uncontrollable. Sufficient trepidation about the content and pace of negotiations with the Palestinians influenced Israeli voters in their May 1996 parliamentary and prime ministerial elections not to give Rabin's successor, Shimon Peres, the opportunity to continue negotiations with the Palestinians. Israelis did not have the faith that Peres would act judiciously and apply sufficient restraint in making strategic concessions to the Palestinians. In an environment of personal insecurity, Likud leader Benjamin Netanyahu was elected prime minister. He interpreted his election mandate as resounding permission to put the brakes on the negotiating process with the Palestinians. For the next three years, Netanyahu insisted on Arafat's full and unconditional cooperation in the security realm before additional territory or prerogative were turned over to him or to his Palestinian authority. In January 1997 and in November 1998, a portion of the city of Hebron and other lands in the West Bank, respectively, were turned over to Palestinian control. Netanyahu's willingness to turn over portions of the land of Israel, something

Begin would never have done, sufficiently alienated core right-wing supporters and other Israeli parliamentarians for them to bring down his government in late 1998. Still in doubt as the May–June 1999 scheduled elections approached was how Israelis and Palestinians would thereafter resolve the difficult, strategic, and emotional issues of water use, the future of the settlements, the final borders of a Palestinian entity, disposition of future Palestinian refugees, and political control and municipal rights in the city of Jerusalem.

Progress in Arab-Israeli peace-making was suspended in the 1980s because of changes in foreign policy priorities and discontinuity in personalities associated with the conflict's management. Other pressing foreign policy issues required Carter's attention, and, within the Middle East, geographic focus of attention shifted eastward. Carter had his hands full with a whole variety of foreign policy issues, including the SALT arms control negotiations and the normalization of relations with China. By the time the Egyptian-Israeli Peace Treaty was signed, major events in the Middle East moved to the Gulf region. The Shah had fallen and Ayatollah Khomeyni returned to Iran. At the end of 1979, American hostages were taken in Tehran, followed by an unsuccessful rescue mission in April 1980 and the negotiations for their release, which took place only minutes after Carter left office on January 21, 1991. The 444 days that the hostages were held consumed much of the White House's attention. In late December 1979, the Soviets invaded Afghanistan, and Carter responded in early 1980 by declaring that "an attempt by any outside force to gain control of the Persian Gulf region will be regarded as an assault on the vital interests of the United States."[108] Unstable politics in the oil-producing regions of the Persian/Arabian Gulf caused oil prices to rise; additional concern for access to oil at reasonable prices was further exacerbated by the outbreak of the Iran-Iraq War in September 1980. A substantial reason for the American economy's downturn in 1979 and 1980 was the high price of oil, which added to the monthly balance of payments deficit, already compounded by high inflation and high mortgage rates.

After Carter's defeat, an absence of continuity in presidential commitment and a change in key personnel in the United States, Israel, and Egypt contributed to a steady decline in attention to the Arab-Israeli conflict. Ronald Reagan did not have the passion, dedication, or personality Carter demonstrated for the issue. Aside from Israel's presence in Lebanon and finding ways to extract American troops safely, there was no immediate penchant to become entwined in furthering Arab-Israeli negotiations. As for others involved in Camp David, Brzezinski returned to academic life and entered the consulting world, and Quandt left the National Security Council for the Brookings Institution. Alexander Haig succeeded Vance as secretary of state and told autonomy negotiator Sol Linowitz in early 1981 that the new administration was going to go slowly in the Middle East. Haig himself lasted only until June 1982, when he was replaced by George Schultz. Gone also from official Washington were Sisco and Saunders. Atherton became U.S. ambassador to Egypt, replacing Eilts. Lewis was still at his ambassadorial post in Tel Aviv. Dayan resigned and was replaced by Yosef Burg of the National Religious Party in Israel, who had no interest in having the autonomy talks succeed or in alienating the settlers in the territories. Israeli Defense Minister Weizman, so helpful to Carter at Camp David and as determined as Carter was to work out the difficulties prior to the peace treaty signing, resigned in 1980. Begin held on to the defense minister's portfolio for fourteen months until he appointed former General Ariel Sharon, a hawk in the advocacy of building, not withdrawing, Israeli settlements (the same Sharon who was in favor of retribution against the Third Army at the end of the October War). By the end of 1981, Sadat was assassinated. Mubarak, the new Egyptian president, had priorities aimed at developing Egypt's relationship with the United States, assuring Israel's full withdrawal from Sinai, rebuilding the Egyptian economy, infrastructure, and military, and repairing relations with the other Arab states. Perhaps Mubarak's last national priority was warming relations with Israel. Indeed, supplying water to an ever-growing population was of greater importance to Mubarak than muzzling an Egyptian press angry at Israeli policies. Not until Arafat visited Egypt at the end of 1982 did Cairo become active again with the Palestinian issue, and then only if it could prevent another Arab state from becoming Arafat's chief counsel. By then Israel's presence in Lebanon dominated inter-Arab affairs. Begin himself resigned from office, to be replaced in September 1983 by Yitzhak Shamir. Having voted against the Camp David Accords, Shamir never annexed the territories but upheld Israel's right to build and expand settlements. In 1988, Shamir offered Palestinians the prospect of elections to a self-governing council in the hopes that it would surpass, neutralize, or compete with Arafat's PLO. After Shamir left office in 1992 in favor of Yitzhak Rabin's second tenure as prime minister, Shamir frequently repeated that his goal as prime minister was never to provide anything more to the Palestinians other than limited autonomy.

Though all of Sadat's political surprises were stunning, his visit to Jerusalem had some of the most immediate and long-term implications. Above all, it transformed the nature of the Arab-Israeli conflict. Yet, his visit became another interim step in the step-by-step process of redefining the Egyptian-Israeli, and therefore Arab-Israeli, relationship. Rather than just a small step like one of the previous disengagement agreements, however, his visit was a giant leap forward; in fact, it was several steps rolled into one. Much like the expulsion of the Soviet advisers from Egypt in July 1972, it was a sudden and unexpected act that reoriented political outlooks, but did not specifically yield, at least immediately, an Arab-Israeli agreement. It was classic Sadat, the actor, on stage, in the spotlight, going it alone. This time, however, Sadat was looking for a commensurate and substantive Israeli reaction. In the previous five years, he had obtained American attention, Israeli interest, and reluctant Israeli trust. Like the surprise of the October 1973 War, the visit carried drama, stimulated diplomatic movement, spawned direct Egyptian-Israeli negotiations, generated emotional responses, and proved again that in order to resolve problems for the next step, American intervention was necessary. Unlike the impact of the Soviet advisers' expulsion in July 1972 or the October War, which had immediate affects on Moscow, Washington, Damascus, Cairo, and Tel Aviv, the Jerusalem visit had a broader range of ramifications. It was an Egyptian national act, but it was also an Arab action. For the remainder of the century, it directly changed the content, nature, and management of the Arab-Israeli conflict; likewise, it influenced Israel's relations with its contiguous neighbors, respective domestic settings, the Palestinians, the American role in Arab-Israeli negotiations, inter-Arab relations and politics, and the region's relationship with the international community. Sadat's goal remained the same as it had since his 1971 proposal to the Israelis to place Egyptian policeman on the east side of the Suez Canal: to roll back Israeli presence in Sinai, and to deepen Egypt's relationship with the United States. Though by no means a military strategist, Begin understood the necessity of exchanging Sinai for the removal of Egypt's war machine against Israel. Reversing the course set by Nasser and the PLO answered in the affirmative the only question that mattered to Begin, "Is it good for the Jews?" In doing so, Begin swapped the strategic depth, airfields, and oil fields of Sinai in order to retain firm control of the West Bank, the Gaza Strip, and Jerusalem. Sadat's trip forced Israel to make a decision about what it would do with the remainder of the territories it obtained in the June 1967 War. Sadat tried to speak for the Palestinians and Jordanians, but he proved unsuccessful at doing so. Neither was willing to transfer to another Arab leader the right of independent or sovereign decision making.

Unlike Sadat in 1977, neither the PLO, Jordan, nor any other Arab state was psychologically prepared to recognize Israel's existence. Therefore, for the subsequent decade, at least, Arab-Israeli negotiations were, with few exceptions, limited, at least in terms of success, to essentially Egyptian-Israeli talks. In 1978, the Palestinians were offered, but refused to accept, the Camp David Accords because their contents promised autonomy or self-government but not a state. Fifteen years later, for a variety of reasons, the PLO accepted a more restrictive form of self-government in secret negotiations with the Israelis in the September 1993 Declaration of Principles, otherwise known as the Oslo Accords. After the 1987 outbreak of Palestinian violence against Israeli occupation, Israeli governments reached the conclusion that they could no longer rule the Palestinian Arab population without intolerable human losses. Israel's three options were (1) to return all of the area to the Jordanians and/or to the Palestinians; (2) retain all the land and absorb the entire Palestinian population into Israel, thereby changing the demographic character of the Jewish state; or (3) retain the land or portions of it but administratively separate themselves from the Palestinian people. Option three, namely Begin's Palestinian autonomy or self-rule idea, was pursued.

In the 1980s, a variety of efforts were made to sort out the Jordanian-Palestinian relationship, both in relation to one another and to the future of the West Bank, the Gaza Strip, and East Jerusalem. At times, King Hussein tried to work clandestinely with Israeli government leaders, but he found it difficult to work with Israeli politicians who were weak politically, often leaked sensitive information to the media, or were more concerned with their own duration in office than with finding a workable process for Jordanian-Israeli negotiations. As for the king himself, sometimes, during the 1980s, he was in the mood and willing to reach an accommodation with Israel through the United States; other times, he preferred dealing with the Israelis directly; and at still other times, he argued that his political options were severely constrained by Arab-world politics. Until the PLO-Jordanian relationship was sorted out in the late 1980s with Jordan stepping aside in July 1988 to allow the PLO to do what was promised them at the Rabat Summit in 1974— namely represent the Palestinians in political negotiations—there was no substantive diplomatic movement in determining the final political status of these territories. When the PLO renounced terrorism and accepted UNSC 242 in late 1988, the United States rewarded it with a dialogue of direct communication through the American ambassador in Tunis. But when the PLO engaged in planning another act of major terrorism against Israel in June 1991 and two months later, when Yasir Arafat embraced Saddam Hussein's invasion of Kuwait, the PLO's relationship with the United States and much of the Arab world soured. During the 1980s and early 1990s, the Palestinian community suffered from political fragmentation, economic decline, worsening relations with major Arab sources of financial support, and the loss of influence and power of the Soviet Union. Fear of the settlement of hundreds of thousands of new Russian Jewish immigrants in the West Bank, coupled with a growing restiveness of the Palestinian population in the West Bank, the Gaza Strip, and East Jerusalem, forced the PLO to do what it thought it would never do—recognize Israel—as it did on September 9, 1993. Arafat and the PLO did not want to negotiate and recognize Israel, but they needed to do so in order to preserve any chance for the development of a Palestinian entity with self-determination in areas that were increasingly overtaken by Israeli settlements.

In 1994, a year after the PLO recognized Israel's existence, Jordan signed a peace treaty with Israel, while the Syrians remained steadfast in their refusal to recognize Israel. Though Damascus too was reluctantly dragged into face-to-face negotiations with Israel, it remained staunch in the view that neither it nor Lebanon would reach an agreement with Israel until Israel unconditionally withdrew from both southern Lebanon and the Golan Heights. In the 1980s, while Egypt was isolated from Arab counsels, other Arab states including Iraq, Syria, and Libya tried to assume the Arab leadership role temporarily vacated by Egypt. With mixed success, each asserted some geographic hegemony over contiguously adjacent lands. By the end of the century, many Arab states had followed the Egyptian, Jordanian, and PLO precedent of managing newly defined relationships with Israel that were somewhere between lukewarm normalization and cold nonbelligerency.

After Sadat's Jerusalem visit, Washington gulped breathlessly, regrouped slowly, and reasserted and then solidified its status as central mediator to the conflict. Though Moscow and the Europeans tried periodically to become equally involved in aspects of the conflict's resolution, neither succeeded. Washington was neither asked nor voluntarily did it relinquish that role. In 1980, the European community's Venice Declaration labeled Israeli settlements in the territories illegal, asked Israel to withdraw from the territories taken in 1967, advocated Palestinian self-determination, and asked that the PLO be associated with future negotiations. In 1996, the European Union reiterated its support for UNSC Resolution 242 of not acquiring territory by force and then went further to state that East Jerusalem should not remain under Israeli sovereignty. These positions thrilled Arab leaders, while Israelis were obviously angered by them and therefore preferred to keep the negotiating locus with the United States. In 1982 after the Israeli invasion of Lebanon, Washington failed in its attempt to patch together an Israeli-Lebanese agreement. In the mid-1980s, State Department officials nobly tried but ultimately could not find suitable Palestinian negotiating partners for Israeli leaders. Later, the Bush administration made efforts to develop confidence-building measures between Palestinians and Israelis that would reduce tensions. These partially succeeded, but they did not result in additional agreements between Arabs and Israelis. After the Gulf War, with Arab-state support that was not there when Carter tried to put the Geneva Conference together, Washington cobbled together the 1991 Madrid Middle East Peace Conference, itself an extraordinary achievement of Secretary of State James Baker. Though Madrid was the venue, the role of Moscow and Europe in shaping the Conference was marginal compared to Washington's role. Moscow and European countries as a unit or separately maintained appearances of participation and consultation in the unfolding diplomacy, but neither were able to block real progress or substantially enhance the pace of negotiations until Norway played its critical role in the secret talks that led to the 1993 PLO-Israeli Oslo Accords. Mediation in Arab-Israeli negotiation remained the preserve of Washington just as Sadat would have wanted it. At three different junctures, Israeli leaders, in continuous search for acceptance from its neighbors, could not reject Arab overtures of recognition: in 1977 after Sadat's visit to Jerusalem; in 1991 with the prospects of Arabs sitting with Israelis at Madrid; and in 1993 with the PLO's recognition of Israel.

Twenty years after the Camp David Accords were signed, the fundamental basis of Arab-Israeli negotiations still remained what it was after the 1967 War: under what circumstances and during what period of time would Israel give back some or all of the Golan Heights, East Jerusalem, the Gaza Strip, and the West Bank? What would Israel receive in return in terms of understandings, agreements, and assurances? In broader historical terms, the Camp David Accords were the long-sought-after declaration of principles, outlining the "third Egyptian-Israeli disengagement agreement," which later became the Oslo Accords. Though not viewed as such at the time, the 1974 and 1975 disengagement agreements were minor in scope and potential impact and were relatively easy to negotiate because they focused on military matters. But they were essential building blocks for developing confidence and testing Egyptian and Israeli intentions. They established the patterns and methods by which the White House would be associated with the negotiating process. If a comparison is made to the earlier disengagement agreements, the Camp David Accords, the Egyptian-Israeli Peace Treaty, the Oslo Accords, and subsequent Oslo implementation agreements, all were more arduous and rancorous to negotiate because they focused on political orientation, ideology, commitment, and defining an exchange of land control for a measure of undefined peace. Kissinger was key to maneuvering the Soviets out of the diplomatic picture, to befriending Sadat, and to convincing the Israelis that agreements between Egypt and Israel were in the interests of the Jewish state. He was not a scholar of inter-Arab politics, but he learned quickly, motivated in great measure by eliminating the oil embargo. Though reluctant to take too many chances, Meir, Rabin, and Dayan tested Sadat's earliest intentions. Critical to the unfolding of the later heroic diplomacy were Sadat, Carter, and Begin. Each made an enormous contribution to creating the foundation necessary to change the Arab-Israeli conflict into a series of Arab-Israeli relationships. At critical junctures, each one jostled and stimulated a process otherwise prone to stagnation. Each took many risks. Each kept the process moving, sometimes elevating it to another level. Each was unconventional, creative, and committed to finding workable conclusions. Vision, not fear of their shadows, guided them. Each toiled precariously in domestic environments that were either shifting, in turmoil, confrontational, or unprepared for the tectonic shifts they made. They were leaders, not managers; statesmen, not timid politicians. In short, what Sadat initiated and acted out, Kissinger harnessed and manipulated, Carter continued, catalyzed, and concluded, and Begin eventually reworked and accepted. While Kissinger and Carter used the power of the Oval Office, Begin and Sadat made unexpected historic compromises. To some extent, each embellished reality to suit his own tactical and strategic purposes. Egyptian-Israeli agreements were not perfect, but the four principals engaged in creating them formed a unique and continuous triangular interaction not witnessed before or since in the quest for Arab-Israeli peace. Their collective heroic diplomacy altered the direction and changed the history of the Arab-Israeli conflict.

APPENDIX

ORAL INTERVIEWS BY THE AUTHOR

Please note that the titles and or positions listed here are not complete biographical entries, nor are they fully representative of the various positions held in public service. In most cases, they reflect the positions and responsibilities corresponding to the 1970s.

KAMAL ABU-JABER, Foreign Minister of Jordan, 1991–1993
Interviewed March 19, 1992, Amman, Jordan

ADNAN ABU-ODEH, Chief of the Hashemite Royal Court, 1973, 1991–1992; Minister of Court and Political Advisor, 1984–1991; and Ambassador of Jordan to the United Nations, 1992–1995
Interviewed July 24, 1992, New York

NABIL AL-ARABI, Egyptian Foreign Ministry official, 1973–present; Counsellor to the Egyptian Mission at the United Nations, 1973; Counsellor to the Egyptian Mission in Geneva, 1974–1976; Legal Adviser and Director Legal and Treaties Department, Egyptian Foreign Ministry, 1976–1978; and Deputy Permanent Representative to the Egyptian Mission at the United Nations, 1978–1981
Interviewed February 26, 1993, Atlanta

MOSHE ARENS, Israeli Foreign Minister and Defense Minister
Interviewed November 16, 1992, Tel Aviv, Israel

ALFRED ROY ATHERTON, JR., participated in U.S-Soviet Middle East negotiations and formulation of Rogers Plan, 1969; Kissinger-Ismail secret meeting in Paris, 1973; mission to Moscow in October 1973 to negotiate UNSC 338; Kissinger Middle East shuttle diplomacy team, 1973–1975; Assistant Secretary of State for Near Eastern Affairs, 1974–1978; Ambassador at Large for Arab-Israeli negotiations, 1978–1979; and U.S. Ambassador to Egypt, 1979–1983
Interviewed July 16, 1992, Washington, D.C., and October 30, 1992, Washington, D.C.

SHLOMO AVINERI, Director-General of the Israeli Foreign Ministry, 1976–1977
Interviewed July 6, 1993, Jerusalem, Israel

ABDEL HALIM AL-BADAWI, Ambassador of Egypt to the United Nations and Egyptian Foreign Ministry official
Interviewed February 28, 1989, Atlanta

HANAN BAR-ON, Deputy Chief of Mission of the Israeli Embassy in Washington, 1975–1979 and Deputy Director General of the Israeli Foreign Ministry, 1979–1987
Interviewed November 12, 1992, and July 8, 1993, Jerusalem, Israel

TAHSIN BASHIR, Press Spokesman for Egyptian President Sadat and Ambassador of Egypt to Canada
Interviewed November 10, 1992, Cairo, Egypt, and July 13, 1993, Cairo, Egypt

USAMAH AL-BAZ, Egyptian Foreign Ministry official, 1973–present; Under-Secretary for Political Affairs and Political Adviser to Egyptian President Mubarak
Interviewed November 9, 1992, Cairo, Egypt

YOSSI BEILIN, Cabinet Secretary to Israeli Prime Minister Yitzhak Shamir and Foreign Minister Shimon Peres, 1985–1989
Interviewed November 15, 1992, Jerusalem, Israel

YOSSI BEN-AHARON, Director-General of Israeli Prime Minister Yitzhak Shamir's Office
Interviewed November 12, 1992, Jerusalem, Israel

ELIAHU BEN-ELISAR, Spokesman for the Israeli Herut Party, 1973–1977; Director-General of the Prime Minister's Office, 1977–1980; Head of the Israeli delegation to the Mena House Talks, December 1977; and Ambassador of Israel to Egypt, 1980–1981
Interviewed November 13, 1992, Jerusalem, Israel, and July 6, 1993, Jerusalem, Israel

ZBIGNIEW BRZEZINSKI, United States National Security Adviser, 1977–1981
Interviewed October 30, 1992, Washington, D.C.

JIMMY CARTER, 39th President of the United States, 1977–1981
Interviewed February 19, 1991, Atlanta, March 19, 1991, Atlanta, and April 23, 1991, Atlanta

YOSSI CIECHANOVER, Director-General of Israeli Ministry of Defense, 1967–1974 and 1977–1984
Interviewed July 5, 1993, Tel Aviv, Israel, and July 30, 1993, New York

WAT T. CLUVERIUS IV, Economic Officer, U.S. Embassy, Tel Aviv, 1969–1971; Political Officer, U.S. Embassy, Tel Aviv, 1971–1972; Israel Desk Officer, State Department, 1973–1976
Interviewed June 27, 1996, Rome, Italy

SIMCHA DINITZ, Ambassador of Israel to the United States, 1973–1979
Interviewed March 20, 1992, Jerusalem, Israel

ABBA EBAN, Ambassador of Israel to the United States, 1950–1959, and Foreign Minister, 1966–1974
Interviewed March 24, 1992, Herzelia, Israel

HERMANN F. EILTS, Ambassador of the United States to Egypt, November 1973–1979
Interviewed April 11, 1991, Boston

AMOS EIRAN, Director-General of Israeli Prime Minister Yitzhak Rabin's Office, 1974–1977
Interviewed June 20, 1998, New York

STUART EISENSTAT, coordinator of domestic and foreign policy issues for Governor Jimmy Carter's presidential campaign, 1975–1976; Domestic Affairs Adviser to President Jimmy Carter, 1977–1981
Interviewed September 14, 1993, Atlanta

EPHRAIM (EPI) EVRON, Assistant Director-General of the Israeli Foreign Ministry during the October 1973 War; Director-General, Israeli Foreign Ministry, 1977–1978; Ambassador of Israel to the United States, 1978–1982
Interviewed March 24, 1992, Ramat Aviv, Israel, and November 15, 1992, Ramat Aviv, Israel

ISMAIL FAHMY, Egyptian Foreign Minister, 1973–1977
Interviewed November 9, 1992, Cairo, Egypt

SHAUL FRIEDLANDER, member of the Israeli Academic Delegation to the 1973 Geneva Conference
Interviewed August 4, 1992, Jerusalem, Israel

MOHAMAD ABD AL-GHANI EL-GAMASY, Chief of Operations of the Egyptian Armed Forces during the October 1973 War; Commander and Chief of Egyptian Army, 1973–1978; Deputy Prime Minister and Minister of War and Production, 1978–1979
Interviewed November 10, 1992, Heliopolis, Egypt

MORDECHAI GAZIT, Director-General of Israeli Prime Minister Golda Meir's and Yitzhak Rabin's Office, 1973–1974
Interviewed March 22, 1992, Jerusalem, Israel
SHLOMO GAZIT, Head of Israeli military intelligence, April 1974–February 1979
Interviewed August 13, 1992, Ramat Aviv, Israel
ASHRAF GHORBAL, Head of the Egyptian interests section under the auspices of the Indian Embassy in Washington, 1968–1972; Deputy to the National Security Council Adviser, Hafez Ismail, 1972–1973; Press Spokesman for the Egyptian Presidency during the October 1973 War; and Ambassador of Egypt to the United States, 1973–1984
Interviewed November 9, 1992, Cairo, Egypt
APRIL GLASPIE, Political Officer, U.S. Embassy in Cairo, November 1973–July 1977; Secretary to Assistant Secretary of State Alfred Atheron, July 1977–September 1978
Interviewed July 28, 1995, Jerusalem, Israel
MORDECHAI GUR, Israeli Military Attaché in Washington prior to the October 1973 War; Head of Northern Command during the October 1973 War; Head of the Israeli delegation to the 1973–1974 Egyptian-Israeli Military Committee Talks; Israeli Chief of Staff, April 1974–April 1978
Interviewed July 7, 1993, Jerusalem, Israel
ALOUPH HAREVEN, Director of Information Division of the Israeli Ministry of Foreign Affairs, July 1970–April 1974; and member of the Israeli delegation to the 1973 Geneva Conference
Interviewed August 2, 1992, Jerusalem, Israel
YEHOSHAFAT HARKABI, member of Israeli delegation to the Rhodes Talks, 1949
Interviewed March 22, 1992, Jerusalem, Israel
HUSSEIN IBN TALAL, King of Jordan, 1953–1999
Interviewed January 11, 1993, Amman, Jordan
ZAKARIA HUSSEIN, Major General in the Egyptian Army and delegate to the Blair House Talks, October 1978
Interviewed November 10, 1992, Cairo, Egypt
FEISAL HUSSEINI, Director of Arab Studies Center
Interviewed November 14, 1992, Jerusalem, Israel
FAWZI AL-IBRASHI, Egyptian participant in the Kilometer 101 Talks; Egyptian Foreign Ministry Legal Adviser, 1973–1993
Interviewed January 5, 1993, Cairo, Egypt
HAFEZ ISMAIL, Egyptian President Sadat's National Security Adviser, September 1971–April 1974
Interviewed January 7, 1993, Cairo, Egypt
YAHIEL KADISHAI, Head of Israeli Prime Minister Menachem Begin's Office and longtime adviser to Menachem Begin, 1977–1983
Interviewed July 2, 1993, Tel Aviv, Israel, and July 5, 1993, Tel Aviv, Israel
ABD AL-HALIM KHADDAM, Foreign Minister of Syria, 1971–1985, and Vice President of Syria, 1985–present
Interviewed July 18, 1993, Damascus, Syria
MUSTAPHA KHALIL, Prime Minister of Egypt, 1978–1980
Interviewed July 14, 1993, Cairo, Egypt
MORDECHAI "REGINALD" KIDRON, member of the Israeli delegation to the 1973 Geneva Conference
Interviewed August 5, 1992, Jerusalem, Israel
WILLIAM B. KIRBY, Deputy Assistant Secretary of State for Near Eastern Affairs; member of the Policy Planning staff; and deputized in several different positions associated with Arab-Israeli negotiations in the 1970s and 1980s
Interviewed July 16, 1992, Washington, D.C.

DAVID A. KORN, Political Officer, U.S. Embassy in Israel, 1967–1971; Office Director for
    Northern Arab Affairs, U.S. Department of State, 1972–1975; Policy Planning Staff
    at the State Department, 1977–1978; participant in several shuttle visits to Middle
    East of Ambassador Roy Atherton in 1978; and Office Director for Israel and Arab-
    Israeli Affairs, Department of State, 1979–1981
    Interviewed October 29, 1992, Washington, D.C.
NAFTALI LAVI, Press Spokesman for Israeli Defense Minister and Foreign Minister Moshe
    Dayan, 1970–1974 and 1977–1979
    Interviewed July 8, 1993, Jerusalem, Israel
SAMUEL W. LEWIS, United States Ambassador to Israel, 1977–1986
    Interviewed February 28, 1992, Washington, D.C.
ABDUL SALAM AL-MAJALI, Chairman of the Jordanian-Palestinian delegation to the Madrid
    Conference and subsequent bilateral talks, 1991–present; Prime Minister and Minis-
    ter of Defense of Jordan, 1993–1995
    Interviewed March 18, 1992, Amman, Jordan
MOSHE MA'OZ, Reservist in Israeli Military Intelligence during the October 1973 War and
    member of the Israeli Academic Delegation to the 1973 Geneva Conference
    Interviewed August 2, 1992, Jerusalem, Israel
TAHIR AL-MASRI, Prime Minister of Jordan, 1991, and Foreign Minister of Jordan, 1984–1988
    and 1991
    Interviewed March 19, 1992, Amman, Jordan
ESMAT ABDEL-MEGUID, Permanent Egyptian Representative to the United Nations, 1972–
    1983; Head of the Egyptian delegation to the December 1977 Mena House Talks
    Interviewed July 14, 1993, Cairo, Egypt
GOLDA MEIR, Prime Minister of Israel, 1969–1974
    Interviewed December 29, 1977, Tel Aviv, Israel
AARON MILLER, member of Policy Planning Staff, U.S Department of State, 1985–present
    Interviewed October 29, 1992, Washington, D.C.
WALID MOUALLEM, Syrian Ambassador to Rumania, 1977–1980; and Syrian Ambassador to
    the United States, 1990–present
    Interviewed July 17, 1993, Damascus, Syria
NIMROD NOVIK, Political Adviser to Prime Minister of Israel and Foreign Minister Shimon
    Peres, 1983–1990
    Interviewed August 16, 1992, Herzelia, Israel
YOSSI OLMERT, Israeli Government Press Spokesman, 1989–1992
    Interviewed September 15, 1992, Detroit
DAN PATTIR, Advisor on Media and Public Affairs to Israeli Prime Minister Yitzhak Rabin's
    and Menachem Begin's Office, 1975–1981
    Interviewed August 3, 1992, Jerusalem, Israel, and August 14, 1992, Tel Aviv, Israel
MOSHE PELED, Israeli Armored Division Commander, led Israeli counterattack against the
    Syrian Army on the Golan Heights during the October 1973 War
    Interviewed August 24, 1995, Atlanta
ROBERT H. PELLETREAU, JR., United States Ambassador to Tunisia; American Interlocutor
    in U.S.-PLO dialogue, December 1988–June 1990; United States Ambassador to
    Egypt, 1991–1993
    Interviewed November 8, 1992, Cairo, Egypt
WILLIAM B. QUANDT, United States National Security Council staff with responsibility for
    the Middle East, 1972–1974 and 1977–1979
    Interviewed May 13, 1992, Washington, D.C.
GIDEON RAFAEL, Ambassador of Israel to the United Nations, 1967; Director-General of the
    Israeli Foreign Ministry, April 1967–December 1971
    Interviewed March 25, 1992, Jerusalem, Israel

ABDEL RAOUF AL-REEDY, Director of International Organizations, 1972–1974; Director of Policy Planning Department of the Egyptian Foreign Ministry, 1977–1979; Mena House delegate, December 1977; and Ambassador of Egypt to the United States, 1984–1992
Interviewed June 10, 1992, Washington, D.C.

ZAID RIFA'I, Prime Minister of Jordan; Prime Minister and Defense Minister of Jordan, 1974–1976
Interviewed January 9, 1993, Amman, Jordan

PETER RODMAN, Member of United States National Security Council Staff and Special Assistant to Henry Kissinger and Brent Scowcroft, August 1969–January 1977; staff member on virtually all of Kissinger's Middle East negotiation and shuttle missions, 1972–1977
Interviewed June 10, 1992, Washington, D.C.

MEIR ROSENNE, Legal Affairs Adviser to the Israeli Foreign Ministry, June 1971–September 1979; Israeli Ambassador to France and later the United States
Interviewed August 6, 1992, Jerusalem, Israel

MOSHE SASSON, Ambassador of Israel to Egypt, 1981–1988
Interviewed August 6, 1992, Jerusalem, Israel

HAROLD SAUNDERS, Middle East Staff member, United States National Security Council, 1961–1974; participant in Secretary of State Henry Kissinger's shuttle missions after the October 1973 War; Deputy Assistant Secretary of State, 1974–1975; Assistant Secretary of State for Near Eastern Affairs, April 1978–January 1981; and participated in drafting the Camp David Accords
Interviewed January 31, 1985, Atlanta, and May 12, 1992, Washington, D.C.

AHMED MAHER EL-SAYEED, Chief of Cabinet to Egyptian Foreign Minister Mohamed Ibrahim Kamel, 1978–1980, and Egyptian Ambassador to the United States, 1992–present
Interviewed July 29, 1993, Washington, D.C.

TALCOTT SEELYE, United States Ambassador to Syria, 1978–1981
Interviewed June 17, 1993, Washington, D.C.

AVRAHAM SELA, Intelligence Officer, Israel Defense Forces, 1970–1980
Interviewed July 30, 1995, Jerusalem, Israel

NABIL SHAATH, Adviser to PLO Chairman Yasir Arafat and Coordinator of Palestinian delegation to the post–Madrid Conference bilateral talks, 1991–1993
Interviewed October 30, 1992, Arlington, Virginia

HERZL SHAFIR, Deputy Chief of Staff of the Israeli Defense Forces; Israeli Military Negotiator with the Egyptians at the Kilometer 101 Talks after the October 1973 War; Delegate and Chief Israeli Signatory to the Syrian-Israeli Military Talks in May–June 1974 and to the Egyptian-Israeli Military Talks in December 1977
Interviewed August 17, 1992, Ramat Hasharon, Israel

ARIYEH SHALEV, Head of Estimates Branch, Israeli Military Intelligence, 1967–1974
Interviewed August 13, 1992, Ramat Aviv, Israel

SHIMON SHAMIR, member of the Israeli Academic Delegation to the 1973 Geneva Conference; Ambassador of Israel to Egypt, 1988–1990, and Ambassador of Israel to Jordan, 1995–1997
Interviewed April 3, 1992, Atlanta

YITZHAK SHAMIR, Prime Minister of Israel, 1983–1992
Interviewed November 16, 1992, Tel Aviv, Israel

FAROUQ AL-SHARA, Foreign Minister of Syria, 1986–present
Interviewed July 18, 1993, Damascus, Syria

MAHMOUD AL-SHARIF, Jordanian Minister of Information, 1991–1993
Interviewed March 19, 1992, Amman, Jordan

OMAR SIRRY, Deputy Chief of Operations in the Egyptian Foreign Ministry during the October 1973 War; Political Adviser to General al-Gamasy during the Kilometer 101 Talks, October–November 1973; and Chief of Cabinet to Egyptian Foreign Minister Ismail Fahmy, 1973–1975
Interviewed January 5, 1993, Cairo, Egypt

JOSEPH SISCO, participant in Secretary of State Henry Kissinger's shuttle missions after the October 1973 War; Assistant Secretary of State for Near Eastern and South Asian Affairs, 1969–1974; and Under-Secretary of State for Political Affairs, 1974–1976
Interviewed February 27, 1992, Washington, D.C.

EPHRAIM SNEH, Governor of Judea and Samaria districts (West Bank), 1985–1987
Interviewed August 17, 1992, Herzelia, Israel

MICHAEL STERNER, Egyptian Desk Officer, State Department, 1969–1974, and Deputy Assistant Secretary of State for Near Eastern and South Asian Affairs, 1977–1981
Interviewed May 13, 1992, Washington, D.C., and June 17, 1993, Washington, D.C.

ROCKY SUDDARTH, Political Officer and Deputy Chief of Mission, United States Embassy, Amman, Jordan, January 1974–July 1979, and Ambassador of the United States to Jordan, 1987–1990
Interviewed October 29, 1992, Washington, D.C.

AVRAHAM TAMIR, Israeli Military Representative to Egyptian-Israeli negotiations from 1973–1988; founder and head of Strategic Planning Branch of the Israeli Defense Forces after the October 1973 War; member of the Israeli delegation to the Egyptian-Israeli Military Committee Talks, January–February 1978
Interviewed November 14, 1992, Tel Aviv, Israel

PATRICK THEROS, Political Officer, United States Embassy, Amman, 1970–1974; Economic Officer, United States Embassy, Damascus, 1976–1980; Deputy Chief of Mission, United States Embassy, Amman, 1987–1991
Interviewed March 31, 1993, Atlanta

SIR BRIAN URQUHART, Under-Secretary General of the United Nations, 1974–1986
Interviewed February 28, 1991, New York

NICHOLIS A. VELIOTES, Special Assistant to the Deputy Secretary of State for Near Eastern and South Asian Affairs, September 1970–1973; Deputy Chief of Mission, United States Embassy, Tel Aviv, July 1973–November 1975; Deputy Director of Policy Planning, Department of State, 1976–March 1977; Deputy Assistant Secretary of State for Near Eastern and South Asian Affairs, 1977–Summer 1978; Ambassador of the United States to Jordan, September 1978–1981; Assistant Secretary of State for Near Eastern and South Asian Affairs, February 1981–1983; Ambassador of the United States to Egypt, November 1983–April 1986
Interviewed September 7, 1995, Washington, D.C.

AHARON YARIV, Head of Israeli Military Intelligence; Special Assistant to the Chief of Staff during the October 1973 War; Head of the Israeli delegation to the Kilometer 101 Talks
Interviewed March 26, 1992, Ramat Aviv, Israel, and August 13, 1992, Ramat Aviv, Israel

MORDECHAI ZIPPORI, Deputy Defense Minister of Israel, 1977–1981
Interviewed July 7, 1993, Jerusalem, Israel

~~~

NOTES

Unless otherwise noted, all interviews were conducted by the author (see Appendix).

CHAPTER I

1. Raphael Israeli, *The Public Diary of President Sadat: The Road to War (October 1970–October 1973)*, part 1 (Leiden: E. J. Brill, 1978), p. 103; *The Public Diary of President Sadat: The Road of Pragmatism (June 1975–October 1976)*, part 3 (Leiden: E. J. Brill, 1979), p. 1258; Yoram Meital, *Egypt's Struggle for Peace Continuity and Change, 1967–1977* (Gainesville: University Press of Florida, 1997), p. 80.
2. Remarks by Joseph Sisco, United States Institute of Peace meeting, April 16, 1991, Washington, D.C.; interviews with Nicholis A. Veliotes, September 7, 1995, Washington, D.C.; and Wat T. Cluverius, June 27, 1996, Rome, Italy.
3. Interview with Usamah al-Baz, November 9, 1992, Cairo, Egypt.
4. Interview with Hafez Ismail, January 7, 1993, Cairo, Egypt.
5. Interview with Usamah al-Baz, November 9, 1992, Cairo, Egypt.
6. Interview with Tahsin Bashir, November 10, 1992, Cairo, Egypt; Mohamed Ibrahim Kamel, *The Camp David Accords* (New York: Metheun Inc., Routledge & Kegan Paul, 1986), p. 109.
7. Interviews with Ashraf Ghorbal, November 29, 1992, Cairo, Egypt; and Hafez Ismail, January 7, 1993, Cairo, Egypt; Mohammed Heikal, *Autumn of Fury: The Assassination of Sadat* (London: Andre Deutsch, 1983), pp. 1–36.
8. Victor Israelyan, *Inside the Kremlin During the Yom Kippur War* (State College: Pennsylvania State University Press, 1995), p. 29.
9. Kamel, *Camp David Accords*, p. 204.
10. Ensio Siilasvuo, *In the Service of Peace in the Middle East, 1976–1979* (New York: St. Martin's Press, 1992), p. 213.
11. Interview with Tahsin Bashir, November 10, 1992, Cairo, Egypt.
12. Interview with David Korn, October 29, 1992, Washington, D.C.
13. Interviews with Nabil al-Arabi, February 26, 1993, Atlanta; and Omar Sirry, January 5, 1993, Cairo, Egypt.
14. Interview with Hafez Ismail, January 7, 1993, Cairo, Egypt.
15. Interview with Omar Sirry, January 5, 1993, Cairo, Egypt.
16. Interview with Mordechai Gazit, March 22, 1992, Jerusalem, Israel.
17. Interview with Michael Sterner, May 13, 1992, Washington, D.C.
18. Interview with Ashraf Ghorbal, November 9, 1992, Cairo, Egypt.
19. Interview with Ahmed Maher El-Sayeed, July 29, 1993, Washington, D.C.
20. Interview with Mohamad Abd al-Ghani el-Gamasy, November 10, 1992, Heliopolis, Egypt.
21. Interview with Ashraf Ghorbal, November 9, 1992, Cairo, Egypt.

22. See Martin Indyk, "To the Ends of the Earth—Sadat's Jerusalem Initiative" (Middle East Papers, Modern Series 1, Center for Middle Eastern Studies, Harvard University, 1984), p. 25.

23. Interview with Peter Rodman, June 10, 1992, Washington, D.C.

24. Interview with Usamah al-Baz, November 9, 1992, Cairo, Egypt.

25. Interview with Ashraf Ghorbal, November 9, 1992, Cairo, Egypt.

26. Interview with Hafez Ismail, January 7, 1993, Cairo, Egypt.

27. Shibley Telhami, *Power and Leadership in International Bargaining: The Path to the Camp David Accords* (New York: Columbia University Press, 1990), pp. 99–106.

28. Mohamed Abdel Ghani El-Gamasy, *The October War Memoirs of Field Marshall El-Gamasy of Egypt* (Cairo: American University in Cairo Press, 1993), p. 186.

29. Interviews with Ashraf Ghorbal, November 9, 1992, Cairo, Egypt; and Nabil al-Arabi, February 26, 1993, Atlanta.

30. Interview with Hafez Ismail, January 7, 1993, Cairo, Egypt.

31. Interview with Zaid Rifa'i, January 9, 1993, Amman, Jordan. See also remarks by Hermann F. Eilts in Kenneth W. Stein (moderator), "The Camp David Accords" (The Carter Presidential Conference, Hofstra University, Hempstead, New York, November 1990).

32. Colin Legum, ed., *Middle East Contemporary Survey, Volume I, 1976–1977* (New York: Holmes and Meier, 1978), pp. 311–12.

33. Interview with Avraham Tamir, November 14, 1992, Tel Aviv, Israel.

34. Interview with Usamah al-Baz, November 9, 1992, Cairo, Egypt.

35. See chapter 4 and Boutros Boutros-Ghali, *Egypt's Road to Jerusalem* (New York: Random House, 1996), pp. 37–42.

36. Interview with Omar Sirry, January 5, 1993, Cairo, Egypt.

37. Interview with Ariyeh Shalev, August 13, 1992, Ramat Aviv, Israel.

38. Israelyan, *Inside the Kremlin,* p. 14.

39. Interview with Abd al-Halim Khaddam, July 18, 1993, Damascus, Syria.

40. Interview with Joseph Sisco, February 27, 1992, Washington, D.C.

41. Interviews with Hafez Ismail, January 7, 1993, Cairo, Egypt; Abd al-Ghani al-Gamasy, November 10, 1992, Heliopolis, Egypt; and Zaid Rifa'i, January 9, 1993, Amman, Jordan.

42. Interview with Zaid Rifa'i, January 9, 1993, Amman, Jordan.

43. Interview with Hafez al-Assad, *Al-Akhbar* (Cairo), September 20, 1993, as quoted in *The Foreign Broadcast Information Service—Near East and South Asia,* September 23, 1993, p. 46.

44. Interviews with Abd al-Ghani el-Gamasy, November 10, 1992, Heliopolis, Egypt, and Abd-Halim Khaddam, July 18, 1993, Damascus, Syria. In April 1972, Sadat told one of his military advisers that his intent was only a "limited war" with Israel. Author's conversation with Egyptian General (Ret.) Ahmed Fahkr, January 5, 1993, Cairo, Egypt; see Alasdair Drysdale and Raymond A. Hinnebusch, Jr., *Syria and the Middle East Peace Process* (New York: Council on Foreign Relations Press, 1991), p. 105, and El-Gamasy, *The October War,* p. 139.

45. See Israelyan, *Inside the Kremlin,* pp. 72–73.

46. Mahmoud Riad, *The Struggle for Peace in the Middle East* (London: Quartet Books, 1981), p. 258; this point was emphatically confirmed in my interview with Abd al-Halim Khaddam, July 18, 1993, Damascus, Syria.

47. Heikal, *Autumn,* p. 50.

48. Interviews with Moshe Ma'oz, August 2, 1992, Jerusalem, Israel: Abd al-Ghani al-Gamasy, November 10, 1992, Heliopolis, Egypt; and Hermann F. Eilts, April 11, 1991, Boston.

49. Interviews with Mordechai Gazit, March 22, 1992, Jerusalem, Israel; and Patrick Theros, March 31, 1993, Atlanta.

50. Interview with Gideon Rafael, March 25, 1992, Jerusalem, Israel.
51. Interview with Zaid Rifa'i, January 9, 1993, Amman, Jordan.
52. Ibid.
53. Interview with Zaid Rifa'i, January 9, 1993, Amman, Jordan. According to Soviet Foreign Ministry sources, when King Hussein made overtures to Sadat and Assad to join the war, Assad welcomed it, but Sadat "flatly rejected it." See Israelyan, *Inside the Kremlin,* pp. 67–68.
54. Interview with King Hussein of Jordan, January 11, 1993, Amman, Jordan.
55. Interviews with Zaid Rifa'i, January 9, 1993, Amman, Jordan, and April Glaspie, July 28, 1995, Jerusalem, Israel; Ismail Fahmy, *Negotiating for Peace in the Middle East* (Baltimore: Johns Hopkins University Press, 1983), pp. 96–98.
56. Interviews with King Hussein of Jordan, January 11, 1993, Amman, Jordan; and Zaid Rifa'i, January 9, 1993, Amman, Jordan.
57. Interview with Hermann F. Eilts, April 11, 1991, Boston.
58. Interview with Epi Evron, March 24, 1992, Ramat Aviv, Israel.
59. Interviews with Epi Evron, March 24, 1992, Ramat Aviv, Israel; and Amos Eiran, June 20, 1998, New York.
60. Interviews with Mordechai Gazit, March 22, 1992, Jerusalem, Israel; and Alouph Hareven, August 2, 1992, Jerusalem, Israel.
61. Interviews with Simcha Dinitz, March 20, 1992, Jerusalem, Israel; Epi Evron, March 24, 1992, Ramat Aviv, Israel; and Aharon Yariv, March 26, 1992, Ramat Aviv, Israel.
62. Interview with Amos Eiran, June 20, 1998, New York.
63. Yitzhak Rabin, *The Rabin Memoirs* (Boston: Little, Brown and Company, 1979), p. 260.
64. Interview with Naftali Lavi, July 8, 1993, Jerusalem, Israel.
65. Interview with Yossi Ciechanover, July 5, 1993, Tel Aviv, Israel.
66. Interview with Yossi Ciechanover, July 5, 1993, Tel Aviv, Israel. Naftali Lavi confirmed the same story of Dayan's proposed resignation.
67. Joseph Goverin, "The Six Day War in the Mirror of Soviet-Israeli Relations, April–June 1967" (research paper no. 61, The Soviet and East European Research Centre, The Hebrew University of Jerusalem, December 1985), p. 24.
68. Interview with Yossi Ciechanover, July 30, 1993, New York.
69. Interviews with Hanan Bar-On, July 8, 1993, Jerusalem, Israel; Naftali Lavi, July 8, 1993, Jerusalem, Israel; and Mordechai Gur, July 7, 1993, Jerusalem, Israel.
70. Interview with Yossi Ciechanover, July 5, 1993, Tel Aviv, Israel.
71. Interview with Yahiel Kadishai, July 2, 1993, Tel Aviv, Israel; see also Moshe Dayan, *Breakthrough: A Personal Account of Egypt-Israel Negotiations* (London: Weidenfeld and Nicolson, 1981), p. 4.
72. Interviews with Yahiel Kadishai, July 5, 1993, Tel Aviv, Israel; Eliyahu Ben-Elisar, July 6, 1993, Jerusalem, Israel; and Naftali Lavi, July 8, 1993, Jerusalem, Israel. Samuel W. Lewis, "Lecture in Honor of Moshe Dayan on the Tenth Anniversary of His Death" (delivered at The Moshe Dayan Center for Middle Eastern and African Studies, The Moshe Dayan Center Library, Tel Aviv, University, Ramat Aviv, Israel, November 17, 1991), p. 3.
73. Interview with Stuart Eisenstat, September 14, 1993, Atlanta.
74. Interview with Yossi Ciechanover, July 5, 1993, Tel Aviv, Israel.
75. Dayan, *Breakthrough,* p. 112.
76. Interviews with Yossi Ciechanover, July 5, 1993, Tel Aviv, Israel; and Mustapha Khalil, July 14, 1993, Cairo, Egypt.
77. Interviews with Mordechai Zippori, July 7, 1993, Jerusalem, Israel; and Ahmed Maher, July 29, 1993, Washington, D.C.
78. See remarks by Menachem Begin, April 11, 1974, and May 20, 1974, in Nataniel Lorch, ed., *Major Knesset Debates,* vol. V (Jerusalem: 1992), pp. 1891–95 and 1915–18.

79. Interviews with Yahiel Kadishai, July 6, 1993, Tel Aviv, Israel; and Eliyahu Ben-Elisar, July 6, 1993, Jerusalem, Israel.

80. Interviews with Epi Evron, November 15, 1992, Ramat Aviv, Israel; and Yahiel Kadishai, July 2, 1993, Tel Aviv, Israel.

81. Interview with Yahiel Kadishai, July 5, 1993, Tel Aviv, Israel.

82. Interviews with Samuel W. Lewis, February 28, 1992, Washington, D.C.; Dan Pattir, August 3, 1992, Jerusalem, Israel; Michael Sterner, June 17, 1993, Washington, D.C.; and Eliyahu Ben-Elisar, November 13, 1992, Jerusalem, Israel.

83. Amos Perlmutter, *Israel: The Partitioned State—A Political History Since 1900* (New York: Charles Scribner's Sons, 1985), pp. 282–83; see also "Begin Only Obstacle, Sadat Says," *Washington Post,* July 23, 1978.

84. Remarks by Husni Mubarak, Cairo Domestic Radio, January 3, 1997, as quoted in *Foreign Broadcast Information Service, Daily Report—Middle East and North Africa,* January 3, 1997.

85. Interview with Epi Evron, March 24, 1992, Ramat Aviv, Israel.

86. Remarks by Menachem Begin, by *Yediot Aharanot,* October 1, 1978.

87. Remarks by Samuel W. Lewis in Kenneth W. Stein (moderator), "The Camp David Accords" (The Carter Presidential Conference, Hofstra University, Hempstead, New York, November 1990). Interview with Samuel W. Lewis, February 28, 1992, Washington, D.C.

88. Henry Kissinger, *Years of Upheaval* (Boston: Little, Brown and Company, 1982), p. 203.

89. Anatoly Dobrynin. *In Confidence: Moscow's Ambassador to America's Six Cold War Presidents* (New York: Times Books, 1995), p. 303.

90. Interview with Peter Rodman, June 10, 1992, Washington, D.C.

91. Interview with Amos Eiran, June 20, 1998, New York.

92. Ibid.

93. Kissinger, *Years,* p. 425.

94. Edward R. F. Sheehan, *The Arabs, Israelis, and Kissinger: A Secret History of American Diplomacy in the Middle East* (New York: Reader's Digest Press, 1976), p. 26.

95. Remarks by Joseph Sisco, United States Institute of Peace meeting, April 3, 1991, Washington, D.C. For additional discussion of the level of distrust and dislike between Kissinger and Rogers, see Walter Isaacson, *Kissinger* (New York: Simon and Schuster, 1992), pp. 195–98, 209–11, and 221–22.

96. Seymour M. Hersh, *The Price of Power: Kissinger in the Nixon White House* (New York: Summit Books, 1983), p. 234.

97. Interview with Peter Rodman, June 10, 1992, Washington, D.C.

98. Richard Valeriani, *Travels with Henry* (Boston: Houghton-Mifflin, 1979), p. 188.

99. Dobrynin, *In Confidence,* p. 306.

100. Interview with Epi Evron, March 24, 1992, Ramat Aviv, Israel.

101. Interviews with Joseph Sisco, February 27, 1992, Washington, D.C.; and Alfred Roy Atherton, Jr., July 16, 1992, Washington, D.C.

102. Interview with Joseph Sisco, February 27, 1992, Washington, D.C.

103. Israelyan, *Inside the Kremlin,* p. 65.

104. Interview with Mordechai Gazit, March 22, 1992, Jerusalem, Israel.

105. Interview with Peter Rodman, June 10, 1992, Washington, D.C.

106. Saadia Touval, *The Peace Brokers: Mediators in the Arab-Israeli Conflict, 1948–1979* (Princeton: Princeton University Press, 1982), p. 230.

107. Interview with Hermann Eilts, April 11, 1991, Boston.

108. Ibid.

109. Interview with Stuart Eisenstat, September 14, 1993, Atlanta.

110. Remarks by Eugene Rostow, United States Institute of Peace meeting, April 3, 1991, Washington, D.C.

111. Interview with Ashraf Ghorbal, November 9, 1992, Cairo, Egypt.

112. Jimmy Carter, *Keeping Faith: Memoirs of a President* (New York: Bantam Books, 1982), pp. 20 and 277; remarks by Harold Saunders in Kenneth W. Stein (moderator), "The Camp David Accords" (The Carter Presidential Conference, Hofstra University, Hempstead, New York, November 1990).

113. Zbigniew Brzezinski, *Power and Principle: Memoirs of the National Security Adviser, 1977–1981* (New York: Farrar Straus Giroux, 1983), p. 97.

114. Interview with Jimmy Carter, February 19, 1991, Atlanta.

115. Carter, *Keeping Faith,* p. 277.

116. Remarks by William B. Quandt, United States Institute of Peace meeting, April 16, 1991, Washington, D.C.

117. Interview with Eliyahu Ben-Elisar, July 6, 1993, Jerusalem, Israel.

118. Remarks by Joseph Sisco and Sol Linowitz, United States Institute of Peace meeting, April 16, 1991, Washington, D.C.; and interview with Michael Sterner, June 17, 1993, Washington, D.C.

119. Remarks by Moshe Dayan, Jerusalem Domestic Service, October 5, 1977, as quoted in *Foreign Broadcast Information Service Daily Report—Middle East and North Africa,* October 6, 1977, p. N4, and in *Ma'ariv,* February 17, 1978.

120. Interview with King Hussein, January 11, 1993, Amman, Jordan.

121. Carter, *Keeping Faith,* p. 53.

122. Remarks by William B. Quandt in Kenneth W. Stein (moderator), "The Camp David Accords" (The Carter Presidential Conference, Hofstra University, Hempstead, New York, November 1990).

123. Interview with Zbigniew Brzezinski, October 30, 1992, Washington, D.C.

124. Interview with Jimmy Carter, February 19, 1992.

125. William B. Quandt, *Camp David: Peacemaking and Politics* (Washington, D.C.: The Brookings Institution, 1986), p. 49.

126. Interview with Amos Eiran, June 20, 1998, New York.

127. Interview with Shlomo Avineri, July 6, 1993, Jerusalem, Israel.

128. Interview with Epi Evron, November 15, 1992, Ramat Aviv, Israel.

129. Nadav Safran, *Israel: The Embattled Ally* (Cambridge: Belknap Press, 1979), p. 569.

130. Interview with Jimmy Carter, March 19, 1991, Atlanta.

131. Interview with Roy Atherton, October 30, 1992, Washington, D.C.

132. Interviews with Epi Evron, November 15, 1992, Ramat Aviv, Israel; and Yossi Ciechanover, July 30, 1993, New York.

133. Interview with Zbigniew Brzezinski, October 30, 1992, Washington, D.C.

134. Interviews with Hanan Bar-On, November 12, 1992, and July 8, 1993, Jerusalem, Israel.

135. Interview with Roy Atherton, October 30, 1992, Washington, D.C.

CHAPTER 2

1   Kenneth W. Stein, *The Land Question in Palestine, 1917–1939* (Chapel Hill: University of North Carolina Press, 1984), pp. 220–21.

2. See Itamar Rabinovich, *The Road Not Taken* (New York: Oxford University Press, 1991); and Avi Shlaim, *Collusion Across the Jordan King Abdullah, The Zionist Movement and the Partition of Palestine* (New York: Columbia University Press, 1988).

3. Interview with Wat T. Cluverius, June 27, 1996, Rome, Italy.

4. Interview with Nicholis A. Veliotes, September 7, 1995, Washington, D.C.; and Gideon Rafael, *Destination Peace: Three Decades of Israeli Foreign Policy—A Personal Memoir* (New York: Stein and Day, 1981), p. 284.

5. Sultan Najib Lutfi, *The Impact of the 1967 War on the Economy of Jordan* (unpublished Ph.D. thesis, George Washington University, 1980), pp. 154–74; and Samir Mutawi, *Jordan in the 1967 War* (New York: Cambridge University Press, 1987), p. 169.

6. Anatoly Dobrynin, *In Confidence,* pp. 160–61.

7. Interview with Wat T. Cluverius, June 27, 1996, Rome, Italy.

8. Daniel Dishon, ed., *Middle East Record* 3, The Shiloah Center for Middle Eastern and African Studies, Tel Aviv University (Jerusalem: Israeli Universities Press, 1967), p. 235.

9. David A. Korn, "The Making of United Nations Security Council Resolution 242," *Pew Cast Studies in International Affairs,* Case 450 (Washington, D.C.: Georgetown University, 1992), p. 12.

10. William B. Quandt, *Peace Process, American Diplomacy, and the Arab-Israeli Conflict Since 1967* (Washington, D.C.: The Brookings Institution, 1993), p. 55.

11. Korn, "The Making of United Nations Security Council Resolution 242," pp. 12–13.

12. Remarks by Joseph Sisco and David Korn, United States Institute of Peace meeting, April 3, 1991, Washington, D.C.

13. Interview with Joseph Sisco, February 27, 1992, Washington, D.C., remarks by Joseph Sisco at the Washington Institute for Near East Policy, August 6, 1997, Washington, D.C., and remarks by Joseph Sisco, *Conference on the October War,* The Middle East Institute, October 9, 1998.

14. Michael O. Wheeler and Kemper V. Gay, *Nuclear Weapons and the 1973 Middle East War,* CSN Occasional Paper Monograph no. 3 (Washington, D.C.: The Center for National Security Negotiations, August 1996), p. 6.

15. Rafael, *Destination Peace,* pp. 231–32.

16. Interviews with Gideon Rafael, March 25, 1992, Jerusalem, Israel; and Alouph Hareven, August 2, 1992, Jerusalem, Israel.

17. Interview with Moshe Dayan by Rami Tal on November 22, 1976, *Yediot Aharanot,* April 27, 1997; and interviews with Naftali Lavi, July 8, 1993, Jerusalem, Israel; and Yossi Ciechanover, July 5, 1993, Tel Aviv, Israel.

18. Interview with Gideon Rafael, March 25, 1992, Jerusalem, Israel.

19. Remarks by Anwar Sadat, October 7, 1977, Cairo Domestic Service, as quoted in *Foreign Broadcast Information Service, Daily Report—Middle East and North Africa,* October 25, 1977, Supplement, p. 26.

20. Remarks by Anwar Sadat, Cairo Domestic Service, February 11, 1971, as quoted in *Foreign Broadcast Information Service, Daily Report—Middle East and North Africa,* February 13, 1971, p. D4.

21. Interviews with Avraham Tamir, November 14, 1992, Tel Aviv, Israel; and Gideon Rafael, March 25, 1992, Jerusalem, Israel.

22. Interview with Gideon Rafael, March 25, 1992, Jerusalem, Israel.

23. Mordechai Gazit, "Egypt and Israel—Was There a Peace Opportunity Missed in 1971?" *Journal of Contemporary History* 32, no. 1 (1997): 97–101.

24. Interviews with Gideon Rafael, March 25, 1992, Jerusalem, Israel; and Nicholis A. Veliotes, September 7, 1995, Washington, D.C.

25. Interview with Avraham Tamir, November 14, 1992, Tel Aviv, Israel.

26. Rafael, *Destination Peace,* pp. 262–77.

27. Interview by *October Magazine* with Anwar Sadat, Cairo, MENA, March 11, 1978, as quoted in *Foreign Broadcast Information Service, Daily Report—Middle East and North Africa,* March 14, 1978, p. D6.

28. Interview with Ariyeh Shalev, August 13, 1992, Ramat Aviv, Israel.

29. Interview with Michael Sterner, May 13, 1992, Washington, D.C.

30. Remarks by William B. Quandt and Joseph Sisco, United States Institute of Peace meeting, April 16, 1991, Washington, D.C.

31. Yoram Meital, *Egypt's Struggle for Peace,* pp. 98–99.

32. Edward R. F. Sheehan, *The Arabs, Israelis, and Kissinger: A Secret History of American Diplomacy in the Middle East* (New York: Reader's Digest Press, 1976), p. 22.

33. Yaacov Ro'i, *From Encroachment to Involvement: A Documentary Study of Soviet Policy in the Middle East 1945–1973* (Jerusalem: Israel Universities Press, 1974), pp. 596–677.

34. For excellent detailed assessments of Soviet attitudes toward Egypt and Egyptian feelings toward the Soviet Union during this period, see Alvin Z. Rubenstein, *Red Star on the Nile* (Princeton University Press, 1977), pp. 275–305; Galia Golan, *Yom Kippur and After: The Soviet Union and the Middle East Crisis* (Cambridge: Cambridge University Press, 1977), pp. 129–68; and Mohamed Abdel Ghani El-Gamasy, *The October War Memoirs of Field Marshall El-Gamasy of Egypt* (Cairo: American University in Cairo Press, 1993), pp. 142–49.

35. Interview with Mohamed Abd al-Ghani el-Gamasy, November 10, 1992, Heliopolis, Egypt.

36. Interview with Hafez Ismail, January 7, 1993, Cairo, Egypt.

37. Henry Kissinger, *Years of Upheaval* (Boston: Little, Brown and Company, 1982), p. 204.

38. Interview with Peter Rodman, June 10, 1992, Washington, D.C.

39. Golda Meir, *My Life* (New York: G. P. Putnam and Sons, 1975), p. 336.

40. Interview with Alouph Hareven, August 2, 1992, Jerusalem, Israel.

41. Interview with Mordechai Gazit, March 22, 1992, Jerusalem, Israel.

42. Interview with Nicholis A. Veliotes, September 7, 1995, Washington, D.C.

43. Mohammed Heikal, *Autumn of Fury: The Assassination of Sadat* (London: Andre Deutsch Limited, 1983), p. 45. Heikal, then the editor of *Al-Ahram,* wrote several articles criticizing the Soviet Union for benefiting from the no-war, no-peace situation between Israel and Egypt.

44. See David Kimche, *The Last Option After Nasser, Arafat and Saddam Hussein: The Quest for Peace in the Middle East* (London: Weidenfeld and Nicolson, 1991), pp. 22–26; Joseph Finklestone, *Anwar Sadat: Visionary Who Dared* (London: Frank Cass, 1996), pp. 91–97; and Mahmoud Riad, *The Struggle for Peace in the Middle East* (London: Quartet Books, 1981), pp. 232–33.

45. Interview with Ashraf Ghorbal, November 9, 1992, Cairo, Egypt.

46. Remarks by Anwar Sadat, *October Magazine,* February 26, 1978, as quoted in *Foreign Broadcast Information Service, Daily Report—Middle East and North Africa,* February 27, 1978, p. D4.

47. Interview with Omar Sirry, January 5, 1993, Cairo, Egypt.

48. Remarks of Moshe Dayan to Hanan Bar-On, from interview with Hanan Bar-On, July 8, 1993, Jerusalem, Israel.

49. "Hussein's Payments only a Part of CIA in Mideast, Extensive and Effective," *Washington Post,* February 22, 1977, pp. A1, A12.

50. Interviews in Washington, D.C., with Joseph Sisco, February 27, 1992; Harold Saunders, May 12, 1992; William B. Quandt, May 13, 1992; Michael Sterner, May 13, 1992; and Peter Rodman, June 10, 1992.

51. Interviews with Peter Rodman, June 10, 1992, Washington, D.C.; and Ashraf Ghorbal, November 9, 1992, Cairo, Egypt; Sheehan, *The Arabs, Israelis, and Kissinger,* p. 22.

52. Interview with Hafez Ismail, January 7, 1993, Cairo, Egypt.

53. Heikal, *Autumn,* p. 46.

54. Interview with Hafez Ismail, January 7, 1993, Cairo, Egypt.

55. Interview with Ashraf Ghorbal, November 9, 1992, Cairo, Egypt.

56. This quotation is taken from two different occasions in October 1977 when Sadat recalled the Kissinger-Ismail meetings. The paragraph cited here is a composite quotation from both reputable sources; see remarks by Anwar Sadat, October 15, 1977, Cairo Domestic Service, as quoted in *Foreign Broadcast Information Service, Daily Report—Middle East and North Africa,* October 17, 1977, p. D9; and text of Sadat's October War Anniversary Interview, October 6, 1977, Cairo Domestic Service, as quoted in *Foreign Broadcast Information Service, Daily Report—Middle East and North Africa Supplement,*

October 25, 1977, p. 41. The details of Kissinger's remarks were confirmed in an interview with Hafez Ismail, January 7, 1993, Cairo, Egypt, and remarks by Ahmed Maher al-Sayed, *Conference on the October 1973 War,* The Middle East Institute, October 10, 1998, Washington, D.C.

57. Interviews with Mohamed Abd al-Ghani el-Gamasy, November 10, 1992, Heliopolis, Egypt; and Hafez Ismail, January 7, 1993, Cairo, Egypt.

58. Interview with Hafez Ismail, January 7, 1993, Cairo, Egypt.

59. Arnaud de Borchegrave, "Next, a 'Shock' by Sadat?" *Newsweek,* April 23, 1973, pp. 36–37.

60. Text of Sadat's October War Anniversary Interview, October 6, 1977, Cairo Domestic Service, as quoted in *Foreign Broadcast Information Service, Daily Report—Middle East and North Africa Supplement,* October 25, 1977, p. 38.

61. Haim Herzog, *The War of Atonement, October 1973: The Fateful Implications of the Arab-Israeli Conflict* (Boston: Little, Brown and Company, 1975), p. 28–29.

62. Lt. General Saad El-Shazly, *The Crossing of Suez* (San Francisco: American Mideast Research, 1980), pp. 201–2.

63. Interview with Moshe Dayan by Rami Tal on November 22, 1976, *Yediot Aharanot,* April 27, 1997.

64. Interview with Nicholis A. Veliotes, September 7, 1995, Washington, D.C.

65. Hussein acknowledged that this meeting took place in a BBC broadcast in May 1998; see *Ha'aretz,* May 17, 1998. Israeli leaders, including General Eli Zeira, head of Israeli military intelligence at the time, General Moshe Peled, the Israeli general who led Israel's forces on the Golan Heights during the October War, and former Israeli Foreign Minister Abba Eban, also acknowledged that such a meeting took place.

66. Remarks by Mordechai Gazit, *Conference on the October War,* The Middle East Institute, October 9, 1998, Washington, D.C.

67. Conversations with General Moshe Peled, Atlanta, August 24, 1995, and Abba Eban, March 13, 1995, Jerusalem, Israel; Eli Zeira, *Milhemet Yom Kippur Mitom Mul Meziot* [The Yom Kippur War Myth Against Reality] (Tel Aviv: Yediot Aharanot, 1993), p. 122.

68. Interview with Ariyeh Shalev, August 13, 1992, Ramat Aviv, Israel.

69. Interview with Epi Evron, March 24, 1993, Ramat Aviv, Israel.

70. Victor Israelyan, *Inside the Kremlin,* p. 3.

71. Ibid., p. 5.

72. Herzog, *The War of Atonement,* p. 51.

73. Interview with Golda Meir, December 26, 1978, Tel Aviv, Israel.

74. Interview with Nicholis A. Veliotes, September 7, 1995, Washington, D.C.; General Avraham Adan, *The Yom Kippur War: An Israeli General's Personal Account* (New York: Drum Books, 1979), pp. 79–80.

75. Interview with Nicholis A. Veliotes, September 7, 1995, Washington, D.C.

76. Herzog, *The War of Atonement,* p. 52.

77. Interview with Yossi Ciechanover, July 30, 1993, New York. Dayan said in an interview published posthumously that in general, Meir "had a problem. . . . [E]verything she would check first of all what the Americans would say." *Yediot Aharanot,* April 27, 1997

78. Edward R. F. Sheehan, *The Arabs, Israelis, and Kissinger,* pp. 27–29.

79. Interview with Esmat Abdel-Meguid, July 14, 1993, Cairo, Egypt.

80. Abba Eban, *Personal Witness: Israel Through My Eyes* (New York: G. P. Putnam's Sons, 1992), p. 523.

81. Interview with Esmat Abdel-Meguid, July 14, 1993, Cairo, Egypt.

82. Dobrynin, *In Confidence,* pp. 289–90.

83. Israelyan, *Inside the Kremlin,* pp. 31, 59.

84. Interviews with William B. Quandt, May 13, 1992, Washington, D.C.; and Michael Sterner, May 13, 1992, Washington, D.C.

85. Interview with Peter Rodman, June 10, 1992, Washington, D.C.
86. Eban, *Personal Witness,* p. 523.
87. Remarks by Roy Atherton, United States Institute of Peace meeting, April 3, 1991, Washington, D.C.; interviews with William B. Quandt, May 13, 1992, Washington, D.C.; and Hafez Ismail, January 7, 1993, Cairo, Egypt.
88. Matti Golan, *The Secret Conversations of Henry Kissinger: Step-by-Step Diplomacy in the Middle East* (New York: Quadrangle, 1976), pp. 63–92.

CHAPTER 3

1. Interviews with Mordechai Zippori, July 7, 1993, Jerusalem, Israel; and Golda Meir, December 26, 1977, Tel Aviv, Israel.
2. General Avraham Adan, *The Yom Kippur War,* p. 87.
3. Ariel Sharon, *Ariel Sharon Warrior: An Autobiography* (New York: Simon and Schuster, 1989), p. 299.
4. Ibid., p. 305.
5. Interview with Shimon Shamir, April 3, 1992, Atlanta; Adan, *The Yom Kippur War.*
6. Interviews with Mohamed Abd al-Ghani el-Gamasy, November 10, 1992, Heliopolis, Egypt; and Omar Sirry, January 5, 1993, Cairo, Egypt. In his interview with me, el-Gamasy emphatically asserted that if it had not been for the "operational hold" imposed upon his troops on October 9 by the commander in chief, Marshall Ahmed Ismail, the Egyptian forces could have gone as far as the Sinai passes even without the missile umbrella that protected them on the east bank of the canal. Ahmed Ismail told Hafez Ismail before the war that Egypt's "immediate objective would be 10 or 12 kilometers east of the canal, but the final objective would be the passes." Interview with Hafez Ismail, January 7, 1993, Cairo, Egypt.
7. Lt. General Saad El-Shazly, *The Crossing,* pp. 245–46.
8. Ibid., pp. 248–51.
9. Discussion with Muhammad al-Baysuni, July 4, 1993, Tel Aviv, Israel.
10. Discussion with Ambassador Muhammad al-Baysuni, July 4, 1993, Tel Aviv, Israel; and remarks by Anwar Sadat, July 10, 1977, *October Magazine,* as quoted in *Foreign Broadcast Information Service, Daily Report—Middle East and North Africa,* July 15, 1977, p. D9.
11. Conversation with General Moshe Peled, August 24, 1995, Atlanta; and Herzog, *The War of Atonement, October 1973,* pp. 96–105.
12. Victor Israelyan, *Inside the Kremlin,* p. 55.
13. Interview with Yossi Ciechanover, July 5, 1993, Tel Aviv, Israel.
14. United States Army Command and General Staff College, *Selected Readings in Tactics: The 1973 Middle East War* (RB 100–2, vol. 1) (Fort Leavenworth, Kansas), August 1976, pp. 3–12.
15. Conversation with Moshe Peled, August 24, 1995, Atlanta.
16. Herzog, *The War of Atonement,* pp. 127–45.
17. Interview with Mordechai Gazit, March 22, 1992, Jerusalem, Israel.
18. El-Shazly, *The Crossing,* p. 274.
19. Interview with Nicholis A. Veliotes, September 7, 1995, Washington, D.C.
20. Edward R. F. Sheehan, *The Arabs, Israelis, and Kissinger: A Secret History of American Diplomacy in the Middle East* (New York: Reader's Digest Press, 1976), p. 33.
21. Interviews with Aulouph Hareven, August 2, 1992, Jerusalem, Israel; and Nicholis A. Veliotes, September 7, 1995, Washington, D.C.
22. Interview with Golda Meir, December 26, 1977, Tel Aviv, Israel.
23. Interview with Wat Cluverius, June 26, 1996, Rome, Italy.
24. Walter Isaacson, *Kissinger* (New York: Simon and Schuster, 1992), pp. 517–23.
25. Interview with Peter Rodman, June 10, 1992, Washington, D.C.

26. Interview with Ariyeh Shalev, August 13, 1992, Ramat Aviv, Israel.
27. Marvin Kalb and Bernard Kalb, *Kissinger* (Boston: Little, Brown and Company, 1974), p. 481.
28. Israelyan, *Inside the Kremlin*, pp. 38, 44, 73.
29. Karen Dawisha, *Soviet Foreign Policy Towards Egypt* (New York: St. Martin's Press, 1979), p. 68.
30. William B. Quandt, "Soviet Policy in the October Middle East War—I," *International Affairs* 53 (July 1977): 386–87.
31. Interview with Hafez Ismail, January 7, 1993, Cairo, Egypt.
32. For a full text of Sadat's speech, see Raphael Israeli, *The Public Diary of President Sadat: The Road to War (October 1970–October 1973)*, part 1 (Leiden: E. J. Brill, 1978), pp. 425–34.

    For several of the dozens of examples of Sadat's repeated use of the October War as the turning point in his interpretation of modern Egyptian history and the central role he obviously played in carrying it out, see his remarks as noted in the index under "October War" in Raphael Israeli's three volumes, *The Public Diary of President Sadat* (Leiden: E. J. Brill, 1978–1979); see also Sadat's remarks made on various occasions as quoted in *Foreign Broadcast Information Service, Daily Report—Middle East and North Africa*, July 8, 1977, pp. D3–D6; July 18, 1977, pp. D3–D10; July 25, 1977, p. D4; July 28, 1978, pp. D6–D7; May 15, 1980, p. D3; and January 2, 1981, pp. D11–D13.

    In subsequent years, the successes claimed from the October War would be recounted by Sadat on almost every public occasion. Just as the July 1952 Revolution became Gamal Abdul-Nasser's key historical benchmark for political legitimation, the October War was of equal, if not more, significance in Sadat's reconstruction of modern Egyptian history. This speech was the first of thousands of public opportunities Sadat would employ to emphasize in the years that followed how the October War had changed Egypt's political direction, restored Egyptian honor, and ennobled Egypt to lead the Arab world.
33. Interviews with Mordechai Gazit, March 22, 1992, Jerusalem, Israel; and Epi Evron, March 24, 1992, Ramat Aviv, Israel.
34. Mahmoud Riad, *The Struggle for Peace in the Middle East* (London: Quartet Books, 1981), p. 269.
35. For a detailed first-person rendition of the "crossing" see Sharon, *Ariel Sharon*, pp. 306–33.
36. Riad, *The Struggle for Peace*, pp. 254–63; El-Shazly, *The Crossing*, pp. 244–70 and 287–303.
37. El-Shazly, *The Crossing*, pp. 291–301. The disagreement with Sadat on the management of information about the war ultimately caused El-Shazly to be relieved of his position and dispatched to London as Egypt's ambassador.
38. Riad, *The Struggle for Peace*, p. 263.
39. Interview with Abd-al Halim Khaddam, July 18, 1993, Damascus, Syria.
40. Kalb and Kalb, *Kissinger*, p. 480. For a more detailed discussion of Kosygin's visit to Cairo and Moscow's policy changes during the war, see William B. Quandt, "Soviet Policy in the October Middle East War—II," *International Affairs* 53 (October 1977): 587–604.
41. Interview with Hafez Ismail, January 7, 1993, Cairo, Egypt.
42. Anwar Sadat, *In Search of Identity: An Autobiography* (New York: Harper and Row, 1977), p. 259; and Israelyan, *Inside the Kremlin*, pp. 105, 109.
43. Israelyan, *Inside the Kremlin*, p. 108.
44. Interview with Ashraf Ghorbal, November 9, 1992, Cairo, Egypt.
45. William B. Quandt, "Soviet Policy in the October Middle East War—II," *International Affairs* 53 (October 1977): 594–95.
46. Israelyan, *Inside the Kremlin*, pp. 68, 97.

47. Interviews with Shlomo Gazit, August 13, 1992, Ramat Aviv, Israel; and Ariyeh Shalev, August 13, 1992, Ramat Aviv, Israel.
48. Sadat contradicts himself about (not) wanting a cease-fire on October 19. See Sadat, *In Search of Identity,* pp. 259, 261.
49. Interview with Patrick Theros, March 31, 1993, Atlanta.
50. Interview with Zaid Rifa'i, January 9, 1993, Amman, Jordan.
51. Israelyan, *Inside the Kremlin,* pp. 131–32.
52. Henry Kissinger, *Years of Upheaval,* p. 546. Interview with Joseph Sisco, February 27, 1992, Washington, D.C.
53. Riad, *The Struggle for Peace,* pp. 253, 262.
54. Ibid., p. 258.
55. Interview with Mordechai Gazit, March 22, 1992, Jerusalem, Israel.
56. Interview with Peter Rodman, June 10, 1992, Washington, D.C.
57. See U. S. State Department "Memorandum of Conversation between General Secretary Leonid Brezhnev and Secretary of State Henry Kissinger at the Kremlin in Moscow," October 20, 1973, Washington, D.C.; and Victor Israelyan. "The October 1973 War: Kissinger in Moscow," *Middle East Journal* (spring 1995): 249–53.
58. Interview with Simcha Dinitz, March 20, 1992, Jerusalem, Israel. Kissinger, *Years,* pp. 546–47.
59. Kissinger, *Years,* p. 548.
60. Interview with William B. Quandt, May 13, 1992, Washington, D.C. The key paragraph from the Brezhnev letter was quoted in "House Ends Study of Nuclear Alert," *New York Times,* April 10, 1974, p. 9.
61. Moshe Dayan, *Moshe Dayan: Story of My Life* (New York: William Morrow, 1976), p. 534.
62. U.S. State Department, "Memorandum of Conversation between General Secretary Leonid Brezhnev and Secretary of State Henry Kissinger at the Kremlin in Moscow," October 20, 1973, Washington, D.C.; and Kissinger, *Years,* p. 550.
63. Kissinger, *Years,* p. 550–51.
64. Israelyan, "The October 1973 War," p. 254–55.
65. U.S. State Department, "Memorandum of Conversation between General Secretary Leonid Brezhnev and Secretary of State Henry Kissinger at the Kremlin in Moscow," October 21, 1973, Washington, D.C.
66. Ibid.
67. Kissinger, *Years,* p. 554; Abba Eban, *Personal Witness,* p. 536.
68. U.S. State Department, "Memorandum of Conversation between General Secretary Leonid Brezhnev and Secretary of State Henry Kissinger at the Kremlin in Moscow," October 21, 1973, Washington, D.C.
69. Interview with Joseph Sisco, February 27, 1992, Washington, D.C.
70. Eban, *Personal Witness,* p. 536.
71. U.S. State Department, "Top Secret Telegram from Henry Kissinger to John Scali" (Moscow 13139), October 21, 1973, Washington, D.C.
72. Israelyan, *Inside the Kremlin,* pp. 143–44.
73. Ibid., p. 149.
74. Ibid., p. 147.
75. Interview with Mordechai Gazit, March 22, 1992, Jerusalem, Israel.
76. Interview with Peter Rodman, June 10, 1992, Washington, D.C.
77. Interview with Abba Eban, March 24, 1992, Herzelia, Israel.
78. Interview with Epi Evron, March 24, 1992, Ramat Aviv, Israel.
79. U.S. State Department, "Memorandum of Conversation between General Secretary Leonid Brezhnev and Secretary of State Henry Kissinger at the Kremlin in Moscow," October 22, 1973, Washington, D.C.

80. Interviews with Epi Evron, March 24, 1992, Ramat Aviv, Israel; and Nicholis A. Veliotes, September 7, 1995, Washington, D.C.
81. Interview with Epi Evron, March 24, 1992, Ramat Aviv, Israel. See also Kissinger, *Years,* pp. 560–61.
82. Interview with Mordechai Gazit, March 22, 1992, Jerusalem, Israel.
83. Interview with Epi Evron, March 24, 1992, Ramat Aviv, Israel; see also Matti Golan, *The Secret Conversations of Henry Kissinger: Step-by-Step Diplomacy in the Middle East* (New York: Quadrangle, 1976), pp. 82–3.
84. Interviews with Epi Evron, March 24, 1992, Ramat Aviv, Israel; and Peter Rodman, June 10, 1992, Washington, D.C.
85. Eban, *Personal Witness,* p. 538.
86. Interview with Epi Evron, March 24, 1992, Ramat Aviv, Israel.
87. Interview with Ariyeh Shalev, August 13, 1992, Ramat Aviv, Israel.
88. El-Shazly, *The Crossing,* pp. 286–87.
89. Dayan, *Moshe Dayan,* p. 544.
90. Interview with Hafez Ismail, January 7, 1993, Cairo, Egypt.
91. Michael O. Wheeler and Kemper V. Gay, *Nuclear Weapons and the 1973 Middle East War,* CSN Occasional Paper Monograph, no. 3 (Washington, D.C.: The Center for National Security Negotiations, August 1996), p. 16.
92. Ismail Fahmy, *Negotiating for Peace in the Middle East* (Baltimore: Johns Hopkins University Press, 1983), p. 30. Hafez Ismail confirms also that they were sent to Egypt. Interview with Hafez Ismail, January 7, 1993, Cairo, Egypt.
93. Dobrynin, *In Confidence,* p. 294.
94. Interview with William B. Quandt, May 13, 1992, Washington, D.C. See also Wheeler and Gay, *Nuclear Weapons,* p. 16.
95. Interview with William B. Quandt, May 13, 1992, Washington, D.C. "House Ends Study of Nuclear Alert," *New York Times,* April 10, 1974, p. 9.
96. Israelyan, *Inside the Kremlin,* p. 173.
97. Interview with Ariyeh Shalev, August 13, 1992, Ramat Aviv, Israel.
98. Interview with Peter Rodman, June 10, 1992, Washington, D.C.
99. Interview with Hafez Ismail, January 7, 1993, Cairo, Egypt.
100. Interview with Naftali Lavi, July 8, 1993, Jerusalem, Israel.
101. Israelyan, *Inside the Kremlin,* pp. 160–83.
102. Dobrynin, *In Confidence,* p. 296.
103. Israelyan, *Inside the Kremlin,* pp. 179–81.
104. Interview with Peter Rodman, June 10, 1992, Washington, D.C.
105. Marvin Kalb and Bernard Kalb, *Kissinger* (Boston: Little, Brown and Company, 1974), p. 489.
106. Dawisha, *Soviet Foreign Policy,* p. 69.
107. Dobrynin, *In Confidence,* p. 297.
108. Interview with Nicholis A. Veliotes, September 7, 1995, Washington, D.C.
109. For a fuller analysis of American decision making during the October 1973 War, see William B. Quandt, *Decade of Decisions: American Policy Toward the Arab-Israeli Conflict, 1967–1976* (Berkeley and Los Angeles: University of California Press, 1977), pp. 165–206.
110. Interview with Simcha Dinitz, March 20, 1992, Jerusalem, Israel.
111. Eban, *Personal Witness,* p. 538.

CHAPTER 4

1. For a full text of Sadat's press conference in Cairo on October 31, 1973, see Raphael Israeli, *The Public Diary of President Sadat: The Road to War (October 1970–October 1973),*

part 1 (Leiden: E. J. Brill, 1978), pp. 434–42. Until his death in October 1981, Sadat propagated the notion of Egypt's untainted victory in the October 1973 War.

2. Remarks by Anwar Sadat, April 18, 1974, as quoted in Raphael Israeli, *The Public Diary of President Sadat:The Road of Diplomacy (November 1973–May 1975)*, part 2 (Leiden: E. J. Brill, 1979), p. 474.

3. Hermann F. Eilts in letter to the author, January 7, 1994.

4. Mohammed Heikal, *Autumn of Fury: The Assassination of Sadat* (London: Andre Deutsch, 1983), pp. 62–63.

5. Interview with Mordechai Gazit, March 22, 1992, Jerusalem, Israel. Aharon Yariv, "On the Way to the Israeli-Egyptian Peace at Kilometer 101" (a lecture presented at The Moshe Dayan Center for Middle Eastern and African Studies at Tel Aviv University, March 30, 1992, Ramat Aviv), p 3. Matti Golan also asserts that Gazit first proposed the idea for direct Egyptian-Israeli military talks; see Matti Golan, *The Secret Conversations of Henry Kissinger: Step-by-Step Diplomacy in the Middle East* (New York: Quadrangle, 1976), p. 93.

6. Interview with Mohamed Abd al-Ghani el-Gamasy, November 10, 1992, Heliopolis, Egypt.

7. Aharon Yariv, "On the Way to the Israeli-Egyptian Peace at Kilometer 101" (a lecture presented at The Moshe Dayan Center for Middle Eastern and African Studies at Tel Aviv University, March 30, 1992, Ramat Aviv), p. 3.

8. Interview with Aharon Yariv, March 26, 1992, Ramat Aviv, Israel. For his interview with me, Yariv reconstructed his recollection of the Kilometer 101 Talks by preparing an outline after consulting a personal diary which he kept of those talks. The most detailed published summary of the Kilometer 101 Talks are found in Golan, *The Secret Conversations,* pp. 93–122.

9. Aharon Yariv, "On the Way to the Israeli-Egyptian Peace at Kilometer 101" (a lecture presented at The Moshe Dayan Center for Middle Eastern and African Studies at Tel Aviv University, March 30, 1992, Ramat Aviv), p. 4.

10. Interview with Aharon Yariv, March 26, 1992, Ramat Aviv, Israel.

11. Interview with Mohamed Abd al-Ghani el-Gamasy, November 10, 1992, Heliopolis, Egypt. El-Gamasy told me that when Dayan died, Israeli radio contacted el-Gamasy to ask for a comment about Dayan. El-Gamasy refused to give such a comment because "there was no need to hurt the Israelis. I did not want to say anything bad about a dead man."

12. Abraham Tamir, *A Soldier in Search of Peace: An Insider's Look at Israel's Strategy in the Middle East* (New York: Harper and Row, 1988), pp. 25–26.

13. Interview with Omar Sirry, January 5, 1993, Cairo, Egypt.

14. Ibid.

15. Interview with Aharon Yariv, March 26, 1992, Ramat Aviv, Israel; and Aharon Yariv, "On the Way to the Israeli-Egyptian Peace at Kilometer 101" (lecture presented at The Dayan Center for Middle Eastern and African Studies at Tel Aviv University, March 30, 1992, Tel Aviv, 1992), p. 7.

16. Interview with Omar Sirry, January 5, 1993, Cairo, Egypt.

17. Interviews with Mohamed Abd al-Ghani el-Gamasy, November 10, 1992, Heliopolis, Egypt; and Omar Sirry, January 5, 1993, Cairo, Egypt. Ensio Siilasvuo, *In the Service of Peace in the Middle East, 1976–1979* (New York: St. Martin's Press, 1992), p. 194.

18. Interview with Omar Sirry, January 5, 1993, Cairo, Egypt.

19. Interview with Mohamed Abd al-Ghani el-Gamasy, November 10, 1992, Heliopolis, Egypt.

20. Interviews with Aharon Yariv, March 26, 1992, Ramat Aviv, Israel; and Mohamed Abd al-Ghani el-Gamasy, November 10, 1992, Heliopolis, Egypt. See also Aharon Yariv,

"On the Way to the Israeli-Egyptian Peace at Kilometer 101" (lecture presented at The Dayan Center for Middle Eastern and African Studies at Tel Aviv University, March 30, 1992, Ramat Aviv), pp. 3–4.

21. Interview with Omar Sirry, January 5, 1993, Cairo, Egypt.
22. Ibid.
23. Interview with Mohamed Abd al-Ghani el-Gamasy, November 10, 1992, Heliopolis, Egypt.
24. Interview with Aharon Yariv, March 26, 1992, Ramat Aviv, Israel.
25. Interview with Mohamed Abd al-Ghani el-Gamasy, November 10, 1992, Heliopolis, Egypt.
26. Interview with Aharon Yariv, March 26, 1992, Ramat Aviv, Israel.
27. Interview with Omar Sirry, January 5, 1993, Cairo, Egypt.
28. Interview with Omar Sirry, January 5, 1993, Cairo, Egypt; Mahmoud Riad, *The Struggle for Peace in the Middle East* (London: Quartet Books, 1981), p. 256. Ismail Fahmy, *Negotiating for Peace in the Middle East* (Baltimore: Johns Hopkins University Press, 1983), p. 36. Sirry claims that the points made in Fahmy's book and repeated here are an accurate recollection of what Sadat dictated to him. Sirry admired Fahmy greatly, because "he was bright, always truthful with Sadat, and always spoke his mind honestly. Fahmy could create accurate strategic analyses very quickly." But on this point of the source of the Egyptian plan taken to Washington, Sirry insists it was not a Fahmy "original."
29. Aharon Yariv, "On the Way to the Israeli-Egyptian Peace at Kilometer 101" (lecture presented at The Moshe Dayan Center for Middle Eastern and African Studies at Tel Aviv University, March 30, 1992, Ramat Aviv), p. 4.
30. Interview with Aharon Yariv, March 26, 1992, Ramat Aviv, Israel.
31. Interview with Meir Rosenne, August 6, 1992, Jerusalem, Israel. That the Israeli government even asked this question of itself of being responsible for the well-being of the Third Army was not a reflection of an ethos that sought to be intentionally malicious. It was, however, indicative of Israel's general negotiating style that would repeatedly resurface during the next two decades. Israel, more than its Arab neighbors, would repeatedly resort to the Western legal tradition of seeking precedent, being as specific as possible, and generally acting in a litigious manner in arguing points of view. This Israeli preference in style had the tendency to slow down the pace of negotiations and anger those who wanted quicker results. Presidents Sadat and Carter were repeatedly vexed by this aspect of Israeli procedure.
32. Interview with Herzel Shafir, August 17, 1992, Ramat Hasharon, Israel.
33. Siilasvuo, *In the Service of Peace,* p. 195.
34. Interview with Mohamed Abd al-Ghani el-Gamasy, November 10, 1992, Heliopolis, Egypt. See also Golan, *The Secret Conversations,* p. 107.
35. Interview with Golda Meir, December 26, 1977, Tel Aviv, Israel.
36. Ibid.
37. Golan, *The Secret Conversations,* pp. 107, 109.
38. Interview with Hermann F. Eilts, April 11, 1991, Boston.
39. Interviews with Aharon Yariv, March 26, 1992, Ramat Aviv, Israel; and Abd al-Ghani al-Gamasy, November 10, 1992, Heliopolis, Egypt.
40. Interview with Mohamed Abd al-Ghani el-Gamasy, November 10, 1992, Heliopolis, Egypt.
41. Interview with Aharon Yariv, March 25, 1992, Ramat Aviv, Israel.
42. Interview with Avraham Sela, July 30, 1995, Jerusalem, Israel.
43. Fahmy, *Negotiating for Peace,* p. 55. There are many places in Fahmy's book that are not fully accurate, and his rendition of events and his influence upon them are not usually corroborated by American, Egyptian, and Israeli sources. Caution should be applied in

using his book as an accurate reference point for when events took place and his personal involvement in making key foreign policy decisions. For example, he wrongfully claimed that the Israelis tried to prevent the Egyptian delegation from reaching Kilometer 101 (p. 38). He claims that, when he met with Kissinger in Washington on October 29, the Israelis were already going back on their promises made during the talks at Kilometer 101 (p. 38), which was not possible because Yariv and al-Gamasy had not yet even made substantive suggestions to one another. He stated that Yariv was a member of the Israeli Cabinet (p. 47) when he negotiated at Kilometer 101, which he was not until April 1974. Fahmy also claimed that the key November 6 meeting between Sadat and Kissinger in Cairo neither lasted long nor "led to new developments" (p. 56). In separate interviews, Atherton, Rodman, Saunders, and Sisco told me that this meeting lasted more than four hours and was crucial in persuading Sadat to accept interim, staged, or phased Israeli withdrawals from Sinai.

An Egyptian diplomat, very familiar with the inner workings of the Foreign Ministry at the time, recalled that Fahmy wanted to show everyone in Egypt that he was at least Kissinger's equal; but at their first luncheon meeting, recalled this diplomat, when Fahmy called out, "Henry, Henry, Henry," Kissinger was not sure who Fahmy was.

44. Interview with Omar Sirry, January 5, 1993, Cairo, Egypt.
45. Interview with Golda Meir, December 26, 1977, Tel Aviv, Israel.
46. Interviews with Aharon Yariv, March 26, 1992, Ramat Aviv, Israel; and Mohamed Abd al-Ghani el-Gamasy, November 10, 1992, Heliopolis, Egypt.
47. Kissinger's enumeration of the six points was in a very different order and less explicit than one of the several Israeli drafts of the six points; see Henry Kissinger, *Years of Upheaval* (Boston: Little, Brown and Company, 1982), p. 641; and Aharon Yariv, "On the Way to the Israeli-Egyptian Peace at Kilometer 101" (lecture presented at The Moshe Dayan Center for Middle Eastern and African Studies at Tel Aviv University, March 30, 1992, Ramat Aviv), pp. 11–12. The six-point agreement was a consensus-made document which Israelis, Egyptians, and Americans participated in drafting.
48. Interviews with Aharon Yariv, March 26, 1992, Ramat Aviv, Israel; and Mohamed Abd al-Ghani el-Gamasy, November 10, 1992, Heliopolis, Egypt.
49. Aharon Yariv, "On the Way to the Israeli-Egyptian Peace at Kilometer 101" (lecture presented at The Moshe Dayan Center for Middle Eastern and African Studies at Tel Aviv University, March 30, 1992, Ramat Aviv), p. 16.
50. Interview with Aharon Yariv, March 26, 1992, Ramat Aviv, Israel. In his own book, Siilasvuo recounted this story accurately, but omitted mention of his anger at being scolded, as suggested by Yariv's rendition. See Siilasvuo, *In the Service of Peace*, p. 201.
51. Golan, *The Secret Conversations*, pp. 116–19.
52. Interview with Abd al-Ghani el-Gamasy, November 10, 1992, Heliopolis, Egypt.
53. Interview with Peter Rodman, June 10, 1992, Washington, D.C.
54. Interview with Abd al-Ghani el-Gamasy, November 10, 1992, Heliopolis, Egypt.
55. Aharon Yariv, "On the Way to the Israeli-Egyptian Peace at Kilometer 101" (lecture presented at The Moshe Dayan Center for Middle Eastern and African Studies at Tel Aviv University, March 30, 1992, Ramat Aviv), pp. 14–16.
56. United States Department of State, Egyptian and Israeli Proposals on Disengagement, Meeting Summaries, "E29A," November 19, 22, 23, and 26, and December 6, 1973.
57. Aharon Yariv, "On the Way to the Israeli-Egyptian Peace at Kilometer 101" (lecture presented at The Moshe Dayan Center for Middle Eastern and African Studies at Tel Aviv University, March 30, 1992, Ramat Aviv), pp. 14–16.
58. Remarks by Anwar Sadat, November 28, 1973, April 18, 1974, and September 15, 1975, as quoted in Israeli, *The Public Diary of President Sadat: The Road to Diplomacy*, pp. 444, 474; and Israeli, *The Public Diary of President Sadat: The Road of Pragmatism*, p. 1044.
59. Interview with Hermann F. Eilts, April 11, 1991, Boston.

60. Kissinger, *Years,* pp. 751–52.
61. Interview with Simcha Dinitz, March 20, 1992, Jerusalem, Israel.
62. Interview with Abba Eban, March 24, 1992, Herzelia, Israel.
63. Interview with Hafez Ismail, January 7, 1993, Cairo, Egypt.
64. Interview with Mordechai Gazit, March 22, 1992, Jerusalem, Israel.
65. Interviews with Hermann F. Eilts, April 11, 1991, Boston; Hafez Ismail, January 7, 1993, Cairo, Egypt; and Brian Urquhart, February 28, 1991, New York. Urquhart was a close aid to Secretary-General Kurt Waldheim during the period of the planning and convocation of the December 1973 Geneva Conference. See also, Kissinger, *Years,* p. 752.
66. Interview with Nicholis A. Veliotes, September 7, 1995, Washington, D.C.
67. Interview with Aharon Yariv, March 26, 1992, Ramat Aviv, Israel.
68. Interview with Peter Rodman, June 10, 1992, Washington, D.C.
69. Interview with Abba Eban, March 24, 1992, Herzelia, Israel.
70. Remarks by Moshe Dayan, *Davar,* November 3, 1977, p. 2.
71. Kissinger, *Years,* pp. 644–45.
72. Interviews with Harold Saunders, May 12, 1992, Washington, D.C.; and Peter Rodman, June 10, 1992, Washington, D.C. Saunders and Rodman have almost identical recollections of Kissinger pleading to Sadat.
73. Interviews with Harold Saunders, May 12, 1992, Washington, D.C.; and Hafez Ismail, January 7, 1993, Cairo, Egypt.
74. Interview with Peter Rodman, June 10, 1992, Washington, D.C.
75. Ibid.
76. Heikal, *Autumn,* p. 68.
77. Interview with Mohamed Abd al-Ghani el-Gamasy, November 10, 1992, Heliopolis, Egypt.
78. Interview with Mordechai Gazit, March 22, 1992, Jerusalem, Israel.
79. Interview with Abd al-Halim Khaddam, July 18, 1993, Damascus, Syria. See also Patrick Seale, *Assad of Syria: The Struggle for the Middle East* (Berkeley and Los Angeles: University of California Press, 1988), pp. 226–27.
80. Interview with Abd al-Halim Khaddam, July 18, 1993, Damascus, Syria.
81. Interview with Brian Urquhart, February 28, 1991, New York.
82. Interview with Abd al-Halim Khaddam, July 18, 1993, Damascus, Syria.
83. Kissinger, *Years,* p. 751.

CHAPTER 5

1. Interview with Joseph Sisco, February 27, 1992, Washington, D.C.; Moshe Dayan, *Moshe Dayan: Story of My Life* (New York: William Morrow and Company, Inc., 1976), p. 501.
2. Remarks by Peter Rodman, United States Institute of Peace meeting, April 16, 1991, Washington, D.C.
3. Henry Kissinger, *Years of Upheaval* (Boston: Little, Brown and Company, 1982), pp. 747, 752.
4. Interviews with Abdel Halim al-Badawi, February 22, 1989, Atlanta; and Abba Eban, March 24, 1992, Herzelia, Israel. Immediately after the 1973 War, Badawi served as a high-ranking bureaucrat in the Egyptian Foreign Ministry in Cairo.
5. Interview with Brian Urquhart, February 28, 1991, New York.
6. Interview with Joseph Sisco, February 27, 1992, Washington, D.C.
7. In my interview with Zaid Rifa'i on January 9, 1993, the former Jordanian Prime Minister recalled a meeting he had with Peter Rodman and National Security Council Adviser Carlucci in 1986. Rodman confided the contents of this secret agreement to

Rifa'i during a conversation that included discussion about a possible reconvened Geneva Conference. Until that meeting in 1986, neither Rifa'i nor King Hussein were aware of that secret agreement. See also interview with Peter Rodman, June 10, 1992, Washington, D.C.

8. Interview with Hermann F. Eilts, April 11, 1991, Boston.

9. Mohamed Heikal, *Autumn of Fury: The Assassination of Sadat* (New York: Random House, 1983), p. 65.

10. Interviews with Zaid Rifa'i, January 9, 1993, Amman, Jordan; and Hafez Ismail, January 7, 1993, Cairo, Egypt.

11. Kissinger, *Years,* p. 747.

12. Ibid., p. 749.

13. Remarks by Peter Rodman, United States Institute of Peace meeting, April 16, 1991, Washington, D.C.; interview with Peter Rodman, June 10, 1992, Washington, D.C.

14. Interview with Fawzi al-Ibrashi, January 5, 1993, Cairo, Egypt.

15. Kissinger, *Years,* pp. 645–46.

16. Ibid, p. 753.

17. Interview with Simcha Dinitz, March 20, 1992, Jerusalem, Israel.

18. Interview with Abba Eban, March 24, 1992, Herzelia, Israel.

19. Interview with Hermann F. Eilts, April 11, 1991, Boston.

20. Galia Golan, *Yom Kippur and After: The Soviet Union and the Middle East Crisis* (Cambridge: Cambridge University Press, 1977), pp. 135–36.

21. Interview with Brian Urquhart, February 28, 1991, New York.

22. Interview with Simcha Dinitz, March 20, 1992, Jerusalem, Israel.

23. Interview with Alouph Hareven, August 2, 1992, Jerusalem, Israel.

24. Remarks by Joseph Sisco, United States Institute of Peace meeting, April 16, 1991, Washington, D.C.

25. Interview with Brian Urquhart, February 28, 1991, New York.

26. Interview with Epi Evron, March 24, 1992, Ramat Aviv, Israel; see also Matti Golan, *The Secret Conversations of Henry Kissinger: Step-by-Step Diplomacy in the Middle East* (New York: Quadrangle, 1976), p. 85.

27. Interview with Mordechai Gazit, March 22, 1992, Jerusalem, Israel.

28. Interview with Abba Eban, March 24, 1992, Herzelia, Israel. In an interview with Mordechai Gazit (March 22, 1992, Jerusalem, Israel), he suggested emphatically, "I was not aware at all that Geneva was considered in the context of the elections, one way or another. In other words, I do not remember hearing if it [the conference] were either good or bad for the elections."

29. Golan, *The Secret Conversations,* pp. 82–89.

30. Interview with Michael Sterner, May 13, 1992, Washington, D.C.

31. Interview with Epi Evron, March 24, 1992, Ramat Aviv, Israel.

32. Interview with Simcha Dinitz, March 20, 1992, Jerusalem, Israel.

33. Interviews with Mordechai "Reginald" Kidron, August 5, 1992, Jerusalem, Israel; and Meir Rosenne, August 6, 1992, Jerusalem, Israel.

34. Interview with Alouph Hareven, August 2, 1992, Jerusalem, Israel; Abba Eban, *Abba Eban: An Autobiography* (New York: Random House, 1977), pp. 545–46.

35. Interview with Shaul Friedlander, August 4, 1992, Jerusalem, Israel.

36. Interview with Shimon Shamir, April 3, 1992, Atlanta.

37. Interviews with Fawzi al-Ibrashi, January 5, 1993, Cairo, Egypt; and Nabil al-Arabi, February 26, 1993, Atlanta.

38. Interview with Nabil al-Arabi, February 26, 1993, Atlanta.

39. Remarks by Peter Rodman, United States Institute of Peace meeting, April 16, 1991, Washington, D.C.

40. Interview with Adnan Abu-Odeh, July 24, 1992, New York.

41. Kissinger, *Years,* pp. 656, 748.
42. Interview with King Hussein, January 11, 1993, Amman, Jordan.
43. Interview with Zaid Rifa'i, January 9, 1993, Amman, Jordan.
44. Interview with King Hussein, January 11, 1993, Amman, Jordan.
45. Iyad Abou with Eric Rouleau, *My Home, My Land* (New York Times Books, 1981), pp. 129–32.
46. Interviews with Harold Saunders, May 12, 1992, Washington, D.C.; and Joseph Sisco, February 27, 1992, Washington, D.C.
47. Moshe Shemesh, *The Palestinian Entity, 1959–1974, Arab Politics and the PLO* (London: Frank Cass, 1988), p. 272.
48. Letter from Hermann F. Eilts to the author, January 7, 1994.
49. Interview with Hermann F. Eilts, April 11, 1991, Boston.
50. Ibid.
51. Interview with Zaid Rifa'i, January 9, 1993, Amman, Jordan.
52. Interview with Adnan Abu-Odeh, July 24, 1992, New York.
53. Interview with Nabil al-Arabi, February 26, 1993, Atlanta.
54. Interview with Zaid Rifa'i, January 9, 1993, Amman, Jordan.
55. "Kissinger Off for Europe and Middle East Today," *New York Times,* December 8, 1973, p. 16, and "Israel Enlarges Atrocity Charge," *New York Times,* December 10, 1973, p. 19.
56. Interviews with Joseph Sisco, February 27, 1992, Washington, D.C.; and Abd al-Halim Khaddam, July 18, 1993, Damascus, Syria.
57. Mahmoud Riad, *The Struggle for Peace in the Middle East* (London: Quartet Books, 1981), p. 277.
58. Interview with Abd al-Halim Khaddam, July 18, 1993, Damascus, Syria.
59. Victor Israelyan, *Inside the Kremlin During the Yom Kippur War* (State College: Pennsylvania State University Press, 1995), p. 214.
60. Riad, *The Struggle for Peace,* p. 272; interview with Abd al-Halim Khaddam, July 18, 1993, Damascus, Syria.
61. Remarks by Peter Rodman, Joseph Sisco, and Richard Murphy, United States Institute of Peace meeting, April 16, 1991, Washington, D.C.
62. Interview with Joseph Sisco, February 27, 1992, Washington, D.C.
63. Interview with Abd al-Halim Khaddam, July 18, 1993, Damascus, Syria.
64. Interview with Joseph Sisco, February 27, 1992, Washington, D.C.
65. Interview with Joseph Sisco, Washington, D.C., February 27, 1992.
66. Interview with David Korn, October 29, 1993, Washington, D.C.
67. U.S. State Department, "Memorandum of Conversation, S/S-7400659." Participants: President Assad of Syria, Foreign Minister Khaddam of Syria, Secretary Kissinger, Assistant Secretary Sisco, Interpreter (Syrian), December 15, 1973, Washington, D.C.
68. Ibid.
69. Ibid.
70. Ibid.
71. Ibid.
72. Ibid.
73. Ibid.
74. Interview with Golda Meir, December 26, 1977, Tel Aviv, Israel.
75. Ibid.
76. Interview with Abd al-Halim Khaddam, July 18, 1993, Damascus, Syria.
77. Interview with Zaid Rifa'i, January 9, 1993, Amman, Jordan. See also Joseph Sisco, "Actors on the Scene: They Are All Still Alive," in *A Fresh Look At the Middle East: War, Peace, or Status Quo* (Washington, 1977), pp. 16–17.
78. The rendition of this conversation was originally provided by Zaid Rifa'i on January 9, 1993, Amman, Jordan, and confirmed in detail with then Foreign Minister Khaddam,

who was present at the Kissinger-Assad meeting. Interview with Abd al-Halim Khaddam, July 18, 1993, Damascus, Syria.

79. Interview with Hermann F. Eilts, April 11, 1991, Boston. Eilts was the newly appointed U.S. ambassador to Egypt at the time. He was told in December 1973 that one of the reasons for Assad deciding not to attend the Geneva Conference was because of pressure he was facing from within his own ruling Ba'ath Party.

80. Interview with Hermann F. Eilts, April 11, 1991, Boston.

81. Remarks by Moshe Dayan, Jerusalem Domestic Service, October 15, 1977, as quoted in *Foreign Broadcast Information Service, Daily Report—Middle East and North Africa,* October 17, 1977, p. N5.

82. Kissinger, *Years,* pp. 1249–50.

83. Interview with Abd al-Halim Khaddam, July 18, 1993, Damascus, Syria.

84. Interviews with Hermann F. Eilts, April 11, 1991, Boston; and Zaid Rifa'i, January 9, 1993, Amman, Jordan.

85. Riad, *The Struggle for Peace,* p. 271.

86. Ibid.

87. Remarks by Syrian President Hafez al-Assad, Middle East News Agency, July 17, 1991, as quoted in *Foreign Broadcast Information Service, Daily Report—Near East and South Asia,* July 22, 1991, p. 37.

88. Interviews with Abd al-Halim Khaddam, July 18, 1993, Damascus, Syria; and Zaid Rifa'i, January 9, 1993, Amman, Jordan.

89. Interview with Hermann F. Eilts, April 11, 1991, Boston. In a separate interview on August 2, 1992, Jerusalem, Israel, Moshe Ma'oz, who attended the 1973 Geneva Conference as an Israeli delegate and who is also an academic specialist on Syria, concurred with Eilts's belief that there were pressures domestically that Assad could not jettison or ignore by choosing to go to Geneva.

90. Remarks by President Hafez Assad, Damascus Domestic Service in Arabic, May 7, 1990, as quoted in *Foreign Broadcast Information Service, Daily Report—Middle East and North Africa,* May 8, 1990, p. 31.

91. Interview with Brian Urquhart, February 28, 1991, New York.

92. Interview with Joseph Sisco, February 27, 1992, Washington, D.C.

93. Remarks by Joseph Sisco, United States Institute of Peace meeting, April 16, 1991, Washington, D.C.

94. Kissinger, *Years,* p. 755.

95. Remarks by William B. Quandt, Harold Saunders, and Joseph Sisco, United States Institute of Peace meeting, April 16, 1991, Washington, D.C. Both Saunders and Sisco were involved in writing the terms of reference for the conference. When asked about its contents and purpose, both had considerable difficulty in recalling that UNSC Resolution 344 even existed!

96. Interviews with Harold Saunders, May 12, 1992, Washington, D.C.; William Quandt, May 13, 1992, Washington, D.C.; and Mordechai Gazit, March 22, 1992, Jerusalem, Israel.

97. Interview with Peter Rodman, June 10, 1992, Washington, D.C.

98. Interview with Brian Urquhart, February 28, 1991, New York.

99. Kissinger, *Years,* p. 795.

100. Eban, *Abba Eban,* p. 547; interview with Brian Urquhart, February 28, 1991, New York.

101. Remarks by President Anwar Sadat to the Israeli Parliament, November 20, 1977, as quoted in *New York Times,* November 21, 1977, pp. 16–17.

102. Interviews with Brian Urquhart, February 28, 1991, New York; and Abba Eban, March 24, 1992, Herzelia, Israel. Eban, *Abba Eban,* p. 547.

103. Interview with Zaid Rifa'i, January 9, 1993, Amman, Jordan.

104. Golda Meir, *My Life* (New York: G. P. Putnam and Sons, 1975), p. 454.

105. Kissinger, *Years*, p. 796.
106. Remarks by Andrei Gromyko, December 21, 1973, as quoted in "Excerpts From the Opening Statements at the Geneva Conference on the Mideast," *New York Times*, December 21, 1973, p. 8.
107. Remarks by Henry Kissinger, December 21, 1973, as quoted in "Excerpts From the Opening Statements at the Geneva Conference on the Mideast," *New York Times*, December 21, 1973, p. 8.
108. This might have been the first time an American official used the term *legitimate* to describe Palestinian interests. By comparison, the Algiers Summit Resolution of the previous month said the PLO "is the sole representative of the Palestinian people." With precision, the Arab Summit addressed the specific issue of representation; with ambiguity, Kissinger addressed the amorphous issue of undefined rights.
109. Fahmy, *Negotiating for Peace*, p. 62. There are many other parts of Fahmy's recollection of the negotiating process that tend to overstate his importance in the process from 1973 until his resignation in November 1977.
110. Interview with Ismail Fahmy, Cairo, October 8, 1977, as quoted in *Foreign Broadcast Information Service, Daily Report—Middle East and North Africa*, October 11, 1977, p. D4.
111. Kissinger, *Years*, p. 797. In his interview with me, Rifa'i readily admitted that his speech at Geneva was harsher in tones than Fahmy's compendium of assaults against Israel.
112. Interviews with Abba Eban, March 24, 1992, Herzelia, Israel; and Zaid Rifa'i, January 9, 1993, Amman, Jordan.
113. Interview with Mordechai Gazit, March 22, 1992, Jerusalem, Israel.
114. Interview with Abba Eban, March 24, 1992, Herzelia, Israel; Abba Eban, *Personal Witness: Israel Through My Eyes* (New York: G. P. Putnam and Sons, 1992), p. 553.
115. Interview with Epi Evron, March 24, 1992, Ramat Aviv, Israel.
116. Remarks by Abba Eban, December 21, 1973, as quoted in "Excerpts From the Opening Statements at the Geneva Conference on the Mideast," *New York Times*, December 22, 1973, p. 8.
117. Interview with Abba Eban, March 24, 1992, Herzelia, Israel; see Golan, *Yom Kippur and After*, p. 166.
118. Interview with Zaid Rifa'i, January 9, 1993, Amman, Jordan.
119. Interview with Hermann F. Eilts, April 11, 1991, Boston.
120. Interview with Abba Eban, March 24, 1992, Herzelia, Israel.
121. Ibid.
122. U.S. State Department, "Middle East Peace Conference," telegram from Henry Kissinger to Department of State, December 23, 1973, Washington, D.C.
123. Ibid.

CHAPTER 6

1. Interview with Epi Evron, March 24, 1992, Ramat Aviv, Israel.
2. Interview with Nabil al-Arabi, February 26, 1993, Atlanta.
3. Interview with Michael Sterner, May 13, 1992, Washington, D.C.
4. U.S. State Department Briefing Paper, "Egyptian-Israel Disengagement Meetings in Geneva—Summary of First Six Sessions between Generals Magdoob and Gur," January 3, 1974 Washington, D.C.; U.S. State Department Six cables from Michael Sterner, Geneva to Department of State, December 27 and 28, 1973, and January 3, 4, 7, and 9, 1974 Washington, D.C.
5. Kissinger, *Years*, p. 800.
6. Kissinger, *Years*, p. 803. Dayan does not give a written version of these discussions with Kissinger in either of his two books, *Breakthrough: A Personal Account of Egypt-Israel*

Negotiations (London: Weidenfeld and Nicolson, 1981); and *Moshe Dayan: Story of My Life* (New York: William Morrow and Company, 1976).

7. Interview with Mordechai Gur, July 7, 1993, Jerusalem, Israel.

8. Memorandum by William B. Quandt, "Possible Disengagement Steps on the Jordanian-Israeli Front and Palestinian Developments," January 10, 1974. Washington, D.C.

9. U.S. State Department, Briefing Paper, "Egyptian-Israeli Disengagement: Phase II, 'E30,'" January 10, 1974. Washington, D.C.

10. Kissinger, *Years,* p. 815.

11. Remarks by Anwar Sadat to a U.S. Congressional delegation, July 13, 1977, as quoted in *Foreign Broadcast Information Service—Daily Report, Middle East and North Africa,* July 14, 1977, pp. D6–D7.

12. Walter Isaacson, *Kissinger* (New York: Simon and Schuster, 1992), p. 548. He correctly concluded from independent sources that "Sadat told Kissinger to seek the best possible numbers he could. Egypt would accept whatever he [Kissinger] could get out of Israel."

13. Mohamed Abdel Al-Ghani el-Gamasy, *The October War Memoirs of Field Marshall El-Gamasy of Egypt* (Cairo: American University in Cairo Press, 1993), p. 335.

14. Kissinger, *Years,* p. 822.

15. Interview with Omar Sirry, January 5, 1993, Cairo, Egypt; El-Gamasy, *The October War Memoirs,* pp. 336–37.

16. Interviews with Abd al-Ghani el-Gamasy, November 10, 1992, Heliopolis, Egypt; and Omar Sirry, January 5, 1993, Cairo, Egypt.

17. Interview with Omar Sirry, January 5, 1993, Cairo, Egypt.

18. Interview with Hafez Ismail, January 7, 1993, Cairo, Egypt.

19. Interview with Abd al-Ghani el-Gamasy, November 10, 1992, Heliopolis, Egypt.

20. El-Gamasy, *The October War Memoirs,* p. 337.

21. Kissinger, *Years,* p. 643.

22. Interview with Abba Eban, March 24, 1992, Herzelia, Israel.

23. U.S. State Department, "Memorandum of Understanding Between the United States Government and the Government of Israel," January 18, 1974, see appendix II, Washington, D.C.; William B. Quandt, *Peace Process, American Diplomacy, and the Arab-Israeli Conflict Since 1967* (Washington, D.C.: The Brookings Institution, 1993), pp. 197–200.

24. Interview with Hermann F. Eilts, April 11, 1991, Boston.

25. Interview with Hafez Ismail, January 7, 1993, Cairo, Egypt.

26. Remarks by Hal Saunders, United States Institute of Peace meeting, April 16, 1991, Washington, D.C.

27. Interview with Ismail Fahmy, November 9, 1992; Cairo, Egypt; Ismail Fahmy, *Negotiating for Peace in the Middle East* (Baltimore: Johns Hopkins University Press, 1983); and Daniel Dishon, "The Web of Inter-Arab Relations," *The Jerusalem Quarterly* 2 (winter 1977): 46–47.

28. *The Jerusalem Post,* January 29, 1974, p. 1.

29. Kissinger, *Years,* p. 885.

30. Remarks by Secretary of State Henry Kissinger, Hearings before the Committee on Foreign Relations United States Senate on Memoranda of Agreements Between the Governments of Israel and the United States, 94th Cong., 1st sess., October 6–7, 1975, p. 207.

31. Stephen F. Ambrose, *Nixon,* vol. 3 (New York: Simon and Schuster, 1991), pp. 292–97.

32. Interview with Harold Saunders, May 12, 1992, Washington, D.C.

33. Interview with Hermann F. Eilts, April 11, 1991, Boston.

34. Ibid.

35. Interview with Peter Rodman, June 10, 1992, Washington, D.C.

36. Separate interviews with Shlomo Gazit and Ariyeh Shalev, August 13, 1992, Ramat Aviv, Israel.
37. Interviews with Hermann F. Eilts, April 11, 1991, Boston, and Abd al-Halim Khaddam, July 18, 1993, Damascus, Syria. Abd al-Halim Khaddam confirmed that there was a commitment on the part of the Arab oil-producing countries "to exercise pressure on the United States of America in order to move for two reasons: move toward disengagement of the forces, and secondly, implementation of the UNSC Resolution 338."
38. Interviews with Roy Atherton, July 16, 1992, Washington, D.C.; and Fawzi Ibrashi, January 5, 1993, Cairo, Egypt. Fawzi Ibrashi agreed with Atherton's assessment.
39. Interview with Hafez Ismail, January 7, 1993, Cairo, Egypt.
40. "Saudi Arabia and Kuwait Give Syria Pledge on Oil Embargo," New York Times, February 5, 1974, p. 3.
41. Interviews with Ariyeh Shalev, August 13, 1992, Ramat Aviv, Israel; and Mordechai Gur, July 7, 1993, Jerusalem, Israel.
42. Interview with Peter Rodman, June 10, 1992, Washington, D.C.
43. Interview with Hermann F. Eilts, April 11, 1991, Boston.
44. On each of the visits I made with President Carter to Damascus, in March 1983, March 1987, and March 1990, we held lengthy meetings with President Assad. Later, when we visited Israel on the same Middle East trips, Israeli officials were invariably interested in learning about our impressions of him. By comparison, for decades Israeli political leaders had conducted hundreds of private meetings with King Hussein and had come to know him well.
45. Interview with Herzl Shafir, August 17, 1992, Ramat Hasharon, Israel.
46. Interview with Golda Meir, December 29, 1977, Tel Aviv, Israel.
47. Interview with Abd al-Halim Khaddam, July 19, 1993, Damascus, Syria.
48. Interview with Yossi Ciechanover, July 30, 1993, New York.
49. Remarks by Joseph Sisco, United States Institute of Peace meeting, April 16, 1991, Washington, D.C.
50. Interview with Hermann F. Eilts, April 11, 1991, Boston.
51. Galia Golan, Yom Kippur and After: The Soviet Union and the Middle East Crisis (Cambridge: Cambridge University Press, 1977), p. 223.
52. Interview with Patrick Theros, March 31, 1993, Atlanta.
53. Interview with Roy Atherton, July 16, 1992, Washington, D.C.
54. Remarks by Harold Saunders, United States Institute of Peace meeting, April 16, 1991, Washington, D.C.
55. Remarks by Peter Rodman, United States Institute of Peace meeting, April 16, 1991, Washington, D.C.
56. Interview with Roy Atherton, July 16, 1992, Washington, D.C. Atherton remembers detailed sessions lasting for four or five hours during the month of negotiations. These meetings required excruciating attention by the note takers and transcribers.
57. Remarks by Peter Rodman, United States Institute of Peace meeting, April 16, 1991, Washington, D.C.
58. Remarks by Joseph Sisco, United States Institute of Peace meeting, April 16, 1991, Washington, D.C. According to UN General Siilasvuo, the negotiations were "seemingly pedantic, over-particular . . . defined in great detail [with] endless distrust [and] continual hair splitting." Siilasvuo, In the Service of Peace, pp. 255–74.
59. Interview with Golda Meir, December 29, 1977, Tel Aviv, Israel.
60. Remarks by Peter Rodman, United States Institute of Peace meeting, April 16, 1991, Washington, D.C.
61. Golan, Yom Kippur and After, p. 224.
62. Interviews with Epi Evron, March 24, 1992, Ramat Aviv, Israel; and Meir Rosenne, August 6, 1992, Jerusalem, Israel.

63. Interview with Herzl Shafir, August 17, 1992, Ramat Hasharon, Israel.
64. Interview with Meir Rosenne, August 6, 1992, Jerusalem, Israel.
65. Ibid.
66. "But Israelis or Syrians Acted to Break Impasse," *New York Times,* May 31, 1974, p. 8.
67. Kissinger, *Years,* p. 1111.
68. Ambrose, *Nixon,* vol.3, p. 348.
69. William B. Quandt, *Decade of Decisions: American Policy Toward the Arab-Israeli Conflict, 1967–1976* (Berkeley and Los Angeles: University of California Press, 1977), pp. 245–56.
70. Ambrose, *Nixon,* vol.3, p. 356.
71. Kissinger, *Years,* p. 1128; and Ambrose, *Nixon,* vol. 3, p. 356.
72. Riad, *The Struggle for Peace,* p. 279.
73. Kissinger, *Years,* p. 1135.
74. Interview with Abd al-Halim Khaddam, July 18, 1993, Damascus, Syria.
75. Quandt, *Decade of Decisions,* p. 248.
76. Interview with Abd al-Halim Khaddam, July 18, 1993, Damascus, Syria.
77. Richard Nixon, *RN: The Memoirs of Richard Nixon* (New York: Filmways Company Publishers, 1978), p. 1015.
78. Ambrose, *Nixon,* vol.3, p. 359
79. Golan, *The Secret Conversations,* pp. 214–17.
80. Interview with Nicholis A. Veliotes, September 7, 1995, Washington, D.C.
81. Kissinger, *Years,* p. 1137.
82. Ibid., p. 1137.
83. Ibid., pp. 1141–42.
84. Interview with Ziad Rifa'i, January 9, 1993, Amman, Jordan.
85. Interviews with William B. Quandt, May 13, 1992, Washington, D.C.; and Ziad Rifa'i, January 9, 1993, Amman, Jordan.
86. Remarks by William B. Quandt, United States Institute of Peace meeting, April 16, 1991, Washington, D.C.
87. Remarks by Harold Saunders, United States Institute of Peace meeting, April 16, 1991, Washington, D.C.
88. Riad, *The Struggle for Peace,* p. 279.
89. Interview with Amos Eiran, June 20, 1998, New York.
90. Ibid.
91. Moshe Shemesh, *The Palestinian Entity, 1959–1974, Arab Politics and the PLO* (London: Frank Cass, 1988), pp. 294–95.
92. U.S. State Department, "Joint U.S. Soviet Communiques Dealing with the Middle East," in *U.S. Policy in the Middle East, December 1973–November 1974,* Special Report No. 12 (Washington, D.C.: Bureau of Public Affairs,1975), pp. 17–18.
93. See Secretary of State Kissinger's statement to the Senate Committee on Foreign Relations, June 7, 1974; see also a discussion with Joseph Sisco, March 27, 1974, U.S. State Department, *U.S. Policy in the Middle East, December 1973–November 1974,* Special Report No. 12,(Washington, D.C.: Bureau of Public Affairs, 1975), pp. 14–16.
94. Reuven Pedatzur, "Coming Back Full Circle: The Palestinian Option in 1967," *Middle East Journal* 49 (Spring 1995): 269–91.
95. Remarks by William B. Quandt, United States Institute of Peace meeting, April 16, 1991, A.M. session.
96. Shemesh, *The Palestinian Entity,* pp. 297–98.
97. Harold Saunders and Cecilia Albin, *Sinai II: The Politics of International Mediation* (paper prepared for the Foreign Policy Institute, School of Advanced International Studies, The Johns Hopkins University, Baltimore, June 1989), p. 37.
98. Shemesh, *The Palestinian Entity,* p. 305.
99. Interview with King Hussein, January 11, 1993, Amman, Jordan.

100. Interview with Nicholis A. Veliotes, September 7, 1995, Washington, D.C.
101. Ismail Fahmy, *Negotiating for Peace in the Middle East* (Baltimore: Johns Hopkins University Press, 1983), p. 99.
102. Interviews with King Hussein, January 11, 1993, Amman, Jordan; and Ziad Rifa'i, January 9, 1993, Amman, Jordan.
103. Interview with Hanan Bar-On, November 12, 1992, Jerusalem, Israel.
104. Interview with King Hussein, January 11, 1993, Amman, Jordan.
105. Interview with Avraham Sela, July 30, 1995, Jerusalem, Israel.
106. Yitzhak Rabin, *The Rabin Memoirs* (Boston: Little, Brown and Company, 1979), pp. 249–50.
107. Remarks by William B. Quandt, United States Institute of Peace meeting, April 16, 1991, Washington, D.C.
108. Remarks by Peter Rodman, United States Institute of Peace meeting, April 16, 1991, Washington, D.C.
109. Kissinger, *Years,* p. 1141.
110. Interview with Ziad Rifa'i, January 9, 1993, Amman, Jordan.
111. As quoted in Golan, *The Secret Conversations,* p. 226; and Walter Isaacson, *Kissinger* (New York: Simon and Schuster, 1992), p. 631.
112. Interview with Amos Eiran, June 20, 1998, New York.
113. Ibid.
114. Interview with Hermann F. Eilts, April 11, 1991, Boston.
115. Saunders and Albin, *Sinai II,* p. 42.
116. Interview with Hermann F. Eilts, April 11, 1991, Boston; Saunders and Albin, *Sinai II,* p. 50.
117. Interview with Omar Sirry, January 5, 1993, Cairo, Egypt.
118. Robert O. Freedman, *Soviet Policy Toward the Middle East Since 1970* (New York: Praeger, 1978), p. 179; see also Fahmy, *Negotiating for Peace,* pp. 142–51.
119. U.S. State Department, "Joint U.S. Soviet Communiqués Dealing with the Middle East," in *U.S. Policy in the Middle East, December 1973–November 1974,* Special Report no. 12 (Washington, D.C.: Bureau of Public Affairs, 1975), p. 18. The full communiqué of the Vladisvostok Summit may also be found in *New York Times,* November 25, 1974.
120. Interview with Hermann F. Eilts, April 11, 1991, Boston.
121. Fahmy, *Negotiating for Peace,* p. 144.
122. Freedman, *Soviet Policy,* pp. 191–95.
123. Interview with Hermann F. Eilts, April 11, 1991, Boston.
124. *Ha'aretz,* December 3, 1974; Quandt, *Decades of Decision,* p. 262.
125. Golan, *The Secret Conversations,* pp. 232–23; "Kissinger Hears Israelis on Sinai," *New York Times,* February 12, 1975, p. 1.
126. Gerald R. Ford, *A Time to Heal* (New York: Harper & Row, 1979), p. 245; remarks by Harold H. Saunders and Peter Rodman, United States Institute of Peace meeting, April 16, 1991, Washington, D.C.
127. Saunders and Albin, *Sinai II,* p. 40.
128. Yitzhak Rabin, *The Rabin Memoirs* (Boston: Little, Brown and Company, 1979), pp. 252, 255.
129. Interview with Hermann F. Eilts, April 11, 1991, Boston. See Saunders and Albin, *Sinai II,* pp. 67–68.
    According to Harold Saunders's personal State Department files, the first formulation that the Israelis accepted that explicitly did not use the term *nonbelligerency* was "Egypt and Israel hereby undertake in the relations between themselves not to resort to the use of force and to resolve all disputes between them by negotiations and other peaceful means. They will refrain from permitting, encouraging, assisting, or partici-

pating in any military, paramilitary, or hostile actions, from any warlike or hostile acts and any other form of warfare or hostile activity against the other party anywhere."

The second formulation agreed upon on March 20 by Israeli negotiators was "Egypt and Israel resolve that the conflict between them shall not be resolved by military means and can only be solved by peaceful means. They hereby undertake not to resort to the threat or use of force against each other and to settle all disputes between them by negotiations and other peaceful means. The parties will give written assurances to the U.S.G. to this effect. They reconfirm their obligation to scrupulously observe the ceasefire on land, sea, and air and to refrain from all military or paramilitary actions against each other and from assisting in military or paramilitary actions against the other party." See Saunders and Albin, *Sinai II,* pp. 67, 72.

130. Rabin, *Memoirs,* p. 254.
131. Saunders and Albin, *Sinai II,* pp. 74–75. Kissinger's admonition to Rabin relating the portent of failure in negotiations was similar in threatening tones, but not in content to the reproach that President Carter delivered to Israeli Foreign Minister Dayan when they negotiated the final contents of the Israeli-U.S. working paper on Geneva of October 4, 1977. See Dayan's recollection of that evening's discussion with Carter in which Carter said, "Understand the significance of our not reaching agreement. You will be isolated from the whole world," *Ma'ariv,* October 13, 1977. This is substantially confirmed by Zbigniew Brzezinski, *Power and Principle: Memoirs of the National Security Adviser, 1977–1981* (New York: Farrar Straus Giroux, 1983), pp. 108–9.
132. Nadav Safran, *Israel: The Embattled Ally* (Cambridge: Belknap Press, 1979), pp. 546–47.
133. Ibid., p. 548.
134. "White House Backs Israel, But it Avoids a Reply to 76 Senators," *New York Times,* May 23, 1975, p. 8.
135. Rabin, *Memoirs,* p. 263.
136. Ibid., pp. 263–65.
137. In their respective memoirs, Ford and Rabin made contradictory claims about whose idea it was for American civilians to monitor the strategic passes. Rabin attributed it to Israel, and Ford gave the credit to Sadat. Tahsin Bashir said Sadat suggested it to Ford in Salzburg. See Ford, *A Time,* p. 308; Rabin, *Memoirs,* p. 268; and interview with Tahsin Bashir, July 13, 1993, Cairo, Egypt.
138. Efraim Inbar, "Yitzhak Rabin and Israeli National Security," BESA Security and Policy Studies no. 25, Bar-Ilan University, Ramat-Gan, Israel, January 1996, p. 13.
139. Interview with Hermann F. Eilts, April 11, 1991, Boston. Remarks by Anwar Sadat before the Egyptian People's Assembly, January 21, 1978, as quoted in *Foreign Broadcast Information Service, Daily Report—Middle East and North Africa,* January 23, 1978, p. D10.
140. Interview with Hafez Ismail, January 7, 1993, Cairo, Egypt.
141. Interview with Abd al-Halim Khaddam, July 18, 1993, Damascus, Syria.
142. Daniel Dishon, "The Web of Inter-Arab Relations," *Jerusalem Quarterly* 2 (Winter 1977): pp. 51–52.
143. Interview with Meir Rosenne, August 6, 1992, Jerusalem, Israel. According to Rosenne, when Israel signed the peace treaty with Egypt in March 1979, a specific date was placed on Washington's commitment to supply Israel with oil.
144. William B. Quandt, *Camp David: Peacemaking and Politics* (Washington, D.C.: The Brookings Institution, 1986), p. 201.
145. Excerpt of letter taken from *Can Israel Survive a Palestinian State* (Jerusalem: 1990). In an interview with Abd al-Halim Khaddam on July 18, 1993; in Damascus, Syria, the Syrian vice president, who in 1975 was Syria's foreign minister, said that it was sixteen years later that Syria learned for the first time about this commitment to Israel. It was revealed to the Syrians during one of Secretary of State Baker's several visits to the Middle East in 1991.

146. Interview with Roy Atherton, October 22, 1992, Washington, D.C.
147. "U.S. Documents Accompanying the Sinai Accord," *New York Times,* September 18, 1975, p. 16.
148. Remarks by Anwar Sadat, February 9, 1978, Cairo Domestic Service, as quoted in *Foreign Broadcast Information Service, Daily Report—Middle East and North Africa,* February 10, 1978, p. D3.
149. Interview with Amos Eiran, June 20, 1998, New York.
150. Rabin, *Memoirs,* p. 290.
151. Interview with Michael Sterner, June 17, 1993, Washington, D.C.
152. Saunders and Albin, *Sinai II,* pp. 113–14.
153. U.S. State Department, text of U.S. reply to a Soviet proposal on reconvening the Middle East peace conference, December 1, 1975, Washington, D.C., *U.S. Policy in the Middle East: November 1974–February 1976, Selected Documents,* no. 4 (Washington, D.C.: Bureau of Public Affairs, 1976), p. 49.
154. Ibid., p. 49.
155. Interview with Hermann F. Eilts, April 11, 1991, Boston.
156. Interview with Nabil al-Arabi, February 26, 1993, Atlanta.
157. Israel Home Service, November 16, 1976, 0505 GMT, as quoted in BBC, *Summary of World Broadcasts,* November 17, 1976, ME/5366/A/3, Moshe Dayan Center for Middle Eastern and African Studies Library, Tel Aviv University, Tel Aviv, Israel.
158. Interview with Golda Meir, December 26, Tel Aviv, Israel.
159. Interview with Shlomo Avineri, July 6, 1993, Jerusalem, Israel.
160. Interview with Yahiel Kadishai, July 5, 1993, Tel Aviv, Israel.
161. Interview with Shlomo Avineri, July 6, 1993, Jerusalem, Israel.
162. Damascus Home Service, November 3, 1976, as quoted in BBC, *Summary of World Broadcasts,* November 5, 1976, ME/5356/A/2, Moshe Dayan Center for Middle Eastern and African Studies, Tel Aviv University, Ramat Aviv, Israel.
163. Interview with Hermann F. Eilts, April 11, 1991, Boston.
164. Remarks by Hermann F. Eilts, "A Symposium on Sadat and His Legacy: Egypt and the World, 1977–1997," The Washington Institute for Near East Policy, November 13, 1997, Washington, D.C.
165. Remarks by Hermann F. Eilts in Kenneth W. Stein (moderator), "The Camp David Accords" (The Carter Presidential Conference, Hofstra University, Hempstead, New York, November 1990); and interview with Hermann F. Eilts, April 11, 1991, Boston.
166. *Tishrin,* December 20, 1976, as quoted in BBC, *Summary of World Broadcasts,* December 22, 1976, ME/5396/A/1, Moshe Dayan Center for Middle Eastern and African Studies, Tel Aviv University, Ramat Aviv, Israel; see also Daniel Dishon, "The Web of Inter-Arab Relations," *Jerusalem Quarterly* 2 (Winter 1977): pp. 57–59.
167. "The Arab Peace Offensive," *Newsweek,* November 29, 1976, p. 45.
168. Interview with Roy Atherton, October 30, 1992, Washington, D.C.
169. Interview with Hermann F. Eilts, April 11, 1991, Boston.

<h2 style="text-align:center">CHAPTER 7</h2>

1. Jimmy Carter, *Keeping Faith: Memoirs of a President* (New York: Bantam Books, 1982), p. 278.
2. Interview with Zbigniew Brzezinski, October 30, 1992, Washington, D.C.
3. Remarks by William B. Quandt, United States Institute of Peace meeting, April 16, 1991, Washington, D.C.
4. Interview with Jimmy Carter, February 19, 1991, Atlanta.
5. Zbigniew Brzezinski, *Power and Principle: Memoirs of the National Security Adviser, 1977–1981* (New York: Farrar Straus Giroux, 1983), pp. 86–87.
6. Interview with Jimmy Carter, February 19, 1991, Atlanta.

7. William B. Quandt, *Camp David: Peacemaking and Politics* (Washington, D.C.: The Brookings Institution, 1986), pp. 40–41.
8. Interview with Shlomo Avineri, July 6, 1993, Jerusalem, Israel.
9. Remarks by Harold Saunders, United States Institute of Peace meeting, April 16, 1991, Washington, D.C.
10. Interview with Epi Evron, November 15, 1992, Ramat Aviv, Israel.
11. Ibid.
12. "Hussein Payments Only a Part CIA in Mideast: Extensive, Effective," pp. 1, A12. *Washington Post*, February 19, 1977; see also Seymour M. Hersh, *The Price of Power: Kissinger in the Nixon White House* (New York: Summit Books, 1983), pp. 215–16.
13. Ben Bradlee, *A Good Life: Newspapering and Other Adventures* (New York: Simon & Schuster Inc., 1995), pp. 424–27.
14. "Hussein Payments Only a Part CIA in Mideast: Extensive, Effective," *Washington Post*, February 22, 1977, pp. 1, A12.
15. Remarks by Harold Saunders, United States Institute of Peace meeting, April 16, 1991, Washington, D.C.
16. Interview with Abd al-Halim Khaddam, July 18, 1993, Damascus, Syria.
17. These meetings are all well summarized in Quandt's *Camp David*, pp. 44–95.
18. Interview with Roy Atherton, October 30, 1992, Washington, D.C.; Yitzhak Rabin, *The Rabin Memoirs* (Boston: Little, Brown and Company, 1979), p. 296.
19. Interview with Shlomo Avineri, July 6, 1993, Jerusalem, Israel.
20. Quandt, *Camp David*, p. 46.
21. Interviews with Amos Eiran, June 20, 1998, New York; and Dan Pattir, August 3, 1992, Jerusalem, Israel; and Hanan Bar-On, July 8, 1993, Jerusalem, Israel.
22. Interview with Jimmy Carter, February 19, 1991, Atlanta; see also Carter, *Keeping Faith*, p. 280.
23. Interview with Hanan Bar-On, November 12, 1992, Jerusalem, Israel.
24. Interview with Shlomo Avineri, July 6, 1993, Jerusalem, Israel.
25. "Clinton, Massachusetts: Remarks and a Question-And-Answer Session at the Clinton Town Meeting," *Public Papers: Carter* 1 (1977): p. 387.
26. Interview with April Glaspie, July 28, 1995, Jerusalem, Israel.
27. Interview with Roy Atherton, October 30, 1992, Washington, D.C.
28. Interview with Nicholis A. Veliotes, September 7, 1995, Washington, D.C.
29. Interview with Jimmy Carter, February 19, 1991, Atlanta.
30. Brzezinski, *Power and Principle*, p. 91.
31. Interview with Jimmy Carter, February 19, 1991, Atlanta.
32. Ibid. It is noteworthy that in his memoirs, *Keeping Faith*, Carter omits any mention of the Clinton town hall meeting or the use of the word "homeland." For Carter, there was almost no concern about breaking such a sensitive diplomatic egg in public. For years afterward, especially after Carter left office, I repeatedly and directly saw how that remark in Clinton, Massachusetts, endowed him with enormous and continued credibility among all Arabs, especially among Palestinians. They viewed him as a true friend who had basic sympathy for their plight, who was willing to oppose Israeli policy in public, and, above all, who was disposed to do so during, not only after, his presidency.
33. See James Reston, "How to Save Israel," *New York Times*, March 24, 1977, p. A9.
34. Remarks by Herman F. Eilts (presented at Conference on Sadat and His Legacy, Egypt and the World, 1977–1997, The Washington Institute for Near East Policy, November 13, 1997, Washington, D.C.).
35. Interview with Jimmy Carter, February 19, 1991, Atlanta.
36. Remarks by Anwar Sadat, February 6, 1978, Cairo Domestic Service, as quoted in *Foreign Broadcast Information Service—Middle East and North Africa*, February 8, 1978, p. D2; interview with David Korn, October 29, 1992, Washington, D.C.; and remarks by Hermann

F. Eilts in Kenneth W. Stein (moderator), "The Camp David Accords" (The Carter Presidential Conference, Hofstra University, Hempstead, New York, November 1990).

37. Interviews with Jimmy Carter, February 19, 1991, Atlanta; and Ashraf Ghorbal, November 9, 1992, Cairo, Egypt. Remarks by Hermann F. Eilts in Kenneth W. Stein (moderator), "The Camp David Accords" (The Carter Presidential Conference, Hofstra University, Hempstead, New York, November 1990).

38. Interview with Jimmy Carter, February 19, 1991, Atlanta; also see Carter, Keeping Faith, p. 310.

39. Remarks by Anwar Sadat, February 6, 1978, Cairo Domestic Service, as quoted in Foreign Broadcast Information Service—Middle East and North Africa, February 8, 1978, p. D2.

40. Interview with Jimmy Carter, February 19, 1991, Atlanta.

41. Remarks by Hermann F. Eilts in Kenneth W. Stein (moderator), "The Camp David Accords" (The Carter Presidential Conference, Hofstra University, Hempstead, New York, November 1990).

42. Interviews with Stuart Eisenstat, September 14, 1993, Atlanta; and Zbigniew Brzezinski, October 30, 1992, Washington, D.C.

43. Interview with Hermann F. Eilts, April 11, 1991, Boston; see also Carter, Keeping Faith, pp. 282–84.

44. Interview with Jimmy Carter, February 19, 1991, Atlanta.

45. Interview with Zbigniew Brzezinski, October 30, 1992, Washington, D.C.

46. Interview with Jimmy Carter, February 19, 1991, Atlanta.

47. Ibid.

48. Quandt, Camp David, p. 56. In Jimmy Carter's The Blood of Abraham: Insights into the Middle East (New York: Houghton-Mifflin, 1985), which I helped write, Carter gives only a partial rendition of the conversation and detail he discussed with Assad in Geneva. Incidently, here again Carter made no mention of his public endorsement of a Palestinian homeland, or his public satisfaction with what he claimed might be Assad's flexibility in future negotiations.

49. Interview with Abd al-Halim Khaddam, July 18, 1993, Damascus, Syria.

50. Interview with Zbigniew Brzezinski, October 30, 1992, Washington, D.C.; and Brzezinski, Power and Principle, pp. 94–95.

51. Interview with Jimmy Carter, February 19, 1991, Atlanta.

52. Carter, Keeping Faith, p. 286.

53. Interview with Nicholas A. Veliotes, September 7, 1995, Washington, D.C.

54. Remarks by William B. Quandt, United States Institute of Peace meeting, April 16, 1991, Washington, D.C.

55. Interview with Zbigniew Brzezinski, October 30, 1992, Washington, D.C.

56. Interview with Samuel W. Lewis, February 28, 1992, Washington, D.C.

57. Interview with Yahiel Kadishai, July 5, 1993, Tel Aviv, Israel.

58. Interview with Eliyahu Ben-Elisar, July 6, 1993, Jerusalem, Israel.

59. Interview with Avraham Sela, July 30, 1995, Jerusalem, Israel.

60. Interview with Eliyahu Ben-Elisar, July 6, 1997, Jerusalem, Israel.

61. Interview with Samuel W. Lewis, February 28, 1992, Washington, D.C.

62. Begin made a point of not taking his new foreign minister, Moshe Dayan, with him on his first visit to the United States. Begin made it clear that he was going to conduct foreign policy and Dayan would be his representative. Begin trusted Dayan, but cautiously, knowing that Dayan "sometimes drew the blanket to cover his ass." Later, in October, after the issuance of the U.S.-U.S.S.R. communiqué and the U.S.-Israeli working paper about Geneva, Begin became less comfortable with what he saw as Dayan's increasing willingness to make decisions without Begin's prior approval. Interviews with Eliyahu Ben-Elisar, November 13, 1992, Jerusalem, Israel; and Epi Evron, November 15, 1992, Ramat Aviv, Israel.

63. Interview with Zbigniew Brzezinski, October 30, 1992, Washington, D.C.
64. Interview with Samuel W. Lewis, February 28, 1992, Washington, D.C.
65. Interview with Jimmy Carter, April 23, 1991, Atlanta.
66. Remarks by Menachem Begin to Knesset, July 27, 1977, as quoted in *Foreign Broadcast Information Service, Daily Report—Middle East and North Africa,* July 28, 1977, p. N2; see also Jerusalem Domestic Service, July 19, 1977, as quoted in *Foreign Broadcast Information Service, Daily Report—Middle East and North Africa,* July 20, 1977, p. N1.
67. Interview with Yahiel Kadishai, July 5, 1993, Tel Aviv, Israel.
68. Moshe Dayan, *Breakthrough: A Personal Account of Egypt-Israel Negotiations* (London: Weidenfeld and Nicolson, 1981), p. 19. Epi Evron, then an adviser to the prime minister on foreign affairs and later Israel's ambassador to Washington, remarked to me on November 15, 1992, that the account in Dayan's memoir, *Breakthrough,* of the events of the summer and fall of 1977 are the most accurate ones that he had read.
69. Remarks by Hafez al-Assad on August 9, 1977, as quoted in *Foreign Broadcast Information Service, Daily Report—Middle East and North Africa,* August 10, 1977, p. H1.
70. Interview with Hafez al-Assad, *Newsweek,* August 1, 1977, p. 30.
71. Dayan, *Breakthrough,* pp. 18–19.
72. Carter, *Keeping Faith,* pp. 290–91.
73. Remarks by Menachem Begin, Jerusalem Domestic Service, July 25, 1977, as quoted in *Foreign Broadcast Information Service, Daily Report—Middle East and North Africa,* July 26, 1977, p. N1.
74. Dayan, *Breakthrough,* p. 21; Carter, *Keeping Faith,* p. 291.
75. Interview with Yahiel Kadishai, July 2, 1993, Tel Aviv, Israel.
76. Interviews with Hanan Bar-On, November 12, 1992, Jerusalem, Israel; Eliyahu Ben-Elisar, November 13, 1992, Jerusalem, Israel; and Moshe Arens, November 16, 1992, Tel Aviv, Israel.
77. Interview with Zbigniew Brzezinski, October 30, 1992, Washington, D.C. See also Brzezinski, *Power and Principle,* p. 101.
78. Remarks by Eliyahu Ben-Elisar (presented at Conference on Sadat and His Legacy, Egypt and the World, 1977–1997, The Washington Institute for Near East Policy, November 13, 1997, Washington, D.C.); and interview with Moshe Arens, November 16, 1992, Tel Aviv, Israel.
79. Interview with Eliyahu Ben-Elisar, November 13, 1992, Jerusalem, Israel. (Ben-Elisar accompanied Begin on this trip to Washington.)
80. Interviews with Yahiel Kadishai, July 5, 1993, Tel Aviv, Israel; and Yitzhak Shamir, November 16, 1992, Tel Aviv, Israel. Yitzhak Shamir, who followed Begin as prime minister, held the same view. He said, "In our view, the withdrawal from Sinai has implemented the demands of 242, of a withdrawal from the occupied territories."
81. Remarks by King Hussein, Baghdad Domestic Service, October 11, 1977, as quoted in *Foreign Broadcast Information Service, Daily Report—Middle East and North Africa,* October 12, 1977, p. A2.
82. Helena Cobban, *The Palestine Liberation Organization: People, Power, and Politics* (London: Cambridge University Press, 1984), pp. 88–90.
83. Interview of Syrian President Hafez al-Assad to *New York Times* senior editor John Oakes, as quoted in *Foreign Broadcast Information Service, Daily Report—Middle East and North Africa,* August 31, 1977, p. H6.
84. Brzezinski, *Power and Principle,* p. 102.
85. Cyrus Vance, *Hard Choices: Critical Years in America's Foreign Policy* (New York: Simon and Schuster, 1983), p. 186. According to Jimmy Carter's recollection, Vance threatened to resign four or five times on issues of principle. He finally did resign over the administration's decision to use force in April 1980, when it tried to rescue the Americans held hostage in Iran.

86. Brzezinski, *Power and Principle,* p. 102.
87. Interview with David Korn, October 29, 1992, Washington, D.C.; Brzezinski, *Power and Principle,* p. 102, and Quandt, *Camp David,* p. 105.
88. Remarks by Anwar Sadat to a U.S. congressional delegation, July 13, 1977, as quoted in *Foreign Broadcast Information Service, Daily Report—Middle East and North Africa,* July 14, 1977, p. D8.
89. Interview with William B. Quandt, May 13, 1992, Washington, D.C.
90. Ismail Fahmy, *Negotiating for Peace in the Middle East* (Baltimore: Johns Hopkins University Press, 1983), pp. 217–18; and Quandt, *Camp David,* pp. 104–7.
91. Quandt, *Camp David,* p. 105.
92. Interview with Epi Evron, November 15, 1992, Ramat Aviv, Israel; see also Dayan, *Breakthrough,* pp. 35–37.
93. Interviews with Yahiel Kadishai, July 5, 1993, Tel Aviv Israel; Eliyahu Ben-Elisar, July 6, 1993, Jerusalem, Israel; and Mordechai Zippori, July 7, 1993, Jerusalem, Israel.
94. Dayan, *Breakthrough,* p. 45. See also Mohamad Ibrahim Kamal, *The Camp David Accords* (New York: Metheun Inc., Routledge & Kegan Paul, 1986), pp. 194–96; and Mark A. Bruzonsky, "Interview with Mohamad Ibrahim Kamel," *The Middle East Journal* 38 (Winter 1984): pp. 85–98.
95. Hassan Tuhami, "Now I Can Speak About the Initiative," *October Magazine,* November 21, 1982, pp. 19–21.
96. Dayan, *Breakthrough,* p. 46.
97. Quandt, *Camp David,* p. 108.
98. Dayan, *Breakthrough,* p. 48.
99. Interviews with Samuel W. Lewis, February 28, 1992, Washington, D.C.; Dan Pattir, August 3, 1992, Tel Aviv, Israel; Moshe Sasson, August 6, 1992, Jerusalem, Israel; Yossi Ciechanover, July 5, 1993, Tel Aviv, Israel; and Naftali Lavi, July 8, 1993, Jerusalem, Israel.
100. Interview with Yahiel Kadishai, July 5, 1993, Tel Aviv, Israel.
101. Interview with Mustapha Khalil, July 14, 1993, Cairo, Egypt.
102. Tuhami, "Now I Can Speak," pp. 19–21.
103. Interview with Eliyahu Ben-Elisar, November 13, 1992, Jerusalem, Israel.
104. Dayan, *Breakthrough,* p. 53.
105. Tuhami, "Now I Can Speak," pp. 19–21.
106. Carter, *Keeping Faith,* p. 294.
107. Remarks by Hermann F. Eilts, "A Symposium on Sadat and His Legacy: Egypt and the World, 1977–1997" (The Washington Institute for Near East Policy, November 13, 1997, Washington, D.C).
108. Interview with Naftali Lavi, July 8, 1993, Jerusalem, Israel.
109. Interview with Hanan Bar-On, November 12, 1993, Jerusalem, Israel.
110. Brzezinski, *Power and Principle,* pp. 105–7.
111. Dayan, *Breakthrough,* pp. 56–64. The details of these meetings with Vance and Carter on September 19, 1977, are the most thorough and penetrating in comparison to other meetings he recounted in his book.
112. Interview with Hanan Bar-On, November 12, 1992, Jerusalem, Israel.
113. Dayan, *Breakthrough,* p. 59.
114. Interview with Naftali Lavi, July 8, 1993, Jerusalem, Israel.
115. William B. Quandt to Zbigniew Brzezinski, "Dayan's Views on Arab-Israeli Peace," October 1, 1977, from the files of William B. Quandt, The Carter Presidential Library Archives, Atlanta.
116. Quandt, *Camp David,* pp. 112–13.
117. Ibid.
118. Dayan, *Breakthrough,* p. 62.

119. Interview with Hanan Bar-On, November 12, 1993, Jerusalem, Israel.
120. Quandt, *Camp David,* pp. 115–16.
121. Interview by Yoel Marcus with Moshe Dayan, *Ha'aretz,* September 29, 1977, pp. 1-2.
122. Remarks by Syrian Defense Minister Mustafa Talas, Damascus Radio, October 7, 1977, as quoted in *Foreign Broadcast Information Service, Daily Report—Middle East and North Africa,* October 7, 1977, p. H1.
123. Brzezinski, *Power and Principle,* pp. 87–88.
124. Interview with Zbigniew Brzezinski, October 30, 1992, Washington, D.C.; and Brzezinski, *Power and Principle,* p. 87.
125. Interviews with Jimmy Carter, February 19, 1991, Atlanta; and Michael Sterner, June 17, 1993, Washington, D.C. Vance was adamant that the communiqué be issued.
126. Interviews with Roy Atherton, October 30, 1992, Washington, D.C.; and Michael Sterner, June 17, 1993, Washington, D.C.
127. Interview with Roy Atherton, October 30, 1992, Washington, D.C.
128. Ibid.
129. Ibid.
130. Interview with David Korn, October 29, 1992, Washington, D.C. See also remarks by Harold Saunders and William B. Quandt in Kenneth W. Stein (moderator), "The Camp David Accords" (The Carter Presidential Conference, Hofstra University, Hempstead, New York, November 1990); interview with William B. Quandt, May 13, 1992, Washington, D.C.
131. Interview with William B. Quandt, May 13, 1992, Washington, D.C.
132. Interview with David Korn, October 29, 1992, Washington, D.C.
133. Interview with Zbigniew Brzezinski, October 29, 1992, Washington, D.C.; and Quandt, *Camp David,* p. 122.
134. Interview with Jimmy Carter, February 19, 1991, Atlanta. It is interesting to note what candidate Carter said in May 1976 about future Soviet involvement in the peace process: "After unpublicized negotiations between us and the Soviet Union, we might jointly make a public proposal of a solution to the Middle East. . . . The Soviet Union is going to have to participate in a forceful way before Syria will be answerable to any productive negotiations with Israel." *Chicago Daily News,* May 8, 1976.
135. Interview with Naftali Lavi, July 8, 1993, Jerusalem, Israel.
136. Remarks by Anwar Sadat in a speech to the Arab Socialist Union Central committee meeting, July 16, 1977, as quoted in *Foreign Broadcast Information Service, Daily Report—Middle East and North Africa,* July 18, 1977, p. D29.
137. Interview with Jimmy Carter, April 23, 1991, Atlanta.
138. Remarks by Moshe Dayan, Jerusalem Domestic Service, November 23, 1977, as quoted in *Foreign Broadcast Information Service, Daily Report—Middle East and North Africa,* November 25, 1977, pp. N1–N11.
139. Interviews with Naftali Lavi, July 8, 1993, Jerusalem, Israel; and William B. Quandt, May 13, 1992, Washington, D.C. Quandt also remembers Dayan saying at this juncture, "It is none of our business."
140. Interview with Michael Sterner, June 17, 1993, Washington, D.C.
141. Interview with Moshe Dayan, *Yediot Aharanot,* October 3, 1977, pp. 1–2.
142. Interview with Eliyahu Ben-Elisar, November 13, 1992, Jerusalem, Israel.
143. Interview with Hanan Bar-On, November 12, 1992, Jerusalem, Israel.
144. Remarks by Yitzhak Rabin, as quoted from Jerusalem Domestic Service in *Foreign Broadcast Information Service, Daily Report—Middle East and North Africa,* October 3, 1977, p. N5.
145. "Statement on Geneva Conference," Cairo Voice of Palestine, as quoted in *Foreign Broadcast Information Service, Daily Report—Middle East and North Africa,* October 3, 1977, pp. A1-A2.

146. Interview with Stuart Eisenstat, September 14, 1993, Atlanta.
147. Interview with Zbigniew Brzezinski, October 30, 1992, Washington, D.C.
148. Interview with Roy Atherton, October 30, 1992, Washington, D.C.
149. Interview with Hanan Bar-On, November 12, 1992, Jerusalem, Israel.
150. Various detailed and rather consistent recollections of this crucial meeting can be found in Brzezinski, *Power and Principle*, pp. 108–9; Dayan, *Breakthrough*, pp. 66–72; and Quandt, *Camp David*, pp. 126–31.
151. See remarks by Moshe Dayan, *Ma'ariv*, October 13, 1977, p. 1. This is substantially confirmed in Brzezinski, *Power and Principle*, pp. 108–9.
152. Interview with Meir Rosenne, August 6, 1992, Jerusalem, Israel.
153. Interview with Zbigniew Brzezinski, October 30, 1992, Washington, D.C.
154. This is not the official text of what was termed "Suggestions for the Resumption of the Geneva Peace Conference." Portions of the text, from which this version was taken, appeared in Dayan, *Breakthrough*, pp. 70–71, and the *Jerusalem Post*, October 13, 1977. For details about the contents of the procedures agreed upon between the Carter administration and Israel for a reconvened Geneva Conference, see remarks by Moshe Dayan, October 11, 1977, Israeli Defense Forces Radio, as quoted in *Foreign Broadcast Information Service, Daily Report—Middle East and North Africa*, October 12, 1977, pp. N3–4.
155. Remarks by Moshe Dayan, Jerusalem Domestic Service, October 11, 1977, and interview with Moshe Dayan, Jerusalem Domestic Service, October 15, 1977, as quoted in *Foreign Broadcast Information Service, Daily Report—Middle East and North Africa*, October 12, 1977, p. N2, and October 15, 1977, p. N3.
156. In a press conference, before delivering a speech to Jewish communal leaders in Atlanta in October 1977, Dayan said that Israel was not going to be picky about the political orientation of Palestinians with whom Israel would negotiate. He said, "Anachnu lo bodkim et hatzizit shelahem" ("We are not going to check their fringes" [to see what they look like]). This was a reference to how Orthodox Jews are measured by the traditional fringes worn under their outer garments. Dayan meant that Israel would not check to see if the Palestinians wore the fringes of the PLO. Later in October and in 1978, Dayan's phrase was liberally translated to, "Israel would not check their passports."
157. See the commentary by Yoel Marcus in *Ha'aretz*, October 11, 1977, p. 11.
158. Interview with Moshe Dayan, Jerusalem Domestic Television Service, October 5, 1977, as quoted in *Foreign Broadcast Information Service, Daily Report—Middle East and North Africa*, October 6, 1977, p. N2.
159. Interviews with Eliyahu Ben-Elisar, November 13, 1992, Jerusalem, Israel; and Epi Evron, November 15, 1992, Ramat Aviv, Israel.
160. Remarks by Anwar Sadat, *October Magazine*, April 9, 1993, as quoted in *Foreign Broadcast Information Service, Daily Report—Middle East and North Africa*, April 10, 1978, p. D8.
161. Interview with Nicholas A. Veliotes, September 7, 1995, Washington, D.C.
162. Remarks by Syrian Foreign Minister Abd al-Halim Khaddam, Damascus Domestic Service, October 24, 1977, as quoted in *Foreign Broadcast Information Service, Daily Report—Middle East and North Africa*, October 25, 1977, p. C2. Sadat confirmed this Syrian attitude in his remarks before the Egyptian People's Assembly on November 26, 1977, as quoted in *Foreign Broadcast Information Service, Daily Report—Middle East and North Africa*, November 28, 1977, p. D9.
163. Interview with Ashraf Ghorbal, November 9, 1992, Cairo, Egypt.
164. Remarks by Jimmy Carter before Emory University students, November 16, 1989, Atlanta.
165. Quandt, *Camp David*, p. 143.
166. Ariel Sharon, *Ariel Sharon: An Autobiography* (New York: Simon & Schuster, 1989), p. 399. Interviews with Meir Rosenne, August 6, 1992, Jerusalem, Israel; and Ashraf Ghorbal, November 9, 1992, Cairo, Egypt. In June 1979 in Ismailiya with Meir Rosenne present,

Sadat told Dayan about the events leading up to his visit to Jerusalem, including discussion about this visit to Romania.

167. Interview with Walid Mouallem, July 17, 1993, Damascus, Syria.

168. Remarks by Nicolae Ceausescu, October 30, 1997, Bucharest Domestic Service; and remarks by Anwar Sadat, October 30, 1977, Cairo, MENA, as quoted in *Foreign Broadcast Information Service, Daily Report—Eastern Europe*, October 31, 1977, pp. H4 and H6, respectively.

169. Interview with Moshe Sasson, August 6, 1992, Jerusalem, Israel. Syrian President Assad claimed that Sadat did not tell the Saudis about his pending trip to Jerusalem. Interview with Hafez al-Assad, *Al-Akhbar* (Cairo), September 20, 1993, as quoted in *Foreign Broadcast Information Service—Near East and South Asia*, September 23, 1993, p. 47.

170. Interview with Mustapha Khalil, July 14, 1993, Cairo, Egypt.

171. Interview with Anwar Sadat on Cairo television, November 4, 1977, as quoted in *Foreign Broadcast Information Service—Near East and South Asia*, November 7, 1977, p. D5.

172. Brzezinski, *Power and Principle*, p. 111.

173. Interview with Zbigniew Brzezinski, October 30, 1992, Washington, D.C.

174. Interview with Anwar Sadat on Cairo television, November 4, 1977, as quoted in *Foreign Broadcast Information Service—Near East and South Asia*, November 7, 1977, p. D7.

175. Remarks by Hermann F. Eilts, "A Symposium on Sadat and His Legacy: Egypt and the World, 1977–1997" (The Washington Institute for Near East Policy, November 13, 1997, Washington, D.C.).

176. Remarks by Anwar Sadat to U.S. congressional delegations, November 12, 1977, and November 15, 1977, Cairo, MENA as quoted in *Foreign Broadcast Information Service—Near East and South Asia*, November 14, 1977, pp. D1–D9, and November 16, 1977, pp. D1–D6.

177. Remarks by Menachem Begin, November 15, 1977, Jerusalem Domestic Service, as quoted in *Foreign Broadcast Information Service—Near East and South Asia*, November 16, 1977, p. N2.

178. Interview with Avraham Sela, July 30, 1995, Jerusalem, Israel.

179. Remarks by Moshe Dayan, Jerusalem Domestic Service, November 16, 1977, as quoted in *Foreign Broadcast Information Service—Near East and South Asia*, November 16, 1977, pp. N1–N13.

180. Remarks by Hermann F. Eilts, "A Symposium on Sadat and His Legacy: Egypt and the World, 1977–1997" (The Washington Institute for Near East Policy, November 13, 1997, Washington, D.C.).

181. Interview with Mustapha Khalil, July 14, 1993, Cairo, Egypt.

182. Interview with Moshe Sasson, August 6, 1992, Jerusalem, Israel.

183. Remarks by Hermann F. Eilts, "A Symposium on Sadat and His Legacy: Egypt and the World, 1977–1997" (The Washington Institute for Near East Policy, November 13, 1997, Washington, D.C.).

184. Interview with Samuel W. Lewis, February 28, 1992, Washington, D.C.

185. Remarks by William B. Quandt, United States Institute of Peace meeting, April 16, 1991, Washington, D.C.; interviews with Samuel W. Lewis, February 28, 1992, Washington, D.C.; Meir Rosenne, August 6, 1992, Jerusalem, Israel; and David Korn, October 29, 1992, Washington, D.C.

186. Interview with Dan Pattir, August 3, 1992, Jerusalem, Israel.

187. Fahmy, *Negotiating for Peace*, pp. 252–84.

188. Interview with Golda Meir, December 29, 1977, Tel Aviv, Israel.

189. Begin "Israel Does Not Wish to Rule and Does Not Want to Disturb or Divide," *New York Times*, November 21, 1977, p. 17.

190. Interview with Golda Meir, December 26, 1977, Tel Aviv, Israel.

191. Remarks by Menachem Begin at the Israeli Parliament, January 23, 1978, as quoted in *Foreign Broadcast Information Service, Daily Report—Middle East and North Africa,* January 24, 1978, p. N1.
192. Interview with Epi Evron, March 24, 1992, Ramat Aviv, Israel.
193. Interview with Samuel W. Lewis, February 28, 1992, Washington, D.C.
194. Remarks by Moshe Dayan, *Jerusalem Post,* November 23, 1977.

CHAPTER 8

1. Remarks by Anwar Sadat, Cairo Domestic Service, November 20, 1977, *October Magazine,* as quoted in *Foreign Broadcast Information Service, Daily Report—Middle East and North Africa,* November 22, 1977, p. D2.
2. Remarks by Mouaffak el-Allaf at the United Nations General Assembly, November 22, 1977, as quoted in "Egypt Leaves U.N. Debate as Syria Attacks Sadat," *New York Times,* November 23, 1977, p. 3.
3. Damascus Domestic Service, November 22, 1977, as quoted in *Foreign Broadcast Information Service, Daily Report—Middle East and North Africa,* November 22, 1977, p. H2.
4. Interview with William B. Quandt, May 13, 1992, Washington, D.C.
5. Remarks by Hermann F. Eilts in Kenneth W. Stein (moderator), "The Camp David Accords" (The Carter Presidential Conference, Hofstra University, Hempstead, New York, November 1990).
6. Interview with William B. Quandt, May 13, 1992, Washington, D.C.
7. Interview with Samuel W. Lewis, February 28, 1992, Washington, D.C.
8. William B. Quandt, *Camp David: Peacemaking and Politics* (Washington, D.C.: The Brookings Institution, 1986), p. 177.
9. Jimmy Carter, *Keeping Faith: Memoirs of a President* (New York: Bantam Books, 1982), pp. 298–300.
10. Interview with Roy Atherton, October 30, 1992, Washington, D.C.
11. For Jabotinsky's remarks on autonomy, see "The Arab Question without Dramatism," in Zev Jabotinsky, *Hazit HaMilhamah shel 'Am Yisrael* (Jerusalem: Lipshutz Press, 1941), pp. 182–92. I am indebted to Yahiel Kadishai for his clear and unambiguous explanation of Begin's concept of autonomy. Interview with Samuel W. Lewis, February 28, 1992, Washington, D.C. See Harvey Sicherman, *Palestinian Autonomy, Self-Government, and Peace* (Boulder: Westview Press, 1993), p. 24.
12. Interview with Epi Evron, March 24, 1992, Ramat Aviv, Israel.
13. Interview with Yossi Ciechanover, July 5, 1993, Tel Aviv, Israel.
14. Interview with Hanan Bar-On, November 12, 1992, Jerusalem, Israel.
15. Interview with Eliyahu Ben-Elisar, November 13, 1992, Jerusalem, Israel.
16. Remarks by William B. Quandt, United States Institute of Peace meeting, April 16, 1991, Washington, D.C.
17. Interview with Samuel W. Lewis, February 28, 1992, Washington, D.C.
18. Carter, *Keeping Faith,* p. 300; see also Mohamed Ibrahim Kamel, *The Camp David Accords* (New York: Metheun Inc., Routledge & Kegan Paul, 1986), p. 82.
19. Colin Legum, ed., *Middle East Contemporary Survey, vol. I, 1976–1977* (New York: Holmes and Meier, 1978), p. 95.
20. Interview with David Korn, October 29, 1992, Washington, D.C.
21. Interview with Eliyahu Ben-Elisar, November 13, 1992, Jerusalem, Israel.
22. Remarks by William B. Quandt, United States Institute of Peace meeting, April 16, 1991, Washington, D.C.
23. Carter, *Keeping Faith,* p. 298.

24. Remarks by Anwar Sadat before the Egyptian People's Assembly, January 21, 1978, as quoted in *Foreign Broadcast Information Service, Daily Report—Middle East and North Africa,* January 23, 1978, p. D5.

25. Interview with Epi Evron, March 24, 1992, Ramat Aviv, Israel.

26. Interview with Eliyahu Ben-Elisar, November 13, 1992, Jerusalem, Israel.

27. Interviews with Samuel W. Lewis, February 28, 1992, Washington, D.C.; Epi Evron, March 24, 1992, Ramat Aviv, Israel; and Roy Atherton, July 16, 1992, Washington, D.C.

28. Interview with Anwar Sadat for Mexican television, January 2, 1978, as quoted in *Foreign Broadcast Information Service, Daily Report—Middle East and North Africa,* January 3, 1978, p. D10.

29. Interviews with Meir Rosenne, August 6, 1992, Jerusalem, Israel; and Samuel W. Lewis, February 28, 1992, Washington, D.C.

30. Interview with Esmat Abdel-Meguid, July 14, 1993, Cairo, Egypt.

31. Interview with Michael Sterner, June 17, 1993, Washington, D.C.

32. Interview with Eliyahu Ben-Elisar, November 13, 1992, Jerusalem, Israel.

33. Interview with Dan Pattir, August 3, 1992, Jerusalem, Israel.

34. Interview with Ezer Weizman, *Ma'ariv,* March 24, 1978.

35. Kamel, *The Camp David Accords,* p. 22.

36. Interview with Michael Sterner, June 17, 1993, Washington, D.C.

37. Kamel, *The Camp David Accords,* p. 24.

38. Remarks by Menachem Begin before the Israeli Parliament, February 15, 1978, as quoted in *Foreign Broadcast Information Service, Daily Report—Middle East and North Africa,* February 16, 1978, p. N3.

39. Avraham Tamir, *A Soldier in Search of Peace: An Insider's Look at Israel's Strategy in the Middle East* (New York: Harper and Row, 1988), p. 18.

40. Moshe Dayan, *Breakthrough: A Personal Account of Egypt-Israel Negotiations* (London: Weidenfeld and Nicolson, 1981), p. 103.

41. Tamir, *A Soldier,* p. 19.

42. Remarks by Menachem Begin, January 19, 1978, as quoted in *Foreign Broadcast Information Service, Daily Report—Middle East and North Africa,* January 19, 1978, p. N15.

43. Tamir, *A Soldier,* pp. 19–20.

44. Remarks by Husni Mubarak, Cairo Domestic Radio, January 3, 1997, as quoted in *Foreign Broadcast Information Service, Daily Report—Middle East and North Africa,* January 3, 1997.

45. Carter, *Keeping Faith,* p. 300.

46. Remarks by William B. Quandt, United States Institute of Peace meeting, April 16, 1991, Washington, D.C.

47. Remarks by Anwar Sadat, Cairo Domestic Service, December 30, 1977, as quoted in *Foreign Broadcast Information Service, Daily Report—Middle East and North Africa,* January 3, 1978, p. D10.

48. Remarks by Yasir Arafat, *London Guardian,* January 3, 1978.

49. "West Bank Mayors Oppose Begin's Plan," Voice of Palestine, December 30, 1977, as quoted in *Foreign Broadcast Information Service—Near East and South Asia,* January 5, 1978, p. A2.

50. Interview with Samuel W. Lewis, February 28, 1992, Washington, D.C.

51. Interview with Roy Atherton, October 30, 1992, Washington, D.C.; and remarks by William B. Quandt, United States Institute of Peace meeting, April 16, Washington, D.C.

52. Remarks by Menachem Begin, January 11, 1978, Paris Domestic Service, as quoted in *Foreign Broadcast Information Service, Daily Report—Middle East and North Africa,* January 12, 1978, p. N1.

53. Interview with Ahmed Maher, July 29, 1993, Washington, D.C.

54. Interview with Moshe Dayan, Jerusalem Domestic Service, December 30, 1977, as quoted in *Foreign Broadcast Information Service, Daily Report—Middle East and North Africa,* January 3, 1978, p. N5. See also Dayan, *Breakthrough,* p. 104.

55. Remarks by General Abd al-Ghani el-Gamasy, 11 January 1978, Cairo, MENA, as quoted in *Foreign Broadcast Information Service, Daily Report—Middle East and North Africa,* January 12, 1978, p. D2.

56. Interview with Moshe Sasson, August 10, 1992, Jerusalem, Israel.

57. Tamir, *A Soldier,* p. 24.

58. Interview with Avraham Sela, July 30, 1995, Washington, D.C.

59. Egypt's six points as presented by President Sadat to the Egyptian People's Assembly, January 21, 1978, as quoted in *Foreign Broadcast Information Service, Daily Report—Middle East and North Africa,* January 23, 1978, pp. D13-D14.

60. Interview with Ahmed Maher, July 29, 1993, Washington, D.C.

61. Kamel, *The Camp David Accords,* p. 58.

62. Ibid., pp. 59–61.

63. Interview with David Korn, October 29, 1992, Washington, D.C.

64. Interview with Roy Atherton, October 30, 1992, Washington, D.C.

65. Interview with Eliyahu Ben-Elisar, July 6, 1993, Jerusalem, Israel.

66. Remarks by Menachem Begin before the Israeli Parliament, January 23, 1978, as quoted in *Foreign Broadcast Information Service, Daily Report—Middle East and North Africa,* January 24, 1978, p. N10.

67. Tamir, *A Soldier,* p. 26.

68. Interview with Ahmed Maher, July 29, 1993, Washington, D.C.

69. Ibid.

70. Quandt, *Camp David,* p. 179.

71. Interview with Eliyahu Ben-Elisar, July 6, 1993, Jerusalem, Israel.

72. Quandt, *Camp David,* p. 179.

73. Interview with Hanan Bar-On, July 8, 1993, Washington, D.C.

74. Remarks by William B. Quandt, United States Institute of Peace meeting, April 16, 1991, Washington, D.C.

75. Carter, *Keeping Faith,* p. 310.

76. Interview with Moshe Dayan, Jerusalem Domestic Service, February 24, 1978, as quoted in *Foreign Broadcast Information Service, Daily Report—Middle East and North Africa,* February 27, 1978, p. N5.

77. Remarks by Ezer Weizman, *Ma'ariv,* March 24, 1978.

78. Quandt, *Camp David,* p. 192.

79. Interview with Harold Saunders, January 31, 1985, Atlanta; and Quandt, *Camp David,* p. 201.

80. Remarks by Harold Saunders, United States Institute of Peace meeting, April 16, 1991, Washington, D.C.

81. Interview with Roy Atherton, October 30, 1992, Washington, D.C.

82. Carter, *Keeping Faith,* p. 315.

83. Interview with Michael Sterner, June 17, 1993, Washington, D.C.

84. Quandt, *Camp David,* p. 206.

85. Remarks by Samuel W. Lewis, United States Institute of Peace meeting, April 16, 1991, Washington, D.C.

86. Interview with Jimmy Carter, February 19, 1991, Atlanta.

87. Zbigniew Brzezinski, *Power and Principle: Memoirs of the National Security Adviser, 1977–1981* (New York: Farrar Straus Giroux, 1983), pp. 253–54; and Quandt, *Camp David,* p. 217.

88. Interview with Eliyahu Ben-Elisar, July 6, 1993, Jerusalem, Israel.

89. Interview with Yahiel Kadishai, July 5, 1993, Tel Aviv, Israel.
90. For extraordinarily insightful reviews of the days at Camp David, see Quandt, *Camp David*, pp. 206–58; and Carter, *Keeping Faith*, pp. 319–429.
91. Quandt, *Camp David*, p. 297.
92. Interview with Nicholas A. Veliotes, September 7, 1995, Washington, D.C.
93. Carter, *Keeping Faith*, p. 397.
94. Remarks by Sol Linowitz and William Quandt, United States Institute of Peace meeting, April 16, 1991, Washington, D.C.
95. Quandt, *Camp David*, p. 263.
96. Interview with Jimmy Carter, April 23, 1991, Atlanta.
97. Carter, *Keeping Faith*, p. 416.
98. Interview with Jimmy Carter, April 23, 1991, Atlanta.
99. Remarks by Sol Linowitz, United States Institute of Peace meeting, April 16, 1991, Washington, D.C.
100. Colin Legum, ed., *Middle East Contemporary Survey, vol. III, 1978–79* (New York: Holmes and Meier, 1980), p. 216.
101. Remarks by Yasir Arafat, March 27, 1979, Baghdad Radio as quoted in *Foreign Broadcast Information Service—Near East and South Asia*, March 28, 1979, p. A3.
102. Remarks by Dr. George Habash, March 27, 1979, Baghdad Voice of Palestine, March 27, 1979, as quoted in *Foreign Broadcast Information Service—Near East and South Asia*, March 29, 1979, p. A9.
103. Remarks by Abd al-Halim Khaddam in *Al-Sharq al Awsat*, March 24, 1979, as quoted in *Foreign Broadcast Information Service—Near East and South Asia*, March 27, 1979, pp. H2–H3.
104. Colin Legum, ed., *Middle East Contemporary Survey, vol. II, 1977–78* (New York: Holmes and Meier, 1979), p. 102.
105. *Akhbar al-Yawm*, March 18 and 27, 1978, as quoted in *Foreign Broadcast Information Service—Near East and South Asia*, March 22 and 31, 1978, respectively.
106. *Al-Jumhuriyah*, March 16, 1978, as quoted in *Foreign Broadcast Information Service—Near East and South Asia*, March 17, 1978.
107. Kenneth W. Stein, "Egyptian-Israeli Relations, 1973–1997," *Israel Affairs* 3, nos. 3–4, (spring–summer 1997); p. 307.
108. Jimmy Carter, *Keeping Faith*, p. 483.

WORKS CITED
AND SUGGESTED
READING

BOOKS

Abou Iyad, with Eric Rouleau. *My Home, My Land.* New York: Times Books, 1981.
Adan, General Avraham. *On the Banks of the Suez.* New York: Presidio Press, 1980.
———. *The Yom Kippur War: An Israeli General's Personal Account.* New York: Drum Books, 1979.
Ajami, Fouad. *The Arab Predicament: Arab Political Thought and Practice Since 1967.* New York: Cambridge University Press, 1981.
Ambrose, Stephen. *Nixon* (vol. 2, 1962–1972). New York: Simon and Schuster, 1989.
———. *Nixon* (vol. 3, 1973–1990). New York: Simon and Schuster, 1991.
Alterman, Jon B. ed., *Sadat and His Legacy Egypt and the World, 1977–1997.* Washington, D.C.: The Washington Institute for Near East Policy, 1998.
Baker, James A., III. *The Politics of Diplomacy Revolution, War and Peace, 1889–1992.* New York: G. P. Putnam's Sons, 1995.
Bar-Siman-Tov. *The Israeli-Egyptian War of Attrition.* New York: Columbia University Press, 1980.
Benziman, Uzi. *Sharon: An Israeli Caesar.* London: Robson Books, 1987.
Ben-Zvi, Abraham. *Between Lausanne and Geneva: International Conferences and the Arab-Israel Conflict.* Boulder: Westview Press, 1989.
Blitzer, Wolf. *Between Washington and Jerusalem: A Reporter's Notebook.* New York: Oxford University Press, 1985.
Boutros-Ghali, Boutros. *Egypt's Road to Jerusalem.* New York: Random House, 1996.
Bradlee, Ben. *A Good Life: Newspapering and Other Adventures.* New York: Simon & Schuster, 1995.
Brzezinski, Zbigniew. *Power and Principle: Memoirs of the National Security Adviser, 1977–1981.* New York: Farrar Straus Giroux, 1983.
Caplan, Neil. *The Lausanne Conference, 1949.* Ramat Aviv: The Moshe Dayan Center for Middle Eastern and African Studies, Tel Aviv University, 1993.
Carter, Jimmy. *The Blood of Abraham: Insights into the Middle East.* Boston: Houghton-Mifflin, 1985.
———. *Keeping Faith: Memoirs of a President.* New York: Bantam Books, 1982.
Cobban, Helena. *The Palestine Liberation Organization: People, Power and Politics.* London: Cambridge University Press, 1984.

Cohen, Eliot A., Michael J. Eisenstadt, and Andrew J. Bacevich. *Knives, Tanks & Missiles: Israel's Security Revolution.* Washington, D.C.: The Washington Institute for Near East Policy, 1998.

Crabb, Cecil V. Jr., and Mulchahy, Kevin V. *Presidents and Foreign Policy Making From FDR to Reagan.* Baton Rouge and London: Louisiana State University Press, 1986.

Dawisha, Karen. *Soviet Foreign Policy Towards Egypt.* New York: St. Martin's Press, 1979.

Dayan, Moshe. *Breakthrough: A Personal Account of Egypt-Israel Negotiations.* London: Weidenfeld and Nicolson, 1981.

———. *Moshe Dayan: Story of My Life.* New York: William Morrow, 1976.

Dishon, Daniel, ed. *Middle East Record,* vol. 3. The Shiloah Center for Middle Eastern and African Studies, Tel Aviv University, Jerusalem: Israeli Universities Press, 1967.

Dobrynin, Anatoly. *In Confidence: Moscow's Ambassador to America's Six Cold War Presidents.* New York: Times Books, 1995.

Drysdale, Alasdair, and Raymond A. Hinnebusch. *Syria and the Middle East Peace Process.* New York: Council on Foreign Relations Press, 1991.

Eban, Abba. *Abba Eban: An Autobiography.* New York: Random House, 1977.

———. *Personal Witness: Israel Through My Eyes.* New York: G. P. Putnam and Sons, 1992.

Fahmy, Ismail. *Negotiating for Peace in the Middle East.* Baltimore: Johns Hopkins University Press, 1983.

Finklestone, Joseph. *Anwar Sadat: Visionary Who Dared.* London: Frank Cass, 1996.

Ford, Gerald. *A Time to Heal.* New York: Harper and Row, 1979.

Freedman, Robert O. *Soviet Policy Toward the Middle East Since 1970.* New York: Praeger, 1978.

El-Gamasy, Mohamed Abdel Ghani. *The October War Memoirs of Field Marshall El-Gamasy of Egypt.* Cairo: American University in Cairo Press, 1993.

Gazit, Mordechai. *The Peace Process 1969–1973: Efforts and Contacts.* Jerusalem: The Magnes Press, 1983.

Golan, Galia. *Soviet Policies in the Middle East.* Cambridge: Cambridge University Press, 1990.

———. *Yom Kippur and After: The Soviet Union and the Middle East Crisis.* Cambridge: Cambridge University Press, 1977.

Golan, Matti. *The Road to Peace: A Biography of Shimon Peres.* New York: Warner Books, 1989.

———. *The Secret Conversations of Henry Kissinger: Step-by-Step Diplomacy in the Middle East.* New York: Quadrangle, 1976.

———. *Shimon Peres: A Biography.* New York: St. Martin's Press, 1982.

Haber, Eitan, Zeev Schiff, and Ehud Yaari. *The Year of the Dove.* New York: Bantam Books, 1979.

Haldeman, H. R. *The Haldeman Diaries: Inside the Nixon White House.* New York: Berkley Books, 1995.

Harkabi, Yehoshafat. *Arab Attitudes to Israel.* Jerusalem: Keter Publishing House, 1972.

———. *Arab Strategies and Israel's Responses.* New York: Free Press, 1977.

Heikal, Mohammed. *Autumn of Fury: The Assassination of Sadat.* London: Andre Deutsch, 1983.

———. *The Road to Ramadan.* New York: Quadrangle Books, 1975.

Hersh, Seymour M. *The Price of Power: Kissinger in the Nixon White House.* New York: Summit Books, 1983.

Herzog, Chaim. *The War of Atonement, October 1973: The Fateful Implications of the Arab-Israeli Conflict.* Boston: Little, Brown and Company, 1975.

Hinnebusch, Raymond A., Jr. *Egyptian Politics Under Sadat: The Post-Populist Development of an Authoritarian-Modernizing State.* Boulder: Lynne Rienner Publishers, 1988.

Hirst, David, and Irene Beeson. *Sadat.* London: Faber and Faber, 1981.

Isaacson, Walter. *Kissinger.* New York: Simon and Schuster, 1992.

Israeli, Raphael. *"I Egypt:" Aspects of President Anwar al-Sadat's Political Thought.* Jerusalem: The Magness Press, 1981.

——. *The Public Diary of President Sadat: The Road to War (October 1970–October 1973).* Part 1. Leiden: E. J. Brill, 1978.

——. *The Public Diary of President Sadat: The Road to Diplomacy, The Continuation of War by Other Means (November 1973–May 1975).* Part 2. Leiden: E. J. Brill, 1979.

——. *The Public Diary of President Sadat: The Road of 84 Pragmatism (June 1975–October 1976).* Part 3. Leiden: E. J. Brill, 1979.

Israelyan, Victor. *Inside the Kremlin During the Yom Kippur War.* State College: Pennsylvania State University Press, 1995.

Jabotinsky, Zev. *Hazit HaMilhamah shel 'Am Yisrael* [War Front of the Jewish People]. Jerusalem: Lipshutz Press, 1941.

Kalb, Marvin, and Bernard Kalb. *Kissinger.* Boston: Little, Brown and Company, 1974.

Kamel, Mohammed Ibrahim. *The Camp David Accords.* New York: Metheun Inc., Routledge and Kegan Paul, 1986.

Kimche, David. *The Last Option After Nasser, Arafat and Saddam Hussein: The Quest for Peace in the Middle East.* London: Weidenfeld and Nicolson, 1991.

Kissinger, Henry. *Years of Upheaval.* Boston: Little, Brown and Company, 1982.

Korn, David. *Stalemate: The War of Attrition and Great Power Diplomacy in the Middle East, 1967–1970.* Boulder: Westview Press, 1992.

Legum, Colin, ed. *Middle East Contemporary Survey, vol. I, 1976–1977.* New York: Holmes and Meier, 1978.

——, ed. *Middle East Contemporary Survey, vol. II, 1977–1978.* New York: Holmes and Meier, 1979.

Linowitz, Sol M. *The Making of a Public Man: A Memoir.* Boston: Little, Brown and Company, 1985.

Lorch, Nataniel (ed.). *Major Knesset Debates,* vol. V. Jerusalem: University Press of America, 1992.

Al-Madfai, Madiha Rashid. *Jordan, the United States and the Middle East Peace Process 1974–1991.* Cambridge: Cambridge University Press, 1993.

Ma'oz, Moshe. *Syria and Israel.* New York: Oxford University Press, 1995.

Meir, Golda. *My Life.* New York: G. P. Putnam and Sons, 1975.

Meital, Yoram. *Egypt's Struggle for Peace, Community, and Change 1967–1977.* Gainesville: University Press of Florida, 1997.

Mutawi, Samir A. *Jordan in the 1967 War.* New York: Cambridge University Press, 1987.

Naor, Arye. *Ktovet 'al Hakir* [Writing on the Wall]. Tel Aviv: Yediot Aharanot, 1978.

Nixon, Richard. *RN: The Memoirs of Richard Nixon.* New York: Filmways Company Publishers, 1978.

Peres, Shimon. *Battling for Peace.* New York: Random House, 1995.

Perlmutter, Amos. *Israel: The Partitioned State—A Political History Since 1900.* New York: Charles Scribner's Sons, 1985.

Quandt, William B. *Camp David: Peacemaking and Politics.* Washington, D.C.: The Brookings Institution, 1986.

——. *Decade of Decisions: American Policy Toward the Arab-Israeli Conflict, 1967–1976.* Berkeley and Los Angeles: University of California Press, 1977.

——. *Peace Process, American Diplomacy, and the Arab-Israeli Conflict Since 1967.* Washington, D.C.: The Brookings Institution, 1993.

Quandt, William B., ed. *The Middle East: Ten Years after Camp David.* Washington, D.C.: The Brookings Institution, 1988.

Rabin, Yitzhak. *The Rabin Memoirs.* Boston: Little, Brown and Company, 1979.

Rabinovich, Itamar. *The Road Not Taken.* New York: Oxford University Press, 1991.

Rabinovich, Itamar, and Haim Shaked. *From June to October, The Middle East Between 1967 and 1973.* New Jersey: Transaction Books, 1978.

Rafael, Gideon. *Destination Peace: Three Decades of Israeli Foreign Policy—A Personal Memoir.* New York: Stein and Day, 1981.

Riad, Mahmoud. *The Struggle for Peace in the Middle East.* London: Quartet Books, 1981.

Ro'i, Yaacov. *From Encroachment to Involvement: A Documentary Study of Soviet Policy in the Middle East 1945–1973.* Jerusalem: Israel Universities Press, 1974.

———. *The U.S.S.R. and Egypt in the Wake of Sadat's July Decisions.* Slavic and Soviet Series, no. 1. The Russian East European Center, Tel Aviv University. Ramat Aviv: n.p., 1976.

Rubenstein, Alvin Z. *Red Star on the Nile.* Princeton: Princeton University Press, 1977.

Sadat, Anwar. *In Search of Identity: An Autobiography.* New York: Harper and Row, 1977.

Safran, Nadav. *From War to War: The Arab-Israeli Confrontation 1948–1967.* New York: Pegasus, 1969.

———. *Israel: The Embattled Ally.* Cambridge: Belknap Press, 1979.

Sasson, Moshe. *Sheva Shanim Beeretz Hamizraim* [Seven Years in the Land of the Egyptians]. Israel: Yediot Aharanot, 1992.

Schiff, Zeev. *October Earthquake, Yom Kippur War 1973.* Tel Aviv: University Publishing Projects, 1974.

Schoenbaum, David. *The United States and Israel.* New York: Oxford University Press, 1993.

Seale, Patrick. *Assad of Syria: The Struggle for the Middle East.* Berkeley and Los Angeles: University of California Press, 1988.

Sharon, Ariel, with David Chanoff. *Ariel Sharon Warrior: An Autobiography.* New York: Simon and Schuster, 1989.

El-Shazly, Lt. General Saad. *The Crossing of Suez.* San Francisco: American Mideast Research, 1980.

Sheehan, Edward R. F. *The Arabs, Israelis, and Kissinger: A Secret History of American Diplomacy in the Middle East.* New York: Reader's Digest Press, 1976.

Shemesh, Moshe. *The Palestinian Entity, 1959–1974: Arab Politics and the PLO.* London: Frank Cass, 1988.

Shlaim, Avi. *Collusion Across the Jordan King Abdullah, the Zionist Movement and the Partition of Palestine.* New York: Columbia University Press, 1988.

Sicherman, Harvey. *Palestinian Autonomy, Self-Government, and Peace.* Boulder: Westview Press, 1993.

Siilasvuo, Ensio. *In the Service of Peace in the Middle East, 1976–1979.* New York: St. Martin's Press, 1992.

Spiegel, Steven L. *The Other Arab-Israeli Conflict Making America's Middle East Policy, From Truman to Reagan.* Chicago: University of Chicago Press, 1985.

Stein, Kenneth W. *The Land Question in Palestine, 1917–1939.* Chapel Hill: University of North Carolina Press, 1984.

Stein, Kenneth W., and Samuel W. Lewis. *Making Peace Among Arabs and Israelis: Lessons from Fifty Years of Negotiating Experience.* Washington, D.C.: The United States Institute of Peace, 1991. (Hebrew version published by The Moshe Dayan Center for the Study of the Middle East and Africa at Tel Aviv University, 1993.)

Stjernfelt, Bertil. *The Sinai Peace Front: UN Peacekeeping Operations in the Middle East, 1973–1980.* New York: St. Martin's Press, 1992.

Susser, Asher. *Double Jeopardy: PLO Strategy Toward Israel and Jordan.* Policy Papers, no. 8. Washington, D.C.: The Washington Institute for Near East Policy, 1987.

———. *In Through the Out Door: Jordan's Disengagement and the Middle East Peace Process.* Policy Papers, no. 19. Washington, D.C.: The Washington Institute for Near East Policy, 1990.

Tamir, Avraham. *A Soldier in Search of Peace: An Insider's Look at Israel's Strategy in the Middle East.* New York: Harper and Row, 1988.

Telhami, Shibley. *Power and Leadership in International Bargaining: The Path to the Camp David Accords.* New York: Columbia University Press, 1990.

Touval, Saadia. *The Peace Brokers: Mediators in the Arab-Israeli Conflict, 1948–1979.* Princeton: Princeton University Press, 1982.

Toward Peace in the Middle East. Report of a Study Group. Washington, D.C.: Brookings Institution, 1975.

Twite, Robin, and Tamar Hermann, ed. *The Arab-Israeli Negotiations.* Tel Aviv: Papyrus Publishing House, 1993.

Valeriani, Richard. *Travels with Henry.* Boston: Houghton-Mifflin, 1979.

Vance, Cyrus. *Hard Choices: Critical Years in America's Foreign Policy.* New York: Simon and Schuster, 1983.

The Washington Institute. *UN Security Council Resolution 242: The Building Block of Peacemaking.* Washington, D.C.: The Washington Institute for Near East Policy, 1993.

Weizman, Ezer. *The Battle for Peace.* New York: Bantam Books, 1981.

Zeira, Eli. *Milhemet Yom Kippur Mitom Mul Meziot* [The Yom Kippur War Myth Against Reality]. Tel Aviv: Yediot Aharnot, 1993.

ARTICLES AND SHORT MONOGRAPHS

Avineri, Shlomo. "Peacemaking: The Arab-Israeli Conflict." *Foreign Affairs* 1 (Fall 1978): 57, 51–69.

Bell, Coral. "The October Middle East War: A Case Study in Crisis Management During Detente." *International Affairs* 50 (October 1974): 531–43.

Bruzonsky, Mark A. "Interview with Mohamad Ibrahim Kamel." *Middle East Journal* 38 (Winter 1984): 85–98.

Caplan, Neil. "Arab-Jewish Relations in Palestine, 1917–1947." *Middle East Focus* 13, 4 (Winter 1991): 2–8, 11.

———. "A Tale of Two Cities: The Rhodes and Lausanne Conferences, 1949." *Journal of Palestine Studies* 21, 3 (Spring 1992): 5–34.

Dishon, Daniel. "The Web of Inter-Arab Relations." *Jerusalem Quarterly* 2 (Winter 1977): 45–59.

Draper, Theodore. "The Road to Geneva." *Commentary* 57 (February 1974): 23–39.

Eban, Abba. "Camp David: The Unfinished Business." *Foreign Affairs* 2 (Winter 1978/79): 57, 348.

Gazit, Mordechai. "Egypt and Israel—Was There a Peace Opportunity Missed in 1971?" *Journal of Contemporary History* 32, 1 (1997): 97–115.

———. "Mediation and Mediators." *Jerusalem Journal of International Relations* 5 (1981): 80–103.

———. "Peacemakers—Mediation in the Arab-Israeli Conflict." In *Negotiations in the Middle East: The Lessons of Fifty Years.* Tel Aviv: The Moshe Dayan Center for Middle Eastern and African Studies, Tel Aviv University, 1993, pp. 91–117.

Goverin, Joseph. "The Six Day War in the Mirror of Soviet-Israeli Relations—April–June 1967." Research Paper, no. 61, The Soviet and East European Research Centre, The Hebrew University of Jerusalem, December 1985.

Handel, Michael I. "The Yom Kippur War and the Inevitability of Surprise." *International Studies Quarterly* 21 (September 1977): 461–502.

Heikal, Mohammed. "Egyptian Foreign Policy." *Foreign Affairs* 56 (July 1978): 714–27.

Hunter, Robert E. "In the Middle of the the Middle East." *Foreign Affairs* 49 (Winter 1971): 137–50.

Inbar, Efraim. "Great Power Mediation: The USA and the May 1983 Israeli-Lebanese Agreement." *Journal of Peace Research* 28 (1991): 71–84.

———. "Yitzhak Rabin and Israeli National Security." *BESA Security and Policy Studies,* no. 25, Bar-Ilan University, Ramat-Gan, Israel, January 1996.

Indyk, Martin. "Detente and the Politics of Patronage: How the October Middle East War Started." *Australian Outlook* 30 (August 1976): 171–96.

———. "To the Ends of the Earth—Sadat's Jerusalem Initiative." *Middle East Papers,* Modern Series 1. Cambridge: Harvard University, Center for Middle Eastern Studies, 1984.

Israelyan, Victor. "The October 1973 War: Kissinger in Moscow." *Middle East Journal* (Spring 1995): 248–68.

Knott, Jack, and Aaron Wildavsky. "Jimmy Carter's Theory of Governing." *Woodrow Wilson Quarterly* 1 (Winter 1977): 49–65.

Korn, David A. "The Making of United Nations Security Council Resolution 242." In *Pew Case Studies in International Affairs,* Case 450. Washington, D.C.: Georgetown University, 1992.

Lipset, Seymour, and William Schneider. "Carter vs. Israel: What the Polls Revealed." *Commentary* 64 (November 1977): 21–29.

Luttwak, Edward N., and Walter Laqueur. "Kissinger and the Yom Kippur War." *Commentary* 58 (September 1974): 33–40.

Parzen, Herbert. "A Chapter in Arab-Jewish Relations During the Mandate Era." *Jewish Social Studies* 29 (October 1967): 203–33.

Pedatzur, Reuven. "Coming Back Full Circle: The Palestinian Option in 1967." *Middle East Journal* 49 (Spring 1995). 269 91.

Perlmutter, Amos. "Crisis Management: Kissinger's Middle East Negotiations (October 1973–June 1974)." *International Studies Quarterly* 19 (September 1975): 316–43.

———. "Israel's Fourth War, October 1973, Political and Military Misperception." *Orbis* 19 (summer 1978): 434–60.

Pierre, Rondot. "Palestine: Peace Talks and Militancy." *World Today* 30 (September 1974): 379–87.

Quandt, William B. "Camp David and Peacemaking in the Middle East." *Political Science Quarterly* 101 (1986): 357–377.

———. "Kissinger and the Arab-Israel Disengagement Negotiations." *Journal of International Affairs* 29 (Spring 1975): 33–48.

———. "Soviet Policy in the October Middle East War–I." *International Affairs* 53 (July 1977): 377–389.

———. "Soviet Policy in the October Middle East War–II." *International Affairs* 54 (October 1977): 587–604.

Reston, James. "How to Save Israel." *New York Times,* March 24, 1977, p. A9.

Roberts, Charles M. "Foreign Policy Under a Paralyzed Presidency." *Foreign Affairs* 152 (Summer 1974): 675–89.

Safty, Adel. "Sadat's Negotiations with the United States and Israel: From Sinai to Camp David." *American Journal of Economics and Sociology* 50 (July 1991): 285–96.

Sheehan, Edward R. F. "How Kissinger Did It—Step By Step in the Middle East." *Foreign Policy* 22 (Spring 1976): 3–70.

Sheffer, Gabriel. "The Images of Arabs and Jews as a Factor in British Policy Towards Palestine (1917–1948)." *Zionism* 1 (Spring 1980): 105–28.

Sherer, John L. "Soviet and American Behavior During the Yom Kippur War." *World Affairs* 141 (Summer 1978): 3–23.

Shlaim, Avi. "Failures in National Intelligence Estimates: The Case of the Yom Kippur War." *World Politics* 28 (April 1976): 348–380.

Smart, Ian. "The Superpowers and the Middle East." *World Today* 30 (January 1974): 4–15.

Stein, Janice Gross. "The Alchemy of Peacemaking: The Prerequisites and Corequisites of Progress in the Arab-Israeli Conflict." *International Journal* 38 (Fall 1983): 531–55.

————. "Prenegotiation in the Arab-Israeli Conflict: Paradoxes of Success and Failure." *International Journal* 44 (Spring 1989): 410–41.

————. "Structures, Strategies and Tactics of Mediation: Kissinger and Carter in the Middle East." *Negotiation Journal* 1 (October 1985): 331–47.

Stein, Kenneth W. "The Arab-Israel Conflict: Making Progress Toward Peace?" *Middle East Insight* 6 (1989): 3–10.

————. (moderator) "The Camp David Accords." Presentation remarks by Hermann F. Eilts, Samuel W. Lewis, William B. Quandt, Harold Saunders, and Daniel Kurtzer, at The Carter Presidential Conference, Hofstra University, Hempstead, New York, November 1990. In Herbert D. Rosenbaum and Alexej Ugrinsky, eds., *Jimmy Carter Foreign Policy and Post-Presidential Years*. Westport, Conn.: Greenwood Press, 1994.

————. "Egyptian-Israeli Relations, 1973–1997." *Israel Affairs* 3, 3–4 (Spring/Summer 1997): 296–320.

————. "The Palestinian Uprising and the Shultz Initiative." *Middle East Review* 21 (Winter 1988–1989): 13–20.

————. "Texture of the Middle East Peace Process." *Middle East Insight* 7 (1990): 14–20.

Tuhami, Hassan. "Now I Can Speak About the Initiative." *October Magazine,* November 21, 1982, pp. 19–21 (in Arabic).

Wheeler, Michael O., and Kemper V. Gay. "Nuclear Weapons and the 1973 Middle East War." *CSN Occasional Paper Monograph, no. 3*. Washington, D.C.: The Center for National Security Negotiations, August 1996.

DOCUMENTS

Carter Presidential Library. National Security Documents, Files of William B. Quandt.

Library of Congress. Congressional Research Service, Foreign Affairs and National Defense Division. *The Search for Peace in the Middle East, Documents and Statements, 1967–1979*. Report prepared for the Subcommittee on Europe and the Middle East of the Committee on Foreign Affairs, U.S. House of Representatives. Washington, D.C.: U.S. Government Printing Office, 1979.

United States Army Command and General Staff College. *Selected Readings in Tactics: The 1973 Middle East War* (RB 100–2, vol. 1). Fort Leavenworth, Kansas: U.S. Army Command and General Staff College, August 1976.

United States Department of State. *U.S. Policy in the Middle East: December 1973–November 1974*. Selected Documents, Bureau of Public Affairs, Special Report, no. 12, 1975.

United States Department of State. *U.S. Policy in the Middle East: November 1974–February 1976*. Selected Documents, Bureau of Public Affairs, Special Report, no. 4, 1976.

United States House of Representatives. *Hearings of the Committee on International Relations on International Security Assistance*. 94th Cong., November 6–February 19, 1976.

United States House of Representatives. *Hearings Before the Special Committee on Investigations of the Committee on International Relations* (The Palestinian Issue in Middle East Peace Efforts). 94th Cong., 1st sess., September 30, October 1, 8, and November 12, 1975.

United States House of Representatives. *Hearings of the Committee on International Relations on the Middle East Agreements and Legislation to Implement the United States Proposal for the Early Warning System in Sinai*. 94th Cong., 1st sess., September 8, 11, 18, and 25, 1975.

United States Senate. *Hearings Before the Committee on Foreign Relations on Memoranda of Agreements between the Governments of Israel and the United States*. 94th Cong., 1st sess., October 6 and 7, 1975.

United States Senate. *Hearings Before the Subcommittee on Foreign Assistance of the Committee on Foreign Relations on Proposed Cash Sale to Egypt of Six C-130 Aircraft and Training of Egyptian Personnel*. 94th Cong., 2nd sess., March 31 and April 2, 1976.

NEWSPAPERS AND SERIALS

Foreign Broadcast Information Service, Daily Report—Middle East and North Africa (MENA), and
  Near East and South Asia, 1977–1998.
Al-Akhbar, 1993.
Al-Jumhuriyah, 1978.
Akhbar al-Yawm, 1973–1979.
Al-Nahar, 1977.
BBC, *Summary of World Broadcasts,* October–December 1976.
Chicago Daily News, 1976.
Davar, 1973–1979.
Ha'aretz, 1973–1979.
Jerusalem Post, 1973–1979.
London Guardian, 1978.
Ma'ariv, 1973–1979.
October Magazine, 1977–1980.
New York Times, 1973–1979.
Newsweek, 1974–1978.
Washington Post, 1973–1979.
Yediot Aharanot, 1973–1979.

INDEX